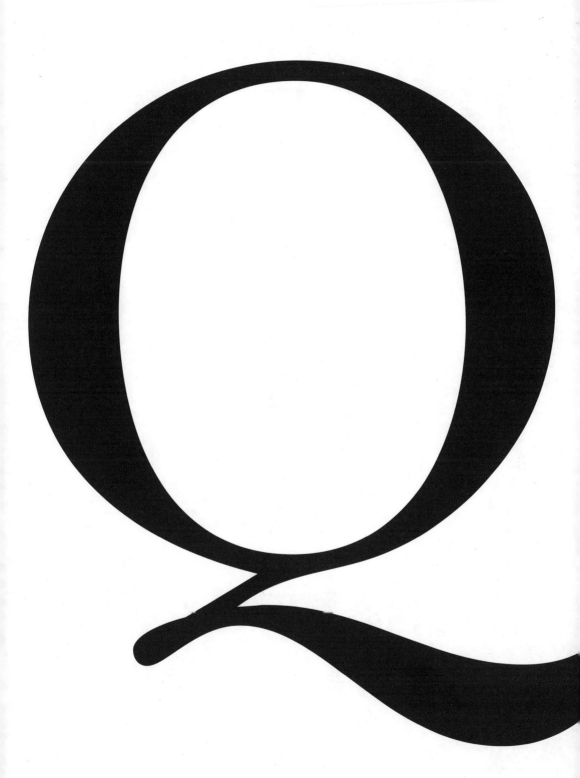

In the series Asian American History and Culture,
edited by Sucheng Chan, David Palumbo-Liu,
& Michael Omi

Q & A
Queer in Asian America
Edited by David L. Eng
and Alice Y. Hom

Temple University Press

Philadelphia

Temple University Press, Philadelphia 19122
Copyright © 1998 by Temple University
All rights reserved. Published 1998
Printed in the United States of America

⊖ The paper used in this publication meets the
requirements of the American National
Standard for Information Sciences – Permanence
of Paper for Printed Library Materials,
ANSI Z39.48-1984

Text design by Richard Eckersley

Library of Congress
Cataloging-in-Publication Data
Q & A : queer in Asian America /
edited by David L. Eng and Alice Y. Hom.
p. cm. – (Asian American history and culture)
Includes bibliographical references.
ISBN 1-56639-639-5 (cloth : alkaline paper). –
ISBN 1-56639-640-9 (pbk. : alkaline paper)
1. Asian American gays – Social conditions.
2. Asian American lesbians – Social conditions.
3. Gays – United States – Identity.
4. Lesbians – United States – Identity.
I. Eng, David L., 1967– .
II. Hom, Alice Y., 1967– . III. Series.
HQ76.3.U5Q4 1998
306.76'6'08995073 – dc21
98-14990

Frontispiece: I. H. Kuniyuki, *Yami No Te II
(The Hand of Darkness)* 1997 version.
A tenth-generation photographically derived
(non–computer made) image, shot in
1986 at a special photo session. Each image
of the series is its own original after
completing its evolution as
a photograph.

Contents

To
the queer Asian American community
&
to our parents, Philip B. Eng and Lucy W. H. Eng
&
Henry M. Hom and Sandy H. Hom

Preface

Q

I. H. Kuniyuki's frontispiece photograph for *Q & A: Queer in Asian America* is a haunting image of butoh dancers that is not quick to legislate what it means to be a queer Asian American. We chose Kuniyuki's striking *Yami No Te II* in particular to avoid proffering what could be immediately apprehended as a predictable or representative image—a group of Asian Americans at a lesbian and gay pride parade, two Asian American queers kissing in the shade of a Chinatown pagoda. We were drawn to Kuniyuki's work because of the quiet ways in which it disrupts the project of representation itself.

Yami No Te II neither prescribes nor mandates how we should see and interpret the convergence of sexuality and race for Asian Americans. Kuniyuki's enigmatic figures emerge and fade—together yet apart. They move at once but not altogether in the same ways, in identical patterns, or in similar directions. Thus, there is ample room to question, to wonder, to admire. This suggestive image highlights the fluid existence of a queer Asian America, underscoring our efforts as editors to present numerous queer Asian American perspectives and identities at the threshold of representation.

At present, a queer Asian America is visibly emerging in the world around us. This collection documents the history of that emergence, contemplates the many closets and disparate corners of queer Asian American existence, and mobilizes some of the various communities claiming this label. As editors, we resist defining, in any absolute manner, the state of a queer Asian America; we prefer instead to throw the question of our multiple identities into the open for contemplation and exploration. This questioning, however, marks only a beginning. By gathering multiple ideas, opinions, and points of view, we hope that this collection also helps to build, shape, and strengthen the community that it seeks to name. With this intent, we offer this book to family, friends, students, and colleagues in our different and overlapping communities.

This project began because Janet Francendese (now editor-in-chief at Temple University Press) and Sucheng Chan (original editor of Temple University Press's Asian American History and Culture series) strongly believed in the need for a collection exploring Asian American lesbian and gay issues. Sucheng Chan proposed this idea to David L. Eng in the summer of 1994. At the suggestion of Elsa E'der, David asked Alice Y. Hom to coedit the project with him in the spring of 1995.

As coeditors of *Q & A: Queer in Asian America*, we have been able to put to good use our combined knowledges of literature and history and gay and lesbian issues, as well as our experiences in community work with different groups and organizations. For bringing us together, and for providing us with sustaining inspiration for this project, we thank Elsa E'der, Sucheng Chan, and Janet Francendese. In addition, we thank Richard Eckersley, Jenny French, and Debby Stuart for their expert design, editorial, and production skills.

This project has also had many other supporters, to whom we owe much gratitude. We are fortunate to have had the extraordinary opportunity of working with these dedicated and wonderful people. First and foremost, we thank the contributors to this collection for their enthusiasm and hard work. We also acknowledge our friends, colleagues, and students at the University of California, Berkeley and Los Angeles; Claremont Graduate University; Columbia University; and places in between. For their personal and intellectual support, our heartfelt thanks go to Karin Aguilar-San Juan, Emilie Bergmann, Marcellus Blount, Judith Butler, Robert Dawidoff, Kim Dillon, Gisele Fong, Judith Goldman, Deena Gonzalez, Ju Hui Judy Han, JeeYeun Lee, Russell Leong, Lisa Lowe, Sanda Lwin, Martin Manalansan, Susette Min, Rosalind Morris, David Palumbo-Liu, Eric Reyes, Vicki Ruiz, Kaja Silverman, Dean Toji, Sophie + Serena + Leti Volpp, and Sau-ling C. Wong.

We also thank the Columbia University Council for Research in the Humanities, which provided summer grants toward the completion of this book.

DAVID L. ENG AND ALICE Y. HOM, *New York City*

Q Q Q Q Q Q Q Q Q Q Q

Introduction
Q & A: Notes on a Queer Asian America
David L. Eng and Alice Y. Hom

Consider the following scenario: A short-haired, butch-looking Asian American lesbian is washing her hands in a public women's restroom.[1] A white woman enters. Startled, she checks the sign on the door and then loudly protests, "This is a women's restroom!" The white woman, assuming that this butch-looking Asian American is a man, claims the restroom as a women's space. Ironically, while it is easy for the white woman to see an emasculated Asian American man in this space of urinary segregation, it is difficult for her to envision a butch Asian American lesbian there.[2]

Let us elaborate. Once, a mutual friend of ours—a Korean American dyke—was washing her hands in a women's restroom when she overheard a conversation behind her. "What's *he* doing here?" one white woman asked another. "Oh, whatever, he probably doesn't read English," her companion replied. In this compounded misreading of both sexual and racial difference—in this restroom as a public site where dominant images of emasculated Asian American men and hyperheterosexualized Asian American women collide—the Asian American lesbian disappears. In both scenarios it is precisely mainstream stereotypes of an effeminized Asian American male (homo)sexuality that affect the ways in which the Asian American lesbian goes unseen and unrecognized.

So how do we consider race, gender, and homosexuality for Asian Americans? It is important to emphasize that this theoretical issue has yet to be broadly interrogated in either Asian American studies or lesbian/gay studies. Clearly, as our two examples indicate, the intersection of racial and (homo)sexual difference produces a set of unsettling representations and curious misreadings notably divergent from those normally associated with mainstream lesbians and gays. And perhaps there is always something curiously queer—something curiously divergent, contradictory, or anomalous—that arises from the crossing of homosexuality and race. In this essay we use the terms "lesbian/gay" and "queer," but we do not mean to imply that they are interchangeable. Although "lesbian/gay" and "queer" often name overlapping constituencies, there are significant political and generational differences between the terms.[3] Here we use "queer" to refer to a political practice based on transgressions of the normal and normativity rather than a straight/gay binary of heterosexual/homosexual identity. The various meanings of these transgressions, divergences, contradictions, and anomalies—how and for what ends they are produced—are addressed herein.

The twenty-six chapters in this collection include essays, personal narratives, roundtable discussions, and illustrations that engage, analyze, mark, and, in turn, help foster the growth of the movement that we call "queer Asian American studies." The emergence of this field has not been smooth or even. The academy has yet to recognize queer Asian American studies as viable and necessary. Nevertheless, as these various chapters attest, queer Asian American studies is a growing intellectual field and a vibrant social movement with serious cultural, economic, and political concerns.

This collection includes a wide spectrum of authors (academics, activists, artists, community organizers, lawyers, and a practicing minister) from a variety of disciplines (ethnic and postcolonial studies, literature and history, visual culture and cinema, cultural and women's studies, law and religion, and anthropology and sociology). These authors combine disparate theoretical fields of knowledge to explore the multiple convergences of race, gender, and homosexuality for queer Asian Americans in innovative and compelling ways. From discussions of immigration and asylum to political organizing and coalition building, from essays on the problems of identity-based politics and vexed notions of "home" to coming-out narratives and critiques of transnational space, these chapters not only chart the state of a queer Asian America but also propose for further investigation a rich set of theoretical questions, current topics, and critical thoughts for political action.

Queer Asian America

Without the Asian American lesbian and gay activists, writers, and scholars who, during the last three decades of the twentieth century, worked and organized both inside and outside various social movements—feminism, civil rights, Third World liberation, Vietnam War protests, black power, and gay liberation—it would be impossible to imagine a queer Asian America today. Two historical circumstances in particular made the current rise of queer Asian American studies possible. First was the formation and proliferation of various Asian American lesbian/gay organizations in U.S. metropolitan centers circa the 1980s. These included Boston Asian Gay Males and Lesbians (1979), Asian Pacific Lesbians and Gays (Los Angeles, 1980), Association of Lesbian and Gay Asians (San Francisco, 1981), Asian Lesbians of the East Coast (New York, 1983), Asian Pacific Lesbians and Friends (Los Angeles, 1983), Gay Asian Rap (Los Angeles, 1984), Gay Asian Pacific Alliance (San Francisco, 1988), Gay Asian Pacific Support Network (Los Angeles,

1988), Asian Pacifica Sisters (San Francisco, 1989), and Gay Asian Pacific Islander Men of New York (1990). The second historical circumstance was the publication of Asian American lesbian writers, such as Willyce Kim, Barbara Noda, Kitty Tsui, Canyon Sam, and Merle Woo during the 1970s and 1980s. Their work helped to give shape to a public and recognizable Asian American lesbian subject within larger feminist circles.[4] The cultural production, political activism, social cohesion, and support networks established by these lesbian and gay Asian American organizations and authors have been integral to our emergence into the domain of the visible—our ability to come out, as it were, into view. These organizations and authors have been crucial to our growing empowerment within larger Asian American and mainstream lesbian/gay communities.

In the last years of the twentieth century, as Asian American studies approaches its thirtieth anniversary in the academy, we are at a theoretical crossroads widely acknowledged by scholars in this and other disciplines.[5] Various critical mobilizations from feminist, poststructuralist, and queer quarters have worked to trouble the rather static cultural nationalist conception of racial identity around which Asian American studies was originally formed (the assumed but unspoken subject of the field was male, heterosexual, working class, American born, and English speaking).

From a queer studies point of view, to insert questions of sexuality, sexual identification, and sexual orientation into our concept of Asian American identity would immediately help to dislodge a static, outdated, and exclusively *racial* notion of who "we" are. Queer identity does not fit comfortably in the broadly polarized (and heterosexist) nationalist/nativist or assimilationist/feminist debate that has shaped Asian American studies and propelled analyses of Asian American racial formation during the 1980s and 1990s.[6] To recognize that Asian Americans are never purely, or merely, racial subjects is a crucial task in the rapidly shifting 1990s political terrain of (post)identity politics and multicultural and diversity management. As Asian American queers, we neither relate nor conform well to implicitly heterosexual models of Asian American identity. Therefore, we need to articulate a new conception of Asian American racial identity, its heterogeneity, hybridity, and multiplicity—concepts that have, after all, underpinned the Asian American moniker from its very inception.[7]

In the late 1990s, we are at a fertile historical moment to witness the emergence of a distinct and visible queer Asian American identity. We are queer, lesbian, gay, bisexual, and transgendered Asian Americans who are willing to engage actively in the discourses of both Asian American and queer politics but unwilling to bifurcate our identities into the racial and the sexual. This is also a historical moment, however, in which racism, sexism, and homophobia—as well as their multiple convergences—are tangibly evident from day to day. Political debates on affirmative action, immigration exclusion, English-only initiatives, multicultural curricula, universal health care, abortion, gay marriage, queer parenting, homosexuals in the military, and antigay legislative initiatives serve to complement an increasing tide of physical violence against people of color and against queers.[8] The emergence of a queer Asian American social movement comes only in the face of, perhaps even in spite of, this virulent backlash.

Certainly the notion of oppositionality is not unfamiliar to those invested in Asian American, women's, or lesbian/gay grassroots and academic movements. The formation of the Asian American movement, second-wave feminism, and modern gay liberation in the late 1960s and early 1970s occurred at a political moment not dissimilar to the 1990s.[9] Indeed, because so many of our present-day political conceptions about and oppositions to racism, sexism, and homophobia trace their roots to this common historical period, it is crucial to consider the historical connections between these movements—not only how they continue to shape our contemporary notions of racism, sexism, and homophobia but also how they relate to and frame one another.

It is interesting to note, for instance, that the fact that the Stonewall riots were led in part by African American and Latino drag queens has only recently been marked by historians and cultural critics.[10] However, this important fact should not be merely appended to the historical revisions of the event. On one hand, it challenges scholars in lesbian/gay studies to reconsider how racial difference may have provided the constitutive framework through which the modern gay movement emerged and gained its coherence. On the other hand, it demands the need for ethnic studies scholars to integrate into their institutional canons what has hitherto been a watershed event of only the lesbian/gay movement. This integration of queer sexuality is one that will undoubtedly have widespread implications for the historiography of both fields, bringing to bear a number of pressing issues: how race and queerness intersect at cross purposes in the articulation of historical events such as the Stonewall riots; how racial difference is sublimated into and masked by questions of sex and sexual difference in the narrating of history, the writing of literature, and the production of subjects and cultures; how race and queerness merge—how they collide—in the fields of the psychic, the social, and the material.

Stonewall provides an intellectual caveat for those of us in Asian American and lesbian/gay studies to search for the interrelation between race and sexuality at all times, even in those instances where their separability may at first seem self-evident. In Asian American studies we have produced powerful and convincing scholarship, for example, on bachelor societies and prostitutes, on model minorities and refugee communities. It is imperative for us to remember, however, that such scholarship is not just a critique of racial and class formation but also, simultaneously, a critique of sexuality.[11] To invoke, for instance, the historical phenomenon of paper sons[12] is to discuss implicitly issues that have everything to do with queerness, homosexuality, and homosociality: the notion of deviant and normative sexuality; the question of real and imagined paternity; the anxieties of patrilineal transmission; the historical, material, and psychic configurations of juridically procured male communities; the state-impelled displacement of biological filiation to communal affiliation.

The recent scholarship of Asian American cultural critics such as Lisa Lowe provides a careful consideration of the numerous competing social differences that work to produce historical and contemporary versions of minoritized Asian American subjects.[13] In *Immigrant Acts,* Lowe discusses how nineteenth- and twentieth-century historical processes of immigration exclusion and legal definitions of citizenship link to form a racialized, gendered Asian American subject before the law. She notes that

> racialization along the legal axis of definitions of citizenship has also ascribed "gender" to the Asian American subject. Up until 1870, American citizenship was granted exclusively to white male persons; in 1870, men of African descent could become naturalized, but the bar to citizenship remained for Asian men until the repeal acts of 1943–1952. Whereas the "masculinity" of the citizen was first inseparable from his "whiteness," as the state extended citizenship to nonwhite male persons, it formally designated these subjects as "male," as well. (11)

Lowe analyzes the juridical mechanisms by which Asian American immigrant laborers were barred at once not only from institutional and social definitions of "maleness" but also from normative conceptions of the masculinity legally defined as "white" (for example, normative heterosexuality, nuclear family formations, entitlement to community). In this manner, Lowe's work highlights the need for Asian American studies scholars to understand that legal and cultural discourses on "deviant" sexuality do not affect only those contemporary Asian American subjects who readily self-identify as queer, lesbian, gay, bisexual, or transgendered; they affect a much larger Asian American constituency as well—regardless of sexual identity or identifications—whose disavowed status as legitimate or proper subjects of the U.S. nation-state render them abnormal as such. We must emphasize that this is a "queer" formation that traces its historical roots backward to shifting twentieth-, nineteenth-, and eighteenth-century legal definitions of the U.S. nation-state and the imagined formations of its citizenry.

During the past several years, we have noticed an increasing attention to (what, perhaps, can even be described as an incipient integration of) issues specific to queer sexuality in new Asian American scholarship, in panel presentations at Asian American studies conferences, in Asian American critical and literary journals, and in Asian American classroom curricula. But this critical attention is far from sustained; it is, instead, sporadic and divided. An illustrative, though certainly not singular, example comes from the pages of *Amerasia Journal,* through the juxtaposition of two special issues, "Dimensions of Desire: Other Asian and Pacific American Sexualities: Gay, Lesbian, and Bisexual Identities and Orientations" in 1994 (Leong) and "Thinking Theory in Asian American Studies" in 1995 (Omi and Takagi).[14]

In the lead article of the 1994 issue of *Amerasia Journal,* "Maiden Voyage: Excursion into Sexuality and Identity Politics in Asian America" (1–17), Dana Y. Takagi takes up many of the topics discussed in this introduction, eloquently arguing for the need to start recognizing different sexual practices and identities that also lay claim to the label "Asian American." By doing so, she insists, we can begin to rethink and to reevaluate "notions of identity that have been used, for the most part, unproblematically and uncritically in Asian American studies" (2) since its formation in the early 1970s around the politics of cultural nationalism. Takagi suggests that we ought to be talking seriously about queer sexuality and Asian American studies together because of the continued "theoretical trouble we encounter in our attempts to situate and think about sexual identity *and* racial identity" at once (2).

In the 1995 issue of *Amerasia Journal,*—which was devoted to exploring the state of theory on the twenty-fifth anniversary of Asian American studies—Michael Omi and Dana Takagi (in the role of guest coeditors) note in their introduction:

> The waning of radical political movements in the 1980s had attendant effects on theory and politics within Asian American studies. We feel that the absence of a sustained and coherent radical theory of social transformation led to a retreat to more mainstream, discipline-based paradigmatic orientations. Contributing

to this trend was the increasing "professionalization" of the field in academic settings, the demands of tenure and promotion for faculty members, and the entrance of newcomers to the field trained in specific disciplines who had not participated in the new social movements of the previous decades. The result of this has been the contraction of space for dialogue across the disciplines—one which could have critically interrogated disciplinary boundaries and fostered cross-disciplinary perspectives. (xiii)

Omi and Takagi are correct in their suggestion that the 1980s marked a demonstrable shift in Asian American social activism and in the Asian American studies movement. Unquestionably, the apotheosis of capital and the dismantling of labor during this decade under the United States's Reagan administration and Britain's Thatcher administration led Asian American studies concomitantly to shift away from and to rethink traditional class-based critiques of race. Yet we should emphasize that, rather than being considered a dearth or waning of radical political movements, this shifting away from and rethinking of traditional class-based analyses could be considered a displacement of progressive Asian American activism and analyses of Asian American racial formation into different, new, and unanalyzed realms.

As two queers who came of age in the age of AIDS, in the age of Asian American lesbian/gay activism, and in the age of Reagan/Bush multicultural politics, we would like to suggest that the 1980s marked a historical period in which gender studies, AIDS activism, divestment, and multiculturalism helped to transform Asian American studies in useful ways. Taken together, these interconnected social movements altered our view of the academy, the world outside it, and the ways in which we perceive the interaction of these two realms. We believe that Takagi's earlier exhortation to rethink "notions of identity that have been used, for the most part, unproblematically and uncritically in Asian American studies" was made possible by the theoretical work done in critical race theory and in postcolonial, gender, and lesbian/gay studies (in various disciplines throughout the humanities and social sciences) during the 1980s.

The rich theoretical work done collectively in these various fields and disciplines has not only helped to foster our sustained analysis of identity in Asian American studies but has also shaped our current critique of Asian American identity politics and the politics of coalition building.[15] Indeed, the 1980s could be seen as that historical period in which multiple political agendas and competing theories of sexual identification came to inform our sense of Asian American racial formation and identity. The cross-disciplinary work done at this time was the theoretical root of the now familiar inter-rogation of cultural nationalism in Asian American studies as a plat-form equating political efficacy with similarity and unity (mascu-line, heterosexual, and working-class) rather than with particularity and difference as the basis for social action. And because of the cross-disciplinary work and the proliferation of theoretical scholar-ship on race, gender, and (homo)sexuality in the 1980s, we can as-sert that the state of Asian American studies in the late 1990s has expanded, rather than contracted, to include hitherto unimagin-able intellectual perspectives, scholarly angles, and progressive politics.

The 1980s introduced newcomers trained in specific disciplines into the field of Asian American studies and witnessed the increas-ing "professionalization" of Asian American studies within the acad-emy. This contemporary dispersal—which is institutionally promis-ing for the current expansion of Asian American studies beyond the West Coast and beyond the enclave of ethnic studies departments—does not compromise the social movements of the previous decades that made it possible. Rather, it provides the necessary intellectual and institutional space for us to rethink a 1960s model of the grass-roots academic/activist against new social agendas and queer for-mations of oppositional Asian American subjectivities. Failure to take on this task risks the reinscription of a static cultural national-ist model of identity as the originary ideal for efficacious political action—a dubious model that both feminists and queers in the field have struggled to deconstruct.

Accounts of our past shape our present-day politics in powerful ways, and to know the roots of our history is to understand what makes our present existence possible. To posit any one historical model as the proper mechanism of living out our political and so-cial lives is limiting. Political progress is not about the valorization of a static past but about reconstituting that past, transforming the contemporary, and imagining a more livable present and future. Certainly, the current college campus resurgence of Asian Ameri-can activism—which demands intellectual acknowledgment and political representation in the form of Asian American, ethnic, and American studies programs—attests to salubrious political change and ever-expanding definitions of what it means to be Asian Amer-ican.[16] This wave of renewed political activism is indebted to the his-torical events and activism of the late 1960s and 1970s as well as to the political and theoretical work of the 1980s.

As scholars and activists invested in the emerging field of queer Asian American studies, we must be open to the possibilities for fu-ture significations of queer Asian American studies. This position is not to relinquish our right to claim a strategic "we" when politically necessary. Yet who are "we"? As this collection suggests, queer Asian America demands more than a deviant swerving from the narrow confines of normativity and normative heterosexuality; it requires subjecting the notion of Asian American identity itself to vigorous interrogation. Queer Asian America comprises a vast and disparate group of locations and regions (North America, U.S. territories, Asia, First World, Third World, North and South), nationalities (Chinese, Filipino, Indian, Japanese, Korean, Vietnamese), religions (Buddhist, Catholic, Christian, Hindu, Sikh), generations, and classes. But the political efficacy of this coalitional gathering in no way requires the ossification of either the label "Asian American" or its contents.

For instance, consider the construction of a "we" in discussions surrounding the inclusion or exclusion of Pacific Islanders in Asian American studies and community organizations. Many activists and academics alike interchange the appellation "Asian American" with "Asian Pacific Islander" (API), "Asian Pacific American" (APA), and other variations. The casual use of "Asian American" as an umbrella term is troubling. Merely adding "Pacific Islander" to an Asian American constituency does not properly address the interests and perspectives of Pacific Islanders. In fact, it helps to obscure the reality of underrepresented Pacific Islanders, while concealing the possibly divergent agendas between these two overlapping groups.[17] Application of affirmative action programs, immigration patterns, sovereignty movements, and citizenship issues are all differently relevant to Pacific Islanders and Asian Americans.[18]

As scholars and activists engaged in queer Asian American studies, how do we then construct identities and communities? We do so by vigilantly insisting that the history of racial and class formation in Asian American studies cannot be understood outside of representations of sexuality and gender and by vigilantly insisting that the end of the twentieth century marks a historical period for rethinking Asian American identity in terms of a shifting queerness, open and continuous in relation to possible and future resignifications.

Aliens in a Queer Nation

What does it mean for those of us in queer Asian American studies to claim membership in (a) Queer Nation?[19] What are the consequences of situating our struggles in terms of the nation or nationhood? What social sacrifices does citizenship in (a) Queer Nation imply—what concessions does that allegiance demand?

As the much cited, popular term "Queer Nation" implicitly suggests, homosexuality is never just about sex or sexuality. Queerness materializes within a concretized space, and it asserts itself in the material realm only through its intersection with a wide range of social differences, frameworks, and locations—the nation being just one of many manifesting sites. In the case of a term such as "Queer Nation," we must ask how ideas of nationhood and citizenship and how questions of domestic and global racism constitute the normative boundaries of a mainstream queer identity—the "typical" queer American citizen.

Thus far, we have focused our commentary on the emerging state of queer Asian American studies. Equally important, however, is the need for those of us invested in both queer and lesbian/gay studies to reevaluate our approaches to the study of sexuality in these fields—to question the insistent privileging of sex and sexuality as its primary and organizing principles. We believe that just as there is much work to be done on issues of sexuality in Asian American studies, serious consideration must be given to sex and sexuality in relation to other types of social alterities—notably race—in queer and lesbian/gay studies.

This type of cross analysis must be highlighted, given the tendency of these fields to imagine, conceive, and define sexuality in rather narrow terms. For instance, the editors of the influential *Lesbian and Gay Studies Reader* describe their primary goal as one in which sex and sexuality are centered and centralized:

> Without attempting to anticipate the outcome of that process [understanding the connections between sexuality and gender], we can still describe lesbian/gay studies by saying that it intends to establish the analytical centrality of sex and sexuality within many different fields of inquiry, to express and advance the interests of lesbians, bisexuals, and gay men, and to contribute culturally and intellectually to the contemporary lesbian/gay movement. (Abelove, Barale, and Halperin xvi)

The editors of this reader neither suggest what these "interests" might look like nor consider how the priorities of their textually unmarked lesbians, bisexuals, and gay men might conflict as a result of substantive or divisive differences modulated by race and class.[20]

For example, current debates on homosexuals in the military and on gay marriage and parenting have been shaped by mainstream lesbian/gay political organizations as an issue of civil rights—equality and parity for (white) lesbians and gays. Mainstream lesbian/gay organizations that configure their political agendas in this way must recognize that this claim on civil rights mimes historical racial civil rights struggles and intersects the current right-wing conservative assault on affirmative action as *special* rights for people of color rather than *equal* rights for all. Far from being immune to similar accusations concerning the coopting of special rights, mainstream lesbian/gay organizations must consider the particular political difficulties and contradictory agendas that national issues like gay marriage and affirmative action pose for individual queers of color who hold multiple affiliations to various political causes and for the politics of coalition building.

From racial, gender, and economic points of view, mainstream gay activists must also carefully reassess their declarations that the age of AIDS has ended.[21] Although it can be argued that the advent of new drug therapies—most notably protease inhibitors—has changed the meaning of an HIV diagnosis from death to illness for certain populations, access to medical care for the vast majority of HIV-positive individuals in the United States (who are not white with private medical insurance) and in other countries is severely limited. Given the fact that cases of HIV transmission and unprotected sex in this country continue to rise for young men of color despite such sanguine pronouncements, mainstream gay organizations must carefully consider the impact of racial, gender, and economic issues in their HIV and AIDS strategies.

Failure to undertake this task compromises the oppositional potentials of queer and lesbian/gay subjectivity. Thus, for example, the editors of *The Lesbian and Gay Studies Reader* focus on tracing the genealogy of gay/lesbian studies to feminism, delineating the field's theoretical debt through this common analogy: what feminism has done for the field of gender, gay/lesbian studies will do for the field of sex and sexuality.[22] But we fear that what gets rescripted in this conceptual alignment of feminism and lesbian/gay studies is the unproblematic positing of the universal (white) subject. As we ask of the coalitional "we" of queer Asian American studies, who are the "proper" subjects of feminism, and who are the "proper" subjects putatively represented by lesbian/gay studies?

It might be useful at this point to invoke the formidable body of scholarship produced by feminists of color such as Gloria Anzaldúa, Rey Chow, bell hooks, Audre Lorde, Chandra Mohanty, Cherríe Moraga, Barbara Smith, and Gayatri Spivak. Throughout the past two decades, these feminists of color, among others, have alerted us to the fact that one becomes a woman not only in opposition to men—not only through the axis of gender—but also along multiple lines of social and cultural differences: race, ethnicity, class, caste, national origin, citizenship, and age. To suggest otherwise would not only flatten out the notion of "woman" but also, in that very same process, center the white European middle-class woman as the unacknowledged and universal subject of feminism.

We might also extend the question of the "subject" of feminism to the field of lesbian/gay studies to suggest that one does not become queer merely through sex or sexuality—that one becomes queer in ways more complex than through simple opposition to a compulsory heterosexual matrix or the repressive machinations of the straight mind. To paraphrase Norma Alarcón, in cultures in which asymmetric race and class relations are a central and organizing principle of society, one may also become a queer in opposition to other queers.[23] To endorse the centralization of sex and sexuality in lesbian/gay studies without serious consideration of how other axes of difference form, inform, and deform the queer subject would be to ignore the corrective theoretical insights of Third World (difference) feminism. The invariable effect would be to cast the white, European, middle-class gay man as the unacknowledged universal subject of lesbian/gay and queer studies.

Our analysis, we must emphasize, does not merely suggest that the unacknowledged subject of lesbian/gay or queer studies is one who might be obliged to struggle against racism, sexism, or class oppression in addition to homophobia. We are not delineating an additive model of social inequity whereby queerness is augmented by supplemental notions of difference. On the contrary, our analysis means to underscore that our very epistemological conception of what it is to be queer cannot be understood without a serious consideration of how social differences such as race constitute our cognitive perceptions of a queer world, how sexual and racial difference come into existence only in relation to one another. To refer once again to our Stonewall example, it seems entirely necessary to ask how and in what ways queerness gains its very legibility and theoretical coherence through its management of racial difference. In this instance, race is not simply contingent—that is, it is not just another oppression that one catalogues onto the centralized term "homosexual." As both this example and our opening analysis of the unseen Asian American lesbian/imagined gay Asian American male indicate, sexuality and race cannot be brought into symmetrical alignment with each other. They are not commensurate oppressions easily catalogued or equated. Instead, the two share a constitutive and dynamic relationship, one whose dialectic combination often yields unrecognized, unacknowledged, and understudied configurations: the invisible Asian American lesbian, the hypervisible Asian American male sissy.

This project of considering race and homosexuality together is all the more urgent in light of the ways in which contemporary queer politics has shaped itself both inside and outside of the academy. As we have suggested through our discussion of AIDS, gay marriage, affirmative action, and terms like "Queer Nation," the potential for mainstream queer politics to recycle unproblematically punitive narratives of race, nation, and colonization is great. This is a recycling that demands sustained theoretical deconstruction. Moreover, the model of consensus to which many mainstream lesbian/gay organizations pay lip service when attempting to build coalitions across racial lines is often appropriated to further mainstream lesbian/gay agendas. The *Miss Saigon* incident is one example. The Lambda Legal Defense and Education Fund in New York organized a major fund-raising event around an arguably racist and sexist play, galvanizing Asian American lesbian and gay groups, as well as progressive Asian American and queer groups on both coasts to protest the show (see Yoko Yoshikawa's Chapter 2). As a political protest visibly dividing and uniting various social, racial, sexual, and political groups along multiple lines of difference and allegiance, the *Miss Saigon* incident exposes the rhetoric of coalition, consensus, and reciprocity in mainstream queer and Asian American politics as one in crisis and in serious need of theoretical and practical reconsideration.

This cooptation again raises complex convergences of racial difference and queer politics, and it brings to our attention the asymmetric social relations that propel our various and disparate causes. For groups like the Lambda Legal Defense and Education Fund and Queer Nation to enlist queers of color—to tout their presence in a public flourish of inclusion—without properly considering what race and ethnicity might entail in terms of their larger political agenda is to say that mainstream lesbian and gay politics desire queers of color on their own terms but are fundamentally unwilling to accommodate themselves to the terms of those others.

It is necessary for queer and lesbian/gay studies to interrogate how the straight mind naturalizes heterosexuality as the only possible, sensible, and desirable organizing principle by which society and social relations can function. It is no less necessary, however, to consider the ways in which this naturalization of heterosexuality comes only through the active management, suppression, and sublimation of other axes of social differences. If queer studies, as Michael Warner insists, "has an effect of pointing out a wide field of normalization, rather than simple intolerance, as the site of violence" (xxvi), we must remember that these processes of normalization most certainly encompass unspecified forms of social violence that have yet to be examined.

One such form of violence, as we have suggested, is the endless capacity of the lesbian/gay and queer movements to displace racial

difference into a matrix of sexual politics. At the end of the twentieth century, we can no longer afford to pitch the terms of our struggles as ones in which sex and sexuality, homophobia and heterosexism are the centralized issues of debate and liberation. We can
no longer accept the notion that considering race and homosexuality together drains the lesbian/gay and queer movements of its
political energies or social efficacies. We can no longer believe that
a desirably queer world is one in which we remain perpetual
aliens—queer houseguests—in a queer nation.

Q & A: An Overview

This book is divided into six parts, containing twenty-six chapters.
The collection closes with a reference section consisting of a selected bibliography and a resource guide of queer Asian American
organizations in the United States.

Part One, "Working Out," provides several concrete analyses of
queer Asian American political practices and movements for social
justice. Emphasizing both personal and collective experiences
around political organizing, these chapters provide critical insights into the problems of negotiating identity politics and coalition building across various generational, social, and spatial differences. Beginning with Karin Aguilar-San Juan's (Chapter 1) call
for a refusal to abandon the utopian project of social justice,
"Working Out" also explores queer Asian American agendas as
they conflict with the political priorities of mainstream lesbian/gay
organizations. From Yoko Yoshikawa's (Chapter 2) look at the politics of organizational fund-raising in relation to the 1991 *Miss
Saigon* benefit to Vera Miao's (Chapter 4) look at the politics of location with reference to New York's Day of Simultaneous Protests,
Part One implores us to think of successful coalition building in
terms of common goals and broad objectives. Ignatius Bau (Chapter 3) rounds out Part One by exploring methods of organizing
widespread coalitional action against right-wing initiatives such as
California's Proposition 187 in the face of seemingly insurmount-
able racial and economic differences.

The question of the queer Asian American body is developed in
Part Two, "Im/Proper Images," which explores the ways in which
normative visual cultures both sustain and undercut the identificatory possibilities for queer Asian Americans. The chapters in Part
Two all address the outer limits of visuality and identification,
whether with dominant images or even—as in Gaye Chan's case
(Chapter 8)—with a dismembered blond mannequin. In the 1990s
queer Asian American artists, as seen in Ju Hui Judy Han's interview
with Marie K. Morohoshi (Chapter 5), have worked diligently to

create a burgeoning body of queer Asian American film and video, while others, as Richard Fung (Chapter 7) shows, have vigilantly strived to deconstruct dominant visual stereotypes that configure queer Asian bodies in singular ways. Victor Bascara (Chapter 6) examines how an explicitly Filipino postcolonial narrative of cultural hybridity—of missionaries and movie makers—structures the very terms of intelligibility for the narrator of Michael Magnaye's video *White Christmas* to come out as "gay."

Part Three, "Keeping Records," investigates the status of personal history and collective historiography in the past conceptions, present configurations, and future incarnations of queer Asian American identity. Nayan Shah (Chapter 9) explores how we might address our continual desire for a concrete history when the overwhelming majority of historical genealogies seem to exclude us. Patti Duncan (Chapter 10) investigates how loss of history and "home" appear as symptom, disease, and pain. Part Three also examines how we approach past historical events to draw meaning for a present-day queer Asian American existence. For example, Eric C. Wat and Steven Shum (Chapter 11) convene an intergenerational group of Asian American gay men of diverse backgrounds and ages to discuss their involvement in political and social organizing in Los Angeles from the 1960s through the 1990s. The essays in Part Three meditate upon the conflicting intersections of the personal and the social, exploring how personal histories are overdetermined by larger narratives of the imperializing nation. As such, JeeYeun Lee (Chapter 12) discusses the attendant problems in our attempts to create a queer Korean American diasporic history and historiography.

Part Four, "Closets/Margins," explores the coming-out process against the social and psychic margins created by naming a queer Asian American identity. Russell Leong (Chapter 13) examines what it means for a man in the age of AIDS to become resigned that he will never find a "home." And Donna Tsuyuko Tanigawa (Chapter 14) explores whether the naming of a queer Asian American identity means inevitable splitting—a multiply fractured identity akin to a linguistic patchwork quilt. Sandip Roy (Chapter 17) explains what it means for us to come out not in the metropolitan centers of New York, Los Angeles, or San Francisco, but in the heart of the Midwest and in geographic margins of isolation. Because images and stories of male to female transsexuals are available more often than female to male experiences and stories, the representation of transgendered sexualities is more often focused on male than on female desire. Consequently, Diep Khac Tran, Bryan, and Rhode (Chapter 15) present a roundtable discussion among "F2M" (female to male) transsexuals. Jennifer Tseng (Chapter 16) presents a study of lesbian and gay male relations in a queer Asian American student organization at the University of California, Los Angeles. Both chapters focus on the process of coming out—the ways in which social groups and categories organize, stage, and discipline the naming of our desires.

Part Five, "Paternity," confronts the widespread stereotype of the Asian American male as "asexual" or "homosexual," what Frank Chin's *Aiiieeeee!* group of coeditors alarmingly labels as the "emasculated sissy" syndrome and what filmmaker Richard Fung (in Chapter 7's exploration of visual stereotypes) has noted as the persistent conflation of "Asian and Anus" in a Western cultural imaginary. The essays in Part Five, such as joël barraquiel tan's opening narrative (Chapter 18), explore not only the vexed identifications—lost and found—that we have with our own marked and fallible fathers but also the (dis)identifications that we undergo in relation to normative paternal symbols, religious and literary. You-Leng Leroy Lim (Chapter 21) examines whether one can find solace in religious faith outside of paternal judgment and fundamentalism and inside of difference. Focusing on the representation of Asian American and conventional white male bodies in literature by Frank Chin (Daniel Y. Kim's Chapter 19), Sui Sin Far (Min Song's Chapter 20), and David Henry Hwang (David L. Eng's Chapter 22), several chapters in Part Five carefully trace the ways in which symbolic identification with the name of the (white) father and his attendant demands—compulsory heterosexuality, whiteness, and the cohesion of the U.S. nation-state—can never quite be sustained, continually bleeding into a desire for the (white) father.

Part Six, "Out Here and Over There," focuses on queer Asian American identity in relation to diasporic concerns. The post-1965 demographic shift of the Asian American population from a U.S.-born to an ascendant model of immigrant identity calls for the reevaluation of a 1970s model of cultural nationalism (and its concomitant focus on domestic concerns) in order to reconsider transnational issues in Asian American cultural debates and criticism.[24] Part Six explores how considering queerness and diaspora together might allow us to trace the formation of U.S. racism and (neo)imperialism in both a domestic *and* a global context. Justin Chin (Chapter 23) examines what it means to come out "over there" where there are supposedly no queers to speak of. Mark Chiang (Chapter 24) explores how we read diasporic texts such as Ang Lee's *Wedding Banquet* in relation to national and cultural prohibitions against homosexuality, as well as in relation to transnational issues of global capital and the exploitation of Third World women. Ju Hui Judy Han (Chapter 25) investigates how an Asian American queer becomes a spy/suspect in his/her own "homeland." Jasbir K. Puar (Chapter 26) concludes the collection by examining whether the theoretical combination of diaspora with queerness necessarily yields a more perfect union or whether it (un)wittingly participates in the complicit rescriptings of nationalist projects (such as Hindu or Sikh religious separatism).

Collectively, these essays delineate what we hope will be recognized as a strong and vibrant queer Asian America.

NOTES

1. Our example is derived from conversations with Ju Hui Judy Han, whose current in-progress project, "Home Is Where the Shit Is," serves as its inspirational model.

2. We certainly do not mean to suggest that all short-haired, butch-looking Asian American women are lesbians.

3. We use "lesbian/gay" to describe the largely identity-based, post-Stonewall (see note 10) political and academic movements that arose in response to the dominant pathologizing medico-juridical discourse on the "homosexual." In its publicness, Rosalind Morris suggests, the notion of gay is often conflated with the issue of same-sex practices—practices that are often thought to be symptomatic of identity.

We distinguish "lesbian/gay" from the term "queer," which we consider to eschew a political platform based exclusively on sexual identity, sexual practices, and the polarization of homo- and heterosexuality. As Michael Warner points out, the term "'queer' gets a critical edge by defining itself against the normal rather than the heterosexual" (xxvi). Initially a designation causing terror and shame, "queer" in contemporary usage has been resignified in a rather capacious context—one that can be used simultaneously to discuss the politics of the personal, to question a spectrum of personal identities, to act against normalizing ideologies, and to resist the historical terror of social phobia and violence. We must remember that "lesbian/gay" and "queer" are not mutually exclusive terms. As Morris points out, gayness might constitute ideal, though not exclusive, grounds for queer practices, and, as Warner points out, queers can often be "lesbian and gays in other contexts—as for example where leverage can be gained through bourgeois propriety, or through minority-rights discourse, or through more gender-marked language (it probably won't replace lesbian feminism)" (xxviii).

While "queer" has been used as shorthand for a population of individuals with a stake in non-normative, oppositional politics, the term also homogenizes and thus erases certain racial and gendered differences (such as lesbian feminism).

4. See, for instance, Willyce Kim's *Curtains of Light* (1970), *Eating Artichokes* (1972), *Under the Rolling Sky* (1976), *Dancer Dawkins and the California Kid* (1985), and *Dead Heat* (1988); Barbara Noda's *Strawberries* (1979); Kitty Tsui's *Words of a Woman Who Breathes Fire* (1983); and Merle Woo's *Yellow Woman Speaks* (1986). Canyon Sam, Kitty Tsui, and Merle Woo were also members of Unbound Feet, a collective of six Asian American women writers and performers, which formed in 1979.

5. See, for instance, Wong 1–27 and the *Amerasia Journal* issue in which her article appears.

6. See Cheung 234–51 and E. Kim 68–93.

7. See Lowe, "Heterogeneity, Hybridity and Multiplicity" 22–44.

8. The most recent examples of anti-immigrant and multicultural backlash legislation in California are Proposition 187 and Proposition 209 (the so-called California Civil Rights Initiative). On the national level there is the Defense of Marriage Act, signed by Bill Clinton; the Immigration Reform and Immigrant Responsibility Act (H.R. 2022); and the *Rohmer vs. Colorado* decision, adjudicating Colorado's Second Amendment.

9. For a history of the rise of the Asian American studies movement, see Wei; for a study of Asian American coalition, see Espiritu; for a study of political organizing in the 1990s, see Aguilar-San Juan. Martin Duberman's *Stonewall* provides a brief history of the homophile movement preceding Stonewall and, based on six life histories, the events leading up to and following the riots. See also Deitcher.

10. There are various accounts of the flash points of the 1969 Stonewall riots. It is safe to say, however, that the numerous and diverging accounts attest to the fact that the start of the riot could not be attributed to any one cause or individual. African American and Puerto Rican drag queens, street kids, and butch lesbians all had a hand in the moment. See Duberman, Faderman, and D'Emilio.

11. Jennifer Ting's "Bachelor Society" 271–79 provides a convincing critique of the conflating of the sojourner and bachelor-community myths to produce a heterosexually deviant Chinatown ghetto. See also Wong, "Ethnicizing Gender" 111–29.

12. The phenomenon of paper sons occurred as a result of the 1906 San Francisco earthquake and fires, which burned down City Hall, destroying birth records. Consequently, Chinese male immigrants in the United States could claim citizenship, both becoming and having "paper sons." See Kingston. See also Chan's *Asian Americans* and Takaki's *Strangers from a Different Shore* for more detailed historical analyses of the phenomenon. In *Island*, Lai, Lim, and Yung record the poetry and history of Chinese immigrants during Angel Island detention.

13. The analysis of Lowe, Takagi, and Omi that follows is a condensed version of an argument elaborated in Eng's "Out Here and Over There" 31–52.

14. A recent example of critical work in Asian American studies is Leong's *Asian American Sexualities* anthology, which is a revised version of the 1994 special *Amerasia Journal* issue on gay and lesbian topics, "Dimensions of Desire." There has also been increased publication of queer novels and poetry and production of lesbian/gay films and videos in the 1990s. See the list of anthologies, fiction, and nonfiction in the Selected Bibliography at the back of this volume. See also Chapter 5, Ju Hui Judy Han's interview with Marie Morohoshi on film and video.

15. See, for instance, Spivak's immensely influential critique of identity politics and "strategic essentialism" in *The Post-Colonial Critic.*

16. Recent student strikes at Columbia University, Princeton University, Northwestern University, the University of Illinois, and the University of Maryland have led to administrative and faculty concessions including the hiring of Asian Americanists. In the University of California system, the dismantling of affirmative action in admission and hiring practices focused debate on the relation of Asian American politics to African American and Chicano concerns.

17. See Kauanui and Han 376–79 and Hall and Kauanui 113–18.

18. This is also true for various Asian American ethnic groups. For example, until the recent dismantling of affirmative action at the University of California, Filipino Americans were eligible for affirmative action programs at Berkeley, but Chinese, Japanese, and Korean Americans were not.

As editors, we have chosen not to use the designation "Asian Pacific Islander" (API). Instead, we encourage further examination of the intersection of and interaction between Asian American and Pacific Islander contexts. However, we have not imposed our views on contributors who use "API" or "APA" in their essays.

19. Queer Nation was the name of the political spin-off group from ACT UP.

20. Although their introduction is rather narrow in its conceptual pitch, the editors of *The Lesbian and Gay Studies Reader* include several essays that focus on the convergence of homosexual and racial differences.

21. See, for example, Sullivan 51–62+ and (for an incisive critique of Sullivan) Harper 5–29.

22. See the introductions to *The Lesbian and Gay Studies Reader* (Abelove, Barale, and Halperin); *Fear of a Queer Planet* (Warner); and "More Gender Trouble," the special issue of *differences* (Butler).

23. See Alarcón 356–69.

24. The issue of the transnational was always part of the field, for instance, in the critical attention of Asian American activists to the Vietnam War and U.S. imperialism in Asia.

WORKS CITED

Abelove, Henry, Michèle Aina Barale, and David M. Halperin, eds. *The Lesbian and Gay Studies Reader.* New York: Routledge, 1993.

Aguilar-San Juan, Karin, ed. *The State of Asian America: Activism and Resistance in the 1990s.* Boston: South End, 1994.

Alarcón, Norma. "The Theoretical Subject(s) of *This Bridge Called My Back* and Anglo-American Feminism." *Making Face, Making Soul: Haciendo Caras.* Ed. Gloria Anzaldúa. San Francisco: Aunt Lute, 1990. 356–69.

Butler, Judith. "Against Proper Objects." Introduction. "More Gender Trouble: Feminism Meets Queer Theory." Special issue. *differences: A Journal of Feminist Cultural Studies* 6.2–3 (Summer–Fall 1994). 1–26.

Chan, Sucheng. *Asian Americans: An Interpretive History.* Boston: Twayne, 1991.

Cheung, King-Kok. "The Woman Warrior Versus the Chinaman Pacific: Must a Chinese American Critic Choose Between Feminism and Heroism?" *Conflicts in Feminism.* Ed. Marianne Hirsch and Evelyn Fox Keller. New York: Routledge, 1990. 234–51.

Chin, Frank, Jeffery Paul Chan, Lawson Fusao Inada, and Shawn Hsu Wong, eds. *Aiiieeeee! An Anthology of Asian American Writers.* Washington, D.C.: Howard UP, 1974. New York: Mentor, 1991.

Deitcher, David, ed. *The Question of Equality: Lesbian and Gay Politics in America Since Stonewall.* New York: Scribner, 1995.

D'Emilio, John. *Making Trouble: Essays on Gay History, Politics and the University.* New York: Routledge, 1992.

Duberman, Martin. *Stonewall.* New York: Plume, 1994.

Eng, David L. "Out Here and Over There: Queerness and Diaspora in Asian American Studies." *Social Text* 52–53 (1997): 31–52.

Espiritu, Yen Le. *Asian American Panethnicity: Bridging Institutions and Identities.* Philadelphia: Temple UP, 1992.

Faderman, Lillian. *Odd Girls and Twilight Lovers: A History of Lesbian Life in Twentieth Century America.* New York: Columbia UP, 1991.

Hall, Lisa Kahaleole Chang, and J. Kehaulani Kauanui. "Same-Sex Sexuality in Pacific Literature." *Asian American Sexualities: Dimensions of the Gay and Lesbian Experience.* Ed. Russell Leong. New York: Routledge, 1996. 113–18.

Harper, Phillip Brian. "The Fetish of Normativity and the 'End of AIDS.'" *Social Text* 52–53 (1997): 5–29.

Kauanui, J. Kehaulani, and Ju Hui Judy Han. "'Asian Pacific Islander': Issues of Representation and Responsibility." *The Very Inside: An Anthology of Writings by Asian and Pacific Islander Lesbian and Bisexual Women.* Ed. Sharon Lim-Hing. Toronto: Sister Vision, 1994. 376–79.

Kim, Elaine. "Such Opposite Creatures: Men and Women in Asian American Literature." *Michigan Quarterly Review* 29 (Winter 1990): 68–93.

Kim, Willyce. *Curtains of Light.* Albany, Calif.: Self-published, 1970.

———. *Dancer Dawkins and the California Kid.* Boston: Alyson, 1985.

———. *Dead Heat.* Boston: Alyson, 1988.

———. *Eating Artichokes.* Oakland, Calif.: Women's P Collective, 1972.

———. *Under the Rolling Sky.* Oakland, Calif.: Maud Gonne, 1976.

Kingston, Maxine Hong. *China Men.* 1980. New York: Vintage, 1989.

Lai, Him Mark, Genny Lim, and Judy Yung. *Island: Poetry and History of Chinese Immigrants on Angel Island, 1910–1940.* Seattle: U of Washington P, 1991.

Leong, Russell, ed. *Asian American Sexualities: Dimensions of the Gay and Lesbian Experience.* New York: Routledge, 1996.

———, ed. "Dimensions of Desire: Other Asian and Pacific American Sexualities: Gay, Lesbian, and Bisexual Identities and Orientations." Special issue. *Amerasia Journal* 20.1 (1994).

Lowe, Lisa. "Heterogeneity, Hybridity and Multiplicity: Marking Asian American Differences." *Diaspora: A Journal of Transnational Studies* 1.1 (Spring 1991): 22–44.

———. *Immigrant Acts: On Asian American Cultural Politics.* Durham, N.C.: Duke UP, 1996.

Morris, Rosalind C. "Educating Desire: Thailand, Transnationalism, and Transgression," *Social Text* 52–53 (1997): 53–79.

Noda, Barbara. *Strawberries.* Berkeley: Shameless Hussy, 1979.

Omi, Michael, and Dana Y. Takagi, eds. "Thinking Theory in Asian American Studies." Special issue. *Amerasia Journal* 21.1–2 (1995).

Sam, Canyon, "Sapphire." *Lesbian Love Stories.* Ed. Irene Zahava. Freedom, Calif.: Crossing, 1989. 261–68.

Spivak, Gayatri. *The Post-Colonial Critic: Interviews, Strategies, Dialogues.* Ed. Sarah Harasym. New York: Routledge, 1990.

Sullivan, Andrew. "When Plagues End: Notes on the Twilight of an Epidemic." *New York Times Magazine* 10 Nov. 1996: 52–62+.

Takagi, Dana Y. "Maiden Voyage: Excursion into Sexuality and Identity Politics in Asian America." *Amerasia Journal* 20.1 (1994): 1–17.

Takaki, Ronald. *Strangers from a Different Shore: A History of Asian Americans.* Boston: Little, Brown, 1989.

Ting, Jennifer. "Bachelor Society: Deviant Heterosexuality and Asian American Historiography." *Privileging Positions: The Sites of Asian American Studies.* Ed. Gary Y. Okhiro, Marilyn Alquizola, Dorothy Fujita Rony, and K. Scott Wong. Pullman: Washington State UP, 1995. 271–79.

Tsui, Kitty. *Words of a Woman Who Breathes Fire.* San Francisco: Spinsters, 1983.

Warner, Michael, ed. *Fear of a Queer Planet: Queer Politics and Social Theory.* Minneapolis: U of Minnesota P, 1993.

Wei, William. *The Asian American Movement.* Philadelphia: Temple UP, 1993.

Wong, Sau-ling C. "Ethnicizing Gender: An Exploration of Sexuality as Sign in Chinese Immigrant Literature." *Reading the Literatures of Asian America.* Ed. Shirley Geok-lin Lim and Amy Ling. Philadelphia: Temple UP, 1992. 111–29.

Woo, Merle. *Yellow Woman Speaks.* Seattle: Radical Women, 1986.

in ma and grandma's generation,
we could not do it.
But you are the one
The Generation to do it
All our hopes and dreams
are placed on you

Overleaf: Erica Lee,
I Look the Same But Do Not Taste the Same,
detail photograph, 8 × 10 inches, 1994

1. Going Home

Enacting Justice in Queer Asian America
Karin Aguilar-San Juan

We will, in short, create fictions, not actual cities or villages, but invisible ones, imaginary homelands, Indias of the mind.—SALMAN RUSHDIE, *Imaginary Homelands*

The Problem of Authenticity

It is a funny thing to be writing an essay about going home when, at the moment, there is really no place I call "home." I was born in Boston but eventually left for Providence. I recently moved to southern California, which has always fascinated me. To go westward is, for an Asian American, to go home, in the sense that many Asian Americans have family in California, in Washington state, or farther west, in Hawai'i. But my immediate family is currently scattered around the Midwest.[1]

For many years, I have been concerned with the way we, as Asian American lesbians and gay men, think about going home.[2] Many of us simply cannot do so, at least not openly, because of the intolerance of parents, relatives, or friends who bristle at our "lifestyles." For too many of my friends, going home involves entering a closet of furtive whispers and private pain. Once I went with several AMALGM[3] members to a Boston suburb, where we had been invited by a friend to enjoy a sumptuous Filipino feast with her family. But since our host had not come out to her mother, we disguised ourselves by sitting around the living room in purposeful order: boy, girl, boy, girl. This superficially heterosexual arrangement made home a safe place for our friend, her mother, and ultimately for us. Without feeling threatened, we could continue our meal.

I am wary, here and in general, of portraying Asian American queers as being less able than other people to "go home." Home seems to bring forth intense and mixed feelings for everyone. It is not my intention to reinforce the idea that Asian Americans are somehow more squeamish about homosexuality, or sex, than is any other group. As far as I know, no one has systematically or by any standard measure compared homophobia in various racial and ethnic groups. But it is probably true that we feel that homophobia is most intense at home, wherever we construe that to be, because home matters the most. It seems that for many Asian Americans, home is a place where "Asianness" originates, a place made more compelling by the negation of an Asian American presence elsewhere. Often, we look to the future with anticipation, hoping that the next time we go home, we can be out.

But I do not want to feed into the notion that as *Asian* Americans, we are somehow always foreigners in America, longing for home in another faraway continent. That stereotype conjures up images of exotic aromas and spicy foods and languages that we do not speak (but that somehow we understand through some feat of intergenerational and international memory). Indeed, because of the popular belief that Asian Americans are never really "at home" in America, I find the concept of "going home" so much more interesting to explore.

This essay is a commentary on the difficulties that arise whenever we evoke the notion of "home," "experience," or "community" as a claim to truth,[4] originary places, authenticating devices, or the grounding of metaphors in social movement activism or cultural representation. My shorthand for this issue is the "problem of authenticity," which has been addressed in other ways by other writers, some of whom I cite throughout this chapter. Authenticity is a problem because it suggests that our actions or our representations are true, universal, or just, without explicit criteria by which these actions or representations may be assessed. As I see it, the problem of authenticity particularly confronts communities organized around some aspect of identity. But it is not a problem that is the sole territory of identity politics. Claims to truth are the basis of any social movement; ultimately, the claim to justice is what drives movements for social change. My intention here is to provide some illustrations of the problem of authenticity as I see it, to offer some explanations for why it persists, and to suggest a possible solution. Throughout my discussion, "queer Asian America" is much more than a simple designation of a population group; I use the phrase to refer to the process of building a sense of collectivity, which, in its most utopian moment, strives toward community.

Home

In the winter of 1994, a group of Filipino American lesbian activists in the San Francisco Bay Area established The Beth and Vangie Legal Defense Fund (I refer to this group as the Fund). Beth and Vangie were fired from their jobs in a human rights agency in Manila when they became lovers. They filed a complaint with the Philippine National Labor Relations Commission and sought legal counsel from an organization called the Women's Legal Bureau. A network composed of thirteen lesbian and women's groups in the Philippines formed Advocates for Lesbian Rights (ALERT) to support Beth and Vangie's case against their former employer. The

Fund, established in San Francisco, opened chapters in other cities in order to garner U.S. support for Beth and Vangie in the form of money, petitions, letters of protest, and publicity. By June 1995, the Fund had produced a newsletter, *Breakout,* published an article featuring a Fund activist in a local lesbian newspaper, and collected a sizable sum of money. The Fund appealed to a collective sense of outrage and indignation at the unfair treatment of our two "sisters" in the Philippines.

Beth and Vangie's new relationship had become known among their twelve coworkers through a breach of confidence. Intra-office gossip eventually cost them their jobs and their privacy. Their employer, the Balay Rehabilitation Center, made the following accusations, citing them as reasons for the firing: (1) for Vangie this was an extramarital affair, (2) Beth and Vangie had "flaunted" the affair in the office, and (3) Beth and Vangie had lobbied for support. Balay also dismissed the four board members who had abstained from the decision to fire the two women.

I was fortunate to attend a benefit party for the Fund on one evening that summer. I had already spent the first part of that day "becoming Filipino" in San Francisco: accompanied by a good friend who helped me practice my broken Tagalog, I had visited a farmers' market full of Filipino shoppers and, later, helped my friend prepare a huge pot of chicken *adobo* and several pans of *inihaw ng bangus* (grilled milkfish) to take to the benefit party. Having spent my day this way perhaps increased my sensitivity to the complex dynamics that can sometimes inform U.S. organizing around issues in the Philippines. At several points during the house party, I became concerned with the way the Fund was positioning itself vis-à-vis Beth and Vangie and, by extension, vis-à-vis lesbian rights in the Philippines (let alone the rest of Asia).[5]

The primary purpose of the party was to collect money. People were invited to donate anywhere from $6 to $50 at the door. Food was free, but soda, beer, and wine were sold at a makeshift bar at the back of the patio. The atmosphere was congenial, and I think most of us were happy to be contributing to a worthy cause. When the night finally turned cold, we congregated inside the house, and the Fund members presented the story of Beth and Vangie. The story was punctuated by quotations from a letter written by Balay's director, Flora Arellano, to a San Francisco human rights commissioner named Jeannette Lazam. The letter seemed full of half-baked excuses for institutionalized homophobia. Arellano suggested, for instance, that Balay could not be homophobic, since Beth had been hired—and even promoted—despite Balay's knowledge of her sexual orientation. Arellano also implied that Beth and

Vangie's relationship was somehow in conflict with Balay's "family systems approach." Finally, Arellano referred to Vangie's husband and daughter as "the aggrieved party," whose rights were being unjustly overlooked. At that moment, I felt embarrassed for Arellano, and for the state of lesbian (and gay) rights in the Philippines in general. Maybe other people felt the same way; by the end of the evening, the Fund had collected $1,000.

It seemed that Balay's understanding of discrimination had missed the boat entirely. Several years ago in the United States, proponents of the Second Amendment to Colorado's state constitution saw gay rights as "special rights." In a sense, they wanted to restrict gay men and lesbians from the equal protection clause of the U.S. Constitution. When the Supreme Court struck down the amendment, it was a gay rights victory, but not because gay people won special rights. In fact, the Court did not have to recognize anything "special" about homosexuality in order to rule that the Constitution protects all citizens from discrimination, regardless of sexual orientation or any other criteria.[6] In the excerpts from Arellano's letter, I did not detect any statement showing recognition of the meaning of homophobia. Arellano's reference to Vangie's husband and daughter as the party whose rights had somehow been violated sounded to me a lot like Colorado's Second Amendment or, worse, like the Christian Right's obsession with protecting the "sanctity" of the nuclear family. Still, many Filipino families are, if not sacrosanct, at least closely knit, so I could imagine a lot of hurt feelings among the friends and relatives of the people at Balay.

Later I picked up a copy of Arellano's letter. Once I had read it more closely, I felt troubled by the ease with which we had demonized Balay the night of the party. Certain choice phrases had been taken out of context, allowing Arellano—and the Philippines in general—to be portrayed as culturally repressive and backward. The way we had jumped scale from the relatively small personal interactions among the Balay staff to the international correspondence between Arellano and Lazam to the organizational efforts of the Fund to protect "lesbian rights in Asia" made me nervous. I felt that we (as supporters of the Fund, San Francisco's Filipino dyke community, and possibly even all queer-friendly Americans) had endowed ourselves with all the powers of self-actualization and enlightenment that traditionally have been associated with modernity and Western civilization.

Worsening my fears about the missionary zeal I thought I glimpsed that evening, a friend paraphrased for me a comment that she had overheard during the party: "If worse comes to worst, we'll just bring Beth and Vangie here." I'm not sure whether "here" meant the apartment, the city, or the country. But, in any case, the words encapsulated in my mind the fantasy of "home" as a safe haven for lesbians. It was a loaded statement, full of misleading implications. It was as if we could build our community simply by kidnaping and bringing "home" oppressed queers from all over the world.

The idea of bringing Beth and Vangie here might have been only a silly fantasy in the heart of one overly zealous activist. The fantasy is interesting, though, because of what I see as its colonial impulse: the desire to extend to Beth and Vangie all the freedoms and the luxuries we are thought to enjoy as lesbians in the United States.[7] I wondered to myself, with some sarcasm, *Could we be assuming that every lesbian in the Philippines wants a chance to be out in the Mission[8] and to be free to eat hippie-style tofu, fly a rainbow flag, wear freedom rings, and march under an "international" banner every year at the Gay Parade?*

Lost in the zealousness is a sense of community participation and struggle. What makes living in the Mission and marching at the Gay Parade so thrilling is not (I hope) the opportunity to buy more queer paraphernalia. I suspect that what makes it possible, even for a moment, to fantasize about queer life in the United States is that there are debates and discussions among lesbians and gay men that allow us to build a sense of shared purpose. When it is good (for example, when our daily lives are unencumbered by stereotypes and hostility), it can be really good. When it is bad (for example, when someone gets fired or loses custody of his or her kids), it can be made better by the efforts of people who come together to fight for recognition. For me, what makes "home" a desirable metaphor is the utopian prospect of building a community. Such interaction always involves a bit of insecurity and uncertainty. That, to me, is the joy of queer social life.

Truly, I do not know where in the world Beth and Vangie would be the happiest. Perhaps no place would be absolutely wonderful—or absolutely bad. But I would have been happier at the Fund benefit if we had engaged in a more thoughtful group discussion about home, family, homophobia, and colonialism. That night, I was concerned about the implication that our sense of lesbian freedom is universal. I do not want to be implicated in what seems a condescending gesture of showing lesbians in the Philippines the "true" path to freedom. This is a gesture I have associated with those U.S. feminists who reinscribe colonialist relations by subordinating the experience of Filipina feminists to the rubric of Third World feminism, thereby preserving the evidently neutral territory of feminism for themselves.

In some respects, the effort to support Beth and Vangie meshes curiously with the political trajectory of the Filipino colonial subject. In this trajectory, the Philippines is our first home, our starting point—but America is our final destination. The margin and the center are in this way clearly demarcated. By viewing Asia as the site of a denial of lesbian rights and America as the site of their defense and assertion, the Fund organizers verged dangerously close to reproducing a colonial myth. Coming out as coming home to the United States would be a sapphic twist on that myth.

Experience

growing up / for a long time / lost childhood
we began writing in secret
when confession, communion, confirmation
confession
taught us to lie

—ELSA REDIVA E'DER, "La Puente"

Just the other day, a young Filipino American man invited me to contribute to an anthology on Filipino American politics. He explained that he and his colleagues have become frustrated with the lack of Filipino American voices in public life and public discourse, an omission that seems particularly egregious given the relative size of the Filipino population in the United States (in 1990 we were the second largest Asian American group). He and I chatted briefly on the phone about the kinds of issues he would like to see covered in the book. Then he said (and I paraphrase), "And, if I'm not mistaken, you're a lesbian, right? Because right now, we don't have anyone writing about that." There was something so final in his designation of me that I was caught off guard. I thought to myself, *He's right, isn't he? What kind of lesbian am I, anyway? Am I the kind of lesbian he means?*

In retrospect, I take no offense at his comment, which I see as an honest invitation to talk about what it means to be a lesbian, a Filipina American lesbian, an activist, and so on. But there is an implication in the question "You *are* a lesbian, right?" that being a lesbian (whatever was meant by that) commands an authenticity of experience—not just any experience, but one that is, from a heterosexual perspective, a marginalized and mysterious experience. By answering, "Yes" to his question, I would be asserting myself, making myself known, validating the life I have so far lived. By answering, "No," I would be disavowing a category called "the lesbian experience." In the end, no matter how I answered the question, something would be deeply wrong.

The appeal to an authentic experience is one way that Asian American lesbians and gay men confer upon ourselves the power of knowledge. Jeffrey Escoffier notes in his essay "Community and Academic Intellectuals: The Contest for Cultural Authority in Identity Politics" that knowledge, whether based in community or in academia, helps to legitimate certain representations and interpretations of political and social life. The knowledge we gain by experiencing queer Asian American community life is devalued in the public sphere, a sphere where Asian Americans are either gangsters or businessmen, hustlers or whores, and none of them is in control of his or her own sexuality. For this reason, acknowledging our experience in terms of our sexuality is a central part of our community-building processes.

At the same time, however, appealing to an authentic experience can make a misleading claim to truth. Feminist historian Joan W. Scott explores this problem in her essay "The Evidence of Experience." She points out that in seeking to give voice to a silenced category of people, we may fail to reveal the reasons for that silencing in the first place. As she puts it, "The evidence of experience then becomes evidence for the fact of difference, rather than a way of exploring how difference is established, how it operates, how and in what ways it constitutes subjects who see and act in the world" (399–400).

I decided not to contribute to the anthology on Filipino American politics, mostly because I am still thinking through my position with regard to Filipino American studies and, more generally, with regard to the Filipino American community. Still, I worry that my contribution to the book could have served as a "lesbian fact" in a larger collection of "facts" about Filipino American life. In that case, nothing about the points of view of the three editors (who are all Filipino American men) would have needed further interrogation: every perspective would have been construed to have an equally objective basis. The truth is that including my voice (or the voice of any other writer with a claim to the lesbian experience) inadvertently reveals that all perspectives are not given equal footing. But by adding a voice from the margins, what never gets air time is the social process by which certain categories (for example, Filipino American life) are assumed to be "central" while others (for example, Filipino American *lesbian* life) are located "naturally" on the margins.[9]

In using this example to launch my criticism of the appeal to an authentic experience, I should be clear: the broadening of perspective, even one based on the "evidence of experience," is not a worthless endeavor. But I think, along the lines presented by Scott, that incorporating a marginalized perspective in a larger work that does not ask *why certain perspectives are marginalized to begin with* is not sufficient. In my mind, this approach—and I am not assuming that the anthology in my example will inevitably exemplify it—lends itself to cooptation by the status quo.

Ironically, by speaking up, we can marginalize ourselves. The danger of the appeal to authenticity is that even when individuals who feel marginalized shape the agenda, the idea of a center—whether out there or in here—can come alive. In the past few years, several collections of writing have been published that showcase some dimension of the Asian American queer experience. One of these is Sharon Lim-Hing's *The Very Inside: An Anthology of Writing by Asian and Pacific Islander Lesbian and Bisexual Women.* I like the eponymous title poem by Indigo Chih-Lien Som; it sends a warm shiver up my back. The last part of it goes

> for you I will jump & stay
> up there like a hollywood special effect
> . . . .
> I will not come
> down, but cry scratching at your starry
> kitchen table until I have written a love
> song for you
> . . . .
> a song that tastes
> like your very inside (188)

It is not out of a lack of appreciation for this poem or for any of the other one hundred pieces included in the book that I make this link to the problem of authenticity. It is, instead, to ask a question about the general project to publish queer Asian American anthologies (like Lim-Hing's or the collection in which this chapter is included): what do we (for instance, Asian and Pacific Islander lesbian and bisexual women) expect to find by looking at (or, in this case, tasting) the "very inside"? Presumably, there *is* a truth there,[10] one to which "we" have special, privileged access because it belongs to "us." But are there not many "truths" to be found by traveling into and across the contours of our Asian and Pacific Islander lesbian and bisexual worlds? My point in stating this rhetorical question is that no single "truth"—no matter how internal to our social circles or our individual psyches—can serve as a central authenticating principle for all of us. Indeed, this essay is an attempt to ground queer Asian America in a way that does not require these multiple truths to be collapsed into one overarching reality.

Lim-Hing's collection (and others like it) makes a gesture toward inclusivity that in my mind suggests an authenticating claim. The long subtitle, *An Anthology of Writing by Asian and Pacific Islander Lesbian and Bisexual Women,* is necessitated by that gesture, since any shorter combination of words would presumably leave out a portion of our world. The impulse of the anthology *The Very Inside* is to extend itself toward the universe.[11] But that is the same impulse, extended from some other originating point, by which Asian and Pacific Islander lesbian and bisexual women were cast as outsiders in the first place.

The problem of authenticity arises whenever some dimension of experience is left out despite a concerted effort to include everyone.[12] In the end, no matter how inclusive we try to be—as editors of collections or as activists in social movements—at some point the line we draw must be exclusive of someone, because it is not possible to anticipate the infinite variety of human experiences or the social and historical circumstances that surround us. I see two ways around this problem. The first is simply to acknowledge the lines that we draw. The second calls for deeper transformation, a world without lines. I would bet that in practice we will—and must—draw some lines. But I hope that we can also imagine a more ideal world, where those lines won't matter. That image should remind us that our work—building a sense of collectivity, moving toward justice—is never really done.

Community

We are gay and straight and bisexual, older and younger, differently able and temporarily able-bodied; and we share an unquenched hope for the survival and sanity of the human community. Believing that no single people can survive being only for itself, we want a base from which to act on our hope.—ADRIENNE RICH, "If Not with Others, How?"

How we, as gay men and lesbians who trace our roots to Asia, think about "home" and "experience" matters most when we try to designate the boundaries of our queer Asian American community.[13] Asian American history makes efforts toward queer community—especially those that depend on a notion of home and family—particularly vexing. Asian Americans often have been treated as perpetual foreigners, seen as outsiders no matter how many generations ago the first immigrants arrived. That is why the distinction between Asian and Asian American is often lost on non–Asian Americans. Over the past century, Asian American community building has been shaped by state-regulated labor markets, exclusion acts, antimiscegenation policies, internment, and resettlement.[14] When queer Asian America places home, the family, and community into question, it does so against a historical backdrop that is already littered with such questions.

As if blind to these questions, queer Asian Americans often draw lines in the sand, by referring to "original" places or to "real" feelings in an effort to fix the location, shape, and meaning of community— and our own positions within it. Such references often seem urgent, inescapable, and even desirable; they signal who is "in" (and who is not) and provide guidelines for community building (including the creation of community institutions, the planning and carrying out of community events, outreach to newcomers, and joint activities with other community groups). In my view, the problem of authenticity arises when community-building efforts among Asian American lesbians and gay men treat "home" or "experience" as preordained facts and thus mimic the exclusive and hierarchical frameworks that make efforts toward visibility and recognition necessary in the first place.

At a recent meeting of LAAPIS (Los Angeles Asian Pacific Islander Sisters), women wrestled to draw some lines in the sand. But I'm not sure anyone saw it that way. One of the reasons for calling the meeting was to discuss the possibility of hosting a weekend retreat for Asian American[15] lesbian and bisexual women from around the United States. (In recent years, at least two such retreats have been held in other cities.) Naturally, the discussion turned to where the retreat would be held and who would be invited to it. I saw lines being drawn in two ways: geographically, as women tried to assess the relationship of Los Angeles to other regions of the country; and socially, as they considered the place of transgendered people in the LAAPIS community. The lines matter, because some people are more free to cross them than others are.

Speaking of crossing lines, I recently moved to the Los Angeles area, which has fascinated me for many years. One of the things that most astounds me about the region is how people relate to geographic space. Everyday activities like working, shopping, and socializing take most people onto major freeways, far beyond the neighborhoods where they reside. Not owning a car, one resident told me, is an indication that you are living below the poverty line. Taking a bus, something I used to do on a regular basis in Boston, is an all-day commitment in Los Angeles.

So I was surprised to discover that, despite the regional habit of driving everywhere (even to the corner store), people who live in Los Angeles rarely visit nearby Orange County. Orange County has a reputation as a politically conservative and culturally sterile place. Basically, they say, it's boring. A recent series on Irvine in the *Orange*

County Register reported that it's a city of beige homes, an aptly colorless image. Apparently, upper- and middle-class white people (and the Asian Americans who can afford to join them) live there because they think it is safer and quieter than Los Angeles.

I make frequent trips to Orange County, because I am doing research on Vietnamese American community building. The region is important to me, because almost half of the entire Vietnamese American population lives there, many concentrated in the working-class city of Westminster. There is a feeling among the people I have interviewed in Orange County that Los Angeles is very far away. The social distance between residents of Los Angeles and Orange County appears to be mutually reinforced for economic, political, racial, and cultural reasons.

When a LAAPIS member asked if women from Orange County would participate in the retreat, I thought about this social distance. In a way, San Francisco and even New York City seemed a lot closer to many of the women in the room than Orange County did. At least in theory, many Asian American lesbians and bisexual women (not to mention gay men) must live there. I think LAAPIS could gain a lot by outreach to Orange County. For example, O Môi, a Santa Ana–based Vietnamese American organization, has found it critical to hold at least a few group events in Orange County. Because the LAAPIS women did not seem to recognize the class issues associated with car ownership, they may have overlooked the fact that some people, even if they want to join, may find Los Angeles physically inaccessible.[16]

Another argument for groups like LAAPIS to pay attention to Orange County is that Orange County can be a closet. For those Asian Americans in Orange County who feel comfortable coming out only when they are away from home, where friends and family won't know, Los Angeles offers a safe haven. Efforts to make them welcome would surely be appreciated.

The issue of participation in LAAPIS events by transgendered people (TGs) is another example of drawing lines in the sand. Who gets included in community often depends on who is there to advocate for themselves. In O Môi, TGs participated right from the start, not out of an abstract principle about inclusion but because people were there to fight for themselves. When O Môi members (mostly lesbians and bisexual women) got together to hash out what they had in common besides being Vietnamese, one person suggested, "It's about feeling like a woman." So when another person declared, "But I don't feel like a woman," the problem of authenticity (to use my terminology) reared its ugly head. After all, what on earth does it mean to "feel like" a woman?

The exclusion of TGs from queer Asian America—whether by intent or by oversight—indicates to me that the body is not necessarily the site of home. "Feeling like" a woman or a man is a good way to put it, because the phrase suggests that the appeal to an authentic experience cannot depend on biological categories (understood by most people as "natural" ones) but, instead, more aptly refers to a subjective expression of desire.[17] Bringing TGs into the picture not only problematizes gender and sexuality; it points to ways that gender and sexuality have become naturalized, almost normalized, dimensions of social life, even in queer Asian America.

When I realized how complicated gender and sexual identity are, I wondered for a moment why I bother to call myself a lesbian. Didn't I mean to be more transgressive—perhaps a bit more queer? It seems that lesbian and gay organizing is just the tip of a very huge iceberg. If queer Asian America is interested in challenging the confining categories of gender and sexuality imposed upon us by the status quo, then queer Asian American activists are going to have to do something about the ways that those categories are enforced on us and on other people. I think we must continually reconsider the bases upon which we include some people—but not others—in our community and cultural work.

In the end, O Môi members decided that their commonality lies in "object choice" (that is, a love for women). It's not always a satisfying choice: when butch lesbians face off against female-to-male TGs, who gets called "sir" can be a seriously touchy issue. Unlike O Môi, LAAPIS has come up with a different proviso regarding transgendered people. They want to include only male-to-female TGs, their argument being that the organization is for women or, presumably, people who want to live as women.

Either way, a can of worms has been opened. Evidently, every solution raises ambivalent feelings, even among the TG community. I suspect there is no "correct" solution, and my intention here is not to offer one. Instead, I want to caution against belittling the issues of inclusion and exclusion—for example, treating transgenderism as a personal predicament only. If queer Asian America has learned nothing else, it has learned that the challenge to sexual normativity is always more than a personal dilemma. The norm of heterosexuality is a social fact that guides hierarchical social practice. Thus, Lorber warns, "Even if some future utopia were not gendered, sexuality is likely to be organized with norms of appropriateness, if not with moral strictures, in the service of community interests. . . . Whoever has the power in the community will be influential in determining what sexualities will have moral hegemony" (79).

Enacting Justice in Queer Asian America

We who occupy the interstices—whose very lives contain disparate selves—
are, of necessity, at home among groups that know little of each other. . . .
We have a deep hunger for a place in which we can be, at one and the same
time, whole and part of something larger than ourselves. Our knowledge
and desire may at times bring us to action.—YOKO YOSHIKAWA, "The
Heat Is On *Miss Saigon* Coalition"

Community building in queer Asian America requires vigilance regarding the notions of home and experience, especially regarding
the ways these concepts may close off further discussion about
who's in and who's out of the community and why. (This is not to
imply that there is a model leader or organization that can bypass
the problem of authenticity to bring all of queer Asian America directly to a copacetic destination called "justice.") The stories I tell
in this essay put forth instances in which that discussion should be
encouraged, because—although tireless efforts have produced important results (events held, money raised, networks established,
anthologies published)—the truth claims that are inherent in the
various references to home and experience may pose stumbling
blocks for future community building.

Perhaps there is no way to avoid the problem of authenticity
completely as I have laid it out here. Collective action inevitably
pushes toward exclusive boundaries and universalizing gestures.[18] The purpose of this essay has been to suggest the ways
that those boundaries might be redrawn or those gestures made
less universal. I hope to ameliorate the problem, not to circum-
vent it.

I will not abandon the project of enacting justice. Enacting justice in queer Asian America involves a rearticulation of the utopian
possibilities of community building against the disenabling impulses of the dominant social order. Too many scholars have given
up on this project, preferring instead to "theorize the subject" by
detailing the myriad ways in which we might be thought to exist.
Some of those theories are compelling, but some of them seem
pointless and detached. Worse, some blur important distinctions
between action and negotiation, inclusion and representation,
power and powerlessness. Too many activists have given up as well,
focusing instead on individual expression and narcissistic explorations of victimization, leaving justice and other lofty ideals to the
scholars.

Enacting justice in queer Asian America is a particularly vexing
task, because precisely at the moment in which we wish to speak, the
problem of authenticity prevents us from doing so. We resist label-

ing; yet without a label, how can our views and perspectives be given a meaningful context? Ironically, we need to fix ourselves as a stable (read: knowable, nameable, solid) community in order to point a finger at the practices and ideas that deny us that stability from the start.

Like many others who refuse the privileges associated with heterosexuality, queer Asian Americans come out and go home only at the risk of great loss, sometimes terror, even death. Gestures toward home and family seem both necessary and impossible: necessary for a sense of completion, impossible because family requires heteronormativity. Yet, because no closet can be home, there is no choice for queer Asian America but to push toward the other side. Much is at stake in building a queer Asian American community. Precisely because of the high price at which queer Asian America purchases a sense of home, our motivation toward building community and enacting justice must be even stronger.

NOTES

Acknowledgments: This essay has several originating moments. In the summer of 1995, I attended a benefit fundraiser for Beth and Vangie, two lesbians in the Philippines who were fired for being gay. The event sparked for me a series of questions about the notion of "home," which became part of the substance of this essay. Months later, I wrote a short review (161–64) of *The Very Inside*, edited by Sharon Lim-Hing, for *Amerasia Journal*. The many varied pieces in that book struck me as desirous, in some way, of home. In the spring of 1996, as a graduate teaching assistant, I gave a guest lecture in a class called Social Movements and Social Change at Brown University. My talk focused on what I termed "the problem of authenticity," a concept that became the analytical framework for this essay. I thank all of the individuals who helped me to develop these thoughts in any or all of these originating moments.

1. When my grandmother Ramona Aguilar recently passed away in the Philippines, I decided to dedicate this essay in memory of her. I often wonder what trail I might trace back to her.

2. I direct my discussion of home primarily toward Asian American studies, where the questions of home and family, home and colonialism are already framed in terms of race and nation. If I were to direct the discussion toward queer studies, I would want to anticipate the issue of Asian American specificity, by making reference to home not as the originating point for our "difference" (from a white norm) but as a place from which Asian Americans are always already negated, made invisible, excluded. But that is a topic for another essay.

3. AMALGM stands for the Alliance of Massachusetts Asian Lesbians and Gay Men. The Boston-based group is currently called QAPA, the Queer Asian Pacific Alliance.

4. Professor Bob Lee of Brown University introduced me to this concept, which he used to describe the potential dissonance between historiography and history as it is "actually" lived.

5. I do not intend to diminish the importance of the support for Beth and Vangie or to portray my views of the campaign as superior to or more informed than those held by anyone else. This narrative is intended only to illustrate how the idea of "home" can be evoked in organizing for social change.

6. I thank David L. Eng for the Second Amendment example.

7. This is not to deny the observation, made by several Fund members that night, that Asian American lesbians are subject to racism. Still, the fantasy implies that being queer in the racist "Amerika" is still better than being queer in the Philippines.

8. The Mission is a predominantly Latino neighborhood in San Francisco, where quite a few lesbians and gay men of color live.

9. Some activists still talk about the "double" and "triple" oppression of women and lesbians of color. The idea that each label adds another layer of oppression sometimes unintentionally reinforces white heterosexuality as the norm and everything else as marginal. I hope that queer Asian American activists reevaluate the idea of layers of oppression, perhaps starting at "home."

10. After a fire destroyed Gertrude Stein's neighborhood in Oakland, California, she is said to have remarked, "There is no there, there."

11. This is only to suggest one possible reading of the anthology's overall message. A more thorough discussion can be found in my recent review of the book in *Amerasia Journal* (161–64).

12. In fact, transgendered people (including cross-dressers and transsexuals) are not included, a matter that I address herein.

13. I am grateful to Susette Min for helping me to tie this section into the rest of the chapter.

14. For an in-depth discussion of the legal history behind Asian immigration, see Hing. For insights into labor migration and its effects on community building, see Chan.

15. I have purposely dropped the term Pacific Islander here; the inclusion of Pacific Islanders as part of the queer Asian American community puts a different twist on the problem of authenticity that would require extensive argument. Unique historical relationships to the United States and to Asia tie Pacific Islanders (especially indigenous peoples) to a set of debates over tradition and cultural experience that are particularly charged. For an important discussion of the way Hawai'i has been portrayed as a timeless mystery, see Buck.

16. I am indebted to writer and organizer Diep Khac Tran for these insights.

17. In her book *Paradoxes of Gender,* feminist sociologist Judith Lorber points out that the male female gender dichotomy is so entrenched in our political, legal, and ideological frameworks that we can hardly es-

cape it, even when reality begs to differ. In a chapter provocatively entitled "How Many Opposites? Gendered Sexuality," Lorber explores the
multiple statuses we assign to people on the basis of anatomical features
and gendered social roles. On the basis of genitalia alone, there are
five—not two—sexes: unambiguously male, unambiguously female,
hermaphrodite, male-to-female transsexual, and female-to-male transsexual. Lorber sees (at least) three sexual orientations: heterosexual,
homosexual, and bisexual. And she sees many more categories of gender displays, emotional bonds, group affiliations, and sexual practices.

18. I thank Joshua Gamson for his comments on this point.

WORKS CITED

Aguilar–San Juan, Karin. "Review of *The Very Inside*." *Amerasia Journal* 22
(1996): 161–64.

Buck, Elizabeth. *Paradise Remade: The Politics of Culture and History in
Hawai'i*. Philadelphia: Temple UP, 1993.

Chan, Sucheng. *Asian Americans: An Interpretive History*. Boston: Twayne,
1991.

Escoffier, Jeffrey. "Community and Academic Intellectuals: The Contest
for Cultural Authority in Identity Politics." *Cultural Politics and Social
Movements*. Ed. Marcy Darnovsky, Barbara Epstein, and Richard
Flacks. Philadelphia: Temple UP, 1995. 20–34.

Hing, Bill Ong. *Making and Remaking Asian America Through Immigration
Policy 1850–1990*. Stanford: Stanford UP, 1993.

Lim-Hing, Sharon, ed. *The Very Inside: An Anthology of Writing by Asian and
Pacific Islander Lesbian and Bisexual Women*. Toronto: Sister Vision, 1994.

Lorber, Judith. *Paradoxes of Gender*. New Haven: Yale UP, 1994.

Scott, Joan W. "The Evidence of Experience." *The Lesbian and Gay Studies Reader*. Ed. Henry Abelove, Michèle Aina Barale, and David M.
Halperin. New York: Routledge, 1993. 397–415.

2. The Heat Is On *Miss Saigon* Coalition
Organizing Across Race and Sexuality
Yoko Yoshikawa

The heat is on in Saigon
The girls are hotter 'n hell
One of these slits here
Will be Miss Saigon
God, the tension is high
Not to mention the smell

—Opening lyrics to *Miss Saigon*

Demonstration #1, 6 April 1991

Someone up there was rooting for us. It was perfect weather for a demo—cool, caressing, fresh—as good as spring evenings get in New York City. Moving toward the theater, we were a huge, motley mass of five hundred or so, waving signs, chanting—loud, formidable, tough. This was *the* place to be seen and to see if you were a lesbian or gay man of color politically active in the local gay and lesbian community, a white gay man or lesbian committed to fighting racism and sexism, or a leftist Asian or Pacific Islander anywhere along the sexual continuum. We, the organizers, were ecstatic. Not until that moment did we know how much support we would gather in our protest of the Lambda Legal Defense and Education Funds's *Miss Saigon* benefit.

Months before, members of the Asian Lesbians of the East Coast (ALOEC) and of Gay Asian and Pacific Islander Men of New York (GAPIMNY) had learned that two major lesbian and gay community institutions were planning to use *Miss Saigon,* Cameron Mackintosh's Broadway musical, as their annual fund-raiser extravaganzas. One of them was the Lambda Legal Defense and Education Fund (LLDEF), a national law organization that champions lesbian and gay rights. The other was New York City's Lesbian and Gay Community Services Center. We felt outraged at these plans, as we saw *Miss Saigon* as the latest in a long line of Western misrepresentations of Asians, perpetuating a damaging fantasy of submissive "Orientals," self-erasing women, and asexual, contemptible men. As Asians and Pacific Islanders who experience the racism and sexism showcased in *Miss Saigon,* we called upon Lambda to drop the fund-raiser. Lambda, however, citing its fiscal bottom line, refused to do

Reprinted from *The State of Asian America: Activism and Resistance in the 1990s*, ed. Karin Aguilar-San Juan (Boston: South End Press, 1994), with permission from the publisher, South End Press, 116 Saint Botolph Street, Boston, MA 02115.

so. Undaunted, we formed a coalition and organized two demonstrations, the first on 6 April 1991 against the Lambda fund-raiser, and the second on 11 April, the opening night of the show.

On 6 April a block or so before the theater, we were stopped by police, intent on keeping us where we could not fully see or be seen by the theatergoers. The rumor was that Tom Stoddard, then–executive director of LLDEF, had warned the police that he expected a large demonstration—and possibly violence. While we moved, amoeba-like, across the street to face the theater, the cops closed in. They hauled away six men, two of whom were monitors and active coalition organizers.[1]

The arrests infuriated us. We considered them an excessive exercise in intimidation. In effect, Stoddard drew a line between "law and order"—Lambda's well-dressed, overwhelmingly white, mainly male donors—and us, mostly yellow and brown-skinned, kept at bay by the cops.

Just minutes before 8 P.M., two donors gave their $100 tickets to us. A quick huddle, and Milyoung Cho and I decided to use the tickets for an impromptu act of civil disobedience. We took off into the enemy zone. Whispering in a deserted bathroom, we hastily planned our action.

The opening number was dazzling—and loud. The musical opens in a brothel in Saigon, where prostitutes vie for the title *Miss Saigon*. U.S. soldiers buy raffle tickets; Miss Saigon will be the prize. But I was not following the songs—this lusty dance of glistening legs and dark breasts, of ogling eyes and lathered lips in uniform mesmerized me. It pulled me in, as soft porn will. But I also felt sickened and alienated. The show was designed to seduce, flooding the senses with a 3-D fantasy—specifically targeted at a heterosexual western man's pleasure center.

Rumor had it that Jonathan Pryce, a Caucasian British man and leading actor, was close to a nervous breakdown, unnerved by all the controversy and criticism of his role as a Vietnamese pimp. We sat and nervously waited specifically for him. As Pryce entered the set and launched into song, we blasted into ours—deliberate discord, whistling, yelling at the top of our lungs: "This play is racist and sexist; Lambda is racist and sexist!"

Kicked out and back on our side of the street, Milyoung addressed the crowd via bullhorn, saying that what we did in there was only possible because of everyone out here—our demonstration moved two donors to rethink their support of Lambda. With their tickets we brought the coalition's rage from the streets into the theater. It was as though Milyoung and I had acted as the claws of a large, potent animal, infiltrating the theater's inner sanctum and ripping away all illusions of innocence. The roar that swept over us as we, unscathed and exultant, emerged from the theater, was a roar of sheer power, concentrated and raw.

Setting the Stage, December 1990

Aluminum plans were half-filled with pad thai, kim chee, chirashi-zushi, egg rolls. When I walked into my first coalition meeting, about two dozen people were on the futon couch and all over the floor, eating, talking, digesting. I felt shy and intimidated. Most of the women were members of ALOEC, the men from GAPIMNY. The men were mostly young, good-looking, and physically entangled—arms flung around shoulders, legs entwined, one man leaning back into another's embrace, and someone's hands playing idly in another's long hair. This easy physical intimacy between Asian and Pacific Islander men moved me: I had seen men on the streets of Shanghai leaning into each other, close, but never here, in this country.

By then, *Miss Saigon* was already notorious for casting Pryce in a role that called for an Asian or Eurasian actor. In London, Pryce had been acting in yellow-face, with prosthetically altered eyelids and tinted makeup. In the summer of 1990, as advanced sales for the show's Broadway run were racking up millions of dollars, Actors' Equity, the U.S. actors' union, called for the "engineer" to be recast with an Asian American when the show moved to New York. The media labeled the union's demand "artistic censorship," and rallied to support Mackintosh, the producer. When Mackintosh threatened to keep *Miss Saigon* off Broadway entirely, Actors' Equity backed down, unwilling to endanger the profits and jobs *Miss Saigon* would offer.

Our discussion after that first meeting centered on the show's theme and lyrics. Our faces were somber as Gene Nakajima summarized the plot and quoted some of the words used to describe Asians: "greasy Chinks" and "slits." *Miss Saigon* is the opera *Madame Butterfly,* created by Giacomo Puccini in 1904, updated and reworked for post–Vietnam War popular consumption. In *Madame Butterfly,* a U.S. naval officer settles in Nagasaki, Japan, with a lovely courtesan known as Madame Butterfly (Chocho-san). Promising to return soon, he sets sail, and she scans the harbor daily, rejecting all other suitors while she waits. Years go by. One day his ship sails in, and he disembarks with his new, white wife on his arm. Madame Butterfly cannot bear the sight and kills herself.

In a memo submitted in late February 1991, Angelo Ragaza, then a former temporary worker at Lambda, urged his coworkers to examine the "orientalist" significance of both the opera and the musical:

Westerners, bent on expanding their empires until there remained no territory left to expand into, were particularly interested in complex, centrally controlled Asian societies. These societies tended to be more tricky to infiltrate, politically and
commercially. Among them, Japan was, and remains, perhaps the
most notorious. . . .

Butterfly is a woman who can only exist for a man, not for or
by herself. She symbolizes a Japan who cannot join the modern
world without America's "help," and an "East" which has no identity without the benediction of the West. Everything about Butterfly's demise sublimates Western frustration about Eastern im-
penetrability. From her defloration by an American military
official to her ritual suicide with a dagger, Butterfly's tragic death
reasserts the primacy of Western virility and, in the mind of the
spectator, erases the challenges to that virility posed by the East.
Put another way, "Madame Butterfly" is constructed on wishful
thinking. (6–7)

Miss Saigon portrays the doomed romance of a U.S. soldier,
Chris, and a Vietnamese prostitute, Kim. In Saigon, Chris meets
Kim at a brothel. They spend one night together and fall in love.
The next day, U.S. forces abruptly pull out of Vietnam, and Chris is
forced to leave without her. He returns three years later with his
white, U.S. wife, Ellen, to look for Kim and the son Chris conceived
with her. Kim, meanwhile, ever faithful to Chris, was forced to flee
Vietnam after killing a loathsome government official who was
pressing her to marry him. Kim finally is reunited with Chris in
Bangkok, only to die in his arms, having killed herself so that Chris
and Ellen will raise her son in the United States.

Virtually the entire twentieth century—and its myriad assaults on
the cult of white male supremacy—separates *Madame Butterfly* from
Miss Saigon. During that period, East Asian nations have forced
Western nations to contend with them as military and economic
peers: with North Korea and North Vietnam (and the dreaded
shadow of Communist China) as Cold War enemies, and with
Japan, former Axis aggressor, recently refashioned as a global financial heavyweight. In this postcolonial era, the West is no longer
unquestionably supreme. These developments have led to a nostalgia for white European racial and cultural supremacy. *Miss Saigon*
resurrects a myth that serves the Western empire in the late twentieth century: abandoned by the white man, the "Oriental" woman
will voluntarily self-destruct.

True, *Miss Saigon* is only a night's entertainment. A few hours of
froth—at $100 a pop—will not a racist make. With the proper dose
of irony and detachment, a viewer could perhaps be humored by

this show. But is it harmless? Hardly. "Miss Saigon" is yet another name to add to the roster of pop culture stereotypes: Suzy Wong, Charlie Chan, Fu Manchu, "Chink," and "Gook." *Miss Saigon* contributes to an entrenched system of racist and sexist images that straitjackets relationships between Asians and Westerners. This system is backdrop to increasing incidents of violence against Asians and Asian Americans across the United States, and paves the way for exploitation in massage parlors, mail-order bride businesses, and Asia-based tourist industries where women, children, and sometimes men are sold as commodities.

At stake in *Miss Saigon* is how those who control the means of representation and reproduction choose to define people of color and non-Western cultures, and to what ends. *Miss Saigon* rewrites the Vietnam War, pulling a sentimental love story from the carnage of carpet bombing, My Lai, and Agent Orange like a rabbit from a hat. Vietnam becomes just another exotic backdrop, good for a shot of nightclub sleaze and a real live helicopter liftoff. Mackintosh and company spiced the racism of "Madame Butterfly"—a white man's wet dream—with the endorphin-pumping antics of Rambo and came up with a new version of an old story of exploitation to feed into the money-making machines of Broadway. The bottom line is profit, and in a racist and patriarchal society, pliant, self-effacing geisha girls and despicable Asian pimps and traitors sell quite profitably.

While we organized against *Miss Saigon* that winter, the United States, led by President George Bush, invaded Iraq. The rhetoric employed by Bush and company to drum up support for the war sheds light on how *Miss Saigon* falls in with a national syndrome: simplistic beliefs about other cultures and non-Christian "natives" rationalize imperialism and aggression. Via mass media, Operation Desert Storm sold us glory and glitz, yellow ribbons and "smart" bombs, of an "all-American" winning team, out in the desert, fighting the good fight against the dark, ungodly, and upstart Saddam Hussein. Similarly, by serving up racist images of Asian servility, powerlessness, and depravity, *Miss Saigon* prepares the palate for the neoimperialist policies advocated by former President Bush. Racist pop culture stifles the possibilities of understanding or compassion across racial or national lines.

The Coalition's Organizational Roots

Dozens of other groups no doubt discussed organizing initiatives in other overheated apartments all over the city that December 1990. A good number probably never saw the light of day. Our effort, however, weathered the winter, took root, and burst into bloom in spring. The Broadway production of *Miss Saigon* certainly merited public criticism and debate. It was our organizing that brought the problematic themes of the play itself to the public eye.

That first potluck heralded a new political alliance between a number of mostly young New York City Asian lesbians and gay men. Before the inception of GAPIMNY, a year or so before, there had been no organization of politically active gay men to match and work with ALOEC. The GAPIMNY-plus-ALOEC combination had vigor: we knew we were pushing open a new and unique space, making community for those who have been marginalized as queers in a straight world, and Asians in a white one. As we came together across gender, we developed an openness toward difference and a flexible negotiating style that served us in good stead as we built our coalition.

A key factor was that we had enough lead time (from December to February) to develop cohesion and strength as a core group. By no means was that easy. After the first couple meetings, Mini Liu, Milyoung, and I would rush through the cold streets of Chinatown, heading for the subway back to Brooklyn, and kvetch about "those men": how fractious and immature "they" were, how "they" did not know how to conduct themselves in a meeting.

As time went by, relations improved. Our meetings became more efficient, although they were always long and frequent. We began to work as a team and to take on organizational roles. James Lee, for example, was archivist and point-person for all flyers, press releases, and our expanding database. I facilitated meetings. Those among us with long histories as activists in the New York Asian American community provided much-needed level-headedness and pragmatic knowledge. A number of the "younger" members had been influenced by queer activism generated in response to the AIDS epidemic. There was an in-your-face, no-shit style to our confrontations and organizing that has always been a characteristic of ACT UP.

Right up until early March, we focused on convincing Lambda and the Community Services Center to cancel their use of *Miss Saigon* as a fund-raiser, not on protesting the play itself. We called on the gay and lesbian community to deal with its institutional racism, and those who responded were men and women, mostly of color, committed to creating a community in which all lesbians and gay men, regardless of color, could find safe haven. They gave our struggle breadth and force. The core group pulled on various threads of friendships and working relationships in the community, and our coalition grew strong at the center of those tangled skeins.

From our base in the lesbian and gay community, we gathered the force and momentum to make our issue visible. We did not go beyond that community until late February, when we decided to take on *Miss Saigon*'s official opening. Only after we were sure that we wanted to make our position on *Miss Saigon* known to the general public, did we actively reach out to Asian and Pacific Islander communities in New York.

I flung myself into this undertaking. It fed a deep hunger in me for community and challenge. All of us in the core group had to deal with the question of how, and in what, do we ground ourselves as the coalition and its goals grew. We learned that we could depend on each other and find our strength there. We recognized in one another a stubborn, outlaw cunning and resilience, knotted ourselves a rope of sometimes grudging but usually wry affection, and tied ourselves in. It was when my grip on that rope loosened that I most likely found myself drowning.

Confronting Lambda, 19 February 1991

As Lambda's fund-raiser was scheduled for April, and the Center's was not until October, our first goal was to persuade Lambda to cancel its benefit. In December, we wrote a letter to Lambda in which we set forth our concerns about *Miss Saigon* and called upon it to discontinue the fund-raiser. The organization responded with a civil but unequivocal no. We arranged a meeting to discuss the issue further.

On 19 February, seven people from Lambda's board, staff, and management met with about a dozen of us, at a long table. Encircling us, along the walls, sat people that we had invited to attend: friends, lovers, and allies from lesbian and gay men of color organizations, and progressive Asian groups.

We stated our position in an opening statement:

What does it mean for Lambda, a civil rights organization that claims to represent *all* Gay men and Lesbian women, to meet its annual budget with images of us as prostitutes and pimps, "greasy Chinks" and "slits"? . . .

We call upon you to recognize that Lambda's use of a racist and sexist play is blatantly hypocritical and unprincipled. The monies you raise from *Miss Saigon* will disappear by the end of your fiscal year, but we contend every day with the exploitative and dehumanizing stereotypes and violence perpetuated by *Miss Saigon*.

We call upon Lambda to recognize its responsibility as an organization of cutting-edge civil rights litigation, to put itself on the line for anti-sexist, anti-racist activism, in solidarity with all of us committed to social change. (ALOEC and GAPIMNY)

The meeting was contentious. Tom Stoddard, Lambda's executive director, explained that it was difficult to pull out, as Lambda had already invested in the fund-raiser, and it was counting on the proceeds, which would be 10 percent of its annual budget. We countered that *Miss Saigon* could ultimately cost Lambda far more in terms of its standing in the gay community. One (white male) board member, volunteered his opinion that *Miss Saigon* is not racist—a (white) friend saw it in London and said so. Carol Buell, another board member, began a sentence with: "Well, when *Miss Saigon* is dead and buried . . ." and Milyoung interrupted, "Men yell 'Suzy Wong' at me in the streets now and that came out twenty years ago!" Ron Johnson, an African American board member, spoke soothingly, sympathetically, of "your pain," and proposed awareness-raising forums on racism for Lambda's donors to be offered in conjunction with the fund-raiser. Tsuhyang Chen, a member of our group, shouted the words "Faggot!" "Dyke!" and asked, in the shocked silence, how they would feel if people were paying money to hear those words used to describe gay men and lesbians. Why, then, is it so hard for you to understand our position vis-à-vis a play in which Asians are called "greasy Chinks" and "slits"?

The meeting was the galvanizing kick we needed to move our campaign up to the next level. Lambda refused to cancel, and we began planning our demonstration for its fund-raiser. Those members of the community who participated in that first meeting with Lambda became the first and most stalwart members of our multiracial coalition. Coming face-to-face with Lambda's resistance and creating a forum for our anger pulled the core group of Asian and Pacific Islander lesbians and gay men together as nothing had before.

It was as though all the reasons anyone ever participates in political organizing were made evident during that meeting. We formed a group that we could trust, solidly knit in our understanding of the issues and goals, but loose and diverse enough to allow a range in tactics (some people on our side of the table were more confrontational than others). I felt that I could step out, and risk speaking beyond what I would ever have been able to say alone, because I was with allies who would hear me and be there to back me up if I could not go on. Many of us who are marginalized by virtue of our color and sexual orientation must silently swallow racist or homophobic remarks, institutionalized bigotry, violence, and the threat of violence, almost daily. What we swallow twists our bowels, poisons our bodies, affects our loves and lives. Collectively, for once, we set up a situation in which we could say, *directly* to the people who angered and hurt us, what they were doing and how they were accountable.

A few days after our meeting, Stoddard let us know by fax that Lambda would not cancel its fund-raiser. The core group of Asians met to discuss our next step, and, hot with anger, we decided to storm Stoddard's office. We marched in, about a dozen strong, and crowded around his desk. The discussion was angry, polarizing, intense. That half-hour had a totemic significance for me; it was as though, talking to and facing that red-faced, loud-voiced figure across the desk, I was standing up to all the white male authority I had ever bowed to in silence before. Stoddard's face metamorphosed to my father's face, as I broke the taboos instilled so well in me as eldest daughter of immigrant Japanese: do not disobey; do not talk back.

Building a Coalition Within the Lesbian and
Gay Community, February to March 1991

Lambda attempted to address our concerns by sending its donors a copy of the statement we had presented at the first meeting and offering refunds to those who wished to return their tickets. This did not satisfy us, and we launched a two-pronged strategy: continue pressuring Lambda to cancel, and greet its theatergoers with a demonstration if it did not.

Our meetings and committees became multiracial. Members of ACT UP, Brooklyn Women's Martial Arts, Gay Men of African Descent, Kambal sa Lusog, Las Buenas Amigas, Latino Gay Men of New York, Men of All Colors Together, Other Countries, Queer Nation, Salsa Soul Sisters, South Asian Lesbians and Gay Men, We Wah and Bar Chee Ampe, among others, joined.

We had meetings and phone conversations with the staff at Lambda. Seven staffpersons, all women, signed a letter to the board and management urging them to reconsider canceling and offering to take salary cuts to offset any loss of funds that doing so could incur. Lambda's public education coordinator, a Latina activist named Mariana Romo-Carmona, resigned in protest.

On the other coast, California's Gay Asian and Pacific Alliance and Asian Pacifica Sisters put pressure on Lambda's Los Angeles office.

In support of our struggle, Audre Lorde, an African American lesbian feminist poet who has since passed away, refused to accept the Liberty Award from Lambda and did not attend the presentation ceremony. Her response to Lambda's decision to use *Miss Saigon* was:

> It was a damned foolish, naive, insensitive thing for Lambda to have done, and again, since I understand why it was done, it makes me furious, it makes me furious!
>
> Until the real nugget of what racism and sexism is all about comes through to the white lesbian and gay community, this thing is going to keep happening all over again. Until every single person in every single organization realizes that people of color, gay

or straight, are constantly being misnamed, are constantly being misidentified, and that if you are going to deal with any piece of culture with people of color, you must go to that community and ask: What do you think of this? And that goes from *Dances with Wolves* to *Miss Saigon.* (Lorde)

In March, coalition members met with the board and management from the Lesbian and Gay Community Services Center. This meeting, unlike the one with Lambda, was amicable and productive. The Center is a truly New York City–based organization, with stronger ties and commitment to the local gay and lesbian community. We had more lead time as the Center's benefit was not until October. The Center witnessed the community's anger in response to Lambda's refusal to cancel and decided to pull out.

Our position stirred strong feelings. At our forum on *Miss Saigon* at the Center on 29 March, a stack of anonymous flyers was found outside, accusing the coalition of being homophobic. The *Village Voice*'s only mention of this issue echoed that accusation:

> Aren't you tired of hearing about a show that hasn't opened yet? Tough. The latest on [*Miss Saigon*], which finally begins previews March 23, is that two gay Asian groups—Asian Lesbians of the East Coast and Gay Asian and Pacific Islander Men of New York—are up in arms over the show's racism and sexism. Are they picketing the authors, the directors, the producer, the theater? No, they're criticizing Lambda Legal Defense and Education Fund and the Lesbian and Gay Community Services Center, two of the 250 nonprofit organizations (including the Pearl S. Buck Foundation) selling benefit tickets to *Miss Saigon.* Sounds like sophisticated, more p.c.-than-thou gay-bashing to me. (Shewey)

These comments uncovered a disturbing assumption: when lesbian and gay people of color criticize the white gay male establishment, they are "gay-bashing." This implies that one must be white to be gay. And that Asian lesbians and gay men are close kin to skinheads, cruising the Village, looking for "faggots" and dykes" to beat up.

The divided feelings of the community found outlet in the letters section of *Outweek,* a weekly magazine that ceased publication that summer. Our message was helped by the sharp exchange: the issue was hot, and one way or the other, people gave it thought. *Outweek*'s editors and commentator Michelangelo Signorile lambasted Lambda for its position on *Miss Saigon,* but a number of their readers did not. Some challenged our analysis of *Miss Saigon,* saying that the show actually criticizes U.S. involvement in Vietnam. Others were frustrated or saddened by what they termed infighting, asking why we should do this to Lambda, when it has done so much for all of us in the realm of civil rights.

We found support among lesbian and gay activists of color and white people committed to fighting racism and sexism, because the issue spoke to the unequal distribution of power and privilege within the lesbian and gay community. As they do in mainstream society, white men hold a disproportionate amount of institutional power in the queer community. Gay white men sit on boards or head up a number of community organizations and often help determine priorities and programs. In the allocation of resources such as AIDS funding, or the absence of programs that battle breast cancer, people of color and lesbians have found that their concerns and needs are not automatically given equal shrift.

In calling upon Lambda to withdraw from its benefit, we drew our line: will you claim as your own our concerns as Asians who, like you, belong to this community? In a larger sense, this is what happens in the United States every time a minority group demands a withheld right or attacks the discriminatory status quo. But when members of a marginalized group accuse other members within the same group of marginalizing them, they hit a land mine. Some members of the community may rush to its defense, sounding the alarm that they have been betrayed from within. They fear the community will splinter into ineffectual fragments, or that others will pounce upon this weak link. What, they ask, will happen to the real issue—our struggle for recognition and equal rights in society-at-large?

The core group broke a taboo: we rocked the boat, hard. We would not wait until the larger struggle was won. What use are future gains to us if we are not full members in the community that exists now? What is this "community" anyhow? We transgressed—derailed "the struggle," aired dirty laundry—because we were staking a claim to a community of our making. Those who saw that joined us. Fifteen activists,[2] of color and white, described this undertaking in a letter addressed to Lambda in *Outweek*:

> We repeat our message to you and all other groups where white men dominate: We can no longer give our time and energy and spirit and lives to those who support our oppression by their racism and sexism. We want a movement where we can bring our whole selves—all of our concerns for freedom—to the organizing table.
>
> There is no tyranny of the oppressed; there is simply the strong call for justice and equality from those who increasingly understand that all oppressions are connected and single issue/single oppression approaches will never bring lasting social change. . . .

You are left with many years of work ahead of you to try to figure out how to overcome your current reputation for upholding
a white heterosexual male view of the world, while we are marching toward a new kind of organizing, a deep and true movement
of social change for all of us. ("Letter to Lambda")

*Within the Asian and Pacific Islander
Community, March to April 1991*

The second demonstration piggy-backed the first. We began organizing for it in late February, when we decided that by supple-
menting our original coalition with members of New York's Asian
and Pacific Islander communities, we could ensure a respectable
turnout against the show on opening night. Our plan was to use
opening night as the forum to register publicly our opposition
to the show itself, proving that we were not just gunning for
Lambda.

Our first new ally in this initiative was the Asian Pacific Alliance
for Creative Equality (APACE), an organization of Asian theater
artists who had organized against *Miss Saigon* in 1990 over the casting issue. We were soon joined by others, including Youth for
Philippine Action (YPA), the Coalition Against Anti-Asian Violence, the Japanese American Citizen's League, the Pan Asian
Repertory Theater, the Chinese Progressive Association, and college students' associations.

They pitched in. Veena Cabreros-Sud read an extraordinarily
powerful speech, which she and other YPA members had written for
our forum at the Center. Ding Pajaron launched her own fight to
educate other parents and administrators at her daughter's private
school about *Miss Saigon,* to convince them to cancel their own *Miss
Saigon* fund-raiser. (In the end, the Bank School went ahead with
it.) Lawyers from Asian and Pacific Islander organizations negotiated with the police at the demonstrations and provided counsel.

The Asians and Pacific Islanders we recruited looked to our
coalition and saw leaders who were Asian, as they were. They saw a
struggle that affected them as Asian and Pacific Islander peoples
and joined it. It should have been that simple. But it was not. We
felt threatened. In the lesbian and gay community, Asians and Pacific Islanders had naturally led the opposition against a show that
was racist toward Asians. But now, that role was up for grabs—after
all, they were Asians too.

We in the core group were quick to suspect the new members of
attempting to erase or dismiss the coalition's lesbian and gay origins and membership. We all, as lesbians and gay men, had directly
experienced the conservatism and homophobia of our own Asian

and Pacific Islander communities. Simultaneously, we felt a fierce loyalty toward our multiracial gay and lesbian allies and needed to assert the lesbian and gay roots of the coalition even as we moved away from it.

The closer we came to opening night, the more we were deluged with media requests for interviews. Yet we were divided on the thorny question of who should represent the coalition. There were a few Asians and Pacific Islanders, such as Peter Chow from Asian Cinevision, who were more experienced in presenting a historical and critical perspective on productions such as *Miss Saigon* to the media. However, we were not prepared to give the fleeting space our organizing had wedged in the public eye to people who had not been integral to the organizing since the beginning.

Would they have assuaged our distrust if we had clearly articulated it? Perhaps. On occasion, some of the Asians and Pacific Islanders were impatient with our relative inexperience with the media and decentralized process. There were also those who may have wished to exploit the coalition for their own organization's interest or personal gains. But I recall no outright instances of homophobia.

Our coalition building in the Asian and Pacific Islander community stumbled over sexual identity. They were not gay, and, therefore, they could not belong. We framed our organizing such that there were in essence two separate groups: gay and lesbian, Asian and Pacific Islander—moving toward two distinct demonstrations. Only in the last week and at the demonstrations, when we were all caught up in the power of what we had wrought, did the coalition become truly one.

Demonstration #2, 11 April 1991

The 11 April demo was less tightly organized and attended. It was less multiracial, more Asian, and more sober. We in the core group were still recovering from the first demonstration and found this one anticlimactic. Opening night was on a weekday and started early—6:30 P.M. People straggled in late, having been tied up at work or assuming that the show would start at 8 P.M. The police cordoned off small pieces of pavement, and herded us into small pens, effectively diminishing our collective force. New York Police were around the corner in full regalia, mounted on horses, waiting for their cue to burst onto the scene. As the demonstration was smaller than that of 6 April, the show of police was overkill.

But how the media swarmed! It was a feeding frenzy of cameras and microphones. All the major networks slotted us as their top story on the evening news that night. And then there were CNN, the *Post,* the *Daily News,* the *New York Times* nonlocal edition, National Public Radio, and so on.

Our two minutes of fame consisted of an Asian talking head mouthing a rapid analysis: *Miss Saigon* is racist and sexist in the stereotypes it parades of Asian women and men as either self-sacrificing geishes or slimy pimps. And yes, we are concerned that Cameron Mackintosh hired a white actor for an Asian role, but, to go further still, we call for challenging and three-dimensional roles for Asian actors in the entertainment and theater industry today.

The primary significance of the second demonstration was that we transmitted the collective voices and faces of Asians and Pacific Islanders, contorted with anger, to society at large. We broke through the ceiling that separates the concerns of subcommunities from mainstream awareness and gave those who were watching a glimpse—of just the tip—of an iceberg.

What we managed to say was certainly not untrue or insignificant. It is just that so much was not said. TV framed the event: the Asian community, monolithic, united, rises up to denounce the injuries of Broadway. No mention was made of our organizing process, no questions were asked about who we were. Why should they? They saw our Asian faces.

The further our organizing took us from the lesbian and gay community, the more asserting our sexuality became a political act. To be a lesbian or gay man in a society that is as homophobic and violent as the United States is to fight for your right to live and love when people might want you dead. To be "out" as lesbians and gay men on an issue that affected us as Asians and Pacific Islanders would show others that we *are* everywhere.

But the media was not interested in tackling that aspect of our coalition. At one point an exasperated TV reporter asked James Lee off the air, "What do lesbians and gay men have to do with protesting *Miss Saigon?*" A link between two such groups was too far-fetched for them. Only one piece about the lesbian and gay leadership was ever published in a mainstream paper. Written by Ying Chan, it was buried deep in the *New York Daily News,* and came out days after the demonstration. Peter Kwong wrote an article about our organizing for the *Village Voice* that never saw publication. Both reporters are Asian and have written extensively about New York City's Asian and Pacific Islander communities.

What we were flew directly in the face of mainstream assumptions about Asians. That Korean grocers are racist, that Asians always excel in math, that Oriental women make good wives, for example—those things are known. But nowhere in their roster of stereotypes was a place for angry, articulate, *queer* Asians. It was too much of a stretch for mainstream society to understand that we could be more than their cardboard cutout Asians, that we could instead be complex individuals with divergent sexualities and multiple allegiances—just like them.

Conclusion

What, in the end, did we really do? *Miss Saigon* is still on Broadway. We never seriously thought we could close it down, although some of us certainly fantasized about a few well-placed stink bombs. Lambda vowed to be more sensitive regarding issues that affect people of color. But when Tom Stoddard resigned from his position as executive director, they hired another white man, despite our lobbying efforts for a person of color or a woman.

The coalition, pared down to its lesbian and gay constituency, plowed on for about a year following the demonstrations, pressing various community organizations to address actively the needs and concerns of people of color and women in their decision making, hiring policies, and programmatic emphases. Finally, it just fizzled out. People left town or became involved in other consuming issues: HIV and AIDS, violence against Asians and Pacific Islanders, relationships, their own physical survival.

Our coalition pointed the way to a possible future: where a complex identity is not only valued but becomes a foundation for unity. We who occupy the interstices—whose very lives contain disparate selves—are, of necessity, at home among groups that know little of each other. We know what others do not about reconciling differences in our own lives and the mutable nature of borders. We have a deep hunger for a place in which we can be, at one and the same time, whole and part of something larger than ourselves. Our knowledge and desire may at times bring us to action: we push the parameters of existing communities wide open and cause the struggles of different communities to overlap and meld. In the tangle that ensues, we may also be midwives of vital coalitions.

This can be done only by claiming all of ourselves, with integrity, in community. At the first demonstration, James Lee taped a neon pink triangle to his leather jacket, emblazoned with the words: "San Francisco-born Gay Man of Korean Descent." On any other night, he could have been bashed for that. But that night, his back was covered. Gray-haired Japanese American wives and mothers and brash young white men from Queer Nation marched side by side. Dykes in dreads, campy queens, leftists of all persuasions: we owned Broadway.

NOTES

Acknowledgments: I have not mentioned many people who were important to the coalition. Among them are Bill Burns, June Chan, John Chin, Lei Chou, Sally Covington, Charlie Fernandez, Ben Geboe, Manolo Guzman, Curtis Harris, Scott Hirose, David Housel, Bert Hunter, Marla Kamiya, Don Kao, Ann Kwong, Mini Liu, Ming Ma, John Albert Manzon, Lance McCready, Gene Nakajima, Alice Ro, Robert Vazquez Pacheco, Vondoro Wilson-Corzen, and Lisa Yi.

1. Monitors Haftan Eckholdt and Joe Pressley as well as activists Chris Hansen, Simon Howard-Stewart, Karl Jagbundhansingh, John Kusakabe were charged with disorderly conduct. The police beat both Kusakabe and Pressly, who are men of color.

2. The letter was signed by Beth Richie, Suzanne Pharr, Val Kanuha, Chris Hansen, Helen Zia, Rebecca Cole, Kelly Kuwabara, Sally Cooper, Dion Thompson, Stephanie Roth, Robert Reid-Pharr, Rick O'Keefe, Tony Glover, Manuel Guzman, and Ann Kochman.

WORKS CITED

ALOEC and GAPIMNY. Statements of members. Read by John Manzon and Yoko Yoshikawa. 19 Feb. 1991.

"Letter to Lambda." *Outweek* 1 May 1991: 5.

Lorde, Audre. Personal videotaped interview with June Chan and Mariana Romo-Carmona. 26 April 1991.

Miss Saigon. Libretto accompanying compact disc. Produced by Alain Boublil and Claude-Michel Schöenberg, 1988.

Ragaza, Angelo. Open memo to Lambda. 21 Feb. 1991. 6–7.

Shewey, Don. "Playing Around." *Village Voice* 12 Mar. 1991.

3. Queer Asian American Immigrants
Opening Borders and Closets
Ignatius Bau

The passage of California's Proposition 187 in November 1994 has become a metaphor for the latest historical manifestation of anti-immigrant hysteria sweeping the United States. Proposition 187 denies education, health care, and social services to individuals suspected of being undocumented immigrants by California government officials. For Asian Americans,[1] Proposition 187 causes frightening historical echoes. We know too well the racist history of immigration restrictions against our ancestors in the United States. For those of us who are gay, lesbian, bisexual, transgender, and queer[2] Asian Americans, Proposition 187 also opens a discussion of our multiple identities. We are challenged to raise issues of immigrant rights in the larger gay/lesbian/bisexual/transgender/queer communities, which have also been racist and exclusionary toward us as queers of color. As queer Asian Americans, we can provide critical connections and help build political alliances between Asian American communities and the gay/lesbian/bisexual/transgender/queer communities. As we continue to come out[3] as queer Asian Americans, we can begin to open both borders and closets in all our communities.

Proposition 187 and Anti-Asian Sentiment
Unfortunately, many Asian Americans failed to make the connections between Proposition 187 and the history of anti-Asian sentiment, law, and policy in the United States. Many felt that Proposition 187 was targeted at undocumented immigrants (read: Latinos) and was not an important issue for our Asian American communities. Yet for Asian Americans, the history of U.S. immigration law and policy is a history of exclusion.

The 1882 Chinese Exclusion Act remains one of the few racially based laws upheld by the U.S. Supreme Court. It is not a coincidence that the 1882 Chinese Exclusion Act, backed by the Workingman's Party, also emerged from California. Political agitation by angry white workers about competition from Chinese immigrant workers resulted in the adoption of the 1879 California Constitution, which prohibited Asians from becoming U.S. citizens, from testifying as witnesses in California courts, and from being employed by any California corporation. Subsequent state legislation also denied Asians the right to marry, go to public schools, and own land.

The Chinese Exclusion Act left a legacy of detention and interrogation at Angel Island in the San Francisco Bay and fostered the creation of Chinese "paper sons" claiming U.S. citizenship—the only way for Chinese to enter the United States legally after the 1880s. Many Chinese Americans—and their children, grandchildren, and great-grandchildren—who have been living in the United States under their "paper" identities and names are technically undocumented immigrants.

The laws against Asian immigration remained in effect until 1943. However, it was not until 1965 that Asians were allowed to immigrate to the United States in large numbers. Much of the anti-immigrant sentiment underlying Proposition 187 is racist: anti-Asian and anti-Latino. Although Asian and Latino immigrants constitute less than 20 percent of all immigrants admitted to the United States since 1820, they constitute the majority of immigrants admitted after the 1965 repeal of the exclusionary quotas.Thus, it is not surprising that although the 1990 U.S. Census reported that Latinos made up only 9 percent and Asian Americans only 3 percent of the total population, recent public opinion polls report a widespread belief that "too many" Latino and Asian immigrants are being admitted to the United States. If current immigration, fertility, and other demographic patterns persist, however, the national population will shift to mirror California's 1990 figures: 29 percent Latino and 11 percent Asian American. This demographic shift is threatening on both social and economic levels.

The Racially Polarized Vote on Proposition 187

We can learn some important lessons from the voting patterns that helped pass Proposition 187. Overall, 59 percent of California's voters supported Proposition 187 and 41 percent opposed it. Yet the vote was racially polarized:[4] 63 percent of white voters supported Proposition 187, but 77 percent of Latino voters and 53 percent of Asian American and African American voters opposed it. The opposition among voters of color was overshadowed by the dominance of white voters in the election. Although only 53 percent of California's adults are white, 81 percent of those who voted in the November 1994 California election were white. In fact, the 63 percent of white voters voting for Proposition 187 (from the 81 percent of all voters) would have been sufficient to pass Proposition 187 without even taking into account how people from communities of color voted. More sobering still is the fact that even if one looks at the number of all *eligible* voters in California's communities of color, assuming 100 percent success in voter registration and turnout, which would increase voters of color from under 20 percent to 30 percent of voters, Proposition 187 would *still* have passed if the remaining 70 percent white voters continued to vote 63 percent in favor of the initiative.[5]

Building Coalitions, Claiming Multiple Identities

The principal lesson to be learned from the experience of Proposition 187 is that coalition building is not only good rhetoric but also a political necessity. The only realistic scenario for the defeat of Proposition 187 would have been a reduction in its support among white voters. If we had been more successful in educating, organizing, and mobilizing voters in communities of color (including increasing opposition to the initiative in African American and Asian American communities), we would not have needed a *defeat* of the initiative among white voters; we would have needed only to reduce its level of support. This distinction is crucial, because the messages and strategies used for "winning" are very different from simply reducing support among white voters and increasing the level of opposition in communities of color. Sufficient numbers of white voters could have been reached through other constituent identities, such as through women's, youth, religious, labor, and gay/lesbian/bisexual/transgender/queer communities and organizations. This would have been an alternative to crafting messages and strategies to appease the so-called angry white men. Obviously, the gay/lesbian/bisexual/transgender/queer communities of California include many white voters who could have been reached more effectively during the campaign.[6]

Queer Asian Americans can be critical in such political coalition building. We can organize in both the Asian American and in the gay/lesbian/bisexual/transgender/queer communities. We can fight the homophobia in our Asian American communities by offering political alliances that are critical to the political success of Asian Americans. If Asian Americans acknowledge the political importance of alliances with the gay/lesbian/bisexual/transgender/queer communities, they must also acknowledge and begin to relate to queer Asian Americans. Such coalition building is a personal necessity as we integrate our multiple identities in our multiple communities.

Queer Analyses of Proposition 187

For the gay/lesbian/bisexual/transgender/queer communities in California, Proposition 187 presented a political challenge. While our queer communities certainly know what it is like to come under attack through the ballot initiative process—witness Oregon, Colorado, Maine, and Idaho in recent years and Florida and California in the early years of the gay and lesbian liberation movement—the debate about Proposition 187 seemed irrelevant to most mainstream queers.

In the gay/lesbian/bisexual/transgender/queer communities, there were generally two levels of analysis about Proposition 187 and about immigrant rights issues in general. The first was an analysis of political solidarity based on shared political scapegoating and victimization. In San Francisco, a popular and effective bumper sticker slogan that was used to rally opposition to Proposition 187 in the gay/lesbian/bisexual/transgender/queer communities was "Who's next?" Some campaign workers even made connections between the right-wing forces that sponsored antigay initiatives and the supporters of Proposition 187.[7]

But the second level of analysis about immigrant issues in the gay/lesbian/bisexual/transgender/queer communities goes beyond political solidarity. This level of analysis requires that the gay/lesbian/bisexual/transgender/queer communities acknowledge their racism, and it requires that queer immigrants come out as *undocumented* immigrants. In fact, many queer immigrants are undocumented in the United States precisely because they are queer. It was not until 1990 that Congress repealed the exclusion of queers, who had been considered to have a "psychopathic personality, sexual deviation or mental defect." Our immigration "family reunification" policies do not include or acknowledge queer families. Marrying a U.S. citizen is one way of legalizing immigration status, but same-sex relationships are not recognized as marriage under immigration laws.[8] This often leaves no legal way for a same-sex partner to remain in the United States.

Even our refugee policies are just beginning to recognize the persecution experienced by gay men/lesbians/bisexuals/transgenders/queers around the world. In the past few years, gay men, lesbians, and transgenders have begun to obtain refugee status in the United States based on their persecution for sexual orientation or gender identity.[9]

Many in the gay/lesbian/bisexual/transgender/queer communities are still in the closet about their immigration status. Some have entered into heterosexual marriages in order to remain in the United States, risking detection, criminal prosecution, and deportation for marriage fraud. Others remain undocumented or with false documentation, severely restricting their ability to obtain work, receive government benefits, or travel freely in and out of the United States. When other family members—spouses, children, parents, and siblings—are either dependent on the queer immigrant for their own immigration status or are involved in the interrelationships that hide the undocumented status of the queer immigrant, the stakes become even higher. It is easy to understand why these queer immigrants are afraid of being outed as undocumented immigrants. The risk of deportation is real; the consequences for family members, employers, and others are also very real.

Progressive AIDS activists have also made connections between the denial of public health services (including HIV-prevention education services) under Proposition 187 and the shifting impact of the HIV epidemic from gay white men to communities of color and immigrant communities. Some AIDS activists have warned that if verification of immigration status becomes a requirement for public health services, both anonymous and confidential HIV antibody testing will be eliminated, not just for undocumented immigrants but for all Californians required to provide proof of their immigration status (and therefore their identities) as a condition for HIV antibody testing.[10]

Moreover, until the gay/lesbian/bisexual/transgender/queer communities acknowledge the multiracial and multicultural diversity of our communities, queer immigrants will continue to be invisible and closeted. If Proposition 187 is a proxy for a racist attack on Asian Americans and Latinos, the queer communities must acknowledge that there are queer Asian Americans and queer Latinos in their midst. Yet racial segregation persists in our queer communities, and queers of color often remain invisible. Those of us who are queers of color who are now U.S. citizens or have legal immigration status can afford to speak out about immigrant rights. It is part of our larger struggle against racism and for diversity in the gay/lesbian/bisexual/transgender/queer communities. Immigrant rights will never be part of the queer liberation agenda until we acknowledge queer immigrants and support their struggle for legal recognition and protection.

There is another dynamic that silences queer immigrants, perpetuating the racism in our queer communities. Many in our queer communities in fact do acknowledge queer diversity: as objects of desire. Yet in stereotypical relationships between older white men and younger Asian men, there are often language and culture barriers that prevent queer Asian men from asserting their independence. It is especially difficult for these men to come out about their immigration status, because they often depend on their lovers/partners for economic and other forms of support. Our efforts to raise queer immigrant issues should include the creation of a political and social space in which queer immigrants can speak for themselves.

Proposition 187 presents an opportunity to raise issues of immigrant rights as well as broader issues of racism and diversity in the gay/lesbian/bisexual/transgender/queer communities. These issues will continue to challenge our multiple communities as we continue to claim our multiple identities.[11]

NOTES

1. Because the term "Asian American" is reductionist as a description of our many diverse communities, I use it primarily in a political sense rather than to suggest a unitary or monolithic Asian American identity or community.

2. Similarly, there is no single gay or lesbian or bisexual or transgender or queer community or identity; there are multiple communities and identities. I use "gay/lesbian/bisexual/transgender/queer" in an attempt to be inclusive.

3. Queer Asian activists in Vancouver have suggested that the concept of "facing out together" is more culturally appropriate to describe queer Asian processes of coming out, because of the importance of saving face and of honoring group rather than individual norms in our Asian cultures.

4. I acknowledge the danger in analyzing voting patterns solely by race, yet the clear racial polarization in the Proposition 187 vote seems to support some level of reductionism. Ultimately, however, I argue against this racial reductionism by encouraging coalition building across racial, gender, sexual orientation, religious, and other identities.

5. This projection presumes a radical change from the actual voter registration and turnout, requiring a doubling in the number of voters from the Asian American communities from 4 percent to 8 percent, an increase in the number of Latino voters from 8 percent to 14 percent, and an increase in African American voters from 5 percent to 8 percent of the total number of voters. Even if *all* these voters from communities of color had registered, turned out, and then voted against Proposition 187 in the same proportion as Latino voters did—a dramatic 77 percent—the initiative still would have passed by over 156,000 votes, or 51 to 49 percent. Bau 7–44.

6. I do not know of any estimates or analyses of the actual gay/lesbian/bisexual/transgender/queer vote on Proposition 187.

7. Although groups such as the Traditional Values Coalition did ultimately endorse Proposition 187, immigrant issues were never a priority for the religious right wing in California.

8. There has been some speculation about whether same-sex relationships that are recognized in certain European countries or in Hawai'i might be recognized under U.S. immigration law, which has traditionally recognized marriages that are legally valid in the foreign country or state in which they occurred. This speculation has become moot, however, with the passage of the falsely named Defense of Marriage Act, which defines marriage under all federal laws, including immigration laws, as a relationship between a man and a woman.

9. I am providing legal representation to a Russian lesbian, Alla Pitcherskaia, who is seeking asylum in the United States because she has been persecuted for her sexual orientation and her political activism in support of gay and lesbian rights. Despite lifelong police surveillance,

arrest, interrogation, detention and beating, and the threat of involuntary psychiatric institutionalization as a "cure" for Pitcherskaia's sexual orientation, the Immigration and Naturalization Service (INS) and the U.S. Board of Immigration Appeals have denied her asylum. The Ninth Circuit Court of Appeals recently ruled that Alla Pitcherskaia need not prove the Russian government's intent to punish or harm her and that government efforts to change her sexual orientation involuntarily would constitute persecution (*Pitcherskaia v. INS*). Both the attorney general and the INS have clearly stated in this and other cases that gay men and lesbians can receive refugee status based on persecution because of their sexual orientation.

10. These fears will be heightened if we adopt a national system requiring mandatory reporting of the names of individuals who test HIV-positive. Although public health authorities would seek to protect the confidentiality of a national registry of HIV-positive individuals, there would be enormous political pressure to open the registry to the INS for the purposes of immigration enforcement. Under the 1996 immigration law, even some permanent residents can be denied reentry into the United States if they are identified as HIV-positive.

11. A similar political struggle has emerged over affirmative action. California's Proposition 209, misnamed the "California Civil Rights Initiative," eliminates affirmative action programs based on race, national origin, and gender in public education, government employment, and public contracting. The *Los Angeles Times* exit poll reported that, just as with Proposition 187, 63 percent of white voters favored the initiative in November 1996 and that, similarly, communities of color opposed Proposition 209, with 76 percent of Latinos, 74 percent of African Americans, and 61 percent of Asian Americans in opposition (*Los Angeles Times* A29; see also *San Francisco Examiner* A12 and Yip 8).

Once again, it was not enough simply to organize communities of color to oppose Proposition 209. Although in the two years between Proposition 187 and Proposition 209, the percentage of voters from communities of color increased from 8 percent to 10 percent Latino, from 5 percent to 7 percent African American, and from 4 percent to 5 percent Asian American, the 74 percent white voters still dominated the election (*Los Angeles Times* A29). There had to be more progress to reduce the support—without necessarily winning—among white voters. The opposition of the gay/lesbian/bisexual/transgender/queer communities can be pivotal in these racially divisive initiatives. Yet the challenge is complex, because there is no affirmative action based on sexual orientation. There is barely protection against employment discrimination based on sexual orientation or gender identity, as is highlighted by the U.S. Senate's recent defeat of the Employment Non-discrimination Act.

Similarly, Asian Americans are extremely divided on the issue of affirmative action, with opponents of affirmative action often portraying

Asian Americans—along with whites—as the victims of the failures or excesses of affirmative action. Asian Americans must simultaneously confront the myth of the "model minority" and the reality of the "glass ceiling" in order to articulate a defense of affirmative action—and opposition to measures like Proposition 209—that is relevant to Asian Americans. See Takagi 1–14 and Wang 49–58.

WORKS CITED

Bau, Ignatius. "Immigrant Rights: A Challenge to Asian Pacific American Political Influence." *Asian American Policy Review* 5 (1995): 7–44.

Los Angeles Times, 7 Nov. 1996: A29.

Pitcherskaia v. INS. No. 95-70887. 9th Cir.

San Francisco Examiner, 6 Nov. 1996: A12.

Takagi, Dana. "The Three Percent Solution: Asian Americans and Affirmative Action." *Asian American Policy Review* 6 (1996): 1–14.

Wang, L. Ling-chi. "Being Used and Being Marginalized in the Affirmative Action Debate: Re-envisioning Multiracial America from an Asian American Perpsective." *Asian American Policy Review* 6 (1996): 49–58.

Yip, Althea. "Asian Votes Shift to Left." *Asian Week,* 15 Nov. 1996: 8.

4. Coalition Politics
(Re)turning the Century
Vera Miao

> A critical difference from myself means that I am not i, am within and without i. I/i can be I or i, you and me both involved. We (with capital W) sometimes include(s), other times exclude(s) me. You and I are close, we intertwine; you may stand on the other side of the hill once in a while, but you may also be me, while remaining what you are and what i am not. —TRINH T. MINH-HA, *Woman, Native, Other*

> Thought shifts, reality shifts, gender shifts: one person metamorphoses into another in a world where people fly through the air, heal from mortal wounds. I am playing with my Self, I am playing with the world's soul, I am the dialogue between my Self and *el espíritu del mundo*. I change myself, I change the world. —GLORIA ANZALDÚA, *Borderlands, La Frontera*

The negotiation of a progressive politics requires the acknowledgment of critical differences among people as crucial to both ideological production and political play. This insight in turn recognizes the complicated nature of identity and its formation. If we attempt to formulate a genealogy of the term "difference" and its currency in contemporary discourses, we see that "differences" in the multiple form emerge as instrumental to the process of identity formation largely because of the criticisms of Western feminism made by women of color. Their important, penetrating analyses of the historical privileging of gender as the locus of experience for women unmask the universal Woman of feminism as implicitly white. This stripping away of hegemonic constructions within counterhegemonic discourses shoves differences to the forefront of consideration, permanently shaping the face of feminist politics. Within the construction of identities marked by differences, it follows that the acknowledgment of the multiplicity of identities necessarily molds the shape of political work. In this essay, I focus on the deployment of differences within coalitions and coalitional politics—strategies built on and by the works of feminists of color—as strong forces toward a progressive politics defined by its heterogeneity.

This conceptual push toward differences is ironically parallel to many current cultural criticisms and postmodern theories, discourses often eschewed by some women of color as elitist and politically suspect. However, these discourses, invested in the critique of the unitary subject and the embracing of the partial and conflicted self, have interesting links to the assertions of differences made by women of color. With the current attention being paid to the phenomenon of postmodernism in relation to notions of identity and knowledge, the self has become fractured and split along lines of infinitely unknowable differences. Within these bodies of thought, identities are never conceptualized as singular or containable; rather, they are the arguably incoherent convergences of numerous and sometimes conflicted sites of being. "'I' is, therefore, not a unified subject, a fixed identity, or that solid mass covered with layers of superficialities one has gradually to peel off before one can see a true face. 'I' is, itself, *infinite layers*" (Trinh 94). These "infinite layers" refuse to embody a unified subject or to house a "true face" and therefore refuse the ability to be known in any totalizing way. Framed in this manner, the act of identifying myself as Asian, lesbian, woman—in this collection and in everyday reality—can never adequately convey the complexity of my position. Within the understanding of the self as multiple and shifting, no term, or any varying constellation of terms, can.

This destabilization of subjectivity—this rather messy jumble of identity—immediately prompts a reductive but important query: where do we locate this theory in practice? Even more pressing is this question: how do these theories operate along the margins for people of color, women, and queers—groups whose political struggles have often been necessarily framed in the context of affirming identity rather than unsettling it? What follows is my own cut-and-paste attempt at reconciling the seeming disparity between postmodern-inflected ideas of the fragmented self and the rhetoric of political movements and action that have historically affirmed the notion of both self and community.[1] I locate the site of this reconciliation between theory and practice, ideology and enactment, in the *coalition* as a potentially radical space within which such simplistic binaries of theory and practice are themselves a site of contestation.

The definition of coalition is not a settled issue. I believe that, instead of identifying a unifying factor assumed to be cohesive and distinct, coalitions must use *differences themselves*—those that exist *within and between* each entity—as a starting point. The important distinction lies in the location of commonality in common political goals rather than in identity. This shift from identity politics to the identification of political goals leaves space for differing expressions precisely because it no longer assumes the need for allegiances built on static and uniform identities. Historically speaking, the reliance on identity as a binding force within identity politics is detrimental if based on a simplistic idea of what constitutes identity. Failing to understand that one person can be committed to more than one struggle, or even competing struggles, undermines the potential strength of identity politics: hence, the erroneous belief—on the part of white, middle-class feminism—in a universal Woman and a global sisterhood outside the power matrices of race and class. In a coalition that is defined instead by political goals, the risk of simplified notions of identity is not a discouraging force, because the risk is not taken at the foundational level of political formation. Already defined by its political goals, the coalition does not need the assumption of some intrinsic and essential commonality for effective political work. At the same time, the mobilization of allegiances through common political desires introduces the exciting possibility of political organizations premised on difference. That is, the acknowledgment of the many differing backgrounds, contexts, and histories informs each member's and organization's formation of a particular political goal and hence of the coalition. This is how coalitional politics provides the means by which the complexity of the self is played out in the mobilization of political action. *I change myself, I change the world.*

These questions about coalitional politics in action can be further explored by way of an example. On 25 April 1995—as I positioned myself at the entrance to the Manhattan Bridge during rush hour traffic—I was not actively thinking about the role of coalitions, but I was laying the necessary groundwork for later ruminations. There were twenty-five of us in all, blocking the entrance to this particular heavily traversed commuter exit from Manhattan. Perhaps a dozen more people—legal observers and the press—lined the sides of the road, sharing the curbs with the spectators, who had gathered to watch our act of civil disobedience. The Committee Against Anti-Asian Violence (CAAAV), with support from the National Congress for Puerto Rican Rights, had organized the deliberate block of New York's traffic exits in a public protest against the harsh and deliberately overlooked reality of police brutality and racial violence. Our group—overwhelmingly Asian, many of whom were female and a few queer—was arrested and taken to the New York Police Department's (NYPD) Fifth Precinct in the heart of Chinatown.

What made this particular moment of political mobilization extraordinary was not just the action at the Manhattan Bridge but also concurrent actions throughout the city. In orchestrated synchronicity, the Brooklyn Bridge, the Brooklyn-Battery Tunnel, and the Queens-Midtown Tunnel were also being blocked, causing gridlock and "finger-tapping, heart-pounding delays of up to two hours" (Magaliman and Polner A5). "The Day of Simultaneous Protests" had taken the city and the NYPD by surprise, leading to general chaos, the arrest of 185 demonstrators, and the triumphant post-action declaration, "This city was ours!"[2]

This essay is particularly concerned with the word "ours" and with who constituted "ours" on 25 April. CAAAV was only one of four main organizers of four distinct protests carried out that day: ACT UP mobilized around cuts in funding for public health care and AIDS-related issues, the CUNY (City University of New York) Coalition Against the Cuts protested the severely slashed public education budget, and Housing Works demonstrated against insufficient funding for housing and the homeless—all cuts that were implemented after Republican Mayor Rudolph Giuliani and Republican Governor George Pataki took office. It was both a multipronged attack involving four central political organizations and a multi-issue action, but, most important, it was a *coalition* working toward the common goal of social justice.

The coalitional effort and political struggle did not end after 25 April; instead, it continued in the courtroom. Several of the demonstrators, for example, had been targeted by the police and the court system for reasons including previous arrest records and charges of resisting arrest. Although the majority of the 185 people were offered dismissals, these few were scheduled to be brought up on official charges and "put through the system." In another act of coalition, all 185 arrested protesters agreed that no demonstrator would accept an offer of dismissal unless every single demonstrator was offered one. After several courtroom appearances and considerable drama, the display of strength and political solidarity prevailed; we were all dismissed with no permanent arrest record.

The dynamics of these specific moments of coalition require more attention. It is important to keep in mind, as I recount the events, that among the more than 200 people involved (185 demonstrators in addition to people giving legal support, legal counsel, and press coverage), *only a handful were already acquainted or had had any prior contact with the groups outside their own particular civil disobedience.* This handful was responsible for organizing the actions of 25 April. The majority of demonstrators were first introduced at the *post*-demonstration legal strategy meeting. There we could see each other's faces and hear each other's stories. In essence, it was the combined and coordinated effort and commitment of people who had had no previous interactions that had pulled off this political feat, both on the streets and in the courtrooms. This accomplishment brings into play many interesting questions in terms of both a localized personal response and a larger conceptual structuring of coalitions.

As I sat in the corner with other members of CAAAV and surveyed the room at the post-demonstration meeting, something became immediately obvious: the CAAAV demonstration, which had been made up almost entirely of people of color, also constituted the majority of people of color across all four actions. The other actions were overwhelmingly white, except for the CUNY Coalition Against the Cuts, whose constituency had come in support of New York's public education system, which predominantly served people of color and lower-income populations. ACT UP had a strong and vocal queer presence, which pulled me in different directions as I struggled to ascertain whether this was another moment of personal conflict. On one hand, ACT UP's visible, mainly queer makeup made me wonder: was there space for me as a *queer* Asian woman in CAAAV, whose organizing principle centers on race and racial violence?[3] If I had chosen to work for AIDS and health care issues, would there have been room for my *racial* identity and politics in the queer whiteness of ACT UP? On the other hand, although CAAAV had mentioned homophobic violence as one manifestation of hatred that the group was dedicated to fighting, racial identity and racial violence came through as the bases for their major tenets. Was the "completeness" of my identity being sacrificed in some way by the split in issues between the two groups I focused on and hypothetically chose between—a split that symbolized the tension of juggling the different and often incommensurable facets of my identity?

I answered my own questions with yet another: was it necessary for me to feel complete as an Asian American lesbian to work effectively in this multi-issue action and, still more provocative, *was it even possible?* The pull between CAAAV and ACT UP that I imagined at the post-demonstration triggered questions of identity fissures that registered on both the psychic and the physical levels. Through the very limitations of my body in space, it was physically impossible for me to be at two demonstrations and organizations at the same time: a literal spatial refusal of a reconciled identity. The psychological split symbolized by the members of CAAAV and ACT UP was literally an embodied one, leading to the necessary moment of physically choosing, quite simply, one site or the other.

As shown in this dilemma of choice between two distinct demonstrations in separate locations, the fraught attempts to ground identities are often refused by the demand for the prioritization of some facet of identity over another. In the case of 25 April, my choice to demonstrate against racialized violence was made on the deliberate privileging of racial identity over sexuality. The psychological ramifications of this kind of inevitable choosing between aspects of identity are not uncharted.

For some time now women and lesbians of color have demanded a respect for the specificity of our identities as perpetually occupying the interstitial space of the "Borderlands."[4] Existing simultaneously within several spheres of experience and oppression—as women, as people of color, and as queers—there can be no "home" in the traditional sense of permanence, safety, and even physical location; rather, each potential home site involves some element of both comfort and alienation.[5] Narratives of rejection and disillusionment by many Asian American lesbians and bisexual women, whose exclusion is caused by the homophobia of racial and ethnic communities and the racism of predominantly white queer populations, are only a few painful interventions in prevailing definitions of "home" and "community." As pieces of a puzzle that never quite fit perfectly anywhere, notions of home as the privileged space of comfort and unconditional acceptance are inevitably vexed.

At the same time, the space of community is also a place of rending. Because of the often competing claims of the different aspects of identity and people's unequal access to power, a community built on unproblematic relations and static loyalties is not possible. Instead, temporality and partiality emerge as central themes in the narratives engendered by women and queers of color: moments of acceptance and rejection; celebration and pain; indeed, identity construction and political negotiation as processes that are always dependent on shifting contexts, situations, people, and subjectivities.

Paradoxically, this difficulty to comprehend identities as cohesive and whole is also hard to reconcile with precisely those identities constructed at the peripheries. The assertion of my identity as an Asian American lesbian is based in a rich history of affirming, and indeed essentializing, the different facets of myself along the axes of race, gender, and sexuality. These moves are crucial both politically and personally. In the face of social and institutional rejection of women, people of color, and queers, the belief in the essential self and a common struggle is not a theoretical error; it is a tactic for survival. Emma Pérez makes the following point: "My essentializing positions are often attacked by a sophisticated carload of postmodern, post-Enlightenment, Eurocentric men and women who ride in the back seat, who scream epithets at those of us who have no choice but to essentialize ourselves *strategically and politically* against dominant ideologies that serve only to disempower and depoliticize marginalized minorities" (105, my emphasis).

One must be wary of moves to destabilize essentialized identities and the consequences that this entails for those who necessarily essentialize themselves in their attempts to fashion oppositional strategies. However, if we examine Pérez's own words, the essentialist moves that she makes are self-conscious, strategic, and political, a declaration that illuminates the deliberate and premeditated reasoning behind the moves. It is this important point that paradoxically destabilizes the essentialist foundations of her actions and words as *constructed*. Indeed, this is the paradox that exists in much of the writings and works produced by lesbians of color; identity is often spotlighted as the main source of power—a tactic that is construed and passed as essentialist but that cannot be essentialist, precisely because *it is a tactic*.[6] Moreover, the assertions of identity that are often read as essentialist are those that advocate for multiple positions and subjectivities, ideas reminiscent of "innovative" postmodern claims. For example, queer women of color demand recognition of the specificity of their experience as multiply and simultaneously inscribed by (for example) race, gender, sexuality, class, and ethnicity. The essentialism that would then purportedly mark their subjectivity is also one that defies easy categorization or universal application.

Yet we cannot dismiss the possibilities that the purposeful dissolution of the essential self unfolds. I would argue that these possibilities are especially *politically* important for those who exist outside the power structure of mainstream and dominant society. With differences marking the distance from the hegemonic norms that occupy dominant positions, it becomes politically crucial to acknowledge these differences as foundational to political identifications and, in fact, as useful tools in political struggle. Rey Chow makes the observation that "for the 'third world' feminist, especially, the local is never 'one.' Rather, her own 'locality' as construct, difference . . . means that pressing its claims is always pressing the claims of a form of existence which is, *by origin, coalitional*" (71, my emphasis). This is a new story of origins, one that makes no gesture toward the reductive claims of singular being and cohesive personhood. Chow presents a narrative that denies traditional understandings of the whole self from a singular point of origin, positing instead a perpetual coming into being distinguished by its multiple points of genesis, identification, and departure.

At the same time, the reality of identities forged in the complicated interstices of differences makes recognizing Chow's "third world" feminist as a coalitional entity by origin imperative in the mobilization of a new type of politics. This new type of politics finds its political resources in the very existence of differences. If we examine Chow's claim of a coalitional entity formed as such in the first instance, we recognize this positing of identity construction as paradoxically influenced by the strategic essentialism of multiply "minoritized" subjectivities and postmodern attempts at dissolving the essential and unitary self. This coupling of two seemingly incompatible approaches results in its own hybrid means of tackling political work. It produces the necessary shifting of political ideologies and agendas from a utopic concept of the whole. The partial and localized perspective is instead understood in terms of its political effectiveness. If we follow the logic of differences and multiplicity, the deployment of this localized perspective has far-reaching political consequences. Chow elaborates: "Totality does not refer to a closed 'whole'; rather, it refers to an interdiscursive space in which the articulation of the local struggle already requires the articulation of its implicatedness in other struggles, and vice versa. . . . Instead, the meaning of 'totality' is precisely otherness—a local struggle is 'total' because of its dependence on what is other than itself through the activity of equivalent articulation" (96).

Chow reorders the definition of totality from the assumptions of complete and original wholeness to a totality that is *constituted* by the interaction of its parts. This definitional shift understands totality only in relation to what it is made up of on local levels—hence the conclusion that "'totality' is precisely otherness." If we understand local struggles and their actors to be heterogeneous, it follows that the constitution of totality must be assumed on differences or on the already intersecting points of partialized positions. In other words, acknowledging the numerous investments that each entity necessarily possesses within leads to the entity's participation in struggles that are conceptualized as without. Through this understanding of self and community as sites of multiple inscriptions, we can see an avenue into multi-issue politics. The employment of local struggles would not be revolutionary in the traditional macrolevel sense; instead, it might revolutionize the way we do our work. By using the differences that fracture both the self and us from each other as the stepping stone for new alliances and involvements in varying struggles, political agendas can be accomplished without sacrificing differences. It is a celebration of difference, of otherness; it is an understanding of differences as a *tool* rather than a stumbling block in our political mobilization and organization. In fact, in this framework, progressive work could not proceed without difference: difference becomes the foundation of a new type of identity politics.

This potential for a radical method of approaching political work was contained in the coalitional steps of 25 April. The manifesto presented by CAAAV stated, "Today we join together with people, communities, and organizations *we have never worked with before*" (my emphasis). This observation, made in the other statements of purpose as well, hit home the uniqueness of this particular political moment. The coming together of four seemingly disparate groups signaled the possibility of a new type of coalitional politics in its specific organization. I mentioned earlier that, outside of a handful of organizers, there was no cross communication between the four actions. In fact, each of the four demonstrations was largely independent from the outset. Thus, the establishment of trust between people who had had no prior contact was quite momentous. What then was the connection that linked us together? What had enabled the establishment of this type of trust, which had played such a figurative role in both the day of civil disobedience and the show of solidarity in the courtroom? How did trust build between people and organizations that had never worked with or even known each other before?

Because this trust was born specifically out of coalition—from identifying a common political goal, even across the complicated terrain of differences—it was not the type of trust normally associated with words like "build." There was no time to attempt to build trust; trust was assumed, because it had to be assumed for any work to be accomplished. That is the new definition of trust that coalitions engender: trust as temporary and inevitably unstable. This by no means diminishes the strength in that moment of trust. The bond that was temporarily created by the political actions of 25 April, for example, triumphed in courtroom proceedings, a victory that illustrates the strength that can exist even outside of permanence. In fact, the very temporality that defines the coalition allows it to work effectively. Papusa Molina declares, "Coalitions are necessary as long as we keep in mind that they are temporary, formed with specific goals in mind, and they need to be disbanded as soon as the objective is achieved" (329).

It is precisely this temporality that makes coalitions particularly important for groups that are marginalized or "minoritized" by dominant ideologies and institutions. Understanding identities as fragmented or conflictual, existing on several valences and registers simultaneously, produces a type of disjunctured politics that finds its investments in many different sites and struggles at the same time. In her essay, "U.S. Third World Feminism: The Theory and Method of Oppositional Consciousness in the Postmodern World," Chela Sandoval explores the radical possibilities and power housed in the multiple subjectivities of the Third World feminist, which "provide repositories within which subjugated citizens can either occupy or throw off subjectivities in a process that at once both enacts and yet decolonizes their various relations to their real conditions of existence. This kind of kinetic and self-conscious mobility of consciousness is utilized by U.S. third world feminists as they identify oppositional subject positions and enact them *differentially*" (11, Sandoval's emphasis). This notion of oppositional positions enacted differentially speaks to a type of political mobilization and action indebted to the existence of differences as the source of its "mobility of consciousness." The kinetic quality that Sandoval identifies among U.S. Third World feminists is precisely a result of the multiple points of identification that mark her as such. In fact, those multiple points provide the tools with which she can act effectively and *subversively* by understanding herself as a site of numerous subjectivities that can be deployed tactically for any given situation. This constant movement refuses the endorsement of dangerously static notions of identity and employs that very "instability" politically. With this in mind, Sandoval goes on to say, "What U.S. Third World feminists demand is a new subjectivity, a political revision that denies any one ideology as the final answer, while instead positing a *tactical subjectivity* with the capacity to recenter depending upon the kinds of oppression to be confronted" (14). Sandoval's notion of tactical subjectivity promises a type of politics that uses differences and internal contradiction to achieve political goals. In fact, it acknowledges the power and radical potential that exists within each one of us as a multiple being precisely because of our ability to position and reposition ourselves in many different struggles. Otherness and difference are now reconceptualized not as obstacles to avoid but as powerful diving boards from which to jump into the political fray.

The use of tactical subjectivity also opens up the coalition as an appropriate space to begin enacting an oppositional consciousness. Understanding that each entity is invested in many different political struggles and agendas allows us to build alliances and bridges to other entities and organizations—thus CAAAV's understanding that its fight to combat the racial violence of police brutality is connected to ACT UP's fight for health care funding for people living with HIV and AIDS. Here the common connection was the general goal for justice within a progressive agenda; as CAAAV's manifesto declared, "Today marks a historical moment: all over the city, we are working for justice, we are fighting for our lives." The understanding that life-threatening issues exist in many different spheres and that, in fact, those spheres overlap and interact propelled the Day of Simultaneous Actions.

Using this understanding as a point of departure, we can return to an earlier question: was it necessary and possible for me to represent myself adequately and complexly within the parameters of the coalition of 25 April? Once again I answer a question with a question: how *could* I have represented myself in my full complexity, and, in fact, what is my full complexity?

I began this chapter by arguing against a notion of the complete self as a method that self-consciously attempts to make allowances for individuation and specificity. I believe that by opening up potential spaces in grassroots political action, these theoretical moves *enabled* me to work in the coalition of 25 April. The very moment of crisis—that split between Asian American and lesbian represented by CAAAV and ACT UP—defines identity and the coalition and, in fact, allows them both to function. In other words, it is the nature of coalitions to organize around prioritized issues, but that is precisely so because it is also one of the most powerful and radical ways to enact a *multi*-issue, complex, and, indeed, postmodern political agenda. After all, in the process of enacting a tactical subjectivity, a position that would seem to work effectively within coalitional politics, one's own prioritized issue can neither remain the same at any given time nor exist within the static lines of "my issue, your issue." Not only is consciousness kinetic and mobile, as Sandoval points out, but goals, issues, and priorities are also in perpetual motion in the same political moment. This acknowledgment of the process of identity produces a reading of the coalition as a realm where, for instance, the self-conscious and "essentialized" identity politics found among some lesbians of color does not shut down the articulation of difference, disparity, and contradiction.

But one must remain cautious about celebrating difference too much. My ideas about the paradox of the self as translated into a specific area of political mobilization are by no means either uncontested or unproblematic in and of themselves. For instance, advocating unpredictable differences and contingent identities as a politically effective perspective is not universally supported. For many people, the belief in the true and whole self is still the most radical means to enact oppositional positions in everyday life and political struggles.

Recall the racial makeup of the four groups involved in the protests of 25 April: the preponderance of people of color in my demonstration and the glaring lack of people of color in the others. It is important to register that the theories and conceptual frameworks I have worked through are written predominantly by and about women of color, Third World feminists, and lesbians of color. In fact, I am both troubled and exhilarated by the production of these ideas around identity and its implication in politics as well as by my own use of these conceptual frameworks in exploring the dynamics of the coalition of 25 April. What does it mean to attribute these notions of tactical subjectivity and political mobility to people and groups *inside and outside* the circles of women, feminists, and lesbians of color when each person is invested in power structures in differing ways? How can I afford not to? How does each person involved in the demonstration of 25 April operate within this schema of internal complication and political negotiation? How can I reconcile the knowledge that people involved in a coalition have different valences of socially sanctioned and institutionalized privilege with the understanding that there nevertheless remains a space for common political footing?

Bernice Johnson Reagon, in her influential words on coalitional politics, expresses herself in this way: "I feel as if I'm gonna keel over and die. That is often what it feels like if you're *really* doing coalition work. Most of the time you feel threatened to the core and if you don't, you're not really doing no coalescing" (356). Papusa Molina, along similar lines, defines coalitions as "intellectual/political exercises where individual needs are sacrificed for the cause. . . . When we build coalitions, we forget to take care of ourselves" (329).

The theme of sacrifice defines the coalition experience for these two women and, indeed, for me in the actions of 25 April. At the same time, the degree and intensity of sacrifice is different for each entity involved in the coalition. In other words, by way of identity, some people find themselves sacrificing more in political work than others need to. That is inevitable, given that the self is a multiply inscribed entity within shifting contexts that are, in turn, mediated by a shifting society and power structure. Yet the coalition responds to this complication, not with a pat solution but by posing a challenging question: in addition to the inherently shifting quality of the entities involved in coalitional work, does not the very space of political work irrevocably alter, impress, and transform the entity?

As Lisa Tessman argues, "Our 'given' identities do not simply dictate our politics (as some identity politics imply); *our identities are themselves formed through our politics,* since our political practice is itself an arena of (re)habituation or reconstitution of identity" (78, my emphasis). The process of coalition building and production is premised on the acknowledgment of common political struggles, even with people and issues not usually clumped together. So, for instance, the organizations and the people from differing backgrounds and histories that banded together on 25 April were, while coalescing, also transforming their own politics and their own subjectivities. These transformations open up the possibility for a future of politics that, although unforeseeable, has great potential, because "this remaking of ourselves in the coalition community does not decrease our differences; rather, it increases the hybridity within all of us" (Tessman 80).

While reflecting on the events of 25 April, a friend expressed her disappointment in the outcome, believing that however much chaos we had created in New York City, the message had not been powerful enough. Indeed, there was no utopic resolution. Racial violence and homophobic violence continue, as does the destruction of the city's public health care system. Moreover, New York's public education system will probably be decimated in the very near future, and homelessness remains an epidemic. Yet the desire for revolutionary change does not and cannot stem from one moment of political upheaval, or even from several. It is, instead, an often arduous, painful, and frustrating *process*—one that by no means involves only coalition. Rather, I believe, coalition is an instrumental and important figure within a political agenda defined only by its ability to redefine and to be everywhere at once. That means that politics is always essentialist and constructivist, radical and conservative, physical and textual, active and latent, and, in the process, always breaking down these dualisms. This multifront, multistrategy approach introduces the space for differences for further elaboration. It does what we have not been able to do quite successfully—put difference, in all its endless manifestations, to work for us.

NOTES

1. I am referring to communities that form around identifying common factors—factors often asserted as biological and therefore immutable, for instance, black people, women. This particular type of community formation creates its own kind of formidable strength, politically and personally; however, it also creates its own flaws, as seen, for example, in the history of U.S. feminism's empowering and conflicted relationship with women across race, class, and sexuality.

2. This was the joint assertion made by the organizers and participants directly after 25 April. It came from the statement of purpose issued for the entire action as well as in both the ACT UP and CAAAV manifestos, whose defiant declaration, "This city was ours!" functioned as a rallying cry both for political action and against oppression by figures like Mayor Rudolph Giuliani, Governor George Pataki, and the New York Police Department.

3. CAAAV was by no means monolithically straight; in fact, there were several self-identified Asian American queers involved. The conflict is grounded more in the assertions of racial identity by CAAAV members at the post-demonstration legal strategy meeting and the declarations of queer sexuality that characterized ACT UP members.

4. This term is borrowed from Gloria Anzaldúa's *Borderlands*.

5. Though, as a friend noted, one has to question the existence of a home for anyone, not just the "minoritized" positions that I call attention to here. The disparity lies in the traditional sense of home used here—one that exists primarily within a safety that enjoys institutional and social power. Hence, as one crude example, the figure of the

straight, white male has a less conflicted access to and concept of home and his community than do those considered to be minorities.

6. Diana Fuss's *Essentially Speaking*, an insightful and provocative analysis of the relationship between essentialism and social construction debates in contemporary criticisms, was particularly useful to me in this analysis.

WORKS CITED

Anzaldúa, Gloria. *Borderlands, La Frontera*. San Francisco: Aunt Lute, 1987.

CAAAV. Manifesto. 25 April 1995.

Chow, Rey. *Writing Diaspora: Tactics of Intervention in Contemporary Cultural Studies*. Bloomington: Indiana UP, 1993.

Fuss, Diana. *Essentially Speaking*. New York: Routledge, 1989.

Magaliman, Jessie, and Rob Polner. "Budget Protest Traps Thousands." *New York Newsday*, 26 April 1995, early ed.: A4–5.

Molina, Papusa. "Recognizing, Accepting and Celebrating Our Differences." *Making Face, Making Soul: Haciendo Caras*. Ed. Gloria Anzaldúa. San Francisco: Aunt Lute, 1990. 326–31.

Pérez, Emma. "Irigiray's Female Symbolic in the Making of Chicana Lesbian *Sitios y Lenguas* (Sites and Discourses)." *The Lesbian Postmodern*. Ed. Laura Doan. New York: Columbia UP, 1994. 104–17.

Reagon, Bernice Johnson. "Coalition Politics: Turning the Century." *Home Girls: A Black Feminist Anthology*. Ed. Barbara Smith. New York: Kitchen Table Women of Color, 1983. 356–68.

Sandoval, Chela. "U.S. Third World Feminism: The Theory and Method of Oppositional Consciousness in the Postmodern World." *Genders* 10 (Spring 1991): 1–24.

Tessman, Lisa. "Beyond Communitarian Unity in the Politics of Identity." *Socialist Review: Arranging Identities* 1–2 (1994): 55–83.

Trinh T. Minh-ha. *Woman, Native, Other: Writing Postcoloniality and Feminism*. Bloomington: Indiana UP, 1989.

5. Creating, Curating, and Consuming Queer Asian American Cinema

An Interview with Marie K. Morohoshi

Ju Hui Judy Han with
Marie K. Morohoshi

Introduction

Marie K. Morohoshi is the former associate director of the annual San Francisco International Asian American Film Festival (SFI-AAFF) presented by the National Asian American Telecommunications Association (NAATA). This article is derived largely from a bibliographical essay Morohoshi originally prepared for this collection while she was still a NAATA staff member. Since then, she has traveled to Hong Kong to work as the associate producer for Ruby Yang's *Citizen Hong Kong* and is currently the conference coordinator for the Fifth International Film Financing Conference in San Francisco. After interviewing Morohoshi about her original essay I reshaped the essay and interview into a conversation between the two of us.

As interviewer, my objectives are to (1) provide a general overview of queer Asian/Asian American cinema, (2) explore the vital relationship between media and activism, and (3) discuss the politics and processes of festival programming. For those who are unfamiliar with the demanding hours and intensive work required to organize a film festival, it may seem as though films and videos miraculously appear at an annual festival. Queer Asian American programs often function as a natural venue for community gathering, where activists and others come together. During the two or three hours of moving images, in that moment of coalescence of different groups, the potential for queer Asian American activism seems nearly tangible.

Festivals function, then, as many things at once: they are simultaneously a site of artistic expression and appreciation, social activity, political resistance, intellectual discussion, and commercial exchange. They provide an opportunity for artists to seek funding and wider distribution. They provide a forum for exchanging political information and engaging in debates. Film festivals are certainly invaluable in building a critical mass of people who can be counted on to participate in cultural community life.

I am troubled, however, by the colonial metaphor of discovery that is deeply embedded in the construction of these spectacles: curators set out to seek new work, compete with each other over acquisition, and proudly showcase their "discoveries." Is it possible to recognize the complex and local specificities of those films and videos—which come from so many different continents and countries—that mark themselves with a self-conscious homosexual agency? By naming them "queer" by U.S. standards, are we complicit in a colonial agenda? If so, what colonial act are we committing? Should an Asian American programmer searching for queer Asian films be scrutinized any differently from, for instance, a white, gay curator who searches for that rare Third World flick? Many of these questions lie outside the scope of this interview, but some are provisionally addressed here.

If we consider that media makers and audiences act as producers and consumers in the market of images, we must also remember, as an indispensable part of the equation, that funders and curators function as distributors. Through my conversation with Morohoshi, an exhibition curator, I hope to challenge the producers, viewers, and distributors of media to engage critically with both the images and the processes through which the images are delivered. In the queer Asian American community, whose coherence is articulated repeatedly through the imagined pronoun "we" and various projects of self-representation, who is (re)presenting whom and by what means?

Interview

Han: Tell me a little about yourself and your background in community work?

Morohoshi: I'm a second-generation J.A. [Japanese American], born and raised on the borders of two LA suburbs—Gardena and Torrance. My initial interest in community organizing sprouted while I was attending Cal State Long Beach and doing white women's studies—I was pretty wrapped up in Marxist feminism and campaigning against the U.S. government's involvement in Central America. It wasn't until the late 1980s, when I moved to San Francisco, that I hooked up with APS [Asian Pacifica Sisters], a nonprofit community organization for Asian American lesbians and bisexual women. I was part of a die-hard core of five or so women who kept the group and its newsletter, *Phoenix Rising,* going for a while.

Han: How did you get involved in doing media work?

Morohoshi: My interest in media/cultural activism was sparked through my community work with APS Although I was still putting in a lot of time for APS, I was harboring feelings about making my own film or video. I got into this media in 1991 when GAPA [Gay Asian Pacific Alliance] and APS were putting together our annual co-gender club at the Box. We realized no one was on top of the visuals, so I asked Pablo Bautista [director of *Fated to Be Queer*] if he wanted to do this with me; neither of us had ever really shot before. We collected and shot a bunch of video stills, did some live action, and edited a half-hour video clip made up of queer Asian American folks in San Francisco. The people who came to the club got off on seeing familiar faces and the events the community had sponsored. In a sense, it was a bigger-than-life visual celebration of the community and the work they had done. From that moment on, I felt inspired to do community work through the moving image, and if not in the production of it, the curation, which is what I'm currently doing.

Living in a society where you're supersaturated with images, it was pretty painful to know that here were these queer Asian American communities sprinkled throughout the United States, but you'd be damned to see any of us on the big screen or on your boob tube at home. I had a strong interest in seeing the queer Asian American community get some playtime and, in the process, empower themselves by having a hand in creating that moving image.

Han: What exactly do you mean by empowerment?

Morohoshi: Empowerment is a process where you go from having very little validation in something—like your existence—[to] having some kind of experience that moves you to a place where you can kick some ass. In terms of making a film, you want to move from empowerment to being in a place of power, where you have access to produce your own work and tell your own story. It's about calling the shots, having the right connections and cash to make the film you want to make. In reality, that's a very tall order. Oftentimes, what a filmmaker has in mind about the project and what [she or he] gets in the end is a compromised or different version of the original piece.

Han: Tell me how you started curating Asian American lesbian and bisexual works.

Morohoshi: Since I was working at FAF [Film Arts Foundation], I was constantly meeting [film] makers and had access to equipment to set up screenings. I was beginning to build my own Rolodex of Asian American lesbian [film] makers, and I thought I should organize a screening for the 1993 APLN [Asian Pacific Lesbian Network] West Coast Retreat in Santa Cruz. I was already involved in coordinating parts of the retreat anyway, and that was the first time I had programmed a lesbian shorts program.

Han: What were some of the works you screened, and how was the screening received at the Santa Cruz retreat?

Morohoshi: A couple of [the works] had played a few months earlier at NAATA's SFIAAFF. One was by Azian Nurudin—a five-minute personal experimental video on S/M sexuality called *Sinar Durjana/ Wicked Radiance.* There was Mari Keiko Gonzalez's *Just A Love Thang Trilogy.* The first one had a very cute Asian American woman, who played the object of desire in this short, steamy personal experimental ditty. We had a couple of documentaries, which weren't necessarily about lesbians but [they] either included lesbians or [were] made by a lesbian . . . like Ann Moriyasu's twenty-three-minute video *Issei Wahine,* which looks at labor and family history of Hawaiian sugar plantation workers through the eyes of Ann's grandmother. Grace Poore screened her work-in-progress, *Voices Heard, Sisters Unseen,* which deals with domestic violence among lesbian and straight couples. Overall, the response was thumbs-up—especially for people who hadn't seen this stuff before. People were asking, "Where can I get copies of these videos?"

Han: Can you give us a little background history about queer Asian American cinema?

Morohoshi: It's difficult to pinpoint when it all started, but a solid body of work has emerged within the past five years. Although works were being made between the early [and] late 1980s, the surge in numbers came in the 1990s, when more Asian American students were enrolling and making films in film school and consumer camcorder sales were at an all-time high. This particular scenario yielded to the prevailing genre called "the personal documentary" or "the personal experimental narrative." A good number of lesbian works defined [themselves] under this category.

Han: What were some of the earlier works?

Morohoshi: The early days saw works from sansei Japanese Canadian lesbian director Midi Onodera, who made *Displaced View* about the Japanese Canadian internment experience during World War II. Richard Fung, in one of the first essays on Asian American queer cinema, wrote, "In *Then/Now,* Onodera's made-for-TV drama, the relationship between a Japanese Canadian woman and her father is temporarily torn apart partly by her career as a writer and partly her love for a woman. At that time [1989], Onodera was perhaps the only Asian lesbian filmmaker in North America who dealt with the issue of her sexuality in [her work]"(63). In 1995, she completed her first feature, *Skin Deep,* which had its world premiere at the Toronto International Film Festival.

On the gay men's side, there's Gregg Araki, who doesn't necessarily identify as an Asian American and doesn't usually use Asian American actors, but he's been successful in making queer films like *The Living End, Totally F***ed Up,* and *Nowhere.* And, of course, as I just mentioned, Toronto-based filmmaker Richard Fung has to his credit *Chinese Characters, Fighting Chance,* and, recently, *Dirty Laundry.*

Han: What do you think is the role of the San Francisco International Asian American Film Festival in fostering Asian American queer cinema?

Morohoshi: The role of the festival is to premiere and launch fresh, new work by, for, and about Asians both in Asia and here in the United States. It's often the only chance for people to see these films and videos, especially queer images. If things work out, a distributor will pick up the work for wider distribution.

Han: When I attended the "It Ain't Easy Being Pretty" shorts program at the 1995 NAATA SFIAAFF, I heard that it took a little extra leg work. Can you tell me more about that?

Morohoshi: Elsa E'der and I were part of the screening committee, and we noticed there was an obvious lack of lesbian content films and videos submitted to the festival. We had to get the word out ourselves and conduct our own preview screenings and curatorial process. If we didn't have the time, [the] energy, or the interest, that queer girls shorts program would have never happened. I'm glad we did it, because we got a lot of community groups involved in throwing a big bash for all the lesbian and bi[sexual] [film]makers following the sold-out screening.

Han: What is your curatorial process?

Morohoshi: Usually for festivals we send out a call for entries and we get anywhere between 150 and 200 entries, but we have no idea what will come in. Basically we filter the randomness and select whatever floats to the top. Even with pieces we really like, sometimes they don't quite fit or resonate with other pieces, so we can't program [them]. Another model is to have a specific topic and then solicit the works that fit the topic. I usually need to solicit specifically for queer Asian American works to make up for the lack in the general pool of submissions.

Han: I attended the closing-night screening of NAATA's 1997 film festival, which presented the West Coast premiere of *Fire,* by Indian Canadian filmmaker Deepa Mehta. What a coup to close the festival with a lesbian film—can you tell me about that?

Morohoshi: I first saw *Fire* when it had its world premiere at the 1996 Toronto International Film Festival. Of all the industry screenings I had attended, *Fire* had the most buzz surrounding it. *Fire* is basically a metaphor for the current conflict between traditional and contemporary India, and the lesbian relationship that develops between Radha [Shabana Azmi] and her sister-in-law, Sita [Nadita Das], signifies the emerging social values and the

changes that are to come. Although it's not pitched as a lesbian
story per se, it's clearly a lesbian film. I knew it would be a crowd
pleaser, but I had no idea how difficult it would be to obtain the
film through the sales agents. We tried to contact Deepa directly,
since Ciby Sales in London wasn't biting, and our only way to get
the film was to go to Deepa herself. But she was in Trivundrum,
a southern and not-so-accessible part of India, and with only days
to go before we had to lock the festival program, the possibility
of getting *Fire* for closing night was very bleak. Literally minutes
before we went into the staff meeting to announce our Plan B
closing-night film, I get this call from India, and it's Deepa saying she's very interested in showing the film at our festival.

It wasn't a big deal for us—for me and the former directors of
the festival, Corey Tong and Paul Yi—to choose a South Asian lesbian film for closing night, although it may have been for other
NAATA staff and a few board members. It was the footwork obtaining the film that was arduous. You may recall, we screened Arthur
Dong's *Coming Out Under Fire,* which had no Asian or Asian American content, but it was made by an Asian American filmmaker. I
think that attests to the fact that we're here to support works by
[film]makers in our communities, and we try to get as many different communities to claim this festival as theirs [as possible].

Han: Nineteen ninety-seven marks the fifteenth year for NAATA's
film festival. Has there been much queer content in past festivals?

Morohoshi: Because one of the main jobs of a film festival is to
showcase new works [that] push the envelope both in form and
content, our past festivals have premiered queer works as they've
emerged. With each year, we've premiered an increasing number of queer works from the Asian diaspora. Over the past few
years we've had very strong queer programming, and I'd argue
that our festival has become a forum where new and emerging
queer Asian and Asian American works are launched. We're also
fortunate to have our festival in March, because that positions us
very early on in the year and gives us leverage to premiere works.

It also makes a big difference to have queer folks on the festival staff, because we're usually the first ones to know about a new
queer production and we attract other queer [film]makers to
submit their works to our festival. In that sense, they don't have
to worry about homophobic hassles from us. If I were to look at
1997's festival staff, screening committee, and intern team, more
than half of us were queer, including the codirector, Corey Tong.
What are you going to do when a bunch of queers run the show!

Han: I've heard that filmmakers have had to choose between the
Frameline Gay and Lesbian Film Festival and your festival, be-

cause Frameline has a submissions requirement that all works must be West Coast premieres. Has this created some tension between the two organizations, and, if so, what efforts have been made to address this issue?

Morohoshi: That's a good point to bring up, because this has been a perceived problem, and I do believe some [film]makers have opted to screen their works at the Frameline festival. But as of last year, or at least to my knowledge, Corey and I and the programmers at Frameline have been collaborating a great deal. In fact, we've given the West Coast or U.S. premieres for gay Asian films like *Where Is My Love?* from Taiwan, *Broken Branches* from Korea, and *Like Grains of Sand* from Japan, and Frameline was interested in screening these films—and they did so—even though we had screened [them] three months earlier. I hear Frameline is also screening *Fire*, and I know they'll have a successful turnout, because we sold out the big house at the Kabuki [Theater], and people were upset they didn't get tickets. If anything, I think we're collaborating more, because the caliber of films we present [is] strong and [they] deserve at least another public screening. Actually, that brings up another point: if you don't catch these films at the film festivals, you may risk never seeing them, because chances are quite slim that they'll be picked up for major theatrical distribution. If anything, they'll get a limited run at an art house theater.

Han: Do you distinguish between Asian and Asian American works?

Morohoshi: Well, the distinction is getting blurrier and blurrier. For example, Shu Lea Cheang complicates the whole question. Here's a lesbian from Taiwan, who grew up in New York City where she started making videos, and has gone on to Tokyo and produced videos with the Japanese dykes there. Her *Fingers and Kisses* features Japanese dykes, and it's funded by Japanese money, but that's not Cheang's home. Cheang also uses the moving image without spoken or written words very well, which helps transcend national boundaries. Another example is Toichi Nakata [*Osaka Story*], who is Korean Japanese, raised in Japan, but who is making films in London right now. So how do you begin to regionalize a filmmaker and [his or her] works?

Han: What kind of lesbian works have come out of Asia?

Morohoshi: That's a tough one to answer. Without making gross generalizations—but I guess I am—Asia is still relatively closeted, and you have to be pretty out to be making lesbian films and videos. This whole notion of being closeted and being very out or coming out is a Western way of defining same-sex relationships. On one hand, you've got feature films coming out of Hong

Kong or China, like *Twin Bracelets* and *The East Is Red;* they have the great gender bender thing going on throughout the film or a subtext that is so "clearly" lesbian that it can't be anything but lesbian. But who's writing and who's looking? Intention and perception are oftentimes two different things, as was the case for *Twin Bracelets.* Everyone pegged it as a lesbian film, but the director/screenwriter said the two main characters were not written as if they were lovers.

However, if you look at some of the recent works from Japan, they're clearly lesbian. Over the past couple of years, the queer communities in urban Japan have been very vocal, and they're documenting the times. For example, *One Shadowless Hour* is a half-hour documentary on Tokyo lesbian activists and their participation in the second Tokyo Gay and Lesbian Parade, plus there are videos such as *Closets Are for Clothes* and *Tamago,* which are short narratives looking at lesbian lives. Pratibha Parmar has been one of the most out, highly visible, and prolific lesbian filmmakers. Her past works include *Sari Red; Flesh and Paper; Khush; Memsahib Rita; Double the Trouble, Twice the Fun;* and *Jodie.* Last time I heard, she was going to make an Asian lesbian feature, so we'll have to wait for that. Actually, I'm not as up to speed with all the lesbian works from Asia as I should be.

Han: What do you make of gay Asian men in Asian queer cinema?

Morohoshi: Well, what's new? Men in Asia have had more access to equipment, resources, and power to make feature films. In general, gay Asian men tend to make feature films, as opposed to most Asian American gay men and lesbians, who tend to make videos. Again, it's about resources. Pieces like Hisayasu Sato's *Muscle* opened the 1994 San Francisco Lesbian and Gay Film Festival; Toichi Nakata's British/Japanese production, *Osaka Story,* showed theatrically in England, Japan, and Korea to tremendous critical review. There has also been Ryosuke Hashiguchi's *Like Grains of Sand,* an amazing story about a high school student falling in love with his best friend; *Heaven-6-Box* and *I Like You, I Like You Very Much,* by Hiroyuki Oki; *Beautiful Mystery;* and Jo-Fei Chen's *Where Is My Love?* Park Jae-ho's *Broken Branches* was touted as the first gay film to emerge out of South Korea. Most of these films were showcased at the San Francisco International Asian American Film Festival.

Han: What kind of queer Asian American aesthetic has emerged from this growing body of work?

Morohoshi: Well, if we look to the United States, the early- to mid-1990s saw the production of an unprecedented range and number of low-budget videos. With short personal experimental narratives leading the way, we're finally beginning to experience what it's like to see ourselves on screen. In assessing independent lesbian film, it seems that experimental films and mixed genres lend themselves more readily than documentaries or narratives to exploring possibilities for the visual expression of lesbian desire.

Han: Who are some talented filmmakers whose works we should watch out for?

Morohoshi: Without listing a long string . . . , here are some talented film- and videomakers. Trac Vu's *My First Year* shows a lot of promise. Ming Ma has quite a few videos under his belt, including *There Is No Name for This* and *Slanted Vision;* Nguyen Tan Hoang has pumped out a few shorts, *Forever Jimmy! Love Letters, Maybe Never,* and *Seven Steps to Sticky Heaven,* all of which screened at various film festivals; and Shani Mootoo [*Her Sweetness Lingers*] from Canada also has done some good work. Quentin Lee also comes to mind. We've shown his works in the past, including *Flow,* and [we] gave his debut feature film, *Shopping for Fangs* (a collaboration with Justin Lin), its world premiere. *Shopping for Fangs* has been described as a "generasian-x"-genre-hopping thriller that takes place in megatropolis Los Angeles, and it stars a cast of Asian Americans who don't necessarily identify themselves as such. Aside from their physicality, nothing about them points to the fact that they're of Asian extraction—no food references, no f.o.b. accent, no family involvement; it's just a bunch of young folks who happen to be Asian and some of whom are queer. The two main characters—one girl, one boy—are both lonely and looking for love, and they're both queer, but their sexual identities are incidental to the story. I find that refreshing, because it doesn't subscribe to a particular Asian American or queer culture of thought—it's just honest and real.

BOOK CITED

Fung, Richard. "Center the Margins." *Moving the Image: Independent Asian Pacific American Media Arts.* Ed. Russell Leong. Los Angeles: UCLA Asian American Studies Center, 1991. 62–67.

SELECTED FILMOGRAPHY/VIDEOGRAPHY

This listing includes films and videos of interest in addition to those cited in the text.

Anxiety of Inexpression and the Otherness Machine. Quentin Lee, director. 53 min. U.S.A, 1992.

Asian and Pacific Islander Lesbian and Bisexual Network. Kris Lee, director. Videocassette. 4 min. U.S.A., 1996.

The Asian Heat in Me. Kimberly SaRee Tomes, director. Videocassette. 1.5 min. U.S.A.

Beautiful Mystery. Nakamura Genji, director. 35 mm. 60 min. Japan, 1983.

Beyond/Body/Memory. Neesha Dosanjh, director. Videocassette. 5 min. Canada, 1993.

Black Haired and Black Eyed. Julie Whang, director. Super 8 mm. 9 min. U.S.A., 1995.

Bolo Bolo. Gita Saxen and Ian Rashid, in conjunction with the Alliance for South Asian AIDS Prevention and Toronto Living with AIDS, producers. 30 min. Canada, 1991.

BOMgAY. Riyad Vinci Wadia and Jangu Sethna, directors. Videocassette. 11 min. India, 1996.

Bottom. Terry Chiu, director. Videocassette. 7 min. U.S.A., 1994.

Broken Branches. Park Jae-ho, director. 35 mm. 96 min. South Korea, 1995.

Bugis Street. Yeung Fan, director. English and Chinese with English subtitles. 35 mm. 100 min. Singapore, 1996.

Channath (Desire). Lily K. Gupta, director. Videocassette. 4 min. U.K., 1995.

Chinese Characters. Richard Fung, director. Videocassette. 22 min. Canada, 1986.

Christopher's Chronicles: Christopher Does Dallas—Chapter One. Christopher Lee and Elise Hurwitz, directors. Videocassette. 10 min. U.S.A., 1997.

Closets Are for Clothes. Dezu, director. Videocassette. 21 min. Japan, 1995.

The Colour of Britain. Pratibha Parmar, director. Videocassette. 58 min. U.K., 1994.

Coming Home. Shu Lea Cheang with Superdyke, directors. Videocassette. 5 min. Japan, 1995.

Coming Out, Coming Home: Asian and Pacific Islander Family Stories. Hima B, director. Videocassette. 30 min. U.S.A., 1995.

Coming Out Under Fire. Arthur Dong, director. 35 mm. 71 min. U.S.A, 1994.

Cut Sleeve. N. A. Diaman, director. 24 min. Philippines, 1992.

Darkness Before Dawn. Wu Feng, director. Chinese with English subtitles. Videocassette. 84 min. People's Republic of China, 1996.

Darwish. Shafeeq Velani, director. 12 min. U.K., 1994.

Delilah. Tanya Mahboob Syed, director. 16 mm. 12 min. U.K., 1995.

Dirty Laundry. Richard Fung, director. Videocassette. 30 min. Canada, 1996.

Displaced View. Midi Onodera, director. Canada, 1988.

The Doom Generation. Gregg Araki, director. U.S.A., 1995.

Double the Trouble, Twice the Fun. Pratibha Parmar, director. U.K.

Dream Girls. Kim Longinotto and Jano Williams, directors. 16 mm. 50 min. Japan/U.K., 1993.

The East Is Red. Ching Siu-tung and Raymond Lee, directors. 95 min. Hong Kong, 1993.

Fated to Be Queer. Pablo Bautista, director. 25 min. U.S.A., 1992.

Fierce Detail. Helena Goldwater, director. 16 mm. 3 min. U.K., 1995.

Fighting Chance. Richard Fung, director. Videocassette. 29 min. Canada, 1990.

Fingers and Kisses. Shu Lea Cheang with Superdyke, directors. Videocassette. 4 min. Japan, 1995.

Fire. Deepa Mehta, director. 35 mm. 104 min. Canada, 1996.

Fish and Chips. Justin Lin, director. 16 mm. 12 min. U.S.A., 1996.

Flesh and Paper. Pratibha Parmar, director. Videocassette. 26 min. U.K., 1990.

Flow. Quentin Lee, director. 16 mm. 80 min. U.S.A., 1995.

Forever Jimmy! Nguyen Tan Hoang, director. Videocassette. 6 min. U.S.A., 1995.

Forever Linda! Nguyen Tan Hoang, director. Videocassette. 12 min. U.S.A., 1996.

Fresh Kill. Shu Lea Cheang, director. 80 min. U.S.A., 1993.

Fuckin' Chink. Margarita Alcantera, director. Videocassette. 5 min. U.S.A., 1996.

G.O.M. Kirby Hsu, director. Videocassette. 9 min. Canada, 1994.

Ground Bloom Flower. Gay Natsu, director. Videocassette. 2 min. U.S.A., 1997.

Heaven-6-Box. Hiroyuki Oki, director. 16 mm. 60 min. Japan, 1995.

Her Sweetness Lingers. Shani Mootoo, director. Videocassette. 12 min. Canada, 1994.

High Tech Rice. Joanne L. Cabatu and Ekaterina Mirkin, directors. 16 mm. 24 min. U.S.A./Russia, 1996.

Hindustan. Gita Reddy and David Dasharath Kalal, directors. Videocassette. 3 min. U.S.A., 1995.

Hu-Du-Men. Shu Kei, director. 35 mm. 90 min. Hong Kong, 1996.

Hysterio Passio. Quentin Lee, director. 16 mm. 2 min. U.S.A., 1994.

I Like You, I Like You Very Much. Hiroyuki Oki, director. Japan.

Isaak. Nick Deocampo, director. 35 mm. 10 min. Philippines, 1994.

Issei Wahine. Ann Moriyasu, director. 23 min. 1991.

Jareena: Portrait of Hijda. Prem Kalliat, director. Videocassette. 25 min. 1990.

Jodie: An Icon. Pratibha Parmar, director. Videocassette. 24 min. U.K., 1996.

Julpari. Swati Khurana and Leith Murgai, directors. Videocassette. 21 min. U.S.A., 1996.

Junky Punky Girlz. Nisha Ganatra, director. Videocassette. 12 min. U.S.A., 1995.

Khush. Pratibha Parmar, director. 16 mm. 24 min. U.K., 1991.

Kore. Tran T. Kim-Trang, director. Videocassette. 17 min. U.S.A., 1994.

Letter from Home. Shaffiq Essajee, director. Videocassette. 12 min. U.S.A., 1995.

Lick. Hima B. and Eliza Barrios, directors. Videocassette. 10 min. U.S.A., 1995.

Like Grains of Sand. Ryosuke Hashiguchi, director. Japanese with English subtitles. 35 mm. 129 min. Japan, 1995.

The Living End. Gregg Araki, director. U.S.A., 1992.

Lonely Hearts Club. Yee Chih-Yen, director. 16 mm. 110 min. Taiwan, 1995.

Love Letters 1 and 2 (for Julian; Love, Hoang). Nguyen Tan Hoang, director. Videocassette. 3 min. U.S.A., 1996.

Love Song for Persis K. David Kalal, director. Videocassette. 9 min. U.S.A., 1995.

The Love Thang Trilogy. Mari Keiko Gonzalez, director. Videocassette. 12 min. U.S.A., 1994.

Maybe Never (But I'm Counting the Days). Nguyen Tan Hoang, director. Videocassette. 15 min. U.S.A., 1996.

Memsahib Rita. Pratibha Parmar, director. 16 mm. 20 min. U.K., 1994.

A Mermaid Called Aida. Riyad Vinci Wadia, director. Videocassette. 50 min. India, 1996.

Midnight Dancers. Mel Chionglio, director. 35 mm. 118 min. Philippines, 1994.

Muscle. Hisayasu Sato, director. Japanese with English subtitles. 35 mm. 60 min. Japan, 1993.

My First Year. Trac Vu, director. Videocassette. 6 min. U.S.A., 1996.

My New Friends. Tsai Ming-liang, director. Videocassette. 53 min. Taiwan, 1995.

My Sweet Peony. Karin Lee, director. English and Chinese without English subtitles. B&w/color. 30 min. Canada, 1994.

The Network. Kris (Christopher) Lee, director. Videocassette. 5 min. U.S.A.

Not Obsessive . . . Nor Resolved. . . . Eliza Barrios, director. Videocassette. 2 min. U.S.A., 1997.

Nowhere. Gregg Araki, director. 82 min. U.S.A, 1997.

Okoge. Takehiro Nakajima, director. 120 min. Japan, 1992.

One Shadowless Hour. Narusa Sasagawa, director. Videocassette. 29 min. Japan, 1995.

Osaka Story. Toichi Nakata, director. 1995.

Out in Silence and *Not a Simple Story.* Christine Choy, director. 37 min. U.S.A., 1994.

Peach. Christine Parker, director. 16 min. New Zealand, 1994.

Peter Fucking Wayne Fucking Peter. Wayne Yung, director. Videocassette. 5 min. Canada, 1994.

Phantom Pain. Neil Matsumoto, director. 16 mm. 83 min. U.S.A., 1996.

Powerful: Women in the Martial Arts. Akko Nishimura, director. Videocassette. 30 min. U.S.A., 1996.

Preservation of the Song. Carter Matin, director. 16 mm. 32 min. U.S.A., 1995.

Private Wars. Nick Deocampo, director. 16 mm. 60 min. Philippines, 1996.

A Queer Story. Shu Kei, director. Cantonese with English subtitles. 110 min. 35 mm. Hong Kong, 1996.

Recounter. Terry Chiu, director. B&w. 16 mm. 3 min. U.S.A., 1994.

Sari Red. Pratibha Parmar, director. Videocassette. 12 min. U.K., 1998.

Seven Steps to Sticky Heaven. Nguyen Tan Hoang, director. Videocassette. 24 min. U.S.A., 1995.

Sex Warriors and the Samurai. Nick Deocampo, director. 16 mm. 26 min. U.K./Philippines, 1995.

Shades of Grey. Madeleine Lim, director. Super 8 mm. 7 min. U.S.A., 1995.

Shapes of Silences. Christy Collins, director. Videocassette. 18 min. Japan, 1996.

Shinjuku Boys. Kim Longinotto and Jano Williams, directors. 16 mm. 53 min. U.K., 1995.

Shopping for Fangs. Justin Lin and Quentin Lee, directors. 16 mm. 90 min. Canada/U.S.A., 1997.

A Short Film About Us. Rita Smith, director. Videocassette. 7 min. U.K., 1996.

The Silent Thrush. Sheng-fu Cheng, director. 100 min. Taiwan, 1992.

Skin Deep. Midi Onodera, director. 35 mm. 85 min. Canada, 1994.

Slanted Vision. Ming-Yuen S. Ma, director. Videocassette. 50 min. U.S.A., 1995.

Sleeping Subjects. Quentin Lee, director. Videocassette. 28 min. U.S.A., 1993.

Straight for the Money. Hima B., director. Videocassette. 60 min. U.S.A., 1994.

Sunflowers. Shawn Hainsworth, director. Tagolog/Illocano with English subtitles. Videocassette. 50 min. U.S.A., 1996.

Talk of the Town. Lani Tupu, director. Videocassette. 10 min. New Zealand, 1995.

Tamago [Eggs]. Yuko Nagae, director. Japanese with English subtitles. Videocassette. 6 min. Japan, 1995.

Ten Cents a Dance [Parallax]. Midi Onodera, director. 30 min. Canada, 1986.

Then/Now. Midi Onodera, director. Canada.

There Is No Name for This. Ming-Yuen S. Ma and Cianna Pamintuan Stewart, directors. Videocassette. 49 min. U.S.A., 1997.

These Shoes Weren't Made for Walking. Paul Lee, director. 16 mm. 27 min. U.S.A., 1995.

Thick Lips, Thin Lips. Paul Lee, director. 4 min. Canada, 1994.

Time . . . Is All There Is. Suse Bohse, director. Videocassette. 9 min. Germany, 1995.

Toc Storee. Ming-Yuen S. Ma, director. 21 min. U.S.A., 1991.

*Totally F***ed Up.* Gregg Araki, director. U.S.A., 1993.

Trans-National Homing. Kimberly SaRee Tomes, director. Videocassette. 3 min. U.S.A., 1995.

Twin Bracelets. Yu-Shan Huang, director. 100 min. Hong Kong/Taiwan, 1990.

Two or Three Things I Know About Them. Anson Mak, director. 39 min. Hong Kong, 1991.

Vicious. Hima B., director. Videocassette. 5 min. U.S.A., 1996.

Voices Heard, Sisters Unseen. Grace Poore, director.

Where Is My Love? Jo-Fei Chen, director. Chinese with English subtitles. 16 mm. 60 min. Taiwan/U.S.A., 1995.

White Christmas. Michael Magnaye, director. 27 min. Philippines/ U.S.A. 1993.

Who's Looking Now. Dawn Wan, director. Videocassette. 5 min. U.S.A., 1994.

Wicked Radiance. Azian Nurudin, director. Malaysia, 1992.

X-Girl. Mari Keiko Gonzalez, director. Videocassette. 10 min. U.S.A., 1995.

6. "A Vaudeville Against Coconut Trees"
Colonialism, Contradiction, and Coming Out in Michael Magnaye's White Christmas
Victor Bascara

We Filipinos have always known that ours is a complex and contradictory culture. . . . To deal with this cosmic insanity, our humor is black and rich in irony.—JESSICA HAGEDORN, "Imelda Sings Again!"

The law of contradiction in things, that is, the law of the unity of opposites, is the most basic law in materialist dialectics. . . . [It] is the basic law of nature and society and therefore also the basic law of thought. It is the opposite of the metaphysical world outlook. It means a great revolution in the history of human knowledge. According to the viewpoint of dialectical materialism, contradiction exists in all processes of objective things and subjective thought and runs through all processes from beginning to end—this is the universality and absoluteness of contradiction.—MAO TSE-TUNG, "On Contradiction"

"The Hybrid Culture That Produced the Hybrid Me"

Indeed it has become customary, even cliché, to narrate Philippine history as "400 years in a convent and 40 years under Hollywood," as Michael Magnaye does in his award-winning short film *White Christmas*. Blending memoir and ethnography,[1] *White Christmas* lovingly parades contemporary Filipino yuletide rituals as symbolic manifestations of the palimpsest colonizing cultural forces of Spain and the United States. With the feel of a slide show of vacation snapshots, the film rotates through a carousel of images from contemporary Filipino life, under the polite but matter-of-fact (presumably autobiographical) voice-over narration of a middle-class cosmopolitan Filipino. After five years of medical study and work in the United States, the narrator returns to Manila for the holidays, offering us his reflections. His film strings together a litany of cultural contradictions that are almost too easy to read against the trajectory of Spanish and U.S. imperialisms, with their respective religious and celluloid legacies syncretized. We see images of Tinkerbell with the three wise men or Santa Claus flying over the Virgin Mary on her donkey. The narrator remarks, "Our country was colonized by missionaries and moviemakers. Because of this, we have no problems in reconciling spectacle with the sacred."

But ultimately Filipino culture's famed ability to reconcile the spectacle of Tinsel Town with the sacred of the Vatican is not quite the central reconciliation that Magnaye's film articulates. Speaking over a solemn image of Filipinos filing into church, the narrator likens himself to a "bar girl" (prostitute)[2] who diligently attended the 4 A.M. masses: "I am reminded of a bar girl in downtown Manila who would not miss a single mass. She always made sure she had time to change before the early morning service. In many ways, she and I are alike: we both have no problems reconciling our individual worlds with our Catholic faiths. All it takes is one quick costume change." At this point we are provoked to wonder what specifically about Magnaye's "individual world" might present a problem to his Catholic faith.[3] At the end of the film, we learn that the catalogued contradictions in *White Christmas* provide the terms for the narrator's (virtual) coming out as gay. If not for these last few moments, *White Christmas* would have simply been a whimsical reflection on curious postcolonial cultural practices. Instead, *White Christmas* shows how postcoloniality structures the terms of cultural intelligibility for the narrator's sexual orientation. This strategic foregrounding of colonialism in an eventual narrative of coming out sets to work the dynamics of the narrator's identity formation as both gay and Filipino, transforming them in the process.[4] Magnaye's film carefully lays out a framework characterizing Filipino national identity[5] as the process of negotiating the two seemingly contradictory colonial institutions that continue to structure Filipino society so powerfully: the cinema and the Catholic church.

Contradiction is the emblematic feature animating the cultural practices in *White Christmas* and giving these practices their aesthetic coherence. The film produces a space for its narrator that does not wither in the face of contradictions and inconsistencies; on the contrary, the film celebrates these very contradictions as a way of life. From his observations, the narrator concludes that what Filipinos "enjoy the most" is "being themselves by not being themselves." This emphasis on the performative is inclusive of, but not necessarily limited to, a gay subjectivity; however, for better or worse, performance has come to be nearly synonymous with queer.[6] In what Homi Bhabha has called "the ambivalence of colonial discourse" (85), Magnaye's film locates productive moments of contradiction that—through mimicry—articulate the simultaneity of queerness and Filipinoness. Commenting on the transgender revue at the film's end, the narrator offers the basic argument of *White Christmas:*

> The performers are doing what they enjoy the most; being themselves by not being themselves. Just like the snow park at the nearby mall, cross-dressing makes the fantasy accessible. This is what Christmas means to me: it is a time when we can dress up like a bearded white man in a red suit, as a virgin in white, or as Diana Ross in a sequined sarong. This is the hybrid culture that produced the hybrid me. I may never find order in the ritual that is

Christmas, nor will I ever see a neat and tidy image of Santa Claus
on a snow-covered roof. I may not have a pure Christmas or pure
snow, but it does not matter. For even if I will end up with a vaudeville against coconut trees, it is still my vaudeville.[7]

Living with—even reveling in—colonialism's contradictions gives
form to the narrator's ostensibly unnamed queerness, and, conversely, queerness comes to structure what it means for him to live
with colonialism's contradictions. As a coming-out narrative, *White
Christmas* is a suggestive intervention into conceptualizations of the
closet, gay transnational identity, and the function of contradiction
in desire. As a narrative of postcolonial national identity, *White
Christmas* is a suggestive intervention into conceptualizations of the
national subject, the postcolonial state, and the function of contradiction in resistance and community.

Performing a function similar to what LeRoi Jones referred to as
"'swing' from verb to noun" (142–65), Magnaye's film takes "queer"
from verb to adjective to noun.[8] In other words, counter to "the
foundationalist reasoning of identity politics [that] tends to assume
that an identity must first be in place in order for political interests
to be elaborated and, subsequently, political action to be taken"
(Butler, *Gender Trouble* 142), "queer" for *White Christmas* is, strategically, first a practice and only later an identity that viewers are left
to label at their peril. Instead of first announcing his queerness and
then showing practices that are queer because he practices them,
the practices come to give meaning to the overt articulation and valorization of identity positions, such as Filipino or gay, which the
film never explicitly names. Magnaye says "gay" once, in reference
to a favorite bar of his, but he never shows or even refers to any sex
acts.[9] By not claiming an explicit identity position, he is not in danger of being (un)faithful or (ir)responsible to it and its official history. Thus he makes possible the articulation of new and previously
unrecognized narrations of histories and subjects.[10]

"Mak[ing] the Fantasy Accessible"

Panning down from a cloudless sky onto sun-baked hills, nipa huts,
rice paddies, agricultural laborers, and a masticating carabao, the
opening shot of *White Christmas* begins with an acknowledgment of
lack: "I come from a country without snow." The country even
lacked a name: "Ferdinand Magellan and his men landed on the islands in the sixteenth century, and they named it Islas de Filipinas
in honor of King Philip II."

White Christmas thematizes conspicuous absences visually (for example, we never see snow, the United States, or, for that matter,
even Magnaye) and aurally (for example, he never says that he is

gay). The film is composed entirely of footage of the Philippines beneath Magnaye's resigned, almost jaded, voice-over narration. Throughout the film, the visuals set the scene for the narration. We see and hear forms of adaptation—of making the phantasmic accessible—in spite of putative lacks of whiteness, adaptations such as artificial indoor snow and Filipinos in whiteface. The compensations for various lacks illustrate forms of imperialist, heteronormative, and contradiction-saturated discipline. The film then seeks to mine this discipline for its radically subversive potential. In *White Christmas,* contradictions emerge, illustrating what Jean Baudrillard calls "simulacra," the putative original that is always already a copy. The continual repetition and ritualizing of idealized masters lends realness to reality itself.[11] Imperialist discipline produces what Bhabha, in his influential theories of colonial mimicry, calls "a proliferation of inappropriate objects" made "appropriate" through unequal power relations (86). Magnaye's film shows how mimicry functions at a number of levels, from consumptive patterns and export-oriented economic development to Northern Hemisphere meteorological normativity.

The immediate contradiction shown by *White Christmas* is climatological. Located "not far from the equator," the Philippines can never have real snow. "We imported a religion from Spain and a language from America. I wish we also had acquired their climates. We have scorching summers, long monsoons, and volcanic eruptions," he tells us. Yet with the kind of irony that makes the subtropical Philippines a leading site for factories producing the North's winter gloves and ski coats, the narrator has been trained to love Christmas snow that he can never have.[12] Speaking as a *faux naïf,*[13] the narrator satirically expresses consternation at an inflated original not turning out to be all that it was expected to be: "After all those Christmases of white Styrofoam and plastic pine trees, I had my first encounter with real snow. As a child I had visions of powdered snow in Vermont or in Switzerland. I ended up with slush on the lower East Side of Manhattan." Over images of the manufacture of artificial conifer trees he tells us: "Although pine trees are scarce in our forests, the Christmas tree became the centerpiece of any home." For Manila's children, the big attraction at Christmastime is a "snow theme park" imported from, of all places, Australia. "Meanwhile it is still 95°[F] outside." We see a disregarded sign that reads: "Notice: Please wipe your shoes well to preserve cleanliness of snow." Displayed before us are scenes of winter bliss, all under the protective roof of one of Manila's "megamalls": youngsters ice skating, children throwing snow at each other. Then in one of the film's strategic cuts, we see what looks like a barren tundra, which is then jarringly traversed by a jeepney. The narrator explains that this was a village before it was leveled by the ash of Mount Pinatubo's 1991 eruption. "Amidst the confusion, many likened it to a winter wonderland." Even the geological formations seem to join in colonial mimicry.

Through the temporary and spatial mobility afforded by such jump-cutting, the narrator constructs a strategic distance from the images he shows. Although the film is autobiographical, it never shows us its narrator. Rather, he seems to be hovering over the proceedings, firmly positioned behind the camera. Shots linger on Filipino boys—from an assembly of school boys to a boy reading to his classmates to a helmeted boy hobbling on ice skates and being pushed by another boy onto the ice to a boy pouting in the corner at a family reunion to a bored toddler holding money. These and other children seem to act as stand-ins for the subject of *White Christmas*. Although they have yet to unlearn realness, they are surrounded by an unreality. Describing the disappointing first attempt of an electric-powered snow park that was ill-prepared for Manila's notorious brownouts, the narrator says, "The result was a mess of slush and mud. For many children that year, their first encounter with snow was no different from mine. Mothers complained because they had to buy sweaters for the occasion and pay fifty pesos entrance per kid only to be met with slush. Perhaps they too had visions of snow in Vermont." Magnaye was once a naïve boy like the ones we see in his film—felicitous subjects of colonialism.

The narrator shows how various forms of discipline inculcated in his schooling prepared him well for the pleasures of mimicry. Before the narration, we see an image of hundreds of uniformed school boys, hands over their hearts, singing the Philippine national anthem. "For eleven years I went to a private Catholic school for boys," says the narrator. The scene cuts to an image of the same school boys reciting, in unison, call-and-response prayers culminating in the sign of the cross. We see a teacher tapping on her desk with a stick, as students dutifully produce nonsensical doodles. Only then does the narrator recount the routine: "Every morning, after the daily prayers, I would toil through a method called Palmer, doing writing drills of ovals and push-and-pulls to the beat of a human metronome." Repetitive daily discipline of souls, spirits, and hands ensured the proper regulation of students' piety, patriotism, and penmanship.

The content as well as the form of their lessons serve colonial discipline.[14] "An award in excellence in penmanship was as important as a prize in mathematics or grammar," Magnaye tells us. Then we see a grammar lesson: A teacher is saying aloud, and writing on the chalkboard, the sentences "I will go. I want to be a strong man." The narrator shows us how racial discourses found their way into the curriculum: "I followed different sets of characters from two readers. Carlos and Rita tended chickens, and Dick and Jane played with their sleds in the snow." Under the guise of grammar pedagogy, students are fed representations of people of color who labor while white children play in the snow. With which of these contradictory sets of characters would these middle-class boys identify? Probably both. We see a boy at the head of the class, reading aloud to his classmates; he recites a grammar lesson similar to the teacher's: "I hope I could be a strong man. I hope I could go to a town like U.S. I hope I could go to Disneyland. In the year 2000 I wish to have a big house. I would have a big . . . " (he pauses) " . . . car. I want to imagine to have a house like the rich man." The teacher then congratulates her student on performing a good recitation.

The narrator paints a portrait of family life similar to his representation of school, emphasizing the forms of middle-class and heterosexist discipline that it enacts, especially during the holidays. From footage that looks like a home movie, we see the interior of a middle-class house, with family members filing in, milling about, and surveying one another. The narrator describes his mixed success at being a good son: "Unlike my friends, who take me on my own terms, my family lives on expectation. The formula is quite common: intelligent boy graduates from college, then becomes a surgeon, and then marries a nice Filipina. I got the first part right, but frequently story lines have to be rewritten." The camera lingers on a pouting boy curled up in a corner. A woman is trying to comfort him with a Christmas present; he refuses to accept it. "Unlike my nonlinear narrative, the plot of the reunion is almost predictable. It is a time for the giving of gifts and money to kids who would not know the price of a kilo of rice. It is a time when my relatives talk about lucrative business ventures or the right schools. It is a time when my aunts complain about how difficult it is to get hired help these days." We get a shot of a blasé young boy holding an enormous-looking peso note. Then we see Filipino men heartily laughing and sitting around a table. "It is a time for the regulation male bonding, which is something I could never do well no matter how hard I tried. It is a time when I am asked whether I am married or have a girlfriend. Since I am neither, nor will I ever be, I seek solace in the chaos that is Christmas." At this point the dénouement of *White Christmas* begins.

The final sequence of juxtaposed images serves as the culmination of the argument of *White Christmas:* we witness colonial discipline queered. The last image we see from the reunion is the family gathered outside for a group picture taking. We hear someone, probably the person snapping the picture of the family, counting, "1, 2, 3," and then there is a cut. From an image of domestic festivity, we now see a stage where performers—holding a formation of bamboo poles resembling an A-frame house—are about to dance the *tinikling*, an indigenous rural dance, in which performers hop between bamboo poles. Commodified like the hula and popular at U.S. college campus Filipino culture nights,[15] the *tinikling* is reputed to "symbolize the Filipino prancing in and out between clashing cultures, Western and Asian" (Roces and Roces 135). But instead of performing to rural indigenous music, these dancers do the *tinikling* under pulsating lights, to the beat of disco music by Diana Ross. Over the image of the drag revue, the narrator explains, "I hook up with some folks on the other end of my spectrum of friends. We go to our favorite gay bar and are treated to a different kind of show. . . . Just like the snow park at a nearby mall, cross-dressing makes the fantasy accessible." The scene changes. We see a street festival with Filipinos dressed up like New Testament figures, yet the music is still Diana Ross. The film imposes a sort of acoustical cross-dressing. We see the ethos of the gay bar spill out onto the streets of Manila. Or has the public culture of Manila's streets invaded the gay bar? Somewhat utopically, the narrator chooses to emphasize the commonalities of these different public spheres: "This is what Christmas means to me: it is a time when we can dress up like a bearded white man in a red suit, as a virgin in white, or as Diana Ross in a sequined sarong." We see outing at literal, if seemingly incidental, levels in *White Christmas;* indoor realities are juxtaposed to outdoor ones, the less public with the more public. The paradigmatic instance juxtaposes indoor artificial snow with outdoor winter wonderland volcanic ash with memories of "slush on the lower East Side of Manhattan." The film juxtaposes and also links the contained social space of the gay bar with the Manila street festivals. Across the spaces that the narrator inhabits is a consistency of inconsistency.

At an individual level, the narrator's sexual orientation never manifests itself with identity statements. Does this mean that the narrator remains closeted or at least that he is only as queer as he makes Filipino culture out to be? *White Christmas* argues that the speaker's queerness is not the exclusive thing to be outed; rather, Filipino cultural tendencies are shown to be queer, at the very least in the sense of "against the normal" (Warner xxvi). This is not to argue that the outing of a gay individual is at all moot—coming out is an extremely important political act—but rather to situate this individual and his gayness socially and culturally. We then can bring out not only his queerness/gayness but also, from his formative so-journing, his Asian Americanness.[16] Does the narrator have to say explicitly that he is gay to be out? Nonarticulation can be somewhat politically disingenuous but discursively quite generative of mean-ing. The closest the narrator comes to coming out explicitly is when he says that traditional male bonding is something he "could never do well" and that to "marry a nice Filipina," as his family wishes, is something he "will never do." And in the closing moments of the film he goes to his "favorite gay bar" with "the other end of [his] spectrum of friends."[17]

What gives this tenuous spectrum its unity is Magnaye's articu-lation of a cultural national identity. Yet, at the same time, what gives national identity its unity is the pleasure in forms of cross-dressing. The pleasure of a drag show is not unlike the pleasure of a Filipino Christmas parade or mall display or even a Filipino Catholic mass. They all serve as unapologetic moments of failure at being faithful to a putative original. Magnaye's film exults in the pleasure of imperfect repetition: the contradictory state of being oneself by not being oneself. Awareness of the processes of cultural construction only enhances the pleasure. Magnaye draws discipli-nary parallels between learning to speak English—he didn't have to rely on subtitles to hear Dorothy say that there's no place like Kansas—the pedagogy of the Palmer method, and the simulacra-esque and "exotic" naming of Manila's streets: "To my five-year-old mind, New York was not a city in America but a street a few blocks from where I lived." "I lived in a neighborhood of exotic-sounding names," he says over images of streets named New York, Oxford, Annapolis, and Stanford, the faraway institution at which Magnaye made *White Christmas*.

We learn that a hopeful Magnaye did finally come to the United States, only to find that it had been replaced by an imperfect copy. Upon arrival at what might be modern history's most radically un-inhabitable ideal—America—he finds "slush on the lower East Side of Manhattan" instead of snow in Vermont. I suggest that we con-sider his experiences with the contradictions of coming to America to be the narrative for which the film's snow fixation is an allegory. Going to America and finding New York slush intead of pure-white snow is a common narrative, especially in Asian American cultural critique.[18] Just as Magnaye displaces his family's predictable het-erosexual expectations with the other end of his spectrum of friends "who take him on his own terms," he concludes by displac-ing the ideal that America held for him with a new kind of appre-ciation for what he had left behind: a culture of contradiction. The optimistic ending of *White Christmas* fuses a homecoming and a coming out. Upon returning to the Philippines, he can claim this "vaudeville against coconut trees" as his own.[19]

"I May Never Find Order in the Ritual"

Though overtly playful, the implications of the ideas explored in *White Christmas* are far-reaching for critiques of imperialism and heterosexism. Declaring, "I may never find order in the ritual that is Christmas," the narrator asserts his role in giving meaning to the chaos and contradictions that surround him. Reconciling things in contradiction is the responsibility, even the raison d'être, of culture and of ideology and its institutions. And contradictions are the "weakest link" of an ideological formation, the point at which organic totality is most likely to be questioned.[20] In general, contradiction can make visible structures that show the classed, raced, and gendered interests dependent upon the invisibility of that structure. In Marxist parlance the "primary" contradiction for ideology to manage is the "general" contradiction of labor and capital. Put simply, if somewhat reductively, despite the fact that capitalism attempts to transform labor (characterized by its use value) into a commodity (characterized by its exchange value), labor and money are never wholly equivalent. This ultimately exploitive nonequivalence gives rise to the proletariat as a class that is conscious of itself. In any colonial relationship, this "principal" contradiction is undeniable, but its meaning is stretched and transformed, most notably through the gendered racialization of labor.[21]

Contradiction, as a concept usefully outlined by Althusser, can make manifest the weakness of a totalizing ideology—whether it is called modernity, capitalism, imperialism, patriarchy, nationalism, or Christianity—depending on how contradiction is "overdetermined" (95), that is, how it is given social and historical significance.[22] Finding the overdetermination of a contradiction is a way of reading, or rereading, culture. Inaugurating an epistemic or paradigmatic shift, this rereading radically transforms inherited signifying practices and marks both the emergence of a new cultural formation and, hopefully, the waning of the dominant one.[23] In the tradition of Kidlat Tahimik's rereading of "progress" in his landmark film *Perfumed Nightmare,* Magnaye's rereadings of the rituals of Filipino Christmases are similar to what Althusser calls "an accumulation and exacerbation of historical contradictions."[24] Althusser's elaborations of contradiction and overdetermination help us to recognize the historical stakes of the cultural practices in *White Christmas.* To help us get at the specificity of the contestations on display in *White Christmas,* the tactics of subversion elaborated by postcolonial theory (especially Bhabha's notions of hybridity, mimicry, and ambivalence) and queer theory (especially Butler's conceptions of performativity in *Gender Trouble*) help us to codify the strategic standpoint of the subject of *White Christmas* as, I suggest, queer Asian American, although this phrase is never used in Magnaye's film. We the viewers are given the right and the responsibility to provide such labels.

The phenomenon of the various mass mobilizations depicted and described in *White Christmas* demonstrates the operations of contradiction and overdetermination. Contradiction forms and mobilizes populations, but not necessarily in that order: "If . . . contradiction is to become '*active*' in the strongest sense, to become a ruptural principle, there must be an accumulation of 'circumstances' and 'currents' so that whatever their origin or sense (many of them will *necessarily* be paradoxically foreign to the revolution in origin and sense, or even its 'direct opponents'), they '*fuse*' into a *ruptural unity:* when they produce the result of the immense majority of the popular masses *grouped* in an assault on a regime which its ruling classes are *unable to defend*" (Althusser, "Contradiction and Overdetermination" 99).

When Christmas rituals are read as Magnaye reads them—for example, using plastic Christmas trees, thinking of the ash of Mount Pinatubo as a winter wonderland, desiring to "dress up like a bearded white man"—they are a form of mobilization of heterogeneous groups in unified, recognizable action. But unlike the predominantly class-based militant mobilization that Althusser describes, Filipino mobilization seems to be determined more by the mode of consumption than by the mode of production. We mobilize in spite of, even to reproduce, apparent contradictions—religious and secular, economic and cultural—not necessarily to form an assaultive "ruptural unity." In other words, while these rituals may mobilize subjects into unified action, they simultaneously discipline them.[25]

The political stakes of contradiction depend on how contradiction is given meaning or is "overdetermined." "Overdetermination" is the term for how contradiction simultaneously opens and closes possibilities in a social formation: "The 'contradiction' is inseparable from the total structure of the social body in which it is found, inseparable from its formal *conditions* of existence, and even from the *instances* it governs; it is radically *affected by them*, determining, but also determined in, one and the same movement, and determined by the various *levels* and *instances* of the social formation it animates; it might be called *overdetermined in its principle*" (Althusser, "Contradiction and Overdetermination" 101).[26] Contradiction can be overdetermined for the forces of reaction by sliding over into conservative "historical inhibition," or, preferably, it can be overdetermined in the radical direction of "revolutionary rupture" (Althusser, "Contradicton and Overdetermination" 106–7). Overdetermination is important for Magnaye's film, since *White Christmas* presents certain phenomena—Christmas rituals—that simultaneously exacerbate contradiction and inevitably reproduce the conditions of contradiction's production.[27]

Contradiction is there if you have interpretive tools to read it. The narrator mentions how he revised his reading of decorating pine trees to find this practice in contradiction with the spirit of Christmas: "I had no idea what these ornaments meant. All that mattered was the glitter. Years later I would learn that this began as a pagan ritual." The film shows an energetic population already mobilized under certain terms: the economic engine fueled by the majesty of Christmas. The point, then, is to transform the terms of mobilization to exacerbate contradiction in the interests and formation of a radical political program such as gay or national liberation. The political potential for reading an instance of mobilization is staggering: especially from a distance, a street party, an unruly mob, and a demonstration can look quite similar. More likely, all these mobilizations coexist in the same space; overdetermination transforms these mobilizations into a concerted effort.[28]

White Christmas accumulates and aligns contradictions for more radical ends by reading Filipino rituals as mimicry, as subverting hegemony while still necessarily abiding (albeit imperfectly) the rules of hegemony. In the colonial context, mimicry has been convincingly theorized as the instrument for exacerbating contradiction through a kind of parody that is not a simple repetition but a reiteration that seriously undermines the naturalness of the original. Postcolonialism, or perhaps more accurately, anticolonial nationalism,[29] is a discursive field founded on, "'fuse[d]' into a *ruptural unity*" by, the accumulation and exacerbation of historical contradiction. The colonized, by always being deemed somehow unequal to the task of fashioning themselves in the image of the colonizer,[30] exacerbate contradiction: "The success of colonial appropriation depends on a proliferation of inappropriate objects that ensure its strategic failure, so that mimicry is at once resemblance and menace" (Bhabha 86). In *White Christmas* Filipino culture is simultaneously Spanish and American, but it is also the undoing of both cultures, which are strategic failures unapologetically displayed. Yet this exacerbated contradiction is necessarily given historical and political meaning by its overdetermination: "[Mimicry] is a form of colonial discourse that is uttered *inter dicta:* a discourse at the crossroads of what is known and permissible and that which

though known must be kept concealed; a discourse uttered between lines and as such both against the rules and within them."
(Bhabha 89). Such practices are multi-edged; failure to perform
convincingly, instead of subverting their masters, can simply be
read as failure, thereby recontaining these bad copies as proof of
the assumed racial inferiority of the colonized.[31]

Mimicry exposes as contradictory the colonizer's corporeally
and epistemically violent "civilizing mission." Racism makes truly
civilizing the colonized impossible, what psychoanalysis calls the
"radically uninhabitable ideal." Moments of the emergence of anticolonial national consciousness can be read as moments of spec-
tacularly overdetermined contradiction—such as, for Filipino anticolonial nationalist historiography, Spain's execution of the three
reformist friars in 1872.[32] Situated in postcoloniality, Magnaye's
film takes instances of mobilization and reads them for their subversive potential despite, and because of, their historical roots in
colonial discipline. The result, *White Christmas* argues, is a kind of
cross-dressing. Various forms of Christmas cross-dressing, read as
such, are then the exacerbation of contradiction. Judith Butler's
writing has provided the articulation of the political possibilities as
well as the limits instantiated by drag. "For a copy to be subversive
of heterosexual hegemony, it has to both mime and displace its conventions. And not all miming is displacing" ("The Body" 84).

Considering Magnaye's pattern of labor migrations, I have suggested that we view this film as coming from a strategic site we could
call queer Asian America. Asian American and queer are identity
positions that are historically predicated on continual displacement
and continual emergence, because they are articulated through
contradiction and overdetermination, through the accumulation
and exacerbation of contradictions of race and class and of gender
and sexuality. As positions of persistent critique, Asian American
and queer are assumed provisionally, to be heuristically and politically enabling, yet always open-ended. But, in the so-called last instance, we must live in a real and imaginable world. Althusser reminds us that "the lonely hour of the 'last instance' never comes"
("Contradiction and Overdetermination" 113). But, as Stuart Hall
further reminds us, the last instance also never goes away. Therefore, to be strategic and useful, we need to choose a standpoint
from which to take advantage of the emergence of a "ruptural
unity," the emergence of new subjects and their histories.[33] We are
at a fertile moment, compared with discourses of sexual and racialized identity, which is witnessing and producing the emergence of
Asian American queerness that exacerbates contradictions and as-

serts an urgency and positionality for using and discerning this historical agency.[34] Some of the most important new work in cultural studies critically articulates the often violent intersection of discourses of sexuality and postcoloniality.[35] By reading *White Christmas* simultaneonsly as a narrative of coming out and a narrative of national identity, we can give radical new meanings to old phenomena like Christmas.

NOTES

1. From studies of Ilongot headhunters to the "gentle" Tasaday, the Philippines has historically been an extremely fertile site for anthropological fieldwork. For example, see Rosaldo and see Nance. Jessica Hagedorn's acclaimed novel *Dogeaters* playfully cites passages from Jean Mallat's 1846 anthropological study *The Philippines* as a way of reclaiming cultural narrative. For an interesting discussion of how "autoethnography . . . insert[s] a subjective, performative, often combative, 'native I' into ethnographic film's detached discourse," see Muñoz 87.

2. For critical histories of the rise of the sex industry in the Philippines, see Sturdevant and Soltzfus and see *Sin City Diary*.

3. The viewer is likely to be tipped off—even before the first frame is projected—by where an independent short film like *White Christmas* is being viewed. For example, Magnaye's film was screened at various film festivals whose organizational principles categorize the film as gay and lesbian (the Frameline Gay and Lesbian Film Festival) or Asian Pacific American (National Asian American Telecommunications Association's film and video festival).

4. For the most part, film theory has had a quasi-exclusive focus on sexual (as opposed to other kinds of) difference. In recent years, processes of racialization and other forms of subjectification have been given more attention by film scholars who read films through the "grid of multiculturalism." See Shohat 168.

5. The word "Filipino" first referred to the Spanish creole colonizers residing in the islands, differentiating them from the socially superior Spanish-born *peninsulares*. The colonized indigenous peoples referred to themselves by their ethnic groupings (for example, Tagalog, Visayan, and Ilokano), and the Spanish referred to them as "Indios." "Filipino" did not come to refer to the colonized indigenous peoples until the emergence of anticolonial struggles in the late nineteenth century. See Roces and Roces 150–51.

6. Judith Butler has questioned her own overeasy application of *Gender Trouble* for pointing to cross-dressing as subversive: "I think that I may have made a mistake by using drag as the example of performativity, because many people have now understood that to be the *paradigm* for performativity, and that's not the case. I don't think it's *the* exemplary example" (Butler, "The Body" 84). For more on the far-reaching political implications of undermining the subject of politics, see Butler *Gender Trouble*, especially 142–49.

Queer is historically related, but not wholly equivalent, to gay. For a concise outline of differences between gay and queer, see Warner xxvi–xxvii. "For both academics and activists, 'queer' gets a critical edge by defining itself against the normal rather than the heterosexual, and normal includes the normal business in the academy. The universalizing utopianism of queer theory does not entirely replace more minority-based versions of lesbian and gay theory—nor could it, since normal sexuality and the machinery of enforcing it do not bear down equally on everyone, as we are constantly reminded by pervasive forms of terror, coercion, violence, and devastation" (xxvi).

7. This is not to say that cross-dressing is at all equivalent to gay. The category of the *bakla* has been characterized as "a male with a woman's heart" (Tan 88) or as "constructed as having an interstitial position between men and women" (Manalansan, "Searching" 63). Arguably Magnaye's film must struggle against dominant conceptions of Filipino gayness that rely solely on an effeminacy much caricatured in Filipino popular culture.

8. Michael Tan suggestively notes that "Filipinos use gay more often as a noun, rather than as an adjective" (91).

9. For an influential discussion of the distinction between gay identity and gay acts, see Sedgwick. Gayness has been much theorized in relation to anal eroticism (see Bersani 197–222). In the heterosexual matrix of the Philippine context, the distinction between being a *bakla,* a gay, or a man who has sex with men (MSM) has continually hampered HIV prevention. See Tan.

10. For a brilliant discussion of conceptions of history and representation for Asian Americans, see Lowe (especially chaps. 5 and 6).

11. For an incisive analysis of the stakes of realness, see Reddy.

12. In *Irving Berlin's White Christmas* an unseasonably warm and verdant Vermont was the disappointing holiday destination of vaudevillians Wallace (Bing Crosby) and Davis (Danny Kaye).

13. For a discussion of the *faux naïf* in reference to Tahimik's *Perfumed Nightmare,* see Jameson.

14. For discussions of the strategies of colonial education, see Ngugi and see Viswanathan.

15. For an interesting discussion of Filipino American cultural formations, see Gonzalves 129–44.

16. In Pablo Bautista's wonderful video *Fated to Be Queer,* one of the interviewees defined being "out ethnically" as dating within one's ethnic group instead of dating (or being dated by) gay white men. This is not (necessarily) the sense of outing ethnically used here.

17. In conversation, Filipino American writer R. Zamora Linmark described to me a condition among Filipinos that he calls being "bisexual from the neck up." In the United States, as Cherríe Moraga notes in *Loving in the War Years,* progressives might claim this status while being heterosexual "from the neck down." Many gay Filipino men claim bisexu-

ality. "Given that effeminacy is the gold standard for coming out as *bakla* or as 'a gay' . . . it should not be surprising that people opt to remain in the closet, or, to tentatively move into self-identification as bisexual" (Tan 91).

18. Carlos Bulosan's *America Is in the Heart* is a well-known and important Asian American narrative that is critical of the contradiction of American ideals and American realities. Disillusionment with America's unfulfilled promises is a common trope in Asian American history and culture, from nineteenth-century Chinese conceptions of "gold mountain" (see Takaki 79–99) to the smuggled immigrants aboard 1992's ill-fated Golden Venture (see Kwong).

19. Magnaye's film invites us to go back and reinterpret the "original" *White Christmas* to find the ambivalences and contradictions of this idealized text. In the opening scene of *Irving Berlin's White Christmas,* we see a picture of a snow-covered chalet and the words "Christmas Eve, 1944." As the camera pulls back, we see that the backdrop hangs on a stage, with Bing Crosby and (now outed) Danny Kaye in the foreground, dancing in army uniforms and Santa Claus hats. As the camera pulls farther back, we see that this stage is a makeshift platform in war-torn Europe. The two return to the States and thrive on the vaudeville circuit. Early in the film, while performing in Florida at Christmastime, they cross-dress. Keeping in mind the colonization of the entire Western Hemisphere and the genocide of indigenous peoples, we need not look very far to find a vaudeville against coconut trees. Kaye and Crosby go up to Vermont, where it is unseasonably warm, but, of course, it snows on Christmas Eve.

20. Perhaps not coincidentally, the critique of totality is also the project of postmodernism. A Derridean concept such as the "pharmakon," describing that which is simultaneously a cure and a poison, for example, is somewhat analogous to overdetermined contradiction. See Derrida 95–117.

21. As Fanon tells us in *The Wretched of the Earth,* "When you examine at close quarters the colonial context, it is evident that what parcels out the world is to begin with the fact of belonging or not belonging to a given race, a given species. In the colonies the economic substructure is also a superstructure. The cause is the consequence; you are rich because you are white, you are white because you are rich. This is why Marxist analysis should always be slightly stretched every time we have to do with the colonial problem" (40). In having to do with the *neo*colonial problem, this tendency continues, if in different forms: "With so-called decolonization, the growth of multinational capital, and the relief of the administrative charge, 'development' does not now involve wholesale legislation and establishing educational *systems* in a comparable way (to nineteenth-century territorial imperialism). This impedes the growth of consumerism in the comprador countries. With modern telecommunications and the emergence of advanced capitalist economies at the two

edges of Asia, maintaining the international division of labor serves to keep the supply of cheap labor in the comprador countries. Human labor is not, of course, intrinsically 'cheap' or 'expensive'" (Spivak 287–88). For a description of contradiction that integrates imperialism and the transition from feudalism to capitalism, see Mao 229–31.

22. For two excellent assessments of Althusserian "contradiction" and "overdetermination," see Hall 91–114 and Laclau and Mouffe 97–100.

23. "Dominant" and "emergent" have been influentially outlined by Williams 121–27.

24. Althusser's main example of this is the Russian Revolution of 1917, when an incredibly heterogeneous range of interest groups was mobilized to found a proletarian state. See "Contradiction and Overdetermination" 94–98.

25. Michel Foucault is the theorist most associated with notions of discipline. See especially 135–228.

26. Laclau and Mouffe explain how Althusser's conception of overdetermination derives from, and is a materialist revision of, overdetermination in linguistics and psychoanalysis: "The most profound *potential* meaning of Althusser's statement that everything existing in the social is overdetermined, is the assertion that the social constitutes itself as symbolic order. The symbolic—i.e., overdetermined—character of social relations therefore implies that they lack an ultimate literality which would reduce them to necessary moments of an immanent law. There are not *two* planes, one of essences and the other of appearances, since there is no possibility of fixing an *ultimate* plane of signification. Society and social agents lack any essence, and their regularities merely consist of the relative and precarious forms of fixation which accompany the establishment of a certain order" (97–98).

27. "Reproduction of the conditions of production" is the primary function of ideology. See Althusser, "Ideology" 127.

28. Not long after the People Power uprising, Carolina G. Hernandez assessed the situation with understandable optimism: "[The Filipino people] need a vision of the future . . . that could motivate them to action and achievement, provide them with an incentive to make sacrifices they would not otherwise make, and give them an objective toward which their collective efforts could be directed. The Filipino people found that vision and acted on it in four climactic days in February 1986. Amorphous and independent groups disciplined themselves to act in unison. They acted peaceably and with enormous courage. And they stopped what looked like certain bloodshed and mob rule. The future demanded that they not lose sight of what they gained" (196).

29. Benedict Anderson provocatively narrates the emergence of anticolonial nationalisms as having been given form by colonialism: "The paradox of official nationalism was that it inevitably brought what were increasingly thought of and written about as European 'national histories' into the consciousness of the colonized—not merely via occa-

sional obtuse festivities, but also through reading-rooms and class-rooms. . . . The irony is that these histories were written out of a historiographical consciousness which by the turn of the century was, all over Europe, becoming nationally defined" (118). Magnaye's conception of Filipino/sexual identity might lean more in the direction of a culturalism than a nationalism that, in terms of political economy, has the postcolonial state as its end. For accounts of the relationship of nationalisms and sexualities, see Parker et al. 1–18 and Berlant and Freeman 193–230.

30. Not surprisingly, Stanley Karnow's 1989 Pulitzer Prize–winning book on American imperialism in the Philippines is entitled *In Our Image: America's Empire in the Philippines.*

31. Material realities often virtually predetermine this failure. Frantz Fanon presciently critiqued the anticolonial nationalist elite "pseudo-bourgeoisie" for its effete economic mimicking of the colonizers (that is, desires for development) doomed to failure by economic realities. See 96–100.

32. See the magisterial work of Teodoro Agoncillo and the revisionist work of Reynaldo Ileto (98–131).

33. Shyam Selvadurai's recent acclaimed novel, *Funny Boy,* is a story that articulates the emergence of the narrator's sexual orientation, which is ostensibly gay (though that word never appears). Outside of South Asia, the book has been marketed quite heavily in gay and lesbian bookstores. Yet in readings in the United States, the author has strategically pitched the book as primarily about the civil war in Sri Lanka, since that aspect has received little attention.

34. Consider also the work of individual queer Asian Americans, cultural production such as Russell Leong's anthology and the Asian American Writers' Workshop's *Witness Aloud,* as well as the burgeoning number of local and national queer Asian American organizations.

35. For example, see the work of Martin Manalansan IV and Rosalind Morris in anthropology and Gayatri Gopinath in literary studies.

WORKS CITED

Agoncillo, Teodoro. *Philippine History.* Manila: Inang Wika, 1962.

Althusser, Louis. "Contradiction and Overdetermination: Notes for an Investigation." *For Marx.* Trans. Ben Brewster. New York: Verso, 1990. 87–116.

———. "Ideology and Ideological State Apparatuses (Notes Towards an Investigation)." *Lenin and Philosophy and Other Essays.* Trans. Ben Brewster. New York: Monthly Review, 1971. 127–86.

Anderson, Benedict. *Imagined Communities: The Origin and Spread of Nationalism.* 2nd ed. New York: Verso, 1991.

Asian American Writers' Workshop. *Witness Aloud: Lesbian, Gay, and Bisexual Asian/Pacific American Writing.* New York: Asian American Writers' Workshop, 1993.

Baudrillard, Jean. *Simulacra and Simulation.* Trans. Sheila Faria Glaser. Ann Arbor: U of Michigan P, 1994.

Berlant, Lauren, and Elizabeth Freeman. "Queer Nationality." *Fear of a Queer Planet: Queer Politics and Social Theory.* Ed. Michael Warner. Minneapolis: U of Minnesota P, 1993. 193–230.

Bersani, Leo. "Is the Rectum a Grave?" *October* 43 (1987): 197–222.

Bhabha, Homi. "Of Mimicry and Man: The Ambivalence of Colonial Discourse." *The Location of Culture.* New York: Routledge, 1994. 85–92.

Bulosan, Carlos. *America Is in the Heart.* Seattle: U of Washington P, 1973.

Butler, Judith. "The Body You Want." Interviewed with Liz Kotz. *Art Forum* (Nov. 1992): 82–89.

———. *Gender Trouble: Feminism and the Subversion of Identity.* New York: Routledge, 1991.

Derrida, Jacques. "The Pharmakon." *Dissemination.* Trans. Barbara Johnson. Chicago: U of Chicago P, 1981. 95–117.

Fanon, Frantz. *The Wretched of the Earth.* Trans. Constance Farrington. New York: Ballantine, 1963.

Fated to Be Queer. Pablo Bautista, director. National Asian American Telecommunications Associations, 1992.

Foucault, Michel. *Discipline and Punish: The Birth of the Prison.* New York: Vintage, 1979.

Gonzalves, Theo. "'The Show Must Go On': Notes on a Filipino Culture Night." *Critical Mass: A Journal of Asian American Cultural Criticism* 2 (Spring 1995): 129–44.

Hagedorn, Jessica. *Dogeaters.* New York: Pantheon, 1991.

Hall, Stuart. "Signification, Representation, Ideology: Althusser and the Post-structuralist Debates." *Critical Studies in Mass Communication* 2 (June 1985): 91–114.

Hernandez, Carolina G. "Reconstituting Political Order." *Crisis in the Philippines: The Marcos Era and Beyond.* Ed. John Bresnan. Princeton: Princeton UP, 1986. 176–99.

Ileto, Reynaldo C. "Outlines of a Non-linear Emplotment of Philippine History." *The Politics of Culture in the Shadow of Capital.* Ed. Lisa Lowe and David Lloyd. Durham, N.C.: Duke UP, 1997. 98–131.

Irving Berlin's White Christmas. Michael Curtiz, director. Bing Crosby and Danny Kaye, performers. Paramount, 1954.

Jameson, Fredric. *The Geopolitical Aesthetic: Cinema and Space in the World System.* Bloomington: Indiana UP, 1992.

Jones, LeRoi. *Blues People: The Negro Experience and the Music That Developed from It.* New York: Morrow Quill, 1963.

Karnow, Stanley. *In Our Image: America's Empire in the Philippines.* New York: Random. 1989.

Kwong, Peter. *Forbidden Workers: Illegal Chinese Immigrants and American Labor.* New York: New, 1997.

Laclau, Ernest, and Chantal Mouffe. *Hegemony and Socialist Strategy: Towards a Radical Democratic Politics.* London: Verso, 1985.

Leong, Russell, ed. *Asian American Sexualities: Dimensions of the Gay and Lesbian Experience*. New York: Routledge, 1996.

Lowe, Lisa. *Immigrant Acts: On Asian American Cultural Politics*. Durham: Duke UP, 1996.

Mallat, Jean. *The Philippines: History, Geography, Customs, Agriculture, Industry and Commerce of the Spanish Colonies in Oceania*. 1846. Manila: National History Institute, 1983.

Manalansan, Martin, IV. "(Dis)orienting the Body: Locating Symbolic Resistance Among Filipino Gay Men." *Positions: East Asia Cultures Critique* 2 (Spring 1994): 73–90.

———. "In the Shadows of Stonewall: Examining Gay Transnational Politics and the Diasporic Dilemma." *GLQ* (1995): 425–38.

———. "Searching for Community: Filipino Gay Men in New York City." *Asian American Sexualities: Dimensions of the Gay and Lesbian Experience*. Ed. Russell Leong. New York: Routledge, 1996. 51–64.

Mao Tse-tung. "On Contradiction." *Mao Tse-tung: An Anthology of His Writings*. Ed. Anne Fremantle. New York: Mentor, 1962. 214–41.

Moraga, Cherríe. *Loving in the War Years*. Boston: South End, 1983.

Morris, Rosalind C. "Three Sexes and Four Sexualities: Redressing the Discourses on Gender and Sexuality in Contemporary Thailand." *Positions: East Asia Cultures Critique* 2 (Spring 1994): 15–43.

Muñoz, José. "The Autoethnographic Performance: Reading Richard Fung's Queer Hybridity." *Screen* 36 (Spring 1995): 83–99.

Nance, John. *The Gentle Tasaday: A Stone Age People in the Philippine Rain Forest*. New York: Harcourt Brace Jovanovich, 1975.

Ngugi Wa Thiong'o. *Decolonising the Mind: The Politics of Language in African Literature*. London: Currey, 1986.

Parker, Andrew, Mary Russo, Doris Sommer, and Patricia Yaeger, eds. "Introduction." *Nationalisms and Sexualities*. New York: Routledge, 1992. 1–18.

Perfumed Nightmare. Kidlat Tahimik, director and performer. Flower Films, 1977.

Reddy, Chandan. "Passing as Reality, Surpassing Reality: Realness in *Paris Is Burning*." *Burning Down the House*. Ed. Rosemary Marangoly George. Boulder: Westview, forthcoming.

Roces, Alfredo, and Grace Roces. *Culture Shock: A Guide to Customs and Etiquette: Philippines*. Portland, Ore.: Graphic Arts, 1985.

Rosaldo, Renato. *Ilongot Headhunting, 1883–1974: A Study in Society and History*. Stanford: Stanford UP, 1980.

Sedgwick, Eve Kosofsky. *Epistemology of the Closet*. Berkeley: U of California P, 1990.

Selvadurai, Shyam. *Funny Boy*. New York: William Morrow, 1995.

Shohat, Ella. "The Struggle Over Representation: Casting, Coalitions, and the Politics of Identification." Ed. Román de la Capra, E. Ann Kaplan, and Michael Sprinker. *Late Imperial Culture*. New York: Verso, 1995. 166–78.

Sin City Diary. Rachel Rivera, director. Women Make Movies, 1992.

Spivak, Gayatri Chakravorty. "Can the Subaltern Speak?" *Marxism and the Interpretation of Culture*. Ed. Cary Nelson and Lawrence Grossberg. Urbana: U of Illinois P, 1988. 271–313.

Sturdevant, Saundra Pollock, and Brenda Soltzfus. *Let the Good Times Roll: Prostitution and the U.S. Military in Asia*. New York: New Press, 1992.

Takaki, Ronald. *Strangers from a Different Shore: A History of Asian Americans*. New York: Penguin, 1989.

Tan, Michael. "From *Bakla* to Gay: Shifting Gender Identities and Sexual Behaviors in the Philippines." *Conceiving Sexuality: Approaches to Sex Research in a Postmodern World*. Ed. Richard G. Parker and John H. Gagnon. New York: Routledge, 1995. 85–96.

Viswanathan, Gauri. *Masks of Conquest: Literary Study and British Rule in India*. New York: Columbia UP, 1989.

Warner, Michael. "Introduction." *Fear of a Queer Planet: Queer Politics and Social Theory*. Minneapolis: U of Minnesota P, 1993. vii–xxxi.

White Christmas. Michael Magnaye, director. National Asian American Telecommunications Association, 1993.

Williams, Raymond. "Dominant, Residual, and Emergent." *Marxism and Literature*. London: Oxford UP, 1980. 121–27.

7. Looking for My Penis
The Eroticized Asian in Gay Video Porn
Richard Fung

> Several scientists have begun to examine the relation between personality and human reproductive behaviour from a gene-based evolutionary perspective... In this vein we reported a study of racial difference in sexual restraint such that Orientals > whites > blacks. Restraint was indexed in numerous ways, having in common a lowered allocation of bodily energy to sexual functioning. We found the same racial pattern occurred on gamete production (dizygotic birthing frequency per 100: Mongoloids, 4; Caucasoids, 8; Negroids, 16), intercourse frequencies (premarital, marital, extramarital), developmental precocity (age at first intercourse, age at first pregnancy, number of pregnancies), primary sexual characteristics (size of penis, vagina, testis, ovaries), secondary sexual characteristics (salient voice, muscularity, buttocks, breasts), and biologic control of behaviour (periodicity of sexual response, predictability of life history from onset of puberty), as well as in androgen levels and sexual attitudes. (Rushton and Bogaert 259)

This passage from the *Journal of Research in Personality* was written by University of Western Ontario psychologist Philippe Rushton, who enjoys considerable controversy in Canadian academic circles and in the popular media. His thesis, articulated throughout his work, appropriates biological studies of the continuum of reproductive strategies of oysters through to chimpanzees and posits that degree of "sexuality"—interpreted as penis and vagina size, frequency of intercourse, buttock and lip size—correlates positively with criminality and sociopathic behavior and inversely intelligence, health, and longevity. Rushton sees race as *the* determining factor and places East Asians (Rushton uses the word *Orientals*) on one end of the spectrum and blacks on the other. Since whites fall squarely in the middle, the position of perfect balance, there is no need for analysis, and they remain free of scrutiny.

Notwithstanding its profound scientific shortcomings, Rushton's work serves as an excellent articulation of a dominant discourse on race and sexuality in Western society—a system of ideas and reciprocal practices that originated in Europe simultaneously with (some argue as a conscious justification for)[1] colonial expan-

From *How Do I Look? Queer Film and Video,* ed. Bad-Object Choices (Seattle: Bay Press, 1991). Reprinted with permission.

sion and slavery. In the nineteenth century these ideas took on a scientific gloss with social Darwinism and eugenics. Now they reappear, somewhat altered, in psychology journals from the likes of Rushton. It is important to add that these ideas have also permeated the global popular consciousness. Anyone who has been exposed to Western television or advertising images, which is much of the world, will have absorbed this particular constellation of stereotyping and racial hierarchy. In Trinidad in the 1960s, on the outer reaches of the empire, everyone in my schoolyard was thoroughly versed in these "truths" about the races.

Historically, most organizing against racism has concentrated on fighting discrimination that stems from the intelligence—social behavior variable assumed by Rushton's scale. Discrimination based on perceived intellectual ability does, after all, have direct ramifications in terms of education and employment, and therefore for survival. Until recently, issues of gender and sexuality remained a low priority for those who claimed to speak for the communities.[2] But antiracist strategies that fail to subvert the race-gender status quo are of seriously limited value. Racism cannot be narrowly defined in terms of race hatred. Race is a factor in even our most intimate relationships.

The contemporary construction of race and sex as exemplified by Rushton has endowed black people, both men and women, with a threatening hypersexuality. Asians, on the other hand, are collectively seen as undersexed.[3] But here I want to make some crucial distinctions. First, in North America, stereotyping has focused almost exclusively on what recent colonial language designates as "Orientals"—that is East and Southeast Asian peoples—as opposed to the "Orientalism" discussed by Edward Said, which concerns the Middle East. This current, popular usage is based more on a perception of similar physical features—black hair, "slanted" eyes, high cheek bones, and so on—than through a reference to common cultural traits. South Asians, people whose backgrounds are in the Indian subcontinent and Sri Lanka, hardly figure at all in North American popular representations, and those few images are ostensibly devoid of sexual connotation.[4]

Second, within the totalizing stereotype of the "Oriental," there are competing and sometimes contradictory sexual associations based on nationality. So, for example, a person could be seen as Japanese and somewhat kinky, or Filipino and "available." The very same person could also be seen as "Oriental" and therefore sexless. In addition, the racial hierarchy revamped by Rushton is itself in tension with an earlier and only partially eclipsed depiction of *all* Asians as having an undisciplined and dangerous libido. I am re-

ferring to the writings of the early European explorers and missionaries, but also to antimiscegenation laws and such specific legislation as the 1912 Saskatchewan law that barred white women
from employment in Chinese-owned businesses.

Finally, East Asian women figure differently from men both in reality and in representation. In "Lotus Blossoms Don't Bleed," Renee Tajima points out that in Hollywood films

> there are two basic types: the Lotus Blossom Baby (a.k.a. China
> Doll, Geisha Girl, shy Polynesian beauty, et al.) and the Dragon
> Lady (Fu Manchu's various female relations, prostitutes, devious
> madames).... Asian women in film are, for the most part, passive
> figures who exist to serve men—as love interests for white men
> (re: Lotus Blossoms) or as partners in crime for men of their own
> kind (re: Dragon Ladies) (28)

Further:

> Dutiful creatures that they are, Asian women are often assigned
> the task of expendability in a situation of illicit love.... Noticeably
> lacking is the portrayal of love relationships between Asian women
> and Asian men, particularly as lead characters. (29)

Because of their supposed passivity and sexual compliance, Asian
women have been fetishized in dominant representation, and there
is a large and growing body of literature by Asian women on the op-
pressiveness of these images. Asian men, however (at least since Sessue Hayakawa, who made a Hollywood career in the 1920s of representing the Asian man as sexual threat)[5] have been consigned to
one of two categories: the egghead/wimp, or—in what may be analogous to the lotus blossom–dragon lady dichotomy—the kung fu
master/ninja/samurai. He is sometimes dangerous, sometimes
friendly, but almost always characterized by a desexualized Zen as-
ceticsm. So whereas, as Fanon tells us, "the Negro is eclipsed. He is
turned into a penis. He *is* a penis,"[6] the Asian man is defined by a
striking absence down there. And if Asian men have no sexuality,
how can we have homosexuality?

Even as recently as the early 1980s, I remember having to prove
my queer credentials before being admitted with other Asian men
into a Toronto gay club. I do not believe it was a question of a color
barrier. Rather, my friends and I felt that the doorman was genuinely unsure about our sexual orientation. We also felt that had
we been white and dressed similarly, our entrance would have
been automatic.[7]

Although a motto for the lesbian and gay movements has been
"we are everywhere," Asians are largely absent from the images pro-

duced by both the political and the commercial sectors of the main-stream gay and lesbian communities. From the earliest articulation of the Asian gay and lesbian movements, a principal concern has therefore been visibility. In political organizing, the demand for a voice, or rather the demand to be heard, has largely been re-sponded to by the problematic practice of "minority" representa-tion on panels and boards.[8] But since racism is a question of power and not of numbers, this strategy has often led to a dead-end to-kenistic integration, failing to address the real imbalances.

Creating a space for Asian gay and lesbian representation has meant, among other things, deepening an understanding of what is at stake for Asians in coming out publicly.[9] As is the case for many other people of color and especially immigrants, our families and our ethnic communities are a rare source of affirmation in a racist society. In coming out, we risk (or feel that we risk) losing this sup-port, though the ever-growing organizations of lesbian and gay Asians have worked against this process of cultural exile. In my own experience, the existence of a gay Asian community broke down the cultural schizophrenia in which I related, on one hand, to a het-erosexual family that affirmed my ethnic culture and, on the other hand, to a gay community that was predominantly white. Knowing that there was support also helped me come out to my family and further bridge the gap.

If we look at commercial gay sexual representation, it appears that the antiracist movements have had little impact: the images of men and male beauty are still of *white* men and *white* male beauty. These are the standards against which we compare both ourselves and often our brothers—Asian, black, native, and Latino.[10] Al-though other people's rejection (or fetishization) of us according to the established racial hierarchies may be experienced as oppres-sive, we are not necessarily moved to scrutinize our own desire and its relationship to the hegemonic image of the white man.[11]

In my lifelong vocation of looking for my penis, trying to fill in the visual void, I have come across only a handful of primary and sec-ondary references to Asian male sexuality in North American rep-resentation. Even in my own video work, the stress has been on de-constructing sexual representation and only marginally on creating erotica. So I was very excited at the discovery of a Vietnamese Amer-ican working in gay porn.

Having acted in six videotapes, Sum Yung Mahn is perhaps the only Asian to qualify as a gay porn "star." Variously known as Brad Troung or Sam or Sum Yung Mahn, he has worked for a number of different production studios. All of the tapes in which he appears are

distributed through International Wavelength, a San Francisco—
based mail-order company whose catalog entries feature Asians in
American, Thai, and Japanese productions. According to the owner
of International Wavelength, about 90 percent of the Asian tapes are
bought by white men, and the remaining 10 percent are purchased
by Asians. But the number of Asian buyers is growing.

In examining Sum Yung Mahn's work, it is important to recognize the different strategies used for fitting an Asian actor into the
traditionally white world of gay porn and how the terms of entry are
determined by the perceived demands of an intended audience.
Three tapes, each geared toward a specific erotic interest, illustrate
these strategies.

Below the Belt, like most porn tapes, has an episodic structure. All
the sequences involve the students and *sensei* of an all-male karate
dojo. The authenticity of the setting is proclaimed with the opening
shots of a gym full of *gi*-clad, serious-faced young men going
through their weapons exercises. Each of the main actors is introduced in turn; with the exception of the teacher, who has dark hair,
all fit into the current porn conventions of Aryan, blond, shaved,
good looks.[12] Moreover, since Sum Yung Mahn is not even listed in
the opening credits, we can surmise that this tape is not targeted to
an audience with any particular erotic interest in Asian men. Most
gay video porn uses white actors exclusively; those tapes having the
least bit of racial integration are pitched to the specialty market
through outlets such as International Wavelength.[13] This visual
apartheid stems, I assume, from an erroneous perception that the
sexual appetites of gay men are exclusive and unchangeable.

A karate *dojo* offers a rich opportunity to introduce Asian actors.
One might imagine it as the gay Orientalist's dream project. But
given the intended audience for this video, the erotic appeal of the
dojo, except for the costumes and a few misplaced props (Taiwanese
and Korean flags for a Japanese art form?), is completely appropriated into a white world.

The tape's action occurs in a gym, in the students' apartments,
and in a garden. The one scene with Sum Yung Mahn is a dream sequence. Two students, Robbie and Stevie, are sitting in a locker
room. Robbie confesses that he has been having strange dreams
about Greg, their teacher. Cut to the dream sequence, which is
coded by clouds of green smoke. Robbie is wearing a red headband
with black markings suggesting script (if indeed they belong to an
Asian language, they are not the Japanese or Chinese characters
that one would expect). He is trapped in an elaborate snare. Enter
a character in a black *ninja* mask, wielding a *nanchaku.* Robbie narrates: "I knew this evil samurai would kill me." The masked figure is

menacingly running the *nanchaku* chain under Robbie's genitals when Greg, the teacher, appears and disposes of him. Robbie explains to Stevie in the locker room: "I knew that I owed him my life, and I knew I had to please him [long pause] in any way that he wanted." During that pause we cut back to the dream. Amid more puffs of smoke, Greg, carrying a man in his arms, approaches a low platform. Although Greg's back is toward the camera, we can see that the man is wearing the red headband that identifies him as Robbie. As Greg lays him down, we see that Robbie has "turned Japanese"! It's Sum Yung Mahn.

Greg fucks Sum Yung Mahn, who is always face down. The scene constructs anal intercourse for the Asian Robbie as an act of submission, not of pleasure: unlike other scenes of anal intercourse in the tape, for example, there is no dubbed dialogue on the order of "Oh yeah . . . fuck me harder!" but merely ambiguous groans. Without coming, Greg leaves. A group of (white) men wearing Japanese outfits encircle the platform, and Asian Robbie, or "the Oriental boy," as he is listed in the final credits, turns to lie on his back. He sucks a cock, licks someone's balls. The other men come all over his body; he comes. The final shot of the sequence zooms in to a close-up of Sum Yung Mahn's headband, which dissolves to a similar close-up of Robbie wearing the same headband, emphasizing that the two actors represent one character.

We now cut back to the locker room. Robbie's story has made Stevie horny. He reaches into Robbie's pants, pulls out his penis, and sex follows. In his Asian manifestation, Robbie is fucked and sucks others off (Greek passive/French active/bottom). His passivity is pronounced, and he is never shown other than prone. As a white man, his role is completely reversed: he is at first sucked off by Stevie, and then he fucks him (Greek active/French passive/top). Neither of Robbie's manifestations veers from his prescribed role.

To a greater extent than most other gay porn tapes, *Below the Belt* is directly about power. The hierarchical *dojo* setting is milked for its evocation of dominance and submission. With the exception of one very romantic sequence midway through the tape, most of the actors stick to their defined roles of top or bottom. Sex, especially anal sex, as punishment is a recurrent image. In this genre of gay pornography, the role-playing in the dream sequence is perfectly apt. What is significant, however, is how race figures into the equation. In a tape that appropriates emblems of Asian power (karate), the only place for a real Asian actor is as a caricature of passivity. Sum Yung Mahn does not portray as Asian, but rather the literalization of a metaphor, so that by being passive, Robbie actually becomes "Oriental." At a more practical level, the device of the dream also allows the producers to introduce an element of the mysterious, the exotic, without disrupting the racial status quo of the rest of the tape. Even in the dream sequence, Sum Yung Mahn is at the center of the frame as spectacle, having minimal physical involvement with the men around him. Although the sequence ends with his climax, he exists for the pleasure of others.

Richard Dyer, writing about gay porn, states that

> although the pleasure of anal sex (that is, of being anally fucked) is represented, the narrative is never organized around the desire to be fucked, but around the desire to ejaculate (whether or not following from anal intercourse). Thus, although at a level of public representation gay men may be thought of as deviant and disruptive of masculine norms because we assert the pleasure of being fucked and the eroticism of the anus, in our pornography this takes a back seat. (28)

Although Tom Waugh's amendment to this argument—that anal pleasure is represented in individual sequences[14]—also holds true for *Below the Belt,* as a whole the power of the penis and the pleasure of ejaculation are clearly the narrative's organizing principles. As with the vast majority of North American tapes featuring Asians, the problem is not the representation of anal pleasure per se, but rather that the narratives privilege the penis while always assigning the Asian the role of bottom; Asian and anus are conflated. In the case of Sum Yung Mahn, being fucked may well be his personal sexual preference. But the fact remains that there are very few occasions in North American video porn in which an Asian fucks a white man, so few, in fact, that International Wavelength promotes the tape *Studio X* (1986) with the blurb "Sum Yung Mahn makes history as the first Asian who fucks a non-Asian."[15]

Although I agree with Waugh that in gay as opposed to straight porn "the spectator's positions in relation to the representations are open and in flux" (33), this observation applies only when all the participants are white. Race introduces another dimension that may serve to close down some of this mobility. This is not to suggest that the experience of gay men of color with this kind of sexual representation is the same as that of heterosexual women with regard to the gendered gaze of straight porn. For one thing, Asian gay men are men. We can therefore physically experience the pleasures depicted on the screen, since we too have erections and ejaculations and can experience anal penetration. A shifting identification may occur despite the racially defined roles, and most gay Asian men in North America are used to obtaining pleasure from all-white pornography. This, of course, goes hand in hand with many problems of self-image and sexual identity. Still, I have been struck by the unanimity with which gay Asian men I have met, from all over this continent as well as from Asia, immediately identify and resist these representations. Whenever I mention the topic of Asian actors in American porn, the first question I am asked is whether the Asian is simply shown getting fucked.

Asian Knights, the second tape I want to consider, has an Asian producer-director and a predominantly Asian cast. In its first scenario, two Asian men, Brad and Rick, are seeing a white psychiatrist because they are unable to have sex with each other.

Rick: We never have sex with other Asians. We usually have sex with
    Caucasian guys.
Counselor: Have you had the opportunity to have sex together?
Rick: Yes, a coupla times, but we never get going.

Homophobia, like other forms of oppression, is seldom dealt with in gay video porn. With the exception of safe-sex tapes that attempt a rare blend of the pedagogical with the pornographic, social or political issues are not generally associated with the erotic. It is therefore unusual to see one of the favored discussion topics for gay Asian consciousness-raising groups employed as a sex fantasy in *Asian Knights.* The desexualized image of Asian men that I have described has seriously affected our relationships with one another, and often gay Asian men find it difficult to see each other beyond the terms of platonic friendship or competition, to consider other Asian men as lovers.

True to the conventions of porn, minimal counseling from the psychiatrist convinces Rick and Brad to shed their clothes. Immediately sprouting erections, they proceed to have sex. But what appears to be an assertion of gay Asian desire is quickly derailed. As Brad and Rick make love on the couch, the camera cross-cuts to the psychiatrist looking on from an armchair. The rhetoric of the editing suggests that we are observing the two Asian men from his point of view. Soon the white man takes off his clothes and joins in. He immediately takes up a position at the center of the action—and at the center of the frame. What appeared to be a "conversion fantasy" for gay Asian desire was merely a ruse. Brad and Rick's temporary mutual absorption really occurs to establish the superior sexual draw of the white psychiatrist, a stand-in for the white male viewer, who is the real sexual subject of the tape. And the question of Asian-Asian desire, though presented as the main narrative force of the sequence, is deflected, or rather reframed from a white perspective.

Sex between the two Asian men in this sequence can be related somewhat to heterosexual sex in some gay porn films, such as those produced by the Gage brothers. In *Heatstroke* (1982), for example, sex with a woman is used to establish the authenticity of the straight man who is about to be seduced into gay sex. It dramatizes the significance of the conversion from the sanctioned object of desire, underscoring the power of the gay man to incite desire in his socially defined superior. It is also tied up with the fantasies of (female) virginity and conquest in Judeo-Christian and other patriarchal societies. The therapy-session sequence of *Asian Knights* also suggests parallels to representations of lesbians in straight porn, representations that are not meant to eroticize women loving women, but rather to titillate and empower the sexual ego of the heterosexual male viewer.

Asian Knights is organized to sell representations of Asians to white men. Unlike Sum Yung Mahn in *Below the Belt,* the actors are therefore more expressive and sexually assertive, as often the seducers as the seduced. But though the roles shift during the predominantly oral sex, the Asians remain passive in anal intercourse, except that they are now shown to want it! How much this assertion of agency represents a step forward remains a question.

Even in the one sequence of *Asian Knights* in which the Asian actor fucks the white man, the scenario privileges the pleasure of the white man over that of the Asian. The sequence begins with the Asian reading a magazine. When the white man (played by porn star Eric Stryker) returns home from a hard day at the office, the waiting Asian asks how his day went, undresses him (even taking off his socks), and proceeds to massage his back.[16] The Asian man acts the role of the mythologized geisha or "the good wife" as fantasized in the mail-order bride business. And, in fact, the "house boy" is one of the most persistent white fantasies about Asian men. The fantasy is also a reality in many Asian countries where economic imperialism gives foreigners, whatever their race, the pick of handsome men in financial need. The accompanying cultural imperialism grants status to those Asians with white lovers. White men who for various reasons, especially age, are deemed unattractive in their own countries, suddenly find themselves elevated and desired.

From the opening shot of painted lotus blossoms on a screen to the shot of a Japanese garden that separates the episodes, from the Chinese pop music to the chinoiserie in the apartment, there is a conscious attempt in *Asian Knights* to evoke a particular atmosphere.[17] Self-conscious "Oriental" signifiers are part and parcel of a colonial fantasy—and reality—that empowers one kind of gay man over another. Though I have known Asian men in dependent relations with older, wealthier white men, as an erotic fantasy the house boy scenario tends to work one way. I know of no scenarios of Asian men and white house boys. It is not the representation of the fantasy that offends, or even the fantasy itself, rather the uniformity with which these narratives reappear and the uncomfortable relationship they have to real social conditions.

International Skin, as its name suggests, features a Latino, a black man, Sum Yung Mahn, and a number of white actors. Unlike the other tapes I have discussed, there are no "Oriental" devices. And although Sum Yung Mahn and all the men of color are inevitably fucked (without reciprocating), there is mutual sexual engagement between the white and nonwhite characters.

In this tape Sum Yung Mahn is Brad, a film student making a movie for his class. Brad is the narrator, and the film begins with a self-reflexive "head and shoulders" shot of Sun Yung Mahn explaining the scenario. The film we are watching supposedly represents Brad's point of view. But here again the tape is not targeted to black, Asian, or Latino men; though Brad introduces all of these men as his friends, no two men of color ever meet on screen. Men of color are not invited to participate in the internationalism that is being sold, except through identification with white characters. This tape illustrates how an agenda of integration becomes problematic if it frames the issue solely in terms of black-white, Asian-white mixing: it perpetuates a system of white-centeredness.

The gay Asian viewer is not constructed as sexual subject in any of this work—not on the screen, not as a viewer. I may find Sum Yung Mahn attractive, I may desire his body, but I am always aware that he is not meant for me. I may lust after Eric Stryker and imagine myself as the Asian who is having sex with him, but the role the Asian plays in the scene with him is demeaning. It is not that there is anything wrong with the image of servitude per se, but rather that it is one of the few fantasy scenarios in which we figure, and we are always in the role of servant.

Are there then no pleasures for an Asian viewer? The answer to this question is extremely complex. There is first of all no essential Asian viewer. The race of the person viewing says nothing about how race figures in his or her own desires. Uniracial white representations in porn may not in themselves present a problem in addressing many gay Asian men's desires. But the issue is not simply that porn may deny pleasures to some gay Asian men. We also need to examine what role the pleasure of porn plays in securing a consensus about race and desirability that ultimately works to our disadvantage.

Though the sequences I have focused on in the preceding examples are those in which the discourses about Asian sexuality are most clearly articulated, they do not define the totality of depiction in these tapes. Much of the time the actors merely reproduce or attempt to reproduce the conventions of pornography. The fact that, with the exception of Sum Yung Mahn, they rarely succeed—because of their body type, because Midwestern-cowboy-porn dialect with Vietnamese intonation is just a bit incongruous, because they groan or gyrate just a bit too much—more than anything brings home the relative rigidity of the genre's codes. There is little seamlessness here. There are times, however, when the actors appear neither as simulated whites nor as symbolic others. There are several moments in *International Skin,* for example, in which the focus shifts from the genitals to hands caressing a body; these moments feel to me more "genuine." I do not mean this in the sense of an essential Asian sexuality, but rather a moment is captured in which the actor stops pretending. He does not stop acting, but he stops pretending to be a white porn star. I find myself focusing on moments like these, in which the racist ideology of the text seems to be temporarily suspended or rather eclipsed by the erotic power of the moment.

In "Pornography and the Doubleness of Sex for Women," Joanna Russ writes:

> Sex is ecstatic, autonomous and lovely for women. Sex is violent, dangerous and unpleasant for women. I don't mean a dichotomy (i.e., two kinds of women or even two kinds of sex) but rather a continuum in which no one's experience is wholly positive or negative. (39)

Gay Asian men are men and therefore not normally victims of the rape, incest, or other sexual harassment to which Russ is referring. However, there is a kind of doubleness, of ambivalence, in the way that Asian men experience contemporary North American gay communities. The "ghetto," the mainstream gay movement, can be a place of freedom and sexual identity. But it is also a site of racial, cultural, *and* sexual alienation sometimes more pronounced than that in straight society. For me sex is a source of pleasure but also a site of humiliation and pain. Released from the social constraints against expressing overt racism in public, the intimacy of sex can provide my (non-Asian) partner an opening for letting me know my place—sometimes literally, as when after we come, he turns over and asks where I come from.[18] Most gay Asian men I know have similar experiences.

This is just one reality that differentiates the experiences and therefore the political priorities of gay Asians and, I think, other gay men of color from those of white men. For one thing we cannot afford to take a libertarian approach. Porn can be an active agent in representing *and* reproducing a sex-race status quo. We cannot attain a healthy alliance without coming to terms with these differences.

The barriers that impede pornography from providing representations of Asian men that are erotic and politically palatable (as opposed to correct) are similar to those that inhibit the Asian documentary, the Asian feature, the Asian experiment film and videotape. We are seen as too peripheral, not commercially viable—not the general audience. *Looking for Langston* (1988), which is the first film I have seen that affirms rather than appropriates the sexuality of black gay men, was produced under exceptional economic circumstances that freed it from the constraints of the marketplace.[19] Should we call for an independent gay Asian pornography? Perhaps I do in a utopian sort of way, though I feel that the problems in North America's porn conventions are manifold and go beyond the question of race. There is such a limited vision of what constitutes the erotic.

In Canada, the major debate about race and representation has shifted from an emphasis on the image to a discussion of appropriation and control of production and distribution—who gets to produce the work. But as we have seen in the case of *Asian Knights,* the race of the producer is no automatic guarantee of "consciousness" about these issues or of a different product. Much depends on who is constructed as the audience for the work. In any case, it is not surprising that under capitalism, finding my penis may ultimately be a matter of dollars and cents.

Discussion

Audience member: You made a comment about perceived distinctions between Chinese and Japanese sexuality. I have no idea what you mean.

Richard Fung: In the West, there are specific sexual ambiences associated with the different Asian nationalities, sometimes based on cultural artifacts, sometimes on mere conjecture. These discourses exist simultaneously, even though in conflict, with totalizing notions of "Oriental" sexuality. Japanese male sexuality has come to be identified with strength, virility, perhaps a certain kinkiness, as signified for example by the clothing and gestures in *Below the Belt.* Japanese sexuality is seen as more "potent" than Chinese sexuality, which is generally represented as more passive and languorous. At the same time, there is the cliché that "all Orientals look alike." So in this paradox of the invisibility of difference lies the fascination. If he can ascertain where I'm from, he feels that he knows what he can expect from me. In response to this query about "ethnic origins," a friend of mine answers,

"Where would you like me to be from?" I like this response because it gently confronts the question while maintaining the erotic possibilities of the moment.

Simon Watney: I wanted to point out that the first film you showed, *Below the Belt,* presents us with a classic anxiety dream image. In it there is someone whose identity is that of a top man, but that identity is established in relation to a competing identity that allows him to enjoy sexual passivity, which is represented as a racial identity. It's as if he were in racial drag. I thought this film was extraordinary. Under what other conditions are Caucasian men invited to fantasize ourselves as racially other? And it seems to me that the only condition that would allow the visibility of that fantasy to be acted out in this way is the prior anxiety about a desired role, about top and bottom positions. This film is incredibly transparent and unconscious about how it construes or confuses sexual role-playing in relation to race. And the thrust of it all seems to be the construction of the Asian body as a kind of conciliatory pseudoheterosexuality for the white "top," who has anus envy, as it were.

Fung: I completely agree. The film says too much for its own good by making this racist agenda so clear.

Ray Navarro: I think your presentation was really important, and it parallels research I'm doing with regard to the image of Latino men in gay male porn. I wondered if you might comment a bit more, however, about the class relations you find within this kind of work. For example, I've found a consistent theme running throughout gay, white male porn of Latino men represented as either *campesino* or criminal. That is, it focuses less on body type—masculine, slight, or whatever—than on signifiers of class. It appears to be a class fantasy collapsed with a race fantasy, and in a way it parallels the actual power relations between the Latino stars and the producers and distributors, most of whom are white.

Fung: There are ways in which your comments can also apply to Asians. Unlike whites and blacks, most Asians featured in gay erotica are younger men. Since youth generally implies less economic power, class-race hierarchies appear in most of the work. In the tapes I've been looking at, the occupations of the white actors are usually specified, while those of the Asians are not. The white actors are assigned fantasy appeal based on profession, whereas for the Asians, the sexual cachet of race is deemed sufficient. In *Asian Knights* there are also sequences in which the characters' lack of "work" carries connotations of the housewife or, more particularly, the house boy.

But there is at least one other way to look at this discrepancy. The lack of a specified occupation may be taken to suggest that the Asian actor is the subject of the fantasy, a surrogate for the Asian viewer, and therefore does not need to be coded with specific attributes.

Tom Waugh: I think your comparison of the way the Asian male body is used in gay white porn to the way lesbianism is employed in heterosexual pornography is very interesting. You also suggested that racial markers in gay porn tend to close down its potential for openness and flux in identifications. Do you think we can take it further and say that racial markers in gay porn replicate, or function in the same way as, gender markers do in heterosexual pornography?

Fung: What, in fact, I intended to say with my comparison of the use of lesbians in heterosexual porn and that of Asian male bodies in white, gay male porn was that they're similar but also very different. I think that certain comparisons of gender with race are appropriate, but there are also profound differences. The fact that Asian gay men are *men* means that, as viewers, our responses to this work are grounded in our gender and the way gender functions in this society. Lesbians are *women*, with all that that entails. I suspect that although most Asian gay men experience ambivalence with white gay porn, the issues for women in relation to heterosexual pornography are more fundamental.

Waugh: The same rigidity of roles seems to be present in most situations.

Fung: Yes, that's true. If you notice the way the Asian body is spoken of in Rushton's work, the terms he uses are otherwise used when speaking of women. But it is too easy to discredit these arguments. I have tried instead to show how Rushton's conclusions are commensurate with the assumptions everywhere present in education and popular thought.

Audience member: I'm going to play devil's advocate. Don't you think gay Asian men who are interested in watching gay porn involving Asian actors will get ahold of the racially unmarked porn that is produced in Thailand or Japan? And if your answer is yes, then why should a white producer of gay porn go to the trouble of making tapes that cater to a relatively small gay Asian market? This is about dollars and cents. It seems obvious that the industry will cater to the white man's fantasy.

Fung: On the last point I partially agree. That's why I'm calling for an independent porn in which the gay Asian man is producer, actor, and intended viewer. I say this somewhat halfheartedly, because personally I am not very interested in producing porn, though I do want to continue working with sexually explicit material. But I also feel that one cannot assume, as the porn industry apparently does, that the desires of even white men are so fixed and exclusive.

Regarding the first part of your question, however, I must insist that Asian Americans and Asian Canadians are Americans and Canadians. I myself am a fourth-generation Trinidadian and have only a tenuous link with Chinese culture and aesthetics, except for what I have consciously searched after and learned. I purposely chose not to talk about Japanese or Thai productions because they come from cultural contexts about which I am incapable of commenting. In addition, the fact that porn from those countries is sometimes unmarked racially does not mean that it speaks to my experience or desires, my own culture of sexuality.

Isaac Julien: With regard to race representation or racial signifiers in the context of porn, your presentation elaborated a problem that came up in some of the safe sex tapes that were shown earlier. In them one could see a kind of trope that traces a circular pattern—a repetition that leads a black or Asian spectator to a specific realm of fantasy.

I wonder if you could talk a bit more about the role of fantasy, or the fantasy one sees in porn tapes produced predominantly by white producers. I see a fixing of different black subjects in recognizable stereotypes rather than a more dialectical representation of black identities, where a number of options or fantasy positions would be made available.

Fung: Your last film, *Looking for Langston,* is one of the few films I know of that has placed the sexuality of the black gay subject at its center. As I said earlier, my own work, especially *Chinese Characters* [1986], is more concerned with pulling apart the tropes you refer to than in constructing an alternative erotics. At the same time I feel that this latter task is imperative, and I hope that it is taken up more. It is in this context that I think the current attack on the National Endowment for the Arts and arts funding in the United States supports the racist status quo. If it succeeds, it effectively squelches the possibility of articulating counter-hegemonic views of sexuality.

Just before I left Toronto, I attended an event called "Cum Talk," organized by two people from Gay Asians Toronto and from Khush, the group for South Asian lesbians and gay men. We looked at porn and talked about the images people had of us, the role of "bottom" that we are constantly cast in. Then we spoke of what actually happened when we had sex with white men. What became clear was that we don't play out that role and are very rarely asked to. So there is a discrepancy between the ideology of sexuality and its practice, between sexual representation and sexual reality.

Gregg Bordowitz: When Jean Carlomusto and I began working on the porn project at Gay Men's Health Crisis, we had big ideas of challenging many of the roles and positionings involved in the dominant industry. But as I've worked more with porn, I find that it's really not an efficient arena in which to make such challenges. There is some room to question assumptions, but there are not many ways to challenge the codes of porn, except to question the conditions of production, which was an important point raised at the end of your talk. It seems to me that the only real way to picture more possibilities is, again, to create self-determining groups, make resources available for people of color and lesbians and other groups so that they can produce porn for themselves.

Fung: I only partly agree with you, because I think, so far as is possible, we have to take responsibility for the kinds of images we create, or re-create. *Asian Knights* had a Chinese producer, after all. But, yes, of course, the crucial thing is to activate more voices, which would establish the conditions for something else to happen. The liberal response to racism is that we need to integrate everyone—people should all become coffee-colored, or everyone should have sex with everyone else. But such an agenda doesn't often account for the specificity of our desires. I have seen very little porn produced from such an integrationist mentality that actually affirms my desire. It's so easy to find my fantasies appropriated for the pleasures of a white viewer. In that sense, porn is most useful for revealing relationships of power.

José Arroyo: You've been talking critically about a certain kind of colonial imagery. Isaac's film *Looking for Langston* contains not only a deconstruction of this imagery in its critique of the Mapplethorpe photographs but also a new construction of black desire. What kind of strategies do you see for a similar reconstructing of erotic Asian imagery?

Fung: One of the first things that needs to be done is to construct Asians as viewing subjects. My first videotape, *Orientations* [1984], had that as a primary goal. I thought of Asians as sexual subjects but also as viewing subjects to whom the work should be geared. Many of us, whether we're watching news or pornography or looking at advertising, see that the image or message is not really being directed at us. For example, the sexism and heterosexism of a disk jockey's attitudes become obvious when he or she says, "When you and your girlfriend go out tonight . . ." Even though that's meant to address a general audience, it's clear that this audience is presumed not to have any women (not to mention lesbians!) in it. The general audience, as I analyze *him*, is white, male, heterosexual, middle-class, and center-right politically. So we have to understand this presumption first, to see that only very specific people are being addressed.

When I make my videotapes, I know that I am addressing Asians. That means that I can take certain things for granted and introduce other things in a completely different context. But there are still other questions of audience. When we make outreach films directed at the straight community—the "general public"—in an effort to make lesbian and gay issues visible, we often sacrifice many of the themes that are important to how we express our sexualities: drag, issues of promiscuity, and so on. But when I made a tape for a gay audience, I talked about those same issues very differently. For one thing, I *talked* about those issues. And I tried to image them in ways that were very different from the way the dominant media image them. In *Orientations* I had one guy talk about park and washroom sex—about being a slut, basically—in a park at midday with front lighting. He talked very straightforwardly about it, which is only to say that there are many possibilities for doing this.

I think, however, that to talk about gay Asian desire is very difficult, because we need to swim through so much muck to get to it. It is very difficult (if even desirable) to do in purely positive terms, and I think it's necessary to do a lot of deconstruction along the way. I have no ready-made strategies; I feel it's a hit-and-miss sort of project.

Lei Chou: I want to bring back the issue of class. One of the gay Asian stereotypes that you mentioned was the Asian house boy. The reality is that many of these people are immigrants: English is a second language for them, and they are thus economically disenfranchised through being socially and culturally displaced. So when you talk about finding the Asian penis in pornography, how will this project work for such people? Since pornography is basically white and middle-class, what kind of tool is it? Who really is your target audience?

Fung: If I understand your question correctly, you are asking about the prognosis for new and different representations within commercial porn. And I don't think the prognosis is very good: changes will probably happen very slowly. At the same time, I think that pornography is an especially important site of struggle precisely for those Asians who are, as you say, economically and socially at a disadvantage. For those who are most isolated, whether in families or rural areas, print pornography is often the first introduction to gay sexuality—before, for example, the gay and lesbian press or gay Asian support groups. But this porn provides mixed messages: it affirms gay identity articulated almost exclusively as white. Whether we like it or not, mainstream gay porn is more available to most gay Asian men than any independent work you or I might produce. That is why pornography is a subject of such concern for me.

NOTES

Acknowledgments: I would like to thank Tim McCaskell and Helen Lee for their ongoing criticism and comments, as well as Jeff Nunokawa and Douglas Crimp for their invaluable suggestions in converting the original spoken presentation into a written text. Finally, I would like to extend my gratitude to Bad Object-Choices for inviting me to participate in *How Do I Look?*

1. See Williams.

2. Feminists of color have long pointed out that racism is phrased differently for men and women. Nevertheless, since it is usually heterosexual (and often middle-class) males whose voices are validated by the power structure, it is their interests that are taken up as "representing" the communities. See Smith 162.

3. The mainstream "leadership" within Asian communities often colludes with the myth of the model minority and the reassuring desexualization of Asian people.

4. In Britain, however, more race-sex stereotypes of South Asians exist. Led by artists such as Pratibha Parmar, Sunil Gupta, and Hanif Kureishi, there is also a growing and already significant body of work by South Asians themselves that takes up questions of sexuality.

5. See Gong 37–41.

6. Fanon 120. For a reconsideration of this statement in the light of contemporary black gay issues, see Mercer 141.

7. I do not think that this could happen in today's Toronto, which now has the second-largest Chinese community on the continent. Perhaps it would not have happened in San Francisco. But I still believe that there is an onus on gay Asians and other gay people of color to prove our homosexuality.

8. The term "minority" is misleading. Racism is not a matter of numbers but of power. This is especially clear in situations where people of color constitute actual majorities, as in most former European colonies. At the same time, I feel that none of the current terms is really satisfactory and that too much time spent on the politics of "naming" can in the end be diversionary.

9. To organize effectively with lesbian and gay Asians, we must reject self-righteous condemnation of "closetedness" and see coming out more as a process or a goal, rather than as a prerequisite for participation in the movement.

10. Racism is available to be used by anyone. The conclusion that—because racism = power + prejudice—only white people can be racist is Eurocentric and simply wrong. Individuals have varying degrees and different sources of power, depending on the given moment in a shifting context. This does not contradict the fact that, in contemporary North American society, racism is generally organized around white supremacy.

11. From simple observation, I feel safe in saying that most gay Asian men in North America hold white men as their idealized sexual partners. However, I am not trying to construct an argument for determinism, and there are a number of outstanding problems that are not easily answered by current analyses of power. What of the experience of Asians who are attracted to men of color, including other Asians? What about white men who prefer Asians sexually? How and to what extent is desire articulated in terms of race as opposed to body type or other attributes? To what extent is sexual attraction exclusive or changeable, and can it be consciously programed? These questions are all politically loaded, as they parallel and impact the debates between essentialists and social constructionists on the nature of homosexuality itself. They are also emotionally charged, in that sexual choice involving race has been a basis for moral judgment.

12. See Dyer. In his chapter on Marilyn Monroe, Dyer writes extensively on the relationship between blondness, whiteness, and desirability.

13. Print porn is somewhat more racially integrated, as are the new safe sex tapes—by the Gay Men's Health Crisis, for example—produced in a political and pedagogical rather than a commercial context.

14. Waugh 31.

15. *International Wavelength News.*

16. It seems to me that the undressing here is organized around the pleasure of the white man in being served. This is in contrast to the undressing scenes in, say, James Bond films, in which the narrative is organized around undressing as an act of revealing the woman's body, an indicator of sexual conquest.

17. Interestingly, the gay video porn from Japan and Thailand that I have seen has none of this Oriental coding. Asianness is not taken up as a sign but is taken for granted as a setting for the narrative.

18. Though this is a common enough question in our postcolonial, urban environments, when asked of Asians, it often reveals two agendas: first, the assumption that all Asians are newly arrived immigrants and, second, a fascination with difference and sameness. Although we (Asians) all supposedly look alike, there are specific characteristics and stereotypes associated with each particular ethnic group. The inability to tell us apart underlies the inscrutability attributed to Asians. This "in-

scrutability" took on sadly ridiculous proportions when during World War II the Chinese were issued badges so that white Canadians could distinguish them from "the enemy."

19. For more on the origins of the black film and video workshops in Britain, see Pines 26.

WORKS CITED

Asian Knights. Ed Sung, director. William Richhe Productions, 1985.

Below the Belt. Philip St. John, director. California Dream Machine Productions, 1985.

Chinese Characters. Richard Fung, director. 1986.

Dyer, Richard. "Coming to Terms." *Jump Cut* 30 (Mar. 1985): 27–29.

———. *Heavenly Bodies: Film Stars and Society*. New York: St. Martin's, 1986.

Fanon, Frantz. *Black Skin, White Masks*. London: Paladin, 1970.

Gong, Stephen. "Zen Warrior of the Celluloid (Silent) Years: The Art of Sessue Hayakawa." *Bridge* 8 (Winter 1982–83): 37–41.

Heatstroke. 1982.

International Skin. William Richhe, director. N'wayvo Richhe Productions, 1985.

International Wavelength News 2 (Jan. 1991).

Looking for Langston. Isaac Julien, director. U.K.: Sankofa Film and Video, 1988.

Mercer, Kobena. "Imaging the Black Man's Sex." *Photography/Politics: Two*. Ed. Pat Holland, Jo Spence, and Simon Watney. London: Comedia/Methuen, 1987. Reprinted in *Male Order: Unwrapping Masculinity*. Ed. Rowena Chapman and Jonathan Rutherford. London: Lawrence and Wishart, 1988. 97–164.

Orientations. Richard Fung, director. 1984.

Pines, Jim. "The Cultural Context of Black British Cinema." *Blackframes: Critical Perspectives on Black Independent Cinema*. Ed. Mybe B. Cham and Claire Andrade-Watkins. Cambridge: MIT P, 1988. 26–30.

Rushton, J. Philippe, and Anthony F. Bogaert, "Race versus Social Class Difference in Sexual Behaviour: A Follow-Up Test of the r/K Dimension." *Journal of Research in Personality* 22 (1988): 259–72.

Russ, Joanna. "Pornography and the Doubleness of Sex for Women." *Jump Cut* 32 (Apr. 1986): 38–41.

Said, Edward. *Orientalism*. London: Routledge and Kegan Paul, 1978.

Smith, Barbara. "Toward a Black Feminist Criticism." *All the Women Are White, All the Blacks Are Men, But Some of Us Are Brave: Black Women's Studies*. Old Westbury, N.Y.: Feminist P, 1982). 157–75.

Studio X. International Wavelength, 1986.

Tajima, Renee. "Lotus Blossoms Don't Bleed: Images of Asian Women." *Anthologies of Asian American Film and Video*. New York: Third World Newsreel, 1984. 28–33.

Waugh, Tom. "Men's Pornography, Gay vs. Straight." *Jump Cut* 30 (Mar. 1985): 30–35.

Williams, Eric. *Capitalism and Slavery*. New York: Capricorn, 1966.

8. Lisa's Closet
Gaye Chan

I was eight years old when I began living with a tall, thin, blond, mannequin. My father, an avid collector of all sorts of things, bought her from a department store going-out-of-business sale. He named the mannequin Lisa, after the daughter of my uncle who had emigrated to the United States when he was sixteen. My uncle named himself Glenn.

Lisa stood at the window of our apartment in Hong Kong for years. My father must have thought it funny to have a white woman standing there looking out onto the city. Each week he took a dress from my mother's closet and changed Lisa's outfit. Lisa being taller and more buxom than my mother, the dresses would be shorter, tighter, and inevitably more sexy when Lisa wore them.

In 1968 my family emigrated to the United States and into to the mys-

tical "American suburb." My father named himself Eric. My mother named herself Jean.

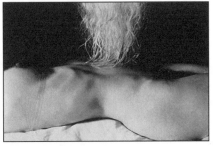

Lisa moved with us to the United States, but she no longer stood at the window. My mother thought it would make a bad impression on the neighbors (a concern that she evidently did not have back in Hong

Kong). So Lisa was relegated to the hallway closet. She stood, it seemed to me at the time, over six feet tall and must have taken up at least half the closet, among winter coats, umbrellas, and other seldom used items. In spite of the fact that the hallway closet was soon named Lisa's closet, each time I opened it Lisa startled and fright-

ened me. She also frightened guests (all of whom were Chinese) who chanced upon her while hanging up their coats.

We moved several times after that. The immodesty of Lisa's stature and rigidity became increasingly burdensome with each move. My mother became impatient with packing, relocating, and storing Lisa. My

father, unwilling to abandon Lisa, tried to appease my mother by making Lisa less obtrusive. He separated parts that would disassemble: her left arm, her right hand, and both her legs at the thighs.

The process of Lisa's coming apart was arguably collaborative until my father, inspired by a "modern art" assemblage he had seen, sawed her torso in half and attached it to a piece of stainless steel that he had salvaged from a construction site. He was thrilled that he had finally discovered a use for it (the stainless steel, of course), and he attempted to make Lisa anatomically correct by adding nipples and genitalia. My father's art project was soon abandoned without ceremony. The only visible result being the license it gave him to further dismantle Lisa. He sawed at her neck, waist, and right shoulder. Thus began Lisa's diaspora.

Being a structural engineer by trade, my father saw immense beauty and pleasure in finding good fits. Lisa was housed in the most unlikely and unexpected (albeit impermanent) places, always moving to yet a better fit. My earlier fears of Lisa's Closet had been substantial yet contained, but with Lisa's new migratory patterns our "chance encounters" became much more frequent and unpredictable.

Lisa was simply everywhere. Her right arm was under my parents' bed. Her hips were behind the bathroom mirror. Her left leg was in the trunk of my parents' car. It seemed as though every time I searched for a lost item or sneaked around secret out-of-the-way places, I came across a dismembered body part (the most memorable being the leg I found under my parents' bed while I was searching for my father's *Playboy* magazines).

I recently asked my father what happened to Lisa. At first he seemed to have forgotten this woman of my youth. When he finally remembered, he was overjoyed that I recalled her in such detail. And although he is not entirely certain, my father thinks that Lisa was thrown away part by part over a period of fifteen years. He says he does not know if any part of her is still with him. His passion for Lisa has evidently been transferred to others of his collections—3M Magic tapes, dismembered calculator innards, milk cartons, garbanzo beans, vitamin bottles . . .

My father asked me why the sudden interest, whether I had "run into Lisa." I could not bring myself to tell him that she and my father were to be the topic of an essay. I feared that this would somehow embarrass him. I realized, though, that the embarrassment is more likely to be my own. In my innocence of sexual matters, Lisa had become an enigma of sexuality, desire, and their ugly sibling, shame.

While Lisa and my sexual innocence have long been left behind, the longing, fear, and shame that were inspired by and contained in Lisa's Closet still hold tremendous fascination for me. This story is one that has evolved in both detail and interpretation over many, many years.

My sister, brother, and I each have very different memories of Lisa. My sister, who is heterosexual, says today that she was extremely offended and disturbed by Lisa. She was offended by the constant presence of what she interpreted as my father's desire. She felt forced, on one hand, to identify with the aestheticized, objectified, and finally dismembered female body and, on the other hand, to be pitted against Lisa's unattainable idealized whiteness. My own reaction to Lisa was complicated by my developing lesbian desire. I am still not entirely sure why I was so embarrassed by my father and Lisa for so long. Was I ashamed to have a father who owned and habitually played with a mannequin? Did I link Lisa with my shame in being a lesbian?

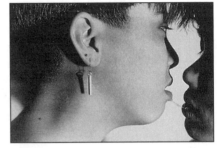

Angel on Folding Chair is a series of photographs that I developed from 1986 to 1988. It was initially inspired by my urge to record, confirm, and speak about my first experiences of unabashed sexual adventure. Besides the pure exhilaration of the experiential, I was interested in the psychological dimensions of finding an identity through the exchange of desire.

Angel on Folding Chair enjoyed a certain amount of acceptance and marketability both in the straight and lesbian worlds, which created a place for me as a rare spokesperson of an "exotic" community to the straight world and also sustained my desirability to the lesbian community as a "glamorous artist." I rode on this perception for a long time. None of my other work has ever enjoyed such popularity.

I suppose it is expected for artists to be suspicious of success, but *Angel on Folding Chair* has also inspired many bouts of shame, doubt, and disillusionment. I began to feel that I was either prostituting myself or pimping my photographs:

What is Angel on Folding Chair?
Who are the angels I am representing?
Are my angels and my father's Lisa manifestations of the same impulse?
Are Lisa and Angel on Folding Chair *symbols/surrogates of straight white male privilege?*

My father, Eric, the collector of things, permeates and permutates my imagination. A few years ago, three years before his retirement, he was laid off by his employer of twenty years when the firm was purchased by an international corporation. Now he spends his time taping together pieces of paper with 3M Magic tape (a huge collection pilfered from his office before his departure) and writing Chinese poetry. He writes of life "like the tides"—of how he attempted but failed to control it. Now he watches the ebb and flow of life on the news and locks his apartment door twenty times a day.

My father showed me his poetry when I showed him my photographs. He said that he didn't understand my work, that it was too sophisticated, too complicated. But to me it was obvious that the themes and the tone of our work mirrored each other.

I started noticing the similarities between my father and me several years ago. These realizations caught me, like most people, by surprise. I registered them with some resistance—the normal resistance of not wanting to be like one's parents, complicated by internalized racism. Mirroring my earlier encounters with Lisa's parts, I am discovering my own, with equal unpredictability and wonderment.

Part Three
Keeping Records

Overleaf: Karen Kimura, *Portrait of Mother*,
xerography and charcoal, one of six
panels, 40 × 30 inches, 1993

9. Sexuality, Identity, and the Uses of History
Nayan Shah

In 1986 Savir Das and Arvind Kumar invented the word "trikon" to break silence and to create a sense of identity for themselves.[1] The lead story of the first issue of the *Trikon*[2] newsletter opened with a dictionary-style definition of the new name, a definition that attempted to translate the symbols of North American/European gay politics into a South Asian language. The definition invoked a particular history of oppression and the transformation of that history into a symbol of gay political assertion:

> **tri-kon** n. (**tri** as in *trim,* **kon** as in *cone*) Sanskrit for triangle. Pink triangles were first used in Nazi concentration camps to identify gay prisoners. Today the sign is embraced by gay men and women not only as a reminder of injustices of the past, but also as a symbol of gay pride. (DAS AND KUMAR 1)

Trikon was one of the first of a half-dozen South Asian lesbian and gay newsletters and support groups that emerged after the mid-1980s in North America, Britain, and India. *Anamika* (United States) started a year before *Trikon; Khush Khayal* (Canada), *Shakti Khabar* (United Kingdom), *Freedom* (India), *Shamakami* (United States), and *Bombay Dost* (India) followed fast on *Trikon*'s heels. These newsletters, which mix politics and desire, have served as forums for articulating identities, shaping community, and sharing the cultural products of South Asian lesbians and gay men. Following *Trikon*'s lead, they have presumed an audience that shares a distinctive yet global identity, a sexual identity that binds the concerns and needs of gay men in Patna and Pittsburgh with those of lesbians in London and Lahore. The desire for community has led to the creation of a global South Asian queer identity, an identity that has fought silence and invisibility in order to emerge.

Silenced in both South Asian patriarchal societies and the white queer communities of North America and Europe, South Asian gays and lesbians have had to invent themselves, often with new words and names of identification. They have appropriated the Hindi and Urdu word *khush,* which means "happy." Some have reconfigured it to mean "gay"; others define it as "ecstatic pleasure."

A version of this essay was first presented at Desh Pardesh: A Conference and Festival Exploring South Asian Culture in the West, Toronto, 6–10, November 1991. It was later published in Rakesh Ratti (ed.), *A Lotus of Another Color: An Unfolding of the South Asian Gay and Lesbian Experience* (Boston: Alyson, 1993).

In 1985 a lesbian collective in the United States used the Sanskrit word *anamika*, meaning "nameless," to address the dearth of names in South Asian languages for relationships between two women. The *Anamika* newsletter folded in 1987. By 1990 a new lesbian collective had formed; as an affirmation of their relationships, the editors named its newsletter *Shamakami*, a Bengali word meaning "desiring one's equal." The appropriation of language has been integral to the invention of identity for South Asian men and women who feel marginalized in dominant South Asian societies. To paraphrase Suniti Namjoshi, words have invented the world of South Asian queer affiliations and social networks (Namjoshi and Hanscombe). They have used language to name themselves and also to address heterosexist oppression.

Many of the essays, stories, poems, and letters that have appeared in these newsletters and other publications have engaged in this politics of assertion. Many self-identified South Asian lesbians and gay men have struggled for representation in both dominant South Asian worlds and dominant white queer worlds. In this struggle they have enlisted history—personal, archeological, and social—to attain visibility and voice. The uses of history have complicated assumptions about the construction of identities and about the project of reclaiming history.

The formation of South Asian queer communities has inspired me to claim an identity, that of a South Asian gay man living in the United States. The narratives, testimonies, and histories produced by self-identified South Asian lesbians and gay men often resonate with my own struggle for identity and desire for community. These powerful resonances have also generated sharp doubts and raised questions about the nature of identity and the creation of culture and community.

Marking Sexual Differences

Identity is about belonging. At its most basic level, identity marks what we have in common with some people and what differentiates us from others. Jeffrey Weeks reminds us that "each of us lives with a variety of potentially contradictory identities. . . . Behind the quest for identity are different, and often conflicting, values. By saying who we are, we are also striving to express what we are, what we believe, and what we desire. The problem is that these beliefs, needs, and desires are often patently in conflict, not only between different communities but within individuals themselves" ("The Value of Difference" 88–89). The cultural production of South Asian lesbians and gay men charts these conflicting identities.

South Asian queers, like other gays and lesbians in North America and Europe, have used coming-out narratives to make sense of their feelings of difference from mainstream society. These narratives follow two general patterns, which seek to explain the process of developing a queer identity. The first explains sexual orientation as originating in adolescence with an awareness of attraction to members of the same sex. The second shows desire developing out of politics.

Narratives following the first pattern often dwell on a first crush or sexual experience. Emotional relationships and sexual experiences often drive self-knowledge and the assumption of a gay/lesbian identity. In a typical narrative strategy, Rahul Mukhopadhyay recalls feelings of tenderness for another boy, which he now interprets as sexual. He describes his feelings for classmate Ali Askar at age nine: "I experienced a warm rush through my body and felt an urgent desire to feel his body close to mine. I wasn't even aware that my feelings were sexual at that time" (1). Later after recounting several high school love affairs with boys, Rahul explains, "I have been gay as long as I can remember. It seems quite immaterial to me to find a reason for homosexuality" (1). Shilpa Mehta experienced a similar sense of same-sex attraction: "Around puberty, I got real conscious that I was attracted to women, not men. Men were my buddies . . . [but] it was women I wanted" ("Silent No More" 3). Shilpa did not act on her desires and have sexual relationships with women until she left Bombay to attend college in the United States.

In the first narrative pattern both men and women define sexual identities through reflections on their objects of desire. However, the second narrative pattern, which describes the movement from political consciousness to sexual identification, seems to be employed by women only. Feminism spurs many self-identified lesbians to articulate their sexual desires. Uma, a New Zealander of Indian descent, fashioned a sexual identity after engaging in battles against sexual discrimination and racism in Australia: "At the university in 1975, I discovered more about sexual discrimination, and felt myself validated at last about this form of oppression. . . . I could read and find out what women around the world were writing—that women who were fighting against sexism called themselves 'feminist.' I then became a 'Black feminist.' . . . I think that my sexuality came more through my politics than anything else. And, of course, because I am a political person, I made my sexuality a political act and came out as publicly as possible" ("Uma" 5).[3]

Kamini Chaudhary also became aware of lesbian relationships and identities by exploring feminism: "I wonder if I had not heard about lesbianism through the women's/feminist literature I was reading, or if I wasn't close friends with a lesbian couple, would I have discovered that loving a woman can be sexual. Was that what was undiscovered and unexpressed with Nazreen?" (1–2). Kamini's refections on her intimate adolescent friendship with Nazreen suggest that politics alone does not explicate the gender differences involved in marking identities. Kamini's choice is one of both pleasure and politics. Kamini's and Uma's narratives suggest that sexual identities and expressions are a choice—pleasure choice—not something prescribed by biology and certainly not by the hypothalamus.[4]

Kamini's knowledge of lesbian relationships informs her reflections about the intimacy between women in India: "I have always loved women. Women friendships in India weren't sexual but they were like love affairs. Drama, trauma, jealousy, intimacy, hugging, holding, touching, and involvement far more intense and complete than any I have experienced in a friendship or relationship with an American" (2). While she marks the romances with Indian women as "more intense and complete" than those she has experienced with American women, through a language of lesbian relationships learned in the United States, Kamini is able to name friendships between women in India "romances."

In most of these coming-out narratives knowledge of relationships and identities as gay and lesbian were acquired by South Asians living in North America, Britain, and Australia. Men and women who have never left South Asia have also developed a sensitivity to gay relationships through European publications, American films, and now newsletters such as *Trikone, Shamakami,* and *Shakti Khabar* that are distributed through personal networks, subscriptions at college campuses, and among the English literate middle and elite classes in major South Asian cities. While sexual experiences may have occurred in Bangladesh or Sri Lanka, the framework to understand and celebrate these experiences as gay and lesbian identities developed in white societies.

These coming-out narratives reveal a shared strategy of reframing the past with present knowledge. Many times these narratives attempt to show a linear progression or the origination of an identity, but often the straight lines tumble into spirals or tangle into webs. In one narrative, memory and desire mix so often with denial and flashes of awareness that the processes of desire and self-understanding can be read in a number of different ways. A woman recounts, "I had my first lesbian relationship when I was 12 years old. I had a crush on a girl in my boarding school which developed into a deep emotional involvement. We would spend hours together, kissing and touching. . . . We had no words to describe what was happening but I remember Rita often saying, 'we love each other but we're not lesbians, are we?' There were all these negative connotations to lesbianism—that it was bad and wrong and that as long as we weren't lesbians, it was O.K." (Anonymous 9). Even at age twelve there were words to name their experiences but perhaps no meanings that celebrated and affirmed their affection; "bad" and "wrong" seemed unlikely adjectives to match their delight. Years later, when she left India to study in the United States, she became a feminist: "Suddenly I had a framework to explain a lot of feelings and frustrations I had been experiencing. . . . I also began to meet women who called themselves lesbians and it was comforting to find that I was not alone, that I wasn't abnormal or weird or crazy. . . . The term 'lesbian' began to acquire many new dimensions for me. It wasn't just about sleeping with women; it was the way in which I defined myself as a woman in relation to other women" (9). Lesbianism no longer meant "bad" sexual acts. To identify as a lesbian was an attempt to claim a community, to share needs and values.

Resisting Silence

Despite the affirmation that may develop from a lesbian and gay identity, many self-identified South Asian lesbians and gay men fear rejection from their families. A South African graduate student in New York writes of the alienation he feels from his family: "I'm an outsider, an outcast in my natural community, a hidden silenced non-person. To participate in the life of my family, I bury my sexuality, my politics, my anger as deeply as possible; I suspect there is a secret dread in my family that I might ultimately shame them horribly" (R.S. 2). This dependence on family and South Asian communities for affirmation has paralyzed many gays and lesbians in South Asian immigrant communities. These communities and families act as a nurturing refuge in environments of racial hostility and cultural misunderstanding. As members of Khush have discovered, "The greatest obstacle to our members' coming out is the fear of losing our ties to our families and communities. We are people whose sense of identity is constructed in a very large part by these institutions" (Rashid 9).

Lesbians and gay men have felt invisible in the South Asian subcontinent as well. Many have felt as helpless as the poet Suniti Namjoshi, who agonizes, in "Because of India," over the impossibility of claiming a queer family, name, or past to make herself socially intelligible (Namjoshi and Hanscombe). Entangled in the feeling of alienation is an acute sense of bewilderment. How does one justify one's own existence when one cannot summon the history or utter a name that describes one's identity. Names creatively appropriated, such as *Khush* and *Shamakami*, may appear to be "mocking translations" (A.V. 4). The possibility of two women loving each other and building a home together in India seems untenable in the face of "defying family" and "ignoring [social] dis-

approval [and] silence" (A.V. 5). Same-sex domesticity under a lesbian identity emerges as the aggressive "preservation of . . . 'American' individualism in Indian society" (A.V. 5).

   In trying to speak and live, we confront the contradictions of our
identities. South Asian heterosexists have often denied the authenticity of queer-identified South Asians by labeling homosexual relationships a white disease, insinuating that our presence in the United
States or Britain has "contaminated our minds and desires" (Khan,
"A White Disease" 1). These heterosexists attempt to use the politics
of race to condemn lesbians and gay men. They perceive queer identities as a threat to the cultural integrity of South Asian immigrants.
The rhetoric is lethal and well understood by immigrants and their
children, who are unceasingly chastised for shedding their "culture"
and acquiring the degenerate and destructive values of white societies. The notion of culture here is like a fossil—solid and petrified.
The conservative ideologies of heterosexist South Asians conflate
queer sexualities with an already well-defined yet adaptable arsenal
of "Western evils"—divorce, alcohol consumption, and drug abuse.
Any unfavorable value is displaced onto a non–South Asian source.
Ironically, these heterosexists unquestioningly accept the historically
"Western" notion that heterosexuality is natural, normal, and biologically correct and that homosexuality is unnatural and perverse.

   Arvind Kumar, editor of *Trikone,* has attempted to address the
pervasive argument that homosexuality is a "Western disease" that
is nonexistent in South Asia. He writes, "The Trikon Archives are
an attempt to prove the perception false. We want to begin documenting the history of gay people in South Asia and their continuing presence. This effort is to validate our existence not only in the
minds of others but also our own. We were present in Ancient India. We were there in Mughal India. And we are very much here in
South Asia now" ("The Trikon Archives" 7). *Shakti Khabar* has also
solicited references to "homosexuals in the history of the subcontinent, particularly in the various religions, i.e., Sikh, Muslim, Hindu,
so that we can prove that homosexuality has nothing to do with the
color of one's skin" (Khan, "Networking in London" 4). Both organizations have begun to build archives and libraries as an act of
representation, validation, and recovery of the past.

What Ever Happened to the Vedic Dyke?

In order to reconcile the conflict between national/racial identity
and sexual identity, several South Asian queers have searched for
"our very own gay tradition." Shivananda Khan, editor of *Shakti
Khabar,* describes the historical presence of homosexuality in South
Asia: "Within the history of the subcontinent there has always been

homosexuality. Sex between those of the same gender is discussed in many Hindu texts and sex manuals. Homosexual activity was also depicted in religious statues" (Khan, "A White Disease" 1). Subodh Mukherjee of Calcutta explores descriptions of Tantric initiation rites, Hindu festivals and sects that celebrated homosexual acts, the descriptions of sodomy in the Kama Sutra, the court customs of Babar, and references to women loving women in the Mahabharata and Ramayana.

Giti Thadani, a lesbian living in New Delhi, has embarked on an archeological project that substantiates Shivananda's claims. Giti's work began with a study of Sanskrit texts: "I set out to read ancient texts, looking for traces of visions of a feminine world which pre-dated patriarchal society. Then I travelled all over India for 3 years, taking photographs of sculptures, temples, and vestiges from those times" (3). Her photographs and summaries of her interpretations are frequently published in South Asian queer newsletters. She interprets the texts, such as the Rig Veda and sculptures that depict sexual acts between women, as revelations of a pre–1500 B.C. feminine world where sexuality was based on pleasure and fertility.

Giti's analysis begs the question "What ever happened to the Vedic dyke?"[5] Giti claims that Aryan invasions dating to 1500 B.C. first began to suppress homosexuality through the emerging dominance of patriarchy. Both sexual systems coexisted, despite fluctuations in relative repression and freedom, until British colonialism, when the destruction of images of homosexual expression and sexual expression in general became more systematic and blatant. Giti argues that Indian middle-class acceptance of Western "homophobia" has encouraged the continued destruction of ancient temple images (Khan, "Giti Thadani" 12).

Subodh Mukherjee also envisions a golden age of sexual tolerance, but he dates the onset of the repression to Mogul rule during the thirteenth century. Since then there has been a gradual erosion of liberal attitudes toward sexuality, "damaging Indian gay culture and forcing it underground" (1). He insists that "by coming out to society as gays, we will thus be only reviving our ancient and varied culture and freeing it from the shackles of unnatural prudery and nauseating morality. . . . For our movement to be successful in India, Indian gays must discard disruptive Western models. In light of our own tradition, we must build a new movement for acceptance of gay love by our society" (3). The irony in Subodh's observations is that although he finds Western models of gay identity disruptive, he still relies on the notion of an "Indian gay" movement, which is itself a Western construct.[6]

This concern about reclaiming the past, this search for the Vedic dyke, makes me think about what I consider history. History is about interpreting the past. We are all writing history by producing new interpretations of the past, and the formation of cultural identities is dynamically related to the project of writing history. The past is not a thing waiting to be discovered and recovered. A "recovered past" cannot secure or fix an identity for eternity. The relationships between identities and histories are fluid and constantly shifting. As Stuart Hall reminds us, "Identities are the names we give to the different ways we are positioned by, and position ourselves within, the narratives of the past" (225). Implicit, then, in the writing of history are the politics of knowledge and the politics of position.

The politics of the South Asian gay and lesbian history are refreshingly self-conscious. Shivananda Khan writes about how we can use the past to buttress our claims, our identities, in the present. We are not then producing a history of Vedic times. We are, at best, using ancient text and sculpture to shade today's meanings of sexual practices:

> As we, living towards the end of the 20th century, fight for our rights to be lesbian or gay, we need to reclaim our historical antecedents, to reconstruct our history, to reinvent the social and philosophical basis that preceded our historical times. If we are to reclaim our own invisible history . . . then we need to explore our temples, our religious sites, reread our Sanskrit texts, truly explore our history with open eyes and go out here and record our history. We must not leave it to the dominant heterosexuals to construct our own history for us. (Khan, "Giti Thadani" 13)

This is precisely where Thadani's work and historical narratives like hers are most exciting. They reconstruct and revise the master narratives of the past, which have sought to erase differences and ignore contested values. The alternative vision they provide can empower us to reclaim and remake both our present world and the understanding of historical contexts that shaped it.

Shivananda, however, goes too far when he interprets Giti Thadani's work as follows: "If we define a lesbian and gay culture as a legitimate space to form same biological gender sexual/emotional relationships that were *socially acceptable* as well as having *high esteem,* . . . it seems therefore that pre-Aryan India had a strong lesbian and gay culture" (Khan, "Giti Thadani" 13, my emphasis). Giti Thadani's work does not prove that same-sex relationships were "socially acceptable" and "highly esteemed" several thousand years ago in some parts of South Asia. The presumption here is that sexuality is a definable and universal activity, ignoring the variety of cultural patterns and meanings.[7] How do we know that a representation of two women embracing meant sex for the historical actors? And even if they did refer to it as sex, does sex have the same meaning as it does for us today?

How does one go about proving that some social practices are acceptable and highly esteemed? What kind of evidence does one need to make those kinds of claims? It is necessary to understand the context, the map of social reality, at the time. Trying to reconstruct the context of second-century India is difficult. Yet we can begin by reading legal texts, religious documents, court texts, and even the placement of the sculpture within architectural complexes. These texts, of course, are usually prescriptive; they provide ideals. They cannot be used to understand attitudes, actual behavior, or motives. We can use these texts and materials to speculate about how people lived and thought. Perhaps, though, the only people we will know anything about are the elite men who wrote and were written about, who endowed temples, and who designed law. These are the conditions of our knowledge of the past. They influence my own skepticism about how much we can know about ancient India.

While the project of reclaiming and reconstructing the past is critical for present political and cultural struggles, let us not read too much of "us" today into the past. We may trap ourselves in the need of a history to sanction our existence. South Asian lesbians and gay men are present now. On that alone, we demand acknowledgment and acceptance.

Sharpening our present political struggles demands an understanding of our current historical context. We can begin by acknowledging that, although there may have been homosexual acts in the past, "what is perhaps relatively new is the idea and development of a 'gay relationship.' " Gay identities and relationships are historically particular to the twentieth century. Gay relationships are not limited to "emotional and sexual bonds akin to marriage between heterosexual couples" (Khan, "A White Disease" 1). Over the past several decades lesbians and gay men have developed a variety of social arrangements and relationships. These relationships have, at moments, allowed some women and men to break out of conventional gender relations and identities.

Recovering histories of both the ancient and recent past challenges us all to understand the possibilities of alternative sexualities and social arrangements. Through mobilizing histories, reappropriating languages, and other cultural strategies, we may be able to gain affirmation and support from South Asian immigrant communities for queer desires and relationships. Simultaneously, these cultural strategies may destabilize the self-definitions of South Asian lesbian and gay communities.

Desiring Community

The claim that lesbians and gay men who can trace their origins to the subcontinent share a common social history and identity has shaped the politics of South Asian queer organizations. While social support groups like Khush have a local focus — for gay men in Toronto—the newsletters presume an international audience. *Shamakami*'s editorial mission is typical of this perspective: "While *Shamakami* will be based in the United States of America, it will strive to promote international networking among South Asian feminist lesbians" ("Shamakami Editorial Policy" 3).

Yet the migration from the subcontinent generated a distinctive South Asian queer identity. The formation of South Asian queer communities has been structured by the post-Stonewall gay liberation movement, experiences of racism, and the development of racial-minority identities in North America and Britain. The experiences that spurred the creation of Shakti are typical: "The main reason for forming a South Asian lesbian and gay group is because of racism and cultural marginalisation. Many white organisations and individuals do not see us as people but as exotic creatures. We want to define our own agenda within a racist climate and not have an agenda imposed by white people" (Editor's Response 13).

Social organizations and networks like Anamika (United States), Trikone (United States), Shakti (United Kingdom), and Khush (Canada), which emerged in the second half of the 1980s, developed a self-conscious policy of developing international contacts with other South Asian lesbians and gay men. Their newsletters consistently provided information, addresses, and news of the other organizations. The groups distribute their newsletters and focus on coverage of lesbian and gay experiences and histories in the subcontinent. Increasingly, gay and lesbian organizations drawing their membership from the urban middle class and elite in India have adopted this international South Asian queer identity. In *Bombay Dost's* first official issue, the editors reprinted a December 1990 article from *The Advocate,* which proclaimed Urvashi Vaid, executive director of the U.S. National Gay and Lesbian Task Force, "woman of the year." The editors noted that Urvashi Vaid's "presence alone does a great deal for us here in India" ("Being Legit" 3).

Despite its fluid application, the construction of this identity has been problematic. In 1989 Khush organized a cultural program, Salaam Toronto. Ian Rashid, one of the organizers, reflects on the problems of self representation and coalition building:

> As a fledgling organization, Khush had wanted to use Salaam Toronto to introduce ourselves to the larger gay/lesbian and South Asian communities. But in many ways the event was primarily for Khush. The members of the group, coming from different parts of the world, wanted to reconcile and reclaim our various ties to our notions of South Asia. . . . Very few of Khush's members are actually South Asian born, the majority coming

from East Africa, the Caribbean, Britain and North America. Constructed around individual memories, mythologies and histories,
Salaam Toronto was trying in some ways to link all of us to a collective sense of source. There seemed a need within Khush to justify the existence of the group beyond our sexual orientation; to
develop a sense of collective as opposed to individual identity. (9)

Ian describes a collective identity that is mitigated by individual
memories and histories, an identity that must be molded from individual particularities and differences to provide some sense of collective "source." Ian shows how we not only presume community and
identity but also create it. This presumed queer South Asian identity
is not singular or static. The organizers of Salaam Toronto form a
coalition of people with different identities, politics, and positions.
The debates, disputes, and labor involved in the process of organizing the event produce new political practices and identities. Since
Salaam Toronto's organization in 1989, South Asian feminists, lesbians, and gay men in Toronto have organized two other cultural
festivals: Desh Pardesh 1990 and Desh Pardesh 1991. Events such
as these are transformative; they can constitute new identities.[8]

Liberating Identity Politics

Although identity emerges from an awareness of difference, articulating an identity can also serve to mask differences. By presuming
a global South Asian queer identity, what do these organizations,
newsletters, and individuals lose or deny? What complexities, diversities, and contradictions are tensely bound in this collective
identity? The differences in experience and understanding that Ian
Rashid describes do more than simply complicate the notion of a
global South Asian queer identity; they draw into question the assumption that these "imagined political communities" (Anderson
15–16) are ideal democracies. The invocation of community tends
to ignore actual inequalities and power relations. These inequalities—often analyzed through categories of gender, class, and race—
within our communities must be addressed.

Some South Asian lesbians have called attention to the way gender inequalities structure organizations like Khush and Trikone,
which are dominated by gay men. Lesbians in North America have
often developed their own networks through the newsletters
Shamakami and *Anamika* or have affiliated themselves with Asian or
black lesbians in order to establish more supportive communities.
Recently, these structural inequalities have been challenged in the
pages of *Trikone*. Mita Radhakrishnan wrote:

> You, Trikone men, have to talk about violence against women and
> what you can do, as gay South Asian males, to stop it. You have to

talk about lesbian invisibility. You have to talk about sexism, and
how you as males are privileged in comparison to us, your South
Asian lesbian sisters. . . . When you say that women have been "underrepresented in Trikone" you have to realize and *take responsibility* for the fact that "underrepresentation" of women doesn't
just "happen" passively. It is the direct result of sexism within the
organization and within individual men. Make *the ending of sexism
one of Trikone's reasons for being.* ("An Open Letter 1)

Editor Arvind Kumar responded by changing Trikone's editorial statement to include a commitment to "ending sexism and discrimination against women in all forms" and specific encouragement of women to "develop [editorial] policy guidelines and
co-edit issues" ("Trikone" 2). These changes in policy and purpose
pleased Mita Radhakrishnan, and she encouraged the readers of
Trikone to "continue the hard but wonderful work of confronting
sexism and other oppressions" ("Letter from Delhi" 2). Although
women continue to contribute to *Trikone,* none of the four issues
since Mita's original letter has had a female coeditor.

There has, though, been even less conversation about class differences and inequalities. Often the subjects of South Asian gay and
lesbian discourse see themselves as undifferentiated, as profoundly
middle-class and educated. There are sometimes nostalgic stories
of young men and women having sex with the servants in their
households in South Asia. As Sharmin Islam relates, "I found
women who worked as domestic help in our house to be a lot
[more] comfortable with me physically than educated women"
(Ahmed and Islam 2).

However, once in Britain or in the United States, there is less
awareness that South Asian lesbians and gay men may experience
differences in class positions and origins. One explanation may be
that race structures so much of our experiences here. In a society
where South Asians are rendered either invisible or alien, South
Asian queer organizations have developed to create safe spaces.
These spaces are defined by race and often displace class differences. Curiously, even racism is not always acknowledged. Sunil
Gupta criticizes Shakti for having a curious lack of self-conscious
politicization, despite the fact that the group is itself defined by
race. He writes, "The pain and anger of daily living the race problem ha[ve] to be recognized" (40).

Race structures organizations and communities not only from the
outside but from the inside as well. Aziz Ahmed sees the presence of
racial consciousness within South Asian communities when he notes
that every South Asian "wants to be as white as possible, or at least
wants to be looked on as being fair. Whiteness has become the cri-

terion for beauty. We are defining ourselves from the perspective of white people. We need to challenge racism not only from white people, but also from our own people" (Ahmed and Islam 5).

I share with Sunil Gupta the belief that talking about the "inherent contradictions and subtle differentiations of colour and background" within queer communities will help us acknowledge and celebrate differences (41). We need not fear that differences or a lack of predetermined "unity" will produce irreconcilable divisions. It will help us develop communities that are stronger and more self-affirming. A global South Asian queer identity does not have to presume a singular set of experiences. It can be about building coalitions and networks of support and understanding.

South Asian lesbian and gay newsletters have served as forums for articulating identities and establishing communities, and they have demonstrated the necessity of identity politics as an important stage in the liberation process. Gathering support is critical for any struggle. In a 1986 issue of *Anamika,* Anu wrote that the individual strategies that "deshi dykes" had developed to deal with the pressures of living contradictory and fragmentary lives were not enough, "for it seems clear to me that any advance will have to be collectively imagined, if we are to escape the stealthy and fugitive-like existence whereby we only dare come out to the tried-and-trusted few" (8). Forums like *Anamika* provide a safe space where one no longer has to fear cruel judgment or retribution. For many, these organizations and networks have transformed their social landscape. Pratibha Parmar recalls that when she first came out, while living in Britain in 1976, "there were very few South Asian lesbians and gays around. We knew we were around and would travel hundreds of miles to meet. Now [in 1990] we have Shakti, a very strong, over 1000 member lesbian and gay group with a newsletter, regular meetings and socials" (Carvahlo 7).

However, the practices of everyday life will not automatically be transformed by the existence of safe spaces, no matter how strong. There were still be parents and relatives, employers and strangers, friends and acquaintances, who may respond to our lives with hostility, misunderstanding, or indifference. But the creation of safe spaces and communities has made a difference. As Ravi relates in a 1987 issue of *Trikone,* "No South Asian will have to embark on this journey of self-discovery and self-affirmation in isolation, but will be able to draw upon a supportive South Asian gay/lesbian *community*" (7). These imagined communities serve a real purpose. They allow us to engage in struggle and self-discovery without feeling alone or alienated.

In inventing identities, creating new subjectivities, and imagining communities, we embark on the creation of "empowerment and political consciousness."[9] These personal, social, and archeological histories are engaged in the act of self-representation. bell hooks explains that the process of becoming subjects "emerges as one comes to understand how structures of domination work in one's own life, as one develops critical thinking and critical consciousness, as one invents new, alternative habits of being" (15). For South Asian lesbians and gay men, as with other silenced groups, self-representation alone cannot liberate us, but breaking silence is the first step in resisting conventional expectations and challenging domination. Jigne Desai of California tantalizes us with the transformations in her own life. She says, "Being Indian and queer, I felt I was the only one. I've always looked at myself as not fitting in. That's changing. Now I'm not afraid to say who I am and what I believe in."

NOTES

Acknowledgments: I am grateful to Ian Rashid, for inspiring me to develop these ideas for Desh Paredesh, and to the following friends, who provided me with invaluable encouragement and critiques: Himani Bannerji, Anne Blackburn, George Chauncey, Mark Haslam, Arvind Kumar, Pratibha Parmar, Hannah Rosen, Rachel Sturman, and Lisa Trivedi.

1. Many newsletter authors, such as Savir Das, have used pseudonyms. Reasons range from protection against interrogation by immigration authorities or exposure in heterosexist communities to the simple exercise of creative license.

2. Trikon changed the spelling of its name to Trikone with the second volume of its newsletter in November 1987, in order to be incorporated as a nonprofit organization in California. Hereafter I use *Trikon* to refer to the newsletter prior to November 1987 and *Trikone* for issues from November 1987 to the present.

3. For a different version of Uma's essay, see "Don't Open Those Lips."

4. The latest development in deducing a biological basis for sexuality is Simon LeVay's hypothesis that differences in the structure of the hypothalamus determine sexual object choice. Like straight women, gay men purportedly have a smaller hypothalamus than do straight men. Scientists and journalists have speculated that lesbians might have a hypothalamic structure similar to that of straight men. LeVay's research follows more than a century of European and American scientific inquiry that has persistently tried to fix a biological cause or measure to putative differences in race, gender, and sexuality. This kind of research has attempted to naturalize social inequalities as the result of differences in human biology and genetics. See also Gibbons.

5. This is a paraphrase of the question raised by feminist historian Uma Chakravarti, "Whatever Happened to the Vedic *Dasi*? Orientalism, Nationalism and a Script of the Past."

6. Subodh Mukherjee's investigation of ancient sexual practices also

relies on the work of Orientalist scholars, particularly the French scholar Alain Danielou. Subodh fails to consider how Danielou's expectations and interpretations of ancient Indian sexuality may have been shaped by pervasive assumptions of Orientalist scholars that India was more primitive, sensual, and eroticized than was repressed, civilized Western Europe. For an examination of Orientalism see Inden.

7. For an elaboration of this argument about sexuality as socially constructed and historically constituted, see Halperin; see also Weeks, *Sex Politics and Society.*

8. Judith Butler discusses the idea that, in order to proceed with political action, coalitional politics need not assume that "identity" is a premise or that "unity" has been reached in advance. Coalitions can then develop and identities can emerge or dissolve depending on the concrete political practices that they comprise.

9. Pratibha Parmar, interviewed in Wong 10.

WORKS CITED

Ahmed, Aziz, and Sharmin Islam. "Breaking the Silence." *Trikone* 3 (Sept. 1988): 2.

Anderson, Benedict. *Imagined Communities: Reflection on the Origin and Spread of Nationalism.* London: Verso, 1983.

Anonymous. "Khayal." *Anamika* 1 (Mar. 1986): 9.

Anu. "Notes from an Indian Diary." *Anamika* 1 (Mar. 1986): 8.

A.V. "A Response to a Room of One's Own." *Shamakami* 2 (Jan. 1991): 4–5.

"Being Legit: Event or Process!" *Bombay Dost* 1 (July–Sept. 1991): 3.

Butler, Judith. *Gender Trouble: Feminism and the Subversion of Identity.* New York: Routledge, 1990.

Carvahlo, Nelson. "Feature Interview. Pratibha Parmar: Fight Back and Struggle (Because You Have To)." *Khush Khayal* 2 (June 1990): 7.

Chakravarti, Uma. "Whatever Happened to the Vedic *Dasi?* Orientalism, Nationalism and a Script of the Past." *Recasting Women: Essays in Indian Colonial History.* Ed. Kumkum Sangari and Sudesh Vaid. New Brunswick, N.J.: Rutgers UP, 1990: 27–87.

Chaudhary, Kamini. "The Scent of Roses: Developing a Sexual Identity." *Trikone* 4 (May–June 1989): 1–2.

Das, Savir [pseud.], and Arvind Kumar. "Our First Time." *Trikon* (Jan. 1986): 1.

Desai, Jigne. Interview. "Out in America." Issue of *Outweek* 105 (3 July 1991).

Editor's Response to Letter from L.N. *Shakti Khabar* 11 (Dec. 1990–Jan. 1991): 13.

Gibbons, Ann. "The Brain as a Sexual Organ." *Science* 253 (30 Aug. 1991): 959–60.

Gupta, Sunil. "Correct Singularities." *Gay Times* (Aug. 1989): 40–41.

Hall, Stuart. "Cultural Identity and Diaspora." *Identity: Community, Cul-*

ture, Difference. Ed. Jonathan Rutherford. London: Lawrence and Wishart, 1990. 222–37.

Halperin David. "Sex Before Sexuality: Pederasty, Politics and Power in Classical Athens." *Hidden from History: Reclaiming the Gay and Lesbian Past.* Ed. Martin Duberman, Martha Vicinus, and George Chauncey, Jr. New York: New American Library, 1989. 37–53.

bell hooks. "The Politics of Radical Black Subjectivity." *Yearning: Race, Gender and Cultural Politics.* Boston: South End, 1990. 15–22.

Inden, Ronald. *Imagining India.* London: Blackwell, 1990.

Khan, Shivananda. "Giti Thadani: Sexuality and Gender in Ancient India." *Shakti Khabar* 15 (Aug.–Sept. 1991): 12–13.

———. "Networking in London." *Trikone* 3 (July 1988): 4.

———. "A White Disease." *Shakti Khabar* 3 (Aug.–Sept. 1989): 1.

Kumar, Arvind. "The Trikon Archives." *Trikon* (Mar. 1986): 7.

———. "Trikone." *Trikone* 5 (May–June 1990): 2.

LeVay, Simon. "A Difference in Hypothalamic Structure Between Heterosexual and Homosexual Men." *Science* 253 (30 Aug. 1991): 956–57.

Mukherjee, Subodh. "Homosexuality in India: A Personal Quest for Historical Perspective." *Trikone* 5 (Jan.–Feb. 1990): 1 + 3.

Mukhopadhyay, Rahul. "Transplanting Roots from India to America." *Trikone* 4 (May–June, 1989): 1–2.

Namjoshi, Suniti, and Gillian Hanscombe. *Felsh and Paper.* Charlottetown, Prince Edward Island: Ragweed, 1986.

Radhakrishnan, Mita. "Letter from Delhi." *Trikone* 5 (July–Aug. 1990): 1–2.

———. "An Open Letter from a South Asian Lesbian to Trikone Men." *Trikone* 5 (May–June 1990): 1–2.

Rashid, Ian. "Out of Home: The Contradictions of Identity. Creating a South Asian Gayness in Toronto." *Rites Magazine* 7 (July–Aug. 1990): 9.

Ravi. "Bits and Pieces." *Trikone* (Sept. 1987): 7.

R.S. "South African, Indian and Gay." Letter. *Trikone* 2 (Nov. 1987): 2.

"Shamakami Editorial Policy." *Shamakami* 1 (1 June 1990): 3.

"Silent No More: A Talk with Shilpa Mehta." *Trikone* 4 (Mar.–Apr. 1989): 3.

Thadani, Giti. Interview. *Lesbian Magazine* (Jan. 1991). Reprinted in *Shakti Khabar* 14 (June–July 1991): 3.

Uma. "Uma." *Connexions.* (Fall 1983): 5.

———. "Don't Open Those Lips." *Mukti* 3 (Spring 1985): 7–10.

Weeks, Jeffrey. *Sex Politics and Society: The Regulation of Sexuality Since 1800.* London: Longman, 1981.

———. "The Value of Difference." *Identity: Community, Culture, Difference.* Ed. Jonathan Rutherford. London: Lawrence and Wishart, 1990. 88–100.

Wong, Lloyd. "Fuck You: This Is Our Home. Claiming South Asian Identity in Britian." Pratibha Parmar interview. *Fuse.* (Summer 1990): 10.

10. history of disease
Patti Duncan

From A Far / What nationality / or what kindred and relation / what blood relation / what blood ties of blood / what ancestry / what race generation / what house clan tribe stock strain / what lineage extraction / what breed sect gender denomination caste / what stray ejection misplaced / Tertium Quid neither one thing nor the other / Tombe des nues de naturalized / what transplant to dispel upon—THERESA HAK KYUNG CHA, *Dictée*

i. "in white layers of memory / in layers of forgetting . . . the object of memory"[1]

>i will lay my body across this divide. i will sustain you.
>i will lay my body across this divide, let you walk across, carry you over.
>movement like water, like wind. like time.
>
>>or memory.
>
>i will lay down my body, tell you: have no fear, you will not hurt me.

ii.

In the foyer of the university library there is a display. Ancient and modern Korean dress. Brightly colored garments hang on white tiers for all to see. The upper body piece of a woman's dress stretched tight, arms held out and pinned down. Trousers with the wide legs spread. Among the articles of clothing hang colored photographs of young Korean women modeling the clothes. Smiling. The former president of the university is now living in Seoul, appointed ambassador. His wife sends home these clothes. The display bears a large plaque with her name.

"Seoul?" one of my professors says out loud during a break from a seminar about feminist theory. "Why would anybody in their right mind *choose* to go there? Poor fool." The students around me laugh. She is talking about the former president.

I remember my mother in a similar dress. She spends hours getting ready, putting it on, fastening the rows of tiny buttons. My sister and I are permitted to help. When she turns around, I fasten a small clasp at her neck. She brushes color across her face carefully, sprays perfume, smoothes curls into the ends of her hair. She is beautiful. One day when we are old enough, as she has promised, she places two large paper-wrapped packages on the bed in her room. My sister and I open them too quickly, and she is upset by our impatience. We pull out miniature versions of her own gown, traditional Korean dresses for women. The colors are red, green, white, banded together. She teaches us methodically how to put them on. So many pieces. There is a correct procedure. I decide to wear mine every opportunity I get.

There are pictures in our family album: me in my Korean gown on stage at the school pageant. My sister playing a large drum at a recital, wearing hers. I am nine and at the piano, accompaniment for the fifth-grade melodrama. All three of us—sister, mother, and me—getting out of the car before a Christmas party. My father must have taken that photograph. My mother holds both our hands; we look like tiny twin versions of her. I wore the dress until the hem had to be let down, until the upper bodice stretched tight across my chest, over a new training bra. I wore it until I could wear only one piece—the upper, outer jacketlike garment, bright colored and made of a shiny silky fabric. I tried to wear it with my skirts, over dresses, with jeans. Until finally my mother took it away from me, packed it up, said, "We will save this now, maybe for your daughter." Her voice was kind then, and she folded it carefully for me.

iii.

My mother was the first daughter of a woman who swore she could tell you the future. This woman, whom I never called Grandmother, claimed that a magic link passed from mother to daughter in her family, and this power had been transmitted through seven generations of women by the time it reached my mother. If the stories are true, then maybe I'm the last link in this chain. Maybe my mother was right when she told me that someday I'd remember.

My mother's mother died of a sickness made worse by malnutrition and poor health care in a village in South Korea, where she'd worked all her life in rice fields. The war claimed the lives of her husband and two sons, and all of her family's possessions, leaving her alone with five daughters and no money. My mother, the oldest daughter, quit school to look for work. She put on heavy makeup to look older than she was and followed the other girls in her village to Seoul, where she worked in a nightclub serving drinks to GIs who asked her if she was looking for a boyfriend. That's where she met my father.

iv.

you are young. younger than i am now. younger than your hands your eyes your worries when i knew you. you look at me look away. recognition. then none. then gone. then fade to black. but you are too young. makeup hides your age this masquerade of years and sex and fear. how old are you? you say you do not know. records burned in a fire, how many years, how long the war? how old do you feel? how old did you need to be? and what i do not know the what you never told me the what i was not supposed to remember.

v.

My father likes to tell stories about how he rescued my mother, helped liberate her people.

When I was a child, I imagined my father a brave man, in uniform, running through lush green with a gun in one hand. My mother would be a frail but beautiful doll-like creature, carried away by this white man who had traveled so far from home to find her and even risked his life to save hers. They are in what appears to be a bomb shelter, cavernous and underground, where my strong father nurses my small and exquisite young mother back to health, having saved her from evil Communists. I suppose I pieced these images together from the stories my father told my sister and me and from all the war movies we watched while growing up. "That's so romantic," my friends used to say when I told them the story about how my parents met. It took me years to realize that by rescuing her, what my father really meant was bringing her to the United States as his war bride.

vi. "narrative shifts, discovers variation"

The summer she turns twelve, her mother develops a serious illness. The girl does not know how to pronounce the name of this disease, does not even understand what it means or what will happen to her mother, her family. Sometimes her mother does not remember things that have happened, things that the girl herself clearly remembers. Sometimes she confuses the girl with her sister, calls them by each other's names, forgets the respective details of their lives. The girl has been told that the disease will affect her mother's memory, her mother's ability to remember. Yet she is not prepared to be forgotten. She is not prepared to be misnamed.

She is no longer required to go to school every day. She is permitted to miss school on a regular basis now, in order to accompany her mother to the hospitals, the doctors, the free clinics. She has a new role in the family, a new function to fulfill. She acts as translator and mediator. Her mother begins to rely on her.

She sits with her mother in waiting rooms. She fills out the forms, endless inquiries into insurance policies, health disorders, histories of disease. She memorizes her mother's social security number.

In small doctors' offices, she translates her mother's words for the doctors and nurses. She does not say, "My mother is speaking English. If you would listen, you would be able to understand for yourself." She does not say, "I barely speak Korean." She learns how to answer their questions without even waiting for her mother's response.

When they go to pharmacies to pick up medication, her mother says out loud, so that the other people in line will hear, that she has to go to the bathroom, or she doesn't feel well and must sit down.

The girl puts on her grown-up face. Holding onto her mother's purse, she has doubled in years. She waits in line for her mother, speaks with the pharmacist and answers his questions, fills out the papers and hands him the check. She learns to write her mother's signature.

At home, in the medicine chest, small bottles of pills are accumulating. Some of them are years old now, others quite new. What the girl knows is that her mother never throws any medication away. Instead she saves it, long after it has expired, in the event that she will one day experience those familiar symptoms of some other disease, some other pain, and she will need its antidote. So when she feels a twinge in her back, she can say, "Oh, this is like my second pregnancy. . . . Where are the pills I had before you were born?" And then she can go find those pills, dated 1969, and swallow one. Because the pain is old, she believes the cure is also. She believes she will stop the pain with her memory. She believes that she can end the pain *because* she remembers. She says, "This ache—in my shoulder—like that time, 1977, when we went to the Grand Canyon and I walked too far. Where are those pills I had?" And then she goes into her bathroom and comes out with a small brown bottle. "Here it is. This will work."

But the girl remembers the trip too. She remembers that her father yelled the entire time, that her mother began to cry. She remembers a fight, that her father stopped the car and made her mother get out. Then he drove on for nearly ten miles before the girl and her sister could make him turn around and go back for their mother. The girl wonders about her mother's loss of memory. She wonders if her mother will ever be able to stop the pain, now that she is forgetting too much. She wonders if she can remember *for* her mother and vows to remember details, dates, and, especially, the pain. Sometimes the girl wakes in the middle of the night and believes that she is going to die. The sickness is no longer her mother's. It belongs to her. Out loud she recites her mother's social security number, over and over.

The pain is growing and, with it, the girl's memory. At school now, she does nothing but try to remember. She remembers her mother's stories about the war: how a country had been split in two; how her mother's father—the girl's grandfather—had been tortured and killed. She has no facts, she has no dates. She makes them up. She makes up her own memories now. If it is her choice, she will create him for herself. She creates him anew. A grandfather constructed as a hero, a great man. He would have saved the country if only he had survived, united the north and the south, and never allowed his own daughter to die of a disease she couldn't even pronounce.

When she is not making up her memories, the girl daydreams that she is dying. Something horrible is happening: leukemia, hepatitis, AIDS. The disease begins somewhere unnoticeable, then spreads all over her body. She believes that she can feel it beginning; there is pain in her hands, in her legs. She daydreams about funerals, going to graveyards. She wonders what she will wear. She wonders what it will feel like. She practices the emotions, alone in her bedroom at night. She practices facial expressions in the mirror: *this is sadness, this is pain, this is remorse, this is the way a good daughter should look when her mother dies.*

In the meantime, she continues going with her mother to hospitals. Once they wait for almost three hours to see a doctor; he is supposed to be "the best." She watches her mother's face as patient after patient continues to walk into the room and is permitted to see the doctor before them. She notices that these people are all white. She watches her mother's hands; they turn, they wring, they curl into fists. When at last they are called into his office, the doctor in his white coat barely looks up. When he speaks to them, he does not acknowledge the girl's mother, except to touch her roughly, to grab her arm, take her pulse, check her heart. He checks her blood pressure as though her arm is not attached to a body. He speaks only to the daughter. He speaks to her as though she is a small child and will not understand. "Your mother is very sick." He pronounces the words slowly, carefully. Maybe he thinks she does not understand English. She does not tell him that she knows no other language. She does not say, "I learned English—only English—so that I would never be confused. That's what my father said." She does not say, "I learned to speak only English, but with a Korean accent. Do you know what that sounds like?"

Instead she remembers the months of speech therapy, with Mrs. Greene, her first instructor in the art of assimilation: how to round out her syllables, soften her "r"s, curve her tongue inside of her mouth. She remembers her father saying, "No more Korean to be spoken in this house. How do you expect them to learn how to speak?" He is in the army and is stationed away, in another country, for several years. While he is away, her mother abides by his rules. She reads her small daughters little golden books in English. She speaks slowly, unsure of herself. The girls imitate her methods and means. They learn to speak slowly and unsure of themselves. They create a language of visual pauses, bilingual glances, flutters of the hand and head. A smile here, a turn there, like mother like daughter, like me. Remember this. The girl does her homework every night, and every night her mother checks it, even though she does not always understand what is written. She takes out her glasses and puts them on, pretends to be reading carefully, gives back the pages saying, "Okay. Do it again."

vii.

At home in the evenings, my mother insisted on family dinners together. She would make "traditional American" meals for us and something Korean for herself. Years ago my father had warned her never to try to make him eat her spicy foods. He complained of the strong smells and stared with dismay and disgust at her jars of kimchee in the refrigerator, yet every Saturday he returned from the grocery store with a huge bag of rice and everything else she had asked him for.

I remember our small kitchen table, where I always sat, pressed against the wall—the smallest one in the smallest space. At dinner my father kept the television on—usually the news or some sports channel. He ate with his eyes on the screen, past my mother's head, occasionally nodding to one of her questions. My older sister sat across from me with a book in her lap. All I could see was the part in her hair, brushed smoothly away from her face. When she raised her face to take a bite, her eyes behind their thick glasses remained focused on the pages down below the table.

Next to me, my mother placed little jars and bowls in front of her—Korean spices and vegetables, sauces and soups. My father was often finished with his entire meal by the time she had set up her own dinner. With chopsticks in her hand, she sampled from each of her dishes, mixing everything with rice from the huge pot she kept plugged in to an outlet on the counter next to her seat. Against the wall, I was trapped. With my father's glazed eyes turned in the direction of the TV screen, and only the top of my sister's head visible, my mother turned all of her attention toward me.

"Eat this," she would say, as she pushed a small roll in my direction. "Push your hair out of your face." "Sit up straight now." "Put your feet back down on the floor." "Now try this," she said. Another roll, this one wrapped in dried seaweed, and another with radishes chopped and mixed with rice, soup with fish and ginger, bulgogi *meat cooked in hot sauce. Everything she pushed my way I ate. With every bite I took, I saw her face light up. She smiled proudly when I finished everything on my plate. Her good girl, she called me. I ate so well.*

viii.

In the doctor's office, when he speaks to her as though she will not understand, she thinks that she has always understood. What the girl actually says to the doctor is, "Yes, sir," while carefully avoiding his eyes. This is what she is supposed to say. This is what she has been taught to say. Her mother is proud to have raised a daughter who is so obedient, so quiet, so sweet. This girl never talks back, she never asks questions, she never protests. She says, "Yes, mother," and she bows her head.

When the doctor says, "You're a very pretty little girl," her face grows warm and she looks down. She notices his hands. They are large and rather fleshy, like her father's hands. He wears a wedding ring on one finger. He puts his hand on her head and touches her long hair. "What pretty hair," he says. "I love Oriental hair, so long and shiny." She looks around to her mother, who only smiles. "Say thank you," her mother tells her. "She so shy," her mother tries to explain to the doctor, who does not seem to hear her. He writes a prescription and hands it to the girl, telling her where to go to have it filled. He says good-bye to the girl, calls her "sweetheart." He says nothing to her mother.

In the car on the way home, the girl's mother curses under her breath. Her knuckles are white on the steering wheel. "Stupid white man! Stupid American!" she says over and over again. For just a moment, the girl does not know who her mother is talking about—the doctor or her father. "He knows nothing," says the mother, who speaks to herself in Korean now, while her daughter stares out the window. When finally the girl looks at her mother, she sees that her mother is crying. She realizes that her mother is sitting on the phone book again, Mountain Bell Yellow Pages. She needs to sit on something to be able to see above the dashboard. Her mother's seat is pressed almost into the steering wheel, and she concentrates hard on the road in front of her.

ix.

To fill the emptiness, the silence, the pause, you will say anything. You say, "I wish you'd let your hair grow long again." You tell me, "*act* like a girl." To take up the waiting, the longing, you feign unknowing. You refuse to remember. Yet you know to wait. You wait.

x.

How will the stories be told, remembered, of childhood and growing up? The images and memories that I've managed to hang onto slip in among the strangest conversations, like fragments of old movies, recurring dreams. Write it like a screenplay, a made-for-TV docudrama: Nancy Kwan plays my mother. Footage from The World of Suzie Wong *stands in as flashbacks of my mother's own early life. (Nobody will notice.) Young Asian American girl grows up among military bases and cross-cultural experiences; she will find reason to question both her racial and sexual identities; she will leave home and come of age in the late 1980s.*

Tell it as a novel. A memoir. An autobiography. A lie. Include photographs for proof. Tell it as the truth. Relay with humor and anecdotes the historical nuances exemplified by generations of women in my family, and the Western myth that Asian women have an unbelievable ability to tolerate great amounts of pain—we are genetically predisposed to endure suffering. In the movie version, any Asian or Asian American actresses will do.

Seeking others among others, I came across the work of Theresa Hak Kyung Cha, Korean American experimental writer, artist, and filmmaker, whose life ended abruptly ("did not die: was robbed of her death")[2] in New York City in 1982, shortly after the publication of Dictée. *"Dear Mother," she wrote. "Nothing has changed, we are at a standstill." Nothing has changed. A stand still. "But you're alive," she reminds me. And you can save your life. You can change your life.*

> To keep the pain from translating itself into memory. She begins each time by charting every moment, the date, the time of day, the weather, a brief notation on the events that have occurred or that are to come. . . . She begins the search the words of equivalence to that of her feeling. Or the absence of it. Synonym, simile, metaphor, byword, byname, ghostword, phantomnation. In documenting the map of her journey.[3]

It is by small acts and insights that change occurs, through a process of critical remembering. By broadening the parameters, pushing the boundaries to their extremes, we reach logical and often illogical conclusions. We begin to alter history. Growing up, I heard too many Asian and Asian American women tell stories of wars and deaths. So often this is all America wants to know or will believe about our lives. The stories they demand are constant and unchanging; the images of us silent, fixed, and suffering.

Grief and loss are the borders of my mother's life. She is constantly reminding me of this. I keep meaning to tell a different story, to somehow change the meanings, change the ending. I keep returning to the stories of my mother, and to the grave of my grandmother.

xi.

i will lay my body across this divide. i will say it again so you will know for sure. now. i will lay my body across this great this continental this divide this difference. i will translate, mediate, i will speak your language and mine too. i will tell you half-truths and you will listen. you will nod your head. do you see that i write within a tradition? do you see that i rebel against that tradition? this history, full of dis-ease, it marks my survival. and yours. there are many sides to the story, many stories within the story, it neither begins nor ends here. i will carry you across. i will write across this divide, i will remember.

mother, we are at a stand . . . still. (do you know what that sounds like?)

NOTES

1. All boldfaced headings in quotation marks are from Cha.

2. Lew 91.

3. Cha 140.

WORKS CITED

Cha, Theresa Hak Kyung. *Dictée*. New York: Tanam, 1982. Berkeley: Third Woman, 1995.

Lew, Walter. *Excerpts from :ΔIKTH/DIKTE for Dictée* (1982). Seoul, Korea: Yeul Eum, 1992.

11. Queer API Men in Los Angeles
A Roundtable on History and Political Organizing
Introduced and edited by Eric C. Wat and Steven Shum

Introduction

"This conversation couldn't have happened ten years ago. Or even five years ago." This comment was expressed by several participants during our roundtable discussion on 27 January 1996. Certainly, political organizing among gay and bisexual Asian and Pacific Islander (API) men is not a recent phenomenon. Even in this small group, two individuals were able to date their own activism to the seventies, when many social-change movements—including Asian American and gay liberation—were at their nascent stage. However, the queer API community in Los Angeles has rapidly increased in size. Even though our community is still relatively young, we are at an exciting and significant moment in its history, where we can begin to talk about the community in terms of generations, exploring how knowledge and experience can be transmitted from one-generation to the next. As always, knowing our history is a prerequisite to both self- and community-empowerment.

In the May 1996 newsletter of the Gay Asian Pacific Support Network (GAPSN), nine community-based support groups are listed for the greater Los Angeles area. Established in 1980 and 1984 respectively, Asian Pacific Gays and Friends—formerly Asian Pacific Lesbians and Gays (APLG)—and GAPSN represent two of the longer established organizations. Now an independent social service agency, Asian Pacific AIDS Intervention Team (APAIT) developed out of APLG in 1987 to address overlooked health concerns within our community. More recently, ethnic-specific support groups have formed to address the specific needs of emerging communities, such as Filipinos, Koreans, and Vietnamese. And, as a result of sexism in our community, women have found the need to create their own spaces, such as Los Angeles Asian Pacific Islander Sisters and the Vietnamese Bisexual, Lesbian, and Transgender group O Môi. Queer API communities have also made headway into mainstream API community organizations. For example, the founding of the Lambda chapter of the Japanese American Citizens League shows the possibility for creating change in a relatively conservative API civil rights organization.[1] In addition, the 1990s witnessed the emergence of queer API student organizations at southern California college campuses, such as the University of California in Los Angeles, Riverside, and Irvine.

More organizations continue to form, based on the changing needs and demographics of our communities. This is especially evident within the last few years. As such, the queer API political landscape is in perpetual flux, and organizing must constantly adapt to these shifts and trends. It is the belief of the editors of this roundtable discussion that the queer API community in Los Angeles can and should place itself within the larger history of progressive organizing for social justice. In fact, as Steven Shum states in the discussion, "There really needs to be a recommitment, among the leadership, to community organizing in whatever form it takes."

In preparing for this discussion, we felt that it was important for different generations of queer APIs to talk about organizing and about how we looked at these issues and concerns differently. Experienced organizers have much to offer younger activists, who themselves bring a renewed sense of energy, commitment, and vision to the movement. We therefore assembled a cross-generational group in order to measure our visions against one another and refine them to be more precise and grounded. The six of us in the roundtable discussion represent many different perspectives; we became involved in the queer API community in various ways and at various stages of our lives.

Clearly, six people cannot speak for an entire community. And this was not our intention. Each roundtable participant alluded to this limitation during the discussion. We are all college educated and come from middle-class backgrounds. We do not face the various language barriers and the lack of employment opportunities that some recent immigrants in our community face. None of us identifies as bisexual or transgendered. We are all men. This editorial decision was made because the pattern of organizing among API lesbian and bisexual women has its own shape and history (although there is co-gender organizing in Los Angeles). And although we refer to an "API" community, the experiences of Pacific Islanders and the particular stereotypes and limitations placed on them cannot easily be encompassed in this broad term.

Though the participants share many commonalties, we are hardly the same. During the discussion, we chose not to focus on what we have in common. Instead, by understanding the specificity of our lives, we hope to begin to see where possibilities lie for future organizing. Anytime we engage each other in our differences—in terms of our experiences and perspectives—our analyses become sharper, even if we continue to disagree. Our roundtable discussion reveals certain themes that, although not universal in their particulars, are nonetheless real and relevant to many community organizers.

And disagree we did. For a significant part of the discussion, the participants struggled over the definition of "political" and its implications for community organizing. Some believe that being political means front line activism—that is, organizing marches and participating in pickets and civil disobedience. Others believe that the political can manifest itself in more subtle forms. Some believe that any queer API organization is political by nature, because it asserts a particular space for those who are marginalized by both the mainstream queer and API communities. Others believe that our politicization is not an automatic reflex; it is a longer process whose development requires conscious effort on the part of our leadership.

This split occurs not only as a function of age and experience but also as a result of our varied political histories and convictions. The older participants, having witnessed the transformation of our political culture into one of conservatism, warn of using political issues too overtly in organizing the community. They remind us that there will always be gay and bisexual men coming out into our community, and these people will always need safe spaces. Our community cannot afford to alienate them. The younger participants, however, having seen a resurgence in student activism in the nineties, are more optimistic about opportunities for incorporating a progressive political analysis into organizing. At our respective college campuses, we see queer API student groups providing safe spaces and, at the same time, using these spaces for educational and organizing purposes. As one of the editors states in the discussion, this optimism might stem from the fact that, when the younger participants became politically active, there was already an established queer API community. They did not start out with nothing. Still, we are reminded that because not everyone in our community has the access to higher education that we have had, we should be cautious about generalizing from our own college experiences.

Organizing is certainly difficult; that much we can agree on. However, as editors of this roundtable, we caution those who use the complexity of our community—for example, the influx of recent immigrants—to explain why organizing APIs is difficult. The argument goes: recent immigrants do not naturally adopt the label, Asian Pacific Islander; they are unfamiliar with, or are denied access to, the political process; they do not feel a part of our history of resistance in this country. To be sure, these issues have practical implications for community organizing. But, as Gil Mangaoang can attest, being a third-generation Filipino American does not automatically mean you will have a certain kind of reinforcement of your identity. As Steven Shum states in the discussion, "We choose to align ourselves with various communities. . . . We may consider ourselves part of the community by simply being, but I think there is a progression—not always forward—but there is a progression where we go beyond simply being, into doing, acting, and resisting." No matter where we were born, it is imperative that we place our work within the larger history of progressive organizing for social justice.

The problem is not the complexity or the diversity of our communities, which is something that we cannot, and do not want to, change anyway. The difficulty in community organizing, we, the editors, believe, lies in how we envision our work. In his article, "The 'Four Prisons' and the Movement of Liberation," Glenn Omatsu provides an alternative analysis of community development from the 1960s to the 1990s. Although his study focuses on the API community in general, it incorporates a political analysis that proves useful in the queer API community as well. Omatsu argues that community-based organizations spawned by the grassroots Asian American movement of the late sixties became bureaucratized and institutionalized in the eighties and nineties, partially in response to the nature of funding.[2] (One can find parallels in the AIDS movement and the subsequent emergence of an AIDS industry.) Instead of giving voice to the voiceless, a class of young professionals has emerged as advocates and spokespeople for the community. In addition, in a decade where the gap between the rich and the poor has widened significantly, the API community has concentrated its attention on basic survival needs, such as jobs, housing, and health care. As mere deliverers of services, political organizers have developed a provider-client relationship with the community, which is sometimes devoid of any organizing and empowering component. The political process became so specialized that we, as political organizers, shielded it from the grass roots, instead of providing them with a critical understanding and organizing skills so that they too could participate. In so doing, we denied them power. Within this context, Mangaoang's call to address the basic needs of the queer API community and to use these survival issues to educate and organize our communities is really a demand that we redefine the political principles behind our work.

One last cautionary note to the readers: the roundtable is made up of six people, some of whom have never worked with each other before. It took us some time to learn how to speak to one another, to learn that we sometimes used the same words to mean different things.[3] We edited out two-thirds of the discussion to avoid repetition and to keep the transcript at a publishable length. And because this conversation, like most, was not entirely linear, we transposed some dialogue in order to clarify the context. The final edited version was submitted to all the participants for approval. As editors, we brought with us some strong convictions and biases, which we believe are evident in the discussion. Editing a manuscript can be a frustrating and sometimes dangerous process. Although we have attempted to represent each participant as fairly as possible, we feel obligated to remind our readers not to treat this roundtable discussion as an unmediated conversation.

Finally, many of us tend to think that some API groups are cultural or social in nature *as opposed to* overtly political. But as Urvashi Vaid, former director of the National Gay and Lesbian Task Force, writes in *Virtual Equality,* the task of transforming our political culture is a war with many fronts "that has room in it for everyone. . . . Rather than defining those groups as cultural and proposing that our mission is to make them political, what if we saw them as the political front line, and organized them in a conscious way to do their cultural work more effectively?" (209). To even begin asking ourselves these questions, we must confront our philosophical and strategic positions more critically. This roundtable discussion is but one attempt.

Roundtable Discussion

Shum: We're at a place right now—here in Los Angeles in 1996—where we can talk about all these queer API organizations we're a part of. Were we to take ourselves back a little in time, these organizations, these safe spaces, did not exist, and the community has undergone some dramatic changes in the interval. These community organizations developed only because there were individuals who understood there was a need, and they decided to push the community. And these organizations grew and thrived. The development of our queer API community and our community's leadership are subjects we need to spend some time talking about.

Goishi: In the fifties, sixties, and somewhat in the seventies, many of us did not know that there were other gay Asians. We were still an oddity. At that point, there was not any structure to bring together Asians who happened to be gay.

Mangaoang: When I came out in the seventies, it was a different political atmosphere. You didn't have the strength of a mature, developed gay movement yet. How then did gay Asians fit in that scenario? That was a real challenge. APIs were subsumed within whatever gay organizations existed then, or we were invisible. There is a whole history of progress that emerged, a whole history of individuals who stepped forward to take those leadership positions.

Goishi: In my case, I never met another gay Asian until I came to L.A. in 1980. I'm sure I'm not the only one who experienced that.

Shum: How did you see yourself developing as a leader then?

Goishi: In my case, I was fortunate in the sense that opportunities to be in leadership positions were there, and I was stupid enough to accept them. [*Laughs.*] I personally didn't think I was a leader for a very long, long time. Or I was a leader only from the standpoint that I happened to be there to raise my hand and say, "yes," and I just had the skills complex to do the work. There was a vision that there wasn't anything being done. Therefore, somebody had to do it, or no one else would.

Cuevas: To be honest, even now, I'm thrown into doing things, and I feel like I don't know what I'm doing. And it's scary. But I come out of the experience learning, and that's the main thing. That's how I build my skills.

Goishi: We assume the leaders will be there, and they will do their thing, and new people will come up. I don't think organizations are doing enough to mentor people into leadership positions. They're often thrown into a sink-or-swim situation. The current leadership here in Los Angeles have not been taking the steps to come up with a program where they encourage people who do show leadership abilities to become leaders. When the end of their term comes up, they're all scrambling for people to assume positions. And they really don't take the opportunity to make sure they have the right people at the right spot, so that the organization can be healthy and move on.

Wat: Do you think there is a leadership vacuum in the queer API community?

Goishi: I'm not sure if it's a leadership vacuum, but I think we are not mentoring leaders so that they can pace themselves and avoid burnout.

Kim: The question about leadership vacuum is not unique to our community. It's a question you hear a lot, whether it be in the mainstream gay and lesbian community or the API community or the African American community. Everywhere people are asking, "Where are our Martin Luther Kings?"

A lot of what I have to say comes from my experience with Gay Asian Pacific Support Network [GAPSN], which I've been involved with for more than three years. I don't know if there is a magical solution to developing leadership. For me, life has been a mentor. You rise to the occasion. In GAPSN, we're always responding to crises, and we don't have enough time to sit back and take stock and try to do the work proactively. We would rely on the same few people—like musical chairs—in terms of leadership positions, and we were just switching chairs, because so few people were becoming involved.

But last year, GAPSN coordinators organized committees where they brought in other people and got them involved in developing agendas and talking through issues. We also asked them to implement some of their ideas, to get their hands dirty. So I was very pleased to see that a majority of this year's board of directors is new. The more people that we got involved, the more of them would volunteer for leadership positions. Leadership development involves going out and identifying people, asking them to just get started. Sooner or later they will see that they have the potential to do more.

Cuevas: It really depends on what kind of space you're talking about. I haven't been that involved in the queer community, because for the issues that I'm involved in I don't find much activity in the queer community—issues like immigration and affirmative action. I wish I saw more activism on these issues in the queer community.

Because of this, I don't feel I have a mentor. Most of the people I work with are straight, and they are my role models. But they're not my mentors. Mentoring is helping someone develop their skills; it's an active process. Also, I am not always out in the API community, because I don't feel safe yet.

Goishi: There are very few spaces in LA where queer Asians can be out. Asian Pacific AIDS Intervention Team [APAIT] is one of those places where I hope it's okay to be who we are because of the work we do. We are a rarity.

Cuevas: I feel I have to earn their respect first, before I can even say I'm gay. The people I work with might be very progressive on many issues, but being out to them is a different matter. So I see the duality in what I do. It gets schizophrenic a lot of times. I don't hide my sexuality, but I'm not completely out either.

Mangaoang: That's a very common phenomenon. When I became politically active, it was not in the gay community. It was within the broader context of the social issues that were confronting our society at the time. Dan [Cuevas] said something that was very important. There is a certain credibility and image that people who find themselves in the forefront project. And when you make the decision to come out, it's a very powerful process, because you are gauged on what you've done. People can't criticize you that much, because you've made a political commitment and other contributions. When this is the context in which you come out, it becomes a stronger statement. He or she happens to have a sexual orientation—fine and good—but that's not the primary identifier.

Wat: This reminds me of how a few of us came out collectively in Asian Pacific Islanders for Immigrant Rights and Empowerment

[API-FIRE], which is a progressive and intergenerational community organization. It was only after we accomplished something and people in the group started coming to us for ideas that we felt we were in sufficient positions of leadership to come out. It was at a dinner after a meeting, and we were talking about some of the racism that we experienced in the West Hollywood Gay Pride Festival. I think it took some by surprise that we were actually at the parade and festival. It's also interesting that Dan [Cuevas], who works in the mainstream API community, can find few mentors. I think there are a lot of queer APIs working in the API community.

Mangaoang: Part of the challenge is not only coming to grips with who we are as gay individuals but also [asking,] How does that fit within the broader fabric of our society? We cannot deal with only being gay in the narrow confines. We are living in a society that is very diverse. That's all too clear. That's part of the challenge of being a leader—it's not just in your own community.

Any community-service organization in L.A. knows that they have to interact with the mainstream organizations. We have to be secure about our identity as Asian people, about what our history and struggles have been in this country. Otherwise, it would be very difficult as gay Asians to move into the mainstream. I think that could be an element of mentoring: to recapture that history, to provide an identity that many of us don't have.

Goishi: This is why I think gay social groups are important. These are the environments where individuals can feel safe and be safe and really blossom into their potential.

Kim: In GAPSN a number of people who were totally in the closet when we first met them are now being very vocal and open about who they are in contexts that you wouldn't [have] expect[ed] a few years ago. People push themselves each day and go out a little more and share their complete selves with their mainstream API coworkers.

Shum: I know that when I was coming out, what was especially helpful was that I knew there was at least one community-based organization that I could go to. Racism within the mainstream gay and lesbian community was a real concern for me. I was an undergraduate at UCLA at the time, and I had heard about GAPSN. But when I went to my first GAPSN meeting, it was a very disorienting experience. I was amazed that there was this large room filled with so many out gay and bisexual API men. But I also came to realize that many of the concerns the group was dealing with were not issues I was dealing with.

Mangaoang: Attracting people has always been the biggest challenge. One of the key points is variety. We can each ask ourselves,

"How did we become involved? What were the issues?" And I would venture a guess that it's probably very diverse. It's what we put on the agenda that attracts a potential member. I don't think there's a formula.

Shum: The strength of our community is certainly our diversity. And our diversity demands that we recognize our distinct needs, but at the same time this diversity needs to be contested. We have these distinct needs and concerns, but there must also exist points where we can organize collectively.

This explains why Mahu, a support group for queer API students, was able to form at UCLA. Not everyone was an American-born Chinese like myself, and not everyone was coming to the space with the exact same concerns. But those of us who were willing to come to the group believed that there was a real need to combat racism within the lesbian and gay community and homophobia within the API community.

Goishi: There's a need to clarify what actually are the needs of our community. I realize that this is a pretty small group. When I was coming out—Gil [Mangaoang] can back me up on this—we knew all the openly gay Asians in town. And today, we can't come near to identifying all of the gay Asians out there. Maybe we could plan to bring together the gay Asian community to discuss how we can work collectively to strengthen all of our organizations.

Mangaoang: The timing is good now for that to occur. A critical mass exists. We didn't have this before. And we know our communities will continue to grow as the number of API's grows in this country and surely here in L.A. It's a good time to look at what we can do—at least have a common perspective. It's hard to say what that common perspective would be.

Shum: Our communities are so difficult to hold together, since there isn't one concern among queer API men—be it social, cultural, or political—that draws everyone together. What's really important is to look at the organizations that already exist and to look at what we would like to see happen. And since we're all community organizers, I'm assuming that this says something about our political ideology.

Wat: I think of a community as a means to do something, rather than an end in itself. For instance, I don't think I'm involved in immigrant rights because I'm a queer Asian but because, as a queer Asian, I know how this can affect me. It's linking the issues. It has to be strategic.

Goishi: I'm trying to relate this discussion to the theme of the roundtable, which I thought was leadership building. How does this fit into bringing the queer API community together?

Wat: Jeff [Kim] brought up GAPSN's committee structure, and I think that's a good example. It shows that how we pattern our institutions has an effect on leadership development. When you decentralize the decision-making power, then more people become involved, and more people become leaders. We have to work on conceiving and building these structures. We have to change them sometimes if they are not working. But all these structures are just means to do something.

Kim: Which is what?

Wat: I think that question is getting really hard to answer at this time, because of the pervasive conservative . . .

Kim: So you mean political stuff.

Wat: Yes.

Kim: Something I learned from being involved in GAPSN is that we would always talk about "We've got to be more political next year." To me, that is in a way being selfish, because you latch onto your own personal development when you say, "I've moved on. So we are going to move the whole organization on." It's important to expand what we're doing as a community but not leave anyone behind. I've seen that happen in other groups, where they moved to the external political side and forgot the internal. That's what we face. We need to work on fixing the organization and being responsive, because the vast majority of our community is mainly interested in the social or relational. Leadership should try to expand their members' horizons but also be mindful that they're serving a community that has different needs. Some people are just coming into it.

Wat: Do you think within these social spaces, then, there exist possibilities for politicization?

Shum: But don't you see the work as political to begin with?

Wat: It's political to begin with, but it also stops at a certain point.

Kim: I think you bring the issues to the leaders in the traditional sense. And they have to find out more about these issues and try to bring an API perspective to them and then bring them back to the general group and try to encourage the group to develop their own stance on these issues. We're not looking at a vacuum.

Wat: Everyone is capable of doing that. Most of us got involved in social organizations at first, but we recognized that there was something not complete about these spaces. And when we look to move on. . . .

Cuevas: There have to be options.

Wat: Right. So who is providing these options? Are *we* providing these options?

Goishi: Everybody needs to progress and keep building on what they've done. Somebody has to be available to continue that process. That's leadership building. As we go on and expand our horizons, we leave behind a structure for people who are coming out. Many of the gay organizations I've seen don't think about this. When they move on, they bring the whole organization. People are left behind, and they eventually drop out and become disillusioned. Or the organization doesn't move fast enough for another group, so these people go off.

Wat: There has to be a formal structure to develop leadership. Skills are easy to learn. You learn by doing; you can't just take a class and then expect to do it. But I think we need to focus on the history of our movement, focus on developing a more progressive political analysis. The social organizations are invaluable, because this is where you can mobilize people. I think there is a general agreement that it's good to move the community beyond just these social spaces and into greater participation in politics.

Goishi: I'm not sure that's true. I'm assuming that you're thinking this is a natural progression from the socialization process to the political arena. I don't think that Asians tend to be political. I think as you progress, you will drop off more people than you take with you.

Mangaoang: I agree with Dean [Goishi] and also much of what Jeff [Kim] has said. There are different levels of participation that people will choose. Some are just going to be comfortable staying at a social level. That doesn't mean that they're necessarily turned off by any political perspective, but we have to give our community the option and not push them. When you start pushing people, they're going to go in the opposite direction. It's not to say that you deny the political history, because that's so very important.

But there are different levels of responsibilities. And that's what leadership is. You will always find those peripheral rings around the leadership body. Depending on how comfortable people feel on those peripheral rings, they are going to move closer in and in. You can't push a person to do that. What we can do is provide that structure.

Wat: I don't mean pushing. There's a fine line between providing structure and options versus pushing. I don't know how we can draw that line, but I do agree people should not be pushed. On the other hand, when we say building a movement, it's always recognizing that there are people who disagree with us, but we should try to get them on our side. Let's have this space for critical debate. Let's look at your point of view and my point of view and the other fifty-six points of view.

Kim: What do you expect to come out of that? A certain community perspective?

Shum: This brings us to something we were talking about earlier—how we come into our communities as APIs or as queers. It's interesting that many believe that we don't have to come out as API. I don't think that's true. We're not born into a community with a certain community perspective. Rather, we choose to align ourselves with various communities at different stages in our lives. Though our ethnicity may be marked from an early age, we have to make a conscious effort to come out as politically progressive within the API community. This parallels, in a way, our coming-out process as gay and bisexual men, how we learn to be more accepting and understanding of our sexual orientation. We may consider ourselves part of the community by simply being, but I think there is a progression—not always forward—but there is a progression where we go beyond simply being, into doing, acting, and resisting.

This may reflect some of the biases of people here at the roundtable, but we need to talk about some vision of our community to enable other people to enter into it, to shape it, or to change it.

Mangaoang: But even that statement is political. I guess that this is the whole point of the discussion. Much of what's been said is very academic. That is not to say it is not important, but for the vast majority of real life scenarios, it's not going to fly, guys. I'm sorry. It's not going to be real. No one is denying that you need to bring that stuff into the community for people to begin to identify, but—take the old analogy—you can take the horse to the water, but the horse has got to be the one to drink. You have to balance bringing in the information but not leaving out the social things.

I'm talking about my own experiences as an old-time organizer/activist back in the seventies, when these were some of the same issues that I remember us talking about. I remember asking how we were going to bring people in, what the key issues were. We recognized that you couldn't go too far, because otherwise you were going to push people away. We couldn't just have one static agenda. I think that's part of the challenge now: how do we continue to grow with our developing community and not lose the perspectives that we have brought with us? You can't always throw the whole agenda out there. I just put a word of caution. If that's the direction, I think you're going to find a very, very small percentage of people who are going to walk the same line.

Shum: But the political analysis is always going to be there. It's something we will keep very close to us. It's our ideals and principles. Whether we want to call it political or personal is another thing. We're going to face a lot of challenges in doing our work. If we're not mindful of these guiding principles, then we're going to stumble into the same old problems.

Goishi: What amazes me is that even though we represent half a dozen agencies at this table, there are all these queer APIs going into West Hollywood, going into the Buddha Lounge,[4] who don't belong to any of our organizations. I would imagine that the vast majority of gay Asians in L.A. do not belong to any organization.

Wat: We can't reach everyone, at least not overnight. We all have to recognize that and not hit ourselves on the head every time we say, "There are people in Buddha Lounge that we don't know and we haven't seen before." The social spaces, even Buddha Lounge, for example, are important to have. But how do we take advantage of the structures that exist? I recognize that there is a tremendous range of ideologies in our communities. Even people who say they don't have one, they do. We have to package our messages in different ways that speak to different people. We can't go out there and preach to people. Yes, I understand that's not going to work. But let's create some spaces where we can talk about these things. I'm not saying that we all have to go out to protests and rallies and register voters. I'm talking about if we understand how immigration, for example, affects our lives, then maybe we will do something about it, even if we don't have the skills yet.

Cuevas: My concern, too, is how we can package some of these basic goals that we as queer API men want to accomplish. Sometimes you have to be political in subtle ways. There's so much stigma attached to being political. When I go to GAPSN meetings, I cannot have a conversation about some of the issues that I'm working on. People don't want to discuss them.

Kim: Are you working toward just talking about issues or forging a consensus? It's easy to talk about issues.

Wat: I don't think we need consensus. I think that's a big myth. I think we need to talk about issues critically. I think consensus could be paralyzing.

Kim: "Critically" meaning what? Does it mean everyone is not thinking enough about these things?

Shum: Or that everyone begins to think like *you* do? [*Laughs.*]

Wat: No. Everyone should begin to think about these issues by sharing their experiences and knowledge to come to their own conclusions. How Mahu does it might be different from GAPSN, which might be different from how APAIT does it with its staff. But even within each organization that does different work, there will be a social space. There was a time when some of us in Mahu volunteered for APAIT— as a group. Not everyone participated, because some people were scared of West Hollywood or they didn't want to be seen there doing AIDS/HIV prevention outreach. But other people eventually became comfortable and joined us. That's what I meant by providing options without taking away the social space.

Goishi: Are you saying that politicization—using your term—should be the goal of our gay API organizations?

Shum: Perhaps we can approach this conversation in another way. As we're talking about providing support and education to our communities, I would say that the work is intrinsically political, because we'll have to talk about basic inequities, systems, and structures that are simply not providing for us when they should be. The work I'm invested in is political because it's more than my own selfish interests. It's political because I'm imagining a future for the larger queer API community. Therefore, everyone at this table is invested in this political work as well.

Wat: A lot of things we do are important. But at the same time, they're like Band-Aids. At what point, however, do we start saying, "Let's not make Band-Aids and talk about why we are being hurt"? That's a longer process that I don't expect to happen overnight or to reach everyone. With the people we've reached already, what can we do?

Kim: Are you saying that leadership is inevitably tied up with politics?

Wat: Leaders need to advocate for the community. But if your constituency is not political, how can you tell politicians that you can mobilize, that they'd better be mindful of this community, because we vote and we pay taxes and give donations? Can you be a leader of a constituency that is not political?

Goishi: I think you can. Sometimes I'm asked by the L.A. Gay and Lesbian Center to represent APIs. And when I take it back to the community, they may not be necessarily politicized in terms of going out and marching. But they would support me and not necessarily think of themselves as part of a political movement.

Wat: They don't have to protest.

Goishi: But they have to come out and support the cause in some way. So our organizations will probably never have full 100 percent participation by our constituents, but they will come out to support the leadership because they feel it's important. That's what you're getting at?

Wat/Cuevas (together): Yes.

Goishi: If that's the case, that probably could be done.

Kim: So what you're saying   be honest about it—you want that constituency to have a certain perspective. You're not just talking about a discussion. You're saying that they have to adopt a certain viewpoint that agrees with you.

Wat: No, if you engage in coalition work, united-front work, you do have to work with people who disagree with you.

Kim: But they only back you up if they agree with you.

Wat: No, it's not so black and white all the time. When we do API-FIRE work, a lot of people have problems, because we have to work with a lot of conservative people. But there are certain points where we can make a united front, especially on immigration issues.

Kim: Then they're agreeing with you on a certain issue. Then it's more than just talking about things political, but getting them to agree on a certain perspective.

Shum: But isn't that part of organizing? Remember that we're only able to have this conversation because the community has developed to a certain point. Community organizing is entirely about political ideology, though it doesn't always have to be couched in these terms. For example, GAPSN calls itself a community-based organization that provides support for gay and bisexual APIs, and many people will not see this work as political work. But I would certainly consider it political, because GAPSN is a space for gay and bisexual APIs to meet, to support one another, and to provide assistance beyond what friends would typically be able to provide.

Kim: Implicit in that statement are certain political issues that we in GAPSN agree on: that if you're going to promote a homophobic agenda, people who identify themselves as gay APIs will rally against you. Or if you're a racist—it's a natural issue for them to agree on.

Shum: I wonder how natural it is, since there are many people of color who don't believe that racism exists or who may not even believe that racism is an issue that we as a community need to do anything about.

Kim: But it's easier to rally people on that issue than, say, affirmative action.

Wat: But there are always going to be issues that are difficult to organize around.

Kim: If your end goal is that the vast majority of the community is in synch with you about certain political issues, that goal might conflict with the general mission of different organizations.

Wat: I think the way you pull people to your side is to engage them in discussion. It's self-defeating to say that we might come up with different positions, therefore we are not going to engage in these discussions.

Shum: How do you see GAPSN developing as an organization then?

Kim: Well, I wish we had a political action coordinator. It's been empty for two years.

Wat: You still engage in politics, though.

Kim: Yes. We haven't polled our members on any particular issue. What we were doing was trying to lead them—not developing consensus, but sharing information. At times, we spoke for the community without having polled everybody in GAPSN. For example, we pushed against Prop[osition] 187.[5]

Wat: Which was hard in the API community.

Mangaoang: Out of curiosity, what was the response from the members on Prop. 187?

Kim: We included information in our newsletter. We talked about it during the business part of some meetings, though we never had a rap discussion on Prop. 187.

Goishi: If the GAPSN membership knew a rap discussion on Prop. 187 was going to take place, how many of them would show up? I think very few would. I don't think our community is at that level of the discussion. I think you'll find some people who are ready to do that, but most people would drop off, because it's just not of their interest or it might be too imposing or they might fear it.

Shum: It doesn't have to be the entire community. There are already members of our community who are invested in this work. Perhaps we can't imagine everyone becoming political. But there really needs to be a recommitment, among the leadership, to community organizing in whatever form it takes. The work needs to be done. The political environment can change so radically that we won't even be able to imagine a queer API community.

Mangaoang: That's a key point that you just hit upon. It's the environment. What's the political climate? During the seventies, it was such a dynamic period you could not help but become politicized. Things were changing so swiftly. It was all around you. In the nineties, we have a different scenario. Jobs are a real critical issue for a lot of folks. We have an economy that's very unstable. So these are some of the basic issues that draw people. We have to look at the climate that we are in now and not create that artificially.

Wat: Because of the pervasiveness of conservatism in the nineties, this is a very different political climate. That's why we need to be more creative in outreaching to people, instead of doing less or being satisfied with less. I think we're at a critical juncture within the queer API community, since there is a critical mass but there are only a handful of organizations. People want to come out to these organizations, and we can take advantage of that. Again, I'm not talking about throwing away what GAPSN or APAIT are doing, because they are doing important work. But somehow add to or personalize the issues. When we talk about affirmative action, it is not just some vague political discussion about what's right or what's wrong, but how it affects people's lives.

Shum: What's especially noteworthy about this conversation about political activism is the different perspectives that are being thrown out. The feeling that political work needs to be done is coming from the younger generation of queer API activists at this table. It's also interesting to hear that this is where much of the optimism for com-

munity organizing among queer APIs is coming from. Maybe it's because we think that there is some more time ahead of us. Maybe it's
because we came out into a community that already existed, and we
think we can take the community further along.

And maybe this is a good time to talk about some of the challenges that we as a community need to face in the near future.

Wat: One of the challenges we have brought up is that the times are
different. We have to organize differently, more creatively. I think
that we need to take certain risks in terms of putting political issues
out there. It might not be successful at first. But I think we need to
start building a foundation for it. Take some risks. Otherwise, it gets
harder and harder.

Kim: The world is getting smaller. Communities can't stay isolated. We
need to build allies. A lot of times, however, it boils down to fatigue
and burnout.

Cuevas: That's why we need more leaders.

Goishi: I think these issues do parallel our movement in APAIT. We're
similarly approaching a point where we have to think about working
with other people-of-color agencies that provide HIV services. Money
is getting tighter. The political environment is not very friendly and
probably will not get any friendlier over the next few years.

Mangaoang: I think one valuable element that could help define some
of the challenges now is to look into the history of the gay Asian
movement and trace some of the benchmarks. What were the key
issues then? How did they develop? What were the challenges that
existed then, and how were they overcome? Unless we recapture
our history, we may recreate the same mistakes as we take up these
new challenges. They're not all that new.

Cuevas: I guess the one thing that kept coming up for me is that activism is a privilege. And we have to realize that. We have to get
down to the basic issues to get people involved.

Shum: Activism shouldn't be the exclusive realm of people who have
gone through college. If that's the case, then what sort of connection is there to the community? What does the queer API community have to offer to low-income, first-generation immigrants? How
does the community provide support and education for us all?

Kim: I think that the challenge is what it's always been, what it's going to be forever. The main challenge is to organize our own community. We have new entrants all the time, whether they are immigrants or people just coming out. And we need to keep
working on bringing them into an awareness of their part in the
community. We're in the business of community building. In a
city like L.A., where there are so many APIs and so many queers,
the challenge is to somehow get more of them involved.

That's why I support the ethnic-specific gay organizations that are working within their own communities, like Barangay or the Gay Vietnamese Alliance. I tried supporting them last year while on the board of GAPSN, but there was some resistance. A lot of times, the only way people are going to understand sexual orientation is through their cultural similarities. Language and trust are big issues. They're not going to go to an English-speaking rap to talk about being gay. More of these groups should form. And their leadership should be mindful of pan-Asian organizing as well.

Goishi: These groups need to be encouraged, because they're going to feed into the GAPSNs and the Mahus and so forth.

Mangaoang: These ethnic-specific organizations can also help their members to understand what is the history of that specific immigrant group in this country and how they had to struggle. Again, we're talking about politicization.

Wat: We're running out of time, and we're just starting to get at some key issues. I know we can't resolve everything in one roundtable discussion, but I'm really surprised—in a good way—at the perspectives that came out in the last couple of hours. It struck me that we didn't share a common language of organizing. Personally, I think struggling to articulate my own understanding of organizing against all these viewpoints has sharpened my approach to this work.

Organization Guide	APAIT	Asian Pacific AIDS Intervention Team
	APANLA	Asian Pacific Americans for a New L.A.
	API/FIRE	Asian Pacific Islanders for Immmigrant Rights and Empowerment
	APLG	Asian Pacific Lesbians and Gays
	GAPSN	Gay Asian Pacific Support Network

PARTICIPANT PROFILES

DAN CUEVAS holds a B.A. in Asian American studies with a specialization in Chicana/o studies from the University of California, Los Angeles. He works for Mabel Teng of the San Francisco Board of Supervisors. His organizing experiences include working for APANLA, a group that organized after the 1992 Los Angeles uprisings and for API/FIRE, where he helped organize a multiracial march in Los Angeles in 1995 to protest anti-immigrant legislation.

DEAN GOISHI, a sansei (third-generation Japanese American) born in Poston, Arizona, has lived in Los Angeles with his partner, Thomas, for sixteen years. He graduated from the University of California, Berkeley. In 1980 he and a group of API gay men formed APLG, one of the few social support organizations for gay Asian men and women at the time.

Goishi serves as the executive director of APAIT, which he cofounded in 1987, and is the primary agency providing HIV/AIDS services to the API communities in Los Angeles.

JEFFREY SEUNGKYU KIM, raised in Chicago, received his law degree from the University of Michigan Law School. He lives in Los Angeles with his partner. Kim has held various leadership positions in GAPSN, an organization that serves and advocates for gay and bisexual API men. Since 1993, he has worked on the legal services staff of the Los Angeles Gay and Lesbian Center, where he coordinates the HIV, Immigration, and Youth Law projects.

GIL MANGAOANG, a third-generation Filipino born in the United States, served in the Vietnam War. In 1971 he returned to college in San Francisco, where he participated in the ethnic studies struggle. Mangaoang's organizing work includes: fighting to stop the eviction of elderly Filipino tenants at the International Hotel; working in the anti-Marcos movement; creating support programs for national liberation efforts in El Salvador; and building houses for sugar cane workers in Cuba. Mangaoang came out in San Francisco in 1975 and has been with his life partner, Juan Lombard, since 1977. They live in Los Angeles, where he is a staff member of APAIT.

NOTES

1. The Lambda chapter is pan-Asian and queer-specific. It was formed in 1995 as a result of the successful organizing of queer and queer-friendly members of the Japanese American Citizens League for a resolution supporting same-sex marriages.

2. See Espiritu 82–111.

3. This is the second of two roundtable discussions. The first discussion—whose participants included Dean Goishi, Jeff Kim, Steven Shum, Eric C. Wat, University of California at Irvine undergraduate student Hoa Su, and Pasadena high school student Kim Ho—was used to tease out certain issues to be focused on in the second discussion.

4. Buddha Lounge is a Los Angeles dance club with a predominantly queer API male clientele.

5. For more on Proposition 187, see Chapter 3.

WORKS CITED

Espiritu, Yen Le. *Asian American Panethnicity: Bridging Institutions and Identities.* Philadelphia: Temple UP, 1992.

Omatsu, Glenn. "The 'Four Prisons' and the Movement of Liberation: Asian American Activism from the 1960s to the 1990s." *The State of Asian America: Activism and Resistance in the 1990s.* Ed. Karin Aguilar-San Juan. Boston: South End, 1994. 19–69.

Vaid, Urvashi. *Virtual Equality: The Mainstreaming of Gay and Lesbian Liberation.* New York: Anchor, 1995.

12. Toward a Queer Korean American Diasporic History
JeeYeun Lee

Looking for a Diasporic Past

I have always had an ahistorical sense of my origins. My parents were not the nostalgic type, the kind I imagined "American" parents to be, always telling stories beginning with "When I was your age." The language gap that grew with the years after my arrival in the United States also contributed to a sense of alienation from a past accessible only through that partially understood tongue. As I search now for a history, I inevitably begin with dilemmas. How do I claim a past that seems both mine and not mine? How do I negotiate a history located in another continent in another tongue? To address these questions, I have found the concept of diaspora useful.

Diaspora has gained much currency in the last decade of the twentieth century, with the convergence of such academic interests as transnationalism, postcolonial studies, and black British cultural studies. With this popularity has come a proliferation of meanings beyond its traditional application to Jewish history, accompanied by attempts to define and classify the concept.[1] Khachig Tölölyan puts forth an expansive definition in his introduction to the first issue of *Diaspora: A Journal of Transnational Studies.* He states, "We use 'diaspora' provisionally to indicate our belief that the term that once described Jewish, Greek, and Armenian dispersion now shares meanings with a larger semantic domain that includes words like immigrant, expatriate, refugee, guest-worker, exile community, overseas community, ethnic community. This is the vocabulary of transnationalism" (4–5).

Shared in this cluster of meanings is the idea of diaspora as the migration and dispersal of a group of people who view themselves as a people by virtue of a common ethnic/national/geographic origin. It is the flip side of the traditional concept of immigration:[2] while immigration focuses on a collective destination, diaspora defines itself by a common origin. For this reason I do not draw much from historical narratives of immigration generated by Asian American studies, which mostly focus on experiences in the United States.[3] This self-conscious Asian American strategy has been necessary and useful for dispelling Orientalist stereotypes of Asians as alien sojourners, and these narratives do constitute an important aspect of my historical contextualization. But as a product of post-1965 migration, in a time when those born outside the United States constitute a growing majority of Asians in the United States,

I am searching for a cross-oceanic history that seems to find a more suitable model in the concept of diaspora.

The history of a diasporic people is about a displaced community looking backward onto another time and another land. Stuart Hall's writings, in particular, have helped me consider how to do this without reifying a homeland. Hall talks about the search for a homeland in the context of diasporic people's present-day constructions of identity and ethnicity, emphasizing how the search is shaped—in fact constituted—by motivations and mediations:

> The homeland is not waiting back there for the new ethnics to re-discover it. There is a past to be learned about, but the past is now seen, and has to be grasped as a history, as something that has to be told. It is narrated. It is grasped through memory. It is grasped through desire. It is grasped through reconstruction. It is not just a fact that has been waiting to ground our identities. ("The Local and the Global" 38)

> The past continues to speak to us. But this is no longer a simple, factual "past," since our relation to it is, like the child's relation to the mother, always-already "after the break." It is always constructed through memory, fantasy, narrative and myth. ("Cultural Identity" 72)

The past is a story, motivated by investments and constituted through modes of representation in the here and now. The following is one aspect of my story, about why the past became diasporic.

A Diasporic Korean ↔ American History

Korean/Americans—no longer there yet not quite here.—LAURA HYUN YI KANG, "Introduction: 'Strewn into Such Assembly' "

I am here because you were there: my location is a direct reflection of nations and peoples shifting and conflicting. It is only with some grasp of the historical relationships between the United States, Korea, and Japan that I can start to tell the significance of my own positionings. I am gradually putting together histories that give some order to a pattern that cannot be explained by the push-and-pull view of immigration. In this model, bad conditions in the "Old World" (for example, poverty, overpopulation, war, and political repression) push people across oceans and continents to good conditions in the "New World" (jobs, education, political stability, and so on). People act as rational individual agents performing cost-benefit analyses on regions of the world. From this point of view, the so-called Third World is an inherently bad and undesirable place to live, and the United States and the rest of the West are the fount of all opportunity and good.

It is precisely these simplistic cause-and-effect models, so seductive to political campaigns, that were mobilized in favor of California's Proposition 187 in 1994[4] and federal immigration and welfare "reform" legislation in 1996. It is precisely these models that absolutely fail to explain current and consistent global patterns of migration. The overwhelming majority—81.5 percent[5]—of emigrating South Koreans come to the United States: why is that so, when there are many other countries in the world with favorable conditions for immigration?

The answer lies in a mesh of historical entanglement whose groundwork was laid in the late nineteenth century and which continues to this day. We are here because you were—and are still—there, economically, politically, culturally. Outside of superficial rhetoric and uninformed public opinion, many people recognize that migration is neither innocent of nor divorced from other global forces. As Ivan Light and Edna Bonacich state, migration "is intimately tied to foreign policy, including economic aid, trade, cultural influence, military assistance, and political interference. U.S. foreign policy in South Korea (as in many other countries) has a direct and indirect impact on the migration of peoples to this country" (125). The many linkages are too involved to explore in detail here, but some lines can be traced sketchily.[6]

Historically, the existence of a South Korea with which the United States could become involved was itself partly a product of U.S. actions. The story begins with the Taft-Katsura Treaty of 1905, a secret agreement between the United States and Japan, in which Theodore Roosevelt agreed not to interfere with Japan's affairs in Korea if Japan did not interfere with U.S. imperialism in the Philippines. With similar agreements from Russia and England, Japan established a protectorate over Korea that year and eventually annexed it as a colony in 1910. Japan's colonial rule was harsh, repressing Korean culture and identity with great force. Koreans fought back, most notably in the March First Movement. This national demonstration and declaration of independence, which began on 1 March 1919, launched two months of demonstrations and protests involving one million Koreans throughout the country. The Japanese brutally suppressed the peaceful uprisings, killing, arresting, and torturing tens of thousands of people.

After having helped to install Japan's colonial domination, the United States and the Allied forces graciously liberated Korea in 1945, only to sacrifice its sovereignty to the strategic interests of the United States and the Soviet Union. The United States proposed, and the Soviet Union agreed, to divide the peninsula at the thirty-eighth parallel after Japan's surrender, presumably in order to oversee the peaceful withdrawal of Japanese troops. However, as Bruce Cumings (*Origins*) and others have revealed, the U.S. government was primarily interested in keeping Korea out of Soviet hands, in order to implement its notion of "security" in the Pacific. That is, the U.S. government's main interest in 1945, which continues to this day, was to establish South Korea firmly as an anticommunist bulwark against the encroachment of the Soviet Union. South and North Korea were thus created as the first—and now nearly the last—site of the Cold War. As Cumings argues, "It is unlikely that there is another country in the world where the United States bears more responsibility for the existing state of affairs" ("Division" 6).

Immediately after liberation, widespread popular organizing sprang up across Korea, demanding a unified independent nation and changes in the unequal class structure left over from the colonial period. The meaning of liberation for those south of the thirty-eighth parallel quickly became a joke, however, as the United States set up a military government, enlisting former Japanese collaborators and other conservative elites, all of whom brutally suppressed the people's demands. Division of the country was concretized by United Nations–sponsored elections in 1948 and cemented into place with the Korean War. As Chungmoo Choi has noted, "What was Korean about the Korean War? Who is the subject of the verb 'to partition'?"

When the "threat" of communism was realized with the "invasion" from the north, the fledgling South Korean government under Syngman Rhee gained crucial endorsement. Jang Jip Choi states that "whereas before the war, the South Korean state had a weak local base of support, the war gave the state an ideological basis for building its legitimacy. Anticommunism, articulated and experienced in everyday life, became the premier motif for ideological legitimization of the South Korean state" (22). It remains to be seen whether democratization under South Korea's current president, Kim Dae Jung, will result in less fervent anticommunism.

The authoritarian dictatorships under Syngman Rhee, Park Chung Hee, Chun Doo Hwan, and Roh Tae Woo all received the blessing and active support of the U.S. government. This support largely took the form of enormous amounts of economic and military aid to the South Korean government, which created linkages that continue to this day. In the 1960s and 1970s, U.S. government aid and private investment financed South Korea's rapid shift to an export-oriented economy, firmly consolidating the country's position in the capitalist world of international trade. U.S. military troops stayed in South Korea after the war, and remain to this day, helping to make the DMZ "the most densely militarized spot in the world" (Abelmann and Lie 52). The United States, which has military bases throughout the country, has also been in official operational control of the South Korean military since 1950 (Abelmann and Lie 81). This close military partnership led South Korea to participate in the Vietnam War, through which South Korea made earnings significant in financing the export-oriented industrialization mentioned above (Byoung-Lo Philo Kim 161). Far from being isolated from each other, military and economic interests for both the South Korean and U.S. governments have served tandem functions in their anticommunist agendas.

All of these developments created several conditions that motivated people to emigrate from South Korea. Lack of personal and political freedoms under the successive dictatorships was a huge incentive for those who could leave to emigrate. The intense drive toward modernization and economic development, and the rhetoric of anticommunism, were used to legitimate the tight control that the government and the Korean CIA held over the population—most notably after Park Chung Hee instituted the Yushin "revitalization" constitution in 1972, which suspended many democratic rights. Those with the means to emigrate came mostly from the newly emerging urban middle class, who found a lack of job opportunities commensurate with their increased levels of education. Light and Bonacich estimate that the majority of Koreans in the United States at the time of their 1980 study were from this urban middle class. Abelmann and Lie also suggest that this sector's search for economic mobility was linked to the desire for democratic rights. They state, "South Koreans wanted personal freedoms to accompany their accumulating commodities: uncensored programs, for example, for their televisions" (68).

Emigration was also encouraged by the Overseas Emigration Law, passed by the South Korean government in 1962 in order to control population growth, alleviate unemployment, earn foreign exchange, and acquire knowledge of advanced technology (Light and Bonacich 103). The very idea of emigration became more conceivable as internal migration within the peninsula grew common. Rapid industrialization led to an unprecedented rural-to-urban migration, creating an entire generation of people uprooted from their hometowns and psychologically detached from the cities in which they now lived. Massive displacement also occurred between 1945 and 1950, when 3.5 million people from North Korea migrated south (Abelmann and Lie 51).

But to explain the choice of the United States—among all other countries—as a destination, the historical and ideological linkages must be taken into account. The intimate military, political, and economic relationships between the two nations have created many points of contact—all opportunities for Koreans to be favorably exposed to the United States. For example, the official view of the United States in South Korea, disseminated and encouraged by the South Korean government, has been that of "colonial liberator and Korean War savior" (Abelmann and Lie 57). Drawn by the common ideology of anticommunism, many South Koreans have looked upon the United States as protector of the free world (as self-proclaimed and dubious as the title may be) and as the site of both economic opportunity and political freedom. They have viewed the United States as a symbol of the economically successful democratic modernity that South Korea has ostensibly been striving for since the 1950s. And as the symbol of a modern Christian nation, the United States has attracted a disproportionate number of Christians among South Korean immigrants (Abelmann and Lie 69–70).[7]

This diasporic part of my story has focused on the role of states: the United States and South Korea. To a large degree this is the product of my sources. The most accessible English-language sources of information about South Korea are in the fields of political science and economics, an overabundance of which analyze the "secret" of East Asian economic success. This body of work, as Hagen Koo notes, tends to "exaggerate the autonomy and strength of the East Asian states and to interpret economic growth in isolation from other political and social changes" (7). From these sources it is hard to distinguish, for both South Korea and the United States, policies that change with the times and individuals who change with regimes. But more than that, it is difficult to see the heterogeneity of those outside the governing bodies, the general populace of South Korea, who are either left out altogether, as passive pawns of industrialization, or discussed as undifferentiated blocs of classes who seem to act with fully formed natural interests. Not evident in readily accessible English-language sources are the brutal realities of the Korean War, colonialism, police-state repression, and industrial labor, as experienced by those subjected to and those complicit in these events. The dilemma of the diasporic search for history in another language, in another land, is that, even if I were able to read them, progressive histories have only recently been able to emerge from the underground.

With the limitations inherent in these sources, it is easy to romanticize Korea as an oppressed, downtrodden homeland, a passive victim of larger nations' interests, which deserves to be sovereign on the basis of its people's millennia-long history. Korean history books open with the foundational myth of the birth of the Korean people in 2333 B.C. According to recorded history, the Korean peninsula has been a unified autonomous state since A.D. 668. With this kind of unity inherent in the national myth, it is difficult to distinguish heterogeneities that would thwart romanticism.

For this reason, I have found Theresa Hak Kyung Cha's *Dictée* a compelling model for narrating a history of a Korean homeland while steadfastly refusing to romanticize it. In *Dictée*, Cha intimately inscribes her personal history with the history of the nation, a diasporic return and reclaiming/rewriting of the homeland. Indeed, Kim and Alarcón's collection of essays about *Dictée* is entitled *Writing Self, Writing Nation*. Laura Hyun Yi Kang notes in that collection, "Identity and personal history for Cha is embedded in other persons and histories. Her own 'story' has a pre-text—the Japanese colonization of Korea and the Korean War. To express herself, she must retell these stories" (79).

In *Dictée* the myth of Korea is not pure, unconditionally heroic, or unmediated. Several essays in *Writing Self, Writing Nation* note Cha's rejection of an easy return to a pure homeland: "The Korean homeland that is longed for is neither recovered nor found. . . . Contestation and home can be located in a simultaneous emergence—that is to say, the contested and the contesting terrain *is* home. Home, in this sense, neither is nor ever can be a settled space. . . . To see home otherwise, as perhaps a final resting place, is to invite the risk of hypostatization and idealization. In *Dictée*, Cha refuses to take the risk and chooses instead to problematize the notion of home." (Shelley Wong 109–110). Cha's home must be problematized because in order to write her diasporic history onto a national past, the complications of conflict, complicity, internalization, and repression must be equally inscribed onto home. Instead of being romanticized, the homeland becomes, in fact, the very site of complexity—of races, nations, genders, and sexualities—complicated in its twisted histories as well as in the desire to tell those stories.

Queering the Homeland

What would a queer version of this diasporic history look like? What would it mean to discuss sexuality as an integral and defining part of this story about governments, wars, capitalism, and migration? How would one go about investigating a queer Korea? And why would this be important?

Reclaiming a history in a diasporic homeland is even more complicated for those of us who are queer. Being multiply displaced makes the process more difficult to research and more fraught with needs and desires. How do people construct a homeland that not only includes but might possibly also even embrace their queer selves? Cherríe Moraga describes such a space for queer Chicanos:

> "Queer Aztlán" had been forming in my mind for over three years and began to take concrete shape a year ago in a conversation with poet Ricardo Bracho. We discussed the limitations of "Queer Nation," whose leather-jacketed, shaved-headed white radicals and accompanying anglo-centricity were an "alien-nation" to most lesbians and gay men of color. We also spoke of Chicano Nationalism, which never accepted openly gay men and lesbians among its ranks. Ricardo half-jokingly concluded, "What we need, Cherríe, is a 'Queer Aztlán.'" Of course. A Chicano homeland that could embrace *all* its people, including its jotería. (147)

Others imagine a reconciliation of homeland and queerness in highly suggestive and creative visual images: Marlon Riggs places a pink triangle on top of a black, green, and red Africa in his film *Anthem;* Trikone, a San Francisco Bay Area organization with a magazine for queer South Asians, uses a similar symbol, in which the outline of the South Asian subcontinent is traced onto a downward-pointing triangle.

Some take on the task of proving an indigenous heritage of same-sex love, relationships, and sexual behavior. For example, an essay by AIDS Bhedhav Virodhi Andolan (ABVA), an AIDS-awareness organization in India, lists evidence of the presence of homosexuality in Indian literary, religious, philosophical, and historical texts. It defiantly states: "We do not need an Alfred Kinsey to discover the rich possibilities of same-sex eroticism and to appropriate these in the form of modern gay sexuality. It's all there in our art, culture, religion, philosophy, and sculpture" (21). And it concludes: "Thus it is clear that homosexuality as a phenomenon is not new to India, and, perhaps because of the religious background of our culture, it has not been an unrelenting tale of oppression and woe" (32–33). Mina Kumar presents an alternative to ABVA's male-centered account by discussing representations of lesbianism in various Indian texts, such as epics and legal codes; she examines them not so much to prove the existence of lesbianism but to analyze the differing attitudes towards lesbianism that are implicit in these texts.

Still others recover a history by conscious construction, using fantasy and myth to reflect on what may or may not be historical "facts." For example, Richard Fung's video *Dirty Laundry* presents simultaneous contemporary and historical narratives to suggest the possibility of homosexuality among Chinese men who built the Canadian railroad in the late nineteenth century. In *When Fox Is a Thousand,* Larissa Lai creates a diasporic tale of women-loving women, spanning continents, times, and species by drawing upon myths and poems of a ninth-century woman poet in China. And although his work does not concern a history relating to a homeland, Isaac Julien's *Looking for Langston* reaches across a diaspora to meditate on a black gay history, which, as Essex Hemphill puts it, "*dare*[*s*] to question history for the names and identities of other black gay men—our ancestors" (182).

These efforts to imagine or recuperate queer presences in diasporic histories have several effects. One is the critique of exclusive ideas about cultural authenticity. Many diasporic communities and communities of people of color in the West explicitly code same-sex desire as a white Western phenomenon, accusing queer people in their midst as selling out, assimilating, or lacking authenticity. Although speaking specifically of South Asian communities, Nayan Shah's observation can apply to others: "The notion of culture here is like a fossil—solid and petrified. . . . Any unfavorable value is displaced onto a non–South Asian source. Ironically, these heterosexists unquestioningly accept the historically 'Western' notion that heterosexuality is natural, normal, and biologically correct and that homosexuality is unnatural and perverse" (see Chapter 9). Gloria Anzaldúa recodes an accusation usually thrown at queers—that we are betraying our people by accepting white Western behavior—and throws it back at mainstream communities of people of color as *their* betrayal of us: "Not me sold out my people but they me. So yes, though 'home' permeates every sinew and cartilage in my body, I too am afraid of going home" (21). By demonstrating an indigenous history of same-sex desire, queers who are diasporic or people of color defy exclusive heterosexist conceptualizations of culture and authenticity.

In addition, queer historical narratives critique heterosexist definitions of community and nation, which rely on simplistic forms of identity politics. Diasporic queers cannot inscribe themselves onto an imagined or real homeland without radically changing its terms, since many forms of nationalism are constructed around assumptions of normative heterosexuality. Marlon Riggs asks, "What time *was* it? Certainly not 'Nation Time,' not for this young, gifted, Black—and queer!—student. No nation, however revolutionary, had dared claim me. No revisionist history, Black, Marxist, or otherwise, dared mention my name" (15).

Jacqui Alexander, in a complex analysis of the co-implications of sexuality, nation, state, decolonization, and transnational capitalism, discusses how and why the states of the Bahamas and Trinidad and Tobago have legislated heterosexist definitions of national identity by criminalizing nonprocreative sexualities, specifically prostitution and lesbian and gay sex. Her argument, as I understand it, is that these states enact such legislation in order to legitimize their authority in the face of economic crises that are actually brought on by processes of neocolonial insertion into transnational capitalism. That is, those who practice prostitution and same-sex behavior are scapegoated to shore up national economic insecurity, their sexuality "disciplined and regulated in order that it might become economically productive" (14). She suggests, as some have noted for other cases, that the state enforces the nation as a larger version of the patriarchal heterosexual family.

Notions of diaspora, too, can rely on heterosexist concepts of kinship and lineage to define community. As a concept, diaspora may be even more prone to myths of reproductive heritage than the nation, whose boundaries can at least be tracked geographically. But if a people is spread over various lands, according to this line of thought, how else can you tell if someone belongs to the diaspora than through a family tree?

Although it does not address diaspora per se, Michael Warner's discussion of "reprosexuality" is useful here. He coins the term to describe "the interweaving of heterosexuality, biological reproduction, cultural reproduction, and personal identity. . . . Reprosexuality involves more than reproducing, more even than compulsory heterosexuality; it involves a relation to self that finds its proper temporality and fulfillment in generational transmission" (9). The idea of generational transmission is central to most conceptions of diaspora. This emphasis on biological reproduction, among other things, naturalizes the boundaries of diasporic community, erasing the ways in which community is actively and selectively imagined, constructed, and maintained. Sau-ling Wong observes that diaspora has "an essentialist core" (17) constituted by a shared origin, in which "the more typical transnational political alliances seem to be those based on 'blood,' as a matter of 'helping one's own'" (18).

One example of this implicitly heterosexist conceptualization of diaspora lies in Paul Gilroy's work. Gilroy uses the notion of diaspora to signify an oppositional affiliation across national borders, a hybrid "changing same," which defies both the essentialism of what he calls "ethnic absolutism" and the deconstructionist position that views identity as utterly contingent. His work focuses on the African diaspora, primarily the descendants of slaves now living in the United Kingdom, the Caribbean, and the United States; these regions, along with Africa, constitute what he calls "the black Atlantic." But, although much of his analysis focuses on change and syncretism within cultures of the black Atlantic, the makeup of this diasporic population seems to be defined solely by biological reproduction and lines of kinship. This is most clearly evident in his failure even to mention the relationship of people of South Asian descent to blackness, despite the existence of political coalitions around blackness in the United Kingdom and the cultural ties of South Asians who have lived in Africa for several generations to other black people of African descent.

This critique has been made by Stefan Helmreich, who believes that Gilroy's unit of the black Atlantic "relies implicitly on an appeal to historical ties of kinship and thus ends up excluding a variety of people who might identify with the black Atlantic experience. . . . Gilroy's analytical frame of the black Atlantic seems to privilege shared heritage—figured through a patriarchal metaphor for inheritance—over hybridity" (246–47). Relying on biological reproduction to define the boundaries of diaspora makes it appear natural, instead of socially constructed, and it not only requires heterosexual reproduction but also sneaks in the patriarchal idea that women are the literal reproducers of the community.[8]

"Blood," "kinship," "lineage": these are all terms that invoke biological reproduction and that form the foundation of most notions of diaspora. Diasporic histories with a queer presence can critique this overwhelming heterosexism and the naturalized equation of kin with diasporic community. They also rework the ground of cultural authenticity and nationalism, uncovering their highly constructed nature and the effort it takes to maintain them as pure and heterosexual. Queerly diasporic narratives of homelands rupture how community is naturalized as heterosexual reproduction, highlighting instead the ways in which cultural authenticity, nation, and diaspora are all actively imagined and maintained in interlocking constructions.

I am not saying that "diaspora," or "nation" for that matter, do not serve useful analytical and political functions, especially in conceptualizing forms and bodies of resistance. Reclaiming biological and cultural lines of heritage have been especially important for peoples forcibly denied knowledge of their histories. However, when diasporic communities are defined solely on these terms, other forms of affiliation cannot be recognized, exclusionary boundaries are fixed in place, and alliances cannot shift to meet the ever-changing forms of hegemony.

Having said that, I think our efforts to reclaim queerness in the homeland need to avoid some common dangers. First, many claim to pursue this effort in order to reconcile "two worlds": the diasporic and the queer. The separation of queer practices and cultural identities is easily labeled as a cultural/ethnic/racial divide, although even for those who are white, being queer usually means leaving home. Rakesh Ratti's introduction to *A Lotus of Another Color* states, "We stand with one foot in the South Asian society, the other in the gay and lesbian world. It is natural then that we should support one another in sorting out these conflicts" (14). The language of "two worlds" homogenizes each side, as if there were not multiple and multiply divided South Asian societies and gay and lesbian (and bisexual and transgender and queer) communities. And, as the quote illustrates, this "binarization" usually sets up the worlds as naturally opposing categories, which must inevitably conflict.

The dichotomy easily lends itself to racist and imperialist uses, specifically the idea that Asian, Third World, or people-of-color cultures are "sadly" more homophobic than are white Western societies. Not surprisingly, this is related to the idea that these cultures are inherently more patriarchal and sexist. This view of the world casts Other cultures as fixed, monolithic, unchanging, backward, and unreasonable, in contrast to an enlightened, modern, liberal humanist Western civilization with an infinite capacity for rational tolerance. It also assumes that homophobia is a single quantifiable phenomenon, with a range of "more" and "less." It is clear to me that these are absurd assumptions, perpetuated by a self-serving white Western pretense to superiority. Carmen Vazquez says, "Challenging homophobia in the Latino community is no more and no less a challenge than it is to challenge it in any other ethnic community" (54). People in Asia, the Third World, or racial minority communities are not *more* homophobic, they are *differently* homophobic, in ways conditioned not only by beliefs, values, and circumstances but also by histories of Western imperialism and U.S. racism.

I am sympathetic to the experience of conflict and division, and I know that two worlds is what it sometimes feels like. I do not think it is necessarily a bad thing to be motivated by pain born of these kinds of experiences. However, I believe that we perpetuate this dichotomy in theory and practice at our own risk and to the detriment of an astute politics.

Second, simply because these accounts challenge the heterosexism of nationalist and diasporic boundaries does not mean that they do not endorse other exclusionary aspects of nationalism and diasporic politics. Being queer does not make us inherently oppositional and radical. Efforts to read queers into the homeland often fail to problematize other aspects of homeland politics, as our eagerness to belong propels us to embrace what is hegemonic in other ways. For example, Jasbir Puar (see Chapter 26) discusses how some constructions of South Asian queerness imitate privileged discourses of the Indian state. In another example, Gayatri Gopinath argues against the claim of some queer theorists that queers in the United States can uniformly challenge national identity by embracing it in the name of nonnormative sexuality: "I would argue that neither [Lisa] Duggan nor [Lauren] Berlant and [Elizabeth] Freeman fully address the particularly vexed relation of many queers of color to the disciplinary and regulatory mechanisms of the state and nation, thereby inadvertently pointing up the severe limitations of any nationalist project, however transgressive" (120).

Although Gopinath is addressing white queers in the United States, I believe that her warning serves equally well for diasporic queers attempting to claim homeland national status, especially when that nation is a state. Diasporas in general may question the reification of nations as states, but they do not constitute an inherent challenge to the existence of states. Khachig Tölölyan notes how diasporic communities can, in fact, uphold the nation-state as a privileged mode of organization: "Transnational communities are sometimes the paradigmatic Other of the nation-state and at other times its ally, lobby, or even, as in the case of Israel, its precursor. . . . Diasporas are sometimes the source of ideological, financial, and political support for national movements that aim at a renewal of the homeland" (5).

Third, attempts to recuperate queers in a diasporic history can, ironically, become ahistorical. Nayan Shah's perceptive essay (see Chapter 9) discusses precisely the motivations for, uses of, and dangers in constructing a queer diasporic history or "'our very own gay tradition.'" He critiques these efforts for using present-day conceptions of queer identities and behaviors to define individuals and actions in the past: "The presumption here is that sexuality is a definable and universal activity, ignoring the variety of cultural patterns and meanings. How do we know that a representation of two women embracing meant sex for historical actors? And even if they did refer to it as sex, does sex have the same meaning as it does for us today? . . . It is necessary to understand the context, the map of social reality, at the time."

The categorization of certain behaviors and identities as "queer," by no means uncontested even in the present, can hardly be extended to all times. There seems to be a growing consensus in queer historiography that historical studies must scrupulously contextualize same-sex behavior.[9] "The forms, content, and context of sexuality always differ. There is no abstract and universal category of 'the erotic' or 'the sexual' applicable without change to all societies.

Any view which suggests otherwise is hopelessly mired in one or another form of biologism, and biologism is easily put forth as the basis of normative attitudes toward sexuality" (Padgug 57). Arguing
for an indigenous queer past has the danger of creating an essential "homosexual" identity, unchanged throughout history, which
may seem liberating in the short term but only boxes us in further.

Finally, recuperating a queer diasporic history can run the danger of applying Western notions of homosexuality and queerness to
non-Western contexts. Same-sex behavior may exist everywhere
and in all cultures, but to categorize it all as part of a global queer
identity formation is arrogantly imperialist. This replicates the uni-
versalism of Western enlightenment thought that demands that cultures be commensurable. Even describing all these disparate acts
under the rubric of "same-sex behavior" may render them overly
similar.

In one of the few essays that discuss "queer" and "diaspora" together, Simon Watney applies diaspora as a metaphor for a global
queer community. Although he pays lip service to "the great diversity of sexual identities through which homosexual desire is acted
upon and lived by different people" (61), he assumes a preexisting
unity of self-identified homosexuals throughout a world that, in his
schema, sometimes seems to refer only to the West. This imperialist move is cemented by his discussion of the sense of relief a queer
person feels upon discovering queers in other countries—speaking, of course, from the viewpoint of the Western traveler: "Even if
one cannot speak the local language, we feel a sense of identification. Besides, we generally like meeting one another, learning
about what is happening to people 'like us' from other parts of the
world" (61). Watney's attitude exemplifies the casual assumption of
global unity that is too often found in the writings and popular conceptions of white Western queers—especially evident in the genres
of travel literature and anthropological writing.

I do not think that those who search for queers in our diasporic
histories approach this level of arrogance, but I do believe that similar assumptions can underlie our efforts. Those of us now living in
the West may have become so comfortable with Western conceptions of queerness and identity that we look for them in our pasts
and, in looking for them, interpret what we find in that mode. Scott
Bravmann makes a similar critique: "I am not suggesting that we
take whatever we want and call it part of 'our' history. To do that is
to fail at understanding the specificities of lesbian and gay historical subjects. For example, efforts to claim the Native American
berdache phenomenon as a traditional gay role reflect this failure. Although such efforts toward incorporation of the *berdache* into les-

bian and gay history have persisted through the 1970s and 1980s, they remain culturally problematic" (74).[10] Although Bravmann's critique addresses predominantly white queer historians, it is acutely applicable to queer diasporic people and people of color living in Western societies. We cannot assume that Western notions of identity and homosexuality apply when we look for queerness in a non-Western homeland.

Why look for a history? Why look for a past? We are driven by longing, by desire, by pain: because we are made to feel insecure about our very existence, because we are afraid to tell our families about our lovers, because we are invalidated by larger society, because we feel like outsiders from too many places, because we have been cut off from historical connection and ancestral roots by various degrees of coercion. For all these reasons and more, history can be a valuable source of validation and legitimization.

However, I think that we have to be careful about how we do this. It is alarmingly easy to fetishize history, to make it into the totalized object of our longings and desires and thus erase the complexities of present agendas. It is imperative to keep in mind what an emphasis on the past erases in addition to what it enables. As Shah puts it, "While the project of reclaiming and reconstructing the past is critical for present political and cultural struggles, let us not read too much of 'us' today into the past. We may trap ourselves in the need of a history to sanction our existence. South Asian lesbians and gay men are present now. On that alone, we demand acknowledgment and acceptance" (see Chapter 9).

It is easy to confuse historical contextualization with a search for origins. Our quest for stories from the past can become archeological excavations adhering to liberal humanist demands for purity, fixity, and origin. We who appear to come from some place else must be singular and knowable, with an identifiable ancestry stretching back in a linear and an uncomplicated manner to the origin. "*Authenticity* as a need to rely on an 'undisputed origin,' is prey to an obsessive *fear:* that of *losing a connection*. Everything must hold together. In my craving for a logic of being, I cannot help but loathe the threats of interruptions, disseminations, and suspensions. . . . A clear origin will give me a connection back through time, and I shall, by all means, search for that genuine layer of myself to which I can always cling" (Trinh 94).

The history of a queer and diasporic homeland is not about the Truth. It is about present-day investments and motivations. It is about present-day mediations, about the necessary interpretation and subsequent representation that go into producing a historical narrative. I believe that there is no "factual" history that waits to be discovered and written about in an impartial manner. Historical sources are not self-evident pieces of fact; historians make many choices about what counts as a source, where to look for sources, how sources are recorded, and how to interpret them as parts of a story. Historical narratives are not timeless truths; they are written by someone who makes choices about modes of representation. A history is not a transparent window into the past.

Similarly, ideas about space and place are stories and constructions. The meanings of spaces do not exist as unchanging truths or as simple facts of nature; they do not spring fully formed into geography books and maps. Rather, geography books, maps, and a host of other mechanisms actively construct meanings of different spaces. Like history, space and place are imagined, mediated, and narrated. Akhil Gupta and James Ferguson discuss how most conceptualizations of space naturalize the equation place = culture = people. They challenge two ways in which this is done: "The first is what we will call the ethnological habit of taking the association of a culturally unitary group (the 'tribe' or 'people') and 'its' territory as natural. . . . A second, and closely related, naturalism is what we will call the national habit of taking the association of citizens of states and their territories as natural. . . . Both the ethnological and the national naturalisms present associations of people and place as solid, commonsensical, and agreed-upon, when they are in fact contested, uncertain, and in flux" (11–12).[11] The location of a people on a land is not a given fact of nature. When we assume that the histories of "our" peoples necessarily lie in one patch of land, we can elide the ways in which this association has come into being and is actively maintained.

We can also make assumptions about the linear movement of diasporas, ignoring that others of the diaspora who have moved through multiple migrations may not identify with the "original" homeland as theirs. Shani Mootoo, a lesbian writer and filmmaker of South Asian descent from Trinidad, says of a South Asian conference in Canada, "I was struck by how everybody kept talking about when they were in India. Today I found myself desperately trying to imagine India so I would not be excluded from the discussion. . . . The truth is a gay Trinidadian, say, of Chinese origin like Richard Fung, probably has more in common with me than most South Asian dykes outside of Trinidad" (6).

When we approach either historical or spatial narratives as "the truth," it is too easy to reify and romanticize "the past" or "the homeland." We can forget that the homeland is not homogeneous, that it is also complex, hybrid, and contradictory. We can forget that the homeland changes too, that it does not exist only in the past. Hall says, "The original 'Africa' is no longer there. It too has been transformed. History is, in that sense, irreversible. We must not collude with the West which, precisely, 'normalises' and appropriates Africa by freezing it into some timeless zone of the 'primitive, unchanging past'" ("Cultural Identity" 76). We can forget a whole range of complexities and difficulties that upset our desire for a neat and knowable past.

Here and now

Migration is a one-way trip. There is no "home" to go back to. There never was. —STUART HALL, "Minimal Selves"

Given these potential pitfalls, I believe that the construction of a queer and diasporic history must be self-consciously strategic. There can be no easy insertion of a queer self into a diasporic past. In the end, I think much of it comes down to the fact that we are located here and now. History is still necessary; we cannot get away from the fundamental necessity of historical grounding and contextualization. But we need to add the perspective of our present locations, the here and now from which we conduct historical searches, narrate these stories, and use them to fulfill our desires.

It is these motivations and mediations that we must recognize and take responsibility for, thus developing a politics of position. "Cultural identities are the points of identification, the unstable points of identification or suture, which are made, within the discourses of history and culture. Not an essence but a *positioning*. Hence, there is always a politics of position, which has no absolute guarantee in an unproblematic, transcendental 'law of history'" (Hall, "Cultural Identity" 72). Simply because queer diasporics, especially those of color, feel multiply oppressed does not mean that we are inherently oppositional, that we hold the final word on the "best" politics of any given situation. We are still accountable for our positioning, for our choices in what we do with the circumstances of our location.

Being accountable to a politics of position means recognizing embedment and complicity. This means acknowledging that for those of us currently located in the West, our narration of a diasporic history is mediated by a Western viewpoint, to the different degrees with which we rely upon Western assumptions and representations. I am not arguing that diasporic peoples should *not* imagine homelands and reconstruct cultural and queer identities or that we are somehow inauthentic in doing so. And I do not mean to imply that Western beliefs form a homogeneous or consistent system. I am simply proposing that our embedment in the structures and thought processes of the West, diverse and contradictory as they are, is not only inescapable but, in fact, *constitutive*. We construct our pasts, identities, and homes *in and through* Western eyes.[12] There is no pure space of marginality in which we stand outside of complicity. Thus the "Korea" in my Korean American identity is shaped partly in and through hegemonic U.S. representations of Korea as an exotic Oriental tourist destination, as the land of irrational violent protest, as the site of an unstable nuclear confrontation;[13] these representations are as equally constitutive of my Korea as are such arguably more firsthand sites of knowledge as my parents' ideas about Korea and my own experiences there.[14]

Developing a politics of position also means being accountable for this location. Rey Chow warns against "the lures of diaspora," telling Third World intellectuals in the West to acknowledge their privileged position in relation to production of knowledge about the homeland. Several white feminists have developed the concept of a politics of location or situated knowledges to come to grips with positions of both relative privilege and oppression. Adrienne Rich sketches a tentative politics of position starting with meanings attached to her physical body and moving outward from there: "I need to understand how a place on the map is also a place in history" (212).[15] Although my location in the United States may reflect the historical actions of states, I have no less of a responsibility to act upon these circumstances. This is why I recently chose to become "naturalized" as a citizen of the United States. As much as I hate to legitimize the existence of the U.S. nation-state and its actions, I realize that I can intervene only by acknowledging my investment in it. The United States is a location for which I need to take responsibility: it would be unconscionably escapist to insist that I do not belong to the United States and that it does not somehow belong to me.

I also believe that in the United States of the 1990s, a politics of location necessitates resignifying immigration. I have been speaking mainly of diaspora, in order to focus attention on the past. Adding a commitment to the here and now means acknowledging a history of immigration. Some theorists whose work focuses on diaspora seem to view the concept of immigration as capable only of its hegemonic connotations of cultural and national assimilation.[16] But in the current political climate, immigration needs to be reclaimed and resignified as a term with more complex meanings. In the arena of popular rhetoric, it is precisely the transnational aspects of immigration that need to be made evident, as politicians and popular media treat immigration as a domestic policy, ignoring the obvious economic and other foreign policies that impact migration. These forces, at least, are not going to take up the language of diaspora any time soon, unless it is to try to send immigrants "home." In this I agree with Inderpal Grewal, who has elaborated how some theorists oppose diaspora to immigration, believing that immigration inherently colludes with discourses of the nation-state. She argues that immigration needs to be rethought instead as a "complex and multivalent category," which can also hold oppositional meanings. Sau-ling Wong makes a similar critique of the current trend toward "denationalization" in Asian American studies, arguing that in spite of the uses of diaspora, political investments in the United States ought to take priority at this time.

Toward Belonging

What, indeed, would a queer Korean American diasporic history look like? What I have presented here is a *framework* for such stories: some historiographic questions to consider, the impact and significance of such a project, a brief consideration of why a Korean American diasporic history exists at all. But I myself have no tales of gay *yangban* scholars and lesbian *kisaeng* entertainers,[17] no suggestive thirteenth-century artwork, no suspicious family trees.

Frankly, I have a hard time imagining what a satisfyingly rich, complex queer Korean American diasporic history would look like: one that did not simply recuperate "gays" and "lesbians" in history, one that closely examined nuances of sexuality over time and investigated the defining impact of sexuality in all aspects of society, one that integrated the impact of migration—one that acknowledged the investments of current day Korean American queers across time and space.

It is no accident that this story is almost inconceivable. Multiple disjunctures combine to create this palpable absence, a feeling that is itself the product of a particular time and place. The sources for my discussion are an example of this stubborn incommensurability of disciplines—Korean studies, Asian American studies, diaspora theory, queer historiography, black British cultural studies, writings by queer people of color—divided into dismally coherent categories marred only by a few happy strays.

Trying to wrap my mind across these divides, facing the simple lack of historical research, I can offer some speculations and questions to start with:

—How have issues of sexuality played a part in South Korean nation formation since the Korean War? Has the national agenda for development driven a kind of compulsory reproduction to produce more workers? Is there perhaps more same-sex behavior among women workers in the free-trade-zone factories, those who would

normally have lived with their parents until marriage? Has capitalism contributed to the emergence of urban gay and lesbian communities in the same way that D'Emilio outlines for the United
States after World War II (100–13)?

—How has sexuality affected migration? Are more women, more
queers and others who feel restricted or rejected more motivated to
migrate? Consider Korean adoptees, whose diaspora is very much a
function of sexuality and class since the Korean War. Consider the
migration of women who married U.S. soldiers, who have been the
source of much chain migration. Look at how migration has re-
plenished Korean communities in the United States in a way that biological reproduction of early-twentieth-century communities could
never have: diaspora fulfills where sexuality fails.

—Consider the older women in the villages of Korea and in Los Angeles's Koreatown, who socialize in circles of *baji-chima* couples—
"*baji-chima*" means, literally, pants-skirt, a term used as a shorthand
for gender roles among women, much as "butch-femme" is used in
the United States. How is it that they identify enough with Western-
style lesbianism to call a talk show featuring Kkiri-kkiri (a lesbian
group in Seoul) but do not feel invested or safe enough to get involved with the group in any way? In this context of gender identification, do nontransgendered gays and lesbians stand out as more
"queer"?

—Were there queers among the leaders of the nationalist movement in Korea and Korean American communities in the 1920s
and 1930s?

—Are there queers in North Korea?

What do sexuality and gender mean in Korea? How can a queer history address both individuals who practiced same-sex behavior and
larger forces of sexuality in society? How can a diasporic history acknowledge both the connections and the ruptures of distance (spatial, temporal, emotional)? Among these interconnections of sexuality, queerness, nation, migration, Korea, and "America," what are
the stories that *I* need?

I look forward to creative responses to these dilemmas and many
queer Korean American diasporic histories to come. I also think
that they are not enough. As necessary as they are, these histories
are only part of a larger project to resignify same-sex desire in Korean and Korean American communities and, indeed, in all communities. We cannot depend solely on histories to justify our existence. Queer and diasporic, wherever we are and whoever we fuck,
the truth is that we always completely belong.

NOTES

Acknowledgments: I extend a big thank-you to David L. Eng, Alice Y. Hom, Jesook Song, Caren Kaplan, and Jasbir Puar for their feedback and encouragement during the writing of this essay.

1. See Safran (83–99), who offers a list of six qualities necessary for a phenomenon to count as a "legitimate" diaspora. See also Clifford (302–38), who attempts a looser "tracking" of diaspora, by examining concepts that overlap (such as borderlands) and oppose (such as indigenous peoples' claims to land).

2. Later in this essay I discuss the need to go beyond this traditional conceptualization.

3. This is changing, as the field of Asian American studies turns to more transnational analyses. For example, see Lye 47–56; Mazumdar 29–44; Okamura 387–400; essays in Omi and Takagi.

4. For more on Proposition 187, see Chapter 3.

5. This figure is from the United Nations 1985 "Demographic Yearbook," cited in Sassen 16.

6. My sources for this quick historical sketch are Abelmann and Lie 49–84; Chan "Introduction" xxi–lx; Jang Jip Choi; Choy 234–43; Cumings, *Origins,* and "Division" 5–16; and Lee.

7. This favorable image has been changing in recent years as the result of an increasing awareness of racism and the limits of economic mobility for immigrants in the United States, according to Abelmann and Lie (79–80). For this and other reasons, the number of Koreans migrating to the United States peaked in the mid-1980s.

8. I acknowledge that it is extremely difficult to avoid discussing diaspora as it is traditionally defined, and, as such, most of my references to Korean and other diasporas in this essay fall into the diaspora = biological lineage equation as well.

9. See, for instance, essays in Duberman, Vicinus, and Chauncey.

10. The term *berdache,* used to describe a situation in some Native American tribes, refers to a person who was born male, took the role of a woman, and, depending on the tribe, was more or less accepted as such. There is a whole body of literature on this topic; see, for example, Roscoe 81–171 and Whitehead 498–527.

11. For further discussion of gendered meanings of space, see Doreen Massey.

12. Here I paraphrase the title of Chandra Talpade Mohanty's essay "Under Western Eyes."

13. U.S. political and popular attention to North Korea waxes and wanes. In 1994, when this portion of the essay was being written, there was pointed attention toward North Korea's possible possession of nuclear weapons and its refusal to allow United Nations inspectors to confirm these suspicions.

14. Laura Hyun Yi Kang ("Surprise Yourself") discusses precisely this

issue of how Korean American identity is constituted in and through dominant U.S. representations of Korea.

15. See also Haraway 575–99, Pratt 11–87, and the analysis of Pratt's essay by Martin and Mohanty 191–212.

16. See, for example, Clifford 302–38 (especially 307 and 311).

17. "*Yangban*" is a term that refers to the upper class of Korean society under Confucianism. "*Kisaeng*" is a term that refers to women who entertained men by singing, dancing, and reciting poetry and who also sometimes served as prostitutes.

WORKS CITED

Abelmann, Nancy, and John Lie. *Blue Dreams: Korean Americans and the Los Angeles Riots*. Cambridge: Harvard UP, 1995.

AIDS Bhedhav Virodhi Andolan (ABVA). "Homosexuality in India: Culture and Heritage." *A Lotus of Another Color: An Unfolding of the South Asian Gay and Lesbian Experience*. Ed. Rakesh Ratti. Boston: Alyson, 1993. 21–33.

Alexander, Jacqui. "Not Just (Any) *Body* Can Be a Citizen: The Politics of Law, Sexuality and Postcoloniality in Trinidad and Tobago and the Bahamas." *Feminist Review* 48 (Fall 1994): 5–23.

Anthem. Marlon T. Riggs, director. Frameline Distribution, 1991.

Anzaldúa, Gloria. *Borderlands/La Frontera: The New Mestiza*. San Francisco: Aunt Lute, 1987.

Berlant, Lauren, and Elizabeth Freeman. "Queer Nationality." *Fear of a Queer Planet: Queer Politics and Social Theory*. Ed. Michael Warner. Minneapolis: U of Minnesota P, 1993. 193–229.

Bravmann, Scott. "Telling (Hi)stories: Rethinking the Lesbian and Gay Historical Imagination." *Out/Look* 2.4 (Spring 1990): 68–74.

Cha, Theresa Hak Kyung. *Dictée*. New York: Tanam, 1982. Berkeley: Third Woman, 1995.

Chan, Sucheng. "Introduction." *Mary Paik Lee, Quiet Odyssey: A Pioneer Korean Woman in America*. Ed. Sucheng Chan. Seattle: U of Washington P, 1990. xxi–lx.

Choi, Chungmoo. "Gender and Nationalism in Postcolonial Korea." Articulations of Korean Women Conf. U of California Berkeley. 15 April 1994.

Choi, Jang Jip. "Political Cleavages in South Korea." *State and Society in Contemporary Korea*. Ed. Hagen Koo. Ithaca, N.Y.: Cornell UP, 1993. 13–50.

Chow, Rey. "Against the Lures of Diaspora: Minority Discourse, Chinese Women, and Intellectual Hegemony." *Writing Diaspora: Tactics of Intervention in Contemporary Cultural Studies*. Bloomington: Indiana UP, 1993. 99–119.

Choy, Bong Youn. *A History of the Korean Reunification Movement: Its Issues and Prospects*. Peoria, Ill.: Research Committee on Korean Unification, 1984.

Clifford, James. "Diasporas." *Cultural Anthropology* 9.3 (1994): 302–38.

Cumings, Bruce. "The Division of Korea." *Two Koreas—One Future?* Ed. John Sullivan and Roberta Foss. Lanham, Md.: UP of America, 1987. 5–16.

———. *The Origins of the Korean War: Liberation and the Emergence of Separate Regimes, 1945–1947.* Princeton: Princeton UP, 1981.

D'Emilio, John. "Capitalism and Gay Identity." *Powers of Desire: The Politics of Sexuality.* Ed. Ann Snitow, Christine Stansell, and Sharon Thompson. New York: Monthly Review, 1983. 100–13.

Dirty Laundry. Richard Fung, director. Videocassette. 30 min. Canada, 1996.

Duberman, Martin Bauml, Martha Vicinus, and George Chauncey Jr., eds. *Hidden from History: Reclaiming the Gay and Lesbian Past.* New York: New American Library, 1989.

Duggan, Lisa. "Queering the State." *Social Text* 39 (Summer 1994): 1–14.

Gilroy, Paul. *"There Ain't No Black in the Union Jack": The Cultural Politics of Race and Nation.* Chicago: U of Chicago P, 1987.

Gopinath, Gayatri. "Funny Boys and Girls: Notes on a Queer South Asian Planet." *Asian American Sexualities: Dimensions of the Gay and Lesbian Experience.* Ed. Russell Leong. New York: Routledge, 1996. 119–27.

Grewal, Inderpal. Paper. Ethnic Studies Colloq. U of California, Berkeley, 22 Sept. 1994.

Gupta, Akhil, and James Ferguson. "Beyond 'Culture': Space, Identity, and the Politics of Difference." *Cultural Anthropology* 7.1 (1992): 6–23.

Hall, Stuart. "Cultural Identity and Cinematic Representation." *Framework* 36 (1989): 68–81.

———. "The Local and the Global: Globalization and Ethnicity." *Culture, Globalization and the World-System.* Ed. Anthony D. King. London: Macmillian Educ., 1991. 19–39.

Haraway, Donna. "Situated Knowledges: The Science Question in Feminism and the Privilege of Partial Perspective." *Feminist Studies* 14.3 (Fall 1983): 575–99.

Helmreich, Stefan. "Kinship, Nation, and Paul Gilroy's Concept of Diaspora." *Diaspora: A Journal of Transnational Studies* 2.2 (1992): 243–49.

Hemphill, Essex. "Undressing Icons." *Brother to Brother: New Writings by Black Gay Men.* Ed. Essex Hemphill. Boston: Alyson, 1991. 181–83.

Kang, Laura Hyun Yi. "Introduction: 'Strewn into Such Assembly.'" *Writing Away Here: A Korean/American Anthology.* Ed. Laura Hyun Yi Kang. Oakland: 1994 Korean American Arts Festival Committee, 1994. v–xi.

———. "The 'Liberatory Voice' of Theresa Hak Kyung Cha's *Dictée*." *Writing Self, Writing Nation: Essays on Theresa Hak Kyung Cha's* Dictée. Ed. Elaine H. Kim and Norma Alarcón. Berkeley: Third Woman, 1994. 73–99.

———. "'Surprise Yourself with a Visit to Korea': Inscribing a Politicized Korean/American Ethnicity." Articulations of Korean Women Conf., U of California, Berkeley, 15 April 1994.

Kim, Byoung-Lo Philo. *Two Koreas in Development: A Comparative Study of*

Principles and Strategies of Capitalist and Communist Third World Development. New Brunswick, N.J.: Transaction, 1992.

Kim, Elaine H., and Norma Alarcón, eds. *Writing Self, Writing Nation: Essays on Theresa Hak Kyung Cha's* Dictée. Berkeley: Third Woman, 1994.

Koo, Hagen. "Introduction: Beyond State-Market Relations." *State and Society in Contemporary Korea.* Ed. Hagen Koo. Ithaca, N.Y.: Cornell UP, 1993. 1–11.

Kumar, Mina. "Representations of Indian Lesbianism." *The Very Inside: An Anthology of Writing by Asian and Pacific Islander Lesbian and Bisexual Women.* Ed. Sharon Lim-Hing. Toronto: Sister Vision, 1994. 404–15.

Lai, Larissa. *When Fox Is a Thousand.* Vancouver: P Gang, 1995.

Lee, Ki-baik. *A New History of Korea.* Trans. Edward W. Wagner. Cambridge: Harvard UP for Harvard-Yenching Inst., 1984.

Light, Ivan, and Edna Bonacich. *Immigrant Entrepreneurs: Koreans in Los Angeles, 1965–1982.* Berkeley: U of California P, 1988.

Looking for Langston. Isaac Julien, director. U.K.: Sankofa Film and Video, 1988.

Lye, Colleen. "Toward an Asian (American) Cultural Studies: Postmodernism and the 'Peril of Yellow Capital and Labor.'" *Privileging Positions: The Sites of Asian American Studies.* Ed. Gary Y. Okihiro, Marilyn Alquizola, Dorothy Fujita Rony, and K. Scott Wong. Pullman: Washington State UP, 1995. 47–56.

Martin, Biddy, and Chandra Talpade Mohanty. "Feminist Politics: What's Home Got to Do with It?" *Feminist Studies/Critical Studies.* Ed. Teresa de Lauretis. Bloomington: Indiana UP, 1986. 191–212.

Massey, Doreen. *Space, Place, and Gender.* Minneapolis: University of Minnesota P, 1994.

Mazumdar, Sucheta. "Asian American Studies and Asian Studies: Rethinking Roots." *Asian Americans: Comparative and Global Perspectives.* Ed. Shirley Hune, Hyung-chan Kim, Stephen S. Fugita, and Amy Ling. Pullman: Washington State UP, 1991. 29–44.

Mohanty, Chandra Talpade. "Under Western Eyes: Feminist Scholarship and Colonial Discourses." *Third World Women and the Politics of Feminism.* Ed. Chandra Talpade Mohanty, Ann Russo, and Lourdes Torres. Bloomington: Indiana UP, 1991. 51–80.

Mootoo, Shani. "Baigan Aloo Tabanka Bachanal." Interview with Dipti Ghosh. *Trikone* (Oct. 1994): 5–6.

Moraga, Cherríe. "Queer Aztlán: The Re-formation of Chicano Tribe." *The Last Generation.* Boston: South End, 1993. 145–74.

Okamura, Jonathan Y. "The Filipino American Diaspora: Sites of Space, Time, and Ethnicity." *Privileging Positions: The Sites of Asian American Studies.* Ed. Gary Y. Okihiro, Marilyn Alquizola, Dorothy Fujita Rony, and K. Scott Wong. Pullman: Washington State UP, 1995. 387–400.

Omi, Michael, and Dana Y. Takagi, eds. "Thinking Theory in Asian American Studies." Special issue of *Amerasia Journal* 21.1–2 (1995).

Padgug, Robert. "Sexual Matters: Rethinking Sexuality in History." *Hidden from History: Reclaiming the Gay and Lesbian Past.* Ed. Martin Bauml Duberman, Martha Vicinus, and George Chauncey Jr. New York: New American Library, 1989. 54–64.

Pratt, Minnie Bruce. "Identity: Skin Blood Heart." *Yours in Struggle: Three Feminist Perspectives on Anti-Semitism and Racism.* Elly Bulkin, Minnie Bruce Pratt, and Barbara Smith. Ithaca, N.Y.: Firebrand, 1984. 11–87.

Ratti, Rakesh. "Introduction." *A Lotus of Another Color: An Unfolding of the South Asian Gay and Lesbian Experience.* Ed. Rakesh Ratti. Boston: Alyson, 1993. 11–17.

Rich, Adrienne. "Notes Toward a Politics of Location." *Blood, Bread and Poetry: Selected Prose 1979–1985.* New York: Norton, 1986. 210–31.

Riggs, Marlon T. "Ruminations of a Snap Queen: What Time Is It?!" *Out/Look* 3.3 (1991): 13–19.

Roscoe, Will. "Bibliography of Berdache and Alternative Gender Roles Among North American Indians." *Journal of Homosexuality* 14.3–4 (1987): 81–171.

Safran, William. "Diasporas in Modern Societies: Myths of Homeland and Return." *Diaspora: A Journal of Transnational Studies* 1.1 (1991): 83–99.

Sassen, Saskia. "Why Migration?" *Race, Poverty and the Environment* (Summer 1993): 15–23.

Tölölyan, Khachig. "The Nation-State and Its Others: In Lieu of a Preface." *Diaspora: A Journal of Transnational Studies* 1.1 (1991): 3–7.

Trinh T. Minh-ha. *Woman, Native, Other: Writing Postcoloniality and Feminism.* Bloomington: Indiana UP, 1989.

Vazquez, Carmen. "Bursting the Lavender Bubble." *Out/Look* 4.2 (Fall 1991): 53–55.

Warner, Michael. "Introduction: Fear of a Queer Planet." *Social Text* 9.4 (1991): 3–17.

Watney, Simon. "AIDS and the Politics of Queer Diaspora." *Negotiating Lesbian and Gay Subjects.* Ed. Monica Dorenkamp and Richard Henke. New York: Routledge, 1995. 53–70.

Whitehead, Harriet. "The Bow and the Burden Strap: A New Look at Institionalized Homosexuality in Native North America." *The Lesbian and Gay Studies Reader.* Ed. Henry Abelove, Michèle Aina Barale, and David M. Halperin. New York: Routledge, 1993. 498–527.

Wong, Sau-ling C. "Denationalization Reconsidered: Asian American Cultural Criticism at a Theoretical Crossroads." *Amerasia Journal* 21.1–2 (1995): 1–27.

Wong, Shelley Sunn, "Unnaming the Same: Theresa Hak Kyung Cha's *Dictée.*" *Writing Self, Writing Nation: Essays on Theresa Hak Kyung Cha's* Dictée. Ed. Elaine H. Kim and Norma Alarcón. Berkeley: Third Woman, 1994. 103–40.

Part Four
Closets/Margins

Overleaf: Hanh Thi Pham, *Lesbian Precepts,*
type R photograph, 30 × 40 inches, 1992

13. Litany
Russell Leong

Last year, on a whim, I went to fabled Malibu to attend an afternoon meditation retreat held by the Vietnamese Buddhist teacher and monk Thich Nhat Hanh. I told my lover, Jandro, who was driving a Toyota, "Let me count the number of BMWs and Volvos in the parking lot, and I will tell you the composition of the audience." I was skeptical, even cynical, as a new Buddhist, but Jandro, who is Catholic, let out a big laugh: "Incense or censer—everything looks the same in all that smoke and mumbling!"

We were not the first in the dusty parking lot. Predictably, a convoy of pastel-colored BMWs, Mazda Miatas, and other automobile imports had preceded us. Couples were walking ahead. They were white, mainly, with a few mixed white-Asian couples—average age about thirty-eight. The men were mostly either blond Nordic types, Jewish lawyers, doctors, or movie professionals wearing white cotton or taupe linen shirts with the long sleeves rolled back to the elbows, thin expensive watches, tan slacks, and Birkenstock sandals. The Asian American females, Japanese and Chinese, were lean and toned with shiny black hair cascading over their gauzy Indian tunics and tight leggings—no obvious makeup over their glowing New Age complexions. The half-dozen African Americans who attended were mostly black males with white female companions.

Jandro and I ran into Pama, a Thai friend of mine. She was carrying a multicolored triangular Thai floor pillow. The three of us made our way to the grassy knoll and put down our blankets, pillows, and jackets. Clusters of people around us were already munching on granola bars or swilling bottled water. Many were wearing crystal *malas* or sandalwood rosaries around their necks and New Age healing gems of amethyst, rutilated quartz, or topaz dangling on black leather cords.

Having entirely forgotten about preparing food for the occasion, we had bought a large bag of barbecued potato chips, carbonated drinks, and hot dogs at a roadside stand. As we opened our paper bags, the people around us began to stare out of curiosity or disdain. Others had brought wholesome vegetarian dishes in plastic containers—tofu and grains in assorted forms, cut apples and carrots, and fruit drinks. There we were, perhaps the only Asian three-

An earlier version of this essay was published in *Tricycle: The Buddhist Review* (1993) and reprinted in *Race: An Anthology in the First Person*, ed. Bart Schneider (New York: Crown Books, 1997). Reprinted by permission.

some out of three hundred people, eating the most processed food of all. Pama stared back at them, but soon, embarrassed, she slipped the greasy hot dog out of the bun and ate the bread and relish alone. Jandro and I figured to hell with the vegetarian voyeurs and noisily chomped down the rest of the hot dogs and salty orange-dyed chips.

Next to us a middle-aged Anglo woman began to admire Pama's pillow; she asked where she could buy it—the colors and shape would be perfect for her patio room. Feeling almost pressed to import a line of pillows in decorator colors for this woman and anxious to end the conversation, Pama was literally saved by the bell. The meditation retreat and lecture were about to begin.

Several French and white American monks and nuns wearing traditional gray Vietnamese garb took their places around the dais set up for Thich Nhat Hanh. The French were from Plum Village, the French monastery he had established to do his work outside of Vietnam. The monks and nuns invoked support for the work of Plum Village and talked about the significance of Thich Nhat Hanh's worldwide peace efforts, which had earned him a Nobel prize nomination. They seemed sincere, yet they had obviously spoken these words many times before. After a sitting meditation led by the French nun, an American male aide introduced Thich Nhat Hanh, a slight, smiling man in a brown robe, who appeared direct in manner and unencumbered by his fame or retinue of French and American devotees.

He began to speak. After that hour I remembered only one thing that he had said: his story of flowers and compost. He had remarked that many admire the beauty and fragrance of flowers, yet flowers, by their nature, finally decay: leaf and stamen, filament and anther, pistil and petal all lose moisture, crumple, and fall to the ground. I glanced at the nape of Jandro's smooth neck, imagining my hand caressing it. Jandro loved flowers—buying them, arranging them, bringing them to others as gifts. Listening to the monk, I did not realize that family, friends, and lovers can also flourish, wither, and die. I could not know then that Jandro would leave this world, and me, a few weeks later.

Perhaps it is not surprising that I was drawn to Thich Nhat Hanh, because he was Vietnamese. Vietnam had figured strangely in my life as a young man—in the form of Tet, which is the Vietnamese name for both the lunar New Year celebration and the Communist Offensive during the Vietnam war. I remember protesting the Vietnam war as an American college student, because I could not understand killing women and men who looked like my own relatives.

But even before Tet and Vietnam, as a youth in San Francisco's Chinatown, I had found myself locked in conflict.

I remember the smell of that day clearly, as pungent as the sun on the asphalt of the basketball court beside the Chinatown alley a few blocks from my family's apartment. As the basketball bounced and landed outside the fence, I ran to retrieve it, looking up. From the alley, I could see TV antennae and, at the corners of the painted balconies above, U.S. and Chinese flags unfurling in the breeze.

My white T-shirt was damp with sweat. I loved the body I had inherited, the stockiness, the muscular legs, and even the overlarge forehead above my darting black eyes. My parents, who worked hard, believed that boys like me, who fought right, played fairly, and won at cards, could fend for themselves. Sisters were another story altogether, they thought.

We played in the Presbyterian church courtyard, because in this Asian barrio of four-story walk-ups and small shops, open space was at a premium. Some of us believed in the Father, the Son, and the Holy Ghost. Others came just for the space, the friendship, or to check out the girls who came for the morning English worship on Sundays. We were second- or third-generation offspring of working-class Chinatown families, descended from Cantonese peasants from villages in the Pearl River Delta.

The head of this church was a burly American reverend of Germanic descent, who was like a father to us—especially the boys. He followed a long line of "Jesus men"—the Reverends William Speer, Otis Gibson, Ira Condit—who had come to Chinatown a century before to teach "heathens" how to pray. For these white missionaries, many of whom were previously stationed in Shanghai, Ningbo, and Canton, the Chinatowns of America were the last Chinese settlements left to conquer. Churches and mission houses— Baptist, Congregational, Catholic, Adventist, Presbyterian, and the True Sunshine Mission—duly dotted every third block of my neighborhood.

In a baritone voice, the reverend ruled his Chinatown roost. He had a special way of explaining the variations of love to us using Greek terms: *philia, agape, eros.* Usually he'd take us into his office, a wood-paneled inner sanctum lined with bookshelves and knick-nacks, and explain doctrine and desire to us patiently. Then there were stories of fishermen who dropped their nets on the sand to follow Jesus. Fallen women picked up their lives and children again after meeting him. Monkeys, goats, tigers, and donkeys gingerly stepped onto the giant wooden ark in pairs, fearing the violent sea beneath them. Being saved, in essence, was a matter of faith and grace that could only be accepted, not earned.

After basketball that day, he called me into his office. He whispered *agape* in my ear. It was not his paternal smile or familiar words that disturbed me this time. It was another feeling, which I could not name. Suddenly I felt his body—twice as wide as and whiter than my real Chinese father's—pressed against mine.

His litany worked its way slowly under my skin, soft shrapnel designed for a war I could not win.

"How doth move a missionary's hand?"

"Save me with your hands on my chest and legs. Promise not to tell in the name of him who died to save us all."

Were these my words or his?

"Who moves inside me, plucks ribs, forks intestines, enters esophagus, takes tongue?"

"What is a missionary's hand doing here?"

I grasped the fingers of his hand.

"Where is the shame; what's in a name?"

"What's this evil game?"

My body tailspun like a basketball out of court. I cried foul. The invocation continued.

Flesh versus spirit.

Age versus Youth.

Christian versus Pagan.

Occident versus Orient.

Colonizer versus colonized.

No one could sense my fear through the mashing of mahjong tiles and the buzz of sewing machines in the Chinatown alley. The litany both infuriated and intoxicated me. Mekong machetes sliced their way through bamboo. My legs ran of their own accord, but without a map I was lost. Under his irreverent hands my body slipped.

Like a chipped tile loosened from a Chinatown roof, I fell from the eaves to the ground. I fled the enclave of my youth. Condemned to silence by the Father, Son, and Holy Ghost, I never said a word to my brother, my parents, or my friends. My T-shirt was sweaty and dirty. Even after I had showered and washed the shirt, I could not rid myself of the nameless love and hatred that rose and stuck in my throat. I was estranged from the person I had once been.

Ornamental figurines—plastic mock-ivory statues of Confucius, Buddha, and Kwan-Yin, the goddess of mercy—graced curio shops. None of them would lift a hand to save me, an ordinary boy of no consequence. They were one and the same to me—interchangeable icons and images that could be bought, sold, and used to decorate home altars, television sets, or the mantels of cramped Chinatown apartments. When I left Chinatown, I did not want any more to do with religion or with Asia.

If Christianity betrayed my generation, Buddhism was no less alien to my nature. Buddhism was only something that white poets went to Japan or China to do. They grew beards, wore cotton robes and sandals, and made pilgrimages to Nara and Nepal between the bouts of seventies drugs and sex. They had no relation to me. For the most part, they regarded Asians like me, who were born in the Americas, as inauthentic and immaterial. Our complex history in this country contradicted all their spiritual or aesthetic notions of Orientalness.

But I could not identify with the middle-class Mahayana Buddhist temples in Chinatown either, with their slick gold icons, red carpets, and well-dressed congregations of Asian Americans attending services on Sundays. I did, however, sometimes visit our family association temple, with its lacquered gilt statues of Kwan-Kung, the warrior/guardian of borders and of the seas. The clicking of joss sticks and the sweetish smell of incense burning in front of ancestral wall tablets hooked me in their narcotic way. Whatever moved through me was as intangible as smoke.

During the next two decades, smoke and sex obscured my life. I found myself drifting, craving the dusky embraces of women and men. I steeped myself in alcohol and believed, wrongly, that through another's love or loneness, I could be desired or diminished: one day desired, the next day abandoned—New York, Seattle, Taipei, Hong Kong, Naha, Tokyo, Kyoto, Los Angeles. Streets meshed and merged in five languages then lost me again. I wandered, searching desperately for an identity and a home more hospitable than the one I had left.

In these countries so foreign to my upbringing, I had always found myself unexpectedly alone in temples or gardens. Outside of Kyoto once I found myself at a small Zen temple, the Ohara. Abandoned by the usual groups of Japanese tourists snapping photographs, I was standing alone with the old granite stones in the garden. Then I realized the temple was closing for the day. Even the brown-robed monks had overlooked my silent presence. They smiled when they discovered they had almost locked me in for the night. Maybe I should have stayed there then—joined the ancient noble family of stones—and never left. I remember that stillness, which was not entirely empty. The dusk was filled with the summer noises of shifting branches and evening doves.

Later, and farther south along the archipelago, Formosa emerged like a green turtle from the sea. Taipei, its capital, was still under martial law. No matter, I was a U.S. citizen, invincible, like all arrogant young Americans those days. Like the Chinese and the

Japanese and the French in Indochina before me, I was but the latest American colonizer of native brown bodies. One evening I remember climbing with a friend up the bamboo scaffolding of an unfinished three-story brick building. The floors were piled with dust and debris, and where stairways would eventually connect the floors were just bluish pockets of air. We abandoned ourselves to lust, our feet and slim arms dangling over the edges of darkness. The buzzing of cicadas covered our breathing. Afterward, we climbed down the scaffolding into that Asian city alive with streets, stairs, and signs that led home—but not to mine. There was "no place like home." Yet I never wanted to go home again.

I found love in other places: in alleyways, between palm trees at dusk, in barely furnished rooms, on worn floors and tatami mats. Sometimes I could not tell the sex of my companions, under their powder and paint, until I pressed myself against their legs. I would walk toward or away from people. Other times motorbike drivers would pick me off the streets and carry me to shabby alcoves in pre-World War II Japanese houses. The *mama-san* would leave a bucket of cold water, soap, a brush, and a towel for customers. I would wash and lay naked on the wooden pallet and close my eyes until I felt a stranger's breath on mine.

Some days I would take the bus. On Hsinyi's number 10 bus, I would reach Yuan Wan, the old Taiwanese section of the city, where preserved serpents in glass apothecary jars lined herbalists' storefronts. Kept girls in Japanese wooden and paper houses vied for my money and happiness.

Alongside the bus, Mormon missionaries pedaled on their bicycles, their polyester shirts soured by their large pink bodies, damp with the sweat of faith. As part of their missionary training, they had to spend a year or two in a foreign country in Asia, Africa, or Latin America. They and the Seventh Day Adventists competed for the island's brown souls: Taiwanese mountain aborigines, innocent countryfolk, unrepentant bar girls. For a hundred years, as precise as German clockwork, Western soldiers and missionaries seemed to follow one another in war to Manila, Saigon, Seoul, Taipei.

Three hours to go before the dusk cooled the streets. Outside some of the older Japanese houses, young girls of no more than fifteen or sixteen were dusting the cobblestoned alleys clean, preparing for evening. After dusk, many of these same girls would smear their lips red, anoint their cheeks with rouge, don their thin, cheap cotton dresses, and—urged on by their *mama-san,* who took most of their meager tips—pull and tug at the shirt sleeves of any local man who passed through the alleys. The brothel madam, usually a middle-aged, heavyset brightly made-up apparition in a floral print dress, would curse at her indentured girls.

One time I had gone with a young woman up to her reed-matted cubicle, which was lit by a single bulb. She dipped a white hand towel into a tin basin filled with an astringent mixture of water and vinegar and told me to pull down my pants. I did, and she cleaned my body with the towel before she pulled up her blouse and placed my hand on her small breasts, the size of half-tangerines. I tried to kiss them, but I could not get excited by her naked body—not because of her sex but because of her age. She looked away from me without smiling. I apologized, hurriedly put on my clothes, and left ten dollars on the worn mat.

Anxiously, I paced the cobblestoned streets. I was a character in a film rewinding upon itself over and over again. Yet I could not escape those slender white arms that tugged and pulled at my short-sleeved shirt, at my chest and waist. Painted faces were the ghosts of children entangled in their bondage. They laughed at me in disdain when I ignored their pleas and the harsher cries of the older women who owned their bodies.

I found myself stumbling into a small side-street doorway, partly to escape them. It turned out to be a shelter for sailors and other seafarers, a temple of Tien Hou, goddess of sailors and protector of the seas. I fell, my knees scraping the worn brick floor of the temple. Tears began to blur my vision. I was no different from those teenaged prostitutes. They too had learned to perform acts of love against their feelings.

I too was floating on the sea of desire with no sign of a harbor. When would I return to myself? Where was my home? In Asia? In America?

As a young man in Asia, I could support myself easily in the company of older men or women. Only after I had run out of money and love and was no longer so desirable did I return to the United States. I found odd jobs here and there, in a radio station, as a shipping clerk, as a newspaper assistant, and so forth. So I ended up here in the City of Angels as a middle-aged man, forty-four, in fact. Old ways of living stayed with me, though with a twist: I inexplicably sought out the company of much younger men, like Jandro.

Such desires diluted my prayers to Buddha, who had entered my life relatively late. It was around the time of the Los Angeles riots, as I drove down the Interstate 5 freeway. The sky was smoky from days and nights of bonfires and rampage. It was then that I sought refuge in a Westminster Vietnamese Buddhist temple, called Little Saigon by the locals, which a friend had introduced me to. There, the monk seemed to understand my wordless despair, not only at the state of the city but at the state of my self-destructive life. The burning flames, the temple monk told me, could lead to both ruin and renewal. He told me to look at the world and myself clearly, without judgment.

Once home, I carefully examined my body in the mirror. No longer lean or agile, it was flaccid like those of the nocturnal madams I had encountered in red-lit alleyways years before. I ran my hands over my shoulders, chest, belly, cock, and thighs. Sweat seeped from my skin. The trapped, stale smells of vinegar, sweat, and sex unfolded from the folds of memory. I reached for my bottle of vodka. It was already empty.

I recalled the pummeling of the small hands of nameless girls and boys whose bodies were sold by others. With the palm of my hand, I struck my face, the stinging suddenly bringing back warmth. But their bruises remained hidden within me, buried beneath the skin's surface. At least with this body, older and tougher now, I could shield each face and hand from further pain—even the pain of a lover's death.

For shortly after the Malibu retreat that Jandro and I had both attended, he died unexpectedly. The brushfires and earthquake followed. It was as if the moment I turned my face away, he, the mountains, and the earth turned into dust.

I had no recourse but to return to the temple to which I had fled during the Los Angeles riots. The monk allowed me a forty-nine-day mourning service for Jandro. The forty-ninth day was the Buddhist day of reckoning for the soul of one who has died. At dusk I drove for an hour in the rain to meet his family at the temple. Inside, his mother had tropical orchids and incense for the altar, a three-foot cardboard and papier-mâché replica of a two-story house and square packets of facsimile gold and silver money to burn, as some Chinese from the old country still did. Two of the temple women took the paper items to the patio and set them ablaze with a cigarette lighter.

"Jandro will be richer in his next life," his mother assured herself and me. But no words came to my mouth. I looked into the darkness and light. Smoke, ashes, and darkness engulfed the space. A single, lime-green orchid danced against the orange flames, separated by the thin wall of patio glass. I felt suspended in the shadow and embrace of opposing energies. Pain, pleasure, and prayer melded in that blazing transformation.

All homes in my life have now vanished: paper windows and walls gone up entirely in smoke. A return to home or childhood unsullied by loss and experience was no longer possible. Home was no longer origins, family, or friends. And home was not the transient refuge of another's embrace or the strong arm of religious belief. I glanced down at my two bare hands. Brown skin held intact the veins, bones, and blood. I would let go of the past. I would no longer crave the future. I would live in this moment.

14. Trying fo' Do Anykine to Donna
Fragments of a Prose Work
Donna Tsuyuko Tanigawa

The Piecing Work

I am taking a long time to finish the project. Knots need to be tied, threads cut. The patchwork is not *pau* yet. My task—to take the materialities of my life, language, memory, and body and create a textual piece—is still in progress. I am working on a prosed Japanese crazy quilt, a *yosegire*, in words.

I use the *yosegire*—literally, the sewing together of fragments—as a pattern. I want to design a *local-style* work. I want to wrap something around myself. I collect snatches of leftover fabric and remnants from past literary wreckage, projects started but never finished. My goal is to make an artistic but useful item from my repository of knowledge.

I use articulations of memory for the *yosegire* work. They are like stored boxes with keepsakes, mementos, childhood photos, and comfort foods: *Obaban's* aloha-print blanket, chicken *hekka* with a distinctive *shoyu*-sugar flavor, a picture of a five-year-old me clinging onto Grandpa near his 1969 Dodge sedan. I also use mappings of personal and collective narratives. My mother tongue of pidgin English stitches the work. I rely upon spools and spools of thread given to me throughout my life: sugar plantation pidgin and Japanese broken English, *Waipahu-kine* dialect, near-standard American English. These are strands of experience and memory.

The Language Fragments: Trying fo' Write Donna

For years, I envied (mostly *haole*) people who wrote in *good-kine* English. I combed through my work with a sorely creased copy of Merriss and Griswold's *A Composition Handbook*. I tried to correct syntax and punctuation before my reader did. In graduate school I struggled to write standard American English. I labored over academic prose. An instructor told me, "Say what you want to say." Implicit in his comment was, "Say it in the 'correct' manner." If I did, it would have been in a language that failed to meet academic expectations.

In 1991 I wrote a seminar paper on lesbian feminist theory entitled "The Persistence of Reified Theories in the Academy: Working Towards a Theory à la Tanigawa." My lover said that the seductive postmodern language drowned out my voice. She suggested that I create a theory in *my language*, then translate the ideas into intelligible (read: *haole*) prose.

Previously published under the title "Women in Hawai'i: Sites, Identities, and Voices," *Social Process in Hawai'i* 38 (1997): 62–69. Reprinted by permission.

I was faced with a crucial question: what was my language? After all, I spoke what I thought was English. I was educated in an American school system. So I was ashamed to speak, much less write, in my mother tongue of pidgin English. *Pidgin fo' talk story, not fo' write down.* I acted *haolefied.* As far back as fourth grade at August Ahrens Elementary School, I wanted to speak *good-kine* English.

This is the curse: my father cannot spell. I make him a chart with the numbers o-n-e through t-w-e-l-v-e. He needs the correct spelling to write checks to Kiso's Lumber Store. "T-h-r-e-e, not t-r-e-e, Dad." I blame his so-called learning disability on his *haole* teacher at Kaumakani Camp. She made him repeat first grade, and her words, the following year.

I was unable to write. I was afraid my work stank. I decided to use the metaphor of a *takuan,* a pungent, pickled Japanese turnip, as my theory. I modeled my thoughts after Miss Takuan, the yellow misfit in Akiko Masuda's fable. Like my mentor, I was "not A grade, or B grade, but '*off-grade*'" (n.p., my emphasis). As Masuda recounts, Miss Takuan tried her best and studied hard, but school was difficult. It made me feel contempt for respect.

For my 1992 New Year's resolution I wrote an autobiographical essay, "Pau Trying fo' Be Like One Haole Dyke." This work did not suit academe. *So wot?* After so many years, I found my chastised tongue and painfully returned to the language of my childhood. *Pidgin fo' everyting.* Haunani-Kay Trask helped chart the path: think in my cultural referents, imagine in my world view, disagree, and eventually oppose the dominant ideology (54; see also Thiongo). *No mo' talk hybolic. Rememba wea you wen come from.*

The Memory Fragments: Trying fo' Tink Donna

How do I begin to locate myself? Where am I as a yonsei local lesbian of Japanese ancestry? *I stay trying fo' rememba.* In 1967 my father and his workers built our home on Kahualei Place. We were the first family to live on this dead-end street located on the *mauka* side of Waipahu, later to become a large suburb. My home was a solitary wooden structure surrounded by brick-red dirt and sugarcane fields. Inside the presence of Okabe Grandpa's black lacquer *butsudan.* He spoke, "I'm here" each time I walked through the living room. His spirit lived in a wooden *kanji*-inscribed stick. I lit *senko* and offered food such as *gohan* and fresh water in the evening.

My home is no longer there. The house was sold to an extended Filipino family after my parents divorced. The structure is now painted Royal Hawaiian Pink, and the jalousie windows are adorned with wrought iron bars. *Kalamungay* trees grow where there were once *jabon* fruits.

I need to find the fragments of my geographic self. The physical landscape—my home, my neighborhood, parts of town—has changed. There are few familiar landmarks: the pole where I wiped my sticky *hanabata*, the empty sugar mill. Is memory my only tool? I take a vicarious trip through Tanigawa Grandpa's stories told with plenty of *pupus* and Primo-brand beer: "I stay talking wit' myself now. I like grind. I like eat senbei cookies from Nii Superette. I like one bento box from Hamada's Okazuya. Ono da shoyu pork. I like suck ice cake wit' prune mui from Kawano Store. You know wot, but? No stay anymore. Da places I wen grow up wit'. All change now. Get K-Mart and Eagle Hardware in da middle of town. Ass why hard fo' go back to my small kid days. Only can talk story. Maybe ass' why I like fill my mouth wit' local food. Makes me feel full like I stay back home."

The Body Fragments: Trying fo' Feel Donna

Can I look to myself while I sew the quilt? Can I go from fragments of language and memory to the intimate region of my physical body? Is it possible to use parts of my four-foot-eleven-inch frame for the project? My body, marked with ethnic, gendered, and sexual inscriptions, will become part of the prosed work.

I decide to stitch the surfaces. I mark my Asian features. What colors do I use? What shapes? There's black for my hair and yellow for my skin. I permit myself to use blue for my names, Tsuyuko and Tanigawa—literally, Rain on the Road and River in the Valley. I appliqué roasted almonds for my slanted eyes. I fleck my work with brown *lentigo* spots aged in the sun. I take off, at last, the thin strips of Scotch tape for "double" eyes.

Eight years ago I enrolled in an undergraduate course called The Japanese-American Experience. The class made my skin crawl. I realize that my discomfort grew from my futile efforts to move out of my Japanese skin. The instructor showed a slide of a topless D-cup *haole* woman. The image, he told us, was an "ethnic joke" on flat-chested Japanese women. Guilty, I identified with the woman on the screen. *I take one almost-A-cup. Geez, I like decent-sized chi-chis.* As I stared at the image, I also coveted her eyelids. Each was as broad as a *lychee* leaf. *Plenty room fo' put eye makeup.* I did not want to be known by my ethnic markings.

I converted to Roman Catholicism in my early twenties. Although I was born in a Soto Zen Buddhist household, my *sansei* parents felt it best that I choose my religion. My spiritual quest took me from the Waipahu Hongwanji Temple to a baptism at Saint Alban's Episcopal Chapel to yet another baptism "in the Holy Spirit" at Foursquare Hope Chapel to confirmation classes at the Jesuit Newman Center. I was drawn to contemplative prayer and was to begin a prenovitiate program at a Benedictine monastery in Saint Louis, Missouri. My fascination with religion was, in large part, a desire to transcend my female body. I had again found a way to crawl out of my skin. Today I am comfortable with my ethnic and gendered markings.

There are part of my *yosegire* work that I fear are unattractive, indeed hideous. I deliberate over the discarded fragments, items that I wished would be blown away like sugarcane ash. These are the "forgotten" memories, the ruins of something I tried so hard to burn and destroy—the blocked childhood incidents. I try to locate myself as wreckage of sexual abuse, sites of incest and rape. I want to include these markings: *don't like showers; water on my face, feel drowning, can't breathe; "Don't get too close to me," I tell my lover; the body doesn't forget; the "nasty" followed by rushing water on my two-year-old face; phobia to saliva; can't watch myself brush my teeth; don't like it on my hands, my face, my arms; my mouth a receptable for peters and parts.*

I continue to remember and put into words. I resist the urge to pick at my skin with its numerous scars. I stop adding homemade "tattoos" crafted with a curling iron and styled with a butter knife—self-mutilation. How do I join these pieces?

The Fragments: Trying fo' Pau the Yosegire
The patchwork is not *pau* yet. My prosed Japanese crazy quilt in words is taking a long time. I have only a few completed panels. At first I was disappointed that my project is incomplete. A gentle consolation came when I was at a partial viewing of the AIDS Quilt, sponsored by our local chapter of the Names Project. It did not matter that I was seeing only several of the thousands of panels. What mattered were those quilts at the exhibit. Life quilts, I conclude, are always in progress.

I sit with fragments of the work. It feels good to have something to wrap around myself. I sit on Obaban's *zabuton* and cover myself with the patchwork. My fingers run over the surface. Several threads are uncut. Some are double-knotted. Pieces of *natto* from a past meal are stuck to the seams. There are also snatches of dried and crusted blood. In the frenzy of my sewing, I have stitched fragments of language and memory to my skin. I am marked by the quilt. I notice the open sores, the scars that I inadvertently picked open. Some of them have bled onto the fabric. The quilt becomes marked by my body. The project is not *pau* yet. There will be more sections and more seams. There will be a quilt.

GLOSSARY

anykine: any sort of; any kind of
bento: boxed lunch

butsudan: Buddhist altar
chi-chis: female breasts
gohan: steamed white rice
good-kine: proper; correct
grind: eat
hanabata: nasal mucus; snot
haole: Causasian; white; foreigner
hekka: Japanese stew
hybolic: hyperbolic; exaggerated for effect
jabon: citrus fruit
kalamungay: edible green leaves
kanji: written character
lentigo: frecklelike mark
local-style: in the style or manner of local culture in Hawai'i
lychee: fruit of the litchi tree
mauka: in the direction of the mountains
natto: fermented soy beans
Obaban: Grandmother; affectionate term for female elder
okazuya: delicatessen
ono: delicious; tasty
pau: finished; complete
prune mui: Chinese preserved prunes
pupus: hors d'oeuvres
sansei: third-generation
senbei: Japanese tea cookies
senko: joss sticks; religious incense
shoyu: soy sauce
takuan: pickled turnip
talk story: converse; a conversation
yonsei: fourth-generation
yosegire: crazy quilt
zabuton: cushion; throw pillow

WORKS CITED

Masuda, Akiko. *Miss Takuan.* Hong Kong: International, 1989.

Tanigawa, Donna Tsuyuko. "Pau Trying Fo' Be Like One Haole Dyke." *Sinister Wisdom* 47 (1992): 8–10. Reprinted in *Asian Pacific American Journal* 2 (1993): 96–98.

Thiongo, Ngugi Wa. *De-colonizing the Mind.* London: Heinemann, 1986.

Trask, Haunani-Kay. "Politics in the Pacific Islands: Imperialism and Native Self-determination." In *From a Native Daughter: Colonialism and Sovereignty in Hawai'i.* Monroe, Maine: Common Courage, 1993. 51–77.

15. Transgender/Transsexual Roundtable
Transcribed by Diep Khac Tran
Edited by Diep Khac Tran,
Bryan, and Rhode

On the Terms

"Transgender" (TG) is a general term that includes transvestites, transgenderists, and anyone else who identifies with the gender communities. A transgenderist is a person who identifies with the opposite gender but does not intend to undergo an anatomical change. A transgenderist may not have the body conflict that a transsexual (TS) has. A transsexual is someone who intends to undergo, or has already undergone, a sex-change operation or hormone therapy.

Introduction by Bryan

What makes us, as humans, want to strive and go beyond limits? Are we born with the need to keep learning more about ourselves and the things around us? If so, I'm no different from anyone else who has uttered the phrase "Who am I?" This roundtable discussion changed some of my viewpoints and reaffirmed others. I hope it will help other people as it has helped me. If it did not enhance my understanding of everything about being a transsexual, at least it gave me a path to walk on. Being males trapped in female bodies keeps us prisoners in so many ways, mentally and physically. Everyone has a wall of some kind that blocks his or her way to happiness, something that makes life a struggle each day. For transsexuals, it's being trapped, since the day we were born, in a body that was never meant to be.

For me, I know this to be true: each second of each day, my life has been one misery after another. "Why?" you might ask. I cannot express the inner me, for the outer image prohibits it. "Male," "female," "gay," and "lesbian" are words that have swirled around in my head since the age of seven. Constantly asking these questions, I knew they would pave the road to my very existence. As long as I didn't know who I was, I could never be happy.

One day, I sat on a living room floor with two other people who had gone through experiences similar to my own. I knew that what we discussed could open doors for me or send me screaming back into the closet. Yet I was willing to take that chance. By doing so, I was finally taking my life into my own hands. I was no longer waiting fearfully for society's or my family's ideals to direct my life for me. Sharing the experiences and feelings of what "transgender/

transsexual" mean to Rhode and Phong made a world of difference to me.

With this roundtable discussion I came to understand a little more about what the words "transgender" and "transsexual" mean to me. I realized I'm not alone in my fears and frustration. Although I don't expect everyone to agree with our comments on the issues, I think we can all agree that society must change in order to better understand transgenders and transsexuals. I hope this roundtable discussion can provide a stepping-stone for fellow transgenders to begin their own journeys into the future. For me, it has provided an opportunity to voice my feelings and frustrations about who I am. I now know I'm not alone in my need to change and be understood. I have friends and family who understand me a little better for my speaking out.

ROUNDTABLE

Rhode: I'm twenty-two. I realized I was a TS after coming out as gay. At that time, I didn't really have an understanding of transsexualism. But meeting other TSs has given me a greater understanding of who I am. Right now, I'm contemplating how to "transist" from being the way I am to completing myself. My expectation for this round-table is to get some kind of understanding of where my fellow TSs and TGs are coming from and to see other opinions on and per-spectives of transsexualism, because there are different experiences and definitions of sexualities and genders. It also helps me under-stand where I place myself in society along with other TSs and TGs.

Phong: I'm a twenty-eight-year-old TS. Since I was very young, I wished I was a boy. When I started to hang around gay friends, I thought I was gay too. But there was one difference. When I looked at men, I wanted to be like them. I don't expect anything out of this round-table. It doesn't make any difference to me to talk about TGs or not. People say it's important, but what do they mean by that? Are they going to do anything about it? The reality for me is to try to work it out by myself the best I can.

Bryan: I was born in Vietnam, but I was raised in the United States since the age of four. My expectations for this roundtable [are] to outreach to other TSs and TGs; to be able to talk to other TSs and TGs about their experiences; to learn more about the [sex-change] operation itself; to find other TSs and TGs to associate with; and to find my identity as a TS in this society. I want to find the courage and wisdom to tell my family who I really am.

On Masculinity and Being Male

Rhode: I want to question other TSs about their definition of the male persona. How do you define masculinity? In the past, a lot of my definitions were taken from stereotypes. I thought I would be more accepted if I fit into what was seen as male. A man has to be strong; he's not supposed to cry. He only does outdoor chores and fixes cars. When I moved to college and began living by myself, I had to learn how to maintain my own car as well as how to cook, clean, and pay bills—everything that men think would be women's chores. My definition of what a male should be has changed over time, because it's really not about being accepted; it's about surviving as a TS in society. I have to know the ropes of both the female and male gender[s]. It shouldn't be just a TS issue. I think everyone needs to be flexible. I also believe research that has said people who are more androgynous are more capable of overcoming a lot of the obstacles in life.

Phong: It's the culture that gives people the idea of the roles that you should take on, and every culture has different roles for men and women.

Bryan: Being a TS and figuring out how to cope being in a woman's body, I have a distaste for anything that's considered women's work. I'll take out the trash, because supposedly that's a man's thing. Doing things that are considered manly makes me feel closer to being viewed as a man. I believe in equality when it comes to cleaning house. Everyone has to do something in a household. I wash the dishes, because I don't consider washing dishes women's work. If you eat and you don't cook, you should clean up and help in ways that you can. It's bad enough to constantly live with the knowledge that you're in the wrong sex, but having to do something that would just repeatedly bring it up is even more stressful. I think society is bad, because of the way it represents and stereotypes males and females. A lot of lesbians and gays don't fit these stereotypes. I'm curious about how [gays and lesbians] define maleness.

Rhode: One of the questions posed to me from the straight *and* queer communit[ies] was why we have to convince someone that we're male inside. People run us through a checklist: "You have short hair, okay; you wear male clothes, okay"; if we don't fit *one* thing, then we're not male.

Bryan: Everything has a double meaning for me. When I lift something heavy and someone says, "Oh, you're so strong!" I think, "Are you being funny? Are you saying that I'm strong or that I'm *trying* to be a man?" I do all the hard and physical work because, subconsciously, I think, "This is what a man should do." It's sort of like therapy. I feel good about myself if I do it.

Rhode: My family believes so strongly that I'm a guy that they expect me to be strong. They tell me to help my brother pick up the fridge! I wish I could, but physically I'm still [*whispers*] female. I don't have the testosterone that would give me the strength. It's been stressing me out lately. It's great they think of me in that way, but it puts a lot of pressure on me, because I physically can't do things my brothers and cousins can. When I get started on my hormones, there won't be any of these problems.

Bryan: One time, I was getting a haircut, and some hair got stuck to my face. When I looked in the mirror, I swear to God, I looked really good. I thought, "Oh! That's me!" The woman who was cutting my hair thought I didn't like it, so she brushed it off. One moment of pure joy!

On Sex and the "Forbidden Zone"

Rhode: I know we've been wanting to talk about sex. Bryan, is that what you consider the "forbidden zone?"

Bryan: As long as I'm in this body, I tense up if a hug gets close to the top part or the bottom part of my body. I consider that the forbidden zone. I've never changed my clothes in front of anyone. I was really surprised when I found out you [Rhode] are in a relationship. I've seen talk shows about transsexuals who have relationships, but that's so far removed. I don't personally know any TS who has a relationship. When I heard you have a straight girlfriend, it opened doors for me.

When you're intimate with someone, you're already nervous. You don't know what the other person wants; they don't know what you want. You don't want to go to bed with a bunch of rules: "Wait, before we do something, I want to set down some rules. You can't touch me here; you can't do this. I'll do this; now don't do this." It becomes formal and tasteless. When I want to be with someone, I want to be romantic. Even if I find someone who's safe, there are so many obstacles. It's not just about meeting and getting to know you. It's about them having to know what a TS is and how we interact.

Rhode: I never thought sex could be so stressful until I met my current girlfriend. When I was with my first girlfriend, I came out as being a lesbian. I was only thirteen and hadn't truly realized who I was. When we had oral sex, it was fine. Later on, when I realized my identity, I didn't want to have oral sex. I couldn't have oral sex done on me. I would do it to my partner. That was the time I started using a dildo. I'd strap it on, and we would have intercourse. Even that is still kind of stressful, because you can't feel it. I can feel the pressure on myself, so I'm capable of reaching orgasm, but as far as me being inside, I can't feel it. When I'm penetrating, sometimes I don't know if the dildo came out all the way. Once, while I was in the motion of doing it, the dildo came out. In the excitement of it all, I hadn't realized it. I was still in that thrusting motion when my girlfriend said, "Oh, oh, wait; it's out!" It was really embarrassing. I hope that doesn't happen again. If I had a real penis, I would never be in that situation. A lot of times, I'll have my partner get on top of me instead of me getting on top. It's easier that way, even though it's more difficult to reach orgasm. I literally have to get myself mentally excited in order to come. Is anyone else using any kind of devices?

Phong: No, I never did.

Bryan: I'm a virgin.

Rhode: People ask me when I los[t] my virginity. It's hard for me to answer. I was having sex for years before I actually penetrated. It depends on your definition of sex.

Bryan: When I say I'm a virgin, [I mean] I'm a pure virgin. I've never taken my clothes off to anyone.

Rhode: When I first had sex, I always needed to wear briefs and those thin tank tops that guys wear. Either that or we would close all the blinds, but it was so dark. I hated having sex that way. I've been reading stuff in magazines saying the best, most exciting time is when it's spontaneous. It's morning, and you wake up; when your girlfriend comes home from work or from school and you do it right there and then. We can't do that! I have to go to my damn safe and get my fricking dildo; that breaks the spontaneity and mood of everything. I used to be so into sex, but now I'd rather not have it.

Bryan: I thought I wouldn't find anyone, because I couldn't see anyone touching me there. If I'm with someone, I c[a]n't take off my clothes. Let's say I find someone who's lesbian or bisexual, because they would be more open to accepting it. In the heat of it all, she grabs me or something; it would freak me out. It's constantly in my head. What are the odds of finding a liberal straight woman to date? It's not fair to say to your partner, "I want to do everything; I want you to be naked, but me, oh no." It's one-sided. I just came out, so a lot of Catholic beliefs are still in me. I keep thinking, "It's a sin! It's a sin!"

Rhode: The way we are, we cannot experience the same kind of sexual pleasures that other people can. We have to restrict ourselves, because we don't want our bodies. My girlfriend told me something that helped me a lot. When we were having oral sex, she said whether I had a penis or not, she would still do the same thing to me. It just so happens that I don't have one. She was telling me to just imagine that I do have one and she's doing it to me. She did it a few times, and I said I couldn't take it anymore. It wasn't enough for me. It's really unfair, and I wish to God I can get over it and allow my girlfriend to do me. I wasn't able to overcome that, and she doesn't do it to me orally. When someone goes down on you, it should be really great. For me, it's more painful and stressful.

Phong: When my last girlfriend started doing oral sex on me, I didn't like it. I would get her distracted, and I would do it on her instead. But I didn't tell her. For Bryan, I think you tense up because you haven't met anyone that you feel comfortable enough to be intimate with. When you have someone, the relationship just starts up by itself. You don't realize it until maybe one night when you're sitting right next to each other and it just happens. It comes easier that way than sitting here and thinking, "If she grabs me . . ." It doesn't work that way.

Bryan: I'm old-fashioned, so I would not sleep with someone until we're in a monogamous relationship. You're talking about someone I'm just dating and we're having sex. I believe in making love.

Rhode: I think what's trying to be said here is that when you're with somebody and starting to become intimate, you'll let go a little. You want that person to share her body, and you'll want to share your body too. I experienced that with my current girlfriend. It was hard for me to let go and give myself to her, because she was the straightest woman I'[d] ever met and [had] just c[o]me from a relationship with a man. Slowly, I was able to loosen up, even though I still didn't like her to touch me in certain places. You just have to focus your mind and really believe she is touching you like she would touch a man. Now I'm able to remove my top to really allow her to touch me. She touches me like she touches a man. She doesn't hold my chest area like I would hold her chest area. When you're going out with a straight woman, it happens like that. As far as down there, we do more intercourse than oral sex.

Bryan: Because I dislike certain parts of my body, even if I'm used to someone, I still have certain zones that are forbidden to her. If I change my sex, she can touch me any way she wants. If she's going down on me in this body, what is she going down on? If she's touching me the way I'm touching her, she's thinking of me in that way. I don't have a penis. What is she going for? I couldn't do it if I knew that she [was] making love to me as a woman.

Talking the Talk

Rhode: A friend of mine in Hawai'i has been practicing to lower his high-pitched voice. Especially when you're younger and your body's developing, you can really teach your body to do what you want.

Bryan: I do that sometimes, but I feel so fake when I do it!

Rhode: There's a line between faking it like "Arggh!" [laughs] and practicing your natural deep voice. When you start practicing to deepen you voice, it will become more natural.

Bryan: My friends have told me the one thing that gives me away is my voice. I do my stupid fake voice when someone asks me, "Excuse me, sir. May I have the time?" I hate it when they start out addressing me as sir and end up saying, "Oh, I'm sorry, ma'am," when they hear me talk. Oh, God, that just knocks me down! I usually just show them my watch. I go by military time, so sometimes I still have to explain it to them! I basically mumble the time. She'd say, "Thank you, young man." And I'd mumble, "You're welcome." But the long sentences and the Vietnamese! Vietnamese can tell better than Caucasians that I'm not a male. I don't know why. I go to a Vietnamese store. I don't say a damn thing. I go and point to what I want. *Chi múo'n cái này không?* Oh, God, I hate that word—*chi* is a Vietnamese female term. I'm thinking, "What? What? It must be my looks." The girl I liked in high school used to always tell me, "Oh, you have such nice cheek bones and [such a nice] complexion. You would be so pretty if you let your hair grow." Oh, it just knocked me down more and more. I was thinking, "You got anything else you want to say?" But she didn't know, and I didn't know either, that saying those things affected me in a bad way. She was always touching me, admiring the fact that I was so pretty. But I didn't want to be pretty. You can call me handsome, but don't call me pretty.

Rhode: I think the voice gives us away. Especially you, Bryan—the way you laugh and talk in a playful way. When you laugh, you force your voice to go soprano. That's what I avoid.

Bryan: When I was born, I had a speech problem. People would make fun of me, and what I would do to make up for it was to speak fast. It might surprise you, but I'm slower now than when I was younger. Sometimes when I'm sitting there and eating, I notice that they're looking and really seeing me. Their minds start to churn. It's almost like an imaginary gadget ticking over their heads, "Is that a . . ." I d[o]n't want to deal with that. When I finish chewing, I start to tell them a joke. I don't want to talk a lot, because people say that girls talk a lot. But when I don't talk, they ask me those questions that I don't want to answer. Basically, I fill the silence.

I'm sick and tired of having to tiptoe around the straight community. *We're* the ones who are dealing with this, and yet *we're* tiptoeing around *you* because you can't *handle* it. We have to deal and live with it. Yet *I'm* trying to make your life *comfortable*. Every day of my *life* is uncomfortable for me. You can't accept me for who I am, yet I have to make you feel more comfortable? That's the battle I'm dealing with right now. A part of me wants to keep my silence, because it would cause so much trouble [not to]. A part of me just wants to say that I'm not ashamed.

On the Transition and the Operation

Rhode: FTMs [female to males] in hormone therapy blend in very well, and we have a higher success rate of passing than MTFs [male to females]. With hormones, FTMs have been able to appear to society as men, without having to change their genitals. A lot of my friends have been going through hormone therapy for years and don't even think of changing their genitals. It's too expensive. When you interact with people, they don't see your penis. They see your face. Hormone therapy is enough for them. For MTFs, hormone therapy is not enough. They really have to do a lot of anatomical changes.

Phong: It's much easier for FTMs to pass in society while in hormone therapy. Male hormones help you develop secondary characteristics like a beard. Female hormones work only for reproduction purposes. MTFs have told me that hormones do very little for them. Taking female hormones doesn't change their bodies, because their bodies have already developed through all those years. Once their bones get that big, they're that big. Female hormones are just for the eggs; you don't develop female characteristics from them. For FTMs, once we start taking hormones, our bodies start growing.

Rhode: I'm wondering if that's one of the reasons why there are more MTF operations than FTM. That's really the only way they can change over. For us, we just have to inject those hormones and let our bodies develop naturally.

Bryan: I always thought that it was easier to cut if off than put one on.

Rhode: That's another reason why there are more MTF surgeries than FTM surgeries: it's cheaper. MTF operations start at $10,000. For us, it would cost $100,000. FTMs aren't able to do it as MTFs in terms of complete transition. It's really a socioeconomic problem. Men get paid more than women. FTMs, especially if they're divorced and left with children, are not able to afford it.

Bryan: Some friends say, "If you feel so strongly about it, do it!" Unless I rob a bank or steal from some old lady with a pension, I'm not going to be able to do it! Despite all the technology, there's always a risk. Even though I may hate this body, at least I can urinate.

Rhode: The newly constructed vagina has less of a function than the newly constructed penis. The penis has a lot of physical functions. In order to pass, it has to be flaccid and be able to get erect from the flaccid state. You also have to be able to urinate through it. Since the male urethra is really long, they can just cut it and place it on top of where the opening is supposed to be. FTMs have a certain urethra length, and there's no way to lengthen it. They attach the lining of the intestine to make up the urethra, but a lot of times it won't work.

There are two techniques that FTM transsexuals go through. When they reconstruct the penis, it's called phalloplasty. There's another way that's called clitoral-free op. When you start injecting yourself with hormones, your clitoris will grow. It won't be large enough to have successful intercourse, but it will grow big like an adult's thumb. A lot of my friends are choosing the phalloplasty. They're still young and sexually active.

MTFs retain the sensual/sexual feeling. We don't. If we do feel something, it's nothing sexual at all. It's just like feeling a leg or an arm. The nerve endings of the clitoris don't extend to the surface of the reconstructed penis. What they do is remove the skin of the clitoris to expose the nerves. They cut the muscles of your thighs, and they cosmetically shape it into a penis. The kind of impulses you get from the nerve endings from your arm are different from those from the clitoris. It's a different kind of orgasm; you really have to mentally focus yourself. One thing I'm dreading is the possibility of not being able to reach orgasm. But between orgasm and living this way, I'd rather change over.

Phong: Even though they can change the outside appearance, they cannot do all of the things to make me a real man—like a born man. It could never be like that. I used to look at a man and a woman and think there wasn't much difference besides the shape. Now I'm learning about thousands of parts and mechanisms working together to become one function; it just seems impossible. Even if I go through all that, I w[ill] never be a real man. No matter what they do, it won't work the way it's supposed to. Why go through all that if it's not going to be successful? I guess I just have to be stuck!

Bryan: [People] who lose [a] leg, get a prosthetic limb. It's not their leg, but it gives them the ability to walk. I know I can never be a born male. At least, I'll be able to live the life of a man according to my standards.

Rhode: People "transist" in order to interact with society. The most stressful thing is the way you're constantly made fun of by society. "Transitioning" won't solve a lot of the personal problems I have. It might even give me more personal problems about my body. But it will help me deal with people and questions like "Are you a girl, or are you a boy? What are you?" I won't have to deal with that anymore. I don't intend [to] do surgery until I see all the complications figured out. I'm patient enough to wait that long. There are a lot of things I plan to do to keep me sane for the meantime. Hormone therapy and chest surgery are not that expensive compared to the phalloplasty surgery. Since I'm small chested, the chest surgery I'll undergo is called the "keyhole" surgery. They cut around the areola and remove the fat and the mammary glands. A lot of my friends who've done that should have found a better surgeon. Don't just find a general surgeon; find a plastic or cosmetic surgeon. I have a lot of friends whose nipples are crooked.

Bryan: Can't they correct that?

Rhode: They can't unless you want to pay again. According to medical society, these are experimental techniques. Whatever they do is corrective. You can't go back and have them correct it for free unless it's life threatening, like if they mess up on the urethra canal and you're pissing internally.

Phong: Do the hormones affect your body in any other way? Males who take steroids to get big—their emotions are whacked.

Rhode: This is a bit of caution if you want to "transist." There are a lot of endocrinologists out there who are giving out synthetic testosterone. That's the worst. Anything synthetic will screw up your body. The one you're supposed to use is called Depatestosterone. It increases your libido, and you tend to be more irritable, aggressive. It's as if you're going through menopause and male puberty at the same time. You'll start growing facial hair and feeling fat redistribution within three months. Your body weight will shift to your stomach. Your voice will start deepening within a month.

Bryan: I have a girl's body. I want a guy's body.

Rhode: The rate of these changes depends on your genetics. A Filipino friend of mine stopped having his menstrual cycle in a month. I have another friend who's been going through it for over a month, and he's still having menstruation. On average, it takes three to six months to stop menstruation.

Phong: If a large amount of testosterone will stop my menstrual cycle, do I have to go through the operation they do on women to remove the ovaries?

Rhode: A hysterectomy? When they do phalloplasty, they do everything else. They'll do a hysterectomy. You wouldn't want a penis and ovaries in there. When you take testosterone, there's no turning back. When you start growing the facial hair, there's no turning it off. With MTFs, no matter how much estrogen they take, they'll have facial hair. Your ovaries will shrink to the point where they'll be nonfunctional.

Bryan: I've heard of FTMs or MTFs who take hormones and turn gay. I read this article about this FTM who got a male lover after he changed over. Before he changed over, he was exclusively attracted to women. He never even looked at a man. Once he changed over, all of the sudden, he didn't like women anymore. He wanted to be with men. I don't want to go through all this and find out that I'm gay.

Rhode: That person might have had bi tendencies and thoughts before. Two of my friends who I thought were straight ended up being bi. Your sexual orientation is different from your gender. We don't have any testosterone in our bodies, but still we're attracted to women. I don't think that testosterone causes our sexual orientation.

Bryan: The article said there are a lot of straight TSs who, once they had the operation, became gay. Before the TS in the article changed over, he was only attracted to women and never even thought of being with a man. Once he started taking those hormones, he got all of the symptoms you mentioned. He got really horny, really irritable, and really short-tempered. The only symptom that shocked him was that he became attracted to men instead of women.

Rhode: It's kind of scary when you're dealing with hormones. Hormones control your hypothalamus and pituitary, which control how you think, how you feel—everything. When you start injecting a large amount of hormones your body's not used to, are you going to be the same person? It doesn't just physically alter you; it might change the way you think.

Bryan: I like myself the way I am as a person. I don't want to become moody. But that's part of hormone therapy. When I read about the operation and the side effects, that's another [trap]door that comes down on me. It's already bad enough you have to work so hard to pay for all of this, but to have it backfire on you! Then you'll not only be stressed; you'll be in-between! At least before, you always know you have your mind, it['s] your body that you ha[ve] a problem with. If you take this stuff, it'll screw with your mind too!

Rhode: Along with those changes, there [are] side effects: hypertension, high blood pressure, and heart disease. Hormone therapy will increase your chances of getting any medical condition that you have in your family, especially if it involves your reproductive system.

Bryan: Every time I think about it, it freaks me out. I'm caught between "I hate my body!" and "I don't want to torture my body."

Phong: When you start hormone therapy, don't they want you to [have] psychiatric therapy as well?

Rhode: There are these Harry Benjamin standards that you have to follow. They say you have to have at least three months of psychotherapy, one session per week. Depending on the person, it can take more or less than three months to prepare for hormone therapy. A friend of mine just went to two sessions, and he was able to start hormone therapy. You have to get some kind of written documentation from the psychiatrist stating you are ready to take hormone therapy. There are a lot of endocrinologists who don't require a letter from a psychiatrist. You can go to a psychologist or even a counselor, as long as you've been getting some kind of psychological help. Then the therapy begins.

Phong: Once you have the documents, you don't need to go back?

Rhode: You need to make visits to your endocrinologist once every three months, for checkups and to make sure the hormones aren't giving you any problems. Some of my friends still go back to their psychologists or psychiatrists from time to time to talk. But that's expensive. It's $100 to $150 for an hour session with a psychiatrist.

Bryan: Will my insurance from work cover psychotherapy? Can I go to therapy under another name, like depression?

Rhode: They'll cover that. Still, it's going to be expensive. Expect to pay about $500 on the first meeting with the endocrinologist. After that, per injection, if you have the doctor inject you, [it's] $60 to $70. Later on, if you learn to inject yourself, the medication will cost you $45 to $60 for a vial that lasts three months. After the initial meeting, it's not a lot. Just imagine paying $50 every three months.

Bryan: Once you start taking the testosterone, you stop getting your menstrual cycle, right?

Phong: [*Laughs.*] You're really focused on that, huh?

Bryan: You don't know how bad! I want to make it clear that I love women. I don't look down on them. I just don't want to be one. It's a kick in the butt every day when I'm on it.

Rhode: My girlfriend told me, "Finally I have a boyfriend who can relate!" I used to bring my cousin whenever I had to buy napkins. Now my girlfriend buys them. When I first moved here, I didn't know anyone, so I made my mom buy me a year's supply so I wouldn't have to buy them.

Bryan: What happens when you stop taking testosterone?

Rhode: You can stop, but you can't stop changes that have happened to you. You still keep growing facial hair.

Bryan: Do you get messed up if you stop taking it?

Rhode: Your body has to have some sort of hormone. If you stop testosterone, you have to go back to estrogen. If there are no hormones going through your body, you're really fucked up!

Bryan: Won't your body naturally kick back and produce estrogen?

Rhode: No, your ovaries that produce it are already gone.

On Family

Phong: My family has too many boys, all boys. It's exciting for them to have a daughter. They handle all the things they think a man should do. I don't really have a voice. Since they're older and they're men, they think they're better. It makes me mad, because I don't have the chance to prove myself. I know for the rest of my life, they will never change. Growing up, I held everything back, because I could never voice it with my brothers. I'd rather not say something, because they're not going to listen. So now I have a problem expressing myself anywhere, at work, at school. When I'm with friends, I'm always sitting in the back, not saying anything. That's because I've learned that all my life.

I'm not only the youngest, but I'm also the only daughter. We have six boys; two of them died in the military. That's four boys for one girl. I really had a hard time growing up. I didn't have anyone to talk to. I didn't have anyone with me during my process of coming out and understanding myself. I didn't [have] any gay friends. I had to find out everything, understand everything by myself. I had to find it my own way. That's why now I don't believe in other people helping me. I did everything by myself, and I got to this point. I don't think people can help me now. When I was going through my hardest times, I didn't have anyone to support or help me out. Now I really don't care if I have anyone to help me or not.

Rhode: Are you out to your family members?

Phong: No, they think I'm gay. We never talk about it.

Rhode: How have your brothers been treating you?

Phong: My brothers are very nice to me. I feel my family will never take me as a boy—no matter what I do, no matter how much I change. In their mind[s], they w[ill] still think of me as a little sister.

Rhode: I have one brother who's totally immature and irresponsible. Everyone asks me to do everything. I don't know if it's more that they see as a guy or they see me as more responsible than my brother.

Bryan: Maybe they see in you the son that they wanted but never had. I'm [in] a family of nine: six girls and three boys. There's a Vietnamese superstition that says if you have the same number of boys and girls, then you're really fortunate. The joke between me and my younger sister is that our family is not rich, but we're not poor either, because I'm half-and-half. We never made it to the rich part, because I'm in this body.

My youngest brother always wanted to wear a dress when he was a kid. We thought maybe the gender thing was switched between the two of us. I['d] always dress as a boy when I was small, and he'd always want to put on makeup. My dad would always say, "Oh, God, the two of them—their brain waves should have been switched." But he grew out of it, and they thought I would grow out of it too.

When I told one of my sisters I felt this way, she said she couldn't see me as a male, because it was against her religion. When I change over, what w[ill] I be to her then? What's important to me is how my family will view me after my change. I told them if that would bother them, I would move. I don't want to be away from my family, but I'm willing to leave my family behind and move to another state for their peace of mind. It wasn't their fault I was born this way, so they shouldn't have to deal with it. I'm single, so I'm not really rooted in that sense.

Phong: My second brother wants to be a female. His friends tell us, "Why don't you guys change?" He's a tall, big guy. He's very handsome. Some people think he's gay, but he actually wants to be a female. They say he would be the largest woman and I would be the smallest man in the world!

On the Filipino and Vietnamese Communities

Rhode: Do Vietnamese have a term for transsexuals?

Bryan: The Vietnamese community thinks it's an illness. It thinks we are the worst kind of homosexual. My brother-in-law thinks that the sex you were born in is the sex you're supposed to be. It's your mind that you have to change and not the other way around.

Phong: Vietnamese society puts the TS in the same category as the homosexual. They think, "You're gay. You want to be the opposite sex because you want to be with a woman." Everything besides straight—basically all queers—is homosexual. Transvestites and all that—it's all on one side.

Rhode: In the Filipino community, we have our separate community labels. *Bakla* refers to gay men. *Tibot* is for butch lesbians. For us, there's *pars*. If I take you to a club in San Francisco, you'll see masculine guys like us with their really feminine girlfriends. In the Vietnamese transsexual community, is there a real clear distinction between who's going to be the man and who's going to be the woman in a relationship?

Phong: My friends who are in relationships do all the physical things. You're supposed to serve the woman. When a man dates a woman, you're supposed to be nice and do everything for her. The women go to the market and things like that. When my friends [would] introduce me to one of the girls, they'd say, "You have to get up and get her food and a drink. They'd tell me, "You're not a man, because you don't know how to act like a man." I never knew there were all these things we had to do for women. I never looked at it that way. The women know they have the power to boss you around. When you start dating them, they keep ordering you around. You have to get everything for them.

Rhode: A lot of my friends who have straight partners tell me they love people like us. Since we don't like to be done, we do everything for the women, even sexually. We're very familiar with the female body. We know how to touch a woman. We know how a woman would respond if we were to touch her in these places. Men don't know one damn thing about the female body. They just slobber around down there. The women are really into people like us, because we concentrate so much on pleasing the woman. Also, we have the image of the man, which is what they're attracted to, but we don't have a penis, so they don't have to worry about getting pregnant

On the Queer Community

Phong: My TS friends and I hang out with each other, like a group of friends. We don't belong to any organizations.

Bryan: This is the first time I've met gay and lesbian Vietnamese. I don't dislike the gay community; it's just that people always ask me if I'm [a] lesbian. I could never even say that I'm a lesbian. There was only one time that I questioned if I'm gay, because I want to be with women. But I could never use the term "lesbian." I would always say, "Am I gay?" Then I thought, "If I were, I would be the strangest gay person I've ever known."

Rhode: The gay and lesbian community on my campus didn't know shit from shit. They would ask, "Oh, are you a transvestite?" I initially became active on campus because I felt a great responsibility to educate people. When we had our transsexual panel at my campus, I told the gay and lesbian community that I didn't feel like I belonged. I didn't want to be mistaken for a lesbian or bisexual. When I['d] go to L.A. Pride, people would make that mistake. Yet that was the only place where I felt safe and not threatened.

When I first became active on campus, everyone started addressing the transgender community and transsexual issues. I was able to change the name of our gay and lesbian organization to include transgenders and transsexuals. But when I stopped being active, that was it. Everyone else was gay, lesbian, or bisexual. I can see where the gay, lesbian, and bisexual community is coming from. It's difficult to address an issue they know little about. If you want your issues to be addressed, you have to address them yourself. I no longer expect people to address my issues, especially the gay, lesbian, and bisexual community. If they do, [they're] misaddressed. When they were addressing issues in my community, they also were addressing transvestites. That's not part of the transsexual community. When I stopped being active in the gay association on campus, people thought I was either flaky or lazy. I just wanted to find my own transsexual community. Now I have, and I've been active with [it].

FTMs *are* out there, but they're less obvious. A lot of TSs are mistaken for dykes. But there *is* a big community of FTMs out there. Of course, a lot of the communities that are out there—transsexual, gay, lesbian, or bisexual—are white dominated. Under Construction, the only group I know of that's exclusively for FTM transsexuals in the Southland, has only three Asian participants. They meet once every three months on a Sunday, a whole-day meeting. The others—Androgyny East, Androgyny L.A., Born Free, and other groups that are supposed to be for FTMS, MTFS, and transvestites—are really run by white MTFS. I've visited Androgyny East, and it's all white MTFS.

Bryan: Men, if they feel like they want to do something, go out and do it. Even when MTFS say, "I've become a woman, and I want to do this and that," there's still that male characteristic to go and do it. They state their rights. Men always do that. That's why there are more books about MTFS. For FTMS, they talk about passing. They're regular people. They're not writers. They have regular jobs. And once they pass, they just live their lives.

Rhode: Do you guys feel like you should separate yourselves from the lesbian community? Have you ever experienced being called a dyke or a butch lesbian?

Phong: It has been easier to get acceptance from the gay men's community than the lesbian community. My brother is friends with two other FTMS, so his gay friends are more exposed to the issue. They accept me instantly, saying, "Oh, you're my man!" O Môi was the first time I ever came out as a transgender, outside of my two other transgender friends. Afterward, a couple of my lesbian friends whom I've know for quite a while said, "Why do you want to be a man? Are you crazy? How come we've never heard about it?" They said that I just wanted to get attention. I haven't got any support from the lesbian community.

Bryan: Because most of the people in O Môi are lesbians, a lot of the members thought I was a lesbian too. That bothered me. The group says it's for lesbians, bisexuals, and transgenders, but I haven't heard anything about how it was supporting transgender issues. When I tell members I'm a TS, the first thing they ask me is what that mean[s]. Then their attitude toward me changes. I can feel the gap developing. If I identify as a man, they either don't want to know me or talk about it. Some of them think I'm still in the closet, that I'm so ashamed of being a lesbian that I make myself think I'm TS. You would think the gay and lesbian community would understand difference.

Rhode: I've had a lot of problems with the lesbian community. I understand when lesbian and bisexual women form their own support group, they want their own space *for women*. When someone comes in and identifies as a man, of course they feel you've invaded their space. I was kind of pissed off when I was not welcomed at one of the organizations I really liked, especially because I identified as a straight transsexual. A lot of my TS friends stay with the straight community and hide their past. They don't come out to their friends or coworkers and say, "I was a transsexual in the past." After I change over, I w[ill] still consider myself part of the queer community, because I'm not the mainstream heterosexual person.

NOTE

Diep Khac Tran, a member of O Môi, a Vietnamese lesbian, bisexual, and transgender organization, convened this roundtable discussion. The definitions of the terms were provided by Bryan, Phong, and Rhode, the roundtable partcipants.

16. Mahu
The Gender Imbalance
Jennifer Tseng

Mahu is the queer Asian Pacific Islander student group at the University of California, Los Angeles (UCLA). Since its establishment in 1991, Mahu's organizational purpose has continually evolved with its changing membership. Originally designed to serve lesbian, gay, bisexual, and transgender Asian communities, Mahu has served as a support group, a social group, a rap/discussion group, a political action/outreach alliance, a place to network and exchange information, and a site for identity formation.

"Mahu" is a Hawai'ian term referring to a man who takes on a woman's role in both appearance and behavior.[1] Though the use of the term surely came about in the well-intentioned spirit of reclamation, it is a misnomer for a pangender, pansexual group. This inaccuracy, coupled with the reality of Mahu's skewed gender ratio—of the ten to twelve core members, only two or three at any one time have been women—raises questions: What are the dangers of glossing over such inconsistencies, of failing to acknowledge difference among members of a pangender, pansexual, and panethnic group? How do such failures and inconsistencies obstruct the building of coalitions across sexualities, genders, and ethnicities?

This chapter examines the fluidity of Mahu's organizational purposes and the relationship of those purposes to the gender imbalance of the membership. Despite the group's coed founding body, the gender imbalance has been long-standing and consistent at least since 1993. Interviews with five Mahu members—Clayton, Eric, Erica, Quentin, and Sara—helped me to make distinctions between the group's stated and actual purposes, acknowledge informal hierarchies and informal types of outreach, address concerns relevant to sustaining a panethnic, pansexual, pangender organization, and suggest how Mahu might remedy the gender imbalance.

Drawing on the lesbian and feminist theory of Janice Raymond, Alice Y. Hom, and Lisa Lowe (24–44); David Lopez and Yen Le Espiritu's "Panethnicity in the United States: A Theoretical Framework" (198–224); and ethnographic studies by Kyeyoung Park ("The Cultivation of Korean Immigrants on American Soil" and "Use and Abuse of Race and Culture"), I outline and critique participants' theories about the gender disparity and offer explanations of my own. It becomes clear that a direct correlation exists between gender parity and the political complexities of panethnic, pansexual, and pangender groups and identities, as questions like the following are answered: What is the purpose of Mahu? Where are the women? Who does Mahu serve? Who was it designed to serve? How might Mahu bridge the gap between theory and practice? This essay addresses the limitations of identity-based groups and the need for such groups to face the challenge of negotiating difference.

The Role and Process of the Ethnographer

My initial reason for attending Mahu meetings was to talk with other API (Asian Pacific Islander) women about the issues of invisibility. But I was concerned that there were only two women out of the dozen people present at the first meeting and (not including me) from zero to three women at the meetings that took place during the next three months. Given the skewed gender ratio, I decided to shift the focus of my project to study the group as a whole to learn more about the group's dynamics. This, I reasoned, would help me not only uncover the causes of the gender disparity but also gain insight into queer API women's invisibility in general.

As a queer Asian woman, I would categorize myself loosely as an "insider" in the ethnography process. Though there was a distinction between me and more established core members, in terms of experience and familiarity with the group, my status as a new member was not terribly striking in a group accustomed to seeing new faces every week. Being an insider afforded me certain clear benefits. The drawbacks, though I did identify some, were more difficult to discern.

Perhaps encouraged by my being Asian and queer, most group members participated very willingly, viewing the project as a tool for educating others and for gaining group visibility and legitimacy. During my first meeting, I indicated that I have been out since 1989. Shortly after the meeting one of the group's informal leaders invited me to speak as a Mahu representative on a panel about Asian American sexualities (unfortunately, I was not able to accept). I believe that my willingness to share my coming-out story and my long-standing status as an out queer Asian woman afforded me the group's openness and respect.

There were two apparent drawbacks to my being an insider. The first was that, because of my connection with various queer communities, my interviewees and I had some acquaintances in common, a fact that occasionally caused a conflict of interest. For example, if the respondent was relating a story that involved a mutual acquaintance, she or he might take pains to appear diplomatic and neutral. The second drawback—which may have been a benefit as well—was my Chinese American ethnicity. Most of the informal leadership of

Mahu (with the exception of Sara) is Chinese American, but I may well have chosen those interviews with whom I found I had a good rapport. Despite the group's ethnically diverse makeup, the participant pool was predominantly Chinese American.

Two other notable limitations of my research were the lack of closeted interviewees and the lack of nonmember female API participants. I was, perhaps, more reluctant to pry into closeted members' lives than they were to share. Ironically, the subject of much of this essay is the nonmember female APIs—the invisible women—with whom I never had the opportunity to speak. Nevertheless, I hope that the data herein have allowed me to examine "sympathetically but critically" the group's dynamics (Zinn 210).

Mahu's Organizational Purpose

Four stated or actual purposes stood out among those named by the interviewees: (1) Mahu as a support/rap group, (2) Mahu as a site for identity formation, (3) Mahu as a place to network and exchange information, and (4) Mahu as a political action/outreach alliance. Though members all agreed that Mahu serves as a support and rap group, not everyone agreed for whom it serves that purpose. Although Mahu's function as a site for identity formation was different for each interviewee, some common patterns emerged. Everyone agreed on Mahu's function as a forum for networking and information exchange. And, although each interviewee made reference to Mahu's possible function as a political action/outreach group, opinions about whether Mahu does or doesn't, should or shouldn't serve in that capacity differed greatly.

Male interviewees were especially enthusiastic about Mahu's success as support/rap group, and both male and female participants noted the two-fold nature of the support: that which they received from the group and that which they offered to other group members: "It's no longer help for me. It's helping others. . . . We need to be a support group. I benefit from the satisfaction that I have helped someone by providing my experience, stories—by having one-on-one and providing information" (Clayton). "I think it's basically a support group for people. I'm satisfied with Mahu just being this way" (Quentin). "Being a queer, or more specifically queer API, I didn't feel that sense of community. Mahu provided that" (Eric). Both female interviewees clearly stated that receiving support and finding a forum for discussion were not their primary purposes for attending Mahu meetings: "I know how it feels to be the only woman there, especially if you're just coming out. . . . My reason for being there is not so much to get support, but to be supportive" (Sara). "If I were to go, it would probably be for announcing something or trying to bring something to somebody's attention that would benefit them, not for my own purposes" (Erica). Erica's and Sara's comments raise the question Are these women beyond the need for support, or does Mahu fail to provide them with the support they need?

All five interviewees referred to Mahu as a site for two types of identity formation: forming a positive queer identity and forming positive queer *and* Asian identities, that is, the integration of sexual and ethnic identities. They all agreed that the first identity formation process typically consisted of three phases: (1) coming out, (2) validating a queer Asian identity, and (3) becoming a facilitator, learning to support others. According to the interviewees, Mahu performed a slightly different role in each phase.

The majority of the participants—noting the distinction between the formation of an Asian identity and a queer identity—explained these phases as occurring in a chronological linear fashion. This framing brings to mind similarly constructed notions in the discourse of race and ethnicity, such as the presumption of a linear assimilation process and "the concept of dual personality" which suggests that the Asian American can be broken down into his [or her] American part and his or her Asian part (Chin x). Within the discourse of race and ethnicity, these theoretical constructs have been exposed as limiting and simplistic. It would prove useful to interrogate Asian American queerness in some of the same ways we have interrogated Asian Americanness.

What follows summarizes one version of an identity formation process described by the interviewees. Many people come to the group as closeted queers in an effort to begin their coming-out process: "When I first came to Mahu, that was the first time I decided to really come out . . . when I was gonna go, 'Yea, all right, I'll accept this identity, being queer'" (Sara). Once out of the closet, members seek validation of their newfound identity: "I'm learning that there's this community of really, really great, strong, courageous people. . . . People do live this way, and they enjoy it, and they feel fulfilled in their lives. I think that kept me in Mahu along with everything else" (Eric). It should be noted that although both women encountered this phase, they did not receive their validation from Mahu. During phase two they found support elsewhere: "It was through other organizations, LAAPIS and O Môi,[2] that I became comfortable with that [a lesbian identity] and also the graduate lesbian group on campus" (Sara).

All of the interviewees reached a point where their desire to support others either replaced or augmented their own need for support: "I feel that I have to be there now, to help other people out, to be responsible, to provide information" (Clayton). Both men and women used the group to facilitate their initial coming out.

The men continued to seek validation from the group, but the women turned to all-women groups to strengthen their identities. As the men and women settled into their sexual identities, they began too to develop their identities as facilitators for others.

Because Mahu is API specific, it served as a safe space in which to integrate sexual and ethnic identities. Again, the men were especially enthusiastic about Mahu's role in this phase of their identity formation: "When I was coming out, I couldn't deal with my Chinese self. [With the help of Asian American studies and Mahu,] I think I realized you can be Chinese *and* gay" (Clayton). "[Mahu] helped me to integrate the sexual and the racial identity. . . . Mahu helped me bring those two together" (Eric). Acknowledging sexuality and ethnicity as two separate identities in need of integration, Clayton's and Eric's comments imply that to syncretize them requires effort. Clayton's comment, in particular, indicates that for some queer Asians, coming out of the queer closet necessitates heading back into the ethnic closet, with one coming out masking or even reversing the other. Is it possible to untangle the two as separate identities, or is such compartmentalizing a "sustaining inner resource which keeps the Asian American [queer] a stranger in the country in which he [or she] was born?" (Chin 7). Although there is no definitive answer to this question, it is evident that groups like Mahu can be instrumental in alerting queer Asians to the interrelation or even inextricability of "queerness" and "Asianness."

Erica and Sara both valued the API specificity of Mahu, but neither one credited Mahu as playing a part in integrating their sexual and ethnic identities. Perhaps the inclusion of gender as an element of identity assisted this integration. Erica commented on her undergraduate experience, "I didn't see myself as a woman, even though I went to a woman's college."

Erica's predicament raises several important issues. Some API women may need to come out not only as queer and Asian but also as women. It is interesting to note that perhaps by virtue of being a queer API woman in a predominantly straight, white female setting (a private women's college), Erica failed to see herself as a woman. Gender is heavily coded in this country, and the female gender is typically coded as being white and heterosexual. To be a "real" woman is to be a wife, a mother, the object of male desire, or a combination thereof. For a queer API who perhaps fits none of these requirements of womanhood, her task is then to invent what being a woman is for herself. If this task is a crucial part of coming out for API women, it is likely to require the support of a pangender group like Mahu.

In their description of Mahu as a place to network and exchange information, some interviewees saw it as allowing them to inform others of important events: "I provide information through all the e-mails and stuff" (Clayton). Others used the information themselves: "I definitely have utilized the phone list, the network. I appreciate it" (Erica). All agreed that it is a great way to widen your social circle directly ("I'm dating someone from Mahu" [Quentin]) and indirectly ("Once in a while Sara will introduce me to [someone], 'Oh this woman just joined Mahu; please meet her'"[Erica]).

Although the idea of Mahu as a resource drew agreement from everyone, Mahu's potential as a political action/outreach group drew mixed reactions. Comments ranged from "I think there's a potential for [the new Mahu to become more active" (Eric) to "As long as it doesn't become a Nazi group, that's fine" (Quentin). Clayton liked the idea of Mahu playing the dual role of support group and outreach group but wondered if it was possible: "It's really hard to be a support group and to provide the community with an event or show. . . . People are probably coming out, dealing with issues, and you can't say, 'Okay, now we're going to perform!'" Sara was uncomfortable with active outreach, seeing it as a form of recruiting: "I don't know. This idea of recruiting—what does it really mean? . . . You know, just like those Christian Fellowship people." (I would argue that equating outreach with conversion may stem from an internalization of the homophobic fear that all homosexuals are trying to recruit straight people.) The struggle to articulate the existence of or need for a political agenda was evident.

Challenges of Pangender Groups

Despite some overlap, interviewees cited four main theories about Mahu's gender imbalance: (1) the socialization of women, (2) the relational nature of women, (3) comfort levels/male presence, and (4) discussion topics.

Sara attributed the imbalance to the socialization of Asian women: "Asian women or just women in general are not socialized to be in touch with our sexuality. . . . We don't explore our desires. . . . We . . . accept the role we're expected to play. It's to get married, become a mother, grandmother." In response to the first part of Sara's explanation, I propose that we consider the question Are Asian men socialized to be in touch with their sexuality? I would argue that neither Asian women nor Asian men have been socialized to be in touch with their sexuality. Asian men are portrayed as asexual (bachelors, computer nerds, businessmen, or hard-working coolies), and Asian women's sexuality is usually defined in terms of someone else's desire. Whether they are seen as asexual or sexualized, both Asian men and women face obstacles in learning to "explore [their own] desires." In response to the second part of Sara's comment, I propose that we consider the question What are the traditional expectations of Asian *men*? Are they not expected to succeed financially and head a family, for example? It seems that both men and women are confronted by traditional roles (compounded by model minority expectations) that might restrict coming-out tendencies. Perhaps women's roles, which typically revolve around marriage, are somewhat more heterosexist. Traditional male roles, which privilege both career *and* marriage, at least afford males—regardless of their sexual preference—the option of a career.

The sociological approach proves useful if we expand traditional roles to include stereotypes. For a woman to assert voice and agency at a rap group like Mahu, she must resist the monolithic myth of the silent Asian woman. Further, "stereotypes (Hollywood portrayals of Asian women as exotic, subservient, passive, sexually attractive and available) as well as being inaccurate are ingrained in a heterosexual context which denies the existence of API lesbians" (Hom 15). I would add that stereotypes deny the existence of API women loving women, whether they are lesbian, bisexual, or transgender. Although I critique Sara's suggestion that "women don't explore [their] desires," I agree with her that expectations of silence and heterosexuality may prohibit some API women from participating in groups like Mahu.

Two male respondents suggested the idea that women who join Mahu pair off quickly and then—consumed with their new relationship—drop the group. Clayton commented, "The women get paired up really quickly, and they find their own support." This theory rests on two faulty assumptions, however: (1) these women came to the group to find a date rather than support and (2) their departure from the group signaled a mission accomplished rather than a mission deferred. This theory panders to the essentialist notion that women tend to be more relational than men. Unfortunately, "relationism objectifies women and their relationships in much the same way women become objectified in a hetero-relational context. It defines women always in reference to someone else" (Raymond 161). Finally, of the five participants, the only one who mentioned finding a partner through Mahu was, in fact, male. The implausible implication here is that men can date fellow members and sustain their connection to the group, but women become consumed with their relationships to the extent of severing group ties.

A third theory posed by both male and female participants was the comfort-level theory, presuming that the presence of men hindered women from joining the group. Sara's and Erica's comments support this theory: Sara commented, "I couldn't really relate either, even though I go to the group, 'cause guys were talking. I just didn't feel that comfortable yet." And, recalling the luxury of attending a women's college, Erica said, "Ideally I'd love to be in a woman's environment again. I can't explain it. Once it's coed, once men come into it, it's completely changed." One of Eric's comments supports the theory too: "What would these guys know about being a lesbian or bisexual woman?"

Eric's question leads us to the interviewees' fourth and final theory: that discussion topics exclude women or discourage them from participation. This theory, which turned up in every interview, was met by mixed reactions. Despite Eric's previous question, he commented, "I think meeting topics are set in a way that I don't think privileges male experiences more than female experiences." But Eric's earlier question reveals an important point: freedom to choose a topic of discussion is not the only concern; quality of discussion is crucial too. Quentin's complaint was reminiscent of an anti–affirmative action employer: "It's just so stupid to have a quota, five men here, five women here. . . . It's more about quality; it's not about quantity." I would argue that in a pangender setting, for many women the quality of discussion may hinge on the number of women there to contribute. If there's no one to engage in a dialogue, you can't begin to assess quality.

In my view, the stereotype theory and the discussion-topic theory are the most applicable of the interviewees' four theories. But I have two theories of my own: the class and access theory and the informal outreach/hierarchy theory. It is common knowledge that men generally make more money than women. It was brought to my attention at the last meeting that both Erica and another woman who occasionally attends Mahu have jobs that prevent them from attending regularly. Class standing affects not only access to meetings but access to information as well—especially in the context of Mahu, whose primary mode of networking (e-mail) necessitates access to a computer.

Finally I think it is crucial to acknowledge both informal outreach and informal hierarchies. When asked if efforts had been made to outreach to queer API women, all the male interviewees gave replies similar to Clayton's: "No. Just as there haven't been any efforts to outreach to men." Quentin commented, "We try to do all our publicity both-gender." And Clayton added, "The fliers are posted everywhere." These explanations fail to take into consideration the informal outreach that takes place in any organization. Because the core group is predominantly male, the informal outreach will most likely occur within queer male circles. Four out of five of the interviewees heard about the group through a friend. Failure to acknowledge this outreach echoes the Eurocentric hiring practices that regularly put women and minorities at a disadvantage. Often no "special effort" is made to recruit these applicants, disregarding informal (and often not so informal) networks like the good old white boy's club. If women are missing from Mahu, and have been since 1993, special efforts must be made for the gender imbalance to be remedied. It is not enough to rely on the hope that "when people [women] feel more comfortable, they will come" (Sara). If they are not comfortable yet, how will they become comfortable without a change?

It follows that informal hierarchies must be acknowledged too. As Eric pointed out, "Even though there isn't a set hierarchy, I think there is one. It's benevolent . . . but you still have to worry about those power dynamics." In Mahu power can be translated as having access to resources, experience, confidence, and knowledged. Such power will inevitably influence which discussion topics get to the table, which facilitation styles are used, what the political agenda will be, and what the face of events production will be—all of which influence the likelihood that women will join and remain with Mahu.

Political Agendas and the Limits of Identity Politics

Even though one is part of a group it does not mean automatically that group will defend your beliefs or rights. Other circumstances such as class status, political philosophies, religious beliefs, etc. can affect that working group—ALICE YEE HOM, "Family Matters: A Historical Study of the Asian Pacific Lesbian Network"

In their discussion of pan-Asian ethnicity, Lopez and Espiritu note that "the clearest example of a group that resists panethnic organization are the Filipinos, who are not only (by their count) the largest subgroup but are also the most socioeconomically distinctive" (211–12). Filipinos are separate because of difference, yes, but—more important—because most pan-Asian groups place a premium on East Asian concerns. Filipinos who resist panethnicity do so because it does not necessarily benefit them. Whenever a term encompasses many people, when an umbrella organization uses essentialism strategically to gain power or make change, there is a danger that the concerns of the group's minorities will be subsumed by the concerns of the group's majority. This applies to pangender and pansexual groups as well. The needs of potential Mahu women may be likened to the needs to Filipinos in a pan-Asian context (that Mahu is pan-Asian too is perhaps a topic for another essay). Here a pangender group designed to serve the needs of both men and women in fact serves mostly the needs of men, much in the same way that many pan-Asian groups serve mostly East Asians and their needs. As such, pan-anything organizations often fail to negotiate difference and overlook both informal outreach and informal hierarchies.

The Future of Mahu

Despite Quentin's assertion, "I'm not gonna necessarily feel tremendously guilty because not enough women showed up. . . . It's not really necessary for me to overcompensate for whatever," all five participants voiced a desire to see more of a gender balance. One man even said jokingly that he was "sick of seeing some of the men that are there" (anonymous). At the last meeting, I gave the group an update of my research and introduced the gender disparity as a topic of discussion. The response was overwhelmingly positive, and the discussion was fruitful. Men asked questions and agreed to support efforts to recruit more women, and two women agreed to take on leadership roles. The group proposed three steps to remedy the imbalance:

1. Visit women's studies, queer studies, and Asian American studies classes; take fliers; and invite women to attend.

2. When new women attend, take their phone numbers, and call them for feedback on discussion topics, potential schedule conflicts, and the like. Offer one-on-one support, and remind them of upcoming events and meetings.

3. Design upcoming events to appeal to women.

This is a good start at maximizing the integrity and efficiency of Mahu and lessening the gap between stated and actual purposes.

Conclusion

This chapter examines the issue of queer Asian women's invisibility within Mahu, the queer Asian student group on UCLA's campus. After placing discrepancies between the group's stated and actual organizational purposes in the context of a panethnic, pansexual, pangender group, I conclude that Mahu's gender disparity can be attributed to the existence of informal networks and hierarchies. Though Mahu clearly serves at least four stated or actual functions, it does not necessarily perform them for both men and women. As Lowe warns, oftentimes "a politics based on ethnic identity facilitates the displacement of intercommunity differences between men and women" (28). In order to sustain a truly panethnic, pansexual, pangender organization, in order to lessen the gap between stated and actual organizational purposes, these groups must consider "instead another notion of difference that takes seriously the conditions of heterogeneity, multiplicity and nonequivalence. . . . The most exclusive construction of Asian American identity—which presumes masculinity, American birth, and speaking English—is at odds with the formation of important political alliances and affiliations with other groups across racial and ethnic, gender, sexuality, and class lines" (Lowe 31). In the case of Mahu, if we are to form alliances across gender lines, we must acknowledge differences between male/female comfort levels, the effects of male/female socialization, and male/female access to time and information. Remedying the gender imbalance necessitates active outreach to queer API women. Only after acknowledging the existence of informal networks and hierarchies can we begin to negotiate difference within this panethnic, pansexual, pangender organization and better understand the diverse needs of our diverse communities.

PARTICIPANT PROFILES

CLAYTON is a fourth-year economics major with a specialization in Asian American studies. He is a Chinese American from Hong Kong who identifies as gay. Clayton attends Mahu meetings regularly.

ERIC, a UCLA alumni, is assistant director of Student Community Projects. He is a Chinese American from Hong Kong who identifies as queer. Eric is a former Mahu member.

ERICA, is a first-year graduate student in Asian American studies. She is a one-and-a-half-generation Chinese American and a fourth-generation Asian Australian who identifies as queer. Erica no longer attends Mahu meetings.

QUENTIN is a third-year graduate student in film and television. He is a gay Chinese American from Hong Kong. Quentin attends Mahu meetings regularly.

SARA is a third-year graduate student in sociology. She is a Vietnamese American who identifies as lesbian. Sara attends Mahu meetings regularly.

NOTES

Acknowledgments: I thank Kyeyoung Park and the 200B class, Critical Issues in Asian American Communities, at the University of California, Los Angeles, for encouraging me to discover Mahu in more than just a superficial way, and I thank the members of Mahu—especially those who allowed me to interview them—for making this article possible. I also thank David L. Eng, Alice Y. Hom, Darlene Rodrigues, and Eric C. Wat for their generous feedback.

1. "Mahu," originally a neutral term, acquired negative connotations after the missionary invasion of Hawai'i.

2. LAAPIS stands for Los Angeles Asian Pacific Islander Sisters. O Môi is the Vietnamese lesbian student group at UCLA.

WORKS CITED

Chin, Frank, Jeffrey Paul Chan, Lawson Fusao Inada, and Shawn Hsu Wong, eds. *Aiiieeeee! An Anthology of Asian American Writers.* Washington, D.C.: Howard UP, 1974.

Clayton. Personal interview. 8 Mar. 1996.

Eric. Personal interview. 10 Mar. 1996.

Erica. Personal interview. 10 Mar. 1996.

Hom, Alice Yee. "Family Matters: A Historical Study of the Asian Pacific Lesbian Network." Master's thesis. U of California, Los Angeles, 1992.

Lopez, David, and Yen Le Espiritu. "Panethnicity in the United States: A Theoretical Framework." *Ethnic and Racial Studies* 13 (Apr. 1990): 198–224.

Lowe, Lisa. "Heterogeneity, Hybridity, Multiplicity: Marking Asian American Differences."*Diaspora: A Journal of Transnational Studies* 1.1 (Spring 1991): 24–44.

Park, Kyeyoung. "The Cultivation of Korean Immigrants on American Soil: The Discourse on Cultural Construction." Unpublished paper.

———. "Use and Abuse of Race and Culture: Discourses on Black/ Korean Tension." Unpublished paper.

Quentin. Personal interview. 12 Mar. 1996.

Raymond, Janice. *A Passion for Friends: Toward a Philosophy of Female Affection.* Boston: Beacon, 1986.

Sara. Personal interview. 8 Mar. 1996.

Zinn, Maxine Baca. "Field Research in Minority Communities: Ethical, Methodological and Political Observations by an Insider." *Social Problems* 27 (Dec. 1979): 209–19.

In India the era of kings and queens was long over, and the royal palaces were being converted into five-star hotels. In England the queen was just a dowdy woman living in a drafty palace, presiding over the tattered remains of her empire and her once picture-perfect royal family. But in America, as I tentatively explored my gayness, I started meeting the real queens—drag queens, potato queens, rice queens, and salsa queens. What I needed to find, my friends assured me, was a bona fide curry queen.

The stereotypical image of a curry queen is British, for the Raj-nostalgia cottage industry has ensured that the British fascination with the "jewel in the crown" will live on. The British curry queen is preferably Oxford educated—or has, at the very least, had a public schooling, complete with cold showers and warm blazers—with a nostalgia for Rudyard Kipling and E. M. Forster, thin cucumber sandwiches for tea, and then sex with the natives (maybe with the young liveried waiter at the exclusive white-sahibs-only club). How decadent! But curry queens are not exclusively British. If you look long and hard, ensconced between those American newspaper ads for GAM (Gay Asian Male) and GLM (Gay Latin Male) you can find a curry queen or two on this side of the Atlantic as well.

Once, mistakenly thinking of myself as Asian, I answered an ad for a GAM. After five minutes of pleasant telephone chitchat, the man asked me where I was from. Playing coy, I asked him to guess.

"Thailand?"

"Close, but not quite."

"Indonesia?"

"Wrong direction."

He seemed genuinely puzzled. For him the largest continent ended at the borders of Thailand. I finally told him I was from India.

"Oh, I'm sorry. I, uh, meant, um," he said, and then he hung up.

But other men are more lax about geographical boundaries.

At a bar in Manhattan: "I love Indians, Mexicans, Arabs—you know. I love how brown you are—not boring WASP white. Say, do you speak English?" This guy was really into brown. He loved slim brown boys with black hair and liquid eyes. "Tell me," he said, "is there something in your culture that makes you all so graceful, you know, soft?" Well, so much for that butch look I thought I had per-

This is a substantially reworked and expanded version of an article that appeared in *Shakti Khabar* no. 17 (London, c. 1991), a newsletter for South Asian lesbians and gay men.

fected! But according to him Indian boys and Mexican women have a problem. As soon as they hit twenty-five, they go to pot. It all goes to the waist. "Must be all that rice you eat." Well, when I hit twenty-five, I could still squeeze into my old jeans. But then I suppose I don't count! I live in America and probably indulge in sneaky Westernized things like step aerobics and nonfat yogurt.

The curry queens of yore, those old colonial British sahibs, did it the hard way—they actually followed the spice trail to India. They went there with their big *sola topis* (pith helmets) and their khaki shorts and suffered through the heat and dust and malaria. But at least they went there, like E. M. Forster in India and T. E. Lawrence in the Arabian desert before they wrote about the dark-skinned, exotic natives and their pagan, exciting ways—doubly exciting after those cucumber sandwiches with a spot of tea. And it was no picnic at the seaside for them—Lawrence of Arabia was kidnapped and raped. As for Forster, who knows what really happened in those dark Marabar caves that scared his Miss Quested so in *Passage to India*.

But the American curry queens are in no rush to swat the flies and mosquitos. They know better than to follow mad dogs and Englishmen into the Indian sun. They would much rather have it brought to them, so they don't have to take all those horrible shots and brave the sweaty Indian crowds. Anyway, there isn't a decent gay bar in the whole Indian subcontinent, according to the International Gay Guide. Sometimes I wonder, "What is it about us that so excites these queens?" All that curry flowing in our veins? The smells of bazaars they've seen on the National Geographic specials? The mounds of golden turmeric and red chili powder piled by the roads? Kohl-eyed Indian boys slipping through the dusk, asking, "Massage, sahib?"? We are all that in safely digestible doses, in capsule form. We give them the rush of fantasy India without the diarrhea and the danger: exotic but disinfected.

To be frank, I have nothing against these curry queens. Frequently, in a bar they are the only ones who bother to talk to me, let alone buy me a drink. And in a bar, after standing for one hour with a glassy half-smile feeling so bloody different, I am often glad of *any* attention I get. And then this man comes along and says, "Hi." I feel resurrected, alive. Someone noticed me. So what if I've never seen a Judy Garland film? So what if I am neither blue-eyed nor blond? There's someone smiling at me. And he may be into brown sugar.

If he has seen too much of *Far Pavilions* or *The Jewel in the Crown*, he'll go for the exotic approach. He'll admire your waistline. He'll ask you how long you have been abroad. He'll either compliment you on your English or be delighted by your cute accent. And he'll say he once knew this Indian (or was it Iranian?) guy who cooked these divine curries. And do you know Jamshed—he was from Bombay too. All the while, he will be holding your brown fingers against his white ones and saying, "You know, someday I really want to go to India." So will you be his little palanquin bearer?

There is also what I call the intellectual approach. These guys have perhaps done the Taj Mahal circuit once or seen a documentary on TV: "Did you see that program on the Discovery Channel about that place where you throw corpses in the Ganges river and those crocodiles. . ." Then they will ask you about gay life in India: "So, are there gay bars in India?" Yes, I actually think there are people who have asked the same question to every gay South Asian they have picked up. It is not just conversation making. They honestly can't believe the answer. It seems inconceivable that there could be gay life without gay bars. It seems almost uncivilized. Perhaps they have been to India and wondered how gay men find each other in those teeming hordes of jostling humanity.

People, of course, are individuals, and not everyone follows this set script. It would be foolish to use this essay as a handy litmus test to check whether the guy smiling at you is interested in you as an individual or as Mowgli. It is merely a look at some of the attitudes that I have encountered in America. And really, I have no problems with people who are turned on by the smell of curry. In fact, more strength to them. The roots of this attraction may be a reliving of the empire-builder's arrogance or the wide-eyed adoration of all things Eastern, as in George Harrison. But as long as he doesn't expect me to clean his boots (*jaldi jaldi* [quickly quickly]) or perform levitation to amuse his friends, that's fine with me.

So now if I find someone feigning an interest in India because he is actually interested in me, I don't feel cheated. I feel almost flattered. The next step is, of course, to find out whether he is interested in me or my cute accent and quaint Indianisms, whether I am something to show off along with the other bargains he picked up in India—the ivory chess set and the Kashmiri rug. And more important, am I willing to play along?

Before anyone starts complaining about my typecasting all white men (if they didn't already start complaining five paragraphs back), let me add that there are plenty of men genuinely interested in India. Not every white man is indulging in a little bit of colonialism every time he beds an Indian. Some have devoted their lives to the study of Indian culture. They know more about Sanskrit, Indian history, and population control campaigns than I ever will. They have lived in hovels without electricity, trekked through miles of arid, drought-stricken wastelands, campaigned beside villagers being dis-possessed by an upcoming dam project. I have no reason to doubt their sincerity and genuine concern. My real problem lies with an-other class of curry queen.

He may be 40-plus or 50-plus. And every time he smiles, I won-der, "Am I the second choice?" After you are too old to lure blue-eyed blonds, do you turn to the Third World for your kicks? Did you have that same fascination for brown boys when you were twenty-five? Or is it a newfound passion that appeared with the love han-dles and the spreading bald patch?

I see him in the pages of Asian magazines. He offers his experi-ence, his financial stability, for my youth. He wants me to be slim, smooth, and boyish. I wonder what will happen when I am no longer so slim, no longer so boyish. Will he just put in another ad for "a shy Asian, nineteen to twenty-five, not into the bar scene"? I see white men offering immigration help to young "friendly" Asian and Latino boys. I see little glossy books of naked wet Asian boys, and I wonder about the man who took these pictures using the powerful allure of his wallet to get some poor village boy to shed his clothes. Such a bargain too—given the current exchange rate for dollars! I wonder if that boy knows that for those few dollars, his brown, glistening, teenaged body is stocked on the shelves of gay bookstores all over the West.

It is, of course, undeniable that there is a tremendous amount of ageism in the gay community. Otherwise, why would people need to describe themselves as "forty-five years young" or "forties, looks early thirties"? And if the older white man is on the prowl for easier prey, that is his prerogative. After all, it will ultimately be my deci-sion whether I let myself be lured into his arms. I am sure there are a lot of young Asian men who are genuinely looking for an older white man—perhaps for help with that green card, perhaps be-cause of the financial stability, or perhaps because that is really what turns them on.

But more than the financial stability and immigration assistance, I fear that the white man is offering his whiteness. I have met many Asian men who will not sleep with another Asian. They feel that would be like sleeping with your own sister. They want to experi-ence the American Gay culture; they want to taste something dif-ferent. But I fear that is just whitewash, because, if that were so, there would be far more Asian men dating black men, Latino men, and Arab men.

We have come to this country to lose ourselves in the comforting anonymity of a land where no one knows our names—where our homosexuality (as long as we don't appear on TV) will not cause shame and stigma to rain down on our families. We sometimes even take new names to fit our new identities—Shyamal becomes Sam, and Bhabesh becomes Bob. But the color of our skins is something we cannot hide with new names. In India I have seen women apply layers of herbal paste to coax their skins into lightening a shade. People inspect newborn babies and say, "Hmmm, looks like he'll be quite dark." The princes in our fairy tales were always tall and fair. It is hard for us to celebrate our tropical colors against this barrage of images—images that we buy into and perpetuate, even in India, where we were surrounded by brown-skinned people.

And then I come to America and find this rigid ladder of color with white on top and black on the bottom. And on a ladder there seems to be only one way to go—up. I have heard Indian men refer to African Americans in derogatory, dismissive terms. In a gay bar I once met a young Indian man who took great pride in the fact that the lightness of his skin made many people assume he was Mediterranean. Another Indian man complained that the only people who seemed to be attracted to him were black men. These attitudes seem to be reinforced by the gay community.

My first experience with the gay community was in the Midwest, where the ideals of beauty were corn-fed blue-eyed boys. As the only brown-skinned man in a bar, I became acutely conscious of the color of my skin, in a way I had never been in India. No one had to throw eggs at me. No one had to hurl racial slurs at me. I would just see those eyes look at me and through me and away from me, and I would feel put in my place. What I needed most at that time was attention. If any white man had come along then and offered it to me, I doubt that I could have refused him. All I wanted was to see myself reflected in his eyes as attractive, as desirable. He would make my long journey to America seem worthwhile.

Then one came along. He was a frustrated schoolteacher in a small town—an overweight man in his late thirties, with a closetful of mail-order porn. But he wanted me. He picked me up in his car and took me to his house. He had Chinese food delivered to his home, so his neighbors would not see us together in the restaurant and wonder who I was. I spent the longest night of my life curled up at the edge of his bed watching the flickering images of a blue movie (with the radio on to drown out the sound). He was fascinated by my skin, my hair. I can still hear his heavy breathing as he asked if he could bathe me. I was so scared I could only shake my head. In the morning, as he drove me home, I felt that in some way I had cheated him and let him down. I had wasted his Chinese dinner.

That day I asked myself what in the world I was doing with him when I felt no attraction to him whatsoever. Over the next few months, I would run into him now and then. He always pretended not to recognize me. Perhaps he really did not—perhaps he had never really looked at my face. But I wanted to thank him for setting me free—free from the need for his approval, free from the desperation to have him desire me in order to feel wanted, real. He made me realize that I could say no, that just having him want me was not enough. I had to want him too, and even if no one else looked at me while I nursed that drink on the barstool, it was not the end of the world. I could finally see him for what he really was— a closeted, scared man wanting my brown body to take him on a magic carpet ride far away from a dreary routine of TV dinners and "soft rock with less talk" radio stations.

But I did not come here to give *him* that ride. That was not part of my job. Lying awake in his bed as the flickering images from the video washed over me, I realized he wanted me much, much more than I wanted him. It had taken all my courage to say, "No." But once I did, the roof did not come crashing down. He did not throw me out in the middle of the night. He did not force his heavy blue-and-white-striped pajama-clad body on me. He even drove me home, as he had promised. It was the first time—in negotiating my desire in America—that I felt I had a choice, that my acquiescence didn't have to be taken for granted, that I didn't need to just quietly accept whatever was doled out to me because I was lucky to get anything at all. My doubts, my fears didn't all dissipate at once in the morning sunshine. I didn't swell up with self-confidence overnight. The need to be wanted, to be desired still remained—as it always will.

But sometimes in a crowded bar, a white man I am not attracted to in the least will smile and say I am cute. I just thank him and move on. It is true that I am brown, and he is white. This is his country, and I am the foreigner. But I do not have to be grateful for his attention. I am not in the business of giving magic carpet rides anymore. I have parked my life in America, *his* country. But it is *my* life, parked by *my* choice, and I have a say in it. I do not need him to validate my ticket.

WORKS CITED

Forster, E. M. *Passage to India.* New York: Chelsea, 1987.
Kaye, M. M. *The Far Pavilions.* New York: St. Martin's, 1978.
Scott, Paul. *The Jewel in the Crown.* New York: Avon, 1979.

Part Five
Paternity

Overleaf: Nguyen Tan Hoang, *Camp,*
color photograph, 1993

18. in his arms
joël barraquiel tan

For my Father-Brother,
Dr. Elias Farajaje-Jones who
is six foot seven exactly.

My Father is five foot two exactly.

"How can you expect to ever have a healthy relationship with a man, when you grew up hating your father!" Billy, my best friend, was always talking shit, but this scared me—really scared me.

I danced for Papa once. We were still living in the Philippines. During the barrio fiesta held for Día de Santo Niño, Papa entered me in the children's dance contest. The music started, and Papa began clapping wildly. "Sayaw, hijo, sayaw." Dance, son, dance. His pride fueled my motions. My six-year-old body swayed and twirled gracefully against the crunchy funk of the Sylvers, Sly and the Family Stone, and James Brown. I was imitating the moves that my godmother had taught me, the same moves she had learned from the American broadcasts of *Soul Train*. I mesmerized the barrio crowd with my faraway bumps and my foreign hustle. My dancing made the clapping audience feel America. One by one, judges tapped the contestants, thanked them, and politely escorted them off the dance floor. I won. When the judges pinned a ribbon on my shirt, Papa shamelessly clapped and screamed from the sidelines, "Anak ko yan. Anak ko yan." That's my son! After a few polite congratulations and backslaps from Papa's *kumpadres,* the crowd started heading toward the limbo contest, but I was still dancing. I swayed to Papa's clapping hands. I spun to His stomping feet. It was just Papa and me in an abandoned tent. There was no music, but I was still dancing. I was still dancing for Him.

Tato liked the way I danced. He liked the way I shook my ass. We met at a party. I was dancing with a friend, and He just lurked in the corner, jocking me. I didn't think much of Him when He introduced himself. He kept bringing up the fact that He was 'Rican, as if He knew something about being Puerto Rican that nobody else knew. He wore his jeans tight and bragged about being a fireman. He boasted that no one could tell that He was gay. I couldn't stand Him! Thirteen months later we were living together. He claimed me. He thought that I belonged to Him. Sometimes He would come up from behind, grab my ass, and ask, "Who does that belong to?" I would say nothing and assertively remove His hand. He would giggle with childish delight. I'd pretend to ignore Him. But in my mind, I'd answer Him, "Yours, baby; that's all yours." He was my first love.

I was her son. She once threatened to kill Papa if He ever tried to take me away from her. Papa retaliated by taking me into the backwoods of the provinces for a few days without telling her where I was. You see, I was the favorite pawn for their power struggles. She was frantic with worry, but He brought me back soon enough. When she asked why He would do something like that, He told her that He just wanted to give her a taste of what He was capable of. After all, He was the Father, and *no one* was going to tell Him what to do with His son! Two weeks later, without Papa's knowledge or consent, she sent me to the United States to live with my *lola,* (grandmother). I didn't see Papa for the next ten years.

Billy called and gave me the news as soon as he heard about it. Good *chisme* (gossip) had a way of making Billy's mouth water. "Girl, he said he'd do it, and he did. I think the police are still looking for him!" Talk about crazy ex's! I can't believe He actually set fire to the apartment. I laughed, but I knew Billy wasn't kidding. Tato had threatened to burn the place down if I ever left Him. He called me a few weeks later. I asked Him if He'd burned the bed I'd bought (on credit). He said, "Yup, in fact, that's where I started. That bed has too many memories and too many miles." Calmly, I asked Tato why He'd done it. He replied, "'Cause I told you I would; I told you."

I was her only son. The day she died, I called Papa. I told Him that I needed Him. He was the only parent I had left. I said, "No matter what our relationship has been like, things just have to get better. They just have to." He was the only parent I had left.

Diane was convinced that I defied gay Asian stereotypes, so she wanted to interview me for her column. I told her I didn't think I defied stereotypes. After all, I had a strong mother, an absent father, I subscribe to *Details,* and I have excellent taste. Furthermore, I am not Asian. I am *Pilipino.* She disagreed. She said that I defied the gay Asian stereotype.

Tato grew up in the Rampart District of Los Angeles. This should explain His fetish for Pilipino men. He flatly denied His "thing" for Flips. He said He liked me 'cause I looked hard, like I was straight— almost. He must have gotten off watching all the Satanas homeboys bangin' in the hood. So now I've got this "thing" for 'Ricans. He was my first love.

Papa insists that I am Chinese. He always insists that I'm *Chi-nese.* He came by the day after my mother died to offer His condolences. I took Him to her bedroom and sat on the bed she died on. I moved over and offered Him a seat. He refused, saying that He'd rather stand. Papa always had this thing about being above—on top. He didn't like to look at me eye to eye. He preferred the downward gaze. He is five foot two. He warned me about my mother's family, because, after all, they *are* Pilipinos. He said they were envious and resentful of me because I am *Chi-nese*. I reminded Him that He was half Philipino. He said that didn't matter, because He went to Chinese school in Manila, so that made Him *Chi-nese*. He continued, saying that Pilipinos are jealous, spiteful people. According to Him, I am *Chi-nese* because I am His son. Papa had this thing about being *Chi-nese*. He said *Chi-nese* as if He knew something about being Chinese that nobody else knew. He had this thing about being above—on top. Papa preferred the downward gaze. Papa is five foot two. I am His son. I am six foot one and a half exactly. And furthermore, I am *Pi-li-pi-no*.

I used to think Chinese people were plotting to eat me. Whenever Mama took me to Manila's Chinatown, I would cling tightly to her skirt. The Chinese were so pale—like vampires! They spoke in lunatic tongues and fought over chicken parts. In the marketplace, the women shrieked, and the men hawked up thick gobs of phlegm just inches from my feet. They looked at my small, plump body with hunger and lust. I imagined my chubby legs rolling in ginger and black bean sauce.

Billy said that one way to know if a man loves you is if he eats you out on the first date. I laughed at first but considered the validity of his claim. Well, if that was true, why didn't he return my phone call? Billy shrugged, "I don't know, girl; I'm waiting for a call too!"

Papa accused me of advertising. He said I was too proud. He said I should keep quiet about it. Nobody needed to know. Nobody even suspected. He asked me if I was sure I was gay. He just couldn't understand how. After all, I *looked* and *acted* like a man. He just couldn't understand how. Sternly, Papa warned me that homosexuality is punishable by death in China.

Tato got off on the fact that no one could tell who was fucking who. That part was so important to Him. He is exactly five foot seven, but He tells everybody that He is five foot nine. He never let me fuck Him. Every once in a while, He would let me eat Him out. I would work my way between His cheeks and just rub my thick tongue back and forth until He was moaning like a madman. Just when I'd worked it so that I was positioned for entry, He would stop me just short of penetration. "Not yet," He'd say. "Soon," He'd promise. "Soon."

Tato loved to fuck me. He didn't like to do much more than to fuck me. He equated my labored expressions with victory when He fucked me. I let Him fuck me 'cause I loved Him. I let Him fuck me because I thought that one day He'd get over the macho hype. I let Him fuck me because that's the way I thought true love was giving.

I let Him fuck me because I thought that someday (soon) it would be my turn. Yup, I let Him *fuck* me. I am exactly six foot one and a half. He was my first love.

I am the first son of a first son. My Father is *Chi-nese.* He has seven brothers. Mama sent His youngest brother through school. My Chinese uncle lived with us during the school year. We shared the same room and the same bed. Each night, he would pull the covers over our heads. He would then guide my six-year-old fingers between his legs until his big hard sticky exploded. In turn, he would kiss, bite, and lick my small, plump body. He said that I was so beautiful he was tempted to eat me alive. Twenty years later when I told Papa, He called me a liar. I am the first son of a first son.

I confessed that He was probably the first Chinese Man I'd ever dated. William reminded me of my Father. Over dinner, He boasted about having a big dick. Challenging His arrogance, I asked Him to pull it out, right there, between the salad and the main course. I reassured Him that no one was looking but me. He said He'd be glad to "whip it out" when were we alone. So He took me back to His place. I tried to kiss Him, but I just couldn't seem to get my tongue past His tightly puckered lips. Surrendering, I started to run my hand over the length of His growing cock. He asked me what I thought. I told Him it was all right. He insisted and asked me if I thought it was huge. I told Him that it wasn't huge; He was just short.

Two nights after my mother died, I called Tato. I hadn't spoken to Him in almost four years. After He burned down the apartment and pulled a slew of other stunts when we broke up, I swore to myself that I would never call Him. I told Him that my mother had died. He offered His condolences and asked me if there was anything He could do to make me feel better. I didn't want to be alone, so I asked Him to spend the night. He was the only one who could have possibly made me feel better. He was my first love.

My Father wanted to know why I didn't go to my mother's rosary. I told Him that I'd just found out that Billy tested HIV-positive and that I'd been up all night comforting him. There was just too much going on, and I was exhausted. He was upset because didn't I didn't attend her rosary. He insisted and kept asking why I couldn't go. I repeated the day's harrowing events. Maybe He just didn't hear me, so I told Him again what happened to Billy and how sad it was. After a long pause, He calmly explained that HIV and other horrible things happen only to gays. He said that this was God's way of punishing us. He reminded me that homosexuality is a crime punishable by death in China. He said I was abnormal, unnatural. He accused me of advertising. He said I was too proud. The decibel level of His voice increased with His hateful litany, until He peaked and screamed, *"How could my son be gay?"* He pulled back, surprised by His own intensity and hissed, "You're disgusting. People like you deserve to die from AIDS."

My Father had this thing about being above—on top. My Father preferred the downward gaze.

My Father is five foot two exactly.

19. The Strange Love of Frank Chin
Daniel Y. Kim

To readers who have even a passing acquaintance with the writings of Frank Chin, the inclusion of this chapter in a collection devoted to work by and about Asian American gays and lesbians may seem initially puzzling. Since Chin's work is unapologetically homophobic, it would be difficult for Asian American writers or critics who identify with a progressive queer politics to claim him as one of their own (Chin himself would probably be uncomfortable with the association). Yet the irony is this: few Asian American writers have been as explicitly concerned with male-male desire as has Frank Chin. In his essays, he insists that white racism imputes to the Asian man a "homosexual" desire, and many of his more literary endeavors betray his own intense and loving obsession with an array of iconic American images of (white) manhood.

In the first two sections of this essay, I explore how Chin defines this "homosexual" desire, which he finds embodied in stereotypical figures like Fu Manchu, and I map the relationship of this desire to the intense interracial homoeroticism that structures much of his work. Chin's relation to the stereotype of the "gay" Asian man is fraught, I believe, with a deeply ambivalent identification. Although it is presented in his writings as an image of what Chin is not, it also represents what he believes he has become, what he irremediably feels himself to be: a yellow man who harbors a deep and abidingly strange love for the white man—strange because it is highly eroticized but antisexual, simultaneously libidinal and identificatory. Moreover this love is intimately intertwined with an equally profound hatred that is at once sadistic and masochistic. I suggest that this muddling together of love and hate in Chin's work casts light on a particular problematic that lies at the heart of the Asian American identities many of us live with: self-loathing.

Although my analyses assert the centrality of Chin's own homoerotic desires to his literary vision, they do not attempt to out a latent gay meaning. I do not assume, in other words, that Chin is secretly gay or that his depiction of the homosexual reflects the experiences or desires of men who identify themselves as gay. My intent, instead, is to disclose how a homophobic fantasy about gay male desire fundamentally structures his writings and informs the way he views and represents his own homoerotic desire.[1]

"The White Christian's Racial Wetdream" and the Legacy of Fu
In order to understand the "homosexual" figure that is the object of fascination in much of Chin's work, we need to begin where he

begins. We need to look at those writings that are largely responsible for whatever currency Chin enjoys in Asian American literary and critical circles: his essays, primarily those cowritten in the early seventies with his fellow *Aiiieeeee!* editors, Jeffrey Paul Chan, Lawson Fusao Inada, and Shawn Hsu Wong.[2] In codifying their conception of the Asian American "real," a paramount concern for Chin and his colleagues is the dismantling of "fake"—that is white racist and stereotypical—portrayals of the Asian, which have been disseminated throughout American culture. What is most at stake in the racial stereotype for these writers is a question of manhood, as is apparent in this often cited passage: "The white stereotype of the Asian is unique in that it is the only racial stereotype completely devoid of manhood. Our nobility is that of an efficient housewife. At our worst we are contemptible because we are womanly, effeminate, devoid of all the traditionally masculine qualities of originality, daring, physical courage, creativity. We're neither *straight* talkin' [n] or *straight* shootin'" ("Racist Love" 68, my emphasis). Although this passage apparently refers to depictions of both male and female Asians, it is clear that to Chin and his colleagues the interarticulation of gender and racial stereotypes is something that should most urgently concern Asian men, for it is obviously yellow males who should be most galled by the fact that they are seen as "womanly."

Moreover, by following a commonplace homophobic logic, this passage implies that if Asian men are seen as "effeminate" and "devoid of all the traditionally masculine qualities," they are also seen as gay. Although this aspect of the stereotype is only alluded to in the passage above—through its repetition of the adjective "straight" in describing certain qualities "we" are apparently "devoid of"—another passage, written more than a decade later, states the point explicitly: "It is an article of white liberal American faith today that Chinese men, at their best, are effeminate closet queens like Charlie Chan and, at their worst, are homosexual menaces like Fu Manchu. No wonder David Henry Hwang's derivative *M. Butterfly* won the Tony for best new play of 1988. The good Chinese man, at his best, is the fulfillment of white male homosexual fantasy, literally kissing white ass. Now Hwang and the stereotype are inextricably one" (Chin et al., *The Big Aiiieeeee!* xiii). As King-Kok Cheung and others have pointed out, there is a fairly undisguised misogyny in these essays.[3] And Cheung in particular has noted that "one can detect . . . [a] homophobia" in them as well (237). To extend Cheung's observation, I assert that the homophobia is not simply detectable; it is palpable and central. Moreover, it is intimately bound up with the misogyny, for by disparaging the feminine, these passages denigrate not only women but also men who are in some way "feminine."

For the most part, Chin and his colleagues invoke this generic view of the gay man in order to elaborate their account of the stereotype of the Asian man. Thus they use the terms "homosexual" and "sissy" interchangeably to describe how yellow men are seen from the perspective of white racism: presumably lacking in manhood, "we" are also seen as gay. These writers do assert, however, that a more specific "homosexual" desire is imputed to the Asian man, though their use of the term turns out to be misleading. In the passage quoted above, Chin and his coeditors assert that the "good Chinese man"—the model stereotypes of Fu Manchu, Charlie Chan, and "David Henry Hwang" (whom they confuse with Hwang's dramatic creation, Song Liling, the protagonist of *M. Butterfly*)—expresses his "homosexuality" by "literally kissing white ass." But while the ass is the part of the male body conventionally associated with homosexual pleasure, its invocation in this context has nothing to do with pleasure per se: to want to kiss ass suggests less a desire for sexual gratification than a willingness to grovel, to humiliate, and to subordinate oneself to another man. What passes here for homosexuality is, in fact, a specific subjective response to racism—a yellow man's ready acceptance of his own racial and masculine inferiority and an eagerness to display this subordination by fawning over that man whom our culture deems superior, the white man. These writers homophobically condemn this response—and the men they see as exemplifying it—by invoking the term "homosexual" as an epithet.

If "homosexual" as it is used by Chin and his colleagues is, in fact, a malicious misnomer used to refer to the stereotype of the yellow man, the term is used similarly to describe the desire of the racist white man. By asserting that the image of the gay yellow man is "the fulfillment of white homosexual fantasy," these writers imply that the structure of white racism itself is basically identical to gay white male fantasy. A white man's desire to have his ass kissed by the yellow man, to use their formulation, undoubtedly expresses a racist desire to have one's racial and masculine superiority affirmed; it does not necessarily express, however, a sexual hunger for another man's touch—it is not about gay pleasure or desire.[4] What's pernicious about the analyses offered by these writers is that they *appear* to uncover how stereotypes of race, gender, and sexuality impinge upon one another, but, in fact, they merely deploy the terms "feminine" and "homosexual" as misogynistic and homophobic epithets to condemn the men who, they believe, embrace the hierarchical, stereotypical roles that white racism assigns to them. Women and gay men consequently bear the collateral damage of this strategy.

With this in mind, I turn to Chin's most detailed account of the stereotype, in an essay entitled "Confessions of a Chinatown Cowboy," which shows how Chin fleshes out his vision of the "gay" yellow man through his reading of Hollywood films featuring the evil Dr. Fu Manchu. Here I am less concerned with the ideologies actually "encoded" within the films (to use Stuart Hall's terminology) than with the way Chin, as a reader, "decodes" and finds meaning within them.[5] What he finds, predictably is "homosexuality."

"Unlike the white stereotype of the evil black stud, Indian rapist, Mexican macho," Chin tells us in "Confessions," "the evil of the evil Dr. Fu Manchu was *not sexual, but homosexual*" (66, my emphasis). Although we glimpse even here—in the surreptitious dropping of the crucial prefix "hetero"—an admission that Fu's desire is something not quite "sexual," by calling attention to the stylized manner in which Fu's body is represented, Chin nonetheless insists that the desire *is* sexual: "Dr. Fu, a man wearing a long dress, batting his eyelashes, surrounded by muscular black servants in loin cloths, and with his bad habit of caressingly touching white men on the leg, wrist and face with his long fingernails is not so much a threat as he is a frivolous offense to white manhood" (66). Apparently these films do not merely assign a general faggotry to Fu's body but also highlight a specific gesture his body makes. Fu has the "bad habit of caressingly touching . . . on the leg" the man he desires: the white hero whom Chin calls "the All-Joe American" (66).[6]

Echoing the point we previously examined, Chin asserts that Fu's alleged homosexuality makes perfect sense, since Hollywood films that prominently feature Chinese characters cater to the desires of white men: these movies enact not only racial fantasies of white superiority but also erotic fantasies in which the ideal yellow man is gay. Thus Fu Manchu and Charlie Chan, who are largely interchangeable in this account, "are visions of the same mythic being, brewed up in the subconscious regions of *the white Christian's racial wetdream.* Devil and angel, the Chinese is a sexual joke glorifying white power" ("Confessions" 66, my emphasis). Moreover, "The [homo]sexual 'evil' offered by Fu Manchu to the white race is nothing less than the satisfaction of the white male fantasy of white balls being irresistible" (66). Note that the desire of the normative white male subject as it is portrayed in these movies—for that is what Chin purports to uncover here—appears to be quite scandalous and "perverse," because the desire to feel "irresistible" is quintessentially "feminine": a desire to be desired, to want to be an object of rather than a subject of desire.[7] Moreover, on this account, the white man's wish to see himself as sexually tantalizing is apparently so intense that he conjures up, as his ideal of Asian manhood, a "gay" man who desires him. If Chin appears here to uncover certain cracks in the dominant fiction that constructs normative white male masculinity—to delve into those fissures in which the disavowed and "perverse" are found lurking—he does so only to conclude that all this potential gender trouble is profoundly untroubling to the manhood that "the All-Joe American" embodies.[8] For Chin, the virility of the white man remains intact, even if what he ideally wants to see in the yellow man is a homosexual desire confirming that, yes, indeed, "white balls" are "irresistible."

As suggested by the recent uproar from heterosexual men in the military, the attitude toward Fu's "homosexuality" that Chin attributes to "the All-Joe American" seems patently unrealistic. Leo Bersani has analyzed a typical expression of this masculine protest:

> The *New York Times* reported on April 3, 1993, that a radar instructor who chose not to fly with an openly gay sailor, Keith Meinhold, feared that Meinhold's "presence in the cockpit would distract him from his responsibilities." The instructor "compared his 'shock' at learning there was a gay sailor in his midst to a woman discovering a 'man in the ladies' restroom.'" Note the curious scatological transsexualism in our radar instructor's (let us hope momentary) identification of his cockpit with a ladies' restroom. In this strange scenario, the potential gay attacker becomes the male intruder on female privacy, and the "original" straight man is metamorphosed, through another man's imagined sexual attention, into the offended, harassed, or even violated woman. (*Homos* 16–17)

This stereotypical view of the gay man as a sexual predator expresses the homophobic fear that he will do to the straight man what the straight man does to the woman. So why then is Fu's particular breed of "homosexual" not an object of fear and loathing to "the All-Joe American"? I suggest that it is because Fu's particular desire (as Chin depicts it) is not the one usually invoked in homophobic portraits of the "gay" sexual predator; he is not really a "man."

Thus Chin tells us that despite and, indeed, because of Fu Manchu's desire for "the All-Joe American," he "is not so much a threat as he is a frivolous offense to white manhood." In order to understand this assertion, we need to examine the contrast Chin draws between Fu and other stereotypical male figures of racial menace, "the evil black stud, Indian rapist, [and] Mexican macho": "Instead of threatening white goddess blond bigtits with sexual assault [as those other figures do], Dr. Fu swishes in to threaten the All-Joe American with his beautiful nymphomaniac daughter" ("Confessions" 66). What the image of the darker-skinned rapist represents in white racist fantasy is something that should be familiar to us: his violent, overpotent masculinity and heterosexuality reflect any number of racial and sexual anxieties.[9] Racist fantasies concerning this figure—if they are stripped down to their bodily particulars—assume that if a black/brown/red penis forcefully penetrates a white vagina, all sorts of apocalyptic consequences will follow. In contrast, the thing Fu does not do in this scenario, and thus the thing he cannot be, is related to the thing he does not appear to have. For if the black/brown/red rapist expresses his threatening heterosexuality and manhood with the appropriate organ, Fu expresses his "homosexuality" with something else altogether: he "*swishes in* to threaten the All-Joe American *with his beautiful nymphomaniac daughter*" (my emphasis). *It is through the body of his daughter,* Chin tells us, that Fu enacts his desire, as if the potential penetration of her body by "All-Joe American" would somehow enact the fulfillment of her father's erotic wishes. Chin's insistence on Fu's homosexuality essentially erases the daughter's heterosexual desire by overwriting it as the displaced expression of her father's desire. The image of a yellow female body is made to function as the expression of a yellow male "homosexual" desire.[10]

And if Fu's desire finds form only within the body of a woman, that particular corporeal habitation would then seem to color and shape—to gender—his desire. Fu does not, apparently, wish to do to another man what men are supposed to do to women: he does not harbor the active, masculine "homosexual desire" usually imputed to the "gay sexual predator," the desire to make the straight man take the woman's place. Rather, since it is rendered in the form of his daughter, Fu's desire suggests itself as feminine—his is a passive desire to assume the woman's place, to be used by the (white) man as she is. The interracial "homosexual" desire that the "gay" yellow man harbors, Chin implies here, involves an *identification* with the position of "woman." It is, in other words, a desire to be fucked.[11]

We must, at this point, reiterate that Chin presents his elaborate account of Fu, the Asian "homosexual," as an analysis of *white male* fantasy. Fu is thereby relegated, it would appear, to the domain of the "fake," of the stereotypical. Chin and his colleagues emphasize throughout their writings that the desire Fu embodies has been produced by the structure of white racism and is thus distinct from the Asian American "real," which it covers over. But although these writers insist upon a clear distinction between the "fake" and the "real," this intent to establish a neat binary between "how we are seen" and "how we are"—even at the grammatical level—is always turning against itself. In the phrases they use to describe the stereotype, there is a preponderant use of the first person plural, "we," which is nearly always coupled with a version of the simple predicate "are *x*." So instead of clauses like "we are seen as womanly, effeminate," we find clauses like "we *are* womanly, effeminate."[12] This grammatical insistence on using variations of the sentence "we are *x*" signals a disturbance of the boundary between the "fake" and the "real" and suggests that the stereotype is not simply a fictive image superimposed upon us—one that has been manufactured by white racism—but also an image that expresses something of our actual experiences and identities. This more complicated sense of the stereotype is, in fact, "theorized" by Chin and Chan in "Racist Love," an essay that suggests that we Asian Americans, *as we really are,* have become nearly identical to our stereotypical depiction: "In terms of the utter lack of cultural distinction in America, the destruction of an organic sense of identity, the complete psychological and cultural subjugation of a race of people, the people of Chinese and Japanese ancestry stand out as white racism's only success" (66). The measure of white racism's success as it pertains to Asian Americans, the measure of our capitulation to it, is our identification with its stereotype of us: as a "subject minority," we have been "conditioned to reciprocate [white racism] *by becoming the stereotype* [; we] live it, talk it, embrace it, measure group and individual worth in its terms, and believe it" (66–67, my emphasis). *We have become,* in other words, *what racism says we are.*

Thus the trajectory of critique in these polemical writings travels *through* the stereotype (and the structures of white racism that produce it) and leads to its ultimate target, which turns out to be "us"—because Chin and his colleagues direct their ire not only at the ideology of white racism but also at Asian America. The recurrent use of the pronoun "we" in these jeremiads, furthermore, suggests that their castigation of "us" is also a self-castigation—if "we" Asian Americans have become the stereotype, these writers include themselves in this pronominal grouping and suggest that they too must struggle with the thing they have become.

What these more "theoretical" writings on the stereotype suggest about "the white Christian's racial wetdream" is that Fu's interracial "homosexual" desire, although a product of white racist ideology, also reflects a desire that is "our" own. They suggest that we Asian American men have been taught by white racism to harbor an eroticized desire for the white man. Rendered in terms that are less inflammatory, the insights of Chin and his colleagues do illuminate a very real experience: living in a culture in which racialized masculine hierarchies predominate, a social order that tends to instill in the yellow man both a sense of his own racial and masculine inferiority and a desire to love and be loved—to have his worth affirmed—

by the one our culture deems superior, the white man. But it is not so easy—nor would it be critically just—to separate out from these essays the misogynistic and homophobic intent that so palpably infuses them. In order to convey the humiliation of this predicament—of always feeling inferior to, and perhaps even desiring, the white man—Chin deploys a sexualized vocabulary that essentially equates the experience of racial and masculine debasement with a phantasmic sense of what it must feel like to be the "woman" in an act of sexual intercourse. To love the white man, to want to be the object of his love, is an experience of such horror for Chin that the only image he can conjure up to depict it is a misogynistic and homophobic conception of the sexual act. His image is one in which the "passive" partner is not only being subordinated but also degraded, exploited, and victimized: the one who is fucked (the woman or the gay male "bottom") is also being fucked over.[13]

The misogyny and homophobia that Chin channels into his denunciation of the stereotypical Asian American identity embodied by Fu ends up targeting not only women, gays, and other Asian Americans but also Chin himself. When Chin describes the "good Chinese man" as a "homosexual" who expresses his desire by "literally kissing white ass," he might well be describing himself, for his own work reveals a prodigious capacity for "kissing white ass." Indeed, no other Asian American writer is quite as obsessed with dominant images of *white* masculinity as is Frank Chin.[14]

"Come Back to the Train Ag'in, Frank Honey!"

Let us turn to a text in which Chin's own libidinal obsession with white men and the masculinity they embody becomes dramatically clear. We take up the invitation proffered in his early autobiographical essay, "Riding the Rails with Chickencoop Slim" (80–89),[15] following him onto the imagistic terrain of the railroad. Through this largely celebratory and elegiac account of railway life, he pays loving homage to his white coworkers and to the man he became among them. We might be surprised to discover that the man he was—especially in the texture of his desires—bears no small resemblance to the figure of Fu. A crucial difference emerges, however, between the "homosexual" desire he imputes to the figure of Fu and the interracial homoerotic desire he avows as his own. In Chin's loving relation to the white man, the erotic is, on one hand, distinguished from the sexual and, on the other, shot through with a mimetic or identificatory element. He expresses, in other words, *an interracial mimetic desire*—one that is "consummated" in highly eroticized moments of intersubjective commingling and that promises to garner the yellow man his fair share of male power. But the yellow manhood Chin envisions around this desire never entirely surmounts the legacy of Fu.

At the heart of Chin's account of railway life is a highly lyrical celebration of the moment one feels the massive machinery of the train shudder into motion. To be moved by the train, as Chin makes clear, is to experience a particular corporeal pleasure: "You're moving. Being moved. The sound of the slack being taken up car by car, steel joint by steel joint, is heard crashing at your back; the crash and tug of the first car and each afterward is echoed in the muscles of your back, a sudden blossoming of a dark heat up your back and fading into the muscles of your shoulder and neck, more lightly again, and a hundred times again" (86). What's rendered here as pleasurable by Chin's imagery is the "touch" of this manlike train: the travel of the train's power through gargantuan lengths of serpentine metal and its eventual "blossoming" into the body. The homoerotic quality of this depiction is further emphasized by the repeated references to the back as the site where this exchange of energy take place and by the direction the energy comes from. Indeed this account tends to read *almost* as if it were a paean to gay male sex, to the joys of being rectally stimulated. But although Chin imbues this passage with an intense *eroticism,* he also suggests that the pleasure it depicts is not quite sexual. The "man" to which he is coupled here is, after all, not human but an anthropomorphized technological object. Moreover, although the highly aestheticized imagery used here tends to romanticize and eroticize the contact between man and manlike machine, it also tends to evaporate the literally sexual aspect of the act to which it seems to refer: the passage suggests and yet refrains from expressly alluding to an anal erotic.

The homoerotic intimacy that Chin enjoys with the train engenders, moreover, a secondary form of intimacy between *actual* men. For this eroticized (though not quite sexual) travel of energy from train to man is not a solitary pleasure. Rather, it is shared with the other men in the cab (who are all white): "The loudness of the four engines increases and we sit down heavily into the gathering density of sound, the rising pitch of vibrations and concussive sounds that reach right through the flesh and clutch the heart and deeper into the valves of the heart, the lips of the valve. Through the floor, into our bones, comes the bone brightening sound of the wheels" (86). To move and be moved by the train, Chin tells us, is to hear the train's "dark heat" as "concussive sounds" and to feel that energy as a kind of physical presence. It is a "gathering *density* of sound" capable of "reach[ing] right through the flesh" and "clutch[ing] into the valves of the heart, the lips of the valve" and

palpable enough for the men to "sit down heavily into." The rhythmic power of the train's "thrusting tons" (83) is given a tactile, material, and even erotic sensuousness here—indeed, it is rendered as
a corporeally intrusive force, capable of something like a penetration—and this despite the fact that there is no literally sexual moment of contact.

Furthermore, as the men within the cab experience together the
"touch" of the train—as the "dark heat" of the train "reach[es]"
equally into their innards—they coalesce grammatically into something like one body: thus it is "*we* [who] sit down heavily into the
gathering density of sound" to feel the "clutch" of "the bone brightening sound" within "*the* flesh," "*the* heart," and "*our* bones." This
breakdown of subjective distinction apparently also engenders a
breakdown of *racial* distinction, as the following passage suggests:
"'Caboose to Engine 2509, highball!' comes over the radio. 'Highball, 2509,' the *Chiquita Banana hurdy gurdy* hoghead [Murphy]
says, and you become familiar with new voices of motion in your
flesh. Our bodies are speed-fluent now; they've been overtaken by,
found out by, the dark untranslatable intelligence of violence and
speed" (86, my emphasis). The strange adjectival mass—"Chiquita
Banana hurdy gurdy"—used here to describe Murphy refers (we
find out only later) to the straw hat he wears and to his resemblance
to an organ grinder when he operates the train's machinery. The
presence of these unexplained modifiers, however, seems to raise
the question of Murphy's ethnic and racial identity—is he perhaps
Latino or Italian?—only to render it irrelevant: he is, after all, Irish.
Indeed what difference can race make to these men, when their individual identities have been subsumed by that subjective, corporeal, and grammatical mass, "our bodies"?

The allure that the moment of speed holds for Chin stems from
the eroticized intimacy it engenders between men of different
races, the profound homosocial bond the workers form through
their communal engagement in an almost mythically heroic act of
labor. As the men within the cab work together to control the larger
masculine force of the train, and as they are pleasurably "overtaken
by . . . the dark untranslatable intelligence of violence and speed,"
they become indistinguishable: the matter of race is dissolved into
the universalizing, rhythmic thumping of a massive engine. What
Chin attempts to pry open here is a boundary—however delicate
and unstable—between the homoerotic and the homosexual. He
attempts to imagine a figurative coupling up of male "bodies" that
resembles and is yet somehow different from the more literal coming together of male bodies that occurs in gay male sex. He offers
here a model of interracial, homoerotic intimacy that is distinct

from the "homosexual" relationship depicted in the "white Christian's racial wetdream." He suggests here, in other words, a similarity but also a crucial difference between his own libidinal relation to white men and the "homosexual" desire he derides as Fu's. This difference stems partially from the way the eroticism of this male-male "contact"—although it verges on the threshold of the sexual—never crosses over into it. But Fu's desire, as we have seen, also involves an identification with the feminine—it is given corporeal form in the figure of his daughter. In contrast, Chin's desire involves an identification of a different order altogether.

As the men within the cab become wedded to each other and to the train's machinery, they achieve not only a kind of communion but also a kind of transubstantiation. Chin follows his description of the pleasurable travel of the energy into his own body—the "blossoming" of the train's "dark heat" up his back—with this sentence: "I feel I'm growing large, that my bones and muscles are overwhelming with size and strength" (86). Chin suggests here that this "contact" with the massive machinery of train enables him to appropriate some of its immensity in his own person. And as his body phantasmically "overwhelm[s] with size and strength," so too does his ego, as this earlier passage shows:

> In every engine I rode there was the possibility that I would become the intelligence of its thrusting tons. As I walked out onto the tracks, I would alert myself for the sight of the engine. And I'd say, "Hey, look at me! I'm going to get in that thing and make it do what I want. I'm going to make that thing go!" That was a fact. And that made me more than just a hundred and thirty pound Chinese boy claiming the rails laid by his ancestors. I was about history. *I was too big* for the name of a little man, Frank Chin. No, sir. I was a *thing*: BRAKEMAN! That's the person I remember being, the one I enjoy remembering on the railroad, the image I love. (83–84, my emphasis)

In becoming the "intelligence" that controls that masculine "thing," the train and its "thrusting tons," Chin too becomes "a thing: BRAKEMAN!" He is no longer a "boy," "a little man," but a masculine subject "too big" to be reduced to the markers of his racial identity: the small size of his Chinese body, the historical legacy of his ancestors' labors, and his name. He sees himself as virile, because he sees himself made over in the image of the manlike "thing" he controls; he *identifies with* the train. Thus each man within the cab—as he is "overtaken" by the train's energy and fused with his companions—is presumably, like Chin, transformed into a masculine "thing."

The train, then, plays a key role in the bond that forms among the workers. It functions as an eroticized object of mutual identification, which enables the brotherhood of the rails to function as a kind of Edenic homosocial horde.[16] The train stands in roughly the same relation to all of the men in the cab: it signifies an image of supreme virility with which all of them identify as they are "overtaken" by it and which amalgamates them into a single homosocial corpus. What is described through all of this is a triangulated structure of identification that engenders an eroticized bond between men of different races. In this respect, the technological status of the train is crucial. Because its superhuman massiveness renders it ultimately unattainable as an identifactory ideal, it tends to override any differences between the men who strive to emulate it:[17] "When I was a brakeman, I weighed a hundred and thirty pounds, and using the fireman's lift I could maybe carry my own weight a little ways. My weight combined with the hoghead's [engineer's] would come to less than five hundred pounds. And out there somewhere, black, hot, alive, waiting for use, part beast, part machine, was an iron horse, a three hundred and sixty ton three thousand horsepower locomotive. Me and the hoghead were expected to climb inside that thing and become its intelligence, attach our lives to it, and make it go" (83). Through a kind of corporeal mathematics, Chin emphasizes how the sheer size of the train works to render negligible any bodily distinctions between the white engineer and him: the disparity between his 130 pounds and his companion's 370 is rendered more or less moot when compared with the 360 tons of the train.

To place this in a slightly different context, in "Chickencoop Slim" Chin appropriates a masculine iconography that has been codified in certain texts of "classic" American literature. His portrayal of the homosocial world of the railroad calls to mind, for instance, the multiracial crew of Melville's *Pequod:* it is a vision of a universalizing and eroticized brotherhood that is achieved through the communal participation in an act of labor. Through much of this memoir, Chin engages in a full-throated celebration of this homosocial "utopian" vision. But even as he voices his own desire for homoerotic connectedness that comes in the moment of travel, he intimates (almost in the same breath) that, for the man of color, this desire will always be thwarted. Although that larger manhood, which binds the men together as they identify with it, is represented by the "thrusting tons" of the massive train, it is also given a human name: "No matter how many times you've gone out, how many engines and crummies you've ridden, you get the call, get your orders, are told the train is yours, you pick up your gear, your lantern, and step outside into a low, flat world of heavy iron and steel, and again, as it was the very first time, *it's like John Wayne* stepping outside and turning a commonplace outdoor scene into the West, his West. You take possession" (82, my emphasis). Chin reveals here that the masculine entity that occupies the apex of that triangulated structure of identification and desire is not simply a suprahuman, supraracial technological thing but also a white man. In fact, the image of manhood that the men all try to emulate consists of *two* superimposed images: the masculinized machinery of the train and the iconic figure of the cowboy, which has been produced by the cinematic machinery of Hollywood westerns. To see oneself as a "railroader" is to see oneself, Chin tells us, as "*the steel and iron version* of John Wayne, Gary Cooper" (86, my emphasis).[18]

What begins to trouble this homosocial paradise is the reemergence of the thing that it had appeared to cast out, to transcend: the racial difference between Chin and his white coworkers. Although Chin makes it clear that he sees in Murphy and the rest of his white coworkers a family resemblance to that archetypical figure of American manhood, John Wayne, the "mythic Westerner," he also reveals that the reverse is not true. When Chin looks at himself through the eyes of Murphy, the white engineer, he sees a *different* body, a bodily difference:

> Now and then a strange smile, a look in [Murphy's] eyes, gives him away. His relationship with these engines, like the mythic Westerner's relationship with the perfect machinery of his guns is promiscuous.
> "You're Chinese, huh?" he says. "I thought you were an Indian in that hat." (85)

Murphy sees in Chin not another Murphy—not another incarnation of "John Wayne"—but simply an Other, a man of color, an "Indian." With this "look," the equalizing potential of the identificatory bond is shattered: of the two men, only the white engineer is liable to be mistaken for—to mistake himself for—the hero of a John Ford film. Because of the difference that race makes, Murphy is able to flesh out his mimetic relation to "the mythic Westerner" in a way that Chin cannot, no matter what hat he wears.

Moreover, this passage reveals that Murphy not only enjoys a privileged relation to the image of "John Wayne"; he also exerts a much greater authority over the machinery of the train. If the engineer is to the train as the gunslinger is to his guns—as Chin's analogy suggests—then it is Murphy alone who functions as the train's governing "intelligence." This particular distribution of power is also alluded to in the following passage, which explains Chin's ini-

tial reference to Murphy as the "Chiquita Banana hurdy gurdy hoghead": "In his Chiquita the Banana straw hat, and his hands playing
between the handles of the throttle, the reverser, the brakes, the air
valve, speaking in melodies and rhythms more than words, [Mur-
phy] seems a lot less than a man controlling a finely honed, ugly set
of machines, seems doing something gentler than operating a ca-
tastrophe. There should be a little spider monkey with a fez blink-
ing on his shoulder. There should be the sound of plump-noted in-
nocuous hurdy gurdy music answering the motion of his hands"
(85). While this "racialization" of the Irish Murphy still works to
comic effect, seemingly underscoring the irrelevance of ethnic
identity to the moment of speed, Chin's elaboration of this conceit
emphasizes here the power and authority that the engineer exerts
by himself. It is Murphy *alone* who exerts his calm mastery over the
machinery of the train, much as an organ-grinder operates his
hurdy gurdy. And thus Chin, instead of being an active participant
in the labor of locomotion, is reduced to a passive onlooker. In this
respect, he bears some resemblance to the monkey he imagines on
Murphy's shoulders, a little manlike creature who simply stands and
watches, entranced by a technology that is not under his control,
over which he has no real claim.

This admission on Chin's part—that Murphy in fact controls the
train's "thrusting tons"—puts the text's celebration of the homoerotic pleasure of locomotion in a rather interesting light. The experience that Chin eroticizes involves opening up his identity and
his body to the "dark heat" of the engine: to feel the pleasurable
transfer of the train's power into one's body is to feel that power as
a physically intrusive force, a "gathering density of sound," which
"crash[es]," "clutch[es]" and "reach[es]" into one's innards. If the
agency that controls the machinery of the train turns out to be Murphy, then the homoerotic "contact" he has celebrated is, in the end,
not so different from the "homosexual" contact for which Fu apparently hungers. To be "overtaken by" the physical energy of the
train—to have one's body rendered so pleasurably "speed-fluent"
by it—is, by Chin's tacit admission, to have been "overtaken by"
Murphy, the white man who ultimately controls it.

And in that white man's eyes, let us remember, Chin has
glimpsed a certain "look" that verifies not only a racial but also a
"sexual" truth. Murphy's relationship with the engine, Chin tells us,
recapitulates the "mythic Westerner's relationship with the perfect
machinery of his guns," which is "promiscuous." This curious
choice of adjective emphasizes the quantitative, which is to say
genocidal, dimension of the racist violence with which the figure of
the gunslinger is associated: he kills often and indiscriminately. The

term "promiscuous" also suggests, however, that this violence has a sexual quality to it. Chin implies that the Indian represents for the cowboy an object of both murderous and sexual desires and that the vehicle for the expression of those desires is his gun, the modern counterpart of which is the massive train. What Chin suggests here is something like the following: *if he, the white man, looks at me and sees an Indian, then he wants to destroy me as he did the Indian; and if he wants to kill me, this also means (somehow) that he desires me sexually; and, finally, if the train constitutes the modern equivalent of the gunslinger's weaponry, it is through the train that he will violate my body and murder me, his enemy, his lover.*

We discover again Chin's homophobic tendency to define any scenario anatomizing the racial and masculine subordination of the yellow man to the white as a "homosexual" scenario. Murphy's comment—"You're Chinese, huh? . . . I thought you were an Indian in that hat"—reveals that his acknowledgment of racial difference also expresses a racist disdain. But although "look" might well betray, to put it crudely, a desire to fuck over the man of color, it doesn't necessarily suggest—as Chin implies—a desire to fuck him. The white man's racist gaze is homophobically encoded by Chin as expressing an interracial "homosexual" desire. Murphy does seem to recapitulate the western gunslinger's historical racism, but for Chin he also recapitulates the homophobe's phantasmic vision of the marauding, "promiscuous" gay man cruising for straight meat.

Chin is not content, however, merely to show how even his own desire for bondedness to the white man leads to a "gay" scenario (thereby collapsing the very distinction he has tried to establish between the interracial homo*erotic* contact afforded by the moment of speed and the interracial "homosexual" contact implied in "the white Christian's racial wetdream"). He also raises the homophobic ante by including in "Chickencoop Slim" two set pieces—parables for reading—which assert that to be mingled so pleasurably, body and soul, with the train and the white man who controls it is to face death. In the first piece, which comes very near the beginning of the memoir, he recounts what he calls "the Universal Brakeman's Story," a narrative that warns of the deadly fate awaiting anyone who takes a love of trains too seriously (80). This is the preamble to the "first and best" variant of this story as it was told to Chin (80): "I was brakin' for, why it musta been the I. C., yeah. Sure, it was the Illinois Central and there was this little fella, a switchman, Shannon his name was, tough little bastard, made out of chicken gizzards and spit. Well I'll be damned he don't go and get himself *coupled up, I mean, coupled up*" (81, my emphasis). To be "coupled up," we find out, is to be caught between the couplings of two boxcars and to die a grisly death through dismemberment. The narrator of this story tells Chin how "just for a leetle momentito as the couplings come apart you could see him, how he was, pinched you know. God he died sudden! Like a dam breaking. Blood!" (81). In light of the "couplings" we've been examining thus far, this cautionary tale—in its emphatic repetition of the phrase, "coupled up, I mean, coupled up"—seems to issue a warning against the very pleasures the essay has also celebrated: the pleasurable and intimate "contact" between man and manlike train and between yellow man and white man, which the moment of speed enables. To be so pleasurably "coupled up" to that gigantic masculine "thing," the train, and to the white man, who in fact marshals its dark power, is to face the possibility of a gruesome death.

If Shannon's tale implies the danger of interracial male-male contact, this message is conveyed more explicitly later in the essay, in the "history lessons" Chin's mother passed down to him. Immediately following the passage in which he recognizes the significance of Murphy's "look," Chin recounts his mother's opinion of her son's proletarian exploits, which she sees as all too reminiscent of those of his forefathers: "There'll be no legends or stories or songs about a Chinese brakeman on the SP line. It's very satisfying to my mother because she sees my extraordinarily unsung railroad career as being somehow very Chinese. Like the Chinese who chipped roadbeds out of solid granite at the rate of six inches a day, I achieved anonymity" (85). The history that she sees embodied in the railroad does not tell of heroic yellow men, who assisted whites in carving out a virgin wilderness. Instead, this history tells us that when white and yellow male bodies come together in an act of labor, the destruction of the latter follows: "She believes everything she says, the story about the Chinese being dynamited by the Irishmen. Everyday or so the air violently bloomed the arms and legs of Chinese to make the Irishmen laugh" (85). *To be coupled up with the white man on his terrain,* Chin suggests through his mother's fable, *is to face the utter destruction of your own body.* The inevitable reintrusion of racial difference in the bond between Chin and his white engineer threatens to resurrect the racist violence that was directed by Murphy's Irish ancestors against Chin's ancestors, the "coolies" who built the railroad.

Through this history and through the story of Shannon, Chin issues a homophobic warning against his own interracial homoerotic desire: having confessed his desire for those pleasurable and erotic (though not quite sexual) moments of subjective commingling that the thrill of motion engenders, he depicts that desire as potentially fatal, as leading ultimately to dismemberment and death. To become tethered to the white man in bonds of love, as Chin himself has, is to risk becoming not only a "homosexual" yellow man but also a dead yellow man—to risk meeting the same end as one's coolie forefathers.

Melancholic Manhood

What should be clear by now is a specific fatalism in Chin's work. By putting his own libidinal investment in white men and the manhood they embody on extravagant display in "Chickencoop Slim"—by making evident an underlying similarity between his desire and Fu's—Chin asserts that the ideological structure of white racism exerts a determining force that is nearly total. He suggests that, since practically all of the images representing manhood in our culture are white, an orientation toward those images and the men who approximate them that is not just loving but also erotic is literally inescapable, even for him. Thus his fervent loathing for Fu also expresses a kind of homophobic self-loathing: what he sees and hates in Fu—an eroticized desire for the white man—is something he sees and hates in himself. Moreover, Chin asserts not only the irresistible force of desire—the inability of the yellow man to cease being drawn to that image of manhood that our culture has *defined* as "irresistible"—but also the immovability, the intransigence, of racial difference, the brute social fact that men like Murphy will always look upon a man like Chin and see an "Indian." He dramatizes in his memoir the intensity of his own desire for a homoerotic interracial bondedness only to underscore the inevitability with which this desire is disappointed. In other words, he recounts something like a story of unrequited love.

What does one do, then, when one's love is not returned, when one looks through the eyes of a lover/friend and sees oneself not as an object of identificatory love, but as something other, an object of racist disdain? Chin answers: one gets angry; one hungers for vengeance; one begins to hate the man one also loves. One strives, in other words, to get over it, to assert the object's inadequacy to one's love for it, to mark and mourn that object's loss. And this is the work that Chin does in recollecting his days on the railroad—it is the work of writing and also the work of mourning. As a memoir, "Chickencoop Slim" presents itself as literally memorializing Chin's former relation to the white men who were his companions. Thus the essay appears also to mark the passing of the man Chin used to be—a man who was, in the confusion of his desires, rather Fu-like. This temporal and subjective irony is indeed accentuated by the brief précis with which the essay opens—"A *former* brakeman, *now* a playwright, returns to the freights for one last run" (80, my emphasis)—and by the ironic self-naming in the title, which likewise suggests an inequation between the author, "Frank Chin," and his autobiographical protagonist, "Chickencoop Slim."

In order to trace more precisely the trajectory of Chin's desire as he transforms himself from brakeman to playwright, I turn to the works of Freud that offer, I believe, a surprisingly parallel narrative of subject of development, of how subjectivity itself is formed in relation to a thwarted object choice. Freud's thought is also quite apposite to Chin's in its confused and confusing conception of desire. Freud's works enact, as Mikkel Borch-Jacobsen has shown, a futile struggle to keep desire and identification apart: at the heart of the Freudian subject, there is no real distinction between those two impulses.[19] We have already seen an intermingling of the erotic and the identificatory in Chin's relation to his white coworkers. The white man is for Chin an object of *an eroticized, loving identification* and thus resembles the object with which Freud's "Mourning and Melancholia" begins.[20] Freud describes the protomelancholic object as *simultaneously* "anaclitic"—(an object of properly sexual desire, someone the subject would like to "have") and narcissistic (an object of identification, someone the subject would like to "be"). This murky muddling together of desire and identification offers a fair description of Chin's relation to his white coworkers: he identifies with them, and his identification is saturated with a kind of loving eroticism. The libidinal component of Chin's desire is, however, rendered by him as not quite sexual (not quite a desire to "have" the object) but, instead, a desire for an eroticized connectedness (something like a desire to "be with" the object). But if there is some difference between the *sexualized* identificatory tie to the object that Freud describes in "Mourning and Melancholia" and the *eroticized* identificatory tie Chin describes in "Chickencoop Slim," what's significant is a continuity: both writers not only underscore the importance of the libidinal component of (homo)social bonds; they also describe a similar psychic response in the subject to the rupturing of such bonds, to object loss.

In Freud's narrative, when the object is lost to a protomelancholic subject—either through the object's death or through "all those situations of [the subject's] being wounded, hurt, neglected, out of favour, or disappointed [by or with the object]" ("Mourning and Melancholia" 172)—he is particularly unwilling or unable to transfer his libido to a new object. Instead his "free libido [is] withdrawn into the ego and not directed to another object. It [does] not find application there, however, in any one of several ways, but serve[s] simply to establish an identification of the ego with the abandoned object" (170). Two interrelated processes are involved here: (1) the turning back of libido from the object to the subject or the transformation of object libido into narcissistic *libido—the subject loves himself as he once loved the object* and (2) the identification of the ego with the lost object—*the subject becomes like the lost object.* Because what was loved in the lost object was already an idealized image of the self, it is relatively easy for an aspect of the self to stand in for that lost object through the intensification of an identificatory impulse that was already present. Thus the subject's love for the object is not eradicated. But, instead of being directed toward a person in the world, that love is turned back toward the altered ego, which has been made over in the image of and can now take the place of that lost object.[21] What was once an *intersubjective social relation* has become an *intrapsychic structure.*

Bearing all of this in mind, let us turn to Chin's characterization of the "present" state of his identity in a long passage near the end of "Riding the Rails with Chickencoop Slim":

> In the vastness of speed, you become roomy enough to accept the knowledge that the railroader you believed in, the steel and iron version of John Wayne, Gary Cooper, Westerner you were and still are is no good. The independent, self-reliant, walk-tall common sense, personal-experience-favoring good man doing what a man has to do who built the railroad and made it work a hundred years ago, who led civilization and learned only from his mistakes and shot straight and dealt square, the iron rider, the Marlboro man in this part of the Twentieth century as a real man is racist, bigoted, politically and socially prejudiced against all reform and book learning and finds it difficult to acknowledge the existence of a world beyond the railroad and his home.
>
> The men I worked with in California, with rare exceptions, were just that. Though I didn't think so then, I couldn't then. I guess I became a little like them, in order to survive. I took on their style, accepted their nicknames, maintained an inner stupidity I believed was manly nobility. I'd lie to protect it, give a conductor so drunk he couldn't get on the caboose by himself an arm and my word. And I know that this is my last trip ever as just this man. (86–87)

From the perspective of the man he is now, the writer, Chin looks back on his former identity and freely avows the mimetic, even assimilationist, desire that had driven him to the railroad: as a brakeman, he had not only tried to emulate the white cowboy heroes of Hollywood westerns and cigarette ads; he had also sought to imitate, on a day-to-day level, the masculine styles of the white men who were his companions, men like Murphy.

The present Chin, however, has apparently not entirely repudiated his loving identification with images of white manhood: for his realization that "the Marlboro man in this part of the Twentieth century as a real man is racist, bigoted, politically and socially prejudiced" leads Chin not to renounce that identification but rather to "accept the knowledge that the railroader you believed in, the steel and iron version of John Wayne, Gary Cooper, Westerner you were *and still are* is no good" (my emphasis). Despite his substitution of the second person pronoun for the first, Chin tells us here that he still retains something of his former self—that his mimetic relation to the *ideal* of white manhood embodied by "John Wayne," in fact, persists, though it is charged with a certain ambivalence. What's changed more dramatically, however, is his relation to men like Murphy: he now forswears *a homosocial relation to "the Marlboro Man" as "a real man"* (my emphasis). In this light, we should recall that his memoir warns specifically against—through his mother's "history lesson" and Shannon's tale—the pleasures of interracial "coupling." In other words, Chin has renounced those pleasurable and eroticized moments of *contact* with the white man but not his mimetic desire per se.

Freud's account helps us to understand how the present Chin's persistent identification with "the steel and iron version of John Wayne, Gary Cooper, Westerner" enables him to forgo the very homosocial contact he eroticizes as pleasurable. Although the moment of Murphy's "look" has signaled for Chin the frustration of his desire—the white man's loss as an erotic object—this has not resulted in the cessation of his desire. By continuing to identify himself with "John Wayne," Chin can sublimate the erotic desire he formerly felt for men like Murphy into a narcissistic self-love (that was always there to begin with). He can renounce the highly eroticized *contact* with the white man that railway work requires—he can sustain object loss—because, insofar as he has come to resemble the ideal of white manhood that all the railway workers aspired to, he has, in a sense, made of himself a compensatory love object, a substitute for the man who was desired and in whose image he has been fashioned: "I was a thing: BRAKEMAN! That's the person I remember being, the one I enjoy remembering on the railroad, *the image I love*" (my emphasis). For an interpsychic homosocial relation to the white man as a "real man" he substitutes an intrapsychic narcissistic relation to an idealized image of white manhood housed within himself. Chin can continue to love the heroic (white) railroader as an ideal that he himself now embodies, an ideal that has been memorialized within him. This mechanism of identification enables Chin's love for the white man to remain alive.

Freud tells us, however, that "identification, in fact, is ambivalent from the very first; it can turn into an expression of tenderness as easily as into a wish for someone's removal" (*Group Psychology* 37). It can express simultaneously, in a classically Freudian paradox, both love and hate. The aggressive aspect of identification is structurally related to the process on which it is psychically modeled. Identification involves an "introjection" of the object, "a setting up of the object inside the ego," a process of internalization that signals "a kind of regression to the mechanism of the oral phase" (*The Ego and the Id* 19). The desire to become the Other—identification—as it is described in *Group Psychology*, is intimately bound up with a sadistic and aggressive desire to eat and destroy him: Identification "behaves like a derivative of the first, *oral* phase of the organization of the libido, in which the object that we long for and prize is assimilated by eating and is in that way *annihilated as such*. The cannibal, as we know, has remained at this standpoint; he has *a devouring affection for his enemies* and only devours people of whom he is fond" (37, my emphasis). The identificatory relation toward an object fuses together "affection" for the object and a desire that the object be "annihilated as such."

In a passage that comes near the opening of "Riding the Rails with Chickenkoop Slim," we find that woven through Chin's elegiac praise of his former coworkers are traces of precisely such murderous intent: "More interesting to me are the men, my teachers, the good and bad men, old timers brakemen and switchmen, enginemen *whose kind will soon be extinct*" (80, my emphasis). What is curious about this sentence is its matter-of-fact positioning of these white men on the doorstep of extinction, its prophetic certainty—and this in a text that makes no mention of the historical and material conditions that might bring about their imminent demise (for instance, the shift from the railways to the airways as the dominant means of transporting goods). Without an explanation, the reader is left to wonder if this sentence, in relaying a historical truth, is also expressing a fantasy of revenge.

Later in the essay we find something that looks quite a bit like such a fantasy. While watching one of the older engineers urinate out the door of the moving train, Chin

> wondered how many bodies of engineers, heads bent down and to the right, the tips of the index fingers and thumbs of both hands light-hoisting a penis, have been found by the side of the tracks, near barnyards or anywhere for that matter. It was so easy to see him displaced by sunlight and a complete view of the passing country.
>
> But should he go. Should his clinging to the classic old way of an engineer having no time to mess around with toilets on the engine be his undoing, and he be gone, doing what a man has gotta do, I would be alone. (83)

In each of these passages, which seem to dramatize a homicidal fantasy, we also find a curious suspension: though these men will "soon be extinct," their expected demise remains imminent; though it is "easy" for Chin to imagine them "displaced by sunlight and a complete view of the passing country," they remain poised in the doorway at the moment before their fatal fall. Chin lingers on the experience of anticipation: the looking forward to a murderous consummation that nonetheless remains in a state of deferral. A moment is frozen, in which sadistic intent achieves an almost crystalline temporal purity. What better way is there to keep a murderous hatred alive, to keep it inviolate and chaste, than to memorialize the instant immediately anterior to its consummation—a moment in which the hated object remains forever courting a mortal blow, a mortal blow that is forever captured in the movement of its furious descent?

There is, however, another reason for this suspension, this need to hold in abeyance the unleashing of murderous violence. If Chin has, through identification, become the compensatory object of his thwarted love, it is also true that he has come to resemble the lost object who was and is also an object of sadistic hatred. To kill the Other is also to kill the self that has been made over in its image. Chin's concluding passage neatly dramatizes this predicament, as he presents himself, aptly enough, as part of another interracial male couple: "I turn to a student brakeman named Hughes, who is just completing his first student trip. He's wearing Murphy's overalls. I say, 'You know, Hughes, you can't be too safe on the railroad, especially when you're pulling pins or tying air or anything around the wheels and couplings. Why, I remember a guy who got himself coupled up. That's right. He was a brakeman, see . . .'" (89, Chin's ellipses). In the concluding lines of his memoir, Chin seems to offer "proof" that his love for men like Murphy has been superseded by hate. Having identified himself so thoroughly with them, he is literally able to step into their shoes: he has become one of them and, as a sign of his transformation, begins to recount the narrative that "every man who's ever turned a wheel or pulled a pin has his own version of," "the Universal Brakeman Story" (80). Furthermore, this mimetic transformation is linked with an implicitly aggressive attitude toward the men he formerly loved: Hughes, garbed as he is in Murphy's overalls, appears as a proxy for the man Chin has literally replaced through identification. And to that figure, in the guise of evincing an affectionate concern, Chin tells a tale whose outcome is bodily dismemberment and death, a tale that seems to express, by now, less a warning than a sadistic fantasy.

The key facet of this final image, however, is Hughes and what he represents. Although he clearly stands in for Murphy, he just as easily stands in for Chin: he wears Murphy's overalls, but he, like Chin, is a brakeman. If Hughes symbolizes an object of hatred, we find condensed within him features of both Chin and Murphy. Chin directs his hatred toward a figure who is neither purely an image of the self nor purely an image of the Other; rather, he is an image of both. Chin's aggression toward the white man follows a circuitous route: it fixes on an object that deflects a portion of it back toward Chin. Loathing an Other with whom one has identified begins to look quite a bit like self-loathing. And if the psychic dynamic that begins to emerge from this melancholic narrative seems masochistic, let us turn one final time to Freud's account, which suggests the proximity of melancholic identification to the form of masochism he later termed "moral."

According to Freud, an insistent and excessive expression of "dissatisfaction with the self on moral grounds is far the most outstanding feature" of melancholia ("Mourning and Melancholia" 169); this self-hatred is, at bottom, the displaced expression of a hatred directed at the lost object, the one who was loved and hated and has now gone away: "If one listens patiently to the many and various self-accusations of the melancholia, one cannot in the end avoid the impression that often the most violent of them are hardly at all applicable to the patient himself, but that with insignificant modifications they do fit someone else, some person whom the patient lives, has loved or ought to love. This conjecture is confirmed every time one examines the facts. So we get the key to the clinical picture—by perceiving that the self-reproaches are reproaches against a loved object which have been shifted on to the patient's own ego" ("Mourning and Melancholia" 169). The melancholic, in other words, expresses sadistic hatred of the lost object by berating the portion of the self that has been made over in its image—through a kind of masochism. The altered ego not only serves as the surrogate object for the subject's libidinal desire; it also bears the brunt of the subject's aggressive impulses. The melancholic regression into narcissism, having installed the loved *and* hated lost object within the ego, determines the ultimately masochistic route through which a sadistic hatred of the lost object is expressed. According to Freud, the melancholic is able to batter the object of this loving hatred only by battering that altered portion of the ego that has been made over in its image: If the melancholic's

> object-love, which cannot be given up, takes refuge in narcissistic identification, while the object itself is abandoned, then hate is expended upon this new substitute-object [the altered ego], railing

at it, depreciating it, making it suffer and deriving sadistic gratification from its suffering. The self-torments of melancholiacs,
which are without doubt pleasurable, signify, just like the corresponding phenomenon in the obsessional neurosis, a gratification of sadistic tendencies and of hate, both of which relate to an
object and in this way have both been turned round upon the self.
("Mourning and Melancholia" 172).

Insofar as Chin has come to maintain his own libidinal and identificatory desires by coming to resemble their object—the white
man—he serves as the substitute object not only for his love of the
white man but for his hatred of him as well. And thus his wrath and
anger at the white men with whom he was so intimately coupled
finds expression in a kind of self-contempt. He has become the very
thing he both loves and hates.

Conclusion

Chin's vision of Asian American male subjectivity is admittedly a
harrowing one. But as a descriptive account of the experience of
racism, it expresses a psychic truth that many of us Asian men who
are American-born or -raised must claim as part of our legacy. Chin
confronts the predicament of being yellow and male, of being
formed as masculine subjects, in a culture in which most of the
dominant images of manhood are white. As a result of our racial difference from those images—a difference that suggests that we can
never fully measure up to them—we have come to know the painful
ambivalence that Chin describes with an unmitigated brutality. We
recognize in his writings our own resentment—and perhaps even
our hatred—for those images and the white men who appear to embody them. He reflects back to us the envy this instills in us and discloses within that envy the coexistence of a kind of love: a desire to
be accepted and have our worth validated by the men we also hate,
a desire to be seen by them as one of them. By avowing that the loving desire for the white man he condemns in Fu also belongs to
him—indeed by celebrating that desire through his lyrical remem-
brances of the interracial bondedness that comes in the moment
of speed—Chin invites us to acknowledge that this desire is ours
as well.

We also recognize in his writings the maddening frustration this
desire often breeds. Even in those moments of deep connectedness—when one feels harmoniously coupled with men who seem to
embody the "traditionally masculine values," when one feels accepted as one of them—one might peer into their eyes and see a
certain knowledge: the knowledge of their birthright as white men,
the intimate knowledge of the racial and masculine privilege be-

stowed upon them by this culture because of the color of their skin. We know this frustration as part and parcel of our "assimilation." Through much of our American lives, we have had dangled before us the promise that the racial coloring of our bodies does not matter, that we will be accepted into the fold regardless. Yet, as we are enticed into believing in that color-blind world—a world in which the distinction between a yellow man's 130 pounds and a white man's 370 simply dissolves—we are confronted by glances that tell otherwise. We have known moments like the one Chin describes, moments in which we have looked at ourselves through the eyes of a white friend/lover and seen an Other body—we have been told, in other words, "I thought you were an Indian in that hat."

But what is perhaps most disturbing about the psychic realism of Chin's writings is the masochism it mirrors back to us. It casts light, I believe, on an aspect of our experience that we might not like to acknowledge: the dirty little wars we fight within and among ourselves. For many of us who have come to realize how our supposedly seamless integration into American culture and society has been limited in subtle and devious ways—and who have consequently tried to recover, discover, or create an Asian American identity—we are prone to castigate with an ardor the "white" identities that we see in others and that we see in ourselves. Chin's example suggests that we might express our hatred of the men who seemed to us to personify manhood, the men we have been taught to regard as "irresistible," by directing that hatred at ourselves. It suggests that the moral violence we inflict on our assimilated identities is perhaps intended for the "white man" we glimpse within the shape of our "Americanized" selves, the "white man" we wish to beat out of ourselves but cannot. Although our masochism, in this sense, is the expression of an anger whose proper objects are out there in the world—the dominant images of manhood that hold sway in our culture, the cultural fictions that construct as normative a masculinity that is in fact "promiscuous" in its violence, and the white men who recapitulate the racism of "John Wayne"—we nonetheless direct the anger at ourselves.

It is crucial to note, however, that while Chin's writings are indeed *descriptive* of a kind of self-loathing that I feel as part of our legacy, we must resist the *prescriptive* pull that his writings exert. If the masochism Chin describes is, in fact, an aspect of our psychic reality—one that we should acknowledge—we must find better psychological, cultural, and political strategies for negotiating it than the "solutions" his writings implicitly and explicitly advocate. Having already addressed the homophobia and misogyny that permeate Chin's essays, I can flesh out the remedy that "Chickencoop

Slim" implicitly offers for our woes. The essay moves toward endorsing, on one hand, an intensified assimilation at the level of our identities and, on the other, a form of radical separatism—the combination of which leads, ultimately, to an intensified masochism. If the very shape of our American male identities expresses our ineradicable and loving identification with the white men—real or imaginary—our culture has taught us to honor, then, Chin suggests, *so be it*; but then let that identification express our undying hatred for them as well. As we take their identities into our own—as we emulate them—let them know that this signals our emancipation from any social bond to them. We no longer need their "touch"; we no longer crave a bondedness to them, because we possess, after all, our own assimilated identities that bear their traces. We have taken them into us and need them no longer as "real" men. We make of our assimilated identities memorials to our frustrated love but also deposit upon them the abundance of our hatred. I thus hate you by hating the me I have become in your image. And though I pay the price of hating myself in direct proportion to the degree that I hate you, I am willing to do so for the release of aggression it enables me. And this, ultimately, is the gesture at the heart of Chinian manhood. It is to hate with a passion and with a vengeance the assimilated identity that is one's own.

Thus the man who emerges on the other side of "Chickencoop Slim"—Frank Chin, the writer—will go on to reproduce a body of work in which the most visceral affective component is a relentless masochism. As Elaine Kim has observed of Chin's dramas and early short stories, "Instead of building a new manhood and a new culture . . . through his imaginative writing, Chin creates an overriding sense of the utter futility of the male protagonist's efforts to redefine himself" (186). Kim describes his characters as "alienated adolescents, [who are] incapacitated by the sense of their own impotence," and finds that Chin's own "contempt" for them "leaves the reader with the impression of futility and bored misanthropy" (189). In her estimation, he "accepts his oppressors' definition of 'masculinity'" and then produces a series of male characters who berate themselves for their inability to live up to that definition. As Kim incisively puts it, his writing presents the spectacle of "the Asian American male protagonist squirming helplessly, pinpointed by his own verbal barbs" (187). Michael Soo Hoo, in a review of Chin's more recent collection of short stories, *The Chinaman Pacific and Frisco R.R. Co.*, echoes Kim's characterization of the writer's earlier works: "Throughout the eight stories, Chin presents the condition of Chinese America in an uncompromising state of decay, masochistically prolonged, and involving empty, hollow shells of

people" (175–76). Soo Hoo cites as exemplary of the tone of the
entire volume a story entitled "The Chinatown Kid," which he describes as "like all the stories in the book . . . a tale of horrific isolation and self-contempt" (176). What Chin tends to offer us in his
writings are literary self-portraits of an Asian American masculinity
in ruins, of men who seem only to hate themselves for their inability to be men.

But within this masochism that so palpably infuses his work, Chin
finds something—I believe—that he experiences as "redemptive."
He finds something in these literary exercises of self-flagellation
that gives him, in other words, the illusion of virility, that enables
him to feel like a "man." He finds in this virulent masochism an
equally virulent sadism, and the authorial subject who brings himself into being through the writing of "Chickencoop Slim" is ultimately a sadist to the same degree that he is a masochist.[22] It is not
only true that the moral condemnation he heaps upon myriad objects throughout his writings is also directed at himself; it is also true
that the aggression to which he subjects himself is always directed
at another, at those loathed objects with which he nonetheless identifies: the "fake" Asian American, the "homosexual," the "feminine," the white man, the rest of us. The masculine "redemption"
Chin finds in masochism is located in the paradoxically sadistic violence of the self-inflicted blow, in the insistent battering of the self
that is always a battering of another. Though it reaps a psychic profit
from the expense of aggression it allows, it is a "redemption" that
we need not claim as our own. Through this incessant recirculation
of fury and wrath, Chin seeks to lay his hands on the thing that most
defines manhood in our culture: a "promiscuous" violence.
Though he too must bear its brunt, this violence enables Chin to
see himself as a disfigured, disfiguring copy of the man he loves, the
man he hates, the man he is, "the mythic Westerner," who—as he
himself tells us—is "no good."

NOTES

Acknowledgments: I thank David L. Eng, Greg Forter, Seth Moglen, and
Carolyn Porter for helping me to clarify the status of "homosexuality"
in my analysis as well as for their overall assistance. I also owe a debt of
gratitude to Karen Su and Sau-ling Wong for their invaluable support
and commentary.

1. I realize that, in taking this approach, I risk asserting too discrete
a boundary between what Eve Sedgwick has termed "the homosocial
and the homosexual," a distinction that enables straight men to disavow
a resemblance and continuity between their own desires for male intimacy and the desires of homosexual men (1–20). Within the context of

analyzing and criticizing the homophobia that propels Chin's writings, however, I believe that the greater error would be to consider his representation of homosexuality and his self-tortured account of his own homoerotic desires as necessarily expressive and revelatory of the real thing. Whether Chin's account of yellow male sexuality bespeaks something of the experiences and desires of Asian American men who identify themselves as gay is a pertinent issue, which I leave for other writers to explore.

2. I am referring primarily to the prefaces and introductions written by Chin et al. for the collections of Asian American writings they have edited: *Aiiieeeee! An Anthology of Asian American Writers* and *The Big Aiiieeeee! An Anthology of Chinese American and Japanese American Literature;* see also Chin and Chan's "Racist Love."

3. Cogent feminist critiques of the misogyny in the works of Chin et al. can be found in Kim and in Cheung. Cheung rightly notes that these and similar passages have the effect of "buttressing patriarchy by invoking gender stereotypes, by disparaging domestic efficiency as 'feminine,' and by slotting desirable traits such as originality, daring, physical courage, and creativity under the rubric of masculinity" and by suggesting "a sexist preference for stereotypes that imply predatory violence against women to 'effeminate' ones" (237).

4. The critique of racist ideology that Chin and his colleagues offer owes a debt, I believe, to Frantz Fanon's *Black Skin, White Masks*. In their analyses of the psychological dimensions of racism in America, Chin et al. have translated much of the spirit, if not the letter, of Fanon's account of the various "complexes" he sees in both the French colonizer and the African colonized. Unfortunately, they have also apparently tapped into an underlying homophobia and misogyny in Fanon's analysis. He views homosexuality, in particular, as perverse and repulsive, and his discussions of the topic seem skewed in ways that are quite prescient of the writings of Chin and his colleagues. In certain French medical writings, for instance, Fanon identifies an implicit reifying and eroticizing of black male sexual appetites, and he voices his indignation in homophobic terms: "I have never been able, without revulsion, to hear a *man* say of another man: 'He is so sensual!' I do not know what the sensuality of a man is" (201, Fanon's emphasis). For critiques of the homophobia in Fanon's work, see Fuss 141–65 and Edelman 42–75.

5. See Hall 128–38. Hall asserts that there is a *"lack of equivalence"* between the ideologies encoded within a text—that is, the belief systems of a culture that figure in the production of mass-media texts—and the ideological meanings that actual language communities find in them (131). Though the semiotic approach Hall takes in his "Encoding/Decoding" does not lead him to address directly the psychic determinants of the decoding process—how structures of desire and identification, for instance, work differentially in various communities and in particular individuals—his distinction between encoded ideologies

within a mass-media text and decoded meanings provides a useful analytical tool for my purposes.

6. Contrasting interpretations of the figure of the Asian male villain are forwarded by Kim and by Fung (see Chapter 7). Like Chin, Kim and Fung argue that the Asian man tends to be portrayed as nonmasculine in Western cultural texts. Elaine Kim, however, regards the figure of Fu not as homosexual but "completely asexual" (8), and gay Asian Canadian critic and filmmaker Richard Fung argues in Chapter 7 that the Asian male is represented in cinematic texts as "sometimes dangerous, sometimes friendly, but almost always characterized by a desexualized Zen asceticism. . . . The Asian man is defined by a striking absence down there. And if Asian men have no sexuality," Fung asks, "how can we have a homosexuality?"

7. For a condensed articulation of the larger cultural view of this desire as "feminine," see Freud's "On Narcissism: An Introduction." In one of his more regressive moments, Freud describes the "truest feminine type" of woman as one who is restricted in "developing a true object-love" (69), and can therefore love only narcissistically: "Strictly speaking such women love only themselves with an intensity comparable to that of the man's love for them. *Nor does their need lie in the direction of loving, but of being loved*" (70, my emphasis).

8. Elements of Chin's critique resonate with the theoretical project of Kaja Silverman in *Male Subjectivity at the Margins.* Like Silverman, Chin exposes much that is indeed "perverse" in and possibly subversive of normative white male subjectivity, and he himself embraces a "perverse" subject position in the masochistic model of Asian American manhood that he ultimately comes to champion. He does so, however, not to bury Caesar, as it were, but to praise him. The "perverse" and masochistic masculinity he endorses is entirely compatible (for him) with an experience of virility; furthermore, his ideological critiques all work to demonstrate that white male privilege coexists quite peaceably with its own "perversity." Chin's writings also call to mind Judith Butler's insights in *Gender Trouble,* in that they emphasize the iterability of masculine identity. But although Chin deploys a performative model of gender identity that is formally much like Butler's, he does so toward much different ends. His model of the Asian American masculine subject repeats white male identity with a difference but also with a *vengeance*— his repetition is motivated by a sadistic (though also masochistic) intent. The iterable aspects of normative masculine subjectivity he is most interested in activating are its aggression and violence.

9. See, for instance, Fanon; Kovel; and Williamson.

10. I am indebted to Karen Su, Seth Moglen, and Greg Forter, who helped me to clarify this elision in Chin's analysis—*his* marginalization of the feminine.

11. The model of "homosexual" desire Chin offers here is actually a kind of heterosexuality in drag. It does not imagine a man desiring

a man, but a man who plays the part of a woman desiring a man. For rigorous analysis of how theoretical paradigms of homosexual desire tend to give same-sex desire a foundationally heterosexual shape, see Butler 1–34.

12. Perhaps the most flagrant example of this tendency is found in Chin's essay "Backtalk." Here Chin addresses Asian American masculinity more indirectly, through the issue of language. The passage from "Racist Love" cited earlier asserts that our perceived inability to talk "straight" is primarily a fault of racist vision, a stereotypical fiction. However, in "Backtalk,"—though Chin concludes by asserting that ours is "a backtalking, muscular, singing stomping full blooded language loaded with nothing but the truth" (557)—he nonetheless makes the following statements without any visible qualifiers: "As a people, we are pre-verbal,—afraid of language as the instrument through which the monster takes possession of us. . . . We are a people without a native tongue. . . . We have no street tongue to flaunt and strut the way the blacks and Chicanoes [sic] do. They have a positive, self-defined linguistic identity that can be offended and wronged. We don't" (557).

13. For a succinct analysis of this larger homophobic and misogynistic fantasy about the passive partner in a sexual exchange, in particular the gay male "bottom," see Leo Bersani's "Is the Rectum a Grave?"

14. For discussions of Chin's fascination with white manhood, see Cheung 234–51, Kim (especially 173–214), and Wong (especially 146–53).

15. My sense is that in "Chickencoop Slim" (title used hereafter for this essay), Chin is staking his ambivalent claim to a paradigmatic trope of interracial male bonding that Leslie Fiedler ("Come Back in the Raft Ag'in, Huck Honey") has identified at the heart of much "classic" American literature. As Fiedler has pointed out, the homosocial utopia that white male writers in American relentlessly carve out in the wilderness, far from the "sivilising" influences of women, often consists of an interracial homoerotic couple, in which the white man is the hero and the man of color is consigned to the role of the wife substitute. What we hear in Chin's depiction of the profound connection that he feels to his white coworkers are echoes of the intimacy that develops between Huck and Jim. However, the view from the other end of the raft, or train, is not nearly as rosy as the one we are accustomed to seeing in American fiction.

16. Chin's vision of the social group bears one resemblance to Freud's account in *Group Psychology and the Analysis of the Ego.* The masculine image of the train (and also of "John Wayne" [82]) in Chin's memoir functions much as the image of the leader in Freud's account. The "*primary social group,*" as Freud defines it, "*is a number of individuals who have put one and the same object in the place of their ego ideal and have consequently identified themselves with one another in their ego*" (48, Freud's italics).

17. This identification with an ideal that is impossible to identify with

completely—that is, "an identification with an unassimilable ideal" (213)—is discussed by Mikkel Borch-Jacobsen as an ultimately impossible structure within Freud's theory. It is a structure that—as Freud's writing itself discloses—cannot hold in check the resurgence of a rivalry that is propelled by a murderous desire to take the other's place. See Borch-Jacobsen 127–239.

18. My analysis of Chin's ambivalent appropriation of this particular image of white manhood drew considerably from Sau-ling Wong's graceful analysis of Chin's "Eat and Run Midnight People," a short story that recycles much of the material contained in this earlier memoir. Wong focuses on the historical and ideological determinants of the ambivalence that informs Chin's attempt to create "a Chinese American mobility myth around the symbol of the railroad" through the figure of the brakeman (146). Here I focus on the libidinal, aggressive, and identificatory determinants of that ambivalence itself.

19. Borch-Jacobsen staunchly asserts that what lies at the heart of the human subject is an "altruicidal," ambivalent, and unquenchable *mimetic desire*, in which love and hate, desire and identification, and sadism and masochism are ultimately indistinguishable. His analysis, however, repeats a shortsightedness in the texts from which it draws: within the Freudian drama as Borch-Jacobsen enacts it, the players are given no gender, no sexuality, no creed, and, indeed, no color. They are a uniform homogeneous mass in which the differences that seem to matter in the world of history—the "anatomical" differences of sex and race, for instance—play no part in the ahistorical repetitive cycle of madness to which the sum of human experience is reduced. We are all, in the end, "sons" of the *same* tribe, who war with each other to usurp the place of the father who never was. And since he never was, he has no color, and the differences and inequalities that predetermine who wins and loses this war between rivals—the unending war that is *human* culture, *human* history—are rendered incidental. Despite the universalizing pull his theories exert, there is much to be gained from Borch-Jacobsen's insights, for they cast light upon the specific drama of beleaguered *yellow* manhood that Chin plays out. The part Chin's autobiographical protagonist plays is very much that of the fraternal rival/friend/lover, whom Borch-Jacobsen elucidates so painstakingly and eloquently. But Chin's inescapable knowledge of the difference in skin color between him and his other self, the white man, structures and determines the specific vicissitudes of his mimetic madness. Although Chin depicts his relation to his white coworkers in terms that echo Borch-Jacobsen's conception of the primal mimetic bond, he sees himself as doubly bound. As a yellow man, not only is he inextricably tied to the white man as mimetic double—at once hated rival and beloved friend/lover—but also, bound as he is by the color of skin, he knows that the mimetic desire he harbors must always be frustrated in a way that is not true for his white counterpart.

20. In this analysis of Freud's essay "Mourning and Melancholia," I address an aspect emphasized by Judith Butler in her reading of the essay (57–65). In Freud's account, the subject's melancholic identification with the lost object paradoxically enables both the renunciation and perpetuation of a repudiated desire. This exposes Chin's complex psychic negotiation of the loving and identificatory desire he feels toward the images of white manhood that are predominant in our culture—the simultaneous renunciation/preservation of a homoerotic desire involved in the melancholic identification with those images and its ultimate path to a form of masochism.

21. In *The Ego and the Id,* Freud shows that it is the ego's identification with the lost object that enables it to court affections that the id once lavished upon another: "When the ego assumes the features of the object, it is forcing itself, so to speak, upon the id as a love-object and is trying to make good the id's loss by saying: 'Look, you can love me too—I am so like the object'" (20).

22. My understanding of Chin's masochism draws from Kaja Silverman's analysis of "reflexive masochism." She suggests that this particular form of masochism is "compatible with—indeed, perhaps a prerequisite for—extreme virility" (327). "The reflexive masochist," Silverman suggests, "might indeed as appropriately be designated a 'reflexive sadist'" (324–25). He is a kind of psychic switch-hitter, both batterer and battered. He "suffers/enjoys pain without renouncing activity" (325). My analysis also draws from the much earlier work of Theodor Reik, who asserts that the sadistic impulse, which Silverman identifies in reflexive masochism, is, in fact, the central driving force behind masochism in general. Silverman, however, carefully distinguishes reflexive masochism from another form, "feminine," which she argues is subversive of normative masculinity. Overall, her work and that of other recent psychoanalytic critics and theorists share the common political goal of upending dominant constructions of gender and sexuality. Kaja Silverman, Leo Bersani, and Gilles Deleuze, among others, assert that male "perversions" like masochism illuminate and resist the oppressive ideological fictions that determine the shape of conventional virility. This focus on marginalized male subjectivities has recently come under criticism by Tania Modleski in *Feminism Without Women: Culture and Criticism in a "Postfeminist" Age.* Modleski warns of the political dangers, from a feminist perspective, of assuming a necessary link between the apparent compromising of masculinities and the lessening of patriarchy's hold.

My analysis of Chin's work serves, I hope, to echo the cautionary note that Modleski sounds and also to transpose it to another register. For the example of Chin should not only caution us against a blanket celebration of masochism as undermining dominant constructions of gender and sexuality, it should also make clear that, in negotiating dominant constructions of race and ethnicity, a hatred of the self is not the solution, but rather the problem—and that we should not, as Chin does, confuse the two.

WORKS CITED

Bersani, Leo. *Homos.* Cambridge: Harvard UP, 1995.

———. "Is the Rectum a Grave?" *October* (1987): 197–222.

Borch-Jacobsen, Mikkel. *The Freudian Subject.* Trans. Catherine Porter. 1982. Stanford: Stanford UP, 1988.

Butler, Judith. *Gender Trouble: Feminism and the Subversion of Identity.* New York: Routledge, 1990.

Cheung, King-Kok. "The Woman Warrior Versus the Chinaman Pacific: Must a Chinese American Critic Choose Between Feminism and Heroism?" *Conflicts in Feminism.* Ed. Marianne Hirsch and Evelyn Fox Keller. New York: Routledge, 1990. 234–51.

Chin, Frank. "Backtalk." *Counterpoint: Perspectives on Asian America.* Ed. Emma Gee. Los Angeles: Asian American Studies Center, U of California, 1976. 556–57.

———. *The Chinaman Pacific and Frisco R.R. Co.* Minneapolis: Coffee House, 1988.

———. "Confessions of a Chinatown Cowboy." *Bulletin of Concerned Asian Scholars* 4.3 (1972): 58–70.

———. "Riding the Rails with Chickencoop Slim." *Greenfield Review* 6.1–2 (1977): 80–89.

Chin, Frank, and Jeffrey Paul Chan. "Racist Love." *Seeing Through Shuck.* Ed. Richard Kostelanetz. New York: Ballantine, 1972. 65–79.

Chin, Frank, Jeffrey Paul Chan, Lawson Fusao Inada, and Shawn Hsu Wong, eds. *Aiiieeeee! An Anthology of Asian American Writers.* Washington, D.C.: Howard UP, 1974. New York: Mentor, 1991.

———, eds. *The Big Aiiieeeee! An Anthology of Chinese American and Japanese American Literature.* New York: Meridian, 1991.

Deleuze, Gilles. "Coldness and Cruelty." *Masochism.* Trans. Jean McNeil. 1967. New York: Zone, 1989.

Edelman, Lee. *Homographesis: Essays in Gay Literary and Cultural Theory.* New York: Routledge, 1994.

Fanon, Frantz. *Black Skin, White Masks.* 1952. Trans. Charles Lam Markmann. New York: Grove, 1982.

Fiedler, Leslie. "Come Back to the Raft Ag'in, Huck Honey!" Reprinted in Mark Twain. *Adventures of Huckleberry Finn: An Authoritative Text, Background and Sources, Criticism.* Ed. Sculley Bradley, Richmond Croom Beatty, E. Hudson Long, and Thomas Cooley. New York: Norton, 1977. 413–22.

Freud, Sigmund. *The Ego and the Id.* Ed. James Strachey. Trans. Joan Riviere. New York: Norton, 1962.

———. *Group Psychology and the Analysis of the Ego.* Ed. and trans. James Strachey. New York: Norton, 1959.

———. "Mourning and Melancholia." 1917. *General Psychological Theory:*

Papers on Metapsychology. Ed. Philip Rieff. New York: Collier, 1963. 164–79.

———. "On Narcissism: An Introduction." 1914. *General Psychological Theory: Papers on Metapsychology.* Ed. Philip Rieff. New York: Collier, 1963. 56–82.

———. *Three Essays on the Theory of Sexuality.* Ed. and trans. James Strachey. New York: Basic, 1975.

Fuss, Diana. *Identification Papers.* New York: Routledge, 1995.

Hall, Stuart. "Encoding/Decoding." *Culture, Media, Language: Working Papers in Cultural Studies, 1972–79.* Ed. Stuart Hall, D. Hobson, A. Lowe, and P. Willis. London: Hutchinson, 1980. 128–38.

Hwang, David Henry. *M. Butterfly.* New York: Plume, 1989.

Kim, Elaine H. *Asian American Literature: An Introduction to the Writings and Their Social Context.* Philadelphia: Temple, UP, 1982.

Kovel, Joel. *White Racism: A Psychohistory.* 1970. New York: Columbia, UP, 1984.

Melville, Herman. *Moby Dick.* 1851. Ed. Charles Feildelson Jr. New York: Macmillan, 1985.

Modleski, Tania. *Feminism Without Women: Culture and Criticism in a "Postfeminist" Age.* New York: Routledge, 1991.

Reik, Theodor. *Masochism in Modern Man.* Trans. Margaret H. Beigel and Gertrud M. Kurth. 1941. New York: Grove, 1957.

Sedgwick, Eve. *Between Men: English Literature and Male Homosocial Desire.* New York: Columbia UP, 1985.

Silverman, Kaja. *Male Subjectivity at the Margins.* New York: Routledge, 1992.

Soo Hoo, Michael. Review of *The Chinaman Pacific and Frisco R.R. Co.* by Frank Chin. *Amerasia Journal* 19.1 (1993): 175–76.

Williamson, Joel. *The Crucible of Race: Black-White Relations in the American South Since Emancipation.* New York: Oxford UP, 1984.

Wong, Sau-ling, *Reading Asian American Literature: From Necessity to Extravagance.* Princeton: Princeton UP, 1993.

20. The Unknowable and Sui Sin Far
The Epistemological Limits of "Oriental" Sexuality
Min Song

Sui Sin Far's "The Smuggling of Tie Co" (first published in 1900) literally and figuratively explores the borders that make an identity culturally legible.[1] In this story, Tie Co, a relatively successful Chinese "laundryman," abruptly solicits the help of the snakehead Jack Fabian to move from an unspecified Canadian town to New York City.[2] Halfway through their arduous nighttime crossing, Tie Co reveals a deep romantic attachment to Jack, saying, "I not like women, like men" (*Mrs. Spring Fragrance* 189).[3] As soon as Tie Co utters these words, he realizes that he and Jack are being tracked by the authorities. Impulsively he throws himself off a bridge to erase any evidence of their crime: "Tie Co's body was picked up the next day. Tie Co's body and yet not Tie Co, for Tie Co was a youth, and this body found with Tie Co's face and dressed in Tie Co's clothes was the body of a girl—a woman" (192). Although the discovery of a female body putatively dispels the homosexual meaning in Tie Co's romantic statement, the narrator refuses to concede epistemological clarity about his or her identity. The story ends with a description of Jack as he conducts a revitalized smuggling operation, reflecting deeply "over the mystery of Tie Co's life—and death" (193).

To understand the nature of this "mystery," we must carefully consider the narrator's depiction of Tie Co. He is described as "a nice-looking young Chinaman" (186), who, when talking to Jack, looks at him with a "faint smile on his small, delicate face" (187). When Jack asks in surprise why Tie Co wants to be taken across the Canadian/U.S. border, he refuses to explain. Jack leaves the discussion muttering, "There's no accounting for a Chinaman" (187). We are introduced to Tie Co not only as a "Chinaman," a fact that is repeated frequently in the text, but also as a member of "the laundry of Cheng Ting Lung & Co." (186). The prominent use of the abbreviation for company calls our attention to the name Tie *Co.* The repetition of this abbreviation highlights the corporate nature of Tie Co's identity, one that is defined explicitly by his race, without which he would lack any identity at all at this point in the story. As the word "corporate" suggests, Tie Co's individuality is subsumed by his place within a larger body of relationships. He is culturally legible only as a member of his racial group. His name literally points to the way his individuality is "tied" to a "company" identity.[4] These descriptions not only ascribe a lack of individualizing characteristics to Tie Co's physical appearance and mannerisms but also substitute this lack with stereotypes of the Chinese as silent, inscrutable, mysterious, cloistered, and effeminate.

Tie Co's individuality only begins to emerge during the trip. As Tie Co and Jack approach the bridge, Jack notices that Tie Co is having difficulty keeping up, and, looking "at the lad protectively," he wonders "in a careless way why this Chinaman seems to him so different from the others" (188). Jack detects something vulnerable about him that he wishes to protect, an intangible quality that differentiates Tie Co from his fellow "Chinamen." This quality leads the narrator to stress that Jack's "liking for Tie Co was real; he had known him for several years, and the lad's quick intelligence interested him." Jack deflects the uncomfortable slippage between his wish to protect Tie Co and his perception of Tie Co's growing individuality by asking if he wouldn't prefer to be back in China. When Tie Co preemptorily replies, "No," Jack begins to question him about his familial relations: "Haven't you got a nice little wife at home? . . . I hear you people marry very young." Jack's use of an ethnological form of inquiry ("you people") to draw attention away from the personal nature of their conversation is cut short by Tie Co's response: "I have no wife" (189). Jack proceeds to recontextualize their conversation into something less intimate, and more heterosexually acceptable, by exclaiming, "You confirmed bachelor!" But even this recontextualization is thwarted, since a "confirmed bachelor" can easily be a euphemism for homosexual. Not to be outdone by Jack's evasion, Tie Co remains adamant in his same-sex longing for Jack: "'I like you,' said Tie Co, his boyish voice sounding clear and sweet in the wet woods. 'I like you so much that I want go to New York, so you make fifty dollars. I no flend in New York'" (189). At this clear impasse, as Jack stumbles through a response to Tie Co's naked confession, Tie Co catches sight of men running around in the "gloom" (190). As the authorities close in, relieving Jack of the need to acknowledge the romantic exchange that has just passed between them, Tie Co commits suicide. Superficially, this act effectively erases his inchoate individuality.

Contrary to the early self-effacing depiction of Tie Co, however, Jack Fabian embodies an individualistic, masculine ideal right from the beginning. He is a kind of rogue, whose mercenary exterior hides a generous heart deserving to be cherished. What prevents this generous nature from becoming stereotypically feminine is his rough exterior. He walks "around with glowering looks," (186) because he has no one to take across the border. When Tie Co solicits his help, Jack gladly jumps at the offer of money, only asking half-heartedly why he wishes to be smuggled. Mercenary but hard-working, willingly adventurous if only given the chance, potentially dan-

gerous when idle and restless, Jack not only represents a gendered
but a class-based ideal as well. Jack fits into a Jacksonian tradition of
equating white masculinity with free (as opposed to slave) labor. In
this tradition, working-class men are often perceived as muscular, resentful, violent, and—given the opportunity and the right leadership—ready to unleash their pent-up energies to fulfill revolutionary or (depending on one's politics) self-destructive goals.[5] As
historian David Roediger argues, "Labor appeals often featured calls
to 'men'—a term that was sometimes used without 'working',
'trades', or 'journey' in front of it to refer to wage earners collectively. *Workingman* and *Workingmen's* consistently graced the titles of
labor groups and the mastheads of the labor press. One important
labor newspaper was simply titled *The Man*" (55). Such "appeals"
made it easier to think of "working class" as synonymous with "manli-
ness," both being ideals of sorts because they portend—like Jack's restless "glowering"—violence and heroism.

But because the white working class is traditionally thought to
have been antagonistic to Chinese immigration, it is surprising to
find these class markers attached to someone who "is said to have
'rushed over' to 'Uncle Sam' himself some five hundred Celestials"
(186).[6] Indeed, rather than highlighting some class-based prejudice, Jack's unpolished nature, and the careless way he deals with
other men, enables the narrator to characterize him as a natural
leader, who easily attracts loyalty and directs that loyalty toward
helping the Chinese. These facts are made plain through the narrator's physical description of Jack: "Uncommonly strong in person, tall and well built, with fine features and a pair of keen, steady
blue eyes, gifted with a sort of rough eloquence and of much personal fascination, it is no wonder that we fellows regard him as our
chief and are bound to follow where he leads. With Fabian at our
head we engage in the wildest adventures and find such places of
concealment for our human goods as none but those who take part
in a desperate business would dare to dream of" (184). The description pointedly contrasts Jack's white characteristics, construed as
"male," to the more effeminate descriptions of Tie Co. If Jack embodies some phallic ideal, with his stereotypically Aryan facial features, "rough eloquence," charismatic personality, resistance to do-
mestication, and physical strength, Tie Co represents the absence
of such masculine characteristics against which this ideal becomes
visible.[7] If Jack is figured as an ideal member of the working class
and of the white race, this is done by making Tie Co the opposite.

Tie Co's suicide, however, fails to eliminate the individualizing
qualities that appear after his body is dredged from the river. It is
only at this point in the story that the reader becomes acquainted

with the full extent of Tie Co's individuality. That Tie Co might have been a woman all along, a fact she would have had to keep secret from her fellow immigrants, suggests her lack of integration within the Chinese community system. That she travels toward New York City without knowing anyone there also shows her individuality. It was quite unusual for a Chinese immigrant to travel to the United States without having arranged to be greeted by a network of fellow immigrants and organizations—for a Chinese woman to undertake such a venture was virtually unthinkable. As a Chinese woman, then, Tie Co is as historically singular as one can possibly be.

The use of the first person plural for the narrator further problematizes the contrast between Jack's individualized and Tie Co's "corporatized" identities. The "we" voice is used explicitly on two occasions, and on both occasions it refers to other snakeheads. Jack may be the leader, but he is also a member of this group of smugglers, which makes him subject to some type of corporatized identity. He is not as unusual as the description above makes him appear. Because he fits so neatly into a familiar racial mold, his individuality is like a "shifter," a linguistic term referring to words like "I." As Richard Klein eloquently explains, "This device for expressing the irreducible particularity of my innermost self is universally available to every speaker and is thus the least particular thing in the world" (9). Similarly, Jack's individuality, which is not universally available but is nevertheless available to a large percentage of North America's population, represents an ideal that becomes more debased the more people attain it. Although individuality denotes something special about his character (white, working-class, male), the wide availability of these special qualities actually works to undermine his claims to individuality.

Hence, the dichotomy between Jack's singularity and Tie Co's self-effacement turns out to be anything but a *dichotomy*. Their relationship is much more dynamic and contrapuntal than the word implies. That Tie Co's individuality emerges only during extended contact with Jack, and that Jack's individuality actually begins to recede as a result, suggests how their identities are marked by what Edward Said calls "intertwined and overlapping histories" (*Culture and Imperialism* 18). Although their earlier relationship is characterized as one between the individual "white man" and the corporate "Chinese"—the former denoting free agency and the latter denoting subsumption to a group—their trip across the Canadian/U.S. border equalizes the discrepancies in the relationship. Jack becomes more dependent on his travel companion, while Tie Co becomes more independent of his earlier associations. Jack becomes less individualistic, while Tie Co becomes more so.

Sui Sin Far uses the tension created by this contrapuntal "dichotomy" to weave a tale of gendered Orientalism—a tale that presents the potential undermining of a white heterosexual masculine identity and its presumed right to lead as it comes into contact with alterity, before narratively ensuring its safety once more. Although the conclusion of this tale reasserts the status quo, suggesting its greater permanence, it also results in many notable alterations (not least of which is problematizing Tie Co's corporate identity). Perhaps the most famous exemplar of this tale is Rudyard Kipling's poem "The White Man's Burden," which sings praises to young white men who go overseas among "Oriental" peoples, at great risk to themselves, to perform the higher duties their ideals demand. Edward Said comments on "The White Man's Burden": "Behind the White Man's mask of amiable leadership there is always the express willingness to use force, to kill and be killed. What dignifies his mission is some sense of intellectual dedication; he is a White Man, but not for mere profit, since his 'chosen star' presumably sits far above earthly gain. . . . One became a White Man because one was a White Man; more important, 'drinking that cup,' living that unalterable destiny in 'the White Man's day,' left one little room for idle speculation on origins, causes, historical logic" (*Orientalism* 226–27). These assumptions are characteristic of Jack, as well, whom the "we" narrator calls "the boldest in deed, the cleverest in scheming, and the most successful in outwitting Government officers" (184).

Though Jack's antiestablishment stance is certainly an important facet of his character, the narrator explicitly states that this stance is motivated primarily by a desire for profit—"money is his object" (184). Jack himself reinforces this characterization by saying, "It is merely a matter of dollars and cents, though, of course, to a man of my strict principles, there is a certain pleasure to be derived from getting ahead of the Government. A poor devil does now and then like to take a little out of those millionaire concerns" (184–85). Hence, even while ascribing his motivation to a simple "matter of dollars and cents," Jack concedes a higher motivation for his risky behavior, one driven by a desire to defy a bloated form of authority. He is framed as a kind of working-class hero, one who views profit motive as a form of self-defense, while simultaneously looking forward to defending the underclass, the "poor devil," from the wealthy. Regardless of his identification with the disenfranchised, however, Jack nevertheless embodies the perfection of his race and carries with him the "ontological" assumption of his racial privilege and duty (Said, *Orientalism* 227). He willingly acknowledges the "burden" to perform death-defying acts of heroism for the needy, whether or not they want such aid.

It should be noted that Jack is unemployed at the beginning of the story because the Chinese have developed their own schemes for getting across the border. The first scheme involves "ingenious" lawyers who, for a large fee, procure a "father" who will swear to a "young Chinaman's" birth in the United States. The second scheme involves the "Chinese themselves," who, "assisted by some white men," manufacture "certificates establishing their right to cross the border" and, in this way, cross "over in large batches" (185–86). Both schemes emphasize the Chinese immigrant's agency in asserting, with only minimal help, his own "right to cross the border"— the first implicitly, through the involvement of a Chinese "father," and the second explicitly, through their own initiative. We might expect the narrator to embrace such examples of Chinese initiative, but instead we find that the narrator scorns them: "That sort of trick naturally spoiled our fellows' business, but we all know that 'Yankee sharper' games can hold good only for a short while; so we bided our time and waited in patience" (186). Even though these schemes involve the Chinese helping themselves, the narrator curiously erases their agency, preferring to see the "Yankee" behind the scheming. Perhaps this erasure makes it easier for the narrator to oppose Jack's desire for physical activity with the less masculine activity of manufacturing fake documents. The narrator's disdain for the latter suggests a greater interest in the heroism of Jack's behavior than in what he accomplishes. Even when Tie Co makes his business proposition, he does so to provide Jack with not only money but also an opportunity to exercise his (white) masculinity.

But although Said is certainly persuasive in arguing that the heroic acts committed by white men depend upon a circular assumption of white masculine superiority, he underemphasizes the extent to which contact with nonwhite, nonmasculine "Orientals" endangers the "White Man's" lofty sense of self. After all, the "White Man" in Kipling's poem suffers through great toil, recriminations from peers, hatred from underlings, and finally death. Said also underemphasizes how the disruptive nature of this contact with "Oriental" Otherness is frequently mitigated by the sacrifice of the "Oriental" subject, a happy alternative to the consequences Kipling adumbrates for his "White Man." Despite Kipling's brave posturing in "The White Man's Burden," one predictably finds this mitigating response in many of Kipling's short stories and in the stories by his numerous epigones.

Sacrifice plays an important role in the process by which a normative white, heterosexual, masculine identity maintains its status as the norm. Jack and the other smugglers like him reaffirm their right to rule by defying the law that upholds this right—because the law itself can also bar them from the kind of vigorous, endangering behavior that proves their worth. The existence of such legal barriers is especially noticeable in more settled regions, where the acts of heroism Kipling celebrates are usually less openly tolerated. Accompanied, as these acts are, by violence and greed, established communities understandably seek to foil such heroic, and destructive, impulses, either through prohibition or expulsion. But since their sense of superiority is so dependent upon the Other's inferiority, the sacrifice of the Other needs to be introduced, or the process of revitalization cannot take place and the norm loses its persuasive hold on the reader. Either the "White Man" needs to pay heavy consequences for helping the Other (because he has broken the law), or the Other must die as compensation for the "White Man's" aid.[8]

With the need for payment in mind, then, we might conclude that Tie Co is a cross-dresser, a woman who pretends to be a man to escape the restrictions placed upon her by society. She falls in love with Jack, whose idealized masculinity inevitably draws her out of her protective transvestism for a fleeting moment of frustrated romantic connection. When she realizes her life might endanger the freedom of her white, male beloved, she kills herself: "'Man come for you, I not here, man no hurt you.' And with the words he whirled like a flash over the rail. In another flash, Fabian was after him. But though a first-class swimmer, the white man's efforts were of no avail, and Tie Co was borne away from him by the swift current" (191). Her death becomes another occasion for Jack Fabian to perform an act of heroism at her expense. As in Puccini's *Madame Butterfly,* this sacrifice evokes the reader's sympathy for the loyal East Asian woman. But unlike in *Madame Butterfly,* the sympathy is channeled through Jack's desperation after failing to save Tie Co: "'I think he was out of his head,' replied Fabian. And he fully believed what he uttered" (191). The sacrifice can be seen simultaneously as a tribute to the sanctity of romantic devotion and as a white male's fantasy about the willing subservience of the racialized Other. As persuasive as this interpretation may be, however, I resist it for the moment—not because it is wrong but because other possibilities exist.

If Orientalism is partly the imaginative typification of the East and its subjects as a highly exoticized and subtly treacherous woman, one who tempts the "White Man" from his civilized but enervating way of life (as the previous interpretation suggests), the East's male subjects must also appear effeminate, their representations carrying connotations of both allure and danger. This opens up a whole constellation of sexual possibilities that depend upon the powerful connections between effemination, repulsion, desire, and a same-sex longing. This is true not only for male subjects who live in the East but also for "Oriental" male subjects and their children who live in the United States. These subjects can sometimes occupy an erotically charged cultural zone, where the notion of masculinity curves backward upon itself, confusing desire with identification, representation with ideology, and leading to a form of epistemological collapse. This zone is so charged and threatening that narratively such subjects are eventually sacrificed in order to return integrity to lost boundaries. These narratives reveal how "Oriental" sexuality cannot exist unmarked by the erotic associations perpetuated and disseminated by Orientalism. I am not arguing that such erotic associations exist outside of history; rather, they are intensely subject to causation and historical changes that influence and make use of the ideas governing the representation of individuals and their sexual affiliations.

Staying close to the narrative codes of gendered Orientalism, then, "The Smuggling of Tie Co" concludes with the authorities' release of Jack—Tie Co's sacrifice having erased all evidence of legal wrongdoing. Jack returns to his adventurer life, engaging in a reinvigorated smuggling operation. However, the body recovered from the river is a woman's body that cannot be positively identified as belonging to Tie Co. Recall the passage: "Tie Co's body was picked up the next day. Tie Co's body and yet not Tie Co, for Tie Co was a youth, and this body found with Tie Co's face and dressed in Tie Co's clothes was the body of a girl—a woman" (192). This is an unusually circular description of a relatively simple narrative event. The name "Tie Co" is repeated six times in this short passage, a numbing repetition that calls attention not only to the name but also to its correspondence to the body. The narrator takes great care to refrain from telling the reader whether the body belongs to Tie Co, emphasizing this unwillingness to tell with the phrase "not Tie Co." The narrator refuses not only to make a positive identification but also to reveal much about the body itself, explaining only that it belongs to either a "girl" or a "woman." Which is it? How prominent are the secondary sexual characteristics? This passage severs the name from the body to such an extent that it even becomes difficult to determine the provenance of the name "Tie Co"; after all, it could be a pseudonym picked up to hide his or her identity.

Even while asserting an inability to determine the relationship between the name and the body, the narrator repeats the name obsessively. We might consider this obsessive repetition an attempt at "hailing," what Louis Althusser believes to be the constitutive moment for the subject by an ever pervasive ideology: "Experience shows that the practical telecommunication of hailings is such that they hardly ever miss their man: verbal call or whistle, the one hailed always recognizes that it is really him who is being hailed" (174). In response to this famous discussion on the relationship between subjects and their subordination to ideology, Terry Eagleton argues that "there is no reason why we should always accept society's identification of us as this particular sort of subject. . . . Someone may be a mother, Methodist, houseworker and trade unionist all at the same time, and there is no reason to assume that these various forms of insertion into ideology will be mutually harmonious" (145). Eagleton makes an important point: there is no particular reason why the name "Tie Co" should have any sway over the person who responded to its call at one time. The very fabricated nature of the name (its disconnection from the body that it supposedly somehow describes and its useless materiality once the subject it attached itself to is dead) leads us to consider the extreme conventionality of "hailing" as a process of identification, a means of knowing a subject, a way of "interpellating" (as Althusser terms it) a subjectivity.

One does not want to gloss over the actual influences that certain forms of ideological hailing have on our lives, hailings that label us and demand that we respond to the label. For example, just as the terms used to denote racial difference impact the way we live our lives, so do the terms "heterosexual" and "homosexual." When people call us "gay" or "straight," they expect us to respond to these labels as if they signify something essential about us. In a way, they do: they signify, in shorthand, whether or not we tend to like men or women, opposite-sex or same-sex partners, licit love objects or illicit love objects (as regulated by compulsory heterosexuality). We are expected, even forced, to respond to one hailing or the other. But even with this example in mind, the repetition of the name "Tie Co" in the previous passage calls our attention to the artificiality of the name's existence, to its failure to name anything concrete, to the vanity of any ideological conception that posits its sway over individual lives "too monistically." This way of seeing, according to Eagleton, passes "over discrepant, contradictory ways in which subjects may be ideologically accosted . . . by discourses which themselves form no obvious cohesive unity" (154). The free-floating nature of the name "Tie Co" should warn us to beware of this false way of seeing. It is a way of envisioning ideology as the source of unitary identities unhinged or uncontradicted by other ideological factors, such as the way "gay" or "straight" fails to identify lesbians or the way these binary terms fail to identify those who refuse to allow their desires to be inhibited by such conventional restrictions.

The ontological status of the body also raises questions about the boundaries that make individual racial and sexual identities legible. The narrator asserts that the body is female but does not explain exactly how this claim is made. Who identifies the body as being Tie Co's? Neither the Canadian nor the American authorities would have been able to do so. The only person who could have was Jack, who would not have done so, because it would have incriminated him. There is no evidence of any Chinese characters at hand who could have identified the body. What criteria were used in determining the sex of the body? Did the people who found the body do a genital inspection, or did they identify the sex by looking only at secondary sexual traits? That the narrator could not decide whether the body belonged to a "girl" or a "woman" indicates that secondary sexual traits, such as breasts, were probably underdeveloped, so the body could just as easily have belonged to a boy. Even when the authorities drag Jack out of the river after a failed attempt to save Tie Co's life, they call Tie Co a "boy" (192). Even so, calling Tie Co a "boy" may have been like calling a black man "boy"—a language practice used to keep racial minorities "in their place," to remind them of the social hierarchy between the races. In a society that equates whiteness and male prerogative with social agency, suffrage, and other political power, it is possible that a person lacking these characteristics because of race would also fail to appear male, even at the most intimate physical level. If a genital inspection was conducted and no penis was discovered, perhaps the inability to find proof of Chinese masculinity equaled a literalized inability to see Chinese men as men in a society that effeminizes them. Race, filtered through Orientalist stereotypes, can be so overdetermining that it can supersede gendered identities. The case of David Henry Hwang's *M. Butterfly* comes immediately to mind.[9]

This gender confusion extends to the narrator's description of Tie Co's behavior. After the body is "picked-up" from the river's edge, the narrator immediately goes on to explain, "Nobody in the laundry of Cheng Ting Lung & Co.—no Chinaman in Canada or New York—could explain the mystery. Tie Co had come out of Canada with a number of other youths. Though not very strong he had always been a good worker and 'very smart.' He had been quiet and reserved among his own countrymen; had refused to smoke tobacco or opium, and had been a regular attendant at Sunday schools and a great favorite with Mission ladies" (192). In this passage, the signifier "Tie Co" is attached to the description of a young man with suspiciously feminine characteristics: he is weak, "quiet," vice-free, and religious. Possession of these characteristics undermines the story's previous claim that Tie Co is a Chinese American man. But, even here, the layers of cultural representation insisting upon the Chinese as "wily," inscrutable, feminine, "boyish," and ageless make the gendered markers harder to decode.

We can find examples of such cultural representations, carried to their logical gender-collapsing extreme, throughout the nineteenth century. In 1854, Charles Pickering published *The Races of Man: And Their Geographical Distribution,* an early attempt to catalogue racial differences. In the chapter entitled "The Mongolian Race"[10] he points out, "I have thought to distinguish in the Mongolian race physical traits and a style of feature, at variance in some respects with those of the remaining series of races. One of these peculiarities consists in the occurrence of a feminine aspect in both sexes. In the absence of any striking difference in stature or dress, I have often seen the stranger at a loss to distinguish *men from women*; a difficulty not depending altogether on the absence of beard, and which, so far as my observation extends, does not take place in the other races" (6, emphasis mine). Pickering, in calling attention to the difficulty of differentiating "Mongolian" men from women, insists twice in this short passage that the difficulty is unique to the race. His redundant concern with the singularity of this collapse hints at the sexual confusion caused by an inability to differentiate between genders.

Recent work by gay and lesbian critics has shown how homosexuality becomes detectable as an aberration—something that stands out from the norm and thus invites commentary, ridicule, and demands for conformity. As Diana Fuss puts it, "Homosexuality constitutes . . . an over-presence, an excess, a surplus, or an overabundance" (61).[11] What makes Pickering's observations interesting, then, is the way the collapse of gendered differences among "Mongolians" calls attention to itself as a unique occurrence, one not found in other racial groups. This collapse is a quality that is constituted exactly as an "excess" or "surplus" in Pickering's text. Noticeably, the wording of the collapse does not suggest a mere confusion between men *and* women but an inability "to distinguish men *from* women." In this passage, Pickering is indicating the lack of legible masculinity among a group of men who, as a result, appear like women. This lack gains positive meaning as an aberration among racial norms—an aberration that furthermore attracts excess commentary. The gender confusion suggested by Pickering's observations does not result in a desexualized androgyny; rather, the confusion highlights a general feminization of the Chinese as an Oriental race, which raises the same kind of anxiety and sexual frisson that effeminate gay men raise in our own culture.

Richard Fung begins his influential essay "Looking for My Penis:

The Eroticized Asian in Gay Video Porn" (see Chapter 7) by discussing the controversial figure of Philippe Rushton, whose cur-
rent-day work on racial differences follows on Pickering's heel. According to Fung, Rushton's interests have led him to posit "that
degree of 'sexuality'—interpreted as penis and vagina size, frequency of intercourse, buttock and lip size—correlates positively
with criminality and sociopathic behavior and inversely with intelligence, health and longevity. Rushton sees race as *the* determining
factor and places East Asians (Rushton uses the word *Orientals*) on
one end of the spectrum and blacks on the other." If Fung is fair in
his characterization of Rushton's arguments, we need to view Rushton as a step backward from Pickering's 1854 cataloguing of racial
differences. Pickering presents his ideas as observations that implicitly foreground the subjective nature of the racial differences he
perceives; Rushton attempts to appropriate the authority of scientific methodology, of his profession (psychology), and of his academic standing (at the University of Western Ontario) to make his
claims appear objective. Regardless of these differences, however,
what immediately strikes me when comparing Pickering with Rushton is the continuity of their racial characterizations. Though they
are writing under very different historical circumstances, they both
perceive the "Oriental" as somehow androgynous—in the strict
sense of lacking sexual and gendered differences.

Fung articulates the persistence of these associations by pointing
out how Rushton's schemata oversexualizes black people and un-
dersexualizes Asians. He writes, "So whereas, as Fanon tells us, 'the
Negro is eclipsed. He is turned into a penis. He *is* a penis,'[12] the
Asian man is defined by a striking absence down there. And if Asian
men have no sexuality, how can we have homosexuality?" He adds
two important caveats to this argument. First he posits the existence
of subtle differences between the representation of Asian racial
groups, both in terms of general region (say, between Near East and
Far East) and in terms of national variation (say, between Japanese
and Filipino). Second he argues that representations of East Asian
women and men are different. The former are frequently portrayed
as sexually compliant and expendable, and the latter are alternately
depicted as "egghead/wimp" and "kung fu master/ninja/samurai."
In either case, the Asian male remains sexless. Though I agree
wholeheartedly with Fung's distinction between representations of
East Asian men and women, I would argue that it is still important
to acknowledge the existence, in popular representations, of gender confusion that *explicitly retains a sexual charge*. These confusing
moments often flatten out the sexual differences between Asian
men and women and ignore the national and regional nuances that

Fung finds in representations of Asian (non)sexuality, while keeping open sexual possibilities.

The very presence of Asian men in gay video porn, even in pitifully small numbers, suggests that they are not merely ciphers, placeholders who signify an absence of sexuality. Rather, they are a source of sexual excitement that stems from the fact that they are simultaneously male and feminine—they are, in other words, men who can, like women, be reminded of an inferior social position. As Fung relates, "Released from the social constraints against expressing overt racism in public, the intimacy of sex can provide my (non-Asian) partner an opening for letting me know my place—sometimes literally, as when, after we come, he turns over and asks where I come from" (Chapter 7). Within the confines of such power dynamics, the representation of an Oriental masculinity becomes both feminized and queer. Just as lesbians are frequently invisible in North American culture, so are the sexual relationships between such "Orientals," whether they are heterosexual, homosexual, or bisexual. Thus, this special kind of Oriental sexuality appears most saliently in interracial romances, with confusing results. When such Orientalist representations involve relations between the two men—almost exclusively between Asian and white—we are faced with the potential collapse, or at least rethinking, of our homosexual and heterosexual labels for sexuality *tout court*. I am not arguing for the abolition of these labels—especially considering the importance of the term "homosexuality" in naming same-gender sexuality as a viable sexual option—but I do wish to stress how these labels can preclude the naming of other forms of sexuality, especially across racial boundaries.

Against the backdrop of such epistemological constraints, which seek to delimit sexual possibilities through restrictive labels, it seems reasonable to argue that the narrator's reluctance to name the body in "The Smuggling of Tie Co" operates within the same economy of thought that leads the law to designate sodomy frequently as "a crime without a name." As Lee Edelman points out, this unwillingness to name is related to a desire to defer having to close off sexual possibilities: "In our heterogeneous and often contradictory mythology of homosexuality, 'the love that dare not speak its name' was frequently designated as the crime *inter Christianos non nominandum*, and it was so designated not only because it was conceived as something lurid, shameful, and repellent, but also because it was, and is, conceived simultaneously as something so attractive that even to name or represent it is to risk the possibility of tempting some innocent into a fate too horrible—or too seductive—to imagine" (87). If sodomy is the crime without a name, its very enunciation has the potential both to horrify and to entice; this is a partic-

ularly apt point in relation to Tie Co's body, which is sacrificed just
at the moment on the bridge when Tie Co makes his romantic desire for Jack clear. Tie Co cannot be more explicit about his feelings
without actually naming them, without saying exactly what he desires of Jack. Metaphorically, Tie Co's sacrifice and the resulting
recovery of a nameless body stands in appropriately both for the desire to commit a "crime without a name" and for an inability to
name that desire, an inability to enunciate "the love that dare not
speak its name."

Jack and the narrator are both repelled and tantalized by the sexual possibilities the illegible body creates. "Fabian is now very busy,"
the story concludes. "There are lots of boys taking his helping hand
over the border, but none of them are like Tie Co; and sometimes,
between whiles, Fabian finds himself pondering long and earnestly
over the mystery of Tie Co's life—and death" (192–93). Again, the
narrator ascribes an intangible quality to Tie Co, which makes him
(or her) different from the other "boys." This quality might refer to
Tie Co's gendered identity—the fact that she is, according to the authorities, a biological female, which makes her subtly different from
her Chinese peers—but the narrator's reluctance to present the
emotional connection between Jack and Tie Co as definitively *hetero*-
sexual is clear. We can trace this reluctance to decide on the body's
sexual identity as an unwillingness to give up the sexual possibilities
represented by a body without a name. Because the racialized body
is not quite male, the attraction is not quite homo- or heteroerotic.

But why does racial identity remain fixed, especially when gendered and sexual meanings become unanchored? We can begin to
address this question by thinking about the contrast between Tie
Co's corporatized racial identity, where individual markers are ultimately subsumed into a group meaning, and Jack's normative
racial identity, where membership in the group is paradoxically defined through an individualistic ideal. Before it reasserts this rigid
contrast, "The Smuggling of Tie Co" begins to question the differences between Tie Co and Jack, a process that culminates in Tie
Co's statement of his own sexual desires. Racial identity at this high
contrapuntal moment becomes more problematic as the distinctions between Tie Co and Jack begin to blur: "The second day they
left their horse at a farmhouse, where Fabian would call for it on his
return trip, crossed a river in a rowboat before the sun was up, and
plunged into a wood in which they would remain till evening. It was
raining, but through mud and wind and rain they trudged slowly
and heavily" (188). This is the only description of the border between Canada and the United States in the story. As the two cross
this border, they are plunged into a kind of perpetual dusk. The

crossing of borders literally obscures the boundaries that separate their individual subjectivities from one another. They cross the river at the darkest moment demarcating night and morning; the shade of the trees darkens their movements and faces; the foliage further conceals their discernible traits; and the weather makes it virtually impossible for any observer to distinguish the differences between the two.

Their border crossing textually blurs the differences between man and woman, heterosexual and homosexual, life and death, as it blurs the distinction between two nations already uncomfortably similar in history and language. "Blur," in this context, means not a complete erasure of differences but increased difficulty in plotting the lines that separate them. At this point in the story, Jack makes a heartfelt speech to Tie Co:

> Look here, Tie Co, . . . I won't have you do this for my sake. You have been very foolish, and I don't care for your fifty dollars. I do not need it half as much as you do. Good God! how ashamed you make me feel—I who have blown in my thousands in idle pleasures cannot take the little you have slaved for. We are in New York State now. When we get out of this wood we will have to walk over a bridge which crosses a river. On the other side, not far from where we cross, there is a railway station. Instead of buying you a ticket for the city of New York I shall take train [*sic*] with you for Toronto. (190)

Tie Co inadvertently switches positions with Jack. Instead of being the object of his heroism, whose helplessness must be alleviated through Jack's aid, Tie Co has taken up Jack's burden of unemployment and potential arrest by putting himself at risk. Seen from this perspective, Tie Co's sacrifice becomes an act of racial usurpation, where he displays heroism from the Other's sake, instead of merely being the Other whom Jack must save. If the tale of gendered Orientalism requires some form of sacrifice, it is important to keep in mind that the sacrifice of the Other enables the "White Man" to survive unpunished for his actions and, by detracting from his heroic stance, diffuses the vitalization he has sought through these actions.

The uncertainty of Tie Co's gender is made explicitly only after his act of self-effacement—as if the fact that Tie Co comes close to becoming individualized and having his (or her) extant desires find expression returns to haunt Jack, and the reader, through the fabrication of a sexual mystery. Tie Co's death reestablishes the racial difference between Chinese and white, corporate and individual, foreign and normal, while propelling the gender and sexual orientation of the body to become ludic. Because the sacrifice fixes Tie Co's racial identity at the same time it fixes Jack's, racial identity can act as a kind of fulcrum upon which the other identities teeter—never stabilizing in one position, never having to foreclose one possibility for another, and hence never having to disavow pleasures promised by any one choice. If this arrangement does not have the potential to satisfy, for both Jack and the reader, neither does it have the ability to disappoint or lead to regret. To the end of the story, the sexual possibilities remain open and perilously inviting, like a ghostly reminder—both pleasurable and frustrating—of the price paid for Jack's independence. The mystery reminds him of the sacrifice he, himself, should have made.

Although it is possible, then, to understand why the instability of the body's meaning might resonate convincingly for Jack, it is puzzling that Tie Co's disguise succeeds so well among the other Chinese immigrants. Even after the body is found and identified, the other Chinese men cling to the idea that Tie Co's identity is still a "mystery." They refuse to believe the physical evidence placed before them, clinging to this "mystery," which allows them to deny the possibility that Tie Co successfully disguised herself as a man in their midst. By denying their failure, they do not have to admit the success of the disguise. To admit this success might also call into question their own gendered identities, which—just as for white men—depend upon the immediate visibility of sexual difference.

The obfuscation of such difference leads them to the difficult question What makes them men? If gender is socially constructed, isn't masculinity—in the male-dominated North American society of the time—equal to social agency, some political equality (at least with fellow men), and a sense of belonging to a community of other men? For Tie Co to have entered into such a masculinist society unquestioned would foreground the disenfranchisement of the Chinese man from the larger society's normative identity. Feminization as a process of making one appear more like a woman is not in itself a negative process that should be bemoaned as some kind of loss or as a symbol of disempowerment. But when feminization is made the rationale for, and not the symptom of, greater political marginalization, then it becomes a form of degradation and a process to be combated. Because it is not always easy to tell the difference between rationale and symptom, we might, in this case, find a more appropriate name for the process than "feminization."

NOTES

Acknowledgments: This essay is excerpted from a dissertation project. An earlier version was presented at the 1996 meeting of the Association for Asian American Studies in Washington, D.C. I thank David L. Eng and, especially, Emma Teng.

1. Sui Sin Far is the pseudonym of Edith Maude Eaton, one of the first Chinese American writers to produce sympathetic stories about Chinese Americans and American Chinatowns. See Annette White-Parks's literary biography, *Sui Sin Far/Edith Eaton*.

2. "Snakehead" is a term for smugglers who transport immigrants illegally from one country into another. Most frequently, the term refers to smugglers involved in the traffic of Chinese illegals. The term's negative connotation highlights the unsavory nature of the profession as it is practiced today and as it was undoubtedly practiced in the time of Jack Fabian. See Kwong 256–68.

3. All references to "The Smuggling of Tie Co" are from Sui San Far's *Mrs. Spring Fragrance*.

4. Sui Sin Far was well aware of the literal meaning of names, as is clearly demonstrated by her choice of pseudonym. Literary scholars have been fascinated by the possible design behind this name. Amy Ling suggests that "Sui Sin Far" loosely translated might mean "water fragrant flower" or narcissus, a flower with significant thematic implications for many of the stories in her collection. More commonly known at the time as Chinese lilies, "these small bulbs . . . needed only as shallow bowl of water and rewarded little effort with a cluster of highly performed, modest white flowers, becoming in the dead of winter a symbol of the persistence of life and beauty" (Ling 41).

Elizabeth Ammons warns that "Sui Sin Far" might not be a translation of any specific Chinese phrase; it may be an Anglo-European wordplay. Ammons traces the possible meaning of the name to the English words "sin" and "far" and to the Latin *sui,* which means "of herself": "The phrase might read 'Of sin far herself'. . . . Is the name her first way of stating her subject as an artist, her audacity as a woman of Chinese ancestry in the west to sin far from what is expected of her, to break the commandment of silence imposed upon her as an Asian woman?" (120).

More recently, White-Parks notes that in the earliest published stories the pseudonym was spelled "Sui Seen Far," with "Sui" being a possible family pet name (xvi). The English meaning here makes an explicit claim about Sui Sin Far's authority to speak for other Chinese Americans. Because she has literally "seen far," she is capable of sharing the insights her unique perspective allows.

5. These characteristics could also, but did not, describe male slaves, because the notion of slavery already suggested a capitulation to the wrong kind of leadership.

6. See especially Alexander Saxton's *The Indispensable Enemy,* still one of the most thorough explorations of the tension between the white working class and Chinese immigrants in the nineteenth century.

7. The word "Aryan," which was typically used at the time to describe white people, usually had a positive connotation; it acquired its negative connotations with the rise of Nazism in the mid–twentieth century.

8. In his readings of novels by Joan Didion, Robert Stone, Don

DeLillo, and Thomas Pynchon, John McClure appears to have identified an updated version of what I have called gendered Orientalism and
its need for sacrifices.

9. *M. Butterfly* is Hwang's theatrical adaptation of a love affair between a French diplomat and a Chinese opera star. The male diplomat
claims he was unaware throughout the affair that the performer, who
played a woman on stage, was not, in fact, a woman—even though they
had sex. Compare Moy 115–29 and Eng 131–52.

10. Pickering includes the Chinese and Native Americans under this
heading but separates the Japanese, Southeast Asians, and Pacific Islanders into a category called "Malayan." In order to understand the logic
behind this separation, we must keep in mind that Pickering's is one of
the earliest scientific attempts to measure racial difference. The approach
described "physical differences verbally in terms of facial angles, head
shape, facial configuration, and skin coloring," which led to a great deal
of confusion. Only after such works as Samuel Morton's *Crania Americana*—which measured skull sizes comparatively—were accepted as more
scientifically valid, did Pickering's approach die out (Miller 155; compare
Stanton 90–112). The fact that Pickering published his book after *Crania
Americana* suggests the coexistence, perhaps mutuality, of both approaches to the nineteenth-century scientific study of races. Although
neither approach is considered scientifically valid today, some psychologists continue to behave as if they are. See Gould 50–68.

11. Fuss goes on to show how the logic of "over-presence" is played
out in Freud's understanding of homosexuality among women: "Homosexuality may be 'less glaring' in women than in men, but it is still
'glaring' (lärmend). Freud's choice of the word lärmend (riotous,
noisy, unruly) to describe homosexuality insinuates that the blindness
issues from homosexuality in women and psychoanalysis has 'neglected'
it not because homosexuality is invisible but because, apparently, it is
too visible, too audible, too present" (61).

12. Fung (Chapter 7) quotes Fanon (120).

WORKS CITED

Althusser, Louis. *Lenin and Philosophy and Other Essays.* Trans. Ben Brew-
    ster. London: Monthly Review, 1971.
Ammons, Elizabeth. *Conflicting Stories: American Women Writers at the Turn
    into the Twentieth Century.* Oxford: Oxford UP, 1991.
Eagleton, Terry. *Ideology: An Introduction.* New York: Verso, 1991.
Edelman, Lee. *Homographesis: Essays in Gay Literary and Cultural Theory.*
    New York: Routledge, 1994.
Eng, David L. "In the Shadow of a Diva: Committing Homosexuality in
    David Henry Hwang's *M. Butterfly.*" *Asian American Sexualities: Dimen-
    sions of the Gay and Lesbian Experience.* Ed. Russell Leong. New York:
    Routledge, 1996. 131–52.
Fanon, Frantz. *Black Skin, White Masks.* London: Paladin, 1967.

Fuss, Diana. *Identification Papers*. New York: Routledge, 1995.

Gould, Stephen Jay. *The Mismeasure of Man*. New York: Norton, 1981.

Hwang, David Henry. *M. Butterfly*. New York: Plume, 1989.

Kipling, Rudyard. "White Man's Burden." *Rudyard Kipling's Verse: Definitive Version*. New York: Doubleday, 1940. 321–22.

Klein, Richard. *Cigarettes Are Sublime*. Durham: Duke UP, 1993.

Kwong, Peter. "New York Is Not Hong Kong: The Little Hong Kong That Never Was." *Reluctant Exiles? Migration from Hong Kong and the New Overseas Chinese*. Ed. Ronald Skeldon. Armok, N.Y.: Sharpe, 1994. 256–68.

Ling, Amy. *Between Worlds: Women Writers of Chinese Ancestry*. New York: Pergamon, 1990.

McClure, John. *Late Imperial Romance*. New York: Verso, 1994.

Miller, Stuart. *The Unwelcome Immigrant: The American Image of the Chinese, 1785–1882*. Berkeley and Los Angeles: U of California P, 1969.

Morton, Samuel. *Crania Americana*. Philadelphia: N.p., 1839.

Moy, James. *Marginal Sights: Staging the Chinese in America*. Iowa City: U of Iowa P, 1993.

Pickering, Charles. *The Races of Man: And Their Geographical Distribution*. London: Bohn, 1854.

Puccini, Giacomo. *Madame Butterfly*. New York: Riverrun, 1984.

Roediger, David. *Wages of Whiteness: Race and the Making of the American Working Class*. New York: Verso, 1991.

Said, Edward. *Culture and Imperialism*. New York: Knopf, 1993.

———. *Orientalism*. New York: Vintage, 1978.

Saxton, Alexander. *The Indispensable Enemy: Labor and the Anti-Chinese Movement in California*. Berkeley and Los Angeles: U of California P, 1971.

Stanton, William. *The Leopard's Spots: Scientific Attitudes Toward Race in America 1815–59*. Chicago: U of Chicago P, 1960.

Sui Sin Far. *Mrs. Spring Fragrance*. 1900. Chicago: McClurg, 1912.

———. *Mrs. Spring Fragrance and Other Writings*. Ed. Amy Ling and Annette White-Parks. Chicago: U of Illinois P, 1995.

White-Parks, Annette. *Sui Sin Far/Edith Eaton: A Literary Biography*. Urbana: U of Illinois P, 1995.

21. Webs of Betrayal, Webs of Blessings
You-Leng Leroy Lim

The following is a tale of the stories I learned from my family, culture, and religion, stories that both blessed and wounded me. It is a story about how I am *making a story* of my life. Stories give context and content, and the meaning that is extracted from the retelling becomes, in turn, *the real story*. From this, we make a set of new decisions, and we are off on a whole new path—writing the second chapter. I am aware, however, that not all the meaning that we extract from the retelling necessarily leads us to life-giving journeys of transformation. When the Nazis recast the Versailles Peace Treaty as a stab in the back orchestrated by Jews, that was an example of a retelling and meaning making (racial purity) that led to the annihilation of millions of Jews, homosexuals, and social outcasts. In America the retelling of World War II victories conceals the story of the internment of Japanese Americans. When the process of retelling serves to mask or obscure dimensions of the story, we begin a journey of incoherence, losing touch with our common human need to explore life's multiple layers of meaning and being. What becomes important then is the defense of our particular version of the story, making fundamentalism the only meaningful act that remains.

What is family? Family is the story that a few people, coming together, have decided to make as a group. Unfortunately, in America today, the fundamentalist version of family allows for only one story: a male and a female coming together to produce children. This version, a rather curious form of biological reductionism, betrays the sex obsession of its fundamentalist authors.

I learned from my paternal grandmother that families go beyond mere reproduction. Born during the last years of the Qing Dynasty in Fukien Province, China, Granny had had her feet bound. She never knew her poverty-stricken parents, for they had sold her to my great-grandmother to be nursed. Together, they fled the poverty of a collapsing dynasty by emigrating to Southeast Asia. As a young girl, my grandmother bought a baby boy on the streets of Singapore. Retelling the story, she said, "I wanted to hold and feed him." He became my *ku kong*, or granduncle. When I asked her in a taped interview who her real mother was, she insisted that Great-grandgranny was her real mother, explaining, "She fed me her milk

A slightly revised version of the essay was published in *Our Families, Our Values: Snapshots of Queer Kinship,* ed. Robert Goss and Amy Adams Squire Strongheart (Binghamton, N.Y.: Harrington Park Press, 1997).

and her saliva.[1] Who birthed me is another matter." I learned from her that a family is not about biology alone—especially since her own was a biological fiction—but about intent, care, and choice. Families are stories about our (mis)adventures in relationships.

Family Name
It was a cold New England winter on the eve of the Chinese Year of the Dog. Gathered around me were four friends whom I had invited to be part of my naming ritual.

For some years my parents had been telling me to get rid of my Chinese name, Leng, which means "dragon." My premature birth prevented my parents from consulting the older relatives for a Chinese name, so they named me after my birth year, the Year of the Dragon. With its mythical and imperial significance, the dragon is an auspicious Chinese figure. (The phrase "children of the dragon" is used to mean Chinese people.) When my parents became fundamentalist Charismatic Christians—ironically, as a result of my having become a Christian a few years earlier—they came to believe that the dragon was synonymous with the devil. My argument that the dragon in the Bible is a Hellenistic dragon and therefore a different entity from the Chinese dragon did not persuade them otherwise.

To be urged to change one's name, especially by the parents who bestowed the name, is to be repudiated. But my parents assured me they were doing it out of love, as if love could sufficiently justify the denunciation. Still, the use of love to justify abuse is no surprise, since the need to share "Gospel love" with nonbelievers to justify racial extermination, colonization, and forced conversions has been a part of the Christian tradition. Such love is about power rather than shared life. Refusing to acknowledge their own abusive use of love, fundamentalist Christians have projected their own duplicity onto homosexuals, claiming that homosexual love, even though it is love, does not make homosexuality right. It might be truer to say that fundamentalist Christian "love," while passionate, is neither right nor loving but instead quite cruel and deluding. But this fact must be denied. Nor surprisingly, the socially designated pariah (the homo in this case) carries the blame for the crimes commented by the accusers. Similarly, parents who reject their children may project responsibility onto the children, accusing them, instead, of being unfilial.

In contrast, the fullness of the Biblical tradition tells a story of love that always respects the integrity of those being loved. The Jewish story is of a frustrated God who demands love and obedience from Israel on threat of punishment. Yet in this story, God learns that to compel love is to destroy the free will of humanity that God has created. Thus, Israel's disobedience is met again and again by divine forgiveness rather than by annihilation. The Christian tradition holds that God becomes human and walks the path of love, risking betrayal and death to show that true love must embrace the integrity of those being loved, even if they are one's enemies. This Christian love story shows that love converts by hospitality not hostility. In the early years of this church community, Christian converts recognized themselves as part of a universal family including slave and nonslave, gentile and Jew, and anyone else who would join. God was Father to all of humanity's brothers and sisters. The rite of baptism joined disparate peoples into community, thus repudiating biological familial ties as the sole marker of legitimate human bonding. The redefinition of family, which was contrary to the norms of the dominant Roman society, caused Christians to be labeled as perverts. Yet the early church was simply taking the word of Jesus, who said, "Who is my mother and brother and sister, but the one who does the will of God" (Matt. 12:48–50). America's conservative right wing would consider the Biblical Jesus a nemesis to their family values.

My parents' subconscious message in the name change was not lost on me: "There is a part of you that we have given you that we think is completely evil, and we want to absolve ourselves of it." Dragon = gay = devil. Eventually, after more than a decade in the United States, I returned to Singapore to come out to them. Having set aside a year from Harvard to accompany them through the process, I was met by prayers, the laying on of hands, and the casting out of demons. One night, I found myself sleepless, my body racked by incredible pain. At bedtime, they had asked if they could pray for me "because we love you"—how can a child say no to that? As they prayed for my healing, I was gripped by a fear unlike any I had felt since my teenage evangelical Christian days. I thought, "What if my homosexuality is a curse from the devil?" As I felt myself disintegrating, five years of gay activism and months of therapy went down the drain. I was fourteen again, fearing my passions and hoping that Father God or Mother Church would rescue me. Now my previously estranged parents had finally come to the rescue, and we could all be a happy family! And then a thought came to me: "You are thirty, not fourteen! The pain is not the devil—it's Mom and Dad. You are being possessed by their shit." Getting out of bed, I lit my sage stick and started cleansing my room. "Take back your shame, guilt, and pain. I no longer carry your load or accept your prayers. May everything coming from you return to you." I collapsed onto my bed, sobbing and exhausted. I had taken the first step toward divorcing my parents—at least the Parent in my psyche and soul. The somatic pains disappeared, replaced by a different pain—a heartache that comes with the freedom of acknowledging loss.

Either the Devouring Parent figure (represented by church, culture, Bible, parents, and so on) dies or else we commit suicide, as so many gay, lesbian, bisexual, and transgendered youth have. When the psychic Parent dies, you are not orphaned. You grow up and make your own family.

My friends gathered. We read a passage from the Bible about how Jacob wrestled with the angel of God. The angel blessed Jacob with the new name Israel, but not before maiming his hip. My friends now named me, giving me many names that describe my relationship to them, names that showed me who I had become. Each new name they gave me awakened a part of me, tying different narratives and pathways, and opened my eyes so that I could see myself more fully. Then it was my turn to reclaim "Leng" for myself. I symbolically laid to rest "Leroy," my public name for thirty years, by putting a cross that I had worn since childhood into a box. Out of that box I pulled a dragon medallion that a friend had given me years before but that I had been too ashamed to wear. Then I renewed my baptismal vows and, in the confession of my faith, I regrounded myself in the love of my God. Taking a blade, I cut a cross over my heart. With my blood, I wrote "Dragon" in Chinese characters on a piece of paper and burned it. I stirred the ashes into a bowl of wine and drank the mixture. Years ago, my paternal grandmother had brought home blessed paper from the temples and burned it, dissolving the ashes in water for me to drink, so that I would be protected from evil spirits. Through a similar act, I was reclaiming the blessings of my pagan ancestors, which I had mistakenly renounced in my baptism years before. By marking my body and drinking my own life, I took into myself all the pain—PAIN—and wonder of my life. I felt the unfelt sorrows of the years, and I felt a power surging from within, awakened by the embodied love of God, as found in my family of friends. We ended the morning with a Eucharist celebrated by an Episcopal priest friend. Then we adjourned for a Boston dim sum to celebrate the coming New Year.

To reclaim my name was to recognize a basic goodness that had come to me at birth and that had been miraculously bestowed upon me by my parents, however unconscious their intentions might have been. Yet many of us queer folks, in coming out to our parents, have had to say at some point, "No, of course it's not your fault; you didn't make me gay." Do we mean to say that homosexuality is not a fault or that it is not an inherited gift? Surely homosexuality becomes a fault only when not received as a gift. All that we are—the fire in the belly and the ache in the bones—comes from an unbroken line of millions of years of love making. Call this evolution or the genetic code. But also call this an ancestral gift. Call it God. The wonder of heterosexual union is the new and unique, yet ancient, life form that is born. Because queer people recognize the mysterious gifts of the ancestral line, when we honor our unique selves, we profoundly honor the family and the wonder of heterosexual intercourse. By honoring the name my parents had unconsciously blessed me with, by honoring the dragon—that binatured creature of water and air that prefigured the divine/human Christ—I had come to honor the foundations of my soul and the God who had laid those foundations.

One of the earliest phrases I learned in the first grade in Chinese school was that "a mother's love is the greatest." My mother's courage, resilience, love, and generosity have been enormous in my life. She held a job as a schoolteacher for twenty-five years while suffering from a debilitating medical condition. For twelve of those years, my father was estranged and absent, and as a single parent she supported the two of us and her infirm mother and brother. She taught me English, Mandarin, and Hokkien and imparted to me a sensitivity of soul. One of the earliest stories we learned in Chinese school was that of Mencius, the most influential Confucian scholar of ancient China. Mencius's mother changed residences three times in order to secure for her son a positive moral environment in which he could grow. Once, when Mencius left a task unfinished, she taught him about his moral failing by cutting the cloth she had been painstakingly weaving. Such was her passion. Reflecting on our own mothers, we wrote essays about the greatness of a mother's love, *wei-da de mu-ai*.

A few weeks after my coming out, in the middle of a conversation about the devil's having infiltrated my mind, my mother fell to her knees, speaking in tongues. Screaming, she cursed, "In the name of Jesus, may you never have a male lover."[2] Snap went the scissors across the many woven stands of our relationship. Mother's love may be the greatest, but it need not be life giving.

In returning to Asia, I had had no illusions about the Chinese homophobia—derived from the shame at the loss of "face"—that I might encounter. But I also knew there was Asian permissiveness and tolerance of difference, a live and let live way of dealing with unresolvable conflicts. I was, however, unprepared to face a virulent and bigoted Christianity that smacked more and more of odious American fundamentalism and especially to have it come from the mouths of Chinese pastors—and my parents! The relationship between American fundamentalists and Southeast Asia is a literal one. The local Christian bookstores are filled with tapes and books from fundamentalist U.S. right-wing presses. The local Anglican Church had recruited an ex-gay man from Kansas (oh, Dorothy!) to run Exodus, a ministry started in the United States to "cure" homosexuality.[3] According to my parents and their Assembly of God Church, homosexuality was evidence of the end of time. I realized, however, that apocalyptic Christianity with its millennialism and restoration were the new colonizing cults from the West.[4] With humiliation, I saw that after Singapore's years of political independence from white colonizers, some Singaporean Christians had made this religious imperialism possible by *colluding* in their own religious recolonization.[5]

Love

So why do I remain a Christian?

When I was twelve, and one year into puberty, a schoolteacher friend of my mother's gave me a small storybook. In it, a young American boy with blond tousled hair finds the courage to visit an old lady—reputed to be a witch—who lives down the street from him. In the denouement, she turns out to be a kindly Christian woman. She asks him if he has ever heard of the love of Jesus. No *we* haven't, *we* said. Then she explains that God loved the world so much that God sent his Son Jesus to die for our sins and be our friend. Would *we* like to receive Jesus into our hearts? *Both of us* said yes, and there in my little room, in the sultry tropical heat of a Singaporean afternoon, the immense weight of loneliness was lifted from my shoulders. And welling up from within me came a surging wave of feelings I could barely control.

I had fallen in love with God. I had also fallen in love with my soul mate, that little vulnerable, courageous, and beautiful boy with the tousled blond hair. As much as I have searched for God, I have searched for that boy who first shared my experience of Love. This was the coming of Christ in my life and body. And my relationship with this Mystical Source of Being would *first* carry me into a long painful struggle with the narrow Christian ideology, as represented by the publishers of that little book, *before* I moved beyond it.

Two years after this love encounter with Jesus and the boy with the tousled hair—a love I was beginning to realize was supposed to be incompatible—I found myself at a Charismatic rally held on the grounds of the Anglican Cathedral in Singapore. All around me people were praying with uplifted arms, and strange sounds were coming out of their mouths. Not knowing what to expect, I stepped forward to be blessed by the visiting English evangelist. Instead, the bishop stood before me, asking me what I wanted. I found myself saying, "Ask God to make me more loving." (Becoming loving was my way of gaining love, unlovable as I felt then.) But under my breath I pleaded, "God, don't make me a homosexual." What happened next was beyond my comprehension: a surge of ecstatic, painful, and utterly pleasurable fire coursed through my body, threatening to turn me inside out. My knees buckled, and I found myself lying on the ground sobbing, uttering incomprehensible sounds, feeling somewhat frightened by the power I had experienced but incredibly loved and held. Later I was told that I had—in the jargon of the Charismatics—been baptized in the Holy Spirit. The experience first gladdened me, because I felt that God had been made known to me. Later, as my attraction to boys remained unabated, I started to hate myself. Clearly, if God had touched me with his own presence yet refused to hear my prayer for sexual change, I had to be despicable.

For anyone who has heard coming-out stories, the years of my teenage life, had they not been so painful, might seem terribly clichéd. The sight of a beautiful boy or emotional intimacy with a male friend would delight and terrorize me. Sneaking into the sexuality section of the Christian bookstores, I would furtively search for the chapter on homosexuality, only to find condemnation. Over and over I returned to search for new books, and each time I found myself reading my own death sentence. The books recommended fasting and prayers; I had done all that, and nothing had changed. Perhaps God did not require my prayers as much as my life. After all, had not Jesus said to pluck out your eye if you lusted after a woman? Perhaps I should destroy my body for lusting after men? Too frightened and weary to take my own life, I groveled to please God by becoming more fundamentalist, crusading against my Muslim, Hindu, and Buddhist Singaporean classmates for being devil worshipers and against women for not submitting to men.

I never imagined, when I was fourteen, that my struggle with spirituality and sexuality would take another fourteen years to find peace. At twenty-eight, I went to a retreat for gay men who were integrating their sexuality and spirituality.[6] I found myself breathing deeply after a massage.

*A voice said, "Return to the breath; stay with the present; feel the now." Now it was time to come home, to come home into the present, into myself and into my body. "Brother, breathe in life. Take twenty breaths and hold. Hold and squeeze." I held the last breath, suspending it, squeezing every muscle in my body until I shook in spasms. I held onto the breath, feeling frustration, then sadness, then desperation, until it seemed I was strangling myself. "Release the breath. Release." And still I held on, the loss and the pain sweeping over me—and the rage. I had been trampled by my dear mother, culture, and church. "Forgive us our trespasses as we forgive those who tres-*passed against us," *whispered a voice from somewhere. I let out a scream and let go, surrendering.*

And then the fire surged though me—again, fourteen years later. I saw myself back on the Cathedral grounds. And—like St. Peter, who saw a net with unclean animals descending and heard God's voice saying, "Eat, nothing is unclean" (Acts 10:9–16)—I saw Shiva; Kuan Yin, the boddhisattva of compassion; and a smiling Chinese dragon dancing with Jesus and my old bishop. There is nothing accursed says the Book of Revelations. I understood why God had not answered the prayer I had made at fourteen; God had filled me with love as I had asked, love toward men. I would learn from Carter Heyward, first from her books and then from our personal friendship, that the erotic life is about sharing in the passion of God.

Being gay is like being born with a compass that is oriented East, toward the holy sun of a fiery desire. In the early years you explore the world with this compass, and it is quite wonderful. You realize soon enough that you walk in a world where most people are going a different direction. So you try using the maps that family, religion, and culture have given you. But the maps are written with a different compass orientation, and your trip, far from getting better, gets much worse. Because you trust those who gave you the maps, you blame yourself for getting lost. Looking for the safe pasture promised by the maps, you eventually find yourself looking down a cliff's edge, wishing you were dead.[7]

I have wished for death and have also come close to looking at it. After escaping an avalanche, falling into a snow crevasse, and capsizing into glacial rivers on two climbing expeditions in Alaska I realize I had been acting out my death wish. The death wish came from self-hatred, but it was also my psyche's way of representing my need for transformation. Alaska showed me how. High up in the snows topographical maps are useless; maps at that altitude cannot accurately plot the characteristics of snowdrifts, shifting glaciers, and hidden crevasses, as they change from day to day. Maps show general characteristics, which have to be interpreted with care. We interpreted the "stories" on the maps and then laid them aside. Then we found ourselves relying on each other, on our individually acquired skills, on our instruments and intuition, and on our constant sharing past experiences on other mountains. Skill, insight, wisdom, the gospel, if you will, must come from many sources, not just from maps.

One day, high on the shoulder of Mount Saint Elias (named after Elijah of the still, small voice), I also put aside my religious maps. I burned the homophobic and xenophobic parts of the Bible, praying to God thus, "These words once gave life to your people Israel, but they are now used by the enemies of my people to bring death to us. I return these words to you, that your Word may come forth with life again." Psychically, I had broken both the power of Biblical literalism in my life and the psychic instruments upholding that way of being in my soul.

Biblical literalism or fundamentalism has less to do with being faithful to God than with making sure that we and God are on the same side and that others are not. Biblical fundamentalism, which has soothed and secured the Western conscience during five centuries of colonization, is being adopted by other cultures now, like my own Singapore. In the end, religious fundamentalism's only purpose is to make the world safe for those who are on God's side— a rather curious need, given that God is already on their side. But then, if this annihilating God is believed to be so ready to destroy everyone else, what reason is there to believe he would not do the same to his own? In fact, an Oxford-trained theologian and Pentecostal minister my parents dragged me to see in Singapore had said to me, "Once saved, not always saved." Apparently, given my homosexuality, my baptism and personal experiences of Christ did not guarantee me salvation. So this fundamentalist God demands fundamentalist loyalty but cannot fundamentally province security. What is this but the mafia Father/God of the missionaries and "evangelical Christians," a God who will shoot the kneecaps off his children as a way of "testing and loving" them. Unmask, judge, sentence, and banish the Godfather.

Casting the Web

They had come from across the country in answer to my call to build for me a protective web of sustenance on the eve of my ordination as deacon in the Episcopal Church. These men and women had been part of my journey toward healing in the past. I had written them to say that as much as I looked forward to my ordination and ministry to the hurting peoples of Christ's body, I was afraid that a homophobic church would devour me. Besides, how was I to stay sane working as a leader in a tradition that much of the time has wanted to see me (as a gay man of Chinese descent) destroyed or colonized? Worse still, because of my own fears, wounds, and loneliness, I might betray myself, my gay and lesbian kin, and others God would entrust to me. Would they come to be my web of lovers?

In the diminishing vesper light of an early Cambridge summer, we gathered. We breathed together, we touched, we sang, wearing our skin as clothes. During one part of the long and incredibly lovely evening, two men, lovers for twenty-odd years, sat me down in the middle of the circle. They brought out a bundle of warm orange fabric, cut into long strips but joined at one end. They tied the end around my waist, and each one of the gathered tribe took up the loose ends, so that I was indeed caught within a web. Then one by one they spoke to me. Their words created a mirror that allowed me to see myself in wonderful, grateful multilayered ways. Looking at them, I realized that what I loved in them was also what I had in me. Their words washed over me, soothing, stinging, stirring, and for the first time in my life, I allowed myself to hear and to receive. For so long, the closet had made me fake it. I had thought I had been accepted to Princeton and Harvard by mistake. There had been no words of praise or love I could trust. Now I believed.

Of the many intimate and powerful words branded on my heart, one person's words have stood out, in part because of the profound shadows they have embodied. He said to me, "I hold this strand, Leng, to tell you that sometimes when you tug at this, I may not be at the end, and you will find there is no one there." Eloi, Eloi, lema sabachthani. My God, why have you forsaken me? And looking into this brother's eyes, I saw that this truth too is part of the rhythm of love.

Later that evening, a friend made another cross over the one I had made earlier in the naming ceremony. I would own my pain, and I would also know that my Christ, and his body, the community, have held my pain already—a body stretched beyond the decay of the Christian churches. In letting go, I found spaces opening within, allowing me to welcome my tribe and family.

For myself as a queer man, the return to and of love is an acknowledgment that home will ultimately not be in the family (biological or otherwise), in the church (however welcoming), or even in a lover/boyfriend. These are, at best, oases, places and moments to rest and play. Rather, God is the uncontainable true home, and the self is the hearth and the burning fire.

Remembrance

When I was in kindergarten, my mother dressed me up in an ancient-looking Chinese silk gown (ah! the beginning of drag!) and entered me in a children's fashion show as the young Yueh Fei, the legendary general of the Sung Dynasty. When Yueh Fei was a youth, his mother had the words *"Jin Zhong Bao Guo,"* or "Unfailing Loyalty to Emperor and Country," tattooed on his back. Years later, after being framed by his prime minister, Yueh Fei was executed by the emperor. In memory of this betrayal, Chinese people put two pieces of leavened dough, representing the prime minister and his wife, on two sticks and deep-fry them. A breakfast staple, these *you tiaos*—a pun on the minister's name—can be found everywhere, from Beijing to American Chinatowns.

Who really betrayed Yueh Fei? Could it not have been the emperor? Certainly, the Tiananmen massacre of 1989 is only the most recent in a series of imperial betrayals in the history of the Chinese people. Perhaps it was Mother Culture, whose tattoos/values made Yueh Fei formulaic and unquestioning. Perhaps it was Yueh Fei himself, so conditioned to cultural norms that he did not resist. Nevertheless, when Chinese people eat *you tiaos,* they do not think about the betrayal and retributive rage embodied in the greasy fritters. Time has made the fritters simply a form of sustenance (the cholesterol notwithstanding). Perhaps the question to ask about Yueh Fei is How was he sustained? Was it mother's love? Or was it love of country and people? Or was it love of the father/emperor? Or perhaps it was none of that. Perhaps he just loved, simply.

Chinese people, through the centuries, have interpreted Yueh Fei's love as loyalty. I think of loyalty as a heart that is blindly unquestioning. Yet, loyalty, or *zhong* (忠) in Chinese, shows the pictograph of a heart (心) that is centered (中). This image suggests powerfully to me that beyond terms like loyalty and love, it is a centered heart that sees one through webs of betrayal.

NOTES

1. The metaphor of saliva for the filial connection refers to a practice in which Chinese parents test the temperature of hot food by cooling it in their own mouths before feeding the premasticated fare to a child.

2. The experience was more unnerving than hurtful at the time. In *Pathological Christianity* Gregory Max Vogt relates a similar story, in which a husband facing possible divorce commands his wife, in God's name, to come back to the house.

3. The two founders of Exodus, Michael Bussee and Gary Cooper, have since become ex-ex-gay. After falling in love with each other, they came out a second time. See the video *One Nation Under God,* which documents the problems and deceptions of the ex-gay ministry.

4. Although Michael Moriarty's treatment rests on his Bible-centered ideology, the description of the New Charismatics' focus on dominion, restoration, and apocalyptism is detailed and comprehensive. See 87–182.

5. With the exception of the Phillipines and pockets of Southeast Asia that are strongholds of the old Roman Catholicism established by the Portuese and Spanish, Protestant Christianity is a new religion in Southeast Asia. In Singapore, the majority of Christian adherents are Chinese converts from the Little Traditions of Taoism, Buddhism, and Confucianism. Although a minority race and politically marginal, Chinese people in the Indo-Malayan region are economically better off than the majority population. Singapore is the exception. Chinese people are the dominant race, but they are conscious of the fragility of their political status. This combination of economic prosperity, qualified political confidence, ethnic marginality/dominance, and neophyte devotion makes religious fervor among Chinese Christians (and others who pick up on the tenor) particularly strong. They also mirror the experi-

ences of American fundamentalists and their mix of eschatological certainty, racial (if white) confidence (though that is always perceived as under siege), sense of political marginality/dominance, and conversion fervor.

6. The retreat was offered by The Body Electric School, which was founded in the 1980s as a response to the AIDS crisis for the purpose of helping men work with deeper issues of eros and spirituality.

7. See Leroy Aarons, *Prayers for Bobby: A Mother's Coming to Terms with the Suicide of Her Gay Son,* which tells the story of Bobby Griffith's jump off the edge when the maps betrayed him.

WORKS CITED

Aarons, Leroy. *Prayers For Bobby: A Mother's Coming to Terms with the Suicide of her Gay Son.* San Francisco: HarperCollins, 1995.

Moriarty, Michael G. *The New Charismatics: A Concerned Voice Responds to Dangerous New Trends.* Michigan: Zondervan, 1992.

The New Oxford Annotated Bible, New Revised Standard Version. New York: Oxford UP, 1991.

One Nation Under God. Teodoro Maniace and Francine M. Rzeznik, producers. Distributed by First Run Features, New York. 3Z/Hourglass Productions, 1993.

Vogt, Gregory Max. *Pathological Christianity: The Dangers and Cures of Extremist Fundamentalism.* Indiana: Cross Cultural, 1995.

22. Heterosexuality in the Face of Whiteness
Divided Belief in M. Butterfly
David L. Eng

White is a color—it is a pastel. . . . In a place where it doesn't belong, on Michael, that same pastel remains a flaming signifier.—EVE SEDGWICK, "White Glasses"

In its investigation of sexuality and sexual difference, psychoanalysis has proven to be an indispensable theoretical tool for feminism and queer studies. Does psychoanalysis have something to offer Asian American, ethnic, or critical race studies? Until recently the answer to this question would have been an emphatic "no." Detractors of psychoanalytic theory have justifiably noted that, in its insistent privileging of sexuality as the organizing principle of subjectivity and social difference, psychoanalysis has been notably silent about issues of race. Yet if we are all (to borrow a phrase from Norma Alarcón) "multiply interpellated subjects," then the ways in which feminism and queer studies have traditionally deployed psychoanalytic theory to expose naturalizing discourses of sexual and, in particular, *hetero*sexual difference must be rethought to include a viable account of race as well.

Indeed, as Diana Fuss suggests, psychoanalysis has a material history—one imbricated in a legacy of Western colonialism (141). Thus, we must wonder whether psychoanalytic narratives merely produce an inaugural (hetero)sexual matrix in transhistorical isolation or whether they simultaneously institute an inaugurating set of historicized racial identifications. Are sexual and racial difference articulated only in and through one another? Do sexual and racial difference gain their discursive legibility through some implicit or explicit crossing? Do they come into existence only in relation to one another?

This chapter is an attempt to think out some of the intersections of sexual and racial difference in psychoanalytic theory. It is part of a larger project, *Racial Castration: Managing Masculinity in Asian America*. This is a work-in-progress that explores the critical links between Asian American studies and psychoanalysis by analyzing representations of Asian American masculinity that demand a more complex understanding of the crossings of sexuality and race. As *Racial Castration* challenges the privileged place that sexual difference has traditionally occupied in psychoanalytic theory, it insists that those of us invested in Asian American, ethnic, and critical race studies consider how psychoanalysis might offer a powerful critique

for understanding processes of sexual and racial identification together. To bring together psychoanalysis and Asian American studies in this manner is to consider explicitly the role of sexuality in
racial formation and the role of race in sexual formation.

Let us turn, then, to David Henry Hwang's *M. Butterfly,* a drama
of colonial encounter. In its critique of what Judith Butler describes
as the symbolic order's imperative of heterosexuality *and* whiteness
(*Bodies That Matter*), *M. Butterfly* exposes the production of whiteness as a universal racial category that projects the burden of difference onto the Asian (American) male body; moreover, Hwang's
drama reveals how this production of an unmarked and invisible
whiteness is achieved only through its complicit intersection with a
matrix of compulsory heterosexuality. Focusing on fetishism (perhaps Freud's most privileged mechanism of disavowal and projection ["Fetishism" 214–19]), I refigure this psychic category in terms
of a "racial castration"—one demanding reconsideration of Freud's
paradigm along altered lines of race and psychoanalytic theory in
insistent relation to the political.

Heterosexuality in the Face of Whiteness

For some time now, critics in both cultural and gender studies have
stressed the importance of giving disenfranchised subjects—people
of color, gays and lesbians, women—"voices," full subjectivities, vis-
ibilities in the face of invisibilities.[1] The emergence of marginal subjects from a domain of silence and invisibility into an order of
speech and visibility is crucial. Yet this goal is only one part of a
larger cultural politics of difference, one that must also examine
the discursive mechanisms by which marginal subjects are rendered
speechless and invisible in the first place. Kobena Mercer addresses
this larger political project by insisting that we initiate a critical investigation of whiteness and *its* strategic occlusion from visibility.
For "all our rhetoric about 'making ourselves visible,'" he asserts,
"the real challenge in the new cultural politics of difference is to
make 'whiteness' visible for the first time, as a culturally constructed
ethnic identity historically contingent upon the disavowal and violent denial of difference" (206).[2]

I would like to take up Mercer's challenge of making whiteness
visible, by investigating not only its conditions of possibility but also
its moments of failure. Consider the remarkable closing scene of
David Henry Hwang's Tony Award–winning drama *M. Butterfly,* moments before the demise of the French diplomat. Donning the
robes of the forsaken Japanese geisha Cio-Cio-San (memorialized
by Puccini's 1904 opera *Madama Butterfly* and its numerous antecedents),[3] René Gallimard commits seppuku after uttering these

final words: "There is a vision of the Orient that I have. Of slender women in chong sams and kimonos who die for the love of unworthy foreign devils. Who are born and raised to be the perfect women. Who take whatever punishment we give them, and bounce back, strengthened by love, unconditionally. It is a vision that has become my life" (91). I read this final scene in contrast to the unveiling of opera diva Song Liling's penis at the opening of act 3. Gallimard is so committed to Puccini's *Madama Butterfly* fantasy of "the submissive Oriental woman and the cruel white man" (17) that it is impossible for him to imagine an alternative outcome to this dreary story of heterosexual and racial domination. Indeed, because he cannot relinquish his colonialist fantasy of "slender women in chong sams and kimonos who die for the love of unworthy foreign devils," the white diplomat must "turn somersaults" (60) in order to protect the integrity of his heterosexual farce.

Vigilant in his desire to maintain *this* particular (heterosexual and racial) vision of the Orient, Gallimard is forced to counter the disrobed diva with a transvesting act of his own: now that Song is publicly the "man," Gallimard must become publicly the "woman." "Get away from me!" he orders Song petulantly. "Tonight I've finally learned to tell fantasy from reality. And, knowing the difference, I choose fantasy" (90). Rejecting the psychoanalytic axiom that posits a constitutive relationship between fantasy and reality, the diplomat refuses to accept the "real" world effects of his geisha girl fantasy. He assumes the sartorial role of Cio-Cio-San, thus receding into the imagined realm of his *Madama Butterfly* fantasy by "straightening" his relationship to the exposed Chinese man. He "returns" it once again—in the realm of his imagination and in the domain of the visible—to a phantasmatically normative heterosexual union. This concluding scene is, of course, an ironic reversal of Puccini's dictum, "Death with honor is better than life . . . life with dishonor" (92, Hwang's ellipsis), for the price of Gallimard's phantasmatic sartorial conversion—the death of the white man—is materially high. Gallimard commits suicide, but he dies with his Orientalist fantasy intact and—most important—as a nominal member of the acceptable and acceptably heterosexual.

I would like to isolate a striking visual detail emphasized in this concluding scene, both in Hwang's stage version and in David Cronenberg's film adaptation of the drama. Before Gallimard dons his wig and kimono, he carefully—even methodically—applies a thick layer of white makeup to his face, appearing literally *in whiteface*. Several commentators have read this action as a faithful rendering of the aesthetic protocols of Japanese theater, relating Gallimard's application of whiteface to the traditional makeup of the *onnogata* in Kabuki theater.[4] Majorie Garber, however, expands the possible interpretations of this critical moment by analyzing the diplomat's bad makeup job in the confluence of various ethnic channels:

> The whiteness of the makeup is traditional in Japanese theater as a sign of the ideal white complexion of the noble, who can afford to keep out of the sun, and the pallor of the protected young woman (or trained geisha) even today. We might note that in *Chinese* opera face-painting participates in an entirely different sign system, in which white on an actor's face symbolized treachery, as red does loyalty, yellow, piety, and gold, the supernatural. In this story of spies and treason the Chinese and Japanese significations are at odds with one another, and Song has already warned Gallimard not to conflate the two. (243, Garber's emphasis)

Though Garber's analysis of this scene largely focuses on Gallimard's egregious misreading of disparate Chinese and Japanese national and cultural aesthetics—the conflation of *chong sams* and kimonos—she subsequently appends a final and provocative interpretation: "The white makeup has yet another significance, since [Gallimard] is continually described as a 'white man' throughout the play, even in France, where 'There're white men all around'" (244).[5] Garber proffers a triple reading of Gallimard's bad makeup job through this condensed cultural survey, but I would like to elaborate on her final point: that Gallimard *is* continually described by Song as a "white man"; that the visible face underscoring Gallimard's failures, demise, and swan song appears to us literally *as* a white face; that the Orientalist and heterosexist fantasy for which Gallimard ultimately dies is achieved only *in* the face of whiteness.

Judith Butler proposes that we begin to theorize the compulsory regimes of the symbolic order—the numerous and coercive interpellations by which individuals are rendered legible as "subjects"—through the lens of not only (hetero)sexual but also racial difference. "The symbolic—that register of regulatory ideality—is also and always a racial industry, indeed, the reiterated practice of *racializing* interpellations" (18; Butler's emphasis), she writes in *Bodies That Matter:*

> Rejecting those models of power which would reduce racial differences to the derivative effects of sexual difference (as if sexual difference were not only autonomous in relation to racial articulation but somehow more prior, in a temporal or ontological sense), it seems crucial to rethink the scenes of reproduction and, hence, of sexing practices not only as ones through which a heterosexual imperative is inculated, but as ones through which boundaries of racial distinction are secured as well as contested.

Especially at those junctures in which a compulsory heterosexuality works in the service of maintaining hegemonic forms of racial purity, the "threat" of homosexuality takes on a distinctive complexity. (18)

Butler asks us to consider how sexual and racial norms intersect to produce viable and recognizable subject positions, to consider how homosexual and racial prohibitions underpinning the foundations of the symbolic order interdict a spectrum of repudiated social identities. If the symbolic order is always also a set of racializing norms, it becomes impossible to speak of the heterosexual matrix in isolation from racial distinctions. The articulation of such a "colorless" category would assume a priori the ontological presumption of sexual over racial difference while denying race any constitutive role in the formation of a legible subjectivity.

Moreover, the assumed primacy in this model of the sexual over the racial would imply that sexual difference is, in effect, "*white* sexual difference, and that whiteness is not a form of racial difference" (Butler, *Bodies That Matter* 182, my emphasis). In producing whiteness as an unmarked category, the symbolic order projects the burden of racial difference onto those bodies outside a universalizing discourse of whiteness. In slightly different terms, if the system of compulsory heterosexuality depends on the occlusion of whiteness as a racial category—drawing its discursive potency only in and through this concealed alignment—then it is imperative that we insist on making whiteness emphatically visible as a culturally constructed racial category.

Furthermore, we must begin to consider the multiple ways in which this universalizing of whiteness works to authorize *at one and the same time* the naturalizing power of the heterosexuality—a necessary amendment to the critical ways in which feminism and queer studies have hitherto framed issues of gender and sexuality. To deconstruct a system of compulsory heterosexual privilege (as psychoanalytic critics in feminism and queer studies have worked so hard to do) without considering racial difference, to fail to understand explicitly whiteness through the perspective of a concomitant racialization, would be to concede from the very outset that "whiteness . . . is yet another power that need not speak its name" (Butler, *Bodies That Matter* 182). It would be to allow the pretensions of whiteness as a universalizing racial category to continue unchecked and unqualified.

Granting that the consolidation of the symbolic order is contingent upon a norm of heterosexuality and whiteness, as well as a prohibition against homosexuality and nonwhiteness, we must note that this consolidation has functioned largely as a regulatory standard, hitherto *invisible* within the field of vision and unremarked in discourse. In its "ideal" form, heterosexuality and whiteness maintain their compulsory power by remaining veiled and undisclosed. Even more, they work in collusion with one another, drawing their discursive force only in and through their smooth alignment. If, as Eve Sedgwick says of her friend Michael Lynch (a gay, white male), whiteness somehow "doesn't belong" on him, remaining a "flaming signifier," it is because the crucial—the mandatory—combination of heterosexuality and whiteness has been violated and transgressed ("White Glasses" 255). In his "flaming" queerness, the whiteness of Michael Lynch is suddenly brought into relief, rendered visible and disconcerting.

Consequently, I read Gallimard's phantasmatic sartorial conversion as a frantic attempt to maintain the normative sexual and racial stipulations of the symbolic order, as a desperate effort to maintain heterosexuality in the face of whiteness. Unable to occupy the position of the European imperialist, following Song's morphological disclosure, Gallimard is so invested in heterosexuality and whiteness that he ultimately elects to occupy the position of the "other" to guarantee the structural integrity of his *Madama Butterfly* fantasy. In a grave sense, then, the symbolic appeals of heterosexuality that impel the death of—and Gallimard's death as—Cio-Cio-San can be realized only in a white face. It is, of course, this dual presumption of a (hetero)sexual and racial positioning that the French diplomat vigilantly struggles to maintain but fails miserably to preserve.

Gallimard's self-sacrifice must be read not only as a visible failure of heterosexuality in the face of whiteness but also as a hyperbolic illustration of the homosexual and racial anxieties underpinning the abject yet constitutive borders of the symbolic domain. Nevertheless, the overwhelming majority of commentaries generated by *M. Butterfly* do not account for this complex nexus of (homo)sexual and racial regulation. They focus exclusively on Song Liling's dramatic male-to-female crossing rather than on the possibility of Gallimard's passing between an acceptable white male *heterosexuality* and an abjected white male *homosexuality*. *New York Times* theater critic Frank Rich, for instance, claiming that Hwang is not "overly concerned with how the opera singer . . . pulled his hocus-pocus in the boudoir," dismisses the possibility that Gallimard's blunder over Song's anatomy might be explored through the lens of a "closeted" or "self-denying" homosexuality (C13). Moira Hodgson, in her summary of the drama for *The Nation*, emphatically concurs with Rich's latter point: "Hwang never gets to the bottom of Gallimard's character. He doesn't question whether the Foreign Service officer knew that Song Liling was in fact a man ('It was dark and she was very modest'), nor does he make him into a self-deluded homosexual" (577).

Moreover—in a patent refusal to investigate the (hetero)sexual limits of white male subjectivity—numerous critics focus their attention only on the "multicultural" issues of the drama: Asian American political agendas, assimilation, the model minority myth, artistic license.[6] John Simon's bitter dismissal of *M. Butterfly* in *New York Magazine* attacks Hwang as the "son of affluent Chinese Americans [who] has scores to settle with both America and the new China, the former for making him embarrassed about his ethnicity, the latter for repudiating his bourgeois status and Armani suits" ("Finding Your Song" 117). Deflecting his attention away from the qualities of the drama itself, Simon focuses on the motivations and failures of Hwang as a frustrated, self-loathing Asian American dramatist. Thus he avoids giving any consideration to the failures of conventional white masculinity informing the play.[7]

These asymmetries remain unchallenged by critics, even though Song bluntly reminds Gallimard of these racial and sexual inequities from the very start of the drama. At their first encounter, the opera diva challenges the diplomat's enthusiastic praise of his performance as Cio-Cio-San, responding with this sharp rejoinder, "Consider it this way: what would you say if a blonde homecoming queen fell in love with a short Japanese businessman? He treats her cruelly, then goes home for three years, during which time she prays to his picture and turns down marriage from a young Kennedy. Then, when she learns he has remarried, she kills herself. Now, I believe you would consider this girl to be a deranged idiot, correct? But because it's an Oriental who kills herself for a Westerner—ah!—you find it beautiful" (17). Song's *Madama Butterfly* parable—his cultural inversion of these spurious sexual and racial asymmetries—seems to be a critical point lost on both Gallimard and his commentators.[8]

In this reading of Hwang's drama, I would like to focus on the limits of conventional white masculinity by examining the methods by which symbolic norms and prohibitions coerce Gallimard's phantasmatic allegiance to ideals of heterosexuality and whiteness. What exactly is this "enchanted space" of the prison cell, ruled by the "work of fairies" that Gallimard describes in his opening monologue (2)? What are the queer phantasms that order and control the white diplomat's psychic blunders and material failures? I turn my attentions to Gallimard to consider how he could have failed to know Song's true anatomical sex for over twenty years. "Did Monsieur Gallimard know you were a man?" persists the officious judge, swinging the all-too-familiar juridical gavel as he interrogates the Oriental diva (81). In his desire to categorize and to stabilize the foundational terms of the symbolic order for which he is a citational mouthpiece, the judge's obsessive question emerges as the central concern of the drama. Yet psychoanalysis would tell us that there is no clear-cut answer to the judge's query, that to know and not know, that to *not* see what is apparently there for us to see, is a perfectly explicable condition in the realm of the psyche.

"An Almost Artful Dealing with Reality"

In "The Dissection of the Psychical Personality" (51–71), Freud provides a visual mapping of the structural relations between the ego, the id, and the superego and the psychical territories of the repressed, the unconscious, the preconscious, and the perceptual-conscious systems (70). This "final topography" is an elaboration of a comparatively schematic "late topography" developed in *The Ego and the Id*. In contrast to the late topography in which the ego is seen to occupy a less capacious area of the psyche, the final topography illustrates a definitive expansion of the ego's psychic territory as it comes to occupy areas in the preconscious, the unconscious, and the territory of the repressed. As such, it is notable because it visualizes a point repeatedly underscored in *The Ego and the Id:* a "part of the ego, too—and Heaven knows how important a part—may be unconscious, undoubtedly is unconscious" (9). If the ego is the seat of both (pre)conscious knowledge and unconscious resistance, then the final topography provides us with a visual representation of the divided subject, one who can know and not know at the same time.

The notion of the divided ego is elaborated most fully in one of Freud's posthumously published works, the "Splitting of the Ego in the Defensive Process," written in 1938 (220–23). In this essay, Freud explains that under the sway of a powerful instinctual demand whose satisfaction is threatened by the danger of an encroaching reality, the ego is forced to decide "either to recognize the real danger, give way to it and do without the instinctual satisfaction, or to repudiate reality and persuade itself that there is no reason for fear, so that it may be able to retain the satisfaction" (220). Unable to make this no-win decision, the ego pursues both possibilities simultaneously through a defensive maneuver that results in two "contrary reactions": on one hand, the ego refuses reality and its constraints on instinctual satisfaction; on the other hand, it recognizes the danger of reality and attempts to divest itself of this fear. The "two contrary reactions to the conflict persist," Freud maintains, "as the centre-point of a split in the ego" (221).

In this essay Freud goes on to describe the paradigmatic psychic mechanism for this simultaneous gratification of instinctual demand and obedience to social prohibition as "fetishism." A little boy caught masturbating is subject not only to the threat of castration by the father but also to the frightening sight of female "castration"—the absence of a penis on the girl.[9] Because the little boy is reluctant to give up masturbation, and because the danger of an encroaching reality—the potential loss of his privileged organ—is effective only insofar as the threat of castration by the father is coupled with and reinforced by this frightening visual affirmation of absence, the little boy creates a fetish that disavows the girl's lack and thus circumvents the paternal threat. Consequently, he carries out his denial of female "castration" by finding a substitute that can be projected in its place: a shine on the nose, a plait of hair, an undergarment, a shoe. The fetish serves, then, as a paradigmatic example of divided belief. Its very existence both denies and attests to female "castration": it says that she does and does not have a penis. Freud maintains that the fetish serves as an ingenious mechanism that "almost deserves to be described as [an] artful . . . dealing with reality," by which the little boy confronts the exigencies of psychic life and the redoubtable threats of the father ("Splitting of the Ego" 223). In this way, the little boy not only eludes paternal prohibition but also facilitates a method by which he can continue undisturbed in his gratifying sexual activities.

In both "Splitting of the Ego in the Defensive Process" and "Fetishism," Freud provides us with a model of divided belief and fetishism that explains how Gallimard could at once both know and now know Song's true anatomical sex. Extending for a moment fetishism's logic to the male body, might Gallimard's psychic appraisal of Song's corporeal endowments also fall into simultaneous affirmation and disavowal of castration? Moreover, the defensive splitting of the ego explains how the diplomat could not see on a *conscious* level what he had already perhaps acknowledged on an *unconscious* level: Song's penis. We come to understand, through the diplomat's simultaneous disavowing and affirming of the presence of this male organ, how he could at once be and not be a (self-denying) homosexual.

Although Freud relishes his description of fetishism as a means for instinctual satisfaction and the evasion of paternal constraint, he leaves us with a foreboding caveat: "But everything has to be paid for in one way or another, and the [little boy's] success is achieved at the price of a rift in the ego which never heals but which increases as time goes on" ("Splitting of the Ego" 221). The fetish, which "*almost* deserves to be described as [an] artful . . . dealing with reality" (my emphasis), is secured only at the cost of a split ego whose mis-recognitions grow larger with time. Castration inevitably comes back to haunt the ego in frightening and unpredictable ways. How does this promised homecoming of castration haunt Gallimard in *M. Butterfly?* And what are the social conditions by which the diplomat is first coerced into a state of divided belief?

Lotus Blossom Fantasy

"We were worried about you, Gallimard," reveals an envious Manuel Toulon, ambassador *extraordinaire* of the French Embassy. "We thought you were the only one without a secret. Now you go and find a lotus blossom . . . and top us all" (46, Hwang's ellipsis). In one fell swoop, Toulon assuages his "worries" about Gallimard through the reassuring articulation of the diplomat's heterosexuality. For Toulon, the "secret" of Gallimard's illicit affair with Song Liling is perfectly "straightforward"—filtered, that is, through symbolic imperatives of heterosexuality and whiteness and framed by a historical legacy of colonialism. As a consequence, Gallimard's "secret" is really no secret at all, but a projection of Toulon's *own* Orientalist fantasies of heterosexuality and whiteness: the "secret" affair of the cruel white man and Oriental "lotus blossom."

The *Madama Butterfly* tableau that Toulon imagines is a fantasy reinforcing and reinforced by the foundations of the social order, its demarcation of distinct sexual and racial borders economically and materially fortified by a long history of European imperialism.[10] I must emphasize that Toulon's "recognition" of Gallimard's alleged "heterosexuality" in this scene of economic, political, and cultural domination is facilitated only through the diplomat's perceived "possession" of the Oriental butterfly—the sexual and racial exploitation of the little brown woman upon whom white male subjectivity in the colonial order is built. Indeed, Toulon's (mis)recognition of the diplomat's affair with the Oriental lotus blossom—Gallimard's racialized heterosexuality, as it were—speaks to a colonial structure in which sexual and racial difference gain their full significance only in relation to one another. Ultimately, this lotus blossom fantasy is neither private nor personal but an open secret that is passed down in time from one colonial bureaucrat to another, from one colonial administration to the next. In the process, this lotus blossom fantasy becomes like Puccini's *Madama Butterfly* tableau, the same old story through its continuous reprisals and compulsive rescriptings.[11]

If Toulon's "secret" of the *Madama Butterfly* phantasmatic is less an individual than a collective fantasy of imperial domination, then its articulation serves not merely to describe the conditions of a culturally acceptable heterosexual and white colonial desire but, more important, to produce these symbolic ideals in its very utterance. In this structuring of the social order, colonial ideals of heterosexuality and whiteness acquire their efficacy only in and through a reiterative structure of citationality and through a material structure of the circulation of commodities, capital, and knowledge. As such, Toulon—subject of and subjected to the symbolic norms and prohibitions of the colonial order—becomes an exemplary spokesmodel for this exclusionary order, another cog in the wheel, as it were.[12]

That the presumptuous Toulon and the pontificating judge ("Did Monsieur Gallimard know you were a man?") are scripted by Hwang to be played by the same actor works to underscore their collective psychic and material investment in the colonial regime they mindlessly extol. The very fabric of the social world dramatized in *M. Butterfly* thus gains its psychic and material resilience through the homogenous fantasies of corporate players, like Toulon, and juridical tools, like the judge, whose primary responsibilities to their particular domains of economics and politics involve their repeated interpellations of men like Gallimard into this old boys' network.[13]

The French ambassador's gleeful statement—"We were worried about you, Gallimard. We thought you were the only one without a secret. Now you go and find a lotus blossom . . . and top us all"—is an optative hailing of the bumbling diplomat into a compulsory network of heterosexuality and whiteness and into an economic and political structure of colonial privilege. Hence, the performative utterance by which Toulon makes Gallimard's little "secret" public functions as the reiterative mechanism by which the paternal legacy secures its psychic investments, binds its political entitlements, and guarantees its economic inheritance. How well does Gallimard recite the prescriptive norms of this collective lotus blossom fantasy?

Racial Castration

In "Fetishism," Freud describes the fetish as a psychic process by which the little boy gives the female a penis substitute to disavow her "lack" and difference and to make her "acceptable as [a] sexual object" (216). Freud thus implies that fetishism serves as a compensatory psychic mechanism by which the trauma of female sexual difference is managed and by which heterosexual relations between men and women are normalized. Since fetishes "are easily obtainable and sexual gratification by their means is thus very convenient" (216), Freud offers this process as a typical method for facilitating a normative heterosexuality between the sexes.

Classic fetishism, according to Freud, plays itself out along the lines of sexual difference. The male fetishist refuses to acknowledge female "castration" by seeing on the female body a penis that is not there to see. In *M. Butterfly*, however, we encounter a strange reversal of this psychic paradigm, a curious reconfiguration of the fetish beyond what Freud's essay explicitly offers. With Gallimard we do not witness a denial of sexual difference and lack resulting in the projection onto the female body of a substitute penis that is not there to see. Instead, we encounter the opposite, a "reverse fetishism," so to speak: Gallimard's blatant refusal to see on the body of an Asian male the penis that *is* clearly there for him to see. How might we account for this strange reconfiguration of the fetish and its *avowal* of castration?

At this juncture, it seems necessary to consider racial difference in the formulation of any potential explanation, since in Gallimard's reconfiguration of the fetish, castration is not denied but stringently affirmed—affirmed not at the site of the white woman but at the site of the Asian man. How might this "racial castration"—this curious crossing of castration with race—make possible the heterosexual relationship between the white man and the white woman around whom Freud implicitly centers his discussions? In this particular psychic scenario, what kinds of difference and lack are being denied and rendered invisible?[14]

To begin our exploration, let us turn to an example of racial dynamics offered by Kaja Silverman in *The Threshold of the Visible World*. In her discussion of the different values culturally conferred upon the black and white male penises, Silverman delineates a social structure by which the black penis works to disturb the sexual relations between the white man and white women: "The differentiation of the white man from the black on the basis of the latter's hyperbolic penis consequently reverberates in disturbing ways within the domain of gender. It places the white man on the side of 'less' rather than 'more,' and, so threatens to erase the distinction between him and the white woman. This is the primary reason, I would argue, that the body of the black man disrupts the unity of the white male corporeal ego" (31). The putatively hyperbolic black male penis threatens the unity of the white male ego by placing him in a position of "less" masculine, thereby endangering the structural distinction between him and the white woman.

In *M. Butterfly*, however, we encounter the opposite situation: a white male is placed in a position of "more" masculine through his disavowal of the Asian (American) penis—a triangulating of American race relations beyond the conventional Manichean relationship of black and white.[15] In other words, by psychically denying the penis that is clearly there for him to see, Gallimard castrates the Asian male, placing him in a position of "lesser" masculinity to secure for himself a position of "greater" masculinity. The white diplomat's racial castration of the Asian male works, then, not to disturb but to stabilize the distinction between him and the white woman—a reversal of the psychic anxiety he conventionally faces with the black male body. Indeed, this model of racial castration—of "reverse fetishism" and its denial of the Asian penis—might be seen as an attempt to produce and to normalize heterosexual relations between the white couple. In *M. Butterfly*, racial castration comes to reinforce the very structures of normative fetishism described by Freud: the myth of the "sufficient" white male and the "lacking" white female is upheld and strengthened.

The French diplomat's reconfiguration of Freudian fetishism in this particular manner works less, then, to problematize than to reiterate the prescriptive norms of the colonial order—the emasculation of the Asian male functioning through not only a material but also a psychically enforced Orientalist framework. In this particular example of reverse fetishism, the Asian male is psychically emasculated, foreclosed from an identification with normative heterosexuality so as to guarantee the white male's claim to this location. As such, the potential trauma of sexual difference is not arrested at the site of the female body (as in the case of classic fetishism), but the potential trauma of racial difference is arrested at, disavowed, and projected onto the body of the Asian male. Gallimard's refusal to see the Asian penis before him thus illustrates the complex manner in which Asian, white, and black male identity circulate in a psychic economy of racial as well as sexual differences, gaining their discursive legibility only in relation to one another. In this particular instance, Gallimard's racial denial of Song's penis facilitates the smooth alignment of heterosexuality and whiteness. This is an invisible alignment that, in its refusal to be named, attempts to secure heterosexuality and whiteness as universal norms in a colonial order.

Gallimard's use of "reverse fetishism" as an effort to shore up his flagging masculine position illustrates a definitive instance in which racial difference must be discussed in terms of sexual difference. The diplomat's "racial castration" of Song exemplifies a distinct psychic process by which whiteness and heterosexuality work collectively to articulate and to secure their universal status in relation to a devalued Asian racial positioning. Through Gallimard's psychic revision of classic fetishism, the potential trauma of racial difference is deflected away from the white male body and projected elsewhere. In his continual refusal to apprehend difference, Gallimard's reworking of fetishism both "reveals and sutures the gap in the lived misidentification of difference as the same" and is thus the psychic mechanism "responsible for the production of universalities, harmonies, and gratifications" (Lowe 151). In this manner, conventional white male subjectivity—as well as a normative heterosexual relationship between the (white) sexes—is scripted and sustained through a specified racial distinction and loss.

Anatomical Weenies and Epic Fiction

As described by Freud, the fetish serves to normalize white heterosexual relations on which the paternal legacy is built through a simultaneous denial and affirmation of female "castration" and "lack." Reconfigured by Gallimard, fetishism also manages anxieties of racial difference by facilitating a normative white heterosexual relationship through the affirmation of a castrated Asian male body that serves to reinforce white male sufficiency. However, as we come to see in *M. Butterfly,* this psychic mechanism turns out to be a profound disappointment for the diplomat. *M. Butterfly* qualifies Gallimard's call to normative white masculinity by charting a series of notable (hetero)sexual reversals.

Ambassador Toulon's attempts at interpellating Gallimard into a colonial matrix of whiteness and heterosexuality through their shared lotus blossom fantasy, as well as the diplomat's own attempts to shore up his flagging masculine position through his racial reconfiguration of classic fetishism, are qualified in the course of the drama by a long history of repeated failures with white women: the pinup girl, Helga, and Renée. If the purpose of the Freudian fetish is to remake the (white) female body into a viable sexual object through the denial of the female's sexual difference and the projection of a "penis substitute," then Gallimard's relationships with these three white women come to be marked by a strange psychic reversal: the trauma of "castration" is not neutralized at the site of the female body; instead, it returns to wash over the white male body.

The diplomat's history with white women—before, during, and after his relationship with Song—is highlighted by the continued failure of the heterosexual imperative. In the young Gallimard's *Playboy* fantasies we witness the first instance of this washout, his onanistic activities rapidly short-circuited by uncooperative anatomy:

Gallimard: I first discovered these magazines at my uncle's house. One day, as a boy of twelve. The first time I saw them in his closet . . . all lined up—my body shook. Not with lust—no, with power. Here were women—a shelfful—who would do exactly what I wanted.

The "Love Duet" creeps in over the speakers. Special comes up, revealing, not Song this time, but a pinup girl in a sexy negligee, her back to us. Gallimard turns upstage and looks at her.

Girl: I know you're watching me.
Gallimard: My throat . . . it's dry.
Girl: I leave my blinds open every night before I go to bed.
Gallimard: I can't move.
Girl: I leave my blinds open and the lights on.
Gallimard: I'm shaking. My skin is hot, but my penis is soft. Why?
. . . .
Girl: I can't see you. You can do whatever you want.
Gallimard: I can't do a thing. Why? (10–11)

Within the confines of the avuncular "closet," Gallimard's reactions seem atypical of most pubescent heterosexual men. Although the diplomat's identification with paternal power is definitively aroused, his penis remains permanently soft. On one hand, Gallimard is thoroughly excited by the prospects of phallic control—enthralled by the power to make "women . . . do exactly as I wanted"; on the other hand, he lacks the necessary "equipment" and is racked by anxieties about heterosexual performance. Despite the pinup girl's self-proclaimed inability to return Gallimard's look, the young diplomat is overwrought by seeing and being seen, disturbed by the visible failure of his paternal organ: "I'm shaking. My skin is hot, but my penis is soft. Why? . . . I can't do a thing. Why?" Gallimard, the young voyeur, is thus caught at the peephole, subjected to the power of an unapprehensible gaze.[16] Since the diplomat literally occupies center stage in this scene, the *visible* failure of his organ comes under intense scrutiny, its flaccid presence given our full attention.

As a "queer" adolescent, the diplomat's struggle to identify with the position of the father—with a position of heterosexuality and whiteness—comes to be haunted by the "masculine" dis-ease of his organ. If Gallimard's reconfiguration of fetishism in regard to Song suggests a logic of reversal—the affirmation of the "castrated" Asian male—here, too, we witness a further inversion: castration is not disavowed and projected onto the white female body but emphatically returns to wash over the white male body. Gallimard—the white male and not the white female—becomes the locus of insufficiency. Hence, we witness in this *Playboy* fantasy an incipient pledge to the heterosexual and white paternal order, one strongly qualified by a dissonant trajectory of desire. Penis and phallus work toward opposite ends—a slippage of phallic power from anatomical control.

At this point, it seems appropriate to invoke recent feminist debates on the distinction between phallus and penis and on the displacement of a differential "lack" and "castration" onto the female body. Silverman, for instance, delineates two separate "castrations" experienced by *all* subjects: the entry into language (primal repression) and the paternal metaphor (the Oedipus complex). If primal repression and the paternal metaphor can be shown to be two separate events, Silverman argues, we can understand the Freudian castration complex "as the metaphoric reinscription and containment of a loss which happens much earlier, at the point of linguistic entry—as the restaging with a 'difference' of a crisis which would otherwise prove inimical to masculinity" ("The Lacanian Phallus" 113). Silverman's critique of Freud's inequitable distribution of a prior linguistic castration onto a "lacking" female (and in Song's instance racial) body finds an unwitting ally in Gallimard. The diplomat's inability to place his flaccid penis within a phantasmatic scene of tumescent phallic plenitude suggests that there is nothing inevitable, after all, in the connection between anatomical male penis and symbolic phallus. The diplomat's failures with white women (and Asian men) emphatically illustrate that he is also—and most hyperbolically—a subject of sexual (and racial) lack.

Gallimard's psychosexual inadequacies are further elaborated in his "arranged" marriage to Helga, the Australian ambassador's daughter. Their conjugal union exemplifies the continuous rescripting of a divided allegiance between paternal authority and heterosexual desire. To begin with, the couple's marriage is overshadowed by Gallimard's "vow renouncing love . . . for a quick leap up the career ladder" (14). Moreover, the political and economic position enjoyed by Gallimard through this corporeal union is subsequently qualified by a noticeable absence of progeny, the material failure of what we might call, in a contemporary context, "family values." That their marriage remains childless is, as Helga contends, none of her doing. Gallimard's loyalties to a white and heterosexual symbolic order appear yet again to be undermined by a slippage between the psychic and the material: though he identifies with the privileges of paternal, colonial power, the diplomat is immobilized by the performative requirements this power demands.

This rift between phallic authority and bodily penis finds its most resonant example in Gallimard's interactions with Renée, the assertive Danish coed. If the male René Gallimard's patronym, which invokes one of France's largest publishing houses, indicates an inherited legacy of paternal privilege, his first name qualifies this presumption through its relationship to his female doppelgänger. Renée's presence, perhaps more than that of any other white woman in the drama, works to the utter ruination of Gallimard's identifications with a colonial regime of heterosexuality and whiteness. To begin with, the diplomat's extramarital affair with the Danish coed is marked by a reversal of gender norms—she is a woman who is "*too* uninhibited, *too* willing . . . *too* masculine" (54, Hwang's emphasis, my ellipsis). Furthermore, Renée's discourse on anatomical "weenies" and "epic fiction" attests to the slippage of male penis from symbolic phallus, bringing René Gallimard face-to-face with his lack.

Renée: I—I think maybe it's because I really don't know what to do with them—that's why I call them "weenies."
Gallimard: Well you did quite well with . . . mine.
Renée: Thanks, but I mean, really *do* with them. Like, okay, have you ever looked at one? I mean, really?
Gallimard: No, I suppose when it's part of you, you sort of take it for granted.
Renée: I guess. But, like, it just hangs there. This little . . . flap of flesh. And there's so much fuss that we make about it. Like, I think the reason we fight wars is because we wear clothes. Because no one knows—between the men, I mean—who has the bigger—weenie. So, if I'm a guy with a small one, I'm going to build a really big building or take over a really big piece of land or write a really long book so the other men don't know, right? But, see, it never really works, that's the problem. I mean, you conquer the country, or whatever, but you're still wearing clothes, so there's no way to prove absolutely whose is bigger or smaller. And that's what we call a civilized society. The whole world run by a bunch of men with pricks the size of pins. (*She exits*)
Gallimard (*To us*): This was simply not acceptable. (55–56)

René Gallimard's horrified reaction to the female Renée's disquisition on the separation between anatomical "weenies" and their symbolic manifestations—wars, epic fiction, large buildings—clearly results from her unwelcome incursion into the realm of paternal privilege and her appropriation of its most powerful tool: language. Renée is completely dominant, physically and psychically: in bed she is in charge, quite literally "on top," as Gallimard admits in saying, "You did quite well with . . . mine" (his penis). Outside the bedroom, she assumes a position of discursive authority, vexing the tongue-tied diplomat by running verbal circles around him.

Renée's scaling down of penile presumption, as well as her incisive observations on the "phallacy" of male size and privilege, drives the wedge ever more deeply between bodily penis and symbolic phallus.[17] If the silent "e" that marks the difference in their shared name is that letter whose responsibility is both to signify and to stabilize a relationship of gender, the silent "e" also accounts for a certain unavoidable symbolic "e"-masculation that Gallimard undergoes at the hands of Renée. In his encounters with his female double, the French diplomat cannot avoid confrontation with—he can no longer render invisible—his own heterosexual failures. To the contrary, the diplomat's relationship with Renée comes to epitomize all his interactions with the white women of the drama: castration and lack return to sit squarely on the shoulders of the white male.

A Homosexual and a Fetishist: Rice Queens and Yellow Fever

How might we reconcile Gallimard's curious attraction to the paternal legacy but not to white women and heterosexuality?[18] Can the fetish serve to deny male homosexuality rather than female castration? Can the fetishist be a homosexual?

On the face of it, these questions might seem rather untenable, since Freud claims that it is precisely the fetish that saves the little boy "from being a homosexual by endowing women with the attribute which makes them acceptable as sexual objects" ("Fetishism" 216). Yet the distinct homosexual and fetishistic pathways by which Freud leads the little boy out of the horror of female "castration" are not so straight as to never cross. If the male fetishist creates a penis substitute and projects it onto the body of the female to make her an acceptable sexual object, this projection is entirely necessary, we learn, for the very reason that the little boy holds an incredible narcissistic investment in the corporeal integrity of his male organ: "No, that [female 'castration'] cannot be true, for if a woman can be castrated then his own penis is in danger; and against that there rebels part of his narcissism which Nature has providentially attached to this particular organ" ("Fetishism" 215).

And here Freud implies that the heterosexual man is no more, no less, a (displaced) narcissist who can love only those objects that remind him of himself, can love only those objects endowed with a penis—with the corporeal outline of his own bodily ego. According to this logic of similitude and false equivalences, the female thus becomes substitute for the male body as heterosexuality thus becomes substitute for homosexuality. As such, the homosexual—traditionally excluded from Freud's cast of anaclitic love-objects—would nevertheless be the one love-object holding the greatest psychic cache for the heterosexual man. Not only does the homosexual man reassuringly and faithfully mirror his body back to the heterosexual man; the homosexual man also has a putative reserve of primary narcissism that would be a potent reminder of the renounced libidinal territory the heterosexual man relinquished in his departure from narcissistic to anaclitic love.[19] In this scenario, the simultaneous masculine avowal and disavowal of homosexuality structures the very condition of possibility by which conventional white masculinity is allowed to emerge.

How might this model of fetishism and homosexuality intersect with Gallimard's racial castration of the Asian male? How might the disavowed Asian male penis that Gallimard refuses to recognize on Song's body serve as a displaced representative of a tabooed homosexual and racial desire? The psychic configuration of "reverse fetishism" in *M. Butterfly* suggests that Gallimard's denial of Song's penis works not merely to shore up a heterosexual relation between white man and woman but also to cover up an abjected homosexual desire *for* the Asian male body. In this sense, we might describe this scenario as Gallimard's "passing" between an acceptable white male heterosexuality and an unacceptable white male homosexuality. How might the diplomat's refusal to see the Asian penis before him "pass off" a prohibited homosexual desire *for* it is as a normative heterosexuality in the face of whiteness?

As discussed earlier, the cruel white man and the submissive Oriental lotus blossom mark an imperial narrative of knowledge that is assiduously rescripted and cultivated by the colonial order. Yet this phantasmatic—deployed from Puccini to Ambassador Toulon and the diplomat's numerous anatomical failures with white women—come ultimately to qualify Gallimard's tenuous position (and finally, his life) within the colonial matrix of white heterosexual power. If the *Madama Butterfly* phantasmatic occupies the acceptable side of a colonialist fantasy, the conscious side of authorized desire, how might we describe the unacceptable underside of this fantasy, the unconscious denial of a tabooed desire? To answer these questions we must turn to Hwang's striking afterword to the play in which he offers a possible explanation for the diplomat's state of divided belief—one unnamed in the drama proper:

> Gay friends have told me of a derogatory term used in their community: "Rice Queen"—a gay Caucasian man primarily attracted to Asians. In these relationships, the Asian virtually always plays the role of the "woman"; the Rice Queen, culturally and sexually, is the "man." This pattern of relationships had become so codified that, until recently, it was considered unnatural for gay Asians to date one another. Such men would be taunted with a phrase that implied they were lesbians.
>
> Similarly, heterosexual Asians have long been aware of "Yellow Fever"—Caucasian men with a fetish for Oriental women. I have often heard it said that "Oriental women make the best wives." (Rarely is this heard from the mouths of Asian men, incidentally.) This mythology is exploited by the Oriental mail-order bride trade which has flourished over the past decade.

American men can now send away for catalogues of "obedient, domesticated" Asian women looking for husbands. (98)

According to Hwang, the concepts of "Yellow Fever" and "Rice Queens" are constructed along congruent lines of heterosexual and homosexual submission—the conscious and acceptable as well as the unconscious and abject sides of a colonialist fantasy. The concept of "Yellow Fever" exists squarely within the approved norms and acceptable knowledges of a conventional colonial order working to buttress white male heterosexuality through the possession and exploitation of the "native" brown woman.

Conversely, the suppressed equivalent of this phenomenon is the homosexual "Rice Queen" phantasmatic. This "Rice Queen" fantasy—its entailing attachment to and desire for the Asian male body—exists squarely within the tabooed regions of symbolic prohibitions against homosexuality and nonwhiteness. Its emergence into the domain of visibility would thus bring to bear the abject underside of the symbolic order, an order whose stability is contingent upon not only the disavowal of but also the violent suppression of homosexuality and nonwhiteness. In this light, we might view Gallimard's psychic makeover and denial of Song's penis as serving a dual purpose: Gallimard's castration of the male opera singer could function both as an attempt to buttress his flagging white masculinity and as an effort to remake the unacceptable Asian male body into an acceptable Asian female form for colonial consumption and enjoyment.

This double-sided fantasy explains, then, how the white diplomat's failures with white women might be interpreted through both a heterosexual and a homosexual valence. I would suggest, finally, that we must read Gallimard's state of divided belief through both of these possibilities: a failed heterosexuality in the face of whiteness and an occluded fantasy of homosexual desire. The former serves as a psychic mechanism by which the symbolic norms of heterosexuality and whiteness are shored up and consolidated in Gallimard's colonial world; the latter serves as a psychic mechanism by which symbolic prohibitions against homosexuality and nonwhiteness are suspended and called into question.

In which fantasy—the *Madama Butterfly* or the Rice Queen phantasmatic—does Gallimard hold the most faith? Is the diplomat finally heterosexual or homosexual? This question may ultimately be unanswerable, for in a larger sense Gallimard's putative ignorance concerning Song's anatomical sex suggests a fundamental equivocation as well as fluidity of sexual identification and desire structuring the symbolic order itself. It suggests the ultimate unknowability and therefore unreliability of "sex" and sexual practice as indicators of a psychic "truth" or of an unwavering sexual disposition. In slightly different terms, Gallimard's psychic equivocations over Song's anatomy concede the inevitable failure of symbolic norms and prohibitions to command faithful versions of heterosexuality and whiteness they cannot ultimately produce, enforce, or guarantee.[20]

Nevertheless, if the very conception of our bodily ego and borders of self come to be informed by a threat of symbolic and material punishment—a threat of pain, bodily disintegration, and loss of social identity—it may be that Gallimard's ostensible deferral to a conscious *Madama Butterfly* phantasmatic serves as a mechanism of self-preservation and advanced self-punishment, the compensatory result of an unconscious disavowal of a desired "Rice Queen" phantasmatic. Indeed, Judith Butler writes, the symbolic order marshals an incredible force of coercion: "When the threat of punishment wielded by that prohibition [against homosexuality and nonwhiteness] is too great, it may be that we desire someone who will keep us from ever seeing the desire for which we are punishable, and in attaching ourselves to that person, it may be that we effectively punish ourselves in advance and indeed, generate desire in and through and for that self-punishment" (*Bodies That Matter* 100). Should we read Gallimard's wavering allegiance to normative symbolic interpellations as a rebellion against or as a submission to this advance self-punishment?

Gallimard's "passing" between an acceptable white male heterosexuality and a tabooed white male homosexuality brings with it not only psychic relief but also concrete material rewards. The diplomat's "passing"—whether consciously or finally unconsciously achieved—is reinforced by a corresponding framework of economic and political benefits. As Earl Jackson Jr. observes, gay white males occupy "a peculiar position in a heterosexist society in that, as men (if they are not 'out'), they potentially have full access to the very power mechanisms that repress them and their fellow 'outsiders,' who cannot 'pass,' white women and people of color of any sexual orientation" (121). The political, economic, and cultural stakes are high for the "passing" gay white male: full access to the world of colonial privileges and rewards. In light of these considerable material advantages, could Gallimard's putative ignorance be seen as *conscious* bad faith? Could Gallimard's anatomical blunder be seen as *consciously* self-denying homosexuality encouraged by the likes of Toulon and the pontificating judge? This question—yet another version of "Did Monsieur Gallimard know you were a man?"—may not be answerable. However, unconscious coercion and conscious bad faith often have similar results in the social context of the "real" world. The material rewards of Gallimard's "passing" as heterosexual in Toulon's colonial regime are great—promotion and adulation by others—whereas the consequences of Song's disrobing and Gallimard's exposure as "homosexual" lead to imprisonment, ignominy, and death. Hence, questions of conscious intent to "pass" *must* be considered, for venal complicity in a system of colonial privilege enjoyed by gay white men who do consciously "pass" is an all too familiar phenomenon in both Hwang's context of colonial China and our contemporary Western world.[21]

If, as I have argued throughout this essay, the power of symbolic norms of heterosexuality and whiteness functions largely through the tacit veiling of their collusionary ideals, then rendering visible the "invisible" workings of a compulsory system of both heterosexuality *and* whiteness is an imperative project. Gallimard's "passing" and slippage from normative white masculinity can be used to provide a model by which we can contest the social structures seeming to guarantee an immutable position of privilege to the conventional white male subject. To this effect, I conclude with a final interpretation of fetishism and the heterosexual failure of whiteness: the failure of the fetishizing Ambassador Toulon—the most strongly coded "sufficient" white male subject of the drama—to prevent even himself from falling into the abjected domain of homosexual desire.

The Confidence of the Thing

We come to learn in Freud's essay "Fetishism" that the struggle that impels divided belief and calls for the psychic mechanism of the fetish is not merely the sight of female "castration" but the truly threatening proportions that this visual "castration" takes when coupled with the threatening prohibitions of the father. In this respect, what the little boy struggles against in "Fetishism" is the father himself and the ambivalent attitudes of hatred and love that his paternal authority elicits.

My observations on this father-son drama that underpins fetishism are supported in the Freudian text by an interesting story of denial, which I would describe as the "ur-text" of castration: two young boys who disavow the actual death of their father. Describing one of the youngsters who in all situations "oscillated between two assumptions" of divided belief, Freud observes, "On the one [hand] his father was still alive and hindered him from action, on the other his father was dead and he had the right to regard himself as his successor" (218). The little boy's state of split knowledge thus suggests that the assumption of the paternal position is ultimately an ambivalent process that is never complete. To borrow loosely from the logic of fetishism: the little boy can and cannot be his father.

If the purpose of fetishism is to normalize a relationship between (white) man and woman, then this psychic mechanism serves to encourage and to facilitate the assumption of the father's place, Freud suggests, specifically through the axis of sexuality, by offering the little boy a way into heterosexual desire. In other words, fetishism, by (re)making the female body an acceptable locale for his libidinal investments, encourages the little boy to identify with the heterosexual position of the father, while denying any residual homosexual desire that he may have for him. This psychic process, as we have observed, occurs only by (re)configuring the female body in the guise of the male—by neutralizing the female's sexual difference and "lack." And in this regard, we witness in fetishism a rather overt attempt on the part of the little boy to write out a desire for the father, which is nevertheless curiously preserved in the "male" form that the female body must invariably assume.[22] Consequently, the social order—its system of compulsory heterosexuality—is maintained by a tenuous line between heterosexual identification and a constant promise of resexualized homosexual desire.

In my reading of *M. Butterfly*, I have focused attention on Gallimard as a hyperbolically marginal male figure occupying the borders of conventional white masculinity. The diplomat's shaky relationship to paternal authority is, however, not an anomalous psychic position, but one that *all* white men come to embody—even the strongly coded father figure Ambassador Toulon. In highlighting the phallic failures of white heterosexual masculinity beyond Gallimard, Hwang thus qualifies in general its universalizing impulses. Let us return one last time to this dynamic father-son duo. Promoting Gallimard to vice-consul, Toulon offers a few words of advice to his new protégé:

Toulon: Humility won't be part of the job. You're going to coordinate the revamped intelligence division. Want to know a secret? A year ago, you would've been out. But the past few months, I don't know how it happened, you've become this new aggressive confident . . . thing. And they also tell me you get along with the Chinese. So I think you're a lucky man, Gallimard. Congratulations.

They shake hands. Toulon exits. Party noises out. Gallimard stumbles across a darkened stage.

Gallimard: Vice-consul? Impossible! As I stumbled out of the party, I saw it written across the sky: There is no God. Or, no—say that there is a God. But that God . . . understands. Of course! God who creates Eve to serve Adam, who blesses Solomon with his harem but ties Jezebel to a burning bed—that God is a man. And he understands! At age thirty-nine, I was suddenly initiated into the way of the world. (37–38)

Embracing the psychic contract of Toulon's old boys' network, Gallimard comes to realize that his emotional battering of the Oriental opera diva has been swiftly and richly rewarded. At age thirty-nine, Gallimard's interpellation into the realm of heterosexual and white privilege is rather late. He "matures" only under the tutelage of Toulon, who rewards the late bloomer with an unexpected promotion.

In his enthusiastic response to Toulon, Gallimard begins unwittingly to mime the ambassador's lessons in divided belief, through the aid of Biblical law: "There is no God. Or, no—say that there is a God. But that God . . . understands. Of course! God who creates Eve to serve Adam . . . that God is a man. There is no God. Or, no— say there is a God." The diplomat suggests through Biblical references to Adam and Eve that his promotion to vice consul signals divine acceptance of the lotus blossom fantasy. Yet although the rhetoric of this language of Genesis is meant to lend an eternal vision to Gallimard's symbolic revelations, the fact that this knowledge is "written across the sky" produces a contradictory feeling of transience. The "truths" of this religious law are written on air, and the urgency of Gallimard's newfound confidence in normative white masculinity has no solid foundation.

Are we back in the territory of fetishism? We must note that Toulon and Gallimard's dialogue is firmly embedded in the logic of divided belief, the willful splitting of heterosexual identification from homosexual desire. Invoking yet again the open "secret" of colonial presumption—the possession of the Oriental lotus blossom—Toulon attempts to forestall any psychic equivocation on the part of Gallimard, by installing him in a network of heterosexuality and whiteness through his promotion to vice-consul. Pay attention to the ambassador's words, however: the diplomat's assumption of place within the paternal legacy is contingent upon a "revamped intelligence division." As dictated by Toulon, this contingent division of this intelligence—this knowing and not knowing (of Song's penis, of the existence of a sexist God)—is one that ultimately becomes emblematic of an unstable white masculinity *tout court*.

As such, fetishism's divided belief becomes a privileged psychic linchpin for the maintenance of white male colonial subjectivity as the universal norm. In this regard, we must note that the figure of woman—Eve and Jezebel—explicitly invoked as the heterosexual buttress for the white male subject is finally overshadowed by an occluded homosexual desire. In Toulon's congratulatory words to the vice-consul, the ambassador invariably turns Gallimard into a fetishized object, resexualizing the borders of a prohibited homosexual desire. "You've *become* this new aggressive confident . . . *thing*" (my emphasis), he tells Gallimard. What is the all-powerful "thing" that Toulon euphemistically describes, but the delegated symbol of male privilege and abuse: the anatomical penis as symbolic phallus? How might we interpret Toulon's conflation of penis and phallus? And what does it mean that Gallimard has "*become* this new aggressive confident . . . thing" for Toulon—has *become*, in effect, the phallus for the ambassador?

Mark Chiang suggests that in "becoming the phallus, Gallimard no longer occupies the position of the man, who is possessor of the phallus; he occupies the position of the woman, whose only hope is to be the phallus. . . . Masculinity in this reading would seem to be just as much a fetish, just as much the object of fetishization, as femininity. If Gallimard accedes to the plenitude of heterosexual masculinity, it is by making himself over into the phallus, by becoming a fetish for Ambassador Toulon" ("A White Thing" 5). If, as Lacan argues in "The Signification of the Phallus" (281–91), the male must "have" the phallus and the female must "be" the phallus, then no longer can white masculinity lay claim to having the phallus in *M. Butterfly* once Gallimard has become this privileged signifier.[23] If the male Gallimard can become—is made to *be*—the phallus for Toulon, then masculinity, as Chiang points out, not only "seem[s] to be just as much a fetish, just as much the object of fetishization, as femininity" but the male body itself is (re)made to function for Toulon as the locus of libidinal investment and homosexual desire as well.[24] Gallimard's bodily frame comes to mark the corporeal limits of the ambassador's desire. As such, no longer is a female body— or even an Asian male dressed up as a female—required to "be" the phallus for the white male. Instead, Gallimard can "be" the phallus for Toulon, a homosexual relay of white male object for a white male subject.[25] Undoubtedly, we have returned to a narcissistic psychic terrain in which the normative white male subject sees only himself everywhere he looks.

Toulon's brief litany on Gallimard as "thing" speaks not only to the contradiction of a Lacanian binary—the "having" of the phallus on the part of the male and the "being" of the phallus on the part of the female—but also to the very collapse of the having/being distinction that legitimates normative white male heterosexuality as the universal mode of the social order. In other words, if one can only "have" the phallus as a male, Gallimard's falling out of this naturalized framework suggests that the logic of a compulsory heterosexual matrix requiring that one can either "have" or "be" the phallus is beset by a fundamental contradiction: an irreconcilable state of anxiety over a "having" and a "being" of the phallus that can never be fully surmounted or strictly separated. The French ambassador's configuration of Gallimard as the phallus thus comes to illustrate a nagging yet entirely normative equivocation at the heart of conventional white masculinity: a "having" that can never be fully "had" and a "being" that can never fully "be."

Ultimately, as *M. Butterfly* brilliantly illustrates, borders between heterosexual identification and homosexual desire are hardly clear-cut—they are unable to function in isolation from one another. This brief exchange between the ambassador and the diplomat renders visible the insistent partitioning of heterosexual identification from homosexual desire that underwrites normative white male subjectivity. Furthermore, this masking over of homosexual desire also involves the masking over of "whiteness" as an invisible racial category. The lotus blossom fantasy—Toulon's open "secret" underpinning all the ambassador's exchanges with Gallimard—attests to conventional white male subjectivity's resolute dependence on the maintenance of both a hegemonic whiteness and an occluded racial boundary. And it is this complex crossing of (homo)sexual and racial difference exposed in Gallimard's donning of whiteface that not only marks the extravagant failure of his *Madama Butterfly* phantasmatic but also insists on a sustained investigation of racial difference in psychoanalytic paradigms of sexual difference such as fetishism.

In the final analysis, Gallimard's application of a thick layer of white makeup to his face—his colonization and assumption of the "other's" place—must be read not merely as an attempt to deflect the explicit homosexual implications of Song's penile unveiling but also as the unveiling of whiteness as a fetishistic application itself, as a mask. This relativizing of whiteness as a universal racial category acknowledges the constructedness of both (hetero)sexual and racial categories. It stresses the need to enlarge our critical focus, in Asian American, ethnic, critical race, feminist, and queer studies, by considering—by naming—the ways in which heterosexuality and whiteness work in tandem to secure the symbolic ideals of colonial authority. In applying this white mask to his face, Gallimard's actions acknowledge that one can *be* neither heterosexual nor white, that symbolic ideals of colonial rule demanding compliance to universal norms of heterosexuality and whiteness can only ever be approximated—that they are ultimately unfulfilled and unfulfillable.

In *M. Butterfly*, the "possession" of the lotus blossom phantasmatic exacts an expensive toll on Gallimard, for the fetishistic costs of arresting the trauma of homosexual and racial difference at the site of the Asian male body require a definitive rift in the diplomat's ego, "which never heals but which increases as time goes on" (Freud, "Splitting of the Ego" 221). It is the concerted focus on the attendant sexual and racial crossings of this rift that turns the analytic lens of Asian American and psychoanalytic studies onto heterosexuality and whiteness as universalizing categories for deconstruction in a new cultural politics—and play—of differences.

NOTES

1. Ralph Ellison's novel, *Invisible Man*; Christine Choy's *Out in Silence*, a documentary on AIDS in the Asian Pacific Islander community; and ACT UP's chant of queer affirmation and protest, "We're here; we're queer; get used to it!" are all examples that collectively emphasize— even demand—the need for the disenfranchised subject to emerge into the visible domain.

2. See the recent special issue of the *Village Voice*, "White Like Who? Notes on the Other Race," a compendium of articles discussing "whiteness" as an invisible racial identity.

3. Ping-hui Liao's article "'Of Writing Words for Music Which Is Already Made': *Madama Butterfly, Turandot*, and Orientalism" provides an excellent summary of Puccini's opera and its critical antecedents. According to Liao, the Puccini opera was originally based on *Madame Butterfly*, a drama written by American playwright David Belasco. Belasco had, in turn, adapted the story from a novella by American author John Luther Long. The original storyline is apparently based on the actual suicide of a Japanese geisha, a story notably recorded by the French writer Pierre Loti in *Madame Chrysanthème*.

4. See, for example, Gabrielle Cody's article "David Hwang's *M. Butterfly*: Perpetuating the Misogynist Myth" (24–27) and John Louis DiGaetani's useful interview with the playwright, "*M. Butterfly*: An Interview with David Henry Hwang" (141–53).

5. Here Garber quotes Hwang.

6. See Miriam Horn's review of *M. Butterfly* in which she compares Hwang to African American film director Spike Lee (52–53). For an excellent summary of the material conditions prohibiting the Asian American artist from full participation in mainstream American artistic production, see Sau-ling Cynthia Wong's *Reading Asian American Literature* (especially 166–211).

7. In "An Actor Despairs," which Simon wrote after *M. Butterfly* won the Tony Award, he retracts his earlier statement and responds to the issue of white masculinity: "While sharing in the shame and heartbreak of René Gallimard as embarrassingly well conveyed by Lithgow, I let the quality of the play slip out of my focus" (146). For an analysis of Simon's admission of an uncomfortable identification with Gallimard's failed white manhood, see Pao 1–16.

8. Ted Danson's donning of blackface at the Whoopi Goldberg roast at New York's Friars Club is a particularly egregious example of these spurious asymmetries. See Williams C1. For a similar debate on the use of yellowface by a white actor, see Smith's analysis of the *Miss Saigon* controversy (41–45).

9. I use "castration" in quotation marks here, since one can technically be castrated only when one loses something that one once had. The idea of female "castration" is problematic, since the woman never had a penis to lose in the first place. Freud's conflation of female penis envy (and the notion of clitoris as inferior penis) with loss and "castration" is both slippery and overdetermined. I thank David Hirsch for discussing this problem with me.

10. See, for instance, Said's analysis of colonialism and cultural production in *Culture and Imperialism* (especially chap. 2) for an analysis of French imperialism in the last two centuries.

11. It seems to me that at this juncture the economic metaphors underpinning many of Freud's psychic models ("But everything has to be paid for in one way or another, and this success is achieved at the price of a rift in the ego which never heals but which increases as time goes on") and the economics of imperialism intersect in ways demanding the historicizing of psychoanalysis and the psychologizing of colonialism. That, however, is a project beyond the scope of this essay.

12. For a discussion of gender norms and citationality, see Butler's *Bodies That Matter* (12–16).

13. I do, of course, make ironic reference to this abduction of Gallimard into heterosexuality and whiteness over and against the hysterical accusations of those who would say that homosexuality is given over to the logic of recruitment in its "reproductive" capacities.

14. It is interesting to note that Freud ends "Fetishism" with a gesture toward a "race-psychological parallel" to this psychic mechanism of denial and projection: the Chinese custom of foot binding, of "first mutilating a woman's foot and then revering it" (219). "The Chinese man seems to want to thank the woman for having submitted to castration," Freud claims. Here Freud seems to raise this racial example only to further his assertions on fetishism's role in the anatomical distinction between the (white) sexes.

15. Here I am allowing a certain slippage from "Asian" to "Asian American," not only because Hwang's text functions within the politics of Asian America but also because to many a racist eye Asians and Asian Americans all "look alike."

16. For an explanation of the distinction between "look" and "gaze" as discussed by Lacan, see Kaja Silverman's *Male Subjectivity at the Margins* (chap. 3).

17. This scene suggests that Renée neutralizes the gender of the phallus. As Jane Gallop has noted in *Reading Lacan*, the typographical error concerning the definite article "la" that marks the "phallus" in the French publication of Lacan's "La Signification du phallus" speaks to a breakdown in symbolic structuration: "If the 'phallic signifier is intrinsically neutral,' then the signifier 'phallus,' the word in language, might be either feminine or masculine, epicene" (137).

18. Sedgwick (*Between Men*) argues, for example, that the homosocial order annexes the figure of woman as the conduit through which homosexual desire is channeled.

19. See Freud's discussion of anaclitic and narcissistic love, in which he names homosexuals, females, children, cats, and criminals as exemplary narcissists ("On Narcissism" 68–72). See also Judith Butler's excellent discussion of normative heterosexuality as a melancholic renouncing of homosexual desire in *Gender Trouble* (57–72).

20. A suitable parallel can be drawn from Freud's admonition that although the superego comes about through an abjection of homosexuality, it cannot ultimately enforce this prohibition from which it is produced (*The Ego and the Id*).

21. In an earlier reading of the drama I explored the material conditions around which "Rice Queens" might choose or not choose to "pass." The identitarian bent with which I approached this first reading of *M. Butterfly* remains crucial in debates on identity-based politics (see Eng 93–116). I hope that the current reading provides a supplementary angle by which to merge my two arguments on both a material "real world" and psychoanalytic level.

22. And here we must remember that the "pangs of conscience" (resulting from the little boy's identification with the father through the sublimation of his homosexual desire) are as Judith Butler points out, "nothing other than the displaced satisfactions of homosexual desire" (*Bodies That Matter* 277). These "pangs of conscience," whose duties lie in keeping the little boy from ever acknowledging the prohibited desire for his father, are in no way secure, for they are the direct result of a psychical *conservation* of homosexual desire, not an obliteration of it (Freud, "On Narcissism" 56–82).

23. Lacan writes, "But one may, simply by reference to the function of the phallus, indicate the structures that will govern the relation between the sexes. Let us say that these relations will turn around a 'to be' and a 'to have,' which, by referring to a signifier, the phallus, have the opposed effect, on the one hand, of giving reality to the subject in this signifier, and, on the other, of derealizing the relations to be signified" (289).

24. As Lacan points out, "It should not be forgotten that the organ [the penis] that assumes this signifying function [of the phallus] takes on the value of a fetish" (290).

25. Here homosociality and its exchange of women gives way to a homosexual economy that no longer, for the moment, requires their presence.

WORKS CITED

Alarcón, Norma. "The Theoretical Subject(s) of *This Bridge Called My Back* and Anglo-American Feminism." *Making Face, Making Soul: Haciendo Caras*. Ed. Gloria Anzaldúa. San Francisco: Aunt Lute, 1990. 356–69.

Belasco, David. *Six Plays: Madame Butterfly, Du Barry, The Darling of the Gods, Adrea, The Girl of the Golden West, The Return of Peter Grimm.* Boston: Little, Brown, 1928.

Butler, Judith. *Bodies That Matter: On the Discursive Limits of "Sex."* New York: Routledge, 1993.

———. *Gender Trouble: Feminism and the Subversion of Identity.* New York: Routledge, 1990.

Chiang, Mark. "A White Thing: Fetishism and Paranoia in the Nation." Unpublished paper. Association for Asian American Studies Annual Conf. U of Michigan, Ann Arbor, Apr. 1994.

Cody, Gabrielle. "David Hwang's *M. Butterfly:* Perpetuating the Misogynist Myth." *Theatre* 20.2 (Spring 1989): 24–27.

DiGaetani, John Louis. "*M. Butterfly:* An Interview with David Henry Hwang." *Drama Review* 33.3 (Fall 1989): 141–53.

Ellison, Ralph. *Invisible Man.* New York: Random, 1947.

Eng, David L. "In the Shadows of a Diva: Committing Homosexuality in David Henry Hwang's *M. Butterfly.*" *Amerasia Journal* 20.1 (1994): 93–116.

Freud, Sigmund. "The Dissection of the Psychical Personality." 1933. *New Introductory Lectures on Psychoanalysis.* Trans. James Strachey. New York: Norton, 1965. 51–71.

———. *The Ego and the Id.* 1923. Trans. Joan Riviere. New York: Norton, 1960.

———. "Fetishism." 1927. *Sexuality and the Psychology of Love.* Ed. Philip Rieff. New York: Collier, 1963. 214–19.

———. "On Narcissism: An Introduction." 1914. *General Psychological Theory.* Ed. Philip Rieff. New York: Collier, 1963. 56–82.

———. "Splitting of the Ego in the Defensive Process." 1938. *Sexuality and the Psychology of Love.* Ed. Philip Rieff. New York: Collier, 1963. 220–23.

Fuss, Diana. *Identification Papers.* New York: Routledge, 1995.

Gallop, Jane. *Reading Lacan.* Ithaca: Cornell UP, 1985.

Garber, Majorie. *Vested Interests: Cross-Dressing and Cultural Anxiety.* New York: Harper Perennial, 1992.

Hodgson, Moira. "*M. Butterfly.*" *The Nation* 23 Apr. 1988: 577–78.

Horn, Miriam. "The Mesmerizing Power of Racial Myths." *US News and World Report* 28 Mar. 1988: 52–53.

Hwang, David Henry. *M. Butterfly.* New York: Plume, 1988.

Jackson, Earl Jr. "Scandalous Subjects: Robert Glück's Embodied Narratives." *differences: A Journal of Feminist Cultural Studies* 3.2 (Summer 1991): 112–34.

Lacan, Jacques. "The Signification of the Phallus." 1958. *Écrits: A Selection.* Trans. Alan Sheridan. New York: Norton, 1977. 281–91.

Liao, Ping-hui. "'Of Writing Words for Music Which Is Already Made': *Madama Butterfly, Turandot,* and Orientalism." *Cultural Critique* 16 (Fall 1990): 31–59.

Long, John Luther. *Madame Butterfly; Purple Eyes; A Gentleman of Japan and a Lady; Kito; Glory.* New York: The Century Company, 1898.

Loti, Pierre. *Madame Chrysanthème.* 1887. Paris: Calmann-Levy, 1922.

Lowe, Lisa. *Immigrant Acts: On Asian American Cultural Politics.* Durham, N.C.: Duke UP, 1996.

M. Butterfly. David Cronenberg, director. Geffen Pictures, 1993.

Mercer, Kobena. "Skin Head Sex Thing." *How Do I Look?* Ed. Bad Object Choices. Seattle: Bay, 1991. 169–222.

Out in Silence. Christine Choy, director. 1994.

Pao, Angela. "The Critic and the Butterfly: Sociocultural Contexts and the Reception of David Henry Hwang's *M. Butterfly.*" *Amerasia Journal* (1992): 1–16.

Puccini, Giacomo. *Madama Butterfly: Opera in Three Acts.* 1904 Italian version by Luigi Illica and Giuseppe Giacosa. English version by Ruth Martin and Thomas Martin. New York: Colombo, 1954.

Rich, Frank. "*M. Butterfly,* a Story of a Strange Love, Conflict and Betrayal." *New York Times* 21 Mar. 1988: C13.

Said, Edward W. *Culture and Imperialism.* New York: Vintage, 1994.

Sedgwick, Eve Kosofsky. *Between Men: English Literature and Male Homosocial Desire.* New York: Columbia UP, 1985.

———. "White Glasses." *Tendencies.* Durham, N.C.: Duke UP, 1993. 252–66.

Silverman, Kaja. "The Lacanian Phallus." *differences: A Journal of Feminist Cultural Studies* 4.1 (Spring 1992): 84–115.

———. *Male Subjectivity at the Margins.* New York: Routledge, 1992.

———. *The Threshold of the Visible World.* New York: Routledge, 1996.

Simon, John. "An Actor Despairs." *New York Magazine* 24 Oct. 1988: 145–46.

———. "Finding Your Song." *New York Magazine* 11 Apr. 1988: 117–18.

Smith, Dinitia. "Face Values: The Sexual and Racial Obsessions of Playwright David Henry Hwang." *New York Magazine* 4 Jan. 1993: 41–45.

Village Voice. "White Like Who? Notes on the Other Race." Special issue 18 May 1993: 24–41.

Williams, Lena. "After the Roast, Fire and Smoke." *New York Times* 14 Oct. 1993: C1+.

Wong, Sau-ling Cynthia. *Reading Asian American Literature: From Necessity to Extravagance.* Princeton: Princeton UP, 1993.

Overleaf: Ken Chu, *Sticky Rice,*
mixed media, 15 × 13.5 × 13.5 inches, 1994.
Photo by Becket Logan.

23. Monster
Justin Chin

The first gay people I knew were not called gay at all. They were the drama queens at school, nellie boys who lived for the annual music and drama night, when they would take over an empty classroom to apply layers of makeup, teeter on high heels, and shimmy up tight dresses fit for the trashiest lounge singers on Bras Basah Road. These were the boys destined for the famed Bugis Street, before the government tore the street down and rebuilt it for tourist efficiency. The queens were called fairies, homos, a-quas, ba-pok, derogatory names that scored their effeminancy. But the queens wore these epithets like generals' epaulets, or perhaps more like Joan Collins–inspired shoulder pads. On that one night, dressed in female drag, they sashayed across the basketball court to the auditorium, ignoring the most hostile name callers, flirting with the milder name callers, and wallowing in all the attention.

Out of drag, in their regular school lives, they gave each other girls' names, hung out together, designed dresses in the margins of their textbooks, and flirted shamelessly with the boys on the swim team. They joined the drama club, where they vied for the female roles that would give them an excuse to get into drag and be applauded for it for one brief moment one night of the year. They dreamed of having a sex change; owning a boutique; dating the captain of the swim team; and becoming a fashion designer, model, or stewardess, not necessarily in that order.

The other boys at school either found the queens vastly entertaining or were grossed out by them to the point of violence. I belonged to the former group, but then I had to. I knew I liked boys, but the stigma of being associated with the queens, who were so resoundingly teased and tormented, made me nestle quite firmly in my comfy closet. I was on the swim team; I participated in sports. Still, I had my campy side; the closet door was at least somewhat ajar: I could do a great impersonation of Madonna circa *Like a Virgin,* but somehow the butchness dulled any hostility toward it. I was accepted by the "problem kids," the ones who sat in the back of the class, paid no attention, skipped school, and generally raised hell; we were destined for all kinds of failure, our teachers predicted.

I knew or, rather, discovered to my horror, quite early on that I wasn't entirely heterosexual. In Primary Six, the hormones started to rage through my baby-fat body: pubic hairs started to peek out of my crotch and armpits, my voice started to change, and I was made aware that I had a penis when my brother complained to my mother that I was still running around the house without my pajama bottoms on. The first pangs of homosexuality struck while I was reading a Buck Rogers book. I had strange feelings deep in my gut when the author described Buck's torso. The story involved alien women in primary colors who kidnapped Buck and tried to become impregnated by his seed so that they could propagate their race. These feelings arose again with Harrison Ford as Han Solo on the cover of *GO Magazine*. This time I went one step further: I hid in the bathroom and kissed the magazine's glossy cover. Then the feelings surfaced again. This time it was *Magnum PI,* Friday nights at 9:30 P.M.

My feelings and preoccupations terrified me. I was raised in a decidedly Christian household. The year before, my guardian, who was an elder at the church, had taken in the church secretary, Betty, who was possessed by the devil. Betty needed a place to stay while the church elders prayed over her, so my aunt opened the house to her. The weeks that Betty stayed there were filled with her screaming and with the strange babble of Betty and the elders speaking in tongues, a verbal tussle between God and the devil. To quell our fears, my aunt decided that we should have Bible study and prayer meetings every night. And this we did. We rid the house of anything that might have harbored the devil: images of dragons, phoenixes, tikis, and primitive-looking renderings. We prayed a lot, constantly aware of the devil lurking in every corner.

Still, I couldn't quell these feelings inside me. I wanted so much to see another penis. My father's, my uncle's, celebrities' in a magazine, anyone's. Scanning through my father's medical textbooks (which he stored under my brother's bed) for pictures of penises, I found them in all their diseased glory: bulbous members plagued with syphilis, gonorrhea, and various sores and boils. I was titillated by the sexual details described in Dr. David M. Ruben's *Everything You Wanted to Know About Sex But Were Afraid to Ask.* I looked up the words "penis," "homosexual," and "intercourse" in the dictionary to see what I would find. After figuring out how to masturbate one day when I was trying to put on a makeshift condom, I took to masturbation with a passion. I took great guilt and secret delight in the "Best Body Poll" issue of *Tiger Beat* (Scott Baio won best body; Gregory "Gonzo Gates" Harrison placed a paltry twelfth). I rode around on my bike looking for men without their shirts on.

One day, this man, an ugly-looking fucker, sat beside me on the bus on my way to school. Suddenly without warning, he placed his hand on my crotch and covered his act with my school bag. I was shocked, frightened, and excited at the same time. At my stop, I got off the bus, and he followed me. He said that we could go to the rest room to "play." It never occurred to me to say no. In the toilet stall, he started sucking my nipples, and he sucked my dick. I had no idea what to do. He pushed my mouth to his ugly cold nipple, but I didn't know what he expected of me. Then he tried to force me to suck his dick. I knew what he expected of me then, and when he forced his dick into my mouth, I gagged so hard I started vomiting. Undaunted, he tried to fuck me in the ass. By this time, I was so scared I was on the verge of tears; in fact, I think I *was* crying. Thankfully, he came and he left. I spent a good deal of time locked in the stall, trying to clean up, crying, and praying to God for forgiveness.

All this should have soured me somewhat to men's penises, but it only made me more confused and needful. One day, something happened that changed my life. I discovered that at a urinal I could actually see someone's penis. I was ecstatic and fearful, but I wanted more. Later, in a restroom at a local shopping mall, as I was trying to sneak a peek at penises, a man at the urinal actually turned to me and started playing with himself. The whole world of rest room sex opened itself up to me. I was thirteen years old.

Soon I was spending a great deal of time hanging out in shopping malls, cruising the rest rooms for sexual encounters. My rest room exploits started to be a great burden on my mind. My homosexual longings were the strongest the same year I was confirmed and baptized—a fabulous, *trés* dramatic Brethren immersion baptism. I was wrecked with guilt and spent the better part of the year making deals with God, asking for a sign, ignoring or rationalizing everything I perceived to be a sign, praying for forgiveness, and being obsessed by raging hormones and a seemingly endless supply of dicks. I believed that it was all part of God's test to see if I was sinning. I was. I believed I was destined for hell. I believed in the rapture, in Revelation, a story that had been read to me when I was a mere child. Every time there was a thunder storm, my heart would collapse, and I would fear the rapture—that the good Christ-fearing folk would be snatched up from the earth and the sinners would be left to fight the end of the millennium against the Antichrist.

Those days I fucked a lot. At some point, I distinctly remember that I had lost count of the number of men that I had tricked with. I fucked a lot. I fucked flight attendants on layovers (Quantas seemed to have the most fags), sailors, potbellied tourists, professors, bankers, businessmen all strangers and very few repeats. Some tried to stay in touch; some fell hopelessly in love at first fuck and wanted to marry me, but I didn't know any better. I wanted more. I had no idea what I wanted. And at some point, and I don't particularly remember when, I stopped praying for forgiveness.

I'm also not sure exactly where and when I got the language for who and what I am. I don't remember how I learned the words "gay," "homo(sexual)," "fag," "queen," and so on. I just seemed to have picked it up and understood what it meant the way one picks up language on the periphery of any closet.

The first person that I knew who admitted publicly to being gay was Gary Goh. I met Gary through a mutual friend, someone I had picked up but ended up not having sex with. I was seventeen, in junior college, on the slippery pipeline to my A levels (standardized exams), and failing every subject miserably (E for biology, O for chemistry and physics, and F for math, though I got an A for my general paper). Gary fessed up to being gay during the compulsory National Service. In the military he declared himself "effeminate homosexual," which got him a desk job, a pass to leave every evening, and visits to the staff psychiatrist, who suggested Gary play more sports with his father. At a time when I was coming to the realization that freedoms were fast disappearing, I thought that his bold declaration—Gloria Gaynor's singing "I Am What I Am" paled by comparison—was such a courageous act.

Gary was by no stretch of the imagination an a-qua. He wanted to be a fashion designer; he was involved in the local theatre scene and he designed many a fabulous costume. Today he's made a name for himself as one of Singapore's up-and-coming young designers. I always looked at him as sort of a hero, as someone who lived as he wanted to and made everyone around him accept it or deal with it. He had no qualms about being a flaming queen in public. Once we were out together, and I was so incredibly embarrassed when he started spinning and dancing in the middle of a shopping center simply because the Bananarama tunes wafting out of a shop moved him so. He had balls, that boy did.

Soon I discovered the gay underbelly of Singapore. I started going to gay bars and discotheques. I had gay friends. I fell in love with men who broke my teenaged heart. I met a Swedish psychologist, who became my first boyfriend. (He was rather abusive, wholly narcissistic, and unrelentingly colonial, and the relationship ended miserably. But, God, he was so damn good-looking.) I started being comfortable with my homosexuality. I stopped being wrecked with guilt. I was still struggling with that closet, with being found out by my family, but in school I was the out fag. I was so out that, in retrospect, I'm amazed that I wasn't harassed at all. I believe my immunity from the really horrid harassment other queens faced had to do with my converging butch and queer appearances. My friends, straight girls and really cool straight guys, protected me a lot too. To them, my queerness was incidental to my personality. They accepted me because they'd known me first as this guy who hated and liked the same things and the same people as they did.

The knowledge that I was a fag didn't change their opinions or our friendship.

I left home to come to the United States when I was eighteen. I decided that I really didn't need to tell my family about my sexual orientation. Sure, they had their suspicions; they had even voiced them, but I had always somehow managed to change the subject, much to everyone's relief.

But as the trickle-down theory would have it, my outness in school soon seeped into the home. My brother and some of my childhood friends started to hang out with my friends from junior college. Soon more people than I had bargained for *knew*. They were very careful about bringing up the subject to me, but by this point I wasn't particularly bothered by it anymore. Out of the blue, I got a nice, supportive, and very subtle note from my brother. My best childhood friend was quite miffed that I had not seen fit to tell him sooner.

I don't have any regrets about how I learned to be gay. Perhaps I harbor some romantic notions about the traditional coming out. Perhaps the way I came out is not what we wish for our younger generations: that it consisted of only severe and superficial sexual experiences, without that hesitant first crush, the awkward horseplay behind the barn, and all those other really affirming, charming, and homopositive experiences that you might read about in coming-out books published by gay presses.

I guess I never *really* came out in any sense of the word, whatever that means. After coming to terms with my desires, I simply tried to live my life the best way, and as unapologetically, as I knew how. With that, people came to their own realizations that I was queer. Telling someone that I am gay really holds no appeal to me; it doesn't mean a thing. I would rather that folks see me live and love in the same breath as they do, but in a queer way and in my queer way. And if they find a monster in that, I'll know that it's a monster of grace and beauty.

24. Coming Out into the Global System
*Postmodern Patriarchies and Transnational
Sexualities in* The Wedding Banquet
Mark Chiang

As a film that depicts diasporic Chinese communities in the United States, *The Wedding Banquet* offers one popular mapping of the trajectory of Asian and Asian American sexuality in the global system. Made on a $750,000 budget (minuscule for a major theatrical release), it became the highest-grossing film in Taiwan, with great success in the United States and other international markets. Surpassing *Jurassic Park* as the film with the highest profit ratio in 1993, it catapulted director Ang Lee to international fame. Lee, whose parents are part of the Chinese émigré population of 1949, is a native of Taiwan, who went to college and film school in the United States. Funding, cast, and crew for the film, which was shot on location in the United States with an American production company, came from both sides of the Pacific.

Although the film gives a positive depiction of its gay protagonist, Gao Wai Tung—a Taiwanese businessman living in New York City with Simon, his white lover—its focus on reconciling the conflicts between the competing demands of sexuality and ethnic identity can hardly be regarded as much more than mildly progressive. Nevertheless, the intent of the reading here is not simply to cast judgment on the degree to which the film subverts or capitulates to the "dominant ideology." Rather, this essay seeks to raise the question of context, by asking how, or where, we locate such transnational cultural productions in the first place, a necessary precondition for any attempt at evaluation.

The film opens a space for gay people in homophobic Asian and American communities, but from a slightly different perspective, it also calls to mind the co-optation of the gay male in the reconstruction of Asian patriarchy. This agenda is, in fact, admitted quite openly by the filmmakers. James Schamus, who collaborated with Lee on all three of his films, remarks that "if the [three films] could be said to have a common theme, it is the question of the father, of the role of the patriarch in a world where the patriarchy is under justifiable fire. In one way, *The Wedding Banquet* is very much about making the institution of fatherhood safe for the contemporary world" (xi–xii). *The Wedding Banquet* certainly offers a useful test case for investigating how patriarchies respond to the pressures and tensions of postmodernity and globalization. In this respect, my analysis attempts to respond to Caren Kaplan and Inderpal Grewal's recent call for a transnational feminist cultural studies: "What we need are critical practices that link our understanding of post-modernity, global economic structures, problematics of nationalism, issues of race and imperialism, critiques of global feminism, and emergent patriarchies" ("Transnational Feminist Cultural Studies" 439).[1]

My argument thus proceeds in two directions. First I demonstrate that the complex entanglements of sexual and ethnic identity in *The Wedding Banquet* cannot be read solely from within the frameworks of national culture, either Chinese or American, but must be read across them in a transnational analysis that attends simultaneously to the local and global. Second I register some of the problems that accompany the globalization of sexuality and identity. In particular, I critique certain queer studies formulations of a global gay identity politics, which generalize the challenge that homosexuality poses to national constructions of identity in the global system without fully accounting for the radically different valences of sexuality in relation to transnational capital and postmodernity. My reading centers on two key moments in film: (1) the ill-fated wedding banquet itself, which epitomizes the crisis of the nation-state, whose cause and solution are both encapsulated in (2) the consolidation of the reconfigured family unit at the end of the film. This closure operates not at the level of national culture and identity, but at the level of the global system. In these terms, *The Wedding Banquet* tells us a great deal about the vicissitudes of national/ethnic identity in the era of postmodernity and about the function sexuality serves in mediating between modernity and postmodernity, the nation and transnational capital.

The film opens with Wai Tung's parents pestering him from Taiwan (via transpacific audiocassette) to get married and raise a family. Meanwhile, Wai Tung, who owns some property, is having trouble collecting rent from Wei Wei, a poor Chinese woman artist who is trying to evade the Immigration and Naturalization Service (INS). Simon suggests to Wai Tung that he marry Wei Wei in order to placate his parents, get Wei Wei a green card, and give Wai Tung a tax break in the bargain. Complications predictably ensue, however, when Wai Tung's parents immediately fly to New York for the wedding of their only son. Simon moves out so that Wei Wei can move in, and the reluctant couple try to feign intimacy for the parents. Ultimately, everything works out: Wai Tung succumbs to Wei Wei's charms on their wedding night and produces a son, satisfying his parents' desire for grandchildren, and he retains his relationship with Simon, who manages to come to an understanding, of sorts, with Wai Tung's father.

The international success of *The Wedding Banquet* as a traveling text offers some indication of its capacity to signify in multiple national contexts. And the appeal of the processes of translation and resignification does not only cross cultural and national boundaries; it also attracts an emergent global/transnational culture, which achieves concrete form in the growing cohesion of the global system. One hypothesis that I advance is that the success of independent (that is, non-Hollywood) films in the international art house and film festival circuit is most often tied to that text's proximity to the culture and values of the transnational capitalist class, which constitutes the main audience for these venues. I suggest, therefore, that *The Wedding Banquet* is a transnational allegory, insofar as it ultimately charts the Chinese diaspora's coalescence into the global system of capital.

My analysis centers on Wai Tung's family, the Gaos, as members of one segment of what Leslie Sklair calls the transnational capitalist class, which is transnational insofar as its members "tend to have global rather than local perspectives" (71).[2] This global perspective finds its visual correlate in the film's aesthetic, its mise-en-scène, the most conspicuous quality of which is a kind of generic blankness. It is this generic and formulaic quality of the film that, apart from its main theme of homosexuality, renders the rest of the film nearly transparent. The primary instance of this evaporation of materiality in the film's cinematography is surely the extent to which Manhattan is resolutely stripped of all of its iconic distinctiveness, converting it into the simulacrum of urban space in any number of metropolitan centers around the globe. Fredric Jameson describes this process as a "kind of representational laundering of ideologically marked contents," in which all signs of the socioeconomic system or of ideological struggle must be excised to avoid interference with the consumption of the film product (*Geopolitical Aesthetic* 119).[3]

This characteristic of the cinematography is indicative of the film's seemingly superficial nature, but it seems to me that it is precisely this very generic transparency that proves most indexical of its transnational origins. The transparency of *The Wedding Banquet* stems from its peculiarly deterritorialized signifiers. Therefore, the generic quality of its narrative is in some sense a consequence of the abstraction of the thematic content from its sociohistorical location in specific material contexts. The space that achieves material visibility in the film, in other words, corresponds to the generalized cosmopolitan space constructed by transnational capital and inhabited by transnational subjects. In order to read a text like *The Wedding Banquet*, then we must rematerialize or reterritorialize its signs, by restoring to them some of their concrete ideological and historical density, a project that this essay returns to in its conclusion.[4]

The plot of *The Wedding Banquet* is set in motion by the tension between Wai Tung's sexual desires and his father's nationalist desires. This antagonism is mediated in part through the trope of the closet and its attendant narratives of coming out. Much of the work in queer studies, however, has been oriented toward the critique of gay identity politics, the closet, and coming out, as being defined by bourgeois constructions of identity. This critique has been extended in the work of lesbian and gay scholars in Asian American studies. If coming out is tangled in epistemological knots, as Diana Fuss has elaborated (1–10), these entanglements are multiplied by the geometrical complications of race and ethnicity. David Eng remarks that "coming out for Asian gays involves many irreconcilable choices between aligning oneself with a predominantly white gay community often tainted by overt racism or an ethnic community often marked by cultural homophobia" (9).[5] Eng concludes that "if nothing else, *The Wedding Banquet* illustrates in exacting detail the inevitable compromises that a tortuous, pathological, and unnatural system of compulsory heterosexuality demands from us all" (10).

While I certainly do not disagree with this assessment, the particular configurations of Wai Tung's negotiations of the closet and coming out encode a considerable amount of information about the material and institutional contexts surrounding these acts or performances. Eng's strategic reading of the film attempts to negotiate the mutual exclusions of racial and sexual communities and identities, yet it also operates within a context of U.S. identity politics, which cannot account for the complexities of sexual and ethnic identities in the global system. What is occluded in a national reading is the way in which the closet itself is reconstructed, in the course of the narrative, under the pressure of globalization. From an initial problematic of assimilation, in which it is a question of competing national identities, it gradually becomes a choice between a national and a transnational/global identity.

Let us begin, then, by investigating some of the meanings attached to homosexuality in Asian and Asian American communities, in order to elucidate the cross-reference of race and sexuality in anxieties of assimilation. In the growing literature by lesbian and gay Asian Americans one can find numerous refutations of the persistent charges that homosexuality affects only white people and that being gay means wanting to be white. Eric Wat states that "for most Asian parents, being Asian and being gay are mutually exclusive. It is not only that homosexuality is a forbidden topic in most Asian communities. More significant, there is not a need to talk about 'it' because it is only a *problem* for white people: 'it' is a white *disease*. For example, in Hong Kong, a Westernized colony where a gay community has become more visible in the last few years, the colloquial word for a gay man is simply *gay-loh* (gay fellow)" (155).[6] The underlying narrative about homosexuality here is that it is an effect of Westernization. And the similarities of this conjunction across a number of different national/ethnic contexts suggest that this association has less to do with the homophobia or traditionalism of ethnic communities than with discourses of nationalism and their particular mechanisms for defining and enforcing normative definitions of community and identity. Nayan Shah explains that in some South Asian communities, "the conservative ideologies of heterosexist South Asians equate queer sexualities with an already well-defined yet adaptable arsenal of 'Western evils'—divorce, drinking alcohol, eating meat, or drug abuse. Any unfavorable value is displaced onto a non–South Asian source" (chapter 9). Shah further notes the irony implicit in the rejection of homosexuality as Western, and therefore foreign to the native culture, when such judgments are themselves structured by a Western dichotomization of sexuality.

Sexuality is obviously one important semiotic field in which social relations are negotiated, and the meanings assigned to homosexuality in the West and non-West are implicated in global relations of inequality. Although homosexuality in American culture is primarily perceived as a form of deviance from prescribed *gender* identities—connoting a threat that arises from within national borders—Wat and Shah suggest that for Asian communities in both Asia and the United States, the phantasmic danger that homosexuality poses to national/ethnic identity may supersede other axes of alterity. The figure of the homosexual becomes a sign for the Western domination that enters from without and disrupts the communities' ability to reproduce the structure of social relations. The homophobia that lesbians and gays of color face in their ethnic communities finds its corollary in the racism that they confront in gay communities that are predominantly white. Domestic racism is inevitably tied to the epistemic structures of imperial domination in the international sphere. And the imposition of Western categories of identity—whether in the name of oppression or liberation (it is not always clear which is which)—may restrict alternative codifications and traditions of sexuality in the non-West within the homosexual/heterosexual opposition. Instances of same-sex relations can, of course, be found in almost all cultures, but they may not appear as "homosexuality" outside of Western regimes of sexuality/knowledge.[7]

Against a nationalist homophobia, then, one major function of homosexuality in *The Wedding Banquet* is precisely to contest the demands of national/ethnic identity, by performing the counternaturalization of assimilation or the impure and inauthentic ethnic subject. By utilizing the sign of homosexuality, the film manages to appropriate whatever legitimacy has been achieved by lesbian and gay constructions of homosexual desire as essential, inherent, and therefore "natural." In the first half of *The Wedding Banquet,* sexuality and national/ethnic identity are elaborated together, so that every representation of sexuality is also simultaneously a negotiation of ethnic identity. The narrative of coming out, the other major thematic that derives from the figure of homosexuality in the film (to which we return later in the argument), is also evident here: following the conjunction of sexuality with ethnicity, the trope of the closet also signifies the deviation from ethnic identity that must be covered up. What becomes immediately apparent is that all of the younger generation of Chinese/Taiwanese in the United States are engaged in the masquerade of authenticity insofar as none of them are capable of enacting the forms of tradition that the older generation continually seeks to re-create.

The convergence of these two thematic strands is most obvious in the case of Sister Mao, Wai Tung's "perfect match," according to the Taiwanese dating service in which his parents enroll him. Far from being the good Chinese wife who will bring Wai Tung back into the fold of Chinese tradition, she is actually like Wai Tung. They are both highly educated, Westernized, upper-class Taiwanese. And they both let their parents enroll them in the dating club, because they both have white lovers they don't want their parents to know about. The closet is thus a function of ethnicity as well as sexuality. Per Wai Tung's requirements, Sister Mao is an opera singer, but her training is in Western opera, and she performs for Wai Tung an aria from *Madama Butterfly.* Her name thus activates a certain irony in its subtle connotation of a more authentic Chinese identity, one that seems to belong more to Wei Wei.

If Wei Wei seems closer to tradition, however—in her mainland origins and her familiarity with classical Chinese calligraphy, customs, and manners—she is completely incapable of the "traditional" housekeeping duty of the wife. In fact, we first encounter her in a sweat-drenched tank top, guzzling vodka from the bottle— somewhat excessive signifiers of Westernization, which are later reinforced (in case there was any doubt) by her sexual aggressiveness and her violent, abstract, expressionist-style canvases. It is paradoxically the Western male, Simon, who is most capable of maintaining the domestic space and (re)producing traditional Chinese cuisine, an indication of the loosening of national/ethnic characteristics from any essential ties to race or blood as a consequence of their international commodification in the global economy.

If the signifiers of sexuality establish themata of assimilation, inauthenticity, and masquerade in the first half of the film, they do so against the nationalist assertions of cultural identity posed by the father. In one interview Lee himself explicates the film (which is based on the true story of one of Lee's friends) in terms of the history of Taiwan:

> *The Wedding Banquet* is a comedy about identity. Identity is an issue that for us Taiwanese is central but also rather muted by our short, contradictory history. In the story, cultural, national, family and individual identities all work at cross-purposes with one another. A gay son, naturalized as an American citizen, can't "come out" to his father, a nationalist general who fled the mainland and whose entire family was wiped-out by the communists. If the wedding allows the son to continue to live "free" in America, he is still imprisoned by the weight of a history his father has shaped, a history that—because he won't be "continuing the family name"—will end with him. But, of course, the end of history is only the beginning of our story. The son's fake marriage to a girl from the mainland unites the "two Chinas," but in a new union that isn't quite what the elders were hoping for. (quoted in "Review" 44)

Note that in Lee's remarks, sexuality is conspicuously absent from the various categories of identity, an indication that homosexuality is a sign for the very confusions of identity that the film seeks to resolve. Rather than a form of identity, sexuality is the discourse in which questions of identity are negotiated. Furthermore, the fact that the son is gay seems almost inseparable from the fact that he is "naturalized as an American citizen." If this synopsis seems to pose the contradictions of Taiwanese identity within a typical nationalist problematic—that is, how to get crossed identities to align themselves, to work toward the same purpose, in order to guarantee the unity of the nation—we should note this passage's ambiguous relation to the nation and the subtlety with which nationalism is invoked only in order to be finally evaded.

The very effort to construct a "national allegory" (Jameson, "Third-World Literature" 65–88) is a performative attempt to script a unitary national narrative out of the contradictions and conflicts of Taiwanese society.[8] I suggest that the national allegory of Taiwan in *The Wedding Banquet* refers to the recent history of the transition from an authoritarian state to a liberal democratic one. The watershed moment was the 1986 lifting of martial law and the legalization of opposition parties that followed. The crisis of the patriarch signifies the crisis of the national state and the necessity of coming to terms with the demands of the global system. From the perspective of the nation, therefore, the fantasy evoked in the film may be the possibility of regaining some measure of control over the destabilizing operations of the global system.

As the organizing sign of the film, the wedding banquet is the hinge upon which the narrative pivots from one trajectory to another. It is, in other words, the transitional moment that must be converted from an end into a beginning; it marks a "generic discontinuity" (Jameson, *Political Unconscious* 144) between comedy and melodrama that signals the film's status as a transnational allegory masquerading as a national one, just as the younger generation performs a masquerade of tradition.[9] Marriage is, of course, one of the central institutions of bourgeois society, and the family has long been conceived as analogous to the nation, so the failure of the wedding to effect closure indicates that the nationalist appeal to cultural authenticity is no longer sufficient to mediate the conflicts that are destabilizing the authority of the state in the global system.

If marriage constitutes the end point of traditional comedy in the West—Schamus cites Shakespeare as the locus classicus (ix–xiii)—the scenes of the wedding banquet mark the end of that generic strand in the text: the film suddenly shifts modes and turns into a family melodrama, not the generic form in which the narrative of coming out is usually cast in American culture. (One function of homosexuality in the plot, then, is to obstruct the closure offered by the wedding in favor of the closure presented at the end of the film.) This generic opposition also corresponds to the contrast between the arranged marriage, as one of convenience or expediency, and the marriage of love, which is supposed to typify the bourgeois version—love being the affective glue that binds together the conflictual elements of liberal society.[10] Because these two generic narratives (comedy and melodrama, or sexuality and ethnic identity) are both insufficient, however, the film must seek a new mode of resolution, one that finds its material analogue in the creation of new familial relations.

The inability of the marriage plot to resolve the conflict between Wai Tung and his father over national/ethnic identity reflects the impossibility of appealing to an originary Chinese identity for Taiwan—given the erosion of Nationalist Party (KMT) hegemony. The quest for a new site of reconciliation requires the disarticulation of the nation from the state, that is, the reconstruction of a transnational patriarchal order. The reason for this—at least in the semi-

otic economy of the narrative—is made explicit in the last line that
Wei Wei utters before the film cuts away from the bed where she lies
atop Wai Tung. In response to his anxious question, "What are you
doing?" Wei Wei replies, "I am liberating you." The Chinese word
for "liberate" here is the same one used to denote 1949 as the year
of Liberation, when the Communists forced the Nationalists into
exile on Taiwan (significantly, although inexplicably, this is a line
that is omitted from the English version of the screenplay). The
anxiety expressed in the threat of a reluctant "liberation" is anxiety
over the threat of mainland invasion, which is a very real possibility,
as recent events remind us, but is also the justification used by the
KMT government to legitimate martial law and authoritarian rule.[11]

The trope of liberation thus condenses both the fear of mainland invasion and the KMT state's imposition of a Chinese ethnic
identity upon the heterogeneous population of Taiwan. This was a
scripting of "fictive ethnicity" (Balibar 86–106) that involved tracing genealogies back to their mainland origins, maintaining an entire legislative body composed of representatives of mainland
provinces, and enforcing the use of Mandarin Chinese (the official
dialect of the mainland empire) over the various local Taiwanese
dialects.[12] The source of anxiety, therefore, is no longer simply the
mainland and the Communists, but in some sense the nation itself,
since the demand for national identification is now seen as ema-
nating from both the mainland and KMT states. Liberation also con-
notes, of course, the Western narrative of individual emancipation,
but during the course of the narrative, that emancipation is transposed from the national to the transnational, from the heterosexual to the homosexual. As a gay man, Wai Tung does not simply represent a Western threat to the Chinese nation; rather, he is
eccentric to the nation as such.

The threat of mainland invasion thus serves to obstruct the nationalist resolution, but it does so by legitimating Wai Tung's homosexuality and, therefore, his rejection of his father's effort to im-
pose upon him an essentialized national/ethnic identity in the
form of a heterosexual union. In opposition to the authentic Chinese identity demanded by his father, Wai Tung's homosexuality
stands in for the hybrid, inauthentic state of the Westernized ethnic subject. On a more basic level, though, the wedding fails to resolve the issues, because it rests on a fundamental conflict. The
trope of liberation signals that competing liberations are at stake
here; in other words, Wai Tung and Wei Wei cannot *both* be liberated simultaneously.[13] "Liberation" thus functions as a signifier en-
capsulating the antithetical relation between Wei Wei's escape
from the global underclass of the undocumented, transnational mi-

grant laborer and Wai Tung's evasion of his father's demand for heterosexual reproduction. Between these two forms of liberation, Wei Wei's desire is understood by Wai Tung (and the film) only as ventriloquizing the father's imperative, a conflation that effectively excludes any possibility of autonomy for Wei Wei or release from the dictates of the international sexual division of labor.

The film's resolution, however, depends most intently upon disciplining Wei Wei as the figure of resistance, so that it is only Wai Tung's impregnation of her, which turns out to be the mechanism of his control over her, that allows the ending to take place in a configuration that resolves the conflicts between the men. The consolidation of a transnational patriarchy of capital is fundamentally dependent upon the subordination of women and labor, and women and labor are conflated in the film, so that woman becomes the very sign of labor. Therefore, if we reconstruct the film around Wei Wei as the main protagonist, we suddenly perceive an entirely new narrative, one that details the cooperation of national and transnational patriarchies in the exploitation of labor and the reconciliation of global capital across national borders. This leads us to the recognition of Wai Tung's occupation in the beginning of the film as essentially that of slumlord. Though we are given no other information about his business in the United States for the previous ten years, it certainly appears that he has been profiting from the exploitation of undocumented immigrants like Wei Wei. In this respect, we may begin to suspect that the crisis of legitimation allegorized in the decline of the father is the displacement of a crisis that afflicts the son. Or, rather, these are perhaps interrelated moments in the relation of capital to labor in the global system.

The transformation of Wai Tung into a patriarch, the declared project of the film, can now be seen as fundamentally dependent not so much upon the reconciliation with his father as upon the solicitation of ideological consent from Wei Wei and her submission to his hegemonic dominance. Returning to the first invocation of the trope of liberation in the film, recall that it occurs in the scene when Wai Tung goes to Wei Wei's loft to collect the three months' back rent she owes him. When Wai Tung announces on the intercom that the "evil landlord" has arrived, she refuses to let him in at first, declaring, "The sixth floor has been liberated!" (Lee 124). Although the anxiety provoked by this encounter is played for laughs, I take it to be perhaps the most fundamental sign of what propels that entire narrative. It is not only the national allegory and the drama of sexual identity but also the situation of the transnational capitalist class in the diaspora, which finds itself in the tricky situation of having to negotiate between the demands of "its own" ethnic communities and those of global capital, without the institutional apparatuses of the state to enforce its position.

If the second half of the film consists of two moments of crisis—coming out and abortion—they are both registered through the mother. But it is important to note that they are, in fact, asymmetrical: Wai Tung's reconciliation with Simon depends on Wei Wei's decision to have the baby. This is structured into the very diegesis, since Wai Tung's father's recognition of Simon as "also" his son comes between Wei Wei's demand for a hamburger and her decision to keep the baby. The moment that Wei Wei comes closest to escaping the domination of the global system is stigmatized in the film through the act of abortion; once this possibility is closed off, her subordination is inevitable. Thus, the multicultural, non-heterosexual family formed by Wai Tung and Simon at the end of the film is in sharp contrast to the representation of women's liberation offered to Wei Wei. Although it is unclear what kind of arrangement she and Wai Tung will eventually come to, the decision to keep the baby drastically reduces her options, foreclosing the possibility of withdrawal from the global system. Her dependence upon global capital is vividly dramatized in the act of consuming that quintessential transnational food commodity and symbol of Americanization, the hamburger.

Cynthia Liu has discussed the antagonism between the antihomophobic and feminist discourses in the film, comparing Wai Tung's acquisition of relative personal freedom with Wei Wei's destiny, which is eventually reduced to biology (1–60). Citing Biddy Martin's caution against "antifoundationalist celebrations of queerness [that] rely on their own projections of fixity, constraint, or subjection onto a fixed ground, often onto feminism or the female body, in relation to which queer sexualities become figural, performative, playful, and fun" (Martin 104), Liu argues that *The Wedding Banquet* "purchases queer-positivity and gay Asian male sexual and class mobility at the expense of a 'miring' Asian female ground. Even the queer-positive elements are muted by the film's 'enabling' capitulation to patriarchal and procreative imperatives" (C. Liu 43). Situating this analysis in terms of the global system and postmodernity, however, we can begin to locate this antagonism within the ideological antinomy between modernity and postmodernity, or—to put it in more concrete terms—the nation-state and the global system. The tension between an apparently antihomophobic or homophilic resolution and an antipatriarchal or feminist one is the tension between sexuality and gender as two divergent challenges to the authority of the nation-state. This discontinuity cannot be parsed as one in which sexuality is inherently more or less efficacious a subversion than is gender; rather, we need to attend to who is being recuperated, the first-born son or the working-class woman.

Although the denouement can be read as offering the reconciliations of East and West, or tradition and modernity, or filial duty and individual freedom, the new structure of sexual and familial relations represented seems to exceed the simple resolution of binary oppositions. If the wedding as nationalist resolution is no longer capable of soliciting consent to bourgeois hegemony, we need to elucidate how the reconstituted family unit at the end of the film represents one attempt to imagine a new structure of social relations—one that would be capable of mediating the contradictions and antagonisms in the global systems. The film's ending seems to be striving toward an alteration in the ideological value and structure of the family to signify no longer the unity of the nation, but rather the unity of the global system as embodied in the concrete institution of the transnational corporation, with Wai Tung as the representative of the transnational capitalist class at the apex.[14] Thus in the publicity photo for the film, Wai Tung bends down to embrace Wei Wei on one side and Simon on the other. The baby that Wei Wei carries is the signifier for the vast Chinese labor force, and the money that is exchanged between Wai Tung's father and Simon is the symbol of their common interest as the owners of global capital.

The fact that this is an international confederation means a diminishment of national distinctions, which also entails leveling the opposition of heterosexuality and homosexuality. This opposition, if we are to agree with a number of accounts of gay history, is foundational to the construction of the modern nation.[15] In contrast, Donald Lowe characterizes sexuality in the era of postmodernity in these terms: "Separated from social reproduction, sexuality thus becomes a sign to energize, in effect to sexualize, late-capitalist consumption. The result is a sexual lifestyle, as distinct from the bourgeois assumption of an interiorized sexual identity. No longer respecting the outer/inner, the public/private oppositions, the new sexual lifestyle is subverting the opposition between heterosexual norm and its other, i.e., the so-called homosexual vice. We are verging toward polysexuality, i.e., sexual *differences without* stable sexual *identities*" (127, Lowe's emphasis). Sexual lifestyle rewrites the homosexual/heterosexual opposition, resulting not so much in the dissolution of the closet as in its reconfiguration in response to the material conditions of the global system. The parameters of the closet are redrawn in the noneuclidean geometries of cyberspace, making it increasingly difficult to speak of being in or out, since Wai

Tung is simultaneously both inside and outside in some new and more complex relation of public and private. This remodeling of the closet and of the discourse of sexuality allows the film to pivot from a nationalist problematic of assimilation (competing national identities) to a transnational problematic of global identities. We can discern this shift in the now-naturalized oxymoron of "global citizenship"; one is declaring oneself a "citizen" of what global entity? This hybrid epithet is an acute index of the transitional moment in which—despite all pronouncements to the contrary—the global system has not yet completely formed and the nation has definitely not been superseded.

It is in this conjuncture that gay men and transvestites can become the emblematic embodiments of the transnational subject. Implicit in such figurations, however, is the unexamined universality of the nation-state as the referent of all subjectivity and the location of all forms of domination. To identify any opposition to the nation as inherently liberatory is to restrict questions of power and inequality within a zero-sum binary of domination and emancipation, such that any reduction in one automatically produces an increase in the other. The description of queer transnational subjectivity as a liberation from the limits of the nation reinscribes Enlightenment narratives of universal history and hierarchies of development. This occludes an inquiry into what material conditions enable or produce subject positions outside of or opposed to the nation—for example, global, diasporic, or transnational ones. In the twenty-fifth-anniversary celebrations of Stonewall, for instance, Martin Manalansan notes that the "official" march started not at the Stonewall Inn but at the United Nations. Documents, souvenirs, and artifacts associated with the anniversary demonstrate how "the textualization of Stonewall has changed—from localized descriptions of a police raid on a Greenwich Village bar to globalized descriptions of a revolutionary moment for gays and lesbians everywhere" (427). These proclamations of an "international" lesbian and gay movement risk subsuming heterogeneous forms of sexuality under a gay identity that is implicated in a specifically Western and bourgeois construction of subjectivity, with its themata of voice, visibility, and coming out.

Dana Takagi points to the manner in which ethnicity and sexuality are fundamentally imagined in terms of a linear trajectory of modernization, when she addresses the division separating ethnic communities from gay communities with this analogy: "Imagining your parents, clutching bento box lunches, thrust into the smoky haze of a South of Market leather bar in San Francisco is no less strange a vision than the idea of Lowie taking Ishi, the last of his tribe, for a cruise on Lucas' Star Tours at Disneyland" (6). The ethnographic analogy exemplifies the rhetorical construction of ethnic identity as primitive or premodern against sexuality as the very signifier of (post)modernity. Manalansan provides an important critique of the continuing structural force of such epistemological categories, when he refers to Barry Adam's distinction between anthropological, or historical, homosexuality and "modern" homosexuality as one in which "gay" becomes "synonymous with capitalist expansion." The consequence of this periodization, Manalansan argues, is that "all same-sex phenomena are placed within a developmental and teleological matrix that ends with Western 'gay' sexuality. Non-'gay' forms are seen as archeological artifacts to be reckoned with only when excavating the origins of pan-cultural/pan-global homosexuality" (427–28). The narrative of gay liberation thus reproduces narratives of universal history that gauge the evolution of civilization from tradition to modernity. But in *The Wedding Banquet,* this antinomy takes the form of a hierarchical opposition between sexuality and race, in which the latter constitutes the essential ground for the postmodern play of queerness.

In a discussion of representations of homosexuality in recent Asian film, Chris Berry provides a good example of the pitfalls of queer theory in the international arena. Referring to Lee Edelman's reading of *Fanny Hill,* Berry writes that "just as sodomy confounds male and female, before and behind, I will argue that the sight of homosexuality today in the simultaneously postcolonial and neo-Confucian construction known as East Asia can confound the logic of East and West and of past and present that underpins that construction and that it does so in a manner that constitutes this essay as a project of 'sexual disorientation'" (159). Putting aside the transposition of queer theory from *Fanny Hill* to East Asia, Berry contends that the visibility of homosexuality in Asian popular culture may be capable of destabilizing postcolonial Asian Orientalist constructions of Asian identity—specifically the nominally postnational construction of an East Asian regional identity that would include the Newly Industrializing Countries (the so-called Four Tigers or Dragons: Hong Kong, Singapore, Taiwan, and South Korea).

Although Berry's argument engages a number of the problems outlined here, let us focus on his conclusion that homosexuality may serve to disrupt the consolidation of an East Asian identity that relies on a colonial division of East and West. Listing a number of East Asian films and videos that deal with the topic of homosexuality, Berry writes, "The disparities between these films themselves confound any notion of a common Confucian East Asian identity,

culture, or set of values. However, it is not the range of different representations that I am focusing on here; rather, it is what they all
share, namely, the act of representing homosexuality that is of interest. . . . By making homosexuality visible at all, every one of these
films and videos resists the conservative, government-centered ideologies of collective identity (whether national or regional) that attempt to other homosexuality" (167). One of the principal questions that I have attempted to pose in this essay is precisely the
extent to which the visibility of homosexuality always and everywhere produces resistance or "sexual disorientation." Images of homosexuality may indeed disrupt homophobic nation-state discourses of identity, but the question that Berry fails to pursue is To
what end? What replaces the nationalist ideologies of collective
identity that homosexuality subverts? Berry's statecentric, postcolonial framework restricts his argument within the opposition between homosexuality and the nation that is part of nationalism's
own self-consolidation, occluding an investigation of sexuality as a
component of various transnational practices.

In discussing the case of Singapore, Berry fails to take adequate
account of how the crisis of state paternity—the discursive nexus
through which the Singapore government constructed a Confucian
identity, one that resonates with the phantasmic decline of the patriarch in Lee's films—may have contradictory effects within the de-
centered ideological field of the global system.[16] Homosexuality's
function in the nationalist rhetoric of the Singapore government requires a more complex account than one that simply attends to binaries of East and West, gay and straight. Despite the vast differences
between Singapore and Taiwan, we can discern in their resurgence
of nationalist sentiment and anxieties of identity their common
function in crisis management, in deflecting popular unrest occa-
sioned by the destabilizations of global restructuring. The mobilization of homophobia as part of this tactic, then, cannot simply be
countered with "deviationist" projects that disseminate the subversive sight of homosexuality. Homosexuality (especially in films made
by producers/artists who, like Lee, are not gay) may be visible only
as an ideological mirage of transnational capital and is therefore implicated in a process of globalization in which the nation-state is
complicit and which the return to nationalism seeks to disavow.

The point here is simply that one main political imperative in the
analysis of transnationalism or globalization is to define and specify
the analytical frame within which we are evaluating any particular
object or action. The reconciliation of the nationalist patriarch with
the gay man may indeed be progressive in the context of the normative and regulatory forms of the nation-state, but this political ef-

fectivity cannot be guaranteed or taken for granted in other contexts. My reading of *The Wedding Banquet* suggests that one tendency in the reconstruction of nationalist patriarchies in postmodernity is the recuperation/incorporation of the "homosexual threat"; in fact, this may be one of the signal processes by which nationalist patriarchies become postmodern patriarchies. The politics of sexuality in the global system, then, cannot be directly extrapolated from within the nation. Rosemary Hennessy provides an incisive critique of queer theory's failure to address the commodification of objects and practices rather than their purely semiotic or discursive production. She argues that

> the appropriation of gay cultural codes in the cosmopolitan revamping of gender displays the arbitrariness of bourgeois patriarchy's gender system and helps to reconfigure it in a more postmodern mode where the links between gender and sexuality are looser, where homosexuals are welcome, even constituting the vanguard, and where the appropriation of their parody of authentic sex and gender identities is quite compatible with the aestheticization of everyday life into postmodern lifestyles. In itself, of course, this limited assimilation of gays into mainstream middle-class culture does not disrupt postmodern patriarchy and its intersection with capitalism; indeed it is in some ways quite integral to it. (Hennessy 170).

Similarly, Caren Kaplan and Inderpal Grewal ("Transnational Feminist Cultural Studies") suggest that within the context of the tensions that have developed in the global system between transnational capital and the nation-state, First World advocates of global identity politics risk becoming the unwitting agents of transnational capital in its struggle against the resistances posed by Third World states.

Hennessy argues that the visibility of queer spectacle often serves to detract attention from, or mask, labor and inequality, the process that Jameson refers to in *The Geopolitical Aesthetic* as "representational laundering." Signifying on Chinese American history, though, we might say that the laundry is one of the things that is laundered out; that is, the visibility of Asian American labor in *The Wedding Banquet* is precisely what is erased. We could characterize the aesthetic of the film, then, as a form of visual gentrification, the cinematographic mode that corresponds to Wai Tung's diegetic venture to convert his abandoned industrial building into condos. What must be excluded from the visual field is the actual community that is riven by differences of class, gender, ethnicity, nationality, and sexuality, and Asian American communities are locations of the Third World in the First World where the labor of production that fuels the operations of global capital can still be glimpsed from time to time. If Asian American communities are not visible in the film, however, they still surface through a kind of diegetic Freudian slip, condensed into the heat, humidity, and noise of Wei Wei's loft/work space—conditions that evoke Taipei and a Third World industrial past but also the Third World ethnic enclave in the First World, composed of sweatshops as well as small, paternalistic family businesses.

Therefore, we need to register what is elided in *The Wedding Banquet's* representations of the Taiwanese diaspora in the United States. But the most striking example of the disappearance of the Asian American from the film is one that is literally invisible. The hotel (perhaps the paramount signifier of the film's transnational locations) where the scenes of the wedding banquet were shot sits almost in the center of Flushing, New York, a community that has become one of the largest concentrations of Chinese and other Asian immigrants in the past decade (much like Monterey Park in Los Angeles). Yet despite the fact that Lee drew on the resources of this community both for his first film, *Pushing Hands,* and for *The Wedding Banquet,* there is absolutely no hint in the film of anything that exists outside the hotel. What begins in the film as an apparent conflict between East and West is transformed in the course of the narrative into a conflict between the two halves of the global system, a new division that is apparent in the racialized class polarization of the contemporary United States.[17]

I have emphasized the dimensions of the film that have been expelled from the visual field or forced into the closet. Foremost among these are Asian American communities as the site of class inequalities and the extraction of surplus value, as well as the site of the underclass, which is excluded from production altogether. The restoration of the materiality of those contexts, as against the abstractions and commodification of capital, is one urgent project for an Asian American cultural studies. It can be conceptualized along the lines of Hennessy's definition of "critique" as a "political practice and a mode of reading that establishes the intimate links between the visible and the historical by taking as its starting point a systemic understanding of the social" (176). Cultural analysis in the global system must seek to return to political "consciousness" the Third World as the locus of offshore production no longer apparent in the First World, and it must trace the contradictory flows of sign, image, and commodity in the global system. This project cannot be undertaken unless our analysis is capable of restoring the interconnectedness of multiple vectors of inequality. An Asian American transnational cultural studies must attend to both poles of the local global conjunction, in order to make the multiple erasures of globalization reappear in the field of action.

NOTES

1. See also Kaplan and Grewal, "Introduction" 1–33.

2. The transnational capitalist class, according to Sklair, "consists of those people who see their own interests and/or the interests of their countries of citizenship, as best served by an identification with the interests of the capitalist global system, in particular the interests of the transnational corporations" (8).

3. Jameson suggests, however, that "it would be too simple and functional to impute this particular stylistic motivation . . . to marketing strategies alone and an attention to a potentially international public; or rather, it would be crucial to affirm such base, external motivation, such determination by the extra-aesthetic, as realities in the object-world that ultimately, at some wider level of analysis, always rejoin the subject (and the formal an aesthetic) in unexpected internal ways" (*Geopolitical Aesthetic* 118).

4. In his discussion of the flow of Japanese media and culture into Taiwan, Leo Ching provides an apt analogy for the difficulties of contextualizing narratives and representations in *The Wedding Banquet* (despite its own attempts at invoking national allegories and identities, which are as much marketing devices as plot devices). Ching notes that despite the history of Japanese colonization of Taiwan, the influx of Japanese culture is generally not regarded as cultural imperialism by the Taiwanese in the same way that the influx of U.S. culture is. He accounts for this disparity by suggesting that because much of Japanese cultural production is, in fact, reengineered simulacra of First World, especially U.S. culture, it carries no national ideological or cultural markers. Commenting on Tsan Hung-Chih's analysis of the proliferation of Japanese cultural products in Taiwan, Ching remarks that "Tsan rightly observes that the cultural merchandise imported from Japan is gradually and increasingly discarding the shade of traditional Japanese culture and ethnic character. What is perceived as Japanese cultural products can easily be of American or British origins. Japan simply reassembles and packages other cultural commodities and sells them to other countries" (277). The result is "a repackaged secondhand cultural commodity that has no specific 'national' origin or discernible ideology" (278) and cannot therefore be read as signifying Japanese national or cultural superiority. Shu-mei Shih furnishes corroborating evidence, citing Taiwanese critic Luo Zhicheng's remark that there are no longer any forms of hegemonic thought in Taiwan, because ideology itself has been commodified, a phenomenon somewhat facetiously confirmed by the appearance of an advertising agency named "Ideology" (Shih 155).

5. For other discussions of the problematic of the closet for Asian

American lesbians and gays, see Fung (Chapter 7), Hom 19–32, Manalansan 425–28, and Wat 149–60.

6. See also Hoo 107–12.

7. Rhonda Cobham suggests, for example, that "the existence of the
social category 'homosexuality' within Western discourse makes it virtually impossible for African writers who make use of the novel form to
write about sexual intimacy in their societies without positioning their
narratives in relation to the meanings associated with the 'foreign'
term" (47–48).

8. For critiques of the concept of "national allegory," see Ahmad;
Chow; and L. Liu 37–62.

9. Jameson proposes that the formal configurations of the text can
be read as a "boat of distinct generic messages—some of them objectified survivals from older modes of cultural production, some an-
ticipatory, but all together projecting a formal conjuncture through
which the 'conjuncture' of coexisting modes of production at a given
historical moment can be detected and allegorically articulated" (*Political Unconscious* 99). The juxtaposition of different generic modes
in *The Wedding Banquet*—mainly comedy/farce and family melodrama—articulates the particular conjunction of nationalism and
transnationalism that characterizes Taiwan's position in the global
system.

10. For an example of the relation between romance and nationalism, see Sommer 71–98.

11. The first direct presidential elections in Taiwan, held in March
1996, prompted military exercises by the mainland navy in the Taiwan
Straits and renewed declarations by the communist government that
Taiwan was a province of the mainland.

12. "Although the [KMT] regime acknowledged that Taiwan had
regional particularities, like any other locality in China, the KMT assiduously promoted the idea that the island was the repository and
guarantor of Chinese tradition as well as the mainland's rich diversity. The national political bodies, such as the Legislative Yuan and
National Assembly, kept in place delegates representing mainland
districts even though they were divorced from their constituents. Regional cuisines and operas flourished and native place associations
were established. Popular culture stressed mainland roots, addressing history and life on the mainland, not the island. Politically and to
some extent culturally, then, Taiwan became a microcosm of pre-
1949 mainland China as interpreted by the KMT. Ironically, while
telling its people that Taiwan was an integral part of China, the KMT
forbad contacts with the mainland, establishing in effect a great wall
across the Straits" (Gold 171–72).

13. In Switzerland *The Wedding Banquet* was shown in English, with
the Chinese dialogue dubbed in French. Furthermore, Wei Wei's crucial bedroom line was translated as "Women's liberation!" which was

greeted, at one showing, by a roar of laughter from the audience. I thank Nida Surber for this information.

14. The reconstructed family seems to partake of something like the fantasy that Caren Kaplan describes in her analysis of the Body Shop's "Trade Not Aid" program as the "*representation* of a corporate *replacement* of the nation-state. It appears to be The Body Shop that funds and manages development projects, just as it appears to be The Body Shop that addresses health care, financing, and environmental concerns in its global reach" ("World Without Boundaries" 58–59, Kaplan's emphasis). For a related discussion of the Japan Exchange and Teaching (JET) Program, see Cazdyn 135–59.

15. See Foucault; Halperin; Katz; and Sedgwick.

16. See Heng and Devan 343–64 on the crisis of state paternity in Singapore. See Shih 149–83 on "Orientalizing" constructions of China in Taiwanese media.

17. Steven Gregory describes this race/class polarization as dividing the United States "into two nations, one 'black' and the other 'white,' but the meanings and the socio-spatial terrain of both terms are shifting, as they always have. Whereas the 'underclass,' a hyper-exploited race/gender/class fraction, is emerging as the nodal point in the articulation of postindustrial blackness, 'whiteness' has opened its arms to a gorgeous mosaic of differences, whose inscription in the global economy, rather than the federal census, increasingly defines belonging" (21).

WORKS CITED

Ahmad, Aijaz. *In Theory: Classes, Nations, Literatures.* London: Verso, 1992.

Balibar, Etienne. "The Nation Form: History and Ideology." *Race, Nation, Class: Ambiguous Identities.* Trans. Chris Turner, London: Verso, 1991. 86–106.

Berry, Chris. "Sexual DisOrientations: Homosexual Rights, East Asian Films, and Postmodern Postnationalism." *In Pursuit of Contemporary East Asian Culture.* Ed. Xiaobing Tang and Stephen Snyder. Boulder: Westview, 1996. 157–82.

Cazdyn, Eric. "Uses and Abuses of the Nation: Toward a Theory of the Transnational Cultural Exchange Industry." *Social Text* 44 (1995): 135–59.

Ching, Leo. "Imaginings in the Empires of the Sun:" Japanese Mass Culture in Asia." *Asia/Pacific as Space of Cultural Production.* Ed. Rob Wilson and Arif Dirlik. Durham, N.C.: Duke UP, 1995. 262–83.

Chow, Rey. *Primitive Passions: Visuality, Sexuality, Ethnography, and Contemporary Chinese Cinema.* New York: Columbia UP, 1995.

Cobham, Rhonda. "Misgendering the Nation: African Nationalist Fictions and Nuruddin Farah's *Maps.*" *Nationalisms and Sexualities.* Ed. Mary Russo, Andrew Parker, Doris Sommer, and Patricia Yaeger. New York: Routledge, 1992. 42–59.

Eng, David L. "*The Wedding Banquet:* You're Not Invited and Some Other Ancillary Thoughts." *Artspiral* 7 (1993): 8–10.

Foucault, Michel. *The History of Sexuality, Vol. 1: An Introduction.* Trans. Robert Hurley. New York: Vintage, 1980.

Fuss, Diana. "Introduction: Inside/Out." *Inside/Out: Lesbian Theories, Gay Theories.* Ed. Diana Fuss, New York: Routledge, 1991. 1–10.

Gold, Thomas B. "Taiwan's Quest for Identity in the Shadow of China." *In the Shadow of China: Political Developments in Taiwan Since 1949.* Ed. Steven Tsang. Honolulu: U of Hawaii P, 1993. 169–92.

Gregory, Steven. "Race and Racism: a Symposium." *Social Text* 42 (1995). 16–21.

Halperin, David M. *One Hundred Years of Homosexuality.* New York: Routledge, 1989.

Heng, Geraldine, and Janadas Devan. "State Fatherhood: The Politics of Nationalism, Sexuality, and Race in Singapore." *Nationalisms and Sexualities.* Ed. Mary Russo, Andrew Parker, Doris Sommer, and Patricia Yaeger. New York: Routledge, 1992. 343–64.

Hennessy, Rosemary. "Queer Visibility in Commodity Culture." *Social Postmodernism: Beyond Identity Politics.* Ed. Linda Nicholson and Steven Seidman. Cambridge: Cambridge UP, 1995. 142–83.

Hom, Alice Y. "Stories from the Homefront: Perspectives of Asian American Parents with Lesbian Daughters and Gay Sons." *Amerasia Journal* 20.1 (1994): 19–32.

Hoo, Maurice L. "Speech Impediments." *APA Journal* 2.1 (1993): 107–12.

Jameson, Fredric. *The Geopolitical Aesthetic.* Bloomington and London: Indiana UP and British Film Institute, 1995.

———. *The Political Unconscious: Narrative as a Socially Symbolic Act.* Ithaca, N.Y.: Cornell UP, 1981.

———. "Third-World Literature in the Era of Multinational Capitalism." *Social Text* 15 (1986): 65–88.

Kaplan, Caren. "'A World Without Boundaries': The Body Shop's Trans/National Geographics." *Social Text* 43 (1995): 45–66.

Kaplan, Caren, and Inderpal Grewal. "Introduction." *Scattered Hegemonies: Postmodernity and Transnational Feminist Practices.* Ed. Caren Kaplan and Inderpal Grewal. Minneapolis: U of Minnesota P, 1994. 1–33.

———. "Transnational Feminist Cultural Studies: Beyond the Marxism/Poststructuralism/Feminism Divides." *positions* 2.2 (1994): 430–45.

Katz, Jonathan Ned. *Gay/Lesbian Almanac: A New Documentary.* New York: Harper and Row, 1983.

Lee, Ang. Eat Drink Man Woman/ The Wedding Banquet: *Two Films by Ang Lee.* Woodstock: Overlook, 1994.

Liu, Cynthia W. "'To Love, Honor, and Dismay': Subverting the Feminine in Ang Lee's Trilogy of Resuscitated Patriarchs." *Hitting Critical Mass* 3.1 (1995): 1–60.

Liu, Lydia. "The Female Body and Nationalist Discourse: *The Field of Life and Death* Revisited." *Scattered Hegemonies: Postmodernity and Transnational Feminist Practices.* Ed. Caren Kaplan and Inderpal Grewal. Minneapolis: U of Minnesota P, 1994. 37–62.

Lowe, Donald. *The Body in Late-Capitalist USA.* Durham, N.C.: Duke UP, 1995.

Manalansan, Martin F., IV. "In the Shadows of Stonewall: Examining Gay Transnational Politics and the Diasporic Dilemma." *GLQ: A Journal of Lesbian and Gay Studies* 2.4 (1995): 425–38.

Martin, Biddy. "Sexualities Without Genders and Other Queer Utopias." *diacritics* 24.2–3 (1994): 104–21.

"Review of *The Wedding Banquet.*" *Migration World Magazine* 22.2–3 (1994): 44.

Schamus, James. "Introduction." Eat Drink Man Woman/The Wedding Banquet: *Two Films by Ang Lee.* Woodstock: Overlook, 1994. ix–xiii.

Sedgwick, Eve. *Epistemology of the Closet.* Berkeley and Los Angeles: U of California P, 1990.

Shih, Shu-mei. "The Trope of 'Mainland China' in Taiwan's Media." *positions* 3.1 (1995): 149–83.

Sklair, Leslie. *Sociology of the Global System.* 2nd ed. Baltimore: Johns Hopkins UP, 1995.

Sommer, Doris. "Irresistible Romance: The Foundational Fictions of Latin America." *Nation and Narration.* Ed. Homi K. Bhabha, London: Routledge, 1990. 71–98.

Takagi, Dana Y. "Maiden Voyage: Excursion into Sexuality and Identity Politics in Asian America." *Amerasia Journal* 20.1 (1994): 1–17.

Wat, Eric C. "Preserving the Paradox: Stories from a *Gay-loh.*" *Amerasia Journal* 20.1 (1994): 149–60.

The Wedding Banquet. Ang Lee, director. Samuel Goldwyn, 1993.

25. Incidents of Travel
Ju Hui Judy Han

Q

398

400

THE THING IS, I GREW UP IN SEOUL AND THE CITY IS VERY FAMILIAR. IT JUST TAKES ME A LITTLE WHILE TO REMEMBER...

SO I ASK A LOT OF QUESTIONS TO A LOT OF PEOPLE.

아저씨, EXCUSE ME, 여기요, ER... 이쪽이 THIS WAY, RIGHT?

USUALLY, IT'S THE **DETAILS** THAT GIVE ME AWAY.

LIKE WHEN I ASK HOW MUCH THE BUS FARE IS. OR WHERE A FAMOUS LANDMARK (LIKE A DEPARTMENT STORE) IS.

WHERE?

USUALLY, THEY DON'T THINK I'M FOREIGN.

고맙습니다.

THEY JUST THINK I'M **STUPID**.

I HEARD THIS STORY ONCE... THIS KOREAN AMERICAN WOMAN WAS ACCUSED OF BEING A NORTH KOREAN SECRET AGENT.

OF COURSE, THIS WAS A WHILE AGO.

CONFUSED KOREAN AMERICANS ARE MUCH MORE COMMON THESE DAYS— REGULARS ON SOAP OPERAS, EVEN.

SOMEBODY GOT SUSPICIOUS & TURNED HER IN - SHE HAD ASKED TOO MANY QUESTIONS

LOOKING AROUND THE SUBWAY TRAIN, I SEE WALLS PLASTERED WITH ADS THAT SELL THINGS AND TRENDS.

OFTEN, NEXT TO THE SUBWAY MAP ABOVE THE DOORS, THERE'S A POSTER FROM THE KOREAN CENTRAL INTELLIGENCE AGENCY (KCIA).

THEY ARE EVERY WHERE.

CHARGES OF ESPIONAGE
GUARANTEEING YEARS
IN 5'5" by 5'5" CELLS,
KOREA BOASTS THE
WORLD RECORD FOR THE
LONGEST PRISON
SENTENCE EVER SERVED
— 45 years for ESPIONAGE.

26. Transnational Sexualities
South Asian (Trans)nation(alism)s and Queer Diasporas
Jasbir K. Puar

Recently I organized a panel for submission to the National Association for Ethnic Studies (NAES) 1996 conference, whose theme was "The Ethnic Experience in the United States: Changing Migrations, Changing Borders, and Changing Traditional Ethnic Communities." Four papers exploring the relationships between migration and sexualities made up the panel, which was entitled "Transnational Sexualities: Narrations of Normativity." My paper, which bore the same title as this chapter, elaborated on queer diasporas as political and academic interventions, by using examples from South Asian queer diasporic representations produced in the United States. Not long after my panel submission, the Executive Council of NAES responded, requesting clarification. They were, they explained, "unable to discern a clear relationship between the abstracts and the conference theme." The correspondence referred specifically to my piece, the only paper examining queer issues. It stated, "We were especially challenged to establish such a relationship given the abstract for [this paper]."

Other more obvious, less interesting, and less tangible readings of the NAES response aside (the abstracts were simply bad, for example), a few thoughts occurred to me after the panel had been submitted to and accepted by two other conferences. Perhaps the paper's suitability had been questioned for reasons that reflected my own for embarking on the project. NAES understood the concept of diaspora as having little to do with a discipline that has focused its efforts on elaborating constructions of ethnicity and race within the national borders of the United States. Moreover, it seems entirely plausible that a discipline that has privileged constructions of race and ethnicity often at the expense of gender and sexuality would find these issues of only "additive [ir]relevance." The situation is not helped by the white, and otherwise fraught and exclusionary epistemes, of the term "queer."

In any case, the confusion indicates the necessity for clarifying the linkages between ethnicity and sexuality and—in this essay specifically—the terms "queer" and "diaspora." Envisioning and expanding on queer diasporas as a political and academic intervention not only speaks directly to the gaps around sexuality in ethnic studies, Asian American studies, and forms of postcolonial studies; it also points gay and lesbian studies, queer studies, and even women's studies (which has considered gender more than sexuality) toward the need to disrupt the disciplinary regimes that continually reinvent bodies of theory cohered by singular, modernist subjects.

Thinking through such interventions is no easy task, and it raises many questions. How could/should one "queer" the diaspora(s) or "diasporicize" the queer? How does inclusion/exclusion from diasporas affect queers of color who have relationships to nations other than the United States? How do diasporic subjects construct queer selves through experiences of displacement? What are the connections between diasporas, queers, and modernities? Obviously I cannot even attempt to answer all of these questions here. In this chapter, I turn my attention to South Asian queer diasporic cultural productions. Although these may involve "deterritorializations" of the diasporic kind (Gupta and Ferguson 9)—in that they may reference a multiplicity of spaces of the nation and the state—I argue that they may also offer dynamics of reterritorialization, often in ways that reiterate nationalist terms through transnational paths. The spaces include, among others, Internet lists such as the co-gendered Khushnet[1] and the South Asian Queer Women's Network; organizations such as Trikone, SALGA (South Asian Lesbian and Gay Association), and Shamakami; Bhangra and Hindi musical appropriations; queercentric festivals like Desh Pardesh and Utsav; work by such filmmakers as Pratibha Parmar and Shani Mootoo; and literature from Canada, Britain, the United States, and India.

To illustrate my concerns, I primarily cite a collection of queer South Asian writing edited by Rakesh Ratti, *A Lotus of Another Color: An Unfolding of the South Asian Gay and Lesbian Experience*.[2] My concerns are twofold. The first is that constructions of queer diasporas may inherently rest upon cultural nationalisms via quests for sexual roots and origins. In the case of *A Lotus of Another Color*, this dynamic produces intersections of nationalism and communalism, resulting in an unfragmented and uncontested version of Hindu India. The second concern is that queer diasporic discourses often resituate nationalist centerings of the West as the site of sexual liberation, freedom, and visibility. These diasporic discourses may actually function as recycled domestic perspectives that run the risk of becoming globalizing ones.

Queering the Diaspora, Diasporicizing the Queer

To begin with, it may be useful to lay out the specific contours of the terms "queer" and "diaspora" and the concepts that their historicities, uses, and limits may impart to each other. In debates over the meanings of "queer," the term has been called too narrow, exclusionary, and white and, alternatively, too expansive, unspecific, and nomadic.[3] Similarly, the question of what exactly constitutes a diaspora has also been discussed at length.[4] However, it is not my purpose here to interrogate the meanings of these terms. Rather, I concur with David Halperin's application of Foucalt's work in the context of lesbian and gay activism that it is more useful to pursue the political implications of the varied *deployments* of these terms. James Clifford also advocates examining not only the content of what constitutes a diaspora but in particular the boundaries of that content and what is at stake politically in the where, why, and how of the boundary demarcation (302–38).

As with other concepts that seek to function as concepts of resistance, it is obviously more enticing to discuss what is oppositional about queers and "diasporics" than what is not. Without minimizing the importance of theorizing resistances, however, theorizing complicities is perhaps equally vital in examining mechanisms of power and hegemonies. The genealogies of "queer" and "diaspora" share a particular absence: neither foregrounds complicities with concepts of the nation-state. The term "queer" has historically presumed that its subjects have a fixed relation of inclusion within the nation-state, one that is rarely interrogated. Constructs of diaspora have often been mobilized as a space of transcendence of nation-states, since diaspora allows for alliances across national boundaries and negotiations of multiple national sites.

It is precisely through noting these terms as *relations,* rather than entities, that the exposure of their limitations produces potentially illuminative interactions. This interfacing of "queerness" and "diaspora" critiques the very terms they seek to incorporate, and in which they are incorporated, forcing particular redefinitions of the original terms. The terms "Queer Nation" and "Lesbian Nation," for example, are indicative of what Gayatri Gopinath terms an "uninterrogated assumption of queer citizenship" (120).[5] Whatever resistance to the state has currently been theorized vis-à-vis queer subjectivities has emerged through a presumed trajectory of named subjecthood—citizenship—within the state. This is a trajectory that diasporic queers trouble and complicate through their critique of the white episteme of queerness.

Similarly, constructions of diaspora that hinge upon masculinist constructions of home and travel are, for the most part, inattentive to gender and silent on sexuality. When queer subjects become visible within diasporic contexts, not only does sexuality become a topic of concern but the masculinist paradigms of diaspora are disrupted as well. Conversely, a critique of such paradigms might lead to an understanding of how certain notions of the nation, as Jacqui Alexander notes, "disallow the queer body" (6). Such constructions of diaspora unwittingly recast essentialized notions of nation that they originally claim to destablize. Paul Gilroy, for example, presents music of the black diasporas as counterhegemonic (to the state) and as critiques of capitalism while simultaneously constructing a masculinist nation-building project to include black in the Union Jack.

Clifford is also remarkably optimistic about diasporas as sites of resistance. He claims that "diasporic practices [are] defined and constrained by nation, but they also exceed and criticize them," distinguishing between an immigrant (who assimilates) and a diasporic figure (who "maintains important allegiances and practical connections to a homeland or dispersed community located elsewhere") (311). Clifford rests his diasporic terrain on two masculinist concepts of home (fixed, stable, inclusive, "back there") and travel (physical, direct, safe, and legal) (311). His diaspora privileges a masculine, mobile, middle- or upper-class subject. This subject has the resources to maintain substantial links—including financial investments—to a homeland, and as a postcolonial elite or cultural nationalist, (he) may have other reasons to invest in the "motherland."

Khachig Tölölyan reminds us that although diasporas may be "exemplary communities of the transnational moment," they may also be "the source of ideological, financial, and political support for national movements that aim at a renewal of the homeland" (5). Citing the work of Gabriel Sheffer, Tölölyan asserts, "In such a context, transnational communities are sometimes the paradigmatic Other of the nation-state and at other times its ally, lobby, or even in the case of Israel, its precursor" (5). As such, participation in the nation-state "back home" (financial, political, and so on) does not automatically indicate progressive participation.

A heightened awareness of national boundaries, notions of belonging, and diasporic positionings does not preclude participation in nationalisms, fundamentalisms, and the like; in fact, such awareness may often facilitate them. For example, the quest for homeland in India is often strengthened in first- as well as subsequent U.S.-born generations in response to conflicted relations to the U.S. state; examples of this include the Khalistan and Hindutava movements, both of which receive substantial financial support from diasporic communities. Amit Rai, for instance, notes contradictory diasporic stances in his analysis of Internet participants' responses concerning various Indian cultural newsgroups: "This textual construction of the diaspora can at the same time enable these diasporics to be for 'affirmative action' in the U.S. and against 'reservations' [jobs for disadvantaged castes] in India, to lobby for a tolerant pluralism in the West, and also support a narrow sectarianism in the East" (42). Resistance to the U.S. state may appear obvious, with the collusion/complicity in the construction of Hindu India hidden/effaced through this positioning vis-à-vis "America."

These contradictions are strong reminders that not all diasporas are "good" (in Clifford's sense). Resistances to the U.S. state may be recast in liberalist rhetorics of multiculturalism and inclusion, as with "model minority" discourses. Other critiques have elaborated at length the conservative impulses of South Asian diasporic political and cultural productions, which in the U.S. range from a continued pursuit of model minority status through upward professional mobility to a lack of political organizing with other communities of color around affirmative action and Proposition 187. Particularly important in this regard is the post-1965 history of relatively privileged immigration of South Asian professionals to the United States in comparison with their migration to Canada and Britain.

As Foucault notes, states normalize domination, creating subjects who regulate themselves. This involves a distinction between power relations that operate through oppression and power relations that operate through productive incorporation. In the most pessimistic of political climates, a diaspora could simply be yet another multiculturalist version of a disciplinary incorporative moment of the state, signaling an absorption or containment of specific postmodern versions of community into establishment ideologies. This construction of diaspora may not effectively function as a transnational alternative to local/global binary thinking, in that it reconstitutes, rather than exposes, the nation. Presuming a singular trajectory of marginality to the state renders a totalizing narrative of homogenized oppositionality of diaspora. Instead, as Rai points out, constructions of a diasporic counterpublic sphere must be attentive to its "constitutive contradictions" (31) in order to constantly challenge the reification of a purely oppositional diaspora.

If, then, there is nothing inherently politically progressive or anti-nation about the terms "queer" and "diapsora," one should not presume that the critiques that they bring to each other necessarily sustain a more perfect union or, in this case, a more perfect oppositionality. Does a queer inflection of diaspora render queer diasporic subjectivities more oppositional? One cannot assume that this combination heightens any particular oppositional potential in relationship to the state. My point here is simply that diasporic queers have not only various relationships to different states but indeed different relationships to common states, determined by highly diverse histories of ethnicity, migration, class, generation, gender, and religious identity. These multiple nation-states are, in fact, not randomly assembled but have specific paths that are quite predetermined through their histories. Though the two are linked, there is a distinction between transgressing ideologies of nationhood and transversing national boundaries; one does not inherently indicate the other. Furthermore, a vexed relationship to the state—meaning the disciplinary apparatus of the nation—neither automatically signals nor automatically produces a critique of essentialized notions of nation that construct "belonging" vis-à-vis unwelcome Others.

Queer diasporas are not immune from forms of cultural nationalism; in fact, they may even rely on them. As such, a queer diaspora must be vigilant of the tendency not only to colonize its nondiasporic referents but also to become in and of itself another complicitous "modern regime of sexuality" (Halperin 20). In the case of South Asian queer diasporas, this regime is a privileged signifier of not only North American and European geopolitical spaces but also class, caste, communal identity, and gender.

Lotus of What Color?

Given the dynamics of the South Asian diasporic spaces in the United States sketched herein and the lack of a coherent body of South Asian queer literature,[6] *A Lotus of Another Color* has been understandably popularized as the "first book of its kind." The collection includes poetry, short stories, and coming-out testimonials, the majority by writers—some of whom use pseudonyms—living in the United States.

The main goal of the collection, it appears, is to challenge white, mainstream gay and lesbian communities and South Asian communities to acknowledge that the terms "queer" and "South Asian" are not mutually exclusive. Ratti writes, "We stand with one foot in South Asian society, the other in the gay and lesbian world" ("Introduction" 14). As such, the book is already a response to the need to represent queer diasporic spaces. Any discussion of *Lotus* must acknowledge the difficulties in critiquing a volume that is itself a coming out of sorts and that has been used by many South Asian queers to educate parents and other family members. It becomes important, then, to note for which South Asians this is an effective strategy and for which it is an impossible one.

A reading of *Lotus* might take note of the continuous attempt at "recovery work" and the desire for inclusion in a culturally nationalist version of an Indian nation that remains an unquestioned origin, a reclaimed home, and a "motherland." This static construction of India then becomes the center of a homogenizing, global, South Asian queer identity. Sexual identity is fixed at a singular intersection with the nation, thus effacing multiple axes of identity, oppression, and privilege. These attempts at "recovery work" are connected to the politics of reterritorialization by conventionally unhailed queer bodies. The emotional and political imperative to claim India seems linked to a desire to explode the myth of homosexuality as a Western construct, as a white disease, and as a foreign import. This expulsion of queer brown bodies from nation as well as culture renders complex reterritorializations, precipitated, in some part, by the desire to be reframed within rejected spheres. Ratti mobilizes this tactic to offer "scientific evidence that same-gender attraction is present in all cultures" to disbelieving South Asian communities: "There are images of same-gender individuals in intimate positions on temples in Khajuraho and Konarek in India. Most of these temples were built more than a thousand years ago. There are also references to homosexuality as an alternative expression of sexuality in the Kama Sutra, the ancient Indian text on the diversities of sex. Babar, the founder of the Mughal dynasty in India, is said to have been gay, as was Abu Nawas, a famous Islamic poet. Homosexuality is as native to the Indian subcontinent as heterosexuality and cannot be dismissed as a Western import" ("Introduction" 13).

In *Lotus* there is an implicit understanding of South Asian as reducible to Indian and Indian as equivalent to a Hindu cultural and religious identity. Hindu mythology is labeled as Indian mythology, and Hindu gods and goddesses are named as Indian gods and goddesses. In the introduction, an image of Ardhanarishwara is accompanied by the following description: "Indian mythology not only recognizes the existence of male and female principals within the human body, but honors and defies it in this representation of Lord Shiva as half man, half woman" ("Introduction" 10). Hindu mythology, through its apparent emphasis of unity of the feminine and masculine, is used to justify contemporary South Asian gay and lesbian identities. For example, a bronze statue depicts "two torsos, one female, one male, arising from the same pelvis, emphasizing the unity rather than the dichotomy of the feminine and themasculine" (295), and another photo shows a "painting of a hermaphroditic figure" (133). Pictures of Hindu temple statues of same-sex erotica "prove" that homosexuality is indigenous to Indian culture. The section entitled "Uncovering our Past/Inventing our Present" opens with a photo of a temple carving from the city of Khajuraho, India, with the caption "Two women sharing an intimate touch" (19). Later, the book presents another temple carving from the same city, captioned "Four women engaged in sexual play" (165).

The *Lotus* chapter entitled "Homosexuality in India: Culture and Heritage" was compiled by AIDS Bhedbav Virodhi Andolan (ABVA), a nonprofit organization focusing on AIDS awareness in India. The essay does an archeological sexual excavation of sorts, attempting to show cultural tendencies of (mostly male) homosexuality in the Kama Sutra, Hindu mythology, tantric rituals, religious mysticism (Hindu), and Muslim culture. Referred to often in *Lotus,* the Kama Sutra, which is hailed as the ancient Indian classic on "matters of sex" (22–23), contains references to gay sex, lesbian activity, and eunuchs. The essay reiterates the focus on Hindu mythology through a discussion of "sexual dualism" (24–25), linking this to "universal bisexuality" and the "tantric rite of anal penetration" (26–27). These examples, among others, present a static notion of "Indian" heritage, with a supposed relevance to a collective "we" of South Asian queers, regardless of diversity.

A critique of *Lotus* is actually offered within the pages of the collection itself. And Nayan Shah, in Chapter 9 (this volume), notes the contingency involved in history building, marking the tensions that need to remain between present and past. Shah notes that much of this excavation "presumes that sexuality is a definable and universal activity, ignoring the variety of cultural patterns and meaning." One of the effects of such sexual excavation is that a sectarian version of Hindu India, where religion inflects nationalism, is constructed and reinforced. "India" as an ideological construct and as a nation-state apparatus *is* contested from "within." Maintaining it as a stable, un-challenged category is the equivalent of keeping notions of white America intact. The conflation of India with Hindu identity and Hin-duism "Otherizes" Sikhs and Muslims, and, given the situation of con-temporary politics in India today, this is not merely a question of semantics.

Here is an example: when a contingent of Trikone members marched in the annual India Day parade in Fremont, California, in August 1994 (which celebrates India's independence from the British), once again part of a dynamic of desired visibility and in-clusion, they ran into a booing, hissing crowd of Khalistani Sikhs protesting the march—despite the fact that Trikone's group was carrying a Khalistani flag. Were the Khalistani Sikhs displeased because of the presence of queers or the presence of Indian Na-tionalists? Or perhaps they were displeased because the suppos-edly progressive queers were also Indian Nationalists? Reading this response as a wholly homophobic one, which many who marched did, misses the complexities of colonial and postcolo-nial production of sexualities and sexual practices and how they link to the politics of nationalism and religious identities in the diasporas. Fleshing out the links between colonialism, capitalism, communalism, and normative heterosexuality, which is critical, occurs less than analyses dealing with gender and class. Thus it must be asked: *which sexual subjectivities are more easily mobilized, available, accessible, and visible in this queer diaspora than others and why?*

Diasporic Globalizing

Lotus clearly reflects margin/center dynamics in South Asian diasporic geopolitical locations. Gopinath comments that *Lotus* "maps the lines of exchange and influence between various global South Asian queer organizations, from (among others) Trikone, Shamakami, and SALGA in the U.S., to Khush in Toronto, to Shakti in London, to Sakhi and Bombay Dost in India" (123). Yet note the uneven materiality of these transnational flows: these networks are dominated by "global" cities, elite populations, and urban centers. Writing about *Lotus's* "near invisibility of working class and lower caste South Asians," JeeYeun Lee pinpoints the implications of such invisibility in her review of the book: "This class imbalance seems to reflect the membership in queer South Asian groups in general, which has a significant effect on the development of this emerging global queer South Asian identity" (101).

This concern is particularly relevant, given that South Asians in the United States are historically, as well as currently, in situations of relative privilege compared with those in other Western diasporic locations. This has led to the marginalization, if not the elimination, of literature and other work from locations such as Canada and Britain generated prior to the publication of *Lotus*. In noting the cultural landscapes of these different locales, one sees the varied mechanisms that are disciplining difference. For example, the context of the United States, where (predominantly middle-class) South Asians have been positioned as producers of acceptable and containable difference, is quite different from the context of Britain, where rhetorics of nation(alism) and the language of citizenship clearly exclude (predominantly working-class) Asians.

Such variations in the domestic locales of the South Asian diaspora demand caution. Sau-ling C. Wong warns that in shifting from the domestic to the diasporic, one must take care that the domestic does not pose as diasporic or even become the diasporic (9). My own concern about how one represents location extends this to question when and how the diasporic becomes a globalizing discourse. An important illustration of the difficulties of theorizing diasporic cultural productions in diverse locations is the concept of coming out or being out. In another review of *Lotus,* editor Rakesh Ratti summarizes the purpose of the collection, stating, "This is really an opportunity to make ourselves more visible, and to define ourselves on our own terms" (Sengupta E3). Who is the "ourselves"? Who gets to be visible? The terms of this inclusion are not, contrary to Ratti's statement, "our own terms." (For example, the term "lotus" conjures up all sorts of Orientalist images for me. I am not at all sure, and neither are others I have asked, what the actual significance of "lotus" is in this context.)

This concern with visibility is perhaps reflected by the numerous coming-out narratives in *Lotus.* I do not want to minimize the importance of the narratives; however, I am concerned that the significance and celebration attached to coming out appears to be understood as a conclusion to the linear teleology of a modernist, rational subject emerging unrepressed and therefore as empowered as any white queer. This teleology is dependent, once again, on India as origin but, more significantly, on the West as a place of sexual freedom and liberation.[7]

For example, in the *Lotus* essay "Toward a Global Network of Asian Lesbians," Sharmeen Islam speaks of lesbian invisibility in Asia and the need for "visible and powerful lesbian and gay organizations in Asian countries" (44). In this globalizing discourse, "Asian" becomes a stable category that transcends differences between diasporic and nondiasporic (or differently diasporic) subjects. Islam does emphasize, however, that whereas the "average lesbian in Asia" faces a lack of community, "a dearth of native literature on gay and lesbian lifestyles, few 'out' role models, and little in the way of organizations," Asian women who live in the West face a set of "unique and important daily issues: racism, exile, immigration and deportation threats, cultural isolation, and Western hybridization" (45). But in attempting to clarify the differences between "us and our Asian sisters," Islam sets up a totalizing First World/Third World Binary, which can only be rectified through the globalization of Western privilege: "It is necessary that we collaborate in the liberation of gays and lesbians in Asia; we must take in hand the reins of our destiny and determine our sexuality and politics in our own cultural context. We must pull together a global community that empowers Asian lesbian and gays everywhere" (43).

Kenyan-born British South Asian lesbian filmmaker Pratibha Parmar unwittingly resurrects a similar telos in the *Lotus* interview "Fighting Back: An Interview with Pratibha Parmar." Parmar is clear that homophobia in England is "given expression through actual physical abuse of lesbians and gays on the streets" (Khush 36). As Parmar recounts her childhood experiences of Paki-bashing in

England (35), claiming that Indians in India "know that racism [in England] exists, but they don't really know the extent of it" (39), she constructs an India where everyone "belongs," where questions of race are supposedly not in operation. Yet later she comments that she would not want to live in India, explaining, "As a woman and an out lesbian, I'd find it very difficult. That is the sad reality, especially having talked to lesbians in India and hearing of the ways in which their lives are circumscribed. It is bad enough in England" (40).

It may be that some lesbians' lives are circumscribed in India, but nowhere does Parmar question her own power to define what circumscribing is or seem aware of her own imposition of a metanarrative of outness. When she states, "It is bad enough in England," it appears that she is talking solely about being out, when in reality it is "bad" for all sorts of intersecting reasons, some of which—racism, classism, homophobia, and so on—Parmar actually acknowledges earlier in the interview. It is here that Parmar abandons her earlier proclamations about racism in Britain and forgets that India, for some, is a place of ethnic (as well as class and caste) belonging. This privileging of being out sets forth sexual identity as separate from other identities, or at least as primary and uninflected by other subject positionings. This narrative posits a domestic perspective as a diasporic perspective that becomes a globalizing tendency.

Whereas Islam and Parmar may globalize through their specific modernist desires for liberation and visibility, Gopinath attempts to negotiate diasporic specificities: "What, then, are the implications of privileging sexuality as a primary 'identity' throughout the diaspora? What possible alternative narratives of sexuality may we be shutting down in such a move? How do we allow for the fact that same-sex eroticism exists and signifies very differently in different diasporic contexts, while simultaneously recognizing the common forms of violence that we face everyday because of our sexuality?" (122).

On one hand, Gopinath posits a diasporic rubric that foregrounds the (homo)sexual and a "sexual identity," presuming that "we" face common forms of violence and effacing the forms of violence that "we" face with each other. On the other hand, she is compelled, in an attempt to contest these homogenizing impulses, to grant or "allow" others same-sex eroticism that may signify "differently." This question, then, must be asked: differently from what? In contrast to Parmar's up-front sentiments (I'm here, I'm queer, and I wouldn't want it any other way, racism or not), the acknowledgment and incorporation of difference with which Gopinath is grappling is fraught with difficulties. While the naming of difference cannot be avoided, the desire to "allow" it without posing questions of power differentials unwittingly levels out the sexual-signification playing field.[8]

What must queer diasporic cultural productions attend to in order to comprehend fully their political viability? Theorizing transnational queer diasporas requires both a politics of location and a politics of placelessness. (R. Lee), which must be attentive to colonial mobilizations of sexuality and postcolonial histories of immigration that create and sustain space/place/time. It is critical to note who or what is crossing which "border" in which direction, as well as when and for what purposes. Together, the examples of Islam, Parmar, and Gopinath strongly suggest the necessity of historicizing the demand for desiring a queer diaspora.

The problems of representing location become even clearer when we consider the work of Shani Mootoo, a queer filmmaker and writer of Indian descent, born in Ireland, raised in Trinidad, and now living in Canada. Richard Fung, a Chinese Trinidadian queer filmmaker and writer, notes the dissymmetries in Mootoo's displaced/replaced/displaced subjectivities: "Mootoo doesn't fit in to essential(ist) constructions of what it means to be Irish, West Indian, Canadian, or Indian. She doesn't either look, sound, or act 'right.' Race, language, and culture are the obvious culprits; the 'typical' Canadian woman is white, just as the 'typical' West Indian is black" (162).

Fung goes on to note that, despite the fact that Indians are now the largest ethnic group in Trinidad, their claim to Caribbeanness is "still a matter of contestation. . . . The resulting generalized West Indian identity is inevitably narrated solely in terms of its African heritage" (162). What Fung alludes to, but does not elaborate on, here is that this contested Indian claim to Caribbeanness is ironically mirrored by a Caribbean claim to Indianness. This claim is contested in a North American context, for here Mootoo isn't the 'typical' Indian either. Not only does not she not "look, sound, or act 'right,'" but the genealogies of ethnicity, class, and origin inflect sharply against dominant South Asian spaces as well. Commenting on Desh Pardesh, the annual queercentric, South Asian left conference in Toronto, Mootoo states, "Here at the discussion on racism in the gay and lesbian community, I was struck by how everybody kept talking about when they were in India. Today I found myself desperately trying to imagine India so I would not be excluded from the discussion. . . . The truth is, a gay Trinidadian, say, of Chinese origin . . . probably has more in common with me than most South Asian dykes outside of Trinidad. . . . It is totally against my politics to suggest any kind of pan–South Asian representation" (Ghosh 6).

Here Mootoo points to the difficulties of a politics of diasporic inclusivity, and yet any specificity in naming also has important consequences. Calling her Indo-Trinidadian Canadian or even Indo-Canadian situates her work very differently from calling her South Asian or South Asian Canadian. The terms "South Asian" and "South Asian Canadian" may elide rifts between Indo-Caribbean communities and South Asian communities in Vancouver (where Mootoo lives), Toronto, New York, and Miami. Indo-Caribbeans cannot simply be absorbed or "included" in South Asian diasporic spaces. It must also be acknowledged that Mootoo's positionality vis-à-vis queer politics in South Asian diasporic spaces may have more currency and connection to India than to "back home" in Trinidad, where her work does not circulate widely. Thus, the fact of her "being from" Trinidad does not automatically signal an "inclusion" of Trinidad in the South Asian global queer network, at least not in any material sense, though the imaginary connections can be foregrounded.

Conclusion

As Tölölyan notes, "Diasporas are the emblems of transnationalism because they embody the question of borders" (6). Pursuing this idea, one must remain vigilantly attentive to how, where, when, and by whom or by what those borders are traversed. Given the masculinist, culturally nationalist queer diasporas laid out herein, it is worth asking certain questions. What are the traveling transnational elements that constitute a particular diaspora? What would these transnational linkages look like if women were the subjects? How do women make/make up transnational linkages?

Wong foregrounds the problems of privileging some transnational links in a diaspora over others. In her critique of Lisa Lowe's theorization of hybridity, Wong asks "to what extent a class bias is coded into the privileging of travel and transnational mobility in Lowe's model" (15). She continues, "Lowe's model of identity and cultural formation celebrating is, at least in part, extrapolated from the wide range of options available to a particular socio-economic class, yet the class element is typically rendered invisible" (15). Wong's comments remind us of the irony of constructing a diaspora that forgets that the transnational act of migration for queers, especially those of color, is quite a corporally and visccrally conflictcd cxpcricncc, pcrhaps morc difficult (for those who have access) than logging onto a queer e-mail network in India. Although Wong makes a compelling argument against those who have hailed the end of the era of the nation-state, a return to "America" as a local site may rearticulate a cultural nationalist version of Asian American. In this sense, the political potential of the term "South Asian American" seems even more limited.

After reading my essay, one may wonder why bother theorizing queer diasporas at all. In this initial exploration of transnational sexualities, my critically pessimistic approach has functioned to counter what I have perceived as an overabundance of celebratory discourses on queer subjectivities. This is not to suggest that coalitional politics is not possible or to demean the modes of pleasure and desire that these spaces enable. It is, however, to note that praxis of pleasure and desire are sometimes constructed through problematic politics and that what one might conceive of as oppositional and contestatory in one location may well be complicit and oppressive in another.

In this light, it is certainly worth examining how constructions of diaspora may suggest new formations for queer politics. Though that has not been the focus of this work, some instances come immediately to mind. Asian American lesbian Trinity Ordona, for example, elaborates on the need to understand immigration as a queer issue: "Prop K was a good thing in that it recognizes domestic partners; on the other hand if you are an immigrant and register your relationship, the INS has documented proof that you are an 'undesirable alien.' Was there any discussion about this in the gay community? The only time immigration is seen as a 'Gay community' problem is when HIV-status persons can't get into the country to attend a conference" (Chung et al. 93).

Another case in point might be Queer Nation's "production of a queer counterpublic out of traditional [American] national icons," described by Lauren Berlant and Elizabeth Freeman (214). What would these traditional national icons be for "diasporics," not to mention the questions of which public and for which queers? Berlant and Freeman assert that "disidentification with U.S. nationality is not, at this moment, even a theoretical option for Queer citizens" (197). Are the rhetorical parodic strategies of Queer Nation, "simulat[ing] 'the national' with a camp inflection" (196), possibly transformed through the politics of queer diasporas? Imagine Esta Noche, a gay bar in the Latino/Chicano district of San Francisco, where, on Labor Day, a drag queen performance used the American flag in its parody. This "drag with the flag" and other such performatives suggest complex diasporic counterpublic spheres and the impossibility of belonging to the nation, yet the impossibility of rejecting it.

The demand for evidence as posited through any public strategies of visibility lies at the heart of the paradox that theories of transnational sexualities must negotiate. For some queer immigrants, as Martin Manalansan points out, visibility is not only undesirable but also dangerous (434). For others who are able to participate in emerging queer cosmopolitan elites, the demand for evidence may result in a recourse to roots, culture, origin, and ultimately the nation(s). Thus, one must interrogate not only how the nation disallows certain queers but, perhaps more urgently, how nations produce and may in fact sanction certain queer subjectivities over others.

NOTES

Acknowledgments: I thank David L. Eng for his editorial expertise. As always, I am grateful to Norma Alarcón, Anjali, Arondekar, Marisa Belausteguigoitia, Inderpal Grewal, Caren Kaplan, Eithne Luibheid, and Katherine Sugg for their comments on drafts and for their tremendous support.

1. Khushnet is another example of the dynamics of cultural and religious nationalism. The organizing principle of a sexual identity politics—upon which this cyberspace rests—has been severely disrupted and fractured by discussions on fundamentalism. In the past, debates have shut down on the assumption that fundamentalism has nothing to do with sexualities. This resurrects a disembodied queer subject wholly constructed by sexual desire and ignores the fact that fundamentalisms and their attendant positionings also construct pleasure and praxis. This "safe space," one that is obviously overdetermined in terms of class-privileged access to the Internet, is also dominated by men, and the list has seen extensive upheaval over the issue of gender dynamics.

2. It should be noted that Ratti's collection uses the phrase "gay and lesbian," and this essay uses the term "queer." The long and complicated histories around the terminologies used by South Asian queers and queer groups cannot be rehearsed here. Suffice it to say, however, that these histories reflect the general critiques of the term "queer" as well as the generational biases of these spaces.

3. See, for example, Butler; Duggan 1–14; Hanawa vxi; Muñoz 5–17; and Yarbro-Bejarano 124–35.

4. See, for example, Chow; Clifford 302–38; Gilroy; Grewal 45–74; Hall 222–36; Ong 745–78; and Tölölyan 3–7.

5. Inattention to issues of citizenship has most recently surfaced in the debates on same-sex marriage legislation in Hawaii, which have not examined the implications for queer immigrants, both documented and undocumented.

6. I attempted to compile a list of South Asian queer readings recently, a process that highlighted the difficulties of terminologies, categories, and canons. As expected, I could not find any work under the combined terms "South Asian" and "queer." I had no luck with the terms "gay," "lesbian," "homosexual," and "Indian" either. Even the combination "Indian" and "sexuality" turned up only a few titles. Such searches illuminate various epistemological and methodological positionings in the ways that terms and definitions are consolidated and deployed. Of course, conventional bibliographical searches reflect the

limitations of the institutionalization of disciplines and the packaging of knowledge. The difficulties of compiling such a bibliography reflect particular historical moments in terms of South Asian queer identities.

The ambiguities around the term "South Asian" are notable. Understanding the term as recently political in contemporary Western diasporic locations, I expected to find literature on diasporic populations. But because "South Asian" also has roots in an International Monetary Fund development vocabulary, the term, when used in the search process, revealed mostly economic research on the countries geographically located in South Asia. The fact that the term "South Asian" brought up Southeast Asian studies as well indicates a common confusion between these area studies categories. Also not revealed by the search was the large body of British titles, in which "Asian" is more commonly used (as is the term "black"). Much literature on South Asians in the United States has also historically been umbrellaed under "Asian" and "Asian American." The term "Indian" brought up "Native American" work from various dates, reflecting different circulations and reclamations of this term.

In the process of claiming a canon of sorts, what gets grouped into a body of literature out of necessity of naming becomes rather ambiguous and arbitrary. This process parallels the simultaneous process of (re)claiming and constructing identity by searching for "roots" and "origins." For example, I found John Irving's *Son of the Circus* listed on several South Asian queer reading/resource lists, because the story takes place in India and features one gay Indian man as a minor character. The other side of the picture is the work of Urvashi Vaid, former director of the National Gay and Lesbian Task Force. Very visible in "mainstream" gay and lesbian movements for at least a decade, she rarely—until very recently—talked about being South Asian or espoused a particular brand of cultural identity politics. There have been debates about her status as a role model and about whether she "represents" South Asian queers or not. Aside from whether or not she "belongs" to the "community" (two notions she deconstructs through her own obscure subject positionings), I think these debates point to the shifting natures of and possibilities for certain strands of identity politics. I should also note that I found the majority of the bibliographic information through the Internet.

7. "They Aren't That Primitive Back Home" is the only essay in *Lotus* that details the diverse sexual practices in India, noting how sexual identity in and of itself can be an imperializing privileged category (Kim 92–97).

8. Gopinath mobilizes this diasporic globalizing in what she admits is a "utopic strain." She writes, "There is a profoundly affective quality to the experience of walking into a roomful of queer brown folks lip-synching along to Choli Ke Piche, a phenomenally popular Hindi film song that, as one gay man playfully commented, has done more for the South Asian queer community than any conference or parade ever has" (123).

I would suggest that ethnographies of reception might be useful in further exploring such a claim. How is this song signifying differently in different diasporic locations? How is this song signifying differently to non–Hindi speaking audiences? Again the Hindu subtext of this version of the South Asian diaspora must be flagged.

WORKS CITED

AIDS Bhedbav Virodhi Andolan (ABVA). "Homosexuality in India: Culture and Heritage." *A Lotus of Another Color: An Unfolding of the South Asian Gay and Lesbian Experience*. Ed. Rakesh Ratti. Boston: Alyson, 1993. 21–33.

Alexander, Jacqui. "Not Just (Any) *Body* Can Be a Citizen: The Politics of Law, Sexuality and Postcoloniality in Trinidad and Tobago and the Bahamas." *Feminist Review* 48 (Fall 1994): 5–23.

Berlant, Lauren, and Elizabeth Freeman. "Queer Nationality." *Fear of a Queer Planet: Queer Politics and Social Theory*. Ed. Michael Warner. Minneapolis: U of Minnesota P, 193–229.

Butler, Judith. *Bodies That Matter: On the Discursive Limits of "Sex."* New York: Routledge, 1993.

Chow Rey. *Writing Diaspora: Tactics of Intervention in Contemporary Cultural Studies*. Bloomington: U of Indiana P, 1993.

Chung, Christy, Aly Kim, Zoon Nguyen, and Trinity Ordona with Arlene Stein, "In Our Own Way: A Roundtable Discussion." *Asian American Sexualities: Dimensions of the Gay and Lesbian Experience*. Ed. Russell Leong. New York: Routledge, 1996. 91–99.

Clifford, James. "Diasporas." *Anthropology* 9.3 (1994): 302–38.

Duggan, Lisa. "Queering the State." *Social Text* 39 (Summer 1994): 1–14.

Foucault, Michel. *The History of Sexuality: An Introduction*. Vol. 1. New York: Vintage, 1978.

Fung, Richard. "Bodies Out of Place: The Videotapes of Shani Mootoo." *Women and Performance: A Journal of Feminist Theory* 8:2 (1996): 161–73.

Ghosh, Dipti. "Baigan Aloo Tabanka Bachanal." *Trikone* 9.4 (Oct. 1994): 6–8.

Gilroy, Paul. *There Ain't No Black in the Union Jack: The Cultural Politics of Race and Nation*. Chicago: U of Chicago P, 1991.

Gopinath, Gayatri. "Funny Boys and Girls: Notes on a Queer South Asian Planet." *Asian American Sexualities: Dimensions of the Gay and Lesbian Experience*. Ed. Russell Leong. New York: Routledge, 1996. 119–27.

Grewal, Inderpal. "The Postcolonial, Ethnic Studies, and the Diaspora: The Contexts of Ethnic Immigrant/Migrant Cultural Studies in the U.S." *Socialist Review* 4 (1994): 45–74.

Gupta, Akhil, and James Ferguson. "Beyond 'Culture': Space, Identity, and the Politics of Difference." *Cultural Anthropology* 7.1 (1992): 6–23.

Hall, Stuart. "Cultural Identity and Diaspora." *Identity, Community, Cultural Difference*. Ed. Jonathan Rutherford. London: Routledge, 1990. 222–36.

Halperin, David. *Saint Foucault*. New York: Oxford UP, 1995.

Hanawa, Yukiko. "Introduction: Circuits of Desire." *positions* 2:1 (1994): v–xi.

Islam, Sharmeen. "Toward a Global Network of Asian Lesbians." *A Lotus of Another Color: An Unfolding of the South Asian Gay and Lesbian Experience*. Ed. Rakesh Ratti. Boston: Alyson, 1993. 41–46.

Khush. "Fighting Back: An Interview with Pratibha Parmar." *A Lotus of Another Color: An Unfolding of the South Asian Gay and Lesbian Experience*. Ed. Rakesh Ratti. Boston: Alyson, 1993. 34–40.

Kim. "They Aren't That Primitive Back Home." *A Lotus of Another Color: An Unfolding of the South Asian Gay and Lesbian Experience*. Ed. Rakesh Ratti. Boston: Alyson, 1993. 92–97.

Lee, JeeYeun. "*A Lotus of Another Color*." Book review. *Amerasia Journal* 20.3 (1994): 100–102.

Lee, Rachel. "Re-siting Empire, Resisting Placelessness." Unpublished paper. Association for Asian American Studies Conf. Washington, D.C. June 1996.

Manalansan, Martin F., IV. "In the Shadows of Stonewall: Examining Gay Transnational Politics and the Diasporic Dilemma." *GLQ: A Journal of Lesbian and Gay Studies* 2.4 (1995): 425–38.

Muñoz, José. "Ephemera as Evidence: Introductory Notes to Queer Acts." *Women and Performance: A Journal of Feminist Theory*. 8:2 (1996): 5–17.

Ong, Aihwa. "On the Edge of Empires Flexible Citizenship Among Chinese in Diaspora." *positions* 1:3 (1993): 745–78.

Rai, Amit. "India On-Line: Electronic Bulletin Boards and the Construction of a Diasporic Hindu Identity." *Diaspora: A Journal of Transnational Studies* 4.1 (Spring 1995): 31–58.

Ratti, Rakesh. Ed. *A Lotus of Another Color: An Unfolding of the South Asian Gay and Lesbian Experience*. Boston: Alyson, 1993.

———. "Introduction." *A Lotus of Another Color: An Unfolding of the South Asian Gay and Lesbian Experience*. Ed. Rakesh Ratti. Boston: Alyson, 1993. 11–18.

Sengupta, Somini. "New Collection of Writing Addresses Problems of Gay South Asians." *Los Angeles Times* 112: 21 Apr. 1993. E3.

Tölölyan, Khachig. "The Nation-State and Its Others: In Lieu of a Preface." *Diaspora: A Journal of Transnational Studies* 1.1 (Spring 1991): 3–7.

Wong, Sau-ling C. "Denationalization Reconsidered: Asian American Cultural Criticism at a Theoretical Crossroads." *Amerasia Journal* 21.1–2 (1995): 1–27.

Yarbro-Bejarano, Yvonne. "Expanding the Categories of Race and Sexuality in Lesbian and Gay Studies." *Professions of Desire: Lesbian and Gay Studies in Literature*. Ed. George Haggerty and Bonnie Zimmerman. New York: MLA, 1995. 124–35.

A   A   A   A   A   A   A   A   A   A

Selected Bibliography
Anthologies, Fiction, and Nonfiction
Compiled by Alice Y. Hom

ANTHOLOGIES

Anthologies that are not lesbian, bisexual, or gay specific include lesbian, bisexual, and gay writers and issues.

Bernstein, Robin, and Seth Clarke Silberman, eds. *Generation Q: Gays, Lesbians, and Bisexuals Born Around 1969's Stonewall Riots Tell Their Stories of Growing Up in the Age of Information.* Los Angeles: Alyson 1996.

Carbó, Nick, ed. *Returning a Borrowed Tongue: An Anthology of Filipino and Filipino American Poetry.* Minneapolis: Coffee House, 1995.

Chung, Connie, Alison Kim, and A. K. Lemeshewsky, eds. *Between the Lines: An Anthology of Pacific/Asian Lesbians.* Santa Cruz, Calif.: Dancing Bird, 1987.

Elwin, Rosamund, ed. *Countering the Myths: Lesbians Write About the Men in Their Lives.* Toronto: Women's, 1996.

Francia, Luis H., and Eric Gamalinda, eds. *Flippin': Filipinos on America.* New York: Asian American Writers' Workshop, 1996.

Gates, Beatrix, ed. *The Wild Good: Lesbian Photographs and Writing on Love.* New York: Anchor, 1996.

Gever, Martha, John Greyson, and Pratibha Parmar, eds. *Queer Looks: Perspectives on Lesbian and Gay Film and Video.* New York: Routledge, 1993.

Hagedorn, Jessica, ed. *Charlie Chan Is Dead: An Anthology of Contemporary Asian American Fiction.* New York: Penguin, 1993.

Johnstone, James C., and Karen X. Tulchinsky, eds. *Queer View Mirror: Lesbian and Gay Short Short Fiction.* Vancouver: Arsenal Pulp, 1995.

————. *Queer View Mirror 2: Lesbian and Gay Short Short Fiction.* Vancouver: Arsenal Pulp, 1997.

Kudaka, Geraldine, ed. *On a Bed of Rice: An Asian American Erotic Feast.* New York: Anchor, 1995.

Lee, C. Allyson, and Makeda Silvera, eds. *Pearls of Passion: A Treasury of Lesbian Erotica.* Toronto: Sister Vision, 1995.

Leong, Russell, ed. *Asian American Sexualities: Dimensions of the Gay and Lesbian Experience.* New York: Routledge, 1996.

Lew, Walter K, ed., *Premonitions: The Kaya Anthology of New Asian North American Poetry.* New York: Kaya, 1995.

Lim-Hing, Sharon, ed. *The Very Inside: An Anthology of Writing by Asian and Pacific Islander Lesbian and Bisexual Women.* Toronto: Sister Vision, 1994.

Mason-Joh, Valerie, ed. *Talking Black: Lesbians of African and Asian Descent Speak Out.* London: Cassell, 1995.

Moraga, Cherríe, and Gloria Anzaldúa, eds. *This Bridge Called My Back: Writings by Radical Women of Color.* New York: Kitchen Table—Women of Color, 1983.

I thank the following people for sharing their bibliographies with me: JeeYeun Lee, Eric Estuar Reyes, and Stephanie Tai for her website.

Nelson, Emmanuel S., ed. *Critical Essays: Gay and Lesbian Writers of Color*
New York: Harrington Park, 1993.

Oikawa, Mona, Dionne Falconer, Rosamund Elwin, and Ann Dector, eds.
Out Rage: Dykes and Bis Resist Homophobia. Toronto: Women's, 1993.

Okihiro, Gary Y., Marilyn Alquizola, Dorothy Fujita Rony, and K. Scott
Wong, eds. *Privileging Positions: The Sites of Asian American Studies.* Pullman: Washington State UP, 1995.

Ratti, Rakesh, ed. *A Lotus of Another Color: An Unfolding of the South Asian
Gay and Lesbian Experience.* Boston: Alyson, 1993.

Shervington, Gwendolyn L., ed. *A Fire Is Burning, It Is in Me: The Life and
Writings of Michiyo Fukaya.* Norwich, Vt.: New Victoria, 1996.

Silvera, Makeda, ed. *Piece of My Heart: A Lesbian of Colour Anthology.*
Toronto: Sister Vision, 1991.

Sullivan, Gerard, and Laurence Wai-Teng Leong, eds. *Asia-Pacific Gay
People: Social and Human Services.* New York: Harrington Park, 1995.

"Witness Aloud: Lesbian, Gay, and Bisexual Asian/Pacific American
Writings." Special issue. *APA Journal* 2:1 (Spring–Summer 1993).

Yamaguchi, Lynne, and Karen Barber, eds. *Tomboys: Tales of Dyke Derring
Do.* Los Angeles: Alyson, 1995.

FICTION

Aruna, V. K. "Two Yoginis." *Our Feet Walk the Sky: Women of South Asian
Diaspora.* Ed. Women of South Asian Descent Collective. San Francisco: Aunt Lute, 1993. 278–82.

Asagi, Lisa. "Portraits of Desire." *Hers: Brilliant New Fiction by Lesbian
Writers.* Ed. Terry Wolverton with Robert Drake. Boston: Faber and
Faber, 1995. 91–96.

Bruining, Mi Ok. "Made in Korea." *Writing Away Here: A Korean/Ameri-
can Anthology.* Ed. Hyun Yi Kang. Oakland, Calif.: Korean American
Arts Festival Committee, 1994. 78–81.

———. "Mother's Day, May 10, 1994." *Writing Away Here: A Korean/Amer-
ican Anthology.* Ed. Hyun Yi Kang. Oakland, Calif.: Korean American
Arts Festival Committee, 1994. 43–46.

———. "To Omoni, in Korea." *Making Face, Making Soul: Haciendo
Caras: Creative and Critical Perspectives by Women of Color.* Ed. Gloria Anzaldúa. San Francisco: Aunt Lute, 1990. 153–55.

Chan, Liza C. May. "Woman in Woman." *Albatross* (Fall 1976): 21.

Chin, Christopher M. "Tonight I Laugh at the World." *Amerasia Journal*
17.2 (1991): 89–92.

Chin, Justin. *Bite Hard.* San Francisco: Manic D, 1997.

———. "Cocksuckers' Tango." *Best Gay Erotica 1997.* Ed. Richard
Labonté. Pittsburgh: Cleis, 1997. 57–61.

———. "Goo." *Flesh and the Word 4: Gay Erotic Confessionals.* Ed. Michael
Lowenthal. New York: Plume, 1997. 229–32.

De, Shobha. *Strange Obsession.* New York: Penguin, 1992.

Dinh, Viet. "Yellowtail." *His^2: Brilliant New Fiction by Gay Writers.* Ed. Robert
Drake with Terry Wolverton. Boston: Faber and Faber, 1997. 56–68.

Dunsford, Cathie. *Cowrie*. New York: Spinifex, 1994.

Fletcher, Lynne Yamaguchi. "Turtleback Dreams an Ocean Breathing." *Bushfire: Stories of Lesbian Desire*. Ed. Karen Barber. Los Angeles: Alyson, 1991. 13–27.

Fukaya, Michiyo Cornwell. *Lesbian Lyrics*. New York: Self-published, 1981.

Han, Ju Hui Judy. "crossing." *Writing Away Here: A Korean/American Anthology*. Ed. Hyun Yi Kang. Oakland, Calif.: Korean American Arts Festival Committee, 1994. 2–4.

Kim, Alison. *Mirror Mirror (Woman Woman)*. Santa Cruz, Calif.: Dancing Bird, 1986.

———. "Sewing Woman." *The Forbidden Stitch: An Asian American Women's Anthology*. Ed. Shirley Geok-lin Lim, Mayumi Tatsukawa, and Margarita Donnelly. Corvallis, Ore.: Calyx, 1989. 203.

Kim, Willyce. *Curtains of Light*. Albany, Calif.: Self-published, 1970.

———. *Dancer Dawkins and the California Kid*. Boston: Alyson, 1985.

———. *Dead Heat*. Boston: Alyson, 1988.

———. *Eating Artichokes*. Oakland; Calif.: Women's P Collective, 1972.

———. "Habits." *Bushfire: Stories of Lesbian Desire*. Ed. Karen Barber, Los Angeles: Alyson, 1991. 88–94.

———. *Under the Rolling Sky*. Oakland, Calif.: Maud Gonne, 1976.

Kobayashi, Tomai, and Mona Oikawa. *All Names Spoken: Poetry and Prose*. Toronto: Sister Vision, 1992.

Kraut-Hasagawa, Ellen. "Noise." *Hers²: Brilliant New Fiction by Lesbian Writers*. Ed. Terry Wolverton with Robert Drake. Boston: Faber and Faber, 1997. 140–44.

Lai, Larissa. *When Fox Is a Thousand*. Vancouver: Press Gang, 1995.

Lee, Sky. *Bellydancer Stories*. Vancouver: Press Gang, 1994.

———. *Disappearing Moon Cafe*. Seattle: Seal, 1992.

Linmark, R. Zamora. *Rolling the R's*. New York: Kaya, 1995.

Liu, Timothy. *Burnt Offerings*. Washington, D.C.: Copper Canyon, 1995.

———. *Vox Angelica*. Cambridge, Mass.: Alice James, 1992.

Mootoo, Shani. *Cereus Blooms at Night*. Vancouver: Press Gang, 1997.

———. *Out on Main Street and Other Stories*. Vancouver: Press Gang, 1993.

Namjoshi, Suniti. *Because of India: Selected Poems and Fables*. London: Only Woman, 1989.

———. *The Conversations of Cow*. London: Women's, 1985.

———. *Feminist Fables*. 2nd ed. London: Sheba Feminist, 1990.

Noda, Barbara. *Strawberries*. Berkeley: Shameless Hussy, 1979.

Okita, Dwight. *Crossing with the Light*. Chicago: Tia Chucha, 1992.

Quan, Andy. "How to Cook Chinese Rice." *Queeries: An Anthology of Gay Male Prose*. Ed. Dennis Denisoff. Vancouver: Arsenal Pulp, 1993 102–9.

Revoyr, Nina. *The Necessary Hunger*. New York: Simon and Schuster, 1997.

Rodriguez, Nice. *Throw It to the River*. Toronto: Women's, 1993.

Roy, Sandip. "Black and Blue: A Tale of Mixed Colors." *Men on Men 6: Best New Gay Fiction.* Ed. David Bergman. New York: Plume, 1996. 258–70.

———. "The Smells of Home." *Contours of the Heart: South Asians Map North America.* Ed. Sunaina Maira and Rajini Srikanth. New York: Asian American Writers' Workshop, 1996. 319–25.

Sam, Canyon. "Sapphire." *Lesbian Love Stories.* Ed. Irene Zahava. Freedom, Calif.: Crossing, 1989. 261–68.

Selvadurai, Shyam. *Funny Boy.* New York: William Morrow, 1994.

Seth, Vikram. *The Golden Gate: A Novel in Verse.* New York: Random, 1986.

Som, Indigo Chih-Lien. "Coming Out Dream Series." *Beyond Definition: New Writing from Gay and Lesbian San Francisco.* Ed. Marci Blackman and Trebor Healey. San Francisco: Manic D, 1994. 36–38.

Tan, Cecilia. "Penetration." *Best Lesbian Erotica 1997.* Ed. Tristan Taormino. Pittsburgh: Cleis, 1997. 109–11.

Tsui, Kitty. *Breathless.* New York: Firebrand, 1996.

———. "Give Joan Chen My Number Anytime." *Lesbian Erotics.* Ed. Karla Jay. New York: New York UP, 1995. 62–70.

———. "Why the Milky Way Is Milky." *Lesbian Love Stories.* Ed. Irene Zahava. Freedom, Calif.: Crossing, 1989. 285–97.

———. *Words of a Woman Who Breathes Fire.* San Francisco: Spinsters, 1983.

Villanueva, Chea. *Bulletproof Butches.* New York: Masquerade Books, 1997.

———. *China Girls.* Self-published. Lezzies on the Move, 1991.

———. *Girlfriends.* New York: Outlaw, 1987.

———. *Jessie's Song.* New York: Masquerade Books, 1995.

Vu, Trac. "PreDahmer." *Beyond Definition: New Writing from Gay and Lesbian San Francisco.* Ed. Marci Blackman and Trebor Healey. San Francisco: Manic D, 1994. 22.

Wong, Norman. "Andrew and I." *Men on Men 6: Best New Gay Fiction.* Ed. David Bergman. New York: Plume, 1996. 336–53.

———. *Cultural Revolution.* New York: Persea, 1994.

Woo, Merle. "untitled." *The Forbidden Stitch: An Asian American Women's Anthology.* Ed. Shirley Geok-lin Lim, Mayumi Tatsukawa, and Margarita Donnelly. Corvallis, Ore.: Calyx, 1989. 131.

———. "Whenever You're Cornered, the Only Way Out Is to Fight." *The Forbidden Stitch: An Asian American Women's Anthology.* Ed. Shirley Geok-lin Lim, Mayumi Tatsukawa, and Margarita Donnelly. Corvallis, Ore.: Calyx, 1989. 132–33.

———. *Yellow Woman Speaks.* Seattle: Radical Women, 1986.

Young, Wynn. "Poor Butterfly!" *Amerasia Journal* 17.2 (1991): 113–19.

Yung, Wayne. *Beyond Yellow Fever.* Canada: Pomelo Project.

———. "Brad: December 19, 1992." *Queeries: An Anthology of Gay Male Prose.* Ed. Dennis Denisoff. Vancouver: Arsenal Pulp, 1993. 153–58.

NONFICTION

Aguilar–San Juan, Karin. "Landmarks in Literature by Asian American Lesbians," *Signs* 18.4 (Summer 1993): 936–44.

Almaguer, Tomás, Rüdiger Busto, Ken Dixon, Ming-Yeung Lu. "Sleeping with the Enemy? Talking About Men, Race, and Relationships." *Out/Look* 4.3 (Winter 1992): 30–38.

Altman, Dennis. "Asian Gays." *Outrage: A Magazine for Lesbians and Gay Men* 137 (1 Oct. 1994): 14.

Araki, Gregg. "The (Sorry) State of (Independent) Things." *Moving the Image: Independent Asian Pacific American Media Arts.* Ed. Russell Leong. Los Angeles: U of California Asian American Studies Center, 1991. 68–70.

"Asian Pacific Lesbians, an Invisible Minority." *Asian Week* 13 Mar. 1987: n.p.

"Asians and Gay Porn: Roundtable Talk with Rafael Chang, Sam Chong, Jesse Cortes, Dino Duazo, Dirk Jang, Edward Lim, Tee Lim, Francisco Mattos, Wing Ng, Brent Patterson, Paul Shimazaki and Craig Yee." Chapbook. San Francisco: Studio Shanghai West, 1991.

"Asian Women: Cross Cultural Exchange: Asian Lesbians of the East Coast." *off our backs* (June 1985): 5+.

Bagley, Peter. "Stepping Out: A Look at the Local Asian Gay Scene." *Sampan* 11 (Sept. 1985): 1–2.

Bhattacherya, Rantim. "Out in the Media: Gay and Lesbian Issues Are Finding Greater Expression in the Indian Press." *Trikone* 9.1 (Jan. 1994): 1+

Black, Ian, Tony Ayres, and William Yang. "Gay Asians." *Outrage: A Magazine for Lesbians and Gay Men.* (1 July 1992): 22.

"Boston Asian Gay Men and Lesbians: Up from Invisible." *Gay Community News* 9.33 (1982): n.p.

Bram, Christopher. "Cultural Revolutionary." Interview with Norman Wong. *Lambda Book Report* 4.3 (1 Mar. 1994): 7–10.

Bruining, Mi Ok. "A Few Thoughts from a Korean, Adopted, Lesbian, Writer/Poet, and Social Worker." *Lesbians of Color: Social and Human Services.* Ed. Hilda Hildago. New York: Harrington Park, 1995. 61–66.

Burning Cloud. "Open Letter from a Filipina/Indiana Lesbian." *Lesbians of Color Caucus Quarterly* 1.1 (1979): 12.

Carrier, Joseph, Bang Nguyen, and Sammy Su. "Vietnamese American Sexual Behaviors and HIV Infection." *Journal of Sex Research* 29 (4 Nov. 1992): 547–61.

Chan, Connie S. "Asian Lesbians: Psychological Issues in the 'Coming Out' Process." *Asian American Psychological Association Journal* 12 (1987): 16–18.

———. "Cultural Considerations in Counseling Asian American Lesbians and Gay Men." *Counseling Gay Men and Lesbians.* Ed. Sari Dworkin and Fernando Gutierrez. Alexandria, Va.: American Association for Counseling and Development, 1992. 115–24.

———. "Issues of Identity Development Among Asian-American Lesbians and Gay Men." *Journal of Counseling and Development* 68.1 (Sep.–Oct. 1989): 16–20.

——. "Issues of Sexual Identity in an Ethnic Minority: The Case of Chinese American Lesbians, Gay Men and Bisexual People." *Lesbian, Gay and Bisexual Identities over the Lifespan: Psychological Perspectives.* Ed. Anthony R. D'Augelli and Charlotte J. Patterson. New York: Oxford UP, 1995. 87–101.

Chan, Liza C. May. "A Lesbian/Feminist Assesses Her 'Heritage.'" *Albatross* (Spring 1976): 24–25.

Ching, Tamara. "Stranger in Paradise: Tamara Ching's Journey to the Gender Divide." *A. Magazine* 3.1 (1993): 85–86.

Choe, Margaret Mihee. "Our Selves, Growing Whole." *Closer to Home: Bisexuality and Feminism.* Ed. Elizabeth Reba Weise. Seattle: Seal, 1992. 17–25.

Choi, K. H., T. J. Coates, Joseph A. Catania, and Steve Lew. "High HIV Risk Among Gay Asian and Pacific Islander Men in San Francisco." *AIDS* 9.3 (Mar. 1995): 306–8.

Choi, K. H., Steve Lew, Eric Vittinghoff, and Joseph A. Catania. "The Efficacy of Brief Group Counseling in HIV Risk Reduction Among Homosexual Asian and Pacific Islander Men." *AIDS* 10.1 (Jan. 1996): 81–87.

Chua, Lawrence. "The Fight to Empower: AIDS Activism in Thailand." *Muae: A Journal of Transcultural Production* 1 (1995): 188–93.

——. "The Postmodern Ethnic Brunch: Devouring Difference." *Muae: A Journal of Transcultural Production* 1 (1995): 4–12.

——. "Queer Wind from Asia." *The Nation* 257.1 (5 July 1993): 38–39 +

——. "Speaking Parts: Silence, Masculinity, and the Postcolonial Faggot." *Taking Liberties: Gay Men's Essays on Politics, Culture, and Sex.* Ed. Michael Bronski. New York: Kasak, 1996. 85–94.

Dang, Quang H., "Refug(e)e: Hiding Out." *Out in All Directions: The Almanac of Gay and Lesbian America.* Ed. Lynn Witt, Sherry Thomas, and Eric Marcus. New York: Warner, 1995. 239–41.

DeGuzman, M. "AIDS Among U.S. Pinoys." *Katipunan* 2.12 (1989): 11–12.

——. "I'm Very Hopeful, I'm Not Ready to Die." *Katipunan* 2.12 (1989): 11–12.

Duncan, Patricia L. "Identity, Power, and Difference: Negotiating Conflict in an S/M Dyke Community." *Queer Studies: A Lesbian, Gay, Bisexual and Transgender Anthology.* Ed. Brett Beemyn and Mickey Eliason. New York: New York UP, 1996. 87–114.

Eng, David L. "Out Here and Over There: Queerness and Diaspora in Asian American Studies." *Social Text* 52–53 (1997): 33–52.

——. "Primal Glances: Race and Psychoanalysis in Lonny Kaneko's 'The Shoyu Kid.'" *Critical Mass: A Journal of Asian American Cultural Criticism* 1.2 (Spring 1994): 65–83.

Eng, David L., and Candice L. Fujikane. "Asian American Gay and Lesbian Literature." *The Gay and Lesbian Literary Heritage: A Reader's Com-*

panion to the Writers and Their Works, from Antiquity to the Present. Ed. Claude J. Summers. New York: Holt, 1995. 60–63.

Fung, Richard. "Bodies Out of Place: The Videotapes of Shani Mootoo." *Women and Performance: A Journal of Feminist Theory* 8.2 (1996): 161–73.

———. "Center the Margins." *Moving the Image: Independent Asian Pacific American Media Arts.* Ed. Russell Leong. Los Angeles: U of California Asian American Studies Center and Visual Communications, 1991. 62–67.

"Gay Asians: Many Live in Fear of Discovery." *Asian Week* 15 Mar. 1985: n.p.

Ghosh, Dipti. "Baigan Aloo Tabanka Bachanal." *Trikone* 9.4 (Oct. 1994): 6–8.

Gupta, Sunil. "Black, Brown and White." *Coming on Strong: Gay Politics and Culture.* Ed. Simon Shepherd and Mick Wallis. London: Unwin Hyman, 1989. n.p.

H., Pamela. "Asian American Lesbians: An Emerging Voice in the Asian American Community." *Making Waves: An Anthology of Writings by and About Asian American Women.* Ed. Asian Women United of California. Boston: Beacon, 1989. 283–90.

Hagland, Paul Ee-Nam Park. "On One Hand and the Other." *Out in All Directions: The Almanac of Gay and Lesbian America.* Ed. Lynn Witt, Sherry Thomas, and Eric Marcus. New York: Warner, 1995. 283–84.

Hall, Lisa Kahaleole Chang. "Bitches in Solitude: Identity Politics and Lesbian Community." *Sisters, Sexperts, Queers: Beyond the Lesbian Nation.* Ed. Arlene Stein. New York: Penguin, 1993. 218–29.

Hanawa, Yukiko, ed. "Circuits of Desire." Special issue. *positions: east asia cultural critique* 2.1 (Spring 1994).

———. "Inciting Sites of Political Intervention: Queer 'n' Asian." *positions: east asia cultural critique* 4.3 (Winter 1996): 459–89.

Harris, Virginia, and Trinity A. Ordoña. "Developing Unity Among Women of Color: Crossing the Barriers of Internalized Racism and Cross-Racial Hostility." *Making Face, Making Soul: Haciendo Caras: Creative and Critical Perspectives by Women of Color.* Ed. Gloria Anzaldúa. San Francisco: Aunt Lute, 1990. 304–16.

Hickey, Shannon. "Gay Asians: The Pain of Living a Lie." *East/West* 25 June 1987: n.p.

Hom, Alice Y., and Ming-Yuen S. Ma. "Premature Gestures: A Spectulative Dialogue on Asian Pacific Islander Lesbian and Gay Writing." *Critical Essays: Gay and Lesbian Writers of Color.* Ed. Emmanuel S. Nelson. New York: Haworth, 1993. 21–51.

Jackson, Lidell. "Cultural Objectification: Sexual Refugees: Gay Asian Men Challenge the Stereotypes (Interview with Gene Chang)." *Colorlife! The Lesbian, Gay, Twospirit and Bisexual People of Color Magazine* 1.5 (Mar. 1993): 8–10.

Kanuha, Valli. "Compounding the Triple Jeopardy: Battering in Lesbian of Color Relationships." *Women and Therapy* 9.1–2 (1990): 169–84.

Kase, Alleson. "Asian Lesbians Speak: A Conference Report." *off our backs* 22.8 (Aug. 1992): 8.

KoreAm Journal. "Special Queer Issue." 4.8 (Aug. 1993).

Lee, Jee Yeun. "Why Suzie Wong Is Not a Lesbian: Asian and Asian American Lesbian and Bisexual Women and Femme/Butch/Gender Identities." *Queer Studies: A Lesbian, Gay, Bisexual and Transgender Anthology.* Ed. Brett Beemyn and Mickey Eliason. New York: New York UP, 1996. 115–32.

KoreAm Journal. "Special HIV/AIDS Issue." 4 (Nov. 1993): 10–17.

Lim, Leng Leroy. "The Gay Erotics of My Mother's Stuttering Tongue." *Amerasia Journal* 22.1 (1996): 172–77.

Lim-Hing, Sharon. "Dragon Ladies, Snow Queens and Asian-American Dykes: Reflections on Race and Sexuality." *Empathy* 2.2 (1990): 20–23.

Linmark, R. Zamora. "And This Next Song Is for Everybody." *Muae: a Journal of Transcultural Production* 1 (1995): 150–63.

Manalansan, Martin F., IV. "(Re)locating the Gay Filipino: Resistance, Postcolonialism, and Identity." *Journal of Homosexuality* 26.2–3 (1993): 53–96.

———. "In the Shadows of Stonewall: Examining Gay Transnational Politics and the Diasporic Dilemma." *GLQ: A Journal of Lesbian and Gay Studies* 2.4 (1995): 425–38.

———. "Speaking of AIDS: Language and the Filipino Gay Experience in America." *Discrepant Histories: Translocal Essays on Filipino Cultures.* Ed. Vicente L. Rafael. Philadelphia: Temple UP, 1995. 193–220.

Nakayama, Takeshi. "Asian Pacific Gays Looking for Acceptance." *Rafu Shimpo* 7 Aug. 1990: n.p.

Ng, Vivien. "Homosexuality and the State in Late Imperial China." *Hidden from History: Reclaiming the Gay and Lesbian Past.* Ed. Martin Duberman, Martha Vicinus, and George Chauncey, Jr. New York: Meridian, 1990. 76–89.

———. "Looking for Lesbians in Chinese History." *Queer Representations: Reading Lives, Reading Cultures.* Ed. Martin Duberman. New York: New York UP, 1997. 199–204.

Nguyen, Huong Giang. "A Vietnamese Lesbian Speaks." *Ikon* 9 (1988): 60–63.

Noda, Barbara. "Asian American Women: Two Special Issues of *Bridge*: An Asian American Perspective." *Conditions* 6 (1980): 203–11.

Noda, Barbara, Kitty Tsui, and Z. Wong. "Coming Out: We Are Here in the Asian Community." *Bridge* 7.1 (Spring 1979): 22–24.

Ogasawara, Dale. "Beyond the 'Rice Queen': Different Politics, Varying Identities." *Colorlife! The Lesbian, Gay, Twospirit and Bisexual People of Color Magazine* 1.5 (Mar. 1993): 9+.

Reyes, Eric Estuar, and Gust A. Yep. "Challenging Complexities: Strategizing with Asian Americans in Southern California Against (Heterosex)isms." *Overcoming Heterosexism and Homophobia: Strategies That*

Work. Ed. James T. Sears and Walter L. Williams. New York: Columbia UP, 1997. 91–103.

Reyes, Nina. "Common Ground, Asians and Pacific Islanders Look for Unity in a Queer World." *Outweek* 22 May 1990: 32–37.

Rieko, Nancy, et al. "Letter to Editors re: Lesbians of Color Conference in Malibu, CA." *Lesbians of Color* 8–11 Sept. 1983: 4.

Rodriguez, Felix I. "Understanding Filipino Male Homosexuality: Implications for Social Services." *Men of Color: A Context for Service to Homosexually Active Men.* Ed. John F. Longres. New York: Harrington Park, 1996. 93–113.

Sengupta, Somini. "New Collection of Writing Addresses Problems of Gay South Asians." *Los Angeles Times* 21 Apr. 1993: E2.

Sohng, Sue, and Larry D. Icard. "A Korean Gay Man in the United States: Toward a Cultural Context for Social Service Practice." *Men of Color: A Context for Service to Homosexually Active Men.* Ed. John F. Longres. New York: Harrington Park, 1996. 115–37.

Tsang, Daniel. "Breaking the Silence: The Emergence of the Lesbian and Gay Asian Press in North America." *Bearing Dreams, Shaping Visions: Asian Pacific American Perspectives.* Ed. Linda A. Revilla, Gail M. Nomura, Shawn Wong, and Shirley Hune. Pullman: Washington State UP, 1993. 101–6.

———. "Third World Lesbians and Gay Men: Challenges for the Eighties." *Gay Community News* 9.31 (1982): n.p.

Tsui, Kitty. "Breaking Silence, Making Waves and Loving Ourselves: The Politics of Coming Out and Coming Home." *Lesbian Philosophies and Cultures.* Ed. Jeffner Allen. Albany: State U of New York P, 1990. 49–61.

———. "Who Says We Don't Talk About Sex?" *The Persistent Desire: A Femme-Butch Reader.* Ed. Joan Nestle. Boston: Alyson, 1992. 385–87.

Vaid, Urvashi. "1993 March on Washington Speech." *Out in All Directions: The Almanac of Gay and Lesbian America.* Ed. Lynn Witt, Sherry Thomas, and Eric Marcus. New York: Warner, 1995. 456–59.

———. *Virtual Equality: The Mainstreaming of Gay and Lesbian Liberation.* New York: Anchor, 1995.

Wat, Eric C. "Blood, Thick and Thin." *Out in All Directions: The Almanac of Gay and Lesbian America.* Ed. Lynn Witt, Sherry Thomas, and Eric Marcus. New York: Warner, 1995. 308–10.

Watanabe, Rae N. "Tackling the Misconceptions: An Interview with Na Mamo O Hawai'i." *Island Lifestyle* (Apr. 1995): 16–17+.

Wilkinson, Willy. "Asian Lesbianism as a Political Identity." *Sojourner* (1984): n.p.

Wong, Christine, and Terry Wolverton. "Yellow Queer: An Oral Herstory of Lesbianism." *Frontiers* 4 (Fall 1979): 52–53.

Wong, Lloyd. "Desparately Seeking Sexuality: A Gay Asian Perspective on Asian Men in Film." *Rites* (May 1991): n.p.

Woo, J. M., et al. "The Epidemiology of AIDS in Asian and Pacific Islander Populations in San Francisco." *AIDS* 2 (1988): 473–75.

Woo, Merle. "Recovering." *Bridge: An Asian American Perspective* 6.4 (1978–79): 43–45.

Woo, Merle, Nellie Wong, and Mitsuye Yamada. *Three Asian American Writers Speak on Feminism*. San Francisco: Radical Women, n.d.

Wooden, Wayne S., Harvey Kawasaki, and Raymond Mayeda. "Lifestyle and Identity Maintenance Among Gay Japanese-American Males." *Alternative Lifestyles* 5 (Summer 1983): 236–43.

X.J. "A View on Gay Asians and AIDS." *Fuse Magazine* 15.5 (Summer 1992): 13–15.

Yong, Tse-Hei. "New Mexico APL." *Out in All Directions: The Almanac of Gay and Lesbian America*. Ed. Lynn Witt, Sherry Thomas, and Eric Marcus. New York: Warner, 1995. 284–85.

Yoshizaki, Amanda. "Breaking the Rules: Constructing a Bisexual Feminist Marriage." *Closer to Home: Bisexuality and Feminism*. Ed. Elizabeth Reba Weise. Seattle: Seal, 1992. 155–62.

Yu, Danny. "Stop the Silence: Asians and Homosexuality." *A. Magazine* 1 (Summer 1990): 64.

Resource Guide
Compiled by Alice Y. Hom

ORGANIZATIONS

Asian and Pacific Islander American Health Forum
116 New Montgomery Street, suite 531
San Francisco, CA 94105
415-512-3408

Asian and Pacific Islander Coalition on HIV/AIDS (APICHA)
257 Seventh Avenue, suite 1204
New York, NY 10001-6708
212-620-7187

Asian and Pacific Islander, Queers and Questioning,
Under 25 All Together (AQUA 25)
730 Polk Street, fourth floor
San Francisco, CA 94109
415-292-3400 ext. 316
AQUAkid@aquanet.org
http://www.AQUAnet.org/

Asian and Pacific Islander Wellness Center
Community HIV/AIDS Services
730 Polk Street, fourth floor
San Francisco, CA 94109
415-292-3400
415-292-3404 (fax)
http://www.apiwellness.org/

Asian Lesbian and Bisexual Alliance in Seattle (ALBA)
P.O. Box 14232
Seattle, WA 98114
206-689-6155
albarocks@msn.com
http://www.alba.org

Asian Lesbian Network USA (ALN/USA)
P.O. Box 2594
Daly City, CA 94017-2594
415-626-6441

Asian Lesbians of the East Coast (ALOEC)
P.O. Box 850
New York, NY 10002

Asian Pacific AIDS Intervention Team (APAIT)
605 W. Olympic Boulevard, suite 610
Los Angeles, CA 90015
213-553-1830
213-553-1833 (fax)

Asian Pacific Crossroads, Orange County
The Center OC
12832 Garden Grove Boulevard, suite A
Garden Grove, CA 92843
APXRDS@aol.com
http://members.aol.com/APXRDS/gap.html

Asian Pacific Islander Lesbians and Gays
P.O. Box 826
Portland, OR 97207
503-232-6408

Asian Pacific Lesbian Bisexual Network (APLBN)
P.O. Box 210698
San Francisco, CA 94121
http://expage.com/page/aplbn

Asian Pacific Lesbian, Bisexual, Transgender Network (APLBTN)
aplbtn@hotmail.com
http://userwww.service.emory.edu/~jkim12/aplbtn/homepage2.html

Barangay (gay Filipino association of Los Angeles)
P.O. Box 3744
Hollywood, CA 90078
213-427-3905
http://members.aol.com/APXRDS/frbarang.html

Chingusai (Korean/American gay, lesbian, and bisexual network)
P.O. Box 741666
Los Angeles, CA 90004-1666
213-553-1873
chingusai@writeme.com

Gay Asian Pacific Alliance (GAPA)
P.O. Box 421884
San Francisco, CA 94142-1884
415-387-0466
gapa@slip.net
http://www.slip.net/~gapa/

Gay Asian Pacific Alliance, Hawai'i
P.O. Box 11692
Honolulu, HI 96828

Gay Asian/Pacific Islander Men of New York (GAPIMNY)
Old Chelsea Station
P.O. Box 1608
New York, NY 10113
212-802-RICE (-7423)
gapimny@leftnet.edu
http://207.10.38.2/~gapimny/

Gay Asian Pacific Islander of Chicago (GAPIC)
P.O. Box A-2544
Chicago, IL 60690

Gay Asian Pacific Support Network (GAPSN)
P.O. Box 461104
Los Angeles, CA 90046
213-368-6488
GAPSN@aol.com

Gay Vietnamese Alliance (GVA)
P.O. Box H48
9353 Bolsa Avenue, suite J–K
Westminster, CA 92683
714-449-8027

Japanese American Citizen League/Asian Pacific Islander
Lambda Chapter
P.O. Box 3622
Gardena, CA 90247-7322
310-355-8363

Khush
P.O. Box 53149
Temple Heights Station
Washington, DC 20009

Kilawin Kolektibo (Pinay lesbian and bisexual group)
51 Macdougal Street, Box 236
New York, NY 10012
kilawin@aol.com

Long Beach Gay Asian Pacific (LBGAP)
2017 East Fourth Street
Long Beach, CA 90814

Long Angeles Asian Pacific Islander Sisters (LAAPIS)
P.O. Box 86484
Los Angeles, CA 90086-0484
213-969-4084
LAAPIS@aol.com
http://www.geocities.com/WestHollywood/8878

Older Asian Sisters in Solidarity (OASIS)
P.O. Box 420396
San Francisco, CA 94142
510-482-0787

O Moi Vietnamese Lesbian, Bisexual, and Transgender Network
P.O. Box 3056
Santa Ana, CA 92703
714-418-0180

Queer and Asian
P.O. Box 14153
Seattle, WA 98114
206-689-6103
qasian@drizzle.com
http://www.drizzle.com/~qasian

Queer Asian Pacific Alliance
P.O. Box 543
Prudential Station
Boston, MA 02219
617-499-9531
qapa@geocities.com
http://www.geocities.com/WestHollywood/Heights/SOLO/index.html

South Asian Lesbian and Gay Association (SALGA)
P.O. Box 50
Cooper Station
New York, NY 10276-0050
219-294-2555

South Bay Queer and Asian
175 Stockton Avenue
San Jose, CA 95126
408-345-1268
SBQA@aol.com
http://members.aol.com/SBQA/index.html

Trikone
P.O. Box 21354
San Jose, CA 95151
408-270-8776
trikone@rahul.net
http://www.rahul.net/trikone/
Trikone, Atlanta
http://www.mindspring.com/~trikatl/index.htm

Vietnamese Lesbians, Gays, and Bisexuals
P.O. Box 460626
San Francisco, CA 94146

ELECTRONIC MAILING LISTS

APLB-L (Asian Pacific Lesbian/Bisexual Discussion List)
Subscribers are mostly from the United States, but subscribers from Asia, Australia, Canada, and England also log on. There is no moderator for this list. To subscribe, e-mail the address below.
aplb-approval@queernet.org

Khush (South Asian lesbian, gay, and bisexual mailing lists)
To join the list *automatically,* e-mail the address below. The subject line does not apply. The first line of your message *must* use the following form: subscribe khush [optional e-mail address].
khush-request@husc3.harvard.edu

Korean-Q List (a list for lesbians and bisexual women of Korean descent)
To subscribe, e-mail the address below:
koreanq-approval@queernet.org

QAPA-L (Queer Asian Pacific American Discussion List)
"An electronic mailing list for gay, lesbian, bisexual, transsexual, and queer Asian Pacific American people of all genders. QAPA-L is private (you can only read and post to the list if you've subscribed) and its subscriber list is confidential (only listowner has access to subscriber names and addresses)." To join, send the message "sub QAPA-L your name" to the computerized administrator's address below.
Computerized administrator: listserv@brownvm.brown.edu
Human administrator: qapa-l-request@brownvm.brown.edu

About the Contributors

KARIN AGUILAR-SAN JUAN worked at *dollars & Sense* (a progressive economics monthly) and South End Press (an independent book publisher) for nine and a half years before embarking on a doctoral degree in sociology from Brown University. She edited the anthology *The State of Asian America: Activism and Resistance in the 1990s* (South End Press) and wrote the foreword to *Dragon Ladies: Asian American Feminists Breathe Fire* (South End Press), edited by Sonia Shah. She currently teaches Asian American studies and sociology at the Claremont Colleges.

VICTOR BASCARA lives in New York City, where he is a doctoral candidate in the Department of English at Columbia University.

Born in Hong Kong, IGNATIUS BAU immigrated to the United States with his family as a child. He lives in San Francisco, where he works on health policy issues at the Asian and Pacific Islander American Health Forum. A founder of the Northern California Coalition for Immigrant Rights, Bau was active in the campaign against California's Proposition 187. He is a member of the Gay Asian Pacific Alliance.

BRYAN was born in Vietnam but raised in the United States since the age of four. He is a lover of music and books and enjoys reading science fiction and fantasy. He is also a member of O Môi, a Vietnamese lesbian, bisexual, and transgender network.

GAYE CHAN is associate professor of art at the University of Hawai'i. She is a multi-media artist, whose work has been displayed in solo and group exhibitions throughout the United States since 1979.

MARK CHIANG is assistant professor of English and Asian American studies at the University of Pennsylvania, where he specializes in Asian American literature and twentieth-century American literature and film. He holds a Ph.D. from the University of California, Berkeley. Chiang's current work-in-progress is a book that examines Asian American cultural production within the frameworks of diaspora, transnationalism, and globalization.

JUSTIN CHIN is a writer and performance artist whose solo pieces have been presented nationally. The author of *Bite Hard* (Manic D Press), his writings have also appeared in *Men on Men 5: New Gay Writing* (Plume), *Eros in Boystown* (Crown), *Premonitions: The Kaya Anthology of New Asian North American Poetry* (Kaya), *Best Gay Erotica 1997* (Cleis), and *Flesh and the Word 4* (Plume).

KEN CHU has exhibited internationally in community-based arts organizations, alternative art spaces, and major art institutions. His work has been included in "Brenda and Other Stories: HIV, AIDS and You," "42nd

Street Art Project," "Asia/America: Identities in Contemporary Asian American Art," "The Decade Show: Frameworks of Identity in the 1980s," and "Cultural Currents." In 1990, he cofounded Godzilla: Asian American Art Network, a group of New York–based Asian and Pacific Islander visual artists and arts professionals.

PATTI DUNCAN is a doctoral candidate in the Institute for Women's Studies at Emory University, where she is completing her dissertation on Asian Pacific American feminist writings and reconceptualizations of language and silence. Duncan is a founding member of Asian Pacific Lesbian, Bisexual, Transgender Network (APLBTN) of Atlanta.

DAVID L. ENG is assistant professor of English and comparative literature at Columbia University. His work has appeared in *Amerasia Journal, Camera Obscura, Critical Mass,* and *Social Text.* He is currently completing a manuscript on psychoanalysis and race entitled *Racial Castration: Managing Masculinity in Asian America.* Eng is an active board member of the Asian American Writers' Workshop as well as the Center for Lesbian and Gay Studies (CLAGS).

RICHARD FUNG is a Toronto-based videomaker and writer. He has received several awards for his work—which has been widely screened and published—including McKnight and Rockefeller Foundation fellowships. Fung is a founding member of Gay Asians Toronto.

JU HUI JUDY HAN is an immigrant queerean (queer + Korean) activist and artist in Los Angeles, where she works on a digital community building project at the Getty Institute. She holds a B.A. in English and women's studies from the University of California, Berkeley. Her projects involve issues of social justice, politics of identity, and technology.

NGUYEN TAN HOANG left Saigon, Vietnam, with his family in 1979, when he was nine years old. After spending a year and half in refugee camps in Malaysia, the family arrived in the United States. Hoang grew up in San Jose, California, and received his B.A. in art and art history from the University of California, Santa Cruz, and his M.F.A in studio art from the University of California, Irvine. Hoang is an artist who works in video and photography to investigate the intersection between popular cultural representation of the Asian male body and the formation of an alternative, queer Asian popular culture. His works have been screened at gay and lesbian and Asian American film festivals and displayed at numerous nonprofit exhibition sites.

ALICE Y. HOM is completing her doctoral dissertation on lesbian-of-color activism and community building in Los Angeles and New York, in the Department of History at Claremont Graduate University. Her essays have been published in *Amerasia Journal, The Very Inside: An Anthology of Writing by Asian and Pacific Islander Lesbian and Bisexual Women* (Sister Vision), *Crit-*

ical Essays: Gay and Lesbian Writers of Color (Haworth), and *Privileging Positions: The Sites of Asian American Studies* (Washington State UP). She also volunteers in the following organizations: Asian Pacific AIDS Intervention Team, California Community Foundation's Lesbian and Gay Community Fund, and the National Asian Pacific American Women's Forum.

DANIEL Y. KIM is assistant professor of English and ethnic studies at Brown University. He is currently working on a book tentatively entitled *Race, Writing and Manhood: Ambivalent Identifications and American Literary Identity in Frank Chin and Ralph Ellison*. Kim's essay on Ralph Ellison will be published in a forthcoming issue of *Novel.*

KAREN KIMURA is a Los Angeles native, sansei (third-generation Japanese American) visual artist. She received her M.F.A. in visual art from the State University of New York, Purchase, in 1993. Kimura is the director of community services and women's prevention services at the Asian Pacific AIDS Intervention Team in Los Angeles, where she develops media campaigns and manages the WOW (Women on Women) prevention and education program.

I. H. KUNIYUKI is a Seattle-based visual artist who holds a B.F.A. in photography. Her current artistic interests include distorting time and space.

ERICA LEE received her B.A. from Scripps College and her M.A. in Asian American studies from the University of California, Los Angeles. Her writing has been published in *Asian American Sexualities: Dimensions of the Gay and Lesbian Experience* (Routledge), and her photographic installations have been exhibited at several shows. Among her many current projects is a short film on Asian Pacific Islander dykes.

Born in Tokyo and raised in Korea, Sweden, England, Chicago, and Wilmette, Illinois, JEEYEUN LEE now lives in San Francisco. Her writing has been published in the *APA Journal's* "Witness Aloud: Lesbian, Gay and Bisexual Asian/Pacific American Writings" issue, *Listen Up: Voices from the Next Feminist Generation* (Seal Press), and *Queer Studies: A Lesbian, Gay, Bisexual, and Transgender Anthology* (New York UP).

QUENTIN LEE, raised in Los Angeles and Vancouver, is an independent writer, director, and producer.

RUSSELL LEONG is the editor of *Amerasia Journal* and the collections *Asian American Sexualities: Dimensions of the Gay and Lesbian Experience* (Routledge) and *Moving the Image: Independent Asian Pacific American Media Arts* (University of California, Los Angeles, and Visual Communications). His fiction and poetry have been published in *Charlie Chan Is Dead* (Penguin), *The Open Boat* (Anchor), *Aiiieeeee!* (Anchor), and *Asian American Literature* (Addison-Wesley).

YOU-LENG LEROY LIM was born in Singapore of Chinese parents and educated at the United World College in New Mexico, Princeton University (A.B. 1990), and the Divinity School of Harvard University (M.Div., 1995). An Episcopal priest, he lives in Los Angeles with his partner, Hung Nguyen, and fills his days with cooking, driving, and dreams of snow.

VERA MIAO holds a B.A. in women's studies from Barnard College. She currently resides on the Lower East Side of New York with her lover and their cat. Miao works in the nonprofit sector.

MARIE K. MOROHOSHI has worked on a number of film and video productions, including Pratibha Parmar's *Jodie: An Icon,* Ruby Yang and Lambert Yam's *Citizen Hong Kong,* and Joan Chen's directorial debut, *Xiu Xiu.* Morohoshi, who lives in San Francisco, coordinated the International Film Financing Conference (IFFCON '98), curated for the Tokyo International Lesbian and Gay Film Festival, and is the former associate director of the National Asian American Telecommunications Association's (NAATA) annual San Francisco International Asian American Film Festival.

HANH THI PHAM is a female-to-female lesbian goddess. Her autobiographical work is oral and photographic.

JASBIR K. PUAR, a doctoral candidate in the Department of Ethnic Studies at the University of California, Berkeley, is completing her dissertation on transnational sexualities. She has published essays on diasporic cultural productions, including "Writing My Way 'Home': Traveling South Asian Bodies and Diasporic Journeys" and "Resituating Discourses of 'Whiteness' and 'Asianness' in Northern England: Second Generation Sikh Women and Constructions of Identity," both of which appeared in *Socialist Review.*

RHODE is twenty-two years old. He realized he was a transsexual after coming out as gay. He is currently contemplating how to "transist" from the way he is to complete himself.

SANDIP ROY grew up in Calcutta, India. He is currently the editor of *Trikone,* a quarterly magazine on South Asian lesbian and gay issues. His work, which has appeared in *Christopher Street, India Currents,* and other journals, will be featured in *Men on Men 6* (Plume).

NAYAN SHAH is assistant professor of history at the State University of New York, Binghamton. He is the author of the forthcoming *Contamination and Cleanliness: Epidemics and the Crisis of Race in San Francisco's Chinatown, 1854–1952* (University of California Press). His current research focuses on sexual politics and the South Asian diaspora.

STEVEN SHUM was the founding director of the Lesbian, Gay, Bisexual, and Transgender Resource Center at the University of California, Riverside, which provides social, cultural, and educational programming. It was the first staffed department of its kind in the University of California system. In 1993 Shum graduated Phi Beta Kappa from the University of California, Los Angeles, with a B.A. in English and communication studies.

As an undergraduate, he was a facilitator for Mahu, UCLA's queer API student organization, and the director of Students Honestly Opening Up Together (SHOUT), a community-service program providing peer mentoring to lesbian, gay, bisexual, and questioning high school students. He also helped formulate the curriculum for a student-initiated course called Asian and Pacific Islander Gay, Lesbian, and Bisexual Experiences.

MIN SONG, a doctoral candidate in the Department of English and American Literature at Tufts University, is completing his dissertation on Sui Sin Far and Henry James. Song has taught at both Tufts University and Smith College.

JOËL BARRAQUIEL TAN is a widely anthologized writer, poet, and performance artist. His work has appeared in *On a Bed of Rice: Asian American Erotica Anthology* (Anchor) and *Asian American Sexualities* (Routledge). He is also a dedicated HIV/AIDS, gay and lesbian, and Pilipino cultural activist. He is currently the director of AIDS programs at Asian Health Services in Oakland, California.

DONNA TSUYUKO TANIGAWA is a yonsei (fourth-generation Japanese American) lesbian from Waipahu, Hawai'i. She is a descendant of plantation sugar laborers and holds fast to her mother tongue of pidgin English. Her work has appeared in numerous journals and collections. Currently working toward a graduate degree in English at the University of Hawai'i, Manoa, Tanigawa teaches women's studies at a community college.

DIEP KHAC TRAN is a board member of O Môi, a Vietnamese lesbian, bisexual, and transgender network. She is also a member of the Snazzy Writers' Workshop in Los Angeles.

JENNIFER TSENG'S work appears in *Love's Shadow: Writings by Women* (Crossing Press), *Skin Deep: Women Write on Color, Culture and Identity* (Crossing Press), and *Calyx: Journal of Women's Art and Literature*. Her writing will also be included in the collection *Genesis* and in forthcoming issues of *Amerasia Journal* and *Riksha Magazine*. Tseng recently completed a collection of stories, poems, and fragments, entitled *The S,* for her master's thesis in Asian American studies at the University of California, Los Angeles, where she is currently a lecturer.

ERIC C. WAT is an aspiring conversationalist. He hopes to spend his life (or at least the next few years) organizing, facilitating, transcribing, and editing roundtable discussions. He will soon have the opportunity to begin conversing, as he completes work on his master's thesis: an oral history project of the gay Asian community in Los Angeles during the late 1970s and early 1980s.

YOKO YOSHIKAWA is a nisei (second-generation Japanese American) who grew up on the East Coast and in Japan. In 1992 she moved to California, where she teaches yoga in Oakland.

K. Scott Wong and Sucheng Chan, eds., *Claiming America: Constructing Chinese American Identities during the Exclusion Era,* 1998

Robert G. Lee, *Orientals: Asian Americans in Popular Culture,* forthcoming